THE EU AS A TRANSFORMATIVE LEGAL AND ECONOMIC ORDER

This open access edited collection, the most recent volume in the landmark series Swedish Studies in European Law, takes an ambitious look at the nature and impact of the European Union.

Drawing on expert analysis, it offers a dual perspective by addressing pertinent questions about the constitutional nature of the Union, as well as the evolution of its Internal Market. This approach has never been more timely as the role of the EU in an increasingly turbulent geo-political environment is both important and challenging. Lawyers as well as others will find this an invaluable assessment of the EU and its power to bring about change.

The EU as a Transformative Legal and Economic Order

Essays in Memory of Ulf Bernitz

Swedish Studies in European Law
Volume 22

Edited by
Antonina Bakardjieva Engelbrekt,
Björn Lundqvist and Jaan Paju

•HART•
OXFORD • LONDON • NEW YORK • NEW DELHI • SYDNEY

HART PUBLISHING
Bloomsbury Publishing Plc
Kemp House, Chawley Park, Cumnor Hill, Oxford, OX2 9PH, UK
1385 Broadway, New York, NY 10018, USA
Bloomsbury Publishing Ireland Limited, 29 Earlsfort Terrace, Dublin 2, D02 AY28, Ireland

HART PUBLISHING, the Hart/Stag logo, BLOOMSBURY and the Diana logo are trademarks of Bloomsbury Publishing Plc
First published in Great Britain, 2026

1

A catalogue record for this book is available from the British Library.

Library of Congress Control Number: 2026945375

ISBN: HB: 978-1-50999-337-6
ePDF: 978-1-50999-339-0
ePub: 978-1-50999-338-3

Typeset by Amnet

On behalf of the Bernitz family, we extend our heartfelt thanks for this interesting book in memory of our beloved Ulf. He could not have been happier than engaging with the research and thoughts that the book addresses, topics that he was truly passionate about. We are confident that he, from above, in his friendly and enthusiastic manner will be reading, listening and participating in the discussions and new findings that this publication brings about.

With our warmest thanks
The Bernitz family

Foreword

DAVID GERBER

I AM GRATEFUL FOR the opportunity to write the foreword to this volume of essays dedicated to Professor Ulf Bernitz. I have treasured my long association and friendship with Ulf, and I am very pleased that this volume will soon be published.

From the time I arrived at the Law Faculty of Stockholm University in 1978 until his passing Ulf was a friend and a mentor. He enriched my life on both personal and academic levels.

He welcomed me to the Law Faculty of Stockholm University, opened doors to research resources, included me in research initiatives, supported my teaching and introduced me to scholars and practitioners throughout Scandinavia. He was immensely supportive. At least as important was his warmth and openness. His door was never closed, and we had many conversations of great value to me. After I returned to the US his support and friendship continued, albeit naturally in a somewhat more sporadic fashion. He was a genuine friend and a selfless supporter who often found ways for us to talk and work together.

His scholarship and his vision have also been of great value to me in my own work. His monograph *Marknadsrätt* that appeared in 1969 still stands out in my mind for its deep erudition and the boldness of the vision it represents. It presents a conceptualisation of economic law which was bold and intriguing for me. Competition law in Sweden was at the time of its publication at best a marginal player in Sweden's legal and business worlds. I spoke with numerous lawyers and businesspeople who even in the 1980s and 1990s were either totally unaware of the existence of competition law or acknowledged only having a vague notion of what it might be. Ulf's book confronted that marginality. It explored the history and context of competition law in other countries (European countries and the US primarily) and related them to Sweden's context. Ulf investigated factors in their evolution that shaped these competition law systems and then proceeded to suggest ways in which those factors could support integrating competition law into Swedish institutional and ideological structures to benefit markets and support consumers.

The book helped me to see more clearly how competition law had to be carved out of the dirigistic models that shaped the framework of markets in much of Europe. The contrast with the development of antitrust law in the US was stark. In addition, the book's analysis of the situation in Sweden helped me to recognise the obstacles that stood in the way of competition law achieving a position of greater importance in economic life. Competition law institutions are particularly vulnerable to outside influences in any legal system, so they require the creation of status and support for their authority. Ulf portrayed that process in the Swedish context very effectively. He was not only a bold thinker, but also a highly pragmatic analyst. As competition law became increasingly important on the European continent in the 1970s and 1980s Ulf recognised the potential for these developments to improve the position of competition law in Sweden, and he worked at many levels to give competition law institutions greater independence and status.

Ulf's perspective was always expanding. He was a strong supporter of Nordic cooperation in economic law throughout his entire career. When he realised that the pressure to expand the membership of the EU was intensifying in the early 1990s he saw the opportunity for Sweden to become part of that expansion. He believed deeply in the need for European integration and in the potential value of EU membership for Sweden. He fought hard for Swedish accession and was instrumental in using integration to benefit Sweden's economic interests. His efforts focused on competition law, but they also included many other areas of what he thought of as 'market law', including, for example, the compromises related to the Swedish state monopoly on the sale of (most) alcoholic beverages. His work in this area continued long after Sweden's entry into the EU. His comparative scholarship must have been of great value in strengthening Sweden's negotiating position and in working with other Europeans.

Ulf Bernitz was not only a practical lawyer, but also a political player who understood that he was in a unique position to benefit both Sweden and the causes of economic and political integration in which he believed. He pursued his goals with intensity and good judgement, and we have all profited from his efforts.

My guess is that he would be concerned about the somewhat 'wobbly' situation of the EU in the 2020s, but I have little doubt that he would do all in his power to improve the state of affairs and that he would also be at least hesitatingly confident about the Union's future.

Contents

PART III
THE EU INTERNAL MARKET AS A TRANSFORMATIVE LEGAL AND ECONOMIC ORDER

PART IV
A NEW EU MARKET LAW FOR THE DATA-DRIVEN ECONOMY

PART V
NEW AND OLD CHALLENGES TO EU MARKET LAW: INTELLECTUAL PROPERTY AND COMPETITION LAW

List of Contributors

Helene Andersson is Associate Professor of European Law and a Partner at Advokatfirman Delphi in Stockholm. She obtained her PhD from Stockholm University under the supervision of Professor Ulf Bernitz, writing her doctoral thesis on dawn raids in competition law. Combining academic scholarship with legal practice, she has extensive experience in EU and competition law and has published and lectured widely in the field. Her research and professional work focus particularly on EU competition law, procedural safeguards in competition investigations, and the relationship between EU law and national legal systems.

Antonina Bakardjieva Engelbrekt is Professor of European Law and Board Director of the Institute of European Law at the Faculty of Law, Stockholm University. She was the Chair of the Swedish Network for European Legal Studies (2011-2022). Antonina has been Hauser Global Research Fellow at NYU School of Law, Fernand Braudel Senior Fellow at the EUI, Florence and Visiting Professor at Chicago Kent College of Law. She has published extensively in European and comparative market Law (competition, Intellectual Property and consumer law) with a focus on governance and institutions.

Stefano Boni joined the Court of Justice of the European Union in 2004, while completing his PhD in European Union Law. He has since served primarily as a member of the cabinets of Judges at both the General Court and the Court of Justice. He is the author of several publications in EU law, focusing in particular on procedural law and competition law.

Jens Fejø, dr. jur., professor emeritus. Previously professor in EU competition law and public procurement law at Copenhagen Business School. Previously chair for the Danish Association of European Law and member of various professional councils and boards. Author to a number of academic research books and journal articles.

David J. Gerber is University Distinguished Professor of Law, Emeritus, Illinois Institute of Technology, Chicago, Illinois. He writes primarily in the areas of competition law and comparative law. Among his books are *Law and Competition in Twentieth Century Europe: Protecting Prometheus* (OUP, 2001) and *Competition Law and Antitrust: A Global Guide* (OUP, 2020). His current project is a comparative study of the legal and economic analysis of economic power.

Lars Henriksson is Professor of Law at Stockholm School of Economics (SSE) with a background in economics and law. His research is centred around market law, antitrust and competition law, and market regulation. He was previously appointed to the Research Council of the Swedish Competition Authority and held the position of

General Counsel for the SSE. Henriksson was member of the Board of the Institute of Intellectual Property and Market Law at Stockholm University (2011-2025) and a Non-Government Advisor to the International Competition Network's Unilateral Conduct Working Group (2013). He also has extensive experience as a consultant and expert in legal matters.

Annette Kur is an Affiliated Research Fellow at Max Planck Institute for Innovation and Competition, Munich. She has held positions of affiliated professor at Stockholm University and honorary professor at the University of Munich (LMU). She has been a visiting professor at NYU (Hauser Global Law School Program), at several European universities and at the National University of Singapore (NUS). Professor Kur was President of the International Association for the Advancement of Teaching and Research in Intellectual Property (ATRIP), 2007-2009. She has written extensively in the field of trademark, unfair competition and industrial design law, as well as private international law.

Björn Lundqvist is Professor of Law at Stockholm University. He is the Chair of the Swedish Network of European Legal Studies, Director of the European Law Institute at Stockholm University and Co-Director of ASCOLA (Academic Association of Competition Law) Nordic. Björn has published extensively, both books and articles, on Competition, Data, and IP Law and Policy related issues.

Ulla Neergaard is Professor of EU Law at the University of Copenhagen and, since 2024, Guest Professor at the University of Greenland (Ilisimatusarfik University). She has been a Visiting Professor at the University of Oxford (2015-16). Her academic foundation was established at the EUI, Florence, where she earned her PhD. She has presided over the International Federation for European Law, FIDE (2013-14) and led its 2014 Congress. For over a decade she has chaired the Danish Association for European Law.

Joakim Nergelius is Professor of Law at the University of Örebro, as well as Assistant Professor of European and Comparative Law at the Åbo (Turku) Academy in Finland. He has written extensively on European and Swedish constitutional law.

Sven Norberg is Juris doctor honoris causa at Stockholm University. After service in the Swedish judiciary (last post Judge of Appeal in Svea Court of Appeal) and in the Ministry of Commerce (last post Chief Legal Officer and Permanent Secretary), he became Director Legal Affairs at EFTA. By the entry into force of the EEA (European Economic Area) Agreement in 1994 he became Judge of the EFTA Court. Following Sweden's accession to the European Union in 1995, he served for ten years as Director in DG Competition of the European Commission.

Jaan Paju is Professor of Constitutional Law and Associate Professor of European Law at Stockholm University. His research focuses on the interaction between national constitutional law, European Union law, and social security law, with particular emphasis on Union citizenship, the coordination of social security systems, fundamental rights, and the relationship between national sovereignty and European integration. Since 2021, he has been affiliated with the Faculty of Law at the University of Bergen, where he has served as Professor II. Since 2023, he has also been a member of the Advisory Committee of CENTENOL at the University of Bergen.

Frantzeska Papadopoulou Skarp is Professor of Intellectual Property Law and Head of the IP Law Group of Stockholm University and affiliated professor at Karolinska Institute. Papadopoulou is the Chair of IFIM (Research Institute for Intellectual Property and Market Law). She is the editor-in-chief and founder of the Stockholm Intellectual Property Law Review and a member of the Board of the National Library of Sweden. Papadopoulou is a member of the expert governmental committee on limitations to copyright. She is the author of several books and articles in the field of intellectual property as well as on regulatory rights.

M. Elvira Méndez-Pinedo is a Spanish-Icelandic professor and legal scholar, specializing in European Union and European Economic Area law. After an international career in Spain, France, USA and Luxembourg, she joined the University of Iceland in 2007 where she has been a full tenured professor of European law since 2010. She has written several books and many articles exploring the general authority and effectiveness of EU and EEA law over national (constitutional) laws. Furthermore, she has done extensive research on the protection of consumer rights in the European internal market and Iceland, before and after the financial crisis.

Magnus Strand is an Associate Professor of European law and Senior Lecturer in private law at Uppsala University. His general research background is in commercial EU law and private law. Other research interests are the regulation and governance of digital markets and artificial intelligence.

Hanns Ullrich is honorary professor at the College of Europe, Bruges and associate researcher at Max Planck Institute for Innovation and Competition, Munich. He has previously held positions as Professor at Universität der Bundeswehr, Munich (1985-2004), Chair of Competition Law and Intellectual Property Law at the European University Institute, Florence (2000/2001 and 2003-2006) and visiting professor at College of Europe, Bruges (1991 – 2021). He has served as rédacteur en chef for Revue internationale de droit économique (2003–2012).

Sybe de Vries is Full Professor of Public Economic Law and since 2012 the Jean Monnet Chair at the Europa Institute of the School of Law of Utrecht University. He is visiting professor at the College of Europe (Bruges) and at the University of Trento (Italy). His research and teaching focus on EU Single market law in general, free movement and competition law, the twin green and digital transition of the EU Single Market, and the interconnection between economic law, fundamental rights and public interests. Sybe is co-director of the Utrecht Centre for Regulation and Enforcement in Europe (Renforce).

Nils Wahl is Visiting Professor at Uppsala University, formerly one of Professor Bernitz' doctoral students, and more recently former Judge and Advocate General, Court of Justice of the European Union.

Angela Ward, PhD, is a member of the Bars of Ireland and England and Wales and practices in EU law. She has held various academic posts, including visiting professorships at University College Dublin, Birkbeck College, University of London, and Western Sydney University, and served for nine years as a référendaire at the CJEU in Luxembourg. She is a founding editor of the Cambridge Yearbook of European Legal Studies, and since completion of her PhD studies at the European University Institute, Florence in 1996, has produced around forty publications in diverse subject areas of EU law.

Stephen Weatherill is Jacques Delors Professor of European Law (Emeritus) at the University of Oxford and a Senior Research Fellow of Somerville College.

Thomas Wilhelmsson is Chancellor (emeritus) and Professor of Civil and Commercial Law (emeritus), University of Helsinki. He is Doctor of Laws (Helsinki University), and Doctor honoris causa (Uppsala, Oslo, Tartu and Turku). He has had many good discussions with Ulf Bernitz on EU law and consumer law. His latest book is *Free Movement of Legal Ideas; Towards a Dynamic Europeanisation of Private Law* (Hart Publishing 2024).

Introduction

ANTONINA BAKARDJIEVA ENGELBREKT,
BJÖRN LUNDQVIST AND JAAN PAJU

THIS BOOK WITH ESSAYS in memory of Professor Ulf Bernitz (1936–2022) has a twofold objective. First, it invites leading scholars in European constitutional and economic law to give their perspective on the nature of the European Union as a transformative legal and economic order. In its 70-year long history, the Union has emerged as a unique project of legal, economic and political integration. It has advanced a whole new vision of building a community of states based on interdependence and mutual trust. As a result, the European project has had deeply transformative effects for the institutional and constitutional foundations of the participating Member States, affecting profoundly the work and life conditions of economic actors and citizens.

Second, and as importantly, the book pays tribute to the late Professor Ulf Bernitz and his impressive academic legacy. Through his long and venerable academic career, Professor Bernitz (or simply Ulf as he was to most of us) established himself as a true institution within Swedish law and a leading figure of European law in Sweden, the Nordics and internationally. With his groundbreaking dissertation *Marknadsrätt*, published in 1969, Ulf Bernitz advanced the concept of 'market law' as a distinct field of law comprising rules that govern relations between economic actors, both safeguarding and defining the limits to the main economic freedoms – freedom of competition, of contract and of enterprise (*näringsfrihet*). The discipline's main function was perceived to be to keep competition free and fair, with a firm basis in private rights, and protection of property rights in particular. The concept 'market law' gained traction and was accepted as denoting a separate legal field also in the other Nordic countries. It is distinct from the notion of economic law (*Wirtschaftsrecht* or *droit économique*) as known in continental Europe and stands out as being more precise and taking a more functional approach. Competition, marketing, consumer and intellectual property law are all conceived as parts of market law, thus underlying the common ground and interplay between these legal disciplines. Starting from the late 1960s and throughout his scholarly work, Ulf made noteworthy contributions to each of these legal fields maintaining a leading position not only in Sweden but also in the Nordic region and internationally.

Of particular significance for Ulf's legacy is his contribution to enhancing the impact of European law and promoting European thinking in Sweden. Ulf worked actively for Sweden's accession first to the European Free Trade Association (EFTA), then to the European Union and, thereafter, for introducing and disseminating European law in Swedish legal education and legal practice. He started the Nordic region's first master's programme in European law at the Department of Law of Stockholm University. He was the mastermind behind countless conferences and seminars on European law, founded the Swedish Network for European Legal Studies and launched *Europarättslig Tidskrift* (the *Journal of European Law*) in 1998.

With his breadth of knowledge, Ulf was possibly one of the last renaissance men in Swedish legal academia, and this book is a joint tribute to his extraordinary legacy as a scholar and mentor. The authors of the chapters in the book have all in various ways been inspired and impacted by Ulf's fascination with the law, 'the art of what is good and just' (*ars boni et aequi*) and by his contagious enthusiasm for European law in particular.

PART I. TRIBUTE TO ULF BERNITZ AS A SCHOLAR AND A VISIONARY

The first part of the book contains a few personal testimonies to Ulf's role as an academic and a visionary in the field of EU law and beyond. The contributions focus on his attitude as a scholar and teacher and his curiosity to explore new legal fields with a vision of developing legal systematics and advancing EU legal policy. In his contribution (chapter one), Sven Norberg describes how Ulf played an important role both for the development of Sweden's position vis-à-vis the European Union and for the modernisation of EU competition law in the beginning of the 2000s.

According to Joakim Nergelius (chapter two), Ulf did not only provide a normative vision of how the law should be, but did so with the kind of energy that can only be derived from the joy of developing EU law scholarship. In Nergelius's view, this reflected Ulf's attitude to the academic profession, research and teaching alike. Ulf saw EU law research not merely as a duty or a job, and not even as a call or mission, but as something fun; a stimulating and interesting activity, quite simply. It is in fact very likely that this attitude helped him preserve his unusual intellectual vitality.

In the third chapter, Thomas Wilhemsson reviews Ulf's contribution to the debate on the Europeanisation of contract and consumer law by looking at unfair contract terms law. Contract law is an important part of what one can call the 'economic constitution' of a society. The understanding of contracts is deeply embedded in national legal culture. It is, therefore, an area in which EU law has been clashing with national and Nordic traditions. One of the most important issues in these clashes, according to Wilhelmsson, is the relationship between the principle of *pacta sunt servanda* and the aspiration to combat unfair contract terms and unfair contractual outcomes. This relationship offers an interesting perspective on the transformative role of EU law in its meeting with the Nordic 'tradition'. In a similar way as Norberg and Nergelius, Wilhemsson pays particular respect to Ulf's visionary capacity underlying the optimistic and positive positions taken by Ulf in his attempt to untangle the legal-cultural clashes.

PART II. THE EU AS A TRANSFORMATIVE CONSTITUTIONAL ORDER

The second part of the book focuses on EU constitutional law. As is well known, the complex relationship between EU law and national constitutional frameworks is constantly evolving, requiring adjustment and recalibration of the delicate balance between the principles of EU integration and the sovereignty of Member States. The fact that EU law takes precedence over conflicting national law leads for obvious reasons to tensions between national legal systems and EU law. While the Charter of Fundamental Rights (the Charter) has sought to settle some of these tensions, the Charter has given rise to problems of its own.

In chapter four, in a joint contribution, Nils Wahl and Stefano Boni focus on the application of the freedom to conduct a business in the Charter. The authors highlight this freedom as the important link between EU constitutional law and the Internal Market. The European project, originally a purely economic one, has over time acquired a significantly wider scope, as is apparent from the Charter. This evolution should, in the authors' view, not jeopardise the functioning of an economically sound Internal Market, which is indispensable for any fundamental right to be effective and sustainable in the long run. Article 16 of the Charter, which grants the status of fundamental right to the freedom to conduct a business, is seen as a recognition of the essential role of entrepreneurship and innovation for economic and social development in the EU and for promoting economic growth. Private operators can rely on that Article in order to be protected from undue interference by public authorities. However, undertakings' freedom is not without limits and should, according to the authors, be used in a way which is simultaneously procompetitive and respectful of fundamental rights, and in particular of human dignity. Efficient judicial remedies are seminal for striking a balance when the actors involved cannot themselves find an acceptable solution.

In her contribution (chapter five), Angela Ward discusses the relationship between EU constitutional law and Member State sovereignty focusing on the EU Charter of Fundamental Rights and its much-debated Article 51(1), defining the scope of application of the Charter. Ward proposes a remodelling of Article 51 of the Charter, pairing down (and significantly) the text of Article 51(1), and splitting 51(1) and 51(2) so that the former, as re-cast, would appear at the beginning of the Charter. This indeed groundbreaking proposal is clearly in the spirit of Ulf Bernitz's scholarship. The General Principles of EU law played a significant role in Ulf's research with four extensive anthologies published by Kluwer. Additionally, as a legal expert in the seminal *Åkerberg Fransson* case and in subsequent contributions, he shed light on the important issue of the scope of application of the EU Charter both in reference to the relationship between EU and Member States' law, and regarding the breadth of rights as such.

Ulf emphasised always that EU law is national law. Hence, he initiated *Europarättslig Tidskrift* in 1998 for the good of Nordic academic research in EU law. The Nordic dimension was important for him. From a Nordic co-operation perspective, EU law includes the dichotomy between the EU and the EFTA legal systems, and between EU integration and Nordic co-operation. Maria Elvira Méndez-Pinedo's contribution (chapter six) is within the field. She claims that primacy of EU law has a transnational dimension which is often ignored by its critics (in particular the school of constitutional pluralism). It guarantees the equality of the Member States, but importantly also of EU citizens, before the Treaties. The chapter focuses on the principle of primacy of EU law in the interface between the EU and EFTA legal systems, that is, between a system that embraces the doctrine of primacy and direct effect and one that does not.

PART III. THE EU INTERNAL MARKET AS A TRANSFORMATIVE LEGAL AND ECONOMIC ORDER

The law of the EU Internal Market is the area which to a great extent inspired Ulf's original idea of Market Law as a legal discipline. Starting with the core freedoms of movement of goods, services, people and capital, and based on a system ensuring fair and undistorted competition, the Internal Market has branched out into all the disciplines outlined by Ulf as forming part of Market Law: competition, consumer, intellectual property law and beyond. Internal Market law in all its variations and outgrowths remained at the centre of Ulf's scholarly activity and is also in the focus of the contributions in this part of the book.

In chapter seven, Stephen Weatherill discusses the interface between EU constitutional law and the free trade paradigm. In the early years of the European integration project, the Court of Justice chose to describe the European Community, now Union, as a 'new legal order', labelling it, more recently, an 'ecosystem'. The features usually set forth as being distinctive of this novel legal order (or ecosystem) are the constitutional principles of EU law developed over time by the Court, notably the principles of direct effect and primacy. However, in his chapter, in a more unconventional manner, Weatherill applies the discourse of a new legal order and ecosystem to the law of the EU Internal Market. Seen from this perspective, *Cassis de Dijon* asserts a preference for judge-led integration ahead of legislative harmonisation as a means to discipline technical standards in the EU Internal Market. It stands for a mix of non-harmonised and harmonised sectors in which the former are prioritised. Yet, Weatherill submits that today the priorities have been reversed. The reality of the Internal Market is that in many sectors it operates primarily on a dense legislative foundation, not on litigation before the Court concerning free movement law. This suggests that *Cassis* unleashed a dynamic. Over time, its limitations as a model have become more widely appreciated, and the Internal Market has gradually changed its regulatory shape. Politically driven market regulation at EU level increasingly supplements judge-led deregulation of national markets, highlighting that predictable rules set at EU level facilitate the development of the Internal Market more successfully than ad hoc resort to free movement law.

Ulla Neergaard and Sybe de Vries, in their contribution (chapter eight), critically revisit the foundations of the free movement law regime in light of new developments and challenges. The authors trace the evolution of the Single Market and agree with Letta's diagnosis that the Internal Market is 'fundamentally based on twentieth-century theoretical principles'. In their view, these principles fail to reflect the evolving dynamics of a market increasingly shaped by digitalisation, innovation and uncertainties related to climate change and its impact on society. The authors highlight at least three new developments and challenges that need to be addressed. First, a new economic theoretical thinking, whereby economists search for solutions to the ecological crisis within planetary boundaries and develop ideas about for example degrowth, post-growth or doughnut economics. Second, a changed Treaty context with a stronger focus on public interests and on the objectives of a social market economy in the Lisbon Treaty. Third, a change of the international context and a multitude of crises that the Union is confronted with, which creates tensions between different objectives.

On the basis thereof, Neergaard and De Vries suggest that there may be a need for reconsideration of the present foundations of free movement law in the primary law interpretations of the Court of Justice of the European Union (CJEU). Currently, there is an inherent priority of the interest in free movement, that is, of economic aims, over non-market interests in the free movement regime. Such a hierarchy implies that non-economic aims are only treated as secondary in nature. A rethinking of the Internal Market paradigms is thus in order, to ensure that these paradigms are resilient, future-proof and sufficiently capable to guide European societies in responding to new societal needs and addressing new challenges.

PART IV. THE NEW MARKET LAW FOR THE DIGITAL DATA-DRIVEN ECONOMY

The fourth part of the book links Ulf Bernitz's conceptualisation of 'market law' (*marknadsrätt*, *marknadsret*) as a separate discipline creating framework rules for the free-market economy with the evolving EU rules for the digital, data-driven economy. As mentioned above, when introduced, the concept of market law denoted a legal discipline, which comprised competition law, intellectual property law and unfair competition law, including rules for the marketing of goods and services to consumers. The contributions in this part of the book trace the transformation that the digital economy brings to these and related fields of law.

A large number of the new European regulations in reference to the data-driven economy deal with the establishment, protection and governance of the digital, data-driven 'market'. This market and its participants are protected under 'general' competition law but also by way of general and sector-specific regulations such as the Digital Markets Act, the Platform-to-Business (P2B) and the Free Flow of Non-Personal Data Regulations. Unfair business practices and strategies are reined in by these and other regulations such as the Digital Services Act. Consumers are also protected from various unfair marketing methods used increasingly in distance selling and e-commerce by the rehaul of relevant consumer law instruments through the Modernisation Directive (Directive 2019/2161). New rights have been introduced in the form of for example a publishers' right in the Digital Copyright Directive (Directive 2019/79), and access and transfer rights to data for users in the Data Act as well as in the Digital Markets Act.

This legal development begs the question whether we are witnessing a nascent new legal system in developing, an EU based 'Market Law' for the digital economy, similar to the legal system construed by Ulf in his early scholarship.

Hanns Ullrich focuses in his contribution (chapter nine) on the EU Data Act's rules on access to and use of data. He begins on a note of amazement. In his view, the European Union, when faced with the threat of the EU market becoming ever more dominated by a few giants of a foreign digital industry, seems to have hastened to build a new market law of the data-driven economy, different from the old market law of the 'bricks-and-mortar' economy. In this effort, however, the EU legislature has proceeded by erecting walls before laying the fundament. Reacting to the pressing problem of losing control over the technological direction of its economy and seizing the political opportunities for effective legislation, the legislature's focus has been on subjecting the major new actors on its 'digital market', notably digital service providers, intermediaries and gate-keeping platforms, to particular rules. Yet, however important these specially tailored rules may be for containing the influence and power of some selectively identified market actors, they are peripheral to the regulation of the core of these markets, which is access to and use of their essential resource, namely data. It has long been the case that data may be held and are offered for business re-use by the public sector, but the bulk of economically relevant data originates from within, and is controlled by, the private sector. Therefore, 'harmonised rules on fair access to and use of data' could serve, according to Ullrich, as a solid fundament for the well-functioning of an innovative data-driven economy. This, indeed, is what the EU legislature expects the Data Act to do, but it did not design the rules of the Act accordingly. Therefore, rather than presenting the Data Act's rules on access to and use of data of the private sector in detail, Ullrich's contribution focuses on their conceptual underpinnings and systemic deficits.

Magnus Strand's contribution (chapter 10) complements Ullrich's text, whereby Strand focuses more on Article 13 of the Data Act, the purpose of which is to govern business-to-business contracts on the sharing of data, to ensure that data is shared under fair, reasonable and non-discriminatory terms and conditions. In his contribution, Strand identifies the essential elements of the rule in Article 13 of the Data Act and analyses them in light of the previous *acquis* of EU contract law. He also discusses how Article 13 of the Data Act contributes, as other EU contract law, to the balancing of commercial freedom against other crucial values in a regulated market economy.

In the next chapter (chapter 11), Jens Fejø takes as his starting point the judgment of the EU Court of Justice (ECJ) from 4 July 2023 in the *Facebook* case (Case C-252/21 *Meta/Facebook v Bundeskartellamt*). The contribution highlights the intensive scrutiny exercised by the ECJ of the procedure followed by Facebook for collecting, registering and handling sensitive personal data collected from the company's users and elsewhere. Although the case started as a competition law case, the ECJ's approach extends to a scrutiny that also concerns the General Data Protection

Regulation (GDPR) rules and the interface between competition law and data protection. The contribution puts emphasis on the fact that the strict attitude of the ECJ towards Facebook and similar companies collecting personal data should be placed in a broader context where the European treatment of the big tech companies may be an inspiration for a global approach.

In chapter 12, Helene Andersson addresses a topic of central importance for the enforcement of the new EU digital market law, namely the issue of *ne bis in idem*. The chapter explores whether the introduction of the Digital Markets Act (DMA), and its concurrent application with existing EU competition rules, provides adequate safeguards against double jeopardy. Although the DMA is said to pursue objectives distinct from those of EU competition law, in Andersson's view, the Commission's own reasons for proposing the legislation suggest otherwise. The stated objectives of the DMA proposal, namely preventing higher prices, reduced quality and diminished choice and innovation, mirror closely the concerns addressed by EU competition rules. The overlap is further underscored by the fact that many of the DMA's obligations are directly inspired by recent antitrust cases brought by the Commission against companies now designated as gatekeepers. Given the possibility of parallel investigations under the DMA and competition law, it is essential to determine whether, and under what circumstances, such investigations might be subject to the prohibition against double jeopardy as outlined in Article 50 of the Charter of Fundamental Rights of the European Union ('the Charter'). Andersson reviews the recent case law of the CJEU and the European Court of Human Rights on double jeopardy and finds serious grounds for concern that parallel administrative proceedings under the DMA and competition law may lead to disproportionate results. She concludes that the Commission and national competition authorities must shoulder their responsibilities with care and not overstep the boundaries of their powers.

In her contribution (chapter 13) Bakardjieva Engelbrekt looks into the institutional design of enforcement of the new EU law of the digital economy. She notes the widely recognised trend of centralisation of enforcement powers in the Commission through the Digital Markets Act and the Digital Services Act, but directs her attention to the continued role of decentralised enforcement by national authorities and enforcement networks. The chapter asks in what ways the institutional design of enforcement of the new EU digital law has been influenced by the accumulated experiences from network-based enforcement of the EU Internal Market Law. To answer this question, the chapter offers a retrospect of the history and performance of two enforcement networks with central role for EU Internal Market Law, the European Competition Network (ECN) and the Consumer Protection Cooperation Network (CPC Network). The author reflects on the strengths and weaknesses in the performance of the two networks and seeks to identify reasons for their differential success. When studying the dynamic generated within the networks, besides the opposing dynamics of vertical and horizontal empowerment, Bakardjieva Engelbrekt discerns a pattern of what she labels 'lopsided enforcement'; whereby some Member States and their authorities assume a more central position in the enforcement of relevant EU law, in concerted action with the Commission. Returning to the Digital Services Package, the enforcement architecture is viewed through the prism of past experiences. The emerging institutional design is better understood as consisting of elements of centralised, decentralised and lopsided enforcement, rather than a trend exclusively along one of these directions. The task ahead is finding the right balance between these sometimes conflicting dynamics.

PART V. NEW AND OLD CHALLENGES TO EU MARKET LAW: INTELLECTUAL PROPERTY AND COMPETITION LAW

The contributions in the fifth and final part of the book address some well-established rules and legal doctrines of EU intellectual property and market law and explore how these rules are being reshaped in response to new and old challenges.

In chapter 14, Lars Henriksson revisits the question of justification for antitrust enforcement regarding vertical agreements. The author submits that the issue still remains contentious – especially when a comparison is made between US antitrust law and EU competition law. He finds the continued US distrust vis-à-vis per se rules in antitrust for vertical agreements to stand in stark contrast to the traditional approach in EU/EEA competition law. However, while the old stance in EU law appears to linger on to date, thus sustaining the Atlantic division, a gradual shift in application of the old rules is noticeable. In his chapter, Henriksson compares per se violations with so-called block clauses in the vertical block exemption regulation, focusing on the method under EU law to distinguish certain severe restrictions which by their very nature are deemed anti-competitive agreements from those that may generate restrictive effects *in casu*.

Annette Kur's contribution (chapter 15) deals with the interface between trade mark law and unfair competition law, an area that has figured prominently in Ulf's scholarship. According to Kur, trade mark law and unfair competition law are closely related fields. Overlaps between them have increased since issues which are traditionally considered as part of unfair competition law have been embraced by EU trade mark legislation and its interpretation by the CJEU. The EU Court, moreover, tends to assume a maximum degree of jurisdiction wherever possible. For trade mark law, this means, on the one hand, that its scope is expanded in comparison to pre-harmonised law; on the other hand, it means that greater account must be taken of aspects usually associated with unfair competition, such as flexibility and openness for countervailing interests (something referred to as a 'Trojan horse'-effect). The article traces the relevant issues in the light of CJEU jurisprudence, showing the positive potential of imbuing trade mark law with unfair competition-oriented thinking, but also pointing out the risks and lacunae that still exist.

In the last chapter (chapter 16) Frantzeska Papadopoulou Skarp deals with access to clinical trials data. The special nature but also the exceptional value of clinical trials data has placed it in the centre of a complicated web of legal regulations concerning both transparency and accessibility, as well as its protection under exclusivity regimes. The protection of data selected during clinical trials is of recognised importance. At the same time, guaranteeing transparency that would allow third parties to test the information submitted by the sponsors, and spread data as much as possible in order to make the outmost of clinical trials has recently received the attention of the legislator. The chapter investigates the complications related with these two directions to be taken into consideration by the applicable legal framework, as well as the changes proposed or implemented following the entry into application of the Clinical Trials Regulation in 2022. The author reflects on what can be deducted by the changes both in the actual protection of data and of the rules that govern its accessibility.

On a final note, it is impossible to overstate Ulf's profound influence on the development of market law and EU law – not only as academic disciplines in Sweden, but also across the Nordic countries and internationally. His intellectual legacy continues to shape the field in lasting ways.

We hope that this book serves as a testament to his enduring contribution and as an inspiration to future scholars.

Part I

Tribute to Ulf Bernitz as an Academic and a Visionary

1

Ulf Bernitz: A Tireless Visionary

SVEN NORBERG

I. INTRODUCTION

THIS CHAPTER BUILDS ON the speech I delivered at the conference organised in memory of Ulf Bernitz celebrating his incredible academic achievements. When I was asked by the conference organisers to give a speech, I realised that, among the conference participants, I was probably the one who had known Ulf the longest, actually 60 years. I therefore decided in my tribute to Ulf to try and recall some memories of our cooperation throughout these many years and of the various roles he had been playing. This applies in particular to our contact during the 1970s and 1980s, when I first worked at the Swedish Ministry of Commerce and Trade (*Handelsdepartementet*) and then in the European Free Trade Association (EFTA) and thereafter into the 1990s and 2000s, when I was at the EFTA Court and the EU Commission.

II. MEETING ULF

I first met Ulf during my law studies at Stockholm University in the early 1960s. In 1964 I had asked for a meeting with Professor Seve Ljungman, a highly respected expert in civil law and particularly in the field of intellectual property law. The purpose was to discuss the subject for the final thesis in my law studies. I told Professor Ljungman that I was interested in the field of competition law and wanted to write my thesis in that area. For a moment he looked hesitant, since he obviously would have preferred a subject of intellectual property law. But suddenly he lightened up exclaiming: 'Men vi har ju unge Bernitz, han är mycket lovande! Skulle kandidaten kunna acceptera, att han blev Er handledare?' ('Of course we have the young Bernitz! He is quite promising! Would you accept that he became your tutor?') Since I already knew Ulf, who had just started work on his licentiate thesis, I immediately accepted the proposal.

Rarely or never was a student tutored in such a generous way, as I was by Ulf. I later found out that I was the first student he had tutored.[1] He suggested that I should

[1] By the end of 2020, according to the Head of Archives at Juridicum at Stockholm University, Ulf had tutored or been examiner for 293 such theses and for 83 theses at Master level.

write on *comparative advertising*, a topic of great relevance at the time in Sweden. Ulf knew of course already all interesting and knowledgeable people to contact, which greatly facilitated my work. My thesis was presented in May 1965, and Ulf even arranged for a shorter version of it to be published in *NIR*, the *Nordic Journal on Intellectual Property*.[2] This publication marked the end of the first of many projects that during more than half a century brought the two of us together.

III. MARKET LAW

Through his 1969 doctoral thesis *Marknadsrätt* (*Market Law*),[3] Ulf created a new legal concept, that of 'market law'. Lars Jonson, late President of the Swedish Market Court, in an article in the well-established Swedish law journal *Svensk juristtidning* (*SvJT*) in 2001,[4] stated that the term market law, 'mainly launched by Professor Bernitz, has quite a clear and since long established meaning. Simply expressed, it covers general rules for carrying out of business through framework rules on establishment, marketing and competition as well as consumer protection.'

A. The 1975 Reform in the Field of Market Law

In the summer of 1974, I joined the Ministry of Commerce and Trade where I worked as Legal Adviser closely with Lars Jonson. Among the many legislative projects waiting were those in the field of consumer policy envisaging fundamental changes in Swedish marketing legislation, and in particular the proposal for a new Marketing Act that in autumn 1975 was presented to Parliament.[5] The new enlarged Act contained rules through which business could be obliged to provide such information about the marketed products, which was of particular importance from the consumer point of view. Furthermore, the Act made it possible to prohibit goods that posed a particular risk for hurting a person or property or which clearly were not fit for their main purpose. Injunctions or prohibitions had to be decided by the Market Court after an action by the Consumer Ombudsman, *Konsumentombudsmannen* (*KO*). The Marketing Act, *Marknadsföringslagen* (1975:1418), entered in force on 1 July 1976 with a new organisation, where the *KO* and the Consumer Board (*Konsumentverket*) were merged into one agency with the Director General also being *KO*.

Thereby, a major reform work in the field of consumer law was completed, that had been going on for some decades and built on extensive proposals for new legislation from two Public Committees on Declaration of goods (*Varudeklarationsutredningen*[6]) and on Publicity (*Reklamutredningen*[7]) as well as by *KO* and the Consumer Board.

[2] Sven Norberg, 'Jämförelser i reklam' (1966) (2) *Nordiskt immateriellt rättskydd* (*NIR*) 77 et seq.
[3] Ulf Bernitz, *Marknadsrätt* (Stockholm, 1969) 63.
[4] Lars Jonson, 'Marknadsrätten, särskilt regleringen av reklam' (2001) *SvJT* 291 et seq.
[5] Prop. 1975/76: 34.
[6] SOU 1973:20.
[7] Reklam III SOU 1973:10 and Reklam IV SOU 1974:23.

B. The Association on Market Law

In the public debate during this period Ulf was of course extremely active in various ways. He had, in 1971, founded the Association for Market Law (*Föreningen för Marknadsrätt*), today the Association of Competition and Market Law (*Konkurrens- och Marknadsrättsliga föreningen*). This provided a very efficient forum for profound and lively, mostly evening, discussions with civil servants, practitioners and representatives of business and consumers actively participating. At the same time Ulf was also chairing the Consumer Services commission of inquiry (*Konsumentjänstutredningen*)[8] and was a member of two other Commissions, one on Home sales (*Hemförsäljningskommittén*) and one on Small housing (*Småhuskommittén*).

Another field of great importance, and where the discussions within the Association for Market Law played an important role, was the marketing of tobacco and alcohol. While Finland and Norway had very strict recent legislation prohibiting all publicity for these products in general, Sweden lacked special rules, which now the Parliament requested.[9]

Following a report in 1976 by the Committee on Publicity for Tobacco and Alcohol (*Tobaks- och Alkoholreklamutredningen*),[10] two new laws were adopted in 1978 regarding the marketing of tobacco and alcohol, respectively. But instead of expressing detailed prohibitions these laws laid down the fundamental principle that – due to the health risks linked to the use of these goods – *particular moderation* had to be observed in the marketing thereof. Publicity, to the extent it would be allowed at all, should be strongly restrictive and moderate.

The application of these laws was closely linked to the Marketing Act and was thus to be handled by the *KO* and the Market Court. This provided an order that gradually over the years was developed through the negotiating practices of *KO* and the case law of the Market Court. This functioned extremely well.

IV. THE 1982 COMPETITION ACT

During my seven and a half years in the *Handelsdepartementet* the post as Minister shifted on six occasions following unusually frequent political transitions in Government.[11] It goes without saying that such a turnover of political leadership does not facilitate the work of advancing more innovative legislative projects.

[8] Set up by the Government in 1973 with final proposals in SOU 1979:36.

[9] The appointment of the Committee, Tobaks- och Alkoholreklamutredningen, followed a 1974 request by Parliament and was preceded by an internal contest between the Ministers for Social Affairs (Sven Aspling) and Trade and Commerce (Kjell-Olof Feldt). Finally, Mr Feldt got in charge of the file with Mr Aspling choosing the Chairman of the Committee.

[10] SOU 1976:63 Reklamen för Alkohol och tobak.

[11] In November 1975 from K-O Feldt to C Lidbom (O. Palme Government). In October 1976 S Burenstam Linder (T. Fälldin I Government), in October 1978 to H Cars (Ullsten Government), in October 1979 to Burenstam Linder (Fälldin II) and in May 1981 to B Molin (Fälldin III). Burenstam Linder left in May 1981 and was first succeeded by JE Wikström formally Minister during 16 days.

In the field of antitrust, Sweden had the old 1953 Law against restrictions of competition,[12] which in principle was an abuse law with only two specific prohibitions against price-fixing and bidding cartels. For the rest it fell upon *NO* (*Näringsfrihetsombudsmannen*), the Ombudsman for freedom of business, to negotiate with industry the termination of specific anti-competitive behaviour. If this was not successful *NO* would seek an injunction at the Market Court. After more than 20 years it had become clear that a more effective and sharper competition legislation, especially regarding mergers, was needed. Since the autumn of 1974, a Committee with MPs under the chairmanship of Mr Lars Jonson[13] was working on a review. Among the members was also Ulf. The Competition Committee (*Konkurrensutredningen*) in January 1978 presented a report, New Law on Restrictions of Competition.[14] Apart from two new prohibitions, against price cartels and market sharing agreements, a special order for vetting mergers was also proposed. Thus, if an acquisition was particularly big, or could imply considerable disadvantages from a public interest point of view, *NO* would be able, with his own opinion, to hand over the case to the Government. After having heard the parties, the Government could then prohibit the acquisition, if it would consider that the merger could bring predominant disadvantages of considerable importance from a public interest point of view.

Neither Minister Hadar Cars, who received this proposal, nor his successor Mr Staffan Burenstam Linder had been able to take a stand. I was thus extremely surprised, when the next Minister, Mr Björn Molin, already on his first day in office in May 1981 declared that he absolutely wanted to bring about a reform of the competition legislation, including an order for merger control. However, this had to be done quickly, since there would be elections to Parliament in September 1982.

I was at the time Permanent Secretary and Chief Legal Officer[15] in the Ministry and had just informed Mr Molin that I very likely would leave the Ministry at the end of the year to take up a post at the EFTA in Geneva. He told me that I would not be allowed to leave the Ministry before I had prepared the Government's bill to Parliament on the new competition legislation. At the same time, he underlined that as a political scientist he could not accept the proposal of the Competition Committee, according to which the Government would have in its hand the whole decision on the acquisition control. 'I don't trust politicians', was his explanation.

I replied that it was hardly possible in such a short time both to manage the necessary amendments in the Committee's proposal and in an appropriate way to prepare and process the necessary referrals. So far, the Committee proposals had in wide circles been met with great interest but also a lot of criticism. One would thus have to expect that the same would apply to any principal modification. His reply was: 'Do what you want, but I want to have a proposal for a bill by Christmas! If necessary, you may avail yourself of unconventional methods for preparing the bill.'

This being said, we immediately initiated the work on preparing the draft bill in a working group in the Ministry. Instead of following the traditional method of preparing

[12] Lagen (1953:603) om motverkande i vissa fall av konkurrensbegränsning inom näringslivet.
[13] Permanent Secretary and Chief Legal Officer (Expeditionschef/rättschef) in the Ministry.
[14] SOU 1978:9 Ny Konkurrensbegränsningslag.
[15] Expeditionschef/rättschef.

a draft to be subject to referral for opinions from all interested parties, I suggested that three external experts should be fully initiated in our work. They should in the strictest confidence be kept informed of all working material and all proposals for texts for the bill. In return, the three were asked continuously during the process to share their views and opinions with our working group. Each of the three prospective experts accepted without discussion these conditions. The experts were Lars Jonson, President of the Market Court, Torsten Löwbeer, *NO*, and the law professor Ulf Bernitz.

During the following six months, the Committee proposal was fundamentally reworked, substantively, as well as editorially. In the first place, the merger control procedure was fundamentally changed in the sense that the main responsibility was given to the Market Court. It was furthermore laid down that the whole assessment should be made on the basis of competition law criteria. A system for control of an acquisition of dominance ought to be based on the notion of *harmful effects*, which thus ought to be the basis for a public intervention against the acquisition itself.[16] A decision by the Market Court to prohibit an acquisition or to enjoin an injunction should require a confirmation by the Government. If, however, the latter would not agree with the assessment of the Court, the prohibition would not be approved but would simply become invalid.

Thanks to the excellent cooperation with the three experts, and not the least with Ulf, the draft Bill on a New Competition Act was finished in time on 21 December 1981[17] and I could leave for EFTA and Geneva.

V. EUROPEAN INTEGRATION – EFTA – EC

A. European Economic Space (EES) (later EEA)

At the accession of UK and Denmark to the European Communities (EC) on 1 January 1973, each of the six remaining EFTA countries (Austria, Finland, Iceland, Portugal, Sweden and Switzerland) concluded two Free Trade Agreements (FTAs) with the European Economic Community (EEC) and the European Coal and Steel Community (ECSC), respectively. Hereby, already in 1977, a free trade area was created between the contracting parties.[18]

For a long time, there was uncertainty as to whether a provision in the FTAs might be directly invoked and given effect before national courts. During 1982, however, the European Court of Justice (ECJ) created full clarity on this. In two landmark preliminary rulings, *Kupferberg*[19] and *Polydor*,[20] the Court declared that these FTAs were part of EC law and that provisions therein could have direct effect, if their wording is sufficiently clear and precise.

[16] Cf Prop. 1981/82 :165 p.96

[17] Referral to the Council of Legislation (Lagrådet) 22 December 1981 of proposal for Act of Competition.

[18] For steel and paper, the last tariffs were abandoned at the end of 1983.

[19] Case 104/81 *Hauptzollamt Mainz v C.A. Kupferberg & Cie KGa.A*, judgment 26 October 1982, EU: C: 1982:62.

[20] Case 270/80 *Polydor Ltd and RSO Records v Harlequin Record Shops Ltd and Simons Records Ltd*, judgment 9 February 1982, EU:C:1982:43.

Although the lawyers very soon would realise the importance of this, the EFTA's seasoned trade experts were of the view that in relation to the EC one should rely on the provisions of the General Agreement on Tariffs and Trade (GATT) rather than on those of the FTAs. In the autumn of 1982, however, France introduced a number of protectionist measures.[21] The EFTA states could now, differently from any other Member of GATT, successfully claim that the French measures were in contradiction with the provisions of the FTAs. This experience was essential, when the first Ministerial Meeting between EFTA and EC, held in Luxembourg on 9 April 1984, decided through widened and deepened cooperation together to create a *dynamic EES*.[22] The idea of holding such a first meeting at ministerial level, inter alia, to celebrate the ten years successful implementation of the EC-EFTA FTAs, had in the autumn of 1983 been advocated by Germany and Norway, who then were holding the presidencies of the EC and EFTA, respectively, but was rejected by France. However, the situation changed in January 1984, when these posts were passed on to France and Sweden, respectively. In the ministerial declaration from the Luxemburg meeting, a great number of new areas of cooperation was mentioned. The Secretary-General of EFTA, Per Kleppe,[23] had during the preparations of the meeting insisted that this cooperation should have a name in order for it not to become just one in a series of declarations. This idea immediately pleased the French, and so the term *Espace économique européenne*, *EEE* (European Economic Space, EES) was born.

B. Fundamental Legal Issues of European Law

All these important developments obviously required further discussion among experts and academics. One of the first such occasions was when from 2–4 May 1984 the Finnish Association of European Law[24] organised what was later shown to be a very important seminar at Hanaholmen in Helsinki. There essential issues of European law could be discussed among legal experts and academics from Sweden,[25] Finland[26] and Denmark[27] as well as from the ECJ (the Danish Judge Ole Due) and the EC Commission (the Legal Advisor John Temple Lang and J-F Verstrynge, Member of the Cabinet of the Competition Commissioner). I represented the EFTA Secretariat.[28]

[21] These so-called *French measures* included customs clearance for all electronic goods in Poitiers and the requirement that all imported goods should have labelling and manuals in the French language.

[22] Bull. EC 4-1984, pp 9–14 and Twenty-fourth Annual Report of the European Free Trade Association, Geneva March 1985, pp 53–55.

[23] Austria and Switzerland preferred a bilateral approach and disliked being grouped together with the other EFTA countries. When they thus objected to Mr Kleppe representing EFTA, the Swedish Minister, Mr Mats Hellström, who held the EFTA Presidency, invited the Secretary-General to join the meeting within the Swedish delegation.

[24] Chairman Professor Zacharias Sundström.

[25] Ulf Bernitz, Pernilla Lindh, Hans Stenberg and Jacob Sundberg.

[26] Kari Juotsamo, Kirsti Rissanen and Lena Sund.

[27] Jens Fejö, Klaus Gulman, Ole Lando and Hjalte Rasmussen.

[28] The papers presented at the seminar are published in Zacharias Sundström m.fl.(eds), *EEC Law and Nordic Commercial relations with the Communities*, Publications of the Finnish Association for European Law A n:o 1, (Helsinki, 1985), hereinafter referred to as 'the Seminar Report'.

One of the most active participants was Ulf Bernitz, who in concluding his speech[29] inter alia called *Kupferberg* 'a kind of Christmas present from the European Court to the EFTA countries'.[30] In this context, he declared:

> The *Kupferberg* doctrine, which partially gives the FTAs direct effect within the Community, adds new dimensions to these agreements. They have become much more important from a legal point of view. They now form the basis for legal arguments and interpretation, and cases for judicial decision. The *Kupferberg* case will probably start a legal development concerning the FTAs which we have awaited for many years.[31]

Neither Ulf, nor any other participant, could then have foreseen how right he was in his predictions! Less than 10 years later, the EEA (European Economic Area) Agreement entered into force!

Another subject discussed at Hanaholmen was the interest in negotiating with the EC *a parallel agreement to the 1968 Brussels Convention* on the recognition and execution of judgments in civil cases. I had in the autumn of 1983 informally been asked by a contact in the EC Commission, how the other EFTA countries – following a Swiss request to the Commission – might react to the idea of negotiating such an agreement. Brussels had no interest in entering such an exercise with only the Swiss but might in a wider context. The view in the EFTA Secretariat was that any new form of cooperation with the EC should be welcomed. When I thus sounded out the Nordic capitals, the reply was first positive from Stockholm. The reaction was the same in Oslo, Helsinki and Reykjavik. Vienna had through its Ministry of Justice negotiated a series of bilateral agreements, but there were no objections to other EFTA countries going ahead. However, it became obvious after a while that Swedish industry was very negative.

When this issue was brought up and discussed at the Helsinki seminar, Hans Stenberg, from the Swedish Institute for Foreign Law, declared that Swedish industry preferred arbitration and lacked any interest in a parallel agreement to the Brussels Convention.[32] This was the view held by Professor Lars Hjerner, who had very strong interests in arbitration.

The discussions that followed at Hanaholmen became particularly intense in the sauna. While the female participants were in the neighbouring swimming pool, Ulf declared that it would be extremely strange, if the strongly EC-friendly Swedish industry would be opposed to an EC proposal for cooperation in a new field. This was widely supported in the sauna. Swedish industry also later changed its position.

In the beginning of 1985, the work then started on what in 1988 became the Lugano Convention,[33] concluded by the six EFTA countries and the 12 EC Member

[29] Bernitz, 'Effects of the EEC Free Trade Agreements from the viewpoint of the EFTA-countries', in *Seminar Report*, 317 et seq.

[30] See *Seminar Report*, 332 et seq.

[31] A very critical view was expressed by HJ Rasmussen in a paper 'On the interpretation and direct effects of Community agreements with third countries, especially with the Nordic countries: A case study of incremental judicial lawmaking' in *Seminar Report*, 332 et seq.

[32] H Stenberg, 'EEC enforcement of judgements and the EFTA countries' in *Seminar Report*, 50 et seq.

[33] Convention on Jurisdiction and the Enforcement of Judgments in Civil and Commercial Matters done at Lugano on 16 September 1988.

States.[34] This Convention and especially its Protocol 2 on uniform interpretation of the Convention showed to be particularly important for the institutional solutions finally saving the EEA Agreement.[35]

In view of the perspectives that now were opened for further development of the EC-EFTA relations, it was natural that this first seminar would be followed by many more, in Sweden as well as in many other places in Europe, where not the least Ulf was an extremely active participant.

C. Judicial Protectionism

In an editorial in the *EFTA Bulletin* 4/85, the editor declared that it was not customary for the *Bulletin* to treat legal issues in such detail but here this was necessary. Then followed two articles under the heading 'Judicial protectionism'. One was written by the Swiss law professor Olivier Jacot-Guillarmod and the other by Ulf Bernitz. Both authors agreed that after *Polydor* and *Kupferberg* it was necessary for the EFTA side to take measures in order that *precise and unconditional* provisions of the FTAs could be given direct effect and be applied as national law in national courts.[36]

Kupferberg and *Polydor*, thus, provoked within the EFTA the principal question of the difference between *monists* and *dualists* regarding the traditions of States to treat in their national legal order international agreements that they have entered into. The Nordic EFTA countries Sweden, Finland, Norway and Iceland were all following a dualistic tradition, while Switzerland and Austria were monists.

Since the Delors Commission, in spring 1985, presented its famous *White Paper on the Completion of the Internal Market*,[37] the EFTA side very soon realised that there would be a need for considerably deeper and more profound obligations, if a serious exclusion from and discrimination in the EC Internal Market should be avoided. To this came the decision at a ministerial EC-EFTA Meeting in Reykjavik in June 1986 to qualify the EES as both *dynamic* and *homogeneous*. In order also to prevent the creation of new obstacles through the EC progress in its completion of the Internal Market it was also agreed that the cooperation should progress *in parallel* to developments in the Community.

In order really to be able to discuss all these challenges, it was first required that the EFTA side legally brought their own house in order. This required a forum for in-depth discussions among lawyers of the fundamental legal issues. After strong initial resistance, in spring 1987, the EFTA Ministerial Council finally agreed to create a special Group of Legal Experts (GLE)[38] to study inter alia relevant differences in

[34] The Convention was also referred to as the Parallel Convention, as it in all essentials was identical to the Brussels Convention.

[35] The particularly strong emphasis by the Contracting Parties laid down in this Protocol towards achieving a uniform interpretation of the two Conventions was later reused in the EEA Agreement. More about this in connection with note 49 below.

[36] Since each one was writing from his national perspective the method to reach this goal differed.

[37] European Commission, White Paper on the Completion of the Internal Market, Luxemburg Office for Official Publications of the European Commission 1985, ISBN 92-825-5436-8.

[38] The Head of the Swedish delegation, Mr Jörgen Holgersson, Permanent Secretary and Chief Legal Officer in the Trade Department of the Ministry of Foreign Affairs, was elected Chairman.

the application and interpretation of the FTAs and other Agreements in the EFTA countries and the EC.

At the end of October 1986, Ulf Bernitz wrote in a letter to me that he had a very clever student by name of Nils Wahl, who during two years had been his assistant at the university and who by far was the best one he had had for many years. He had top marks in all subjects and was excellent. Nils was very interested in practising as a trainee at the EFTA. 'In short Nils is a person that it really would be worthwhile for you to invest in and who certainly would prove very useful to you.' Thus, Ulf contributed to Nils joining EFTA, where he as a trainee prepared the fundamental document that during the two following years would serve as the essential basis for the work of GLE.[39] Therein, the differences between monistic and dualistic application of international agreements were extensively and thoroughly presented, for the situation in the EC and in the individual EFTA countries, as well as all relevant case law.[40] The paper even contained a reference to a quote of the Dutch academic Henry. G. Schermers, who regarding the differences between monists and dualists had stated that there was actually no difference, they had the same obligations, only it was much easier to cheat if you were a dualist.

In parallel to the GLE and other technical expert groups working on the realisation of the gradually more and more defined EES, there were a great number of legal seminars held at a national level as well as internationally. In such fora, these big and fundamental issues could be thoroughly discussed among civil servants and practitioners from Government offices, agencies, trade and industry and not the least the academic world.

Of particular importance for the Swedish work were the seminars on EC-EFTA Legal Issues, which from 1985 onwards were organised annually by the Director General of the Board of Commerce, Gunnar Söder. These meetings became decisive for influencing public opinion and gave support for a braver and more progressive European policy. It deserves to be mentioned that we were now treading on, to some extent, mined land.[41] One of the most active participants was not very surprisingly Ulf, who always stimulated the debate with wise interventions and constructive ideas.

There was, however, a difference between ventilating these issues at seminars at home, where everyone more or less knew each other, and to do it at any of the larger European events, where also participants from European universities and various EC institutions played a prominent role. This implied that the thoughts and ideas that the experts were working on could be tested and discussed before any final or locked negotiation positions had been taken.

[39] The paper EFTA/GLE 1/87 had the rather innocent title Differences in the Application and Interpretation of the Free Trade Agreements between the EC and the EFTA countries.

[40] Published by Nils Wahl in a slightly edited version under the heading *The Free Trade Agreements between the EC and EFTA Countries – Their Implementation and Interpretation, A Case Study*, Publications by the Institute for Intellectual Property and Market Law at the Stockholm University, No 44 (Stockholm, 1988).

[41] Since Prime Minister Olof Palme's firm 'no' to a Swedish Membership of the EC in 1971, which was said to be due to the Swedish policy of neutrality, any discussions on closer relations with the Community were unthinkable.

In the summer of 1988 the College of Europe in Bruges organised a big seminar under the headline 'EC and EFTA – More than just good friends?' ('CEE-AELE – Marriage en vue?') Among the participants were several Ministers, EC Commissioners, senior industrialists and senior public officials and practitioners. The academic world was very well represented, inter alia, by Ulf's doctoral student Nils Wahl.

A major seminar was held at the University of Neuchâtel in October 1988.[42] Among the participants were several of the members of the GLE,[43] the Director General of the EC Commission Legal Service Dewost, the Judge and later president of ECJ Rodriguez Iglesias and of course Ulf, whose intervention provoked the impulsive Swiss State Secretary and Chief negotiator Blankart to state:

> If I've correctly understood, it has just been said that in Sweden, the FTA and the Stockholm Convention on EFTA were considered as some sort of 'semi-political soft law'. That leaves me perplexed and gives at the same time the key, I guess, to the marked flexibility of Sweden at the negotiating table.[44]

In his annual statement to the European Parliament in January 1989, the Commission President Jacques Delors raised the question whether the EFTA countries were, as they often claimed, ready together with the EC to create an EES in a new form of institutionally structured association with common organs for decision-making and administration. Thanks to the GLE work above all on direct applicability and direct effect, the EFTA countries could deliver an unequivocally positive answer to the principal issue in Delors' question.[45]

In October 1989, the Irish politician Mary Robinson arranged a seminar in Dublin, 'Creating a European Economic Space: Legal Aspects of EC-EFTA Relations'. Among the around 150 participants were a great number of the negotiators from the EFTA countries, the President of the ECJ Judge Ole Due and a great number of academic European law experts. This was also the first occasion when many EC Member States realised how advanced the work on the EES was. Mary Robinson had invited the embassies of all other EC Member States in Dublin to participate.

In his presentation in Dublin, Ulf Bernitz in particular raised the issue of how far 'the acquis communautaire' regarding the ECJ case law should be taken over in an EES agreement. Referring to *Polydor*, Ulf especially underlined the significance of the wording on 'the scope and purposes of the EES in the preamble' and in the introductory articles of an EES agreement.[46] How right Ulf was became obvious two years

[42] O Jacot-Gillarmod (ed), *L'avenir du libre-échange en Europe: vers un Espace économique européen?* (Zurich, Schultess, 1990).

[43] From Sweden, the Chief Legal officer in the Foreign Trade Department of the Foreign Ministry, later Judge at the EU Court, Ms Pernilla Lindh.

[44] The above-mentioned report para 950.

[45] See declarations from a) Meeting of EFTA Heads of Government in Oslo 14 and 15 March 1989 and b) Informal Ministerial Meeting between the European Community and its Member States and the Member States of EFTA in Brussels 20 March 1989 and c) Ministerial Meeting of the EFTA Council in Kristiansand 13 and 14 June 1989, all in Twenty-ninth Annual Report of the European Free Trade Association, Geneva May 1990.

[46] Mary Robinson and J Findlater (eds), *Creating a European Economic Space: Legal Aspects of EC-EFTA relations*, Papers from the Dublin Conference October 1989, The Irish Centre for European Law Ltd (Trinity College, Dublin 2, 1990) 220.

later, when after the Opinion 1/91 of the ECJ,[47] the EEA Agreement[48] had to be renegotiated before it could be approved by the Court.[49] Thanks to this Agreement, which entered into force on 1 January 1994,[50] it also became possible for Austria, Finland and Sweden to become Members of the EU already a year later on 1 January 1995.

VI. EU: THE MODERNISATION REFORM REGARDING THE APPLICATION OF ARTICLES 85 AND 86

In November 1995, I joined the EU Commission and what was then still DG (Directorate-General) IV, later renamed DG Competition (DG COMP). I was in charge of an antitrust Directorate for all consumer and capital goods with around 30 case handlers and more than 600 ongoing cases. Over 30 years, the notification system under Regulation 17 from 1962 regarding the application of the fundamental antitrust rules, Articles 85 and 86 EC, had created immense problems as to case handling and efficiency.[51] This was most shocking, especially as it was nothing that one ever talked about outside DG IV.

In January 1996, however, an informal working group under the Deputy Director-General Gianfranco Rocca was set up internally in DG IV, where each of the four antitrust directors participated. The work was carried out under the strictest secrecy and was generally referred to as 'Modernisation'. It was decided to apply a '*tabula rasa*' approach and to examine, from the outset, the best way to imagine a new and more efficient order for enforcing the antitrust rules of the Treaty, one that was better adapted to the twenty-first century and to a reality of 25 or more EU Member States.

After little more than a year's work, one of the conclusions of the group was that a prominent part of a future system would be to employ all those resources which existed within national competition authorities, as well as include a decentralised application of Articles 85 and 86 of the EU Treaty. This approach was approved by Karel Van Miert, the Competition Commissioner.

Since the early days of the EC one of the most prominent fora for serious discussions on essential matters of European law has been FIDE (International Federation for European Law). In June 1998 the XVIIth FIDE Congress was convened in Stockholm. Ulf Bernitz had in 1976 taken the initiative of creating the Swedish Association for

[47] Opinion 1/91 ECR [1991] I-6079.

[48] When the formal negotiations were initiated in June 1990, it was decided to accept a proposal from the British PM, Mrs Thatcher, to use the word Area instead of Space, which was more down to earth.

[49] Opinion 1/92 ECR [1992] I-2821. During the renegotiations the wording on homogeneity had been considerably elaborated and strengthened inspired by the language used in Protocol 2 to the Lugano Convention. In the Preamble, for example, a new fifteenth paragraph was added: 'Whereas, in full deference to the independence of the courts, the objective of the Contracting Parties is to arrive at and maintain, a uniform interpretation and application of this Agreement and those provisions of Community legislation which are substantially reproduced in this Agreement and to arrive at an equal treatment of individuals and economic operators as regards the four freedoms and the conditions for competition.'

[50] This one-year delay was caused by a negative referendum in Switzerland on 6 December 1992.

[51] These problems are described in more detail in my article Sven Norberg, 'Making a Virtue of Necessity and at the same time Strengthening European Competition Law Enforcement – How the White Paper on Modernisation came about' (2007) (4) *ERT* 803 et seq.

European Law and he was now also President of FIDE and of the Congress. For each Congress the tradition is to have three main themes for discussion.

Ulf had very strongly advocated and succeeded in making 'National Application of Community Competition Law' one of the main themes of the Congress. My colleague in DG IV, Dr John Temple Lang, was General Rapporteur for this subject that was profoundly discussed during two full days. John also happened to be one of the leading profiles in our Modernisation Group. The discussions at the Congress on the basis of his General Report including 16 national reports, the Swedish one written by Nils Wahl, became very intensive.[52]

The FIDE discussions in Stockholm provided a major contribution to the Commission White Paper on the Modernisation of the Rules of application of Articles 85 and 86, that was adopted a year later on 28 April 1999.[53] The publication of this White Paper was generally perceived as a bolt from a clear sky. Not the least was this the case in Stockholm, where I had been invited by Ulf the same day to present 'recent developments in antitrust' to a larger audience. No one in the audience in Aula Magna had ever expected that the Commission, through such a fundamental reform, would give up its monopoly but also propose a far-reaching decentralisation to the national level of the application of the central competition rules of the EU Treaty. This materialised five years later, when Council Regulation (EC) 1/2003[54] on the implementation of the rules on competition laid down in Articles 81 and 82 of the Treaty entered into force on 1 May 2004, at the same time as the big enlargement of the EU with 10 new Member States from Central and Eastern Europe.

VII. CONCLUSIONS

So far, I have tried, from my perspective as a civil servant during more than 30 years in the Swedish Ministry of Commerce and Trade, the EFTA Secretariat and the EU Commission, to give examples of how the tireless and always optimistic Ulf with great enthusiasm constantly engaged himself in decisive discussions of essential issues in the fields of competition and market law as well as any aspects of European law. His innumerable contributions have been generous as wise and ingenious. Thereby Ulf in a unique way has played an extraordinarily essential role both in Swedish legislative work and in the formation of Swedish European policy.

In addition to this come his enormous contributions as a most inspiring teacher, academic author and visionary tutor for generations of law students. Numerous are the occasions, inside or outside Sweden, when I have met young lawyers, who have proudly told me that they have had Ulf as their professor. I have then been even prouder to be able to reply, that I in any case was the first student that was tutored by Ulf! Ulf Bernitz the tireless visionary!!

[52] See further my article mentioned in note 51, 815–16.

[53] OJEU (C132) 12.5.1999, p 1. When the Amsterdam Treaty entered in force on 1 May 1999 these Articles were renumbered 81 and 82. Today they are 101 and 102 of the TFEU.

[54] OJEU (L1), 4.1.2003, p 1.

2

The Joy of EU Law Scholarship

A Few Words on Ulf's Pragmatic Approach, Passionate Research Interest and Practical Importance

JOAKIM NERGELIUS

THIS VOLUME IN MEMORY of Ulf Bernitz is not only to honour his immense academic work and cherish his legacy, but also to better understand how he was able, for six decades, to produce such a huge amount of books, articles and speeches – as well as numerous teaching and supervisory assignments – that he did, with such outstanding quality. A part of the answer, in my view, is not only his outstanding intellectual qualities, but also his attitude to the academic profession, research and teaching alike. Ulf saw EU law research not merely as a duty or a job and not even as a call or mission, but basically as something fun. A stimulating and interesting activity, quite simply. It is in fact very likely that this fruitful attitude helped to preserve his unusual intellectual vitality and youth, up to a very high age.

Thinking about personal recollections of Ulf, another factor that occurs is his very pragmatic, realistic attitude to various legal issues. I remember in particular the FIDE conference in London in early November 2002, when the first proposal for a new EU constitution had just been presented. Numerous scholars and other attendants were busy discussing different articles and analysing their importance in detail. The issue even became, without previous planning, a conference point all of its own, with panels and spontaneous seminars. Ulf was like myself sceptical and found it premature to pay so much attention to a proposal that was very likely to be changed or even annulled which, as we know, is exactly what happened.

Another similar issue has to do with sources of law, not only from a theoretical perspective. Before and when Sweden joined the EU, quite a few scholars predicted that the Nordic and Swedish judicial tradition of paying much attention to so-called *travaux préparatoires* was going to disappear, since it seemed incompatible with EU law. Ulf, though no supporter of the method of interpreting laws through their preparatory works, was among those who were not convinced, believing that the

European Court of Justice (ECJ) could find a way to respect the Swedish tradition and reconcile it with existing EU law, rather than simply quashing it.[1] Once again he was proven right in a few years,[2] which is worth remembering since he and other Swedish EU law scholars have recently been quite unfairly accused of being 'fanatical' in their support for continued Europeanisation of Swedish law.[3]

From a personal point of view, I found myself on the same, sometimes quite lonely side as Ulf in two somewhat controversial Swedish constitutional and political issues at the turn of the century, concerning the closure of the nuclear reactor Barsebäck[4] and Sweden's non-membership of the euro. In these and other issues, I appreciated his totally independent views extremely much and he was, most of the time, proven to be right in the long run, as now shown for example by the lively discussion on construction of new nuclear reactors. Here, it is also worth noticing that the highly doubtful refusal of the Supreme Administrative Court to ask for a preliminary ruling from the Court of Justice, thus ignoring the so-called CILFIT criteria[5] was, from all practical and principled points of view, disqualified by the ECJ through the famous *Köbler* judgment only a few years later.[6]

Concerning the Economic and Monetary Union (EMU) or euro issue, which has recently been more discussed than ever since the unfortunate referendum in 2003, it is clear that the rules on the economic and monetary union existed in the then EC Treaty when Sweden joined the EU in 1995. Sweden, like other new Member States, adhered to and accepted all existing EU rules (*l'acquis communautaire*) at the time of joining the union, that is, 1 January 1995 (furthermore with few notable exceptions and in the same way as Austria and Finland, who joined simultaneously). It is thus clear that Sweden violates EU law by not participating in the EMU, though the purely legal position of Sweden was somewhat improved through the enactment in 2009 of Article 139 TFEU, according to which Sweden is now formally to be considered as having an exception from the euro. The violation in question has gone on since 1997, when the decision was made not to take part in the so-called third phase of EMU, despite the facts that Sweden met the so-called convergence criteria and did not, like Denmark and previously the UK, enjoy a legally binding exception (which has also not been applied for after the disastrous referendum in 2003). Ulf saw these problems earlier and clearer than any other Swedish or international scholar.[7] The question

[1] See Ulf Bernitz, *Sverige och Europarätten* (Stockholm, Norstedts juridik, 2002) 29. Incidentally, the same position was taken by another of my favourites within Swedish legal science, the late Professor of Jurisprudence in Lund, Aleksander Peczenik. For an overview of the Swedish debate on this important topic at the time of Sweden joining the EU, see Peczenik, *Vad är rätt? Om demokrati, rättssäkerhet, etik och juridisk argumentation* (Stockholm, Norstedts juridik, 1995) 249.

[2] See C-478/99 *Commission v Sweden*, EU:C:2002:281 and C-371/02 *Björnekulla Fruktindustrier* EU:C:2004:275.

[3] See Mikael Mellkvist, 'De fanatiska protokollförarna – En kritisk essä rörande den s.k. "europeiseringen"' (2023) *Svensk Juristtidning* 199.

[4] RÅ 1999 ref. 76.

[5] After the even more well-known *CILFIT* case, 283/81, EU:C:1982:335.

[6] C-224/01 *Gerhard Köbler v Republik Österreich*, EU:C:2003:513.

[7] In chapter 9 of *Sverige och Europarätten* (n 1) the issue is dealt with in a very clearsighted way, in an article published before the ill-fated referendum had even been announced. In particular, he criticised the idea that Sweden after 1995 could decide itself whether to join or not, independent of existing rules.

now is of course how long the current legally, economically and politically unsatisfactory situation may last.

These examples are hopefully enough to show how clearsighted Ulf was and the huge importance that he had not only for Swedish law research, where he has rightly been described as the last great encyclopaedist of law, a rare specialist and expert in many different fields, but also for the public Swedish debate, where he will be greatly missed. For instance, when this contribution was written in 2024, I would very much have liked to hear his views on the rule of law crisis, with the then forthcoming European Parliament elections and the framing of a new Commission.

Finally, however, I would like to return to the research arena. Ulf was indeed a legal polyhistor, an expert not only in EU law but in intellectual property law, competition law, contract and private law, consumer law, constitutional law and many other fields. It is likely that he was in fact the last of his kind. The few memories recalled above do perhaps not reveal this, since they do mainly concern the constitutional area. However, they show that he also had a theoretical interest[8] and that he was not only wise but had a real passion for scholarly and societal matters alike. Few Swedish legal scholars have been equally important.

[8] Here it is natural to refer both to his excellent book *Sverige och Europarätten* from 2002 (n 1) and to the three anthologies on General Principles that were edited from 2000–13 with myself and Xavier Groussot as main co-editors: Ulf Bernitz and Joakim Nergelius (reds), *General Principles of European Community Law* (Alphen aan den Rijn, Kluwer, 2000; Ulf Bernitz, Joakim Nergelius, Xavier Groussot and Cecilia Carner (reds), *General Principles of EC Law in a Process of Development* (Alphen aan den Rijn, Kluwer, 2008); Ulf Bernitz, Xavier Groussot and Felix Schulyok (reds), *General Principles of EU Law and European Private Law* (Alphen aan den Rijn, Kluwer, 2013).

3

Ulf Bernitz, the EU and Nordic Thinking on Contractual Fairness

THOMAS WILHELMSSON

I. INTRODUCTION: ULF BERNITZ AND STANDARD FORM CONTRACTING

In the Nordic countries, the particular challenges related to standard form contracting for a long time attracted little attention.[1] Therefore, the contribution of Ulf Bernitz to bringing this issue on the Nordic legal agenda was pioneering. His two long papers in *Svensk Juristtidning* 1972–1974[2] and, based on them, the first Nordic book on the law of standard form contracts in 1974 became Nordic trendsetters. Not surprisingly, his book has been published already in nine editions,[3] growing in size. By the book, he set an example to be followed by other Nordic scholars.[4]

From the point of view of a Nordic private law scholar, standard form contracting is a self-evident issue in a volume honouring Ulf Bernitz. Not only was he a pioneer in this area, he also contributed to the understanding that the regulation of standard form contracts and of contract law more generally was closely connected with emerging principles of justice in the EU.[5]

The main theme of this volume in memory of Ulf Bernitz is the EU as a transformative legal and economic order, with a focus on its constitutional impact. Contract law is an important part of what one can call the 'economic constitution' of a society. The understanding of contract is deeply embedded in the national legal culture. It is, therefore, an area in which EU law has been clashing with national and Nordic traditions. One of the most important issues in these clashes is the relationship between

[1] A much-cited paper by Curt Olsson at the Nordic lawyers' meeting 1957 was an exception, see Curt Olsson, 'Verkan av avtalsklausuler i standardformulär' in *Förhandlingarna å det tjugoförsta Nordiska Juristmötet I Helsingfors den 22–24 augusti 1957*, Bilaga VI (1959).

[2] Ulf Bernitz, 'Utvecklingen mot en standardavtalsrätt I–II' (1972) 57 *Svensk Juristtidning* 401; (1974) 59 *Svensk Juristtidning* 81.

[3] Ulf Bernitz, *Standardavtalsrätt* 9th edn (Stockholm, Norstedts juridik, 2018).

[4] Including myself: *Standardavtal och oskäliga avtalsvillkor* 3rd edn (Helsingfors, Talentum, 2008).

[5] On his early interest in European principles of justice, see eg Ulf Bernitz and Pär Hallström (eds), *Principles of Justice and the European Union* (Stockholm, Juristförlaget, 1995).

the principle of *pacta sunt servanda* and the aspiration to fight unfair contract terms and unfair contractual outcomes. This issue offers an interesting perspective on the transformative role of EU law in front of a Nordic 'tradition' – and on the optimistic positions taken by Ulf Bernitz in this process.

I will in the following explore the Bernitzian approach to how EU rules on contractual unfairness can and should interact with the Nordic tradition.

II. THE UNFAIR CONTRACT TERMS DIRECTIVE AND NORDIC LAW

As one of the key issues in contract law is how to deal with unfair contract terms, the Unfair Contract Terms Directive (UCTD)[6] is perhaps the most important piece of EU legislation in the area of contract law.

The Directive is built around a general clause in Article 3(1), according to which a term 'shall be regarded as unfair if, contrary to the requirement of good faith, it causes a significant imbalance in the parties' rights and obligations arising under the contract, to the detriment of the consumer'. This has made 'good faith' a joint basic concept of European contract law. This good faith requirement is applicable both in individual disputes, in which an unfair term shall not be binding on the consumer, and in preventive, collective proceedings to prevent the continued use of unfair terms. In this chapter, I will mainly discuss the impact of the UCTD on the contract law assessment of individual disputes and leave the more public law geared application of the collective instruments aside.

There are, however, limitations to the reach of this joint concept. First, as the name and the aim of the Directive show, it is applicable to consumer law only. It reflects a French approach that tends to see rules like those in the Directive as instruments for protecting the weaker contract party. This limitation is also natural, as the EU may not have competence to issue European rules affecting the core of general contract law.

Second, the Directive focuses on standard form contracting. The good faith requirement covers only terms which have not been individually negotiated. In line with this approach there is a further limitation in Article 4(2) according to which the unfairness assessment shall relate 'neither to the definition of the main subject matter of the contract nor to the adequacy of the price and remuneration'. These limitations reflect a German approach[7] to the issue, worrying primarily about the lack of sufficient contractual will to create a binding effect, when standard forms are used.

The Nordic approach is broader. Even though both consumers and standard terms are important legal concepts, they have not been used to delimit the application of the fairness principle. In contemporary discourse on unfair contract terms, the Nordic countries are usually mentioned as the most adjustment-friendly legal orders. To the

[6] Council Directive 93/13/EEC on unfair terms in consumer contracts [1993] OJ L 95/29.

[7] For the German critique against a more broadly applicable proposal, Hans Erich Brandner and Peter Ulmer, 'The Community Directive on Unfair Terms in Consumer Contracts: Some Critical Remarks on the Proposal Submitted by the EC Commission' (1991) 28 *Common Market Law Review* 647.

Nordic more or less similar Contracts Acts[8] was added a general clause in Section 36, according to which courts can modify or set aside not only unfair standardised terms in consumer contracts, but also terms in business-to-business contracts and individually negotiated terms. Such a generally applicable fairness rule goes further than is the case in other European jurisdictions.

Despite these basic differences, however, the Directive did not directly challenge the Nordic approach. According to Article 8, the Directive is a minimum harmonisation directive, allowing the Member States to adopt or retain more stringent provisions. The Nordics could continue to cherish their general fairness approach, and the changes made in Nordic legislation when the Directive was implemented were minor.

The Commission later returned to the issue and proposed turning the Directive into a harmonising (maximum) directive.[9] If the proposal had been accepted, it would have had deep impact on Nordic contract law. It was no surprise that the proposal was met with opposition from the Nordic countries. As many other Member States were also against the proposal, it did not succeed in changing the nature of the Directive. I will not here comment on possible future amendments – in this or other directions – of the Directive, but discuss it, and Ulf Bernitz's comments on it, in its present form.

III. ENDANGERING THE NORDIC TRADITION?

The UCTD opened up new doors, for example in common law, but it is clearly more limited than the Nordic approach to contractual fairness. Because of the minimum character of the Directive, however, no change in the Nordic tradition was required.

Is that all? Is the different Nordic tradition saved by the minimum harmonisation character? The changes at the surface level are small, but what about legal culture?[10] Ulf Bernitz foresaw the Directive to have a greater impact on national cultures: 'in my opinion the Contract Terms Directive will, in the long term, probably have a greater impact on the development of domestic law in the Member States than was originally anticipated'.[11] One should indeed look more closely at possible legal-cultural long-term effects of the Directive when assessing its impact on national law. Some have expressed fears,[12] but Ulf Bernitz gave a positive vision, reflecting his general pro-EU spirit. He claimed, early on, that 'the Directive and its implementation in Swedish

[8] In Sweden, Lag om avtal och andra rättshandlingar på förmögenhetsrättens område (1915:218); in Norway, Avtaleloven (1918/4); in Denmark, Lov om aftaler og andra retshandler på formuerettens område (re-enacted 1986/600); and in Finland, Laki varallisuusoikeudellisista oikeustoimista/Lag om rättshandlingar på förmögenhetsrättens område (228/1929).

[9] Proposal for a Directive of the European Parliament and of the Council on consumer rights, COM(2008) 614 final.

[10] On surface level law and legal culture, see Kaarlo Tuori, *Critical legal Positivism* (Aldershot, Ashgate, 2002).

[11] Ulf Bernitz, 'Swedish Standard Contracts Law and the EC Directive on Contract Terms' (2000) 39 *Scandinavian Studies in Law* 13, 13.

[12] As Bernitz (n 11) 25 underlines, I have belonged to this camp. So also in the shorter version Ulf Bernitz, 'Swedish Standard Contracts Law and the EEC Directive on Contract Terms' (1997) 2 *European Review of Private Law* 213, 220.

law has in certain respects entailed a consolidation and strengthening of consumer protection in the area of standard contract law'.[13]

I will in the following discuss the elements of Ulf Bernitz's vision. How could he assess the impact of the UCTD to be a development of the traditionally fairness-friendly Nordic tradition? And to what extent was he right in making this assessment, in the view of subsequent developments?

When discussing 'the Nordic tradition' one needs to make some *caveats*. First, the fairness principle is not as deeply embedded in legal tradition as one might expect. The fairness principle was developed during the twentieth century by including adjustment clauses in various Nordic laws on particular types of contract, such as the law on insurance contracts.[14] Of great importance was the fairness clause in section 8 of the Acts on promissory notes.[15] Nordic Supreme Courts used these rules by analogy to proclaim the existence of a general fairness rule.[16] This, however, happened only a few years or decades before the legislative adoption of the general clause in the 1970s and 1980s: Sweden 1976, Finland 1982, Norway 1983 and Denmark 1986.[17] Only after the adoption of the express general clause – that also lowered the threshold for adjustment from 'obviously unfair' to pure 'unfair' – one or two decades before the UCTD, the 'tradition' was clearly established. Second, the 'tradition' is perhaps not as jointly Nordic as one could expect. The wordings of the general clauses in the different Nordic countries are not identical. In detail, there is also not so much learning across the borders as one could expect,[18] even though practice has probably developed in a relatively similar way.[19] 'Nordic tradition', in other words, is perhaps not so homogeneous and strongly rooted that the culture would be immune against impulses from the EU. One has to look more closely at the critical issues in order to assess the possible influence on legal-cultural level.

At least three issues are of particular interest when discussing the relationship between the UCTD and the Nordic tradition. As mentioned above, the scope of application of the fairness clause in Nordic law is broader, covering both business-to-business contracts (as well as contracts between private persons) and individually negotiated terms, including the price and the main subject matter of the contract. In addition to these two issues, the Nordic approach to fairness is different also with regard to its temporal perspective on the issue. The assessment of unfairness in the Nordics focuses on the consequences of the application of a term, whilst the UCTD ties the assessment to the more abstract question whether the term was

[13] Bernitz (n 11) 25.

[14] Nordic Insurance Contracts Acts, s 34.

[15] Nordic Promissory Notes Acts, s 8.

[16] In Finland Supreme Court 1974 II 16.

[17] The general clause was introduced in the Nordic Contract Acts by Act 1976:185 (Sweden), Act 956/82 (Finland), Act 1983/160 (Norway) and Act 1986/600 (Denmark).

[18] For example, in his book on standard form contracts Bernitz (n 3) 162–208 mostly relies on Swedish cases. This is relatively typical for both doctrine and case-law on the general clause. Hilde Hauge, 'Unfair Contract terms in Nordic Contract Law' in Torgny Håstad (ed), *The Nordic Contracts Act: Essays in Celebration of its One Hundredth Anniversary* (Copenhagen, Djøf Publishing, 2015) 157, 170 notes that there are different opinions on the similarity of practice: therefore one cannot give a definitive answer to the question whether practice is similar.

[19] Bernitz (n 3) 163 with sources.

unfair at the time of the conclusion of the contract. Some have even considered this movement of the perspective of the assessment from the time of conclusion of the contract to the time of application to be one of the most important symbolic effects of the Nordic general clause.[20]

The first critical issue, the possibility to adjust unfair business-to-business contracts (and contracts between private persons), does not seem to have led to notable clashes between the UCTD and the Nordic approaches. In practice, the differences are perhaps not as big as theory suggests: also in Nordic practice the courts have been fairly restrictive in using the general clause in business-to-business relations, when the parties are equal.[21] But even here some difference remains: 'where parties are on an equal footing' the general clause can be applied 'in exceptional circumstances'.[22] The Nordic general clause can also be used as an instrument for protecting weaker parties in business relations: Ulf Bernitz has written about small business protection.[23] The UCTD does not seem to have changed the Nordic approach to this issue. The impact may rather have worked in the other direction: the Principles of European Contract Law, drafted by the so-called Lando-Commission, extend the rules on adjustment of unfair standard terms to business-to-business contracts.[24] In the same vein Ulf Bernitz has expressly suggested that the UCTD should 'be used analogously and as source of comparison' in other areas than consumer law when one of the parties is in an inferior position.[25]

Perhaps one cannot in this context really even speak about a clash between the UCTD and the Nordic tradition, as business-to-business contracts are outside the scope of the Directive and, therefore, it does not take any stand on these contracts. A clearer difference of approach lies in the limitation of the good faith requirement of the Directive to terms which have not been individually negotiated and, in particular, the exclusion of terms relating to the definition of the main subject matter of the contract or the adequacy of the price from the fairness assessment. These limitations of the good faith requirement are within the general scope of the Directive, covering consumer contracts, and would therefore require similar limitations in national law, if the Directive were not a minimum directive. The pressure on the domestic tradition is here more obvious.

To some extent, one can find similar lines of reasoning in Nordic law as behind the UCTD. Even though the Nordic general clause applies to individually negotiated contract terms, one can assume that the unilaterally standardised quality of a term is an argument for adjustment[26] that lowers the threshold of finding the term unfair. But there is still a difference, which most clearly is uttered in the speciality of the

[20] Kai Krüger, *Norsk kontraktsrätt* (Bergen, Alma Mater Forlag, 1989) 402.

[21] Bernitz (n 3) 172; Ole Lando et al (eds), *Restatement of Nordic Contract Law* (Copenhagen, Djøf Publishing, 2016) 157.

[22] Lando et al (n 21) 155.

[23] Ulf Bernitz, 'The Small Businessman and § 36 of the Swedish Contracts Act' in Steven D Anderman et al (eds), *Law and the Weaker Party: An Anglo-Swedish Comparative Study*, Vol IV (Abingdon, Oxfordshire, Professional Books, 1989) 169.

[24] PECL 4:110. The Draft Common Frame of Reference (DCFR) II.-9:405 suggests a higher threshold for b-to-b contracts.

[25] Bernitz (n 11) 26.

[26] Se eg the Finnish *travaux préparatoires, Regeringens proposition (Government Bill) 247/1981* 16.

Finnish general clause: in Article 36(3) of the Finnish Contracts Act, it is expressly stated that with regard to adjustment of unfair contract terms 'a provision relating to the amount of consideration shall also be deemed a contract term'. This express clause has at least in Finland prevented negative or limiting effects of the UCTD in this respect. With regard to both consumer and business-to-business contracts, the general clause has been used to adjust the price and other individual terms. Also in the other Nordic countries, it still seems clear that an unfair price can be adjusted with reference to the general clause,[27] and the same of course goes for other individually negotiated terms.

In his assessment of the limitation of scope, Ulf Bernitz choses to emphasise a positive feature. He noted that Swedish legislation had lacked a definition of standard contract, which has made it difficult to draw a clear line between different forms of terms. Therefore, he finds it important that the Directive in Article 3 expressly defines a term to be 'not individually negotiated where it has been drafted in advance and the consumer has therefore not been able to influence the substance of the term'. In addition, the Article contains a rule on burden of proof, according to which the seller or supplier has to prove that a standard term has been individually negotiated, if he claims that to be the case. According to Bernitz, one should now see the definition of the UCTD as 'fundamental' with regard to the characterisation of a contract as a standard contract.[28]

The third basic difference between the Nordic and the EU approach relates to the temporal perspective of the assessment of fairness. Nordic law focuses on the consequences of applying a contract as compared to the Directive-based analysis of the contract terms as such. This Nordic speciality may obviously in some cases be advantageous for the consumers, and in other cases work to their detriment. If the application of a term that as such appears as balanced in a particular case would lead to an unfair result, because of the special situation or of changed circumstances, adjustment would be possible according to Nordic law, but not according to the UCTD. But on the other hand, if an originally unfair term leads to less unfair results because of changed circumstances, the Directive would still make it possible for the consumer to challenge the validity of the term, whilst the Nordic approach would probably not. Ulf Bernitz notes, however, that the Directive in both situations leads to the most consumer-friendly result. In the first case, when Nordic law is more advantageous for the consumer, the minimum character of the Directive allows the Nordic solution, whilst in the second case the solution of the Directive has been secured by a small amendment of Swedish legislation.[29] He does not mention the possibility that the Directive in the long run might change the perspective of the Nordic tradition. But is this ideologically important difference really very significant in practice? Anyway, so far such a change of perspective has hardly happened. As will be discussed below in Section V, case-law on the Nordic general clause has rather been more focused on consequences *in casu* and less interested in classifying terms as unfair as such than the legislator had expected.

[27] Hauge (n 18) 166.
[28] Bernitz (n 11) 16–17.
[29] ibid 23.

As to the most important possible threats to the Nordic tradition, it is still hard to find any signs that they would have materialised. At least one cannot claim, looking at the development, that Ulf Bernitz was wrong in not emphasising them, instead of just cheering a few legal-technical advances, like the definition of standard terms.

IV. OR DEVELOPING THE NORDIC TRADITION?

The key question with regard to the role of the UCTD in either improving or reducing Nordic consumer protection obviously relates to the threshold of application of the general clause. How unreasonable or unbalanced should a contract term be, to be hit by the general clause? Does unfairness according to the UCTD cover less or more cases than the Nordic general clauses?

Obviously, this is not possible to assess with any certainty. Even though the Nordic implementation of the UCTD assumes that the Nordic general clauses are at least as advantageous for the consumer as the Directive, this is hard to confirm in practice. In light of the relatively few substantive issues dealt with by the Nordic courts and the Court of Justice of the European Union (CJEU), one cannot really say whether the Nordic level of protection is higher.[30]

The CJEU has anyway supported a continuing relevance of national law, as it usually has left the concrete assessment of whether a term should be regarded as unfair to the national court. According to the landmark case *Freiburger Kommunalbauten*, the CJEU should not rule on the application of the general unfairness criteria to a particular term, as it 'must be considered in the light of the particular circumstances of the case in question'.[31] This means that the deciding court should in its assessment give consideration also to national law.

If one really makes an effort in showing that the UCTD at least in some cases would indicate a lower degree of protection than Nordic law, one could look at the Annex to the Directive that contains an indicative list of terms that may be regarded as unfair (the implementation of the Annex is discussed in the next section of the chapter). Even though the main bulk of the list was considered to contain examples of unfair terms that were familiar also in Nordic law,[32] one may at least doubt whether 'the principle of symmetry' in some of the cases might be detrimental to the protection of the consumer.[33] A consumer who, for example, cancels the contract and according to its terms loses a considerable amount is not really helped by knowing that he could have used the same remedies in the unlikely case that the business would have done the cancelling. The result-oriented rather than term-oriented Nordic law

[30] Hauge (n 18) 166.

[31] Case C-237/02 *Freiburger Kommunalbauten GmbH Baugesellschaft & Co KG v Ludger Hofstetter and Ulrike Hofstetter* ECLI:EU:C:2004:209, para 22.

[32] See eg Bernitz (n 3) 180.

[33] See Thomas Wilhelmsson, *Social Contract Law and European Integration* (Aldershot, Dartmouth, 1995) 201. Such terms are found in the Annex (d) and (f). For example, according to (d), a term is unfair if it has the object or effect of 'permitting the seller or supplier to retain sums paid by the consumer where the latter decides not to conclude or perform the contract, without providing for the consumer to receive compensation of an equivalent amount from the seller or supplier where the latter is the party cancelling the contract'.

would not necessarily have put so much emphasis on the value of a formal balance of the contract, if the consequences of the application do not seem fair. But this is a detail, and as such it does hardly tell very much about the general threshold for adjustment.

The fear that the UCTD would raise the threshold for adjustment from what it was in the fairness-friendly Nordic countries in the first years after the adoption of the Directive might have been realistic. The fact that the CJEU wisely refrained from making concrete assessments of the unfairness of particular terms, however, did soon show that the fear was exaggerated. Then later turns of the case-law of the CJEU brought European law in an even more advanced consumer-friendly direction, strengthening consumer protection in several ways.

This advanced case-law of the CJEU concerns both the substantive standard, the threshold, for applying the general clause and procedural issues related to its application. As to the substance, some elements of a free-standing European doctrine of unfairness have emerged, and these elements are relatively tough on the businesses. The most important one is the Aziz formula. In the *Mohamed Aziz* case the CJEU, after having endorsed the principle that national courts should make the concrete unfairness assessment, went on to define the standard to be used. When applying the 'good faith' test the court must determine 'whether the seller or supplier, dealing fairly and equitably with the consumer, could reasonably assume that the consumer would have agreed to the term concerned in individual contract negotiations'.[34] If taken seriously this standard, focusing on what the consumer could be expected to accept in individual contract negotiations, discussing the term in question, seems relatively strict, perhaps even going further than traditional Nordic doctrine.

The CJEU has also underlined the intended punitive character of the UCTD. The legal consequence of a term being characterised as unfair is that it loses its binding effect completely. The court should not adjust it to a fair level, but totally disregard it, even if the result becomes unfair against the business. For example, if a penalty clause is considered unfair, the court cannot just reduce the amount of the penalty; it cannot apply it at all.[35] There are several other cases emphasising this punitive effect of the Directive.[36] Such cases may be more favourable for the consumer side than the Nordic practice that accepts adjustment of an unfair term to a fair level.[37] Also Ulf Bernitz in his early assessment of the Directive noted how the Directive in this respect is stricter towards the businesses than Nordic law.[38]

[34] Case C-415/11 *Mohamed Aziz v Caixa d'Estalvis de Catalunya, Tarragona i Manresa (Catalunyacaixa)* ECLI:EU:C: 2013:164, para 76.

[35] Case C-488/11 *Dirk Frederik Asbeek Brusse, Katarina de Man Garabito v Jahani BV* ECLI:EU:C:2013:341.

[36] For example, Case C-618/10 *Banco Español de Crédito, SA v Joaquín Calderón Camino* ECLI:EU:C:2012:349, Case C-377/14 *Ernst Georg Radlinger and Helena Radlingerová v Finway a s* ECLI:EU:C:2016:283, and Joined Cases C-154/15, C-307/15 and C-308/15 *Fransisco Gutiérrez Naranjo v Cajasur Banco SAU, Ana Maria Palacios Martínez v Banco Bilbao Vizcaya Argentaria SA (BBVA), Banco Popular Español, SA v Emilio Irles López and Teresa Torres Andreu* ECLI:EU:C:2016:980.

[37] For example, Finnish cases on unfair penalty clauses in most cases only adjust the amount of the penalty, see eg Supreme Court KKO 1938 II 104, 1940 I 15, 1946 II 292, 1951 II 149, 1960 II 95, 1985 II 171 and 1985 II 177 (the cases are not consumer cases though).

[38] Bernitz (n 11) 23.

The almost 'radical' approach to developing consumer protection adopted by the CJEU is even more clearly visible in the multitude of cases concerning procedural issues related to the application of the UCTD. The CJEU has here boldly gone into issues of procedural law that in principle are a territory of national law. In order to make the protection offered by the Directive effective, the Court has downplayed requirements of procedural activity imposed on the consumer by national law. Without going into detail, one can describe the main idea expressed in several detailed contexts that a national court should be able to take into account the possible unfairness of contract terms of its own motion.[39] The consumer protection offered by the Directive should not be hollowed out by procedural omissions that the weaker party, the consumer, may make.

The move by the CJEU was bold not only because it went into a terrain in which EU law was relatively alien, but also because the UCTD does not in any express way indicate the opening of such a path. The strong procedural push, indicating a serious aspiration to make the consumer protection rules effective in practice, certainly was a surprise for many. In Nordic law, a similar expansion of the effect of the general clause into core issues of procedural law, in order to improve the position of the weaker party, was hard to imagine before the new case-law from the UCTD. In Finland, for example, the Supreme Court stated that a lower court should not have adjusted the contract (of its own motion), when the consumer had not demanded adjustment or even expressed any views on the fairness of the terms.[40] Only a small step in the protective direction is found in a case in which the Court accepted adjustment, when the weaker party had expressed views on the fairness of the contract, even though the party had not expressly demanded adjustment.[41] Even this small step, however, was strongly criticised by legal doctrine on procedural law.[42] Now, the Finnish Supreme Court in the landmark case KKO 2015:60 has implemented the CJEU practice requiring national courts to assess the unfairness of contractual terms on their own motion.

The optimistic views of Ulf Bernitz about the UCTD as a piece of European legislation that can contribute to the consolidation and strengthening of Nordic consumer protection seems to have got at least some validation by the case-law of the CJEU during the last two decades. Before finally assessing his foresight, we need to look at yet another issue: the implementation of the Annex of the Directive.

V. THE ROLE OF THE ANNEX

In the legal narrative on the relationship between Nordic law and the UCTD the Annex to the Directive has given rise to interesting case-law. The Annex contains an

[39] The extensive CJEU case-law is described and analysed eg in Geraint Howells, Christian Twigg-Flesner and Thomas Wilhelmsson, *Rethinking EU Consumer Law* (London and New York, Routledge, 2018) 154–62 and Anthi Beka, *The Active Role of Courts in Consumer Litigation: Applying EU Law of the National Courts' Own Motion* (Cambridge, Intersentia, 2018).

[40] Supreme Court, KKO 1992:12.

[41] Supreme Court, KKO 1990:148.

[42] Jyrki Virolainen, 'Åberopsbörda och jämkning av avtalsvillkor' (2006) 142 *Tidskrift, utgiven av Juridiska Föreningen i Finland* 187 with further references.

indicative and non-exhaustive list of unfair terms (a so-called grey list) that describes 17 types of clauses. Even though the grey list reflects some continental approaches, its content – as a grey list, allowing exceptions in particular cases – is for most parts familiar for Nordic law, as mentioned above. The content of the list has not been considered problematic, but the method of implementation.

According to the Nordic governments, an enactment of an indicative list of this kind would not be compatible with the prevailing Nordic legislative tradition. Therefore the Annex was only introduced into Nordic law through the *travaux préparatoires* to the legislation that implemented the UCTD. The terms on the indicative list were enumerated in these preparatory documents, which are considered to be an essential part of the legal sources in Nordic law.

The European Commission did not accept this as a sufficient method of implementation. By only including the Annex, with a commentary, in the statement of reasons for the implementing law, Sweden had not fully implemented the UCTD, according to the Commission. The Commission brought an action against Sweden seeking a declaration that it had failed to fulfil its obligations under the Directive.[43] Even though the action was brought against Sweden alone, the joint Nordic nature of the case was obvious: Denmark and Finland intervened in the case in support of Sweden, and the Court referred to the tradition common to the Nordic countries when it discussed the source value of the preparatory work. In this case, as the list of terms in the Annex is only indicative,[44] the Court accepted the Swedish arguments, according to which preparatory work is considered to be an important aid to interpreting legislation in the Nordic countries, and the application of the Commission was dismissed. It seemed that the Nordic tradition had won a clear victory in the Nordic-EU tension.

But in what respect should one really consider this to be a victory? Was it a good solution to downplay the idea of having an express list of unfair terms? Even though the *travaux préparatoires* are considered to be an essential source of law in the Nordic countries, it is probable that the choice of implementation method at least reduced the source value of the Annex in comparison with what it would have been, if the list had been a part of the adopted legal text. This might also mean that the idea of a term-focused application of the general clause gets less support from the Directive in the Nordic countries.

The Nordic approach to adjustment, focusing primarily on the results of the application of the terms of the contract *in casu*, has the advantage that it aims to achieve the best justice in the individual case, but it has disadvantages as well. The focus on the concrete application reduces the opportunities to use the general clause as an instrument for steering contractual practice. The precedential effect of judgments in which the court has used the general clause becomes relatively limited. The steering effects are left to the collective enforcement of the fairness test (which I am not discussing in this chapter).

The drafters of the Nordic general clauses in the Contracts Acts realised this disadvantage and wished to increase the impact of case-law. According to the Finnish

[43] Case C-478/99 *Commission of the European Communities v Kingdom of Sweden* ECLI:EU:C:2002:281.

[44] Cf the judgment on the failure of Denmark to implement the Equal Pay Directive, Case C-143/83 *Commission of the European Communities v Kingdom of Denmark* ECLI:EU:C:1985:34, para 10.

travaux préparatoires, for example, the courts should in their reasoning expressly state whether the term in question was considered to be unfair as such in the actual type of contract.[45] Also in Sweden there was a push for a more term-oriented application of the fairness rule, even though other views were expressed as well.[46] The recommendations aimed at increasing the precedential effect of judgments concerning unfairness of terms. The courts, in other words, were invited to point out typically unfair terms – to add cases to an imagined list of terms that are not acceptable.

The courts, however, have not followed the wishes of the legislator. Case-law in which a term has expressly been considered typically unfair is scarce. In Finland, for example, the Supreme Court has used such wording when condemning relatively obvious cases of unfairness, like contractual limitations of liability for gross negligence.[47] Also Swedish courts have been very reluctant to develop a term-oriented practice.[48] Maybe a more express enactment of the grey list of the UCTD could have inspired the courts more actively to join the work on developing an expanding list of indicatively unfair terms.

Again, the European-minded Ulf Bernitz saw the opportunities rather than the problems connected with the UCTD. He was of the opinion that the Annex should have been implemented by legislation. He feared that the list implemented in this form, not included in the statute, might easily pass unnoticed when contracts are drafted, clients are counselled and decisions are made.[49] In addition, he had legal queries. One might question whether the Swedish Government overstated the legal position of *travaux préparatoires* for the Court.[50] In other words, according to Bernitz, the Swedish Government might have fooled the Court about the source value of preparatory works!

Ulf Bernitz indeed expected that the UCTD and its grey list could lead to a change of culture that he considered to be a welcome advantage. This change of culture would mean a more term-oriented application of the general clause. Here Bernitz interestingly refers to the German concept of *Fallgruppenbildung*.[51]

This German reference is one sign of Bernitz's Europeanised approach to law. As will be discussed in the following, it is still very topical, even though his prophecy on a growing European case-law produced list of unfair terms does not seem to have come true – yet.

VI. CONCLUSION AND VISION: TOWARDS EUROPEAN LEARNING

The discussion concerning the relationship between the UCTD and the Nordic tradition has often underlined the great differences on the level of principle. In practice, however, the Directive has not led to dramatic changes in Nordic law.

[45] *Regeringens proposition (Government Bill) 247/1981* 12.
[46] See Bernitz (n 3) 170.
[47] Supreme Court KKO 1983 II 91.
[48] Bernitz (n 3) 206–08.
[49] Bernitz (n 11) 22.
[50] Bernitz (n 3) 178.
[51] Bernitz (n 11) 25.

The European-minded Ulf Bernitz consequently emphasised both the similarities between the Directive and Nordic law and the steps towards improvement of Nordic law inherent in the Directive. He recommended the use of the Directive analogously to other than consumer contracts, when there is an imbalance of power; he welcomed the new and broad definition of standard form contracts; and he pointed out the details in which the Directive was clearly to the advantage of the consumers, requiring some (small) changes in domestic Nordic law. In general, he saw the Directive as something that consolidated and strengthened Nordic consumer protection.

Looking at the case-law of the CJEU during the last decades, Ulf Bernitz's pro-European stance seems surprisingly foresighted. The Court has been quite radical in developing the procedural safeguards for the effectiveness of the UCTD. In addition, it has created also substantive formulas, such as the *Mohamed Aziz* test,[52] that seem quite consumer-friendly, as to their wording. History may in this way have proven Ulf Bernitz's very positive assessment of the impact of the Directive on the consumer-friendly Nordic tradition to be more well-founded than many expected.

In his assessment of the Directive, Ulf Bernitz also seemed to regard Europeanisation as a value as such. He predicted that 'there will probably be a successive development of an essentially common European contract law within this central sector'.[53] Even though case-law from the CJEU has not yet had such an effect, as the concrete assessment of the unfairness of clauses has been left to the national courts,[54] *Mohamed Aziz* might be a sign that the Court is more willing to proceed into developing substantive fairness law than before. This remains to be seen. The failure of the Commission to turn the UCTD into a maximum directive indicates the difficulties involved in a development towards a genuinely European concept of contractual unfairness.

There is, however, another way to approach Europeanisation. Rather than harmonising the principles, Europeans can learn from each other in detail. Legal inspiration across borders within the EU could develop domestic legal thinking on the unfairness of particular clauses. The free movement of legal materials, such as domestic case-law and doctrine, across national borders could contribute to Europeanised term-related small narratives on unfairness of contractual terms.[55]

There have been attempts to promote such cross-border learning. After the adoption of the UCTD the Commission sponsored the development of a database on case-law (including administrative decisions and complaint board decisions) concerning unfair contract terms, called CLAB Europa.[56] One of the aims of this database was to give national decision-makers the opportunity to learn from each other when assessing the fairness of particular clauses. Due to several reasons, however, the project did not work: the database contained too many cases, the reports were short

[52] See n 34.

[53] Bernitz (n 11) 26.

[54] According to the approach of *Freiburger Kommunalbauten*, see n 31.

[55] I have attempted to develop such a view on Europeanisation in *Free Movement of Legal Ideas: Towards a Dynamic Europeanisation of Private Law* (Oxford, Hart Publishing, 2024).

[56] CLAB referring to 'clauses abusives'. See on the project Hans-W Micklitz and Malek Radeideh, '*CLAB Europa* – The European Database on Unfair Terms in Consumer Contracts' (2005) 28 *Journal of Consumer Policy* 325.

and sometimes unintelligible, the translations were not always acceptable and the limitations of the materials to be reported were unclear. The project was therefore terminated.

Even though the first project did not succeed, the idea was not bad. New technology makes it possible to create new ways in which fairness can be assessed.[57] Digitalisation and artificial intelligence offer increased opportunities for experimental learning across the borders. Joint fairness-narratives might be good examples of such learning.

Perhaps Ulf Bernitz was right in this aspect as well. Maybe the cross-border use of available source materials and the development of digital tools to process it can contribute to produce Europeanised learning on the fairness of particular clauses. His prediction of a European *Fallgruppenbildung* may have been more to the point than we yet realise.

[57] For example, programs have been developed for searching and identifying potentially unfair clauses in standard form conditions, see Hans-W Micklitz, Przemyslaw Palka and Yannis Panagis, 'The Empire Strikes Back: Digital Control of Unfair Terms of Online Services' (2017) 40 *Journal of Consumer Policy* 367. The listing of unfair terms in digital markets is presented and discussed by Cristina Poncibò, 'The UCTD 30 Years Later: Identifying and Blacklisting Unfair Terms in Digital Markets' (2023) 19 *European Review of Contract Law* 321.

Part II

The EU as a Transformative Constitutional Order

4

Freedom to Conduct a Business: The Search for a Balance that Avoids Undue Interference

NILS WAHL AND STEFANO BONI*

I. INTRODUCTION

Article 16 of the EU Charter of Fundamental Rights (the 'Charter') states that '[t]he freedom to conduct a business in accordance with Union law and national laws and practices is recognised'.

It is well-known that the Charter was proclaimed in 2000 and acquired full legal status on 1 December 2009, with the entry into force of the Treaty of Lisbon. However, as observed by Advocate General Cruz Villalón, the freedom to conduct a business has a long history in EU law. Originally seen as a corollary to the fundamental right to property, it started to exist in its own right in the 1980s, achieving the status of a general principle of European Union law.[1]

As already argued elsewhere,[2] the freedom to conduct a business is of fundamental importance for the future of the EU. The emergence of protectionist trends in many Member States as a reaction to several economic and political crises meant that development of the internal market has been side-lined. However, those crises are, in our view, one of the reasons why it has become even more crucial to protect businesses, which should not be taken for granted even in a (somewhat) capitalistic society. The freedom to conduct a business, because it encourages entrepreneurship and innovation, also promotes economic growth. This growth is essential not only for economic development but also for social development in the EU, especially as it reduces unemployment and creates resources to be used to foster sustainability.[3] Undoubtedly the

* All views expressed in this publication are strictly personal.

[1] Opinion of AG Cruz Villalón in Case C426/11 *Alemo-Herron*, EU:C:2013:82, para. 48.

[2] N Wahl, 'The Freedom to Conduct a Business: a Right of Fundamental Importance for the Future of the European Union' in F Amtenbrink et al (ed), *The Internal Market and the Future of European Integration: Essays in Honour of Laurence W. Gormley* (Cambridge, CUP, 2019).

[3] cf European Union Agency for Fundamental Rights (FRA), *Freedom to conduct a business: exploring the dimension of a fundamental right*, 2015, 3 and 7.

Commission and the EU legislature have taken steps designed to improve the conditions in which new businesses can flourish.[4] However, rules continue to exist – both at the national and EU level – that interfere with the possibility for undertakings to conduct business and hamper cross-border trade. Therefore, it is seminal that private operators can rely on Article 16 of the Charter in order to be sheltered from *undue* interference by public authorities. This contribution can hopefully shed some light on what can be considered as undue.

II. THE SCOPE OF THE FREEDOM TO CONDUCT BUSINESS

As to the scope of freedom to conduct a business, it must be noted that the Explanations Relating to the Charter,[5] which, in accordance with the third subparagraph of Article 6(1) TEU and Article 52(7) of the Charter, have to be taken into consideration when interpreting the Charter,[6] specify that Article 16 is based, first, 'on Court of Justice case-law which has recognised freedom to exercise an economic or commercial activity' as well as 'freedom of contract' and, second, 'on Article 119(1) and (3) [TFEU], which recognises free competition'.

In its subsequent case-law, the Court of Justice, while confirming that the protection afforded by Article 16 of the Charter covers the three aspects referred to in the above-mentioned Explanations (i.e. freedom to exercise an economic or commercial activity, freedom of contract and free competition), made clear that that protection embraces, in particular, the freedom to choose with whom to do business as well as the freedom to determine the price of a service and includes, inter alia, the right for any business to be able to freely use, within the limits of its liability for its own acts, the economic, technical and financial resources available to it.[7]

It might seem that this case-law attributes quite a wide scope to the freedom to conduct a business, so that private operators can run their business without any major interference. Nevertheless, it must be borne in mind that, as emerges from the very wording of Article 16 and as the Court of Justice has consistently underlined, the freedom to conduct a business does not constitute an absolute prerogative, but must, first, be viewed in relation to its function in society and, second, be weighed in the balance with other interests protected by the EU legal order and the rights and freedoms of others. Therefore, that freedom may be subject to a broad range of interventions on the part of public authorities which may, in the public interest, limit the exercise of economic activity. However, as stated in Article 52(1) of the Charter, any limitation on the exercise of the rights and freedoms recognised by the latter must be

[4] eg Regulation (EU) 2019/1150 of the European Parliament and of the Council on promoting fairness and transparency for business users of online intermediation services, [2019] OJ L186/57; Regulation (EU) 2022/1925 of the European Parliament and of the Council on contestable and fair markets in the digital sector and amending Directives (EU) 2019/1937 and (EU) 2020/1828 (Digital Markets Act) [2002], OJ L265/1; Regulation (EU) 2022/2065 of the European Parliament and of the Council on a Single Market For Digital Services and amending Directive 2000/31/EC (Digital Services Act), [2022] OJ L277/1.

[5] [2007] OJ C303/17.

[6] Case C-283/11 *Sky Österreich*, C-283/11, EU:C:2013:28, para. 42.

[7] Case C-124/20 *Bank Melli Iran*, EU:C:2021:1035, paras 78–79.

provided for by law, respect the essence of those rights and freedoms and, in compliance with the principle of proportionality, be necessary and actually meet objectives of general interest recognised by the European Union or the need to protect the rights and freedoms of others.[8]

It follows from the above that, as has been stressed by Advocate General Cruz Villalón, the freedom to conduct a business acts to protect economic initiative and economic activity, obviously within limits but nevertheless ensuring that there are certain minimum conditions for economic activity in the internal market. Thus, the freedom to conduct a business acts as a limit on the actions of the EU in its legislative and executive role as well as on the actions of the Member States in their application of EU law.[9]

III. A BALANCE WHICH IS DIFFICULT TO STRIKE

As has already[10] been submitted, it can be considered that the Court of Justice, while striking a balance between the freedom to conduct a business and other rights and freedoms, has (too) often placed the former at a disadvantage in comparison with other rights.

This was particularly evident in the Court's judgment in *Sky Österreich*, in which the freedom to conduct a business and the freedom of expression and information (Article 11 of the Charter) were particularly at issue.[11] While the public must undoubtedly be ensured access to information of general interest, even if such access can affect the interests of the holder of exclusive broadcasting rights, it is less clear whether the right to access information should extend to commercial sports events.

[8] ibid paras 80–83.

[9] Opinion of AG Cruz Villalón in Case C426/11 *Alemo-Herron*, EU:C:2013:82, para 50.

[10] Wahl, above note 2.

[11] Case C283/11. In this Case, the Court was asked to interpret Directive 2010/13/EU of the European Parliament and of the Council on the coordination of certain provisions laid down by law, regulation or administrative action in Member States concerning the provision of audiovisual media services (Audiovisual Media Services Directive) [2010] OJ L263/15, in the context of exclusive broadcasting of a sporting event. Article 15 of that Directive provides that for short news reports, any broadcaster established in the EU must have access to events of high interest to the public which are transmitted on an exclusive basis by a broadcaster. Such a rule undoubtedly limits the right of the holder of exclusive broadcasting rights to choose with whom and for what price it may wish to enter into an agreement and amounts to inference with the freedom to conduct a business of holders of exclusive broadcasting rights. The Court emphasised that the relevant provision of Directive 2010/13 does not affect the core content of the freedom to conduct a business. In the Court's view, Article 15 of that Directive does not prevent a business activity from being carried out as such by the holder of exclusive broadcasting rights. In addition, it does not prevent the holder of those rights from making use of them by broadcasting the event in question itself for consideration or by granting that right to another broadcaster on a contractual basis for consideration or to any other economic operator. As concerns the assessment of proportionality, the Court considered that the restriction had a legitimate aim, namely to promote pluralism of the media in the production and programming of information in the EU, protected under Article 11(2) of the Charter, that the restriction was appropriate for the purpose of ensuring that the objective pursued was achieved and that no less restrictive measures were available to achieve the objective pursued. Lastly, the Court found that the provision in question ensured a fair balance between the freedom to conduct a business, on the one side, and the fundamental freedom of EU citizens to receive information and the freedom and pluralism of the media, on the other side.

More generally, the freedom to conduct a business has regularly been trumped by the protection of consumers[12] and public health.[13] As to companies active in the information society, it should be noted that, admittedly, in some judgments the Court adopted a more pro-business approach. In *Scarlet*[14] and *UPC*,[15] questions arose regarding the obligations of an internet service provider to take measures in order to limit the appearance of copyrighted material on its website. In both cases, the Court held that the obligations at issue constituted an interference with the right of the internet service provider to conduct a business. This was so, in essence, because of the significant costs and difficulties involved in complying with those obligations. As concerns the balancing of the different interests at stake, however, the Court reached two substantially different conclusions. In *Scarlet*, the Court judged that the obligations weighing on the internet service operators were too far-reaching and costly. Consequently, it found that those obligations constituted an unlawful interference in the freedom to conduct a business. On the other hand, in *UPC*, the Court held that the obligations at issue did not impact on the core of the freedom to conduct a business – and this notwithstanding the considerable costs involved – and could therefore be justified under certain conditions. It follows that, in spite of arriving at different conclusions regarding the lawfulness of the interference, the Court took account of the interests of the operators concerned.

It can be added that, more recently, in *Poland/Parliament and Council*,[16] the Court examined the new liability regime concerning internet service providers set out in Article 17 of Directive 2017/790.[17] In its judgment, it stressed again, as it had done in *UPC*, that in order to respect the freedom of internet service providers to conduct a business and ensure a fair balance between that freedom, the right to freedom of expression and information of the users of their services, and the rights of intellectual property rightsholders, obliging internet service providers to take measures to ensure their services are not used to infringe copyright may require that those service providers be allowed to determine the specific measures to be taken to achieve the result sought. In this way they can choose to put in place the measures which are best adapted to the resources and abilities available to them and which are compatible with other obligations and challenges which they may encounter in the exercise of their activity.

However, in other cases such as *Google Spain*[18] and *Schrems*,[19] where the fundamental rights warranted by Article 7 (Respect for private and family life) and Article 8 (Protection of personal data) of the Charter were at issue, the Court ruled in favour of data protection; notwithstanding the fact that such a result entailed huge costs for the companies involved. One could wonder whether Article 16 should have been

[12] Case C134/15 *Lidl*, EU:C:2016:498.

[13] Case C-544/10 *Deutsches Weintor*, EU:C:2012:52; Case C-477/14 *Pillbox 38*, EU:C:2016:324.

[14] Case C-70/10 *Scarlet*, EU:C:2011:771.

[15] Case C-314/12 *UPC*, EU:C:2014:192.

[16] Case C-401/19 *Poland/Parliament and Council*, EU:C:2022:297, para 75.

[17] Directive (EU) 2019/790 of the European Parliament and of the Council on copyright and related rights in the Digital Single Market and amending Directives 96/9/EC and 2001/29/EC [2019] OJ L130/92.

[18] Case C-131/12 *Google Spain*, EU:C:2014:317.

[19] Case C-362/14 *Schrems*, EU:C:2015:650.

taken into consideration as well, in order to check whether those costs risk making business unsustainable. More generally, in our view, when dealing with situations which could result in heavy obligations imposed on entrepreneurs, public authorities, including the judiciary, should take into account, implicitly at the very least, the need to respect the freedom to conduct a business. In the case-law of the Court, references to Article 16 of the Charter are not very frequent, above all when one bears in mind the economic consequences most Court judgments may have on business.

In more recent case-law, one can nonetheless find some examples which show that the Court, while recognising the relevance of protecting other rights or freedoms, has paid more attention to the freedom to conduct a business.

A first example would be the *PI* case.[20] Here, the referring court asked whether EU law precluded national legislation providing that a commercial establishment, such as a massage parlour, could be closed with immediate effect by a decision of a national authority on the grounds that it suspected prostitution was being practised within that establishment, without the required authorisation; that legislation did not ensure that certain procedural rights were complied with in relation to the person operating that establishment.[21] It is worth noting that the Court, while answering the questions put forward by the national judge, mentioned Article 16 of the Charter of its own initiative and stressed that, according to case-law, that provision refers, inter alia, to Article 49 TFEU, which guarantees the fundamental freedom of establishment.[22]

In its analysis, the Court pointed out that the supply of the alleged services at issue without an authorisation granted by a public authority does not ensure proper control by the competent authorities of these activities within the establishment concerned. Consequently, the provision of those services by persons not subject to specific health requirements and regular checks to detect sexually transmitted diseases was likely to lead to increased health risks, which are covered inter alia by Article 35 of the Charter. On those grounds, the Court recognised that the power for a national authority to close, with immediate effect, a commercial establishment because of a possible unauthorised exercise of a brothel could be justified by overriding reasons in the public interest. However, while determining whether that restriction was proportionate, the Court highlighted that that legislation allowed the closure of an establishment without the stating of any reasons, in fact and in law, in writing and communicated to its addressee, whereas it required that the application for the annulment of a decision on that closure be reasoned by the person concerned. After recalling that the obligation to state reasons is linked to the effectiveness of judicial review and to the right to be heard in all proceedings, which are affirmed by Articles 47 and 48 of the Charter, the Court noted that the requirement that the national administrative authorities state reasons is particularly important in order to determine whether a restriction of the right to conduct a business is justified and proportionate. On those grounds, the Court found that Article 49 TFEU, Article 15(2) and Articles 16, 47 and 52 of the

[20] Case C-230/18 *PI*, EU:C:2019:383.
[21] Case C-230/18 *PI*, paras 22, 24 and 45.
[22] ibid para 54 and case-law cited.

Charter and the general principle of the right to good administration precluded the national legislation at issue.[23]

It seems to us that the Court struck a fair balance between the need to safeguard public health and the protection of business, insofar as it did not accept that a commercial establishment could be closed under conditions which do not assure respect of the right of the person running that business to an effective remedy and to a court, as well as their rights of defence. Admittedly, on the merits, public authorities can find reasons which justify that limits are imposed on a business which can jeopardise public health. However, requiring those authorities to comply with formal requirements while adopting decisions imposing such limits contributes to avoiding undue interference and makes it easier for the entrepreneur in question to evaluate whether it is appropriate to bring an action against such a decision.

A second example is the *Skeyes* case.[24] Here, at the request of the airline Ryanair, a Belgian national judge had ordered Skeyes, the autonomous public undertaking designated, according to Article 8 of Regulation No 550/2004,[25] by Belgian authorities as the exclusive provider of air traffic services for Belgian airspace, to provide those services notwithstanding collective action by its staff, so that air traffic could be operated normally.[26] It must be noted that those services consist especially in ensuring the safety of air navigation. Skeyes having brought third-party proceedings against that order, the national judge asked the Court whether Article 8 of the above-mentioned Regulation must be interpreted as conferring on airspace users, such as airlines, a right to an effective remedy, before the national courts, against the air traffic service provider in order to submit to judicial review any alleged failures by the latter to fulfil its obligation to provide services in the exercise of its powers as a public authority.[27] While answering that question, the Court indicated that, although airlines enjoy rights conferred by the relevant EU secondary law, they are also subject to the rules of EU safety law. Referring to the Opinion of Advocate General Rantos,[28] the Court added that airlines also enjoy the rights and freedoms conferred by EU primary law, including the freedom to conduct a business recognised in Article 16 of the Charter, which had not been mentioned by the national judge in its question. According to the Court, the rights of Ryanair were potentially infringed by a decision to close airspace taken by an air traffic service provider, so that it had the right to an effective remedy as provided for in Article 47 of the Charter. Because of the absence of EU rules governing the matter, it was for the national legal order of each Member State to lay down the detailed procedural rules governing those remedies, provided that those rules are not, in situations covered by EU law, less favourable than in similar situations subject to national law. However, the Court specified that, since the main proceedings concerned a request made on grounds of extreme urgency, the national judge must be able to grant interim relief

[23] ibid paras 71–87 and 91.

[24] Case C-353/20 *Skeyes*, EU:C:2022:423.

[25] Regulation (EC) No 550/2004 of the European Parliament and of the Council on the provision of air navigation services in the single European sky, [2004] OJ L96/10.

[26] Case C353/20 *Skeyes*, paras 1, 2, 17–20.

[27] ibid para 36.

[28] Opinion of AG Rantos in Case C353/20 *Skeyes*, EU:C:2022:20, para 38.

in order to ensure the full effectiveness of the judicial decision to be given on the existence of the rights claimed under EU law.[29]

Again, in our view, the Court found an acceptable balance between, on the one hand, the need to safeguard a general interest such as the respect of safety requirements and, on the other hand, the protection of business, insofar as it stated that undertakings whose economic interests are impaired must have access to effective judicial remedies, including interim measures. In this regard, it should be noted that the lack of such remedies can make the fact of operating a business highly risky. Actually, time-consuming and prolonged litigation is one of the biggest obstacles to business development in several countries. The excessive duration of court proceedings and the ineffective enforcement of final judgments can render judicial protection illusory. For those reasons, the effective possibility to judicially enforce the freedom to conduct a business is seminal in order to make that freedom a reality.[30]

In the same case, the Court was also asked to determine whether Regulation No 550/2004 must be interpreted as precluding not only application of the rules on competition laid down by the FEU Treaty to the provision of air navigation services connected with the exercise of the powers of a public authority, but also the application of rules relating to rights and freedoms of airspace users. The Court confirmed that the Regulation at issue precludes the application of the competition rules to the provision of the above-mentioned services but specified that this circumstance does not entail that the application of the other rights and freedoms is precluded. In this respect, the Court made reference again to the freedom to conduct a business and recalled that this freedom can be limited because of safety requirements, provided that these limitations comply with the conditions set out at in Article 52(1) of the Charter, which had to be verified by the national judge.[31]

As previously indicated, the freedom to conduct a business includes free competition. It is worth noting that the judgment of the Court in *Skeyes* seems to show that this freedom has a scope which does not always overlap with the rules of the FEU Treaty specifically aimed at protecting competition, insofar as Article 16 can apply even when competition rules do not.

IV. LOOKING FOR A BALANCE WHICH DOES NOT HURT WORKERS (AND WORK)

As already pointed out, the freedom to conduct a business comprises contractual freedom. When employment contracts are at issue, it is particularly important that that freedom is exercised, and possibly limited, in such a way that corresponds to an adequate balance between the employers' rights and those of the employees. In this context, one should also raise the question whether the fact of protecting workers is (always) the right way to protect work. It goes without saying that workers are, first and foremost, individuals, so their dignity as human beings cannot be jeopardised by

[29] Case C-353/20 *Skeyes*, paras 45–53.
[30] cf FRA, above note 3, 47 and 48.
[31] Case C-353/20 *Skeyes*, paras 58–68.

the fact that they need to earn a living. Moreover, in a democratic society, workers should be granted high-level protection also as members of a professional category. However, that protection should not be conceived in such a way that it would make it very difficult for a business, first, to be profitable enough to reward entrepreneurs' efforts and, second, to adapt to new challenges that may arise in particular because of changing conditions in a globalised world or because of crises that not even cautious entrepreneurs could have foreseen.

Our view in this respect can be summarised by referring to the position that was expressed by the Advocate General in *AGET Iraklis*,[32] according to which workers are best protected by an economic environment which fosters stable employment. Historically speaking, the idea of artificially maintaining employment relationships, in spite of unsound general economic foundations, has been tested and has utterly failed in certain political systems of yesteryear. It seems to us that the case-law in this field shows that the Court, while striking a balance between the freedom to conduct a business and other freedoms or rights, is less inclined than in other fields to accept restrictions to the former freedom. That does not, however, mean that the Court is not sufficiently protecting workers.

A brief reminder of two cases already commented upon elsewhere[33] could be useful to understand the Court's position. First, in its judgment in *Alemo-Herron*[34] concerning the rights of employees in transfers of undertakings, the Court was asked to interpret Article 3 of Directive 2001/23.[35] That provision states that the new employer (transferee) is bound by the terms and conditions agreed in any collective agreement on the same terms applicable to the previous employer (transferor) under that agreement. The Court had to clarify whether that rule also applied to terms and conditions in an employment contract that referred to collective agreements negotiated and adopted after the date of the transfer (so-called dynamic clauses) without the participation of the transferee.[36]

The Court noted, in particular, that the relevant provisions of EU law do not aim solely to safeguard the interests of employees in the event of a transfer of an undertaking, but seek to ensure a fair balance between the interests of those employees, on the one hand, and those of the transferee, on the other. It stressed that the specific feature of the case resided in the fact that the transfer of the undertaking at issue took place between a legal person governed by public law and a legal person governed by private law. Moreover, the Court emphasised that dynamic clauses such as those at issue in the case before the referring court could limit considerably the room for manoeuvre of transferees, not least in light of the significant adjustments and changes that were necessary in the transfer of an undertaking from the public sector to the private sector.[37] Referring to the freedom to conduct a business, and in particular the

[32] Opinion of AG Wahl in Case C201/15 *AGET Iraklis*, EU:C:2016:429, para 73.
[33] Wahl, above n 2.
[34] Case C426/11 *Alemo-Herron*, EU:C:2013:521.
[35] Council Directive 2001/23/EC on the approximation of the laws of the Member States relating to the safeguarding of employees' rights in the event of transfers of undertakings, businesses or parts of undertakings or businesses [2001] OJ L82/16.
[36] Case C426/11 *Alemo-Herron*, para 20.
[37] ibid paras 25–29.

freedom of contract, the Court held that the transferee's contractual freedom had been seriously reduced to the point that such a limitation was liable to adversely affect the very essence of its freedom to conduct a business. This was so because the transferee had not been able to take part in the negotiation of the collective agreements and assert its interests effectively in the contractual process.[38]

Second, in *AGET Iraklis*,[39] the Court was asked to rule whether EU law precludes national legislation according to which undertakings must secure authorisation from the competent authorities in order to put into effect collective redundancies. In accordance with the relevant national provisions, if the parties taking part in consultations on the projected collective redundancies do not reach agreement, the competent authorities must either decide to extend the consultations or not authorise some or all of the redundancies in question, basing that decision on (1) the conditions in the labour market, (2) the situation of the undertaking and (3) the interests of the national economy. In its judgment, and subject to a number of caveats, the Court emphasised that the national rules can only be allowed to the extent that they do not affect the effectiveness of Directive 98/59[40] on collective redundancies. In examining the national rules in the light of Article 49 TFEU, however, the Court stated that the rules constituted a restriction to the freedom of establishment. In particular, the Court highlighted that a company should be free to determine the nature and extent of the economic activity that it wants to carry out in a given Member State, especially the size of the fixed establishments and the number of workers required for that purpose, and also to scale down, even to zero, its activity in that Member State.[41] Moreover, the Court observed that the national legislation under scrutiny constituted a limitation on the exercise of the freedom to conduct a business enshrined in Article 16 of the Charter. While admitting that those rules may be justified under certain conditions, the Court considered, due to the generality of the rules in question, that those rules did not comply with the requirement of proportionality.[42]

These two judgments, especially the first, have been criticised heavily on the grounds that they gave precedence to freedom to conduct a business over the protection of workers.[43] It is nevertheless submitted that, in *Alemo-Herron* the Court struck

[38] ibid paras 33–35.

[39] Case C-201/15 *AGET Iraklis*, EU:C:2016:972.

[40] Council Directive 98/59/EC on the approximation of the laws of the Member States relating to collective redundancies, [1998] OJ L225/6.

[41] It is submitted that, by referring, at para 53 of its judgment, to para 65 of the Advocate General's Opinion, the Court implicitly accepted his remark according to which a company has the right to leave a Member State, even if this is simply in order to pursue an economic activity in another Member State where it is more profitable.

[42] Case C-201/15 *AGET Iraklis*, paras 44, 53 and 73–104.

[43] S Weatherill, 'Use and Abuse of the EU's Charter of Fundamental Rights: On the Improper Veneration of Freedom of Contract' (2014) 10(1) *European Review of Contract Law* 167; S Giubboni, 'Freedom to Conduct a Business and EU Labour Law' (2018) 14(1) *European Constitutional Law Review* 172; E Gill-Pedro, 'Whose Freedom is it Anyway? The Fundamental Rights of Companies in EU Law' (2022) 18(2) *European Constitutional Law Review* 183. For a different interpretation of the judgment in *AGET Iraklis*, according to which the Court did not follow the liberal approach of the Advocate General see A Fabre, 'Autorisation administrative des licenciements collectifs: la liberté d'entreprise plie mais ne rompt pas . . .' (2017) 2 *Revue de droit du travail* 127; M Markakis, 'Can Governments control Mass Layoffs by Employers? Economic Freedoms vs Labour Rights in Case C-201/15 AGET Iraklis' (2017) 13(4) *European Constitutional Law Review* 724.

a reasonable balance between the interests of undertakings and employees and, in *AGET Iraklis*, although it did not entirely follow a pro-business approach, the Court wisely avoided giving a green light to national measures which, while allegedly aimed at protecting workers, produced legal uncertainty to an extent which was unacceptable to undertakings. As already mentioned, we think that, except perhaps in the short term, employees' interests cannot thrive when employers are put in difficult situations.

Whereas we do not find it appropriate to answer in detail the criticism that those judgments, and the Opinion of the Advocate General in the second, generated, it should be highlighted that the fact of following an alleged liberal approach by no means implies that the freedom to conduct a business, in particular contractual freedom, protects employers when they rely on that freedom in order to act contrary to human dignity.

In this respect, we would like to first mention the *TP* case.[44] The applicant in the main proceedings, J.K., had been working as a self-employed audiovisual editor for seven consecutive years for TP, a Polish public television channel, under successive contracts. After the conclusion of a new employment contract in November 2017 for the following month, J.K. was informed of the cancellation of his shifts that had already been scheduled for that month and no further contract was concluded. A few weeks before those events, J.K. had published a video displaying his homosexuality and calling for tolerance towards same-sex couples. In such circumstances, J.K. brought an action for damages before a Polish judge. The latter had doubts as to the compatibility of Polish law on equal treatment with Directive 2000/78,[45] insofar as the former excludes from its scope the freedom of choice of contracting parties, so long as that choice is not based on sex, race, ethnic origin or nationality. On those grounds, he asked the Court to interpret Article 3(1)(a) and (c)[46] of Directive 2000/78.[47]

First, the Court noted that the conditions for access to any occupational activity, whatever the nature and characteristics of such activity, are covered by Article 3(1)(a) of Directive 2000/78 and, accordingly, fall within the scope of that Directive, provided that that those activities are genuine and are pursued in the context of a legal relationship characterised by a degree of stability. Therefore, that provision covers the refusal, on discriminatory grounds, to conclude a contract for specific work with a contractor engaged in an independent economic activity.[48]

Second, it pointed out that, although Article 3(1)(c) of Directive 2000/78 refers specifically to 'working conditions, including dismissals and pay', a person who has been self-employed may find themselves obliged to stop working due to their

[44] Case C-356/21 *TP* (*Audiovisual editor for public television*), EU:C:2023:9.

[45] Council Directive 2000/78/EC establishing a general framework for equal treatment in employment and occupation [2000] OJ L303/16.

[46] This provision reads as follow: 'Within the limits of the areas of competence conferred on the Community, this Directive shall apply to all persons, as regards both the public and private sectors, including public bodies, in relation to:
(a) conditions for access to employment, to self-employment or to occupation, including selection criteria and recruitment conditions, whatever the branch of activity and at all levels of the professional hierarchy, including promotion;
. . .
(c) employment and working conditions, including dismissals and pay'.

[47] Case C-356/21 *TP*, paras 1, 2, 12–29 and 31.

[48] ibid 32–51.

contractual counterparty and thus be in a vulnerable position comparable to that of an employed worker who has been dismissed. For this reason, TP's decision not to renew that contract for specific work on the ground, according to the applicant, of his sexual orientation, thus terminating the professional relationship between them, falls within the scope of that provision.[49]

Third, and more importantly for the subject matter at issue in this contribution, the Court, after recalling that the Polish law on equal treatment appeared to pursue an objective seeking to protect the freedom to choose a contracting party, which is covered by Article 16 of the Charter, noted that the very fact that that law provided for a number of exceptions to the freedom to choose a contracting party showed that the Polish legislature itself considered that discrimination could not be regarded as necessary for the purposes of safeguarding that freedom in a democratic society. The Court highlighted that there was no reason to make a distinction depending on whether the discrimination concerned is based on sexual orientation or on one of the other grounds expressly referred to in the Polish law. Moreover, the Court underlined that to accept that freedom of contract allows a refusal to contract with a person on the ground of that person's sexual orientation would be tantamount to depriving Article 3(1)(a) of Directive 2000/78 of its practical effect insofar as that provision specifically prohibits any discrimination based on that ground as regards access to self-employment.[50]

In our opinion, the *TP* judgment confirms the fact that workers should not fear that employers are allowed to rely on Article 16 of the Charter in order to use contractual freedom in a way that impinges on their rights as human beings. The Court did not even need to run a proportionality test, because there was no other interest worth protecting against which it could have been necessary to weigh J.K.'s right to equal treatment.

Second, we would like to make reference to the case-law of the Court[51] concerning private workplace regulations which prohibit workers from wearing visible political, philosophical or religious signs in the workplace. In this respect, the Court held that such rules may constitute a difference in treatment that is indirectly based on religion or belief, for the purposes of Directive 2000/78, if it is established – which it is for national judges to ascertain in any individual case brought before them – that the apparently neutral obligation that they encompass results, in fact, in persons adhering to a particular religion or belief being put at a particular disadvantage. However, the Court recalled that such a difference in treatment would nonetheless not constitute indirect discrimination, if it were objectively justified by a legitimate aim and the means of achieving that aim were appropriate and necessary. According to the Court, an employer's desire to display, in customer relations, a policy of political, philosophical or religious neutrality relates to the freedom to conduct a business recognised by Article 16 of the Charter and may be regarded as a legitimate aim, in particular where the employer involves in its pursuit of that aim only those workers who are

[49] ibid paras 52–66.
[50] ibid paras 73–78.
[51] Case C-157/15 *G4S Secure Solutions*, EU:C:2017:203; Joined Cases C804/18 and C341/19 *WABE and MH Müller Handel*, EU:C:2021:594; Case C-344/20 *S.C.R.L. (Religious clothing)*, EU:C:2022:774.

required to come into contact with the employer's customers. At the same time, the Court specified that the mere desire of an employer to pursue a policy of neutrality – while in itself a legitimate aim – is not sufficient, as such, to justify objectively a difference in treatment indirectly based on religion or belief, since such a justification can be regarded as being objective only where there is a genuine need on the part of that employer, which it is for that employer to demonstrate.[52] The Court added that, for that purpose, one should, first, take into consideration, inter alia, the legitimate wishes of those customers and the adverse consequences that that employer would suffer in the absence of that policy and, second, determine whether prohibition on wearing any visible sign of political, philosophical or religious beliefs imposed by an employer is limited to what is strictly necessary, in view of the adverse consequences that the employer is seeking to avoid by adopting that prohibition, and whether that policy of neutrality is genuinely pursued in a consistent and systematic manner.[53]

It seems to us that the burden of proof which lays with the employer is not an easy one to discharge. Therefore, we do not think that the fact that the Court relied on Article 16 of the Charter in order to justify a difference in treatment means that the Court did not find a fair balance between the freedom to conduct a business and the principle of non-discrimination.[54]

While reading together the case-law about signs in the workplace and the judgment in *TP*, one could wonder whether the fact that in the latter the Court adopted a straightforward approach, according to which, in essence, an employer is not allowed to dismiss a worker because of his sexual orientation, whereas, in the signs in the workplace case-law, it followed a more nuanced reasoning, means that Article 16 of the Charter gives entrepreneurs some leeway as to possible discrimination on the ground of religious beliefs, but it does not give them any leeway when other kinds of discrimination are at issue. An endless debate could be held over how privately a religion could or should be displayed in the workplace. However, we think that the main lesson that one should draw from the cases commented above is that Article 16 of the Charter can in no way shelter employers' choices which, while entailing negative consequences on employees, have no impact on business efficiency or its success. When employers' policies may have both a positive impact on business and negative consequences on their employees, Article 16 can play a role in the assessment of the legality of those policies through a strict test meant to preclude any possible abuse.

V. CONTRACTUAL FREEDOM AND COMPETITION LAW

As the freedom to conduct a business includes not only contractual freedom but also free competition, we find it interesting to examine the relation and the possible conflicts between these two aspects of the fundamental rights provided for in Article 16 of the Charter.

[52] Case C-344/20 *S.C.R.L*, paras 37–40 and the case-law cited.
[53] Joined Cases C804/18 and C341/19 *WABE and MH Müller Handel*, paras 65 and 67–69.
[54] A more critical opinion on this case-law can be found in D Martin, 'Cachez ce voile que je ne saurais voir!: l'interdiction de discrimination fondée sur la religion vue par la CJUE' (2018) 4 *Droit social* 314.

It is not difficult to imagine that two or more undertakings could consider that it is more profitable for them to agree on how to share a market instead of competing on it. However, it should be noted that free competition is a *sine qua non* for undertakings *effectively* engaging in business. As the General Court recalled, although anti-competitive practices are very often, at least in the short term, in the individual commercial interest of the undertakings, they are nonetheless illegal.[55] Moreover, according to Article 101(2) TFEU, anti-competitive agreements are automatically void.

Even if all this might seem to be quite simple, insofar as free competition, as enshrined in competition rules provided for in the FEU Treaty, trumps contractual freedom when the latter has been used in an anti-competitive way, a much higher degree of complexity arises when commitments within the meaning of Article 9 of Regulation No 1/2003[56] are at stake, as it is shown by the judgment of the Court in *Groupe Canal+/Commission*.[57]

The US studio Paramount concluded licensing agreements for audiovisual content with the main pay-TV broadcasters of the EU, including Sky and Groupe Canal+. The European Commission opened an investigation into possible restrictions affecting the provision of pay-TV services under the licensing agreements in question, in order to assess the compatibility of those restrictions with Article 101 TFEU and Article 53 of the EEA Agreement. In its statement of objections the Commission expressed concern in particular about two clauses in the licensing agreements which Paramount had concluded with Sky. The purpose of the first clause was to prohibit Sky from responding favourably to unsolicited requests from consumers residing in the EEA but outside the United Kingdom and Ireland to purchase television distribution services, or to limit the possibility of its responding favourably to such requests. The second clause required Paramount, in the context of the agreements which it concluded with broadcasters established in the EEA but outside the United Kingdom, to prohibit those broadcasters from responding favourably to unsolicited requests from consumers residing in the United Kingdom or Ireland to purchase television distribution services, or to limit the possibility of their responding favourably to such requests.

According to the Commission, those agreements, through such clauses, led to absolute territorial exclusivity and were capable of constituting a restriction of competition by object within the meaning of Article 101 TFEU and Article 53 of the EEA Agreement. Paramount offered commitments in order to address the concerns raised by the Commission and stated that it was prepared, inter alia, no longer to comply with or act in order to enforce the clauses, included in the licensing agreements concluded between it and broadcasters such as Groupe Canal+, which led to absolute territorial protection for those broadcasters. The Commission adopted a decision[58] by which it accepted the commitments offered and made them binding, as provided for in Article 9 of Regulation No 1/2003. Paramount then notified Groupe

[55] Case T-50/00 *Dalmine/Commission*, EU:T:2004:220, para 211.

[56] Council Regulation (EC) No 1/2003 on the implementation of the rules on competition laid down in Articles [101 and 102 TFEU], [2003] OJ L1/1.

[57] Case C-132/19 P *Groupe Canal +/Commission*, EU:C:2020:1007.

[58] Commission Decision relating to a proceeding under Article 101 TFEU and Article 53 of the EEA Agreement (Case AT.40023 – Cross-border access to pay-TV).

Canal+ of the terms of those commitments, which implied its intention no longer to ensure compliance with the absolute territorial exclusivity granted to that broadcaster on the French market.[59]

Groupe Canal+ brought an action seeking annulment of the decision at issue, which, after being dismissed by the General Court,[60] was successful in front of the Court of Justice. The latter noted that, in the context of Article 9 of Regulation No 1/2003, the Commission is required to verify commitments offered, not only from the perspective of whether they are appropriate to address its competition concerns, but also with regard to the effect of the commitments on the interests of third parties, so that those third parties' rights are not rendered meaningless. In that context, the Court of Justice considered that the General Court was wrong when it stated that those third parties could ask national courts to enforce their contractual rights without infringing the provisions of Article 16 of Regulation No 1/2003, which prohibits those courts from adopting decisions running counter to an earlier Commission decision on the matter. In fact, the Court highlighted that a decision of a national court requiring an operator to breach its commitments which have been made binding by a Commission decision would clearly run counter to that decision.[61]

In addition, according to the Court, given that the second sentence of Article 16(1) of Regulation No 1/2003 requires national courts to avoid giving decisions which conflict with a decision contemplated by the Commission for the application, inter alia, of Article 101 TFEU, the General Court also erred in law by holding that a national court could declare the relevant clauses compatible with Article 101 TFEU, even though the Commission could still, under Article 9(2) of Regulation No 1/2003, reopen the proceedings and, as it had initially envisaged, adopt a formal decision containing a formal finding that there had been an infringement.[62]

Because of those limits on the jurisdiction of the national courts, the Court of Justice found that the General Court was wrong to hold that the possibility for Paramount's contracting partners to bring an action before the national courts was capable of remedying the effects of Paramount's commitments on the contractual rights of those contracting parties.[63]

Giving final judgment on the matter itself, the Court emphasised the essential character, in the scheme of the licensing agreements in question, of the obligations intended to ensure the territorial exclusivity granted to broadcasters affected by the above-mentioned commitments and reached the conclusion that, by adopting the decision at issue, the Commission rendered meaningless the contractual rights of Groupe Canal+ vis-à-vis Paramount and thereby infringed the principle of proportionality, which entailed the annulment of that decision.[64]

[59] Case C-132/19 P *Groupe Canal+/Commission*, para 5, at which the Court summarised the background to the dispute and the contested decision by quoting the relevant paragraphs of the appealed judgment from the General Court.

[60] Case T-873/16 *Groupe Canal+ v Commission*, EU:T:2018:904.

[61] Case C-132/19 P *Groupe Canal+/Commission*, paras 106–11.

[62] ibid paras 112–14.

[63] ibid paras 116–17.

[64] ibid paras 121–28.

Without entering into debate[65] about what the Court's judgment in *Groupe Canal+/Commission* has meant for the role and the future of Commission's decisions founded on Article 9 of Regulation No 1/2003, we would like to underline that, although the Court did not mention Article 16 of the Charter in that judgment, it dealt with the possible conflict between, on the one hand, the protection of free competition via Commission decisions which make engagements binding and, on the other hand, the rights that a private party holds because of the exercise of its contractual freedom, in such a way that the former cannot totally negate the latter. Such a result is similar to the case-law about Article 16 of the Charter according to which,

> as regards the condition relating to respect for the essence of the freedom to conduct a business, it must be borne in mind that that requirement is potentially infringed, in particular, where an undertaking is deprived of the opportunity to assert its interests effectively in a contractual process.[66]

In essence, a public authority is not allowed to apply competition law in a way that deprives third parties of contractual rights which they hold and leave them without effective judicial remedies. Such a public enforcement of competition law can be considered as an undue interference in business.

VI. CONCLUDING REMARKS

At its very beginning, the European project was essentially an economic one, founded on the progressive creation of a common market characterised by free competition and economic efficiency, so that goods would be produced and services offered in the most economically viable manner. Over time that project has acquired a scope which goes far beyond the economic aspect, as is particularly apparent when reading the Charter, which contains many rights and principles whose nature is not (purely) economic. However, this should simply mean that the original project has been developed further, without jeopardising the functioning of an economically sound internal market, whose existence and continuous improvement are, in our opinion, a *sine qua non* for all other rights and freedoms to be effective and sustainable in the long term.

The fact that the Charter also granted the full status of a fundamental right to the freedom to conduct a business can be seen as confirmation that that freedom continues to play a seminal role in order for the EU to flourish. That right can not only be directly invoked, but also be, as shown by some of the cases mentioned above,[67] referred to by the Court on its own initiative or even taken into consideration implicitly. The freedom to conduct a business should, at the very least tacitly, be taken into account in each situation which could entail significant consequences on the way a business is run. The importance of that freedom should be enhanced also by the EU

[65] VL Idot, 'Concurrence – Engagements en antitrust et principe de proportionnalité' (2021) 2 *Europe* 66; B Keane, 'Commitments, for Better or for Worse?' (2021) 5 *Journal of European Competition Law & Practice* 387; F von Schreitter and M Sura, 'Cut! Verpflichtungszusagen nach dem Canal+-Urteil des EuGH (C-132/19 P)' (2021) 9 *Wirtschaft und Wettbewerb* 488.

[66] Case C-124/20 *Bank Melli Iran*, EU:C:2021:1035, para 87 and the case-law cited.

[67] See text accompanying footnotes 22, 28, 65 and 66 above.

judiciary in at least two ways: first, it should be a pillar in order to make it easier for undertakings to seek remedies against interferences by public authorities; second, judicial decisions should not underestimate their economic consequences.

Through the freedom to conduct a business undertakings can avoid, or at the very least seek remedies against, interference by public authorities which are undue, insofar as they go beyond what is necessary to preserve *other* public interests. It is important to stress the adjective 'other', because, as developed above, it is in the public interest that undertakings are allowed to run their business in the most efficient way, so that they can be economically sound and therefore keep people working for them, or even hire more people, and pay taxes which are necessary in order for public authorities to have the resources needed to provide infrastructures and services.

This is why it is pivotal that every time that public authorities adopt measures which have an impact on the way a business can be run, they ask themselves whether those measures are necessary and whether there could be less invasive measures.

However, undertakings should also be aware that their freedom is not without limits and should be used in a way which is simultaneously procompetitive and respectful of human dignity. It goes without saying that such a balance is not always easy to find. Therefore it is fundamental that effective judicial remedies exist in order to solve as efficiently as possible cases in which the actors involved cannot find themselves an acceptable solution. The freedom to conduct a business is effective in practice only if companies can rely on such remedies. This is why the EU judiciary has given more and more importance to the efficient administration of justice and has been through several internal and structural reforms aimed at improving its functioning.[68]

[68] See Report submitted pursuant to Article 3(2) of Regulation (EU, Euratom) 2015/2422 of the European Parliament and of the Council amending Protocol No 3 on the Statute of the Court of Justice of the European Union <https://curia.europa.eu/jcms/upload/docs/application/pdf/2018-01/en_2018-01-12_08-43-52_183.pdf> and Request submitted by the Court of Justice pursuant to the second paragraph of Article 281 of the Treaty on the Functioning of the European Union, with a view to amending Protocol No 3 on the Statute of the Court of Justice of the European Union <https://curia.europa.eu/jcms/upload/docs/application/pdf/2022-12/demande_transfert_ddp_tribunal_en.pdf>.

5

*From Copper-Fastening Competence to Workable Structural Rule: The Case for Modernising Article 51(1) of the Charter**

ANGELA WARD

I. INTRODUCTION

THE EXPLANATIONS TO ARTICLE 51 of the EU Charter of Fundamental Rights assert, at the outset, that this provision 'seeks to establish clearly that the Charter applies *primarily* to the institutions and bodies of the Union' (my emphasis). Whether the objective of clarity has been achieved is open, however, to debate, given the volume of academic analyses,[1] propelled by a persisting stream of CJEU rulings concerning the, supposedly, subsidiary element of Article 51. It concerns the Member States and provides that the Charter applies to them 'only when they are implementing Union law'.[2]

* An abridged version of this article was published in (2025) *Cambridge Yearbook of European Legal Studies* 1.

[1] Among many see A Rosas, 'When is the EU Charter of Fundamental Rights Applicable at National Level' (2012) 19 (4) *Jurisprudence* 1269. F Fontanelli, 'The Implementation of European Union law by Member States Under Article 51 (1) of the Charter of Fundamental Rights' (2014) 20 *Columbia Journal of European Law* 194; C Matusescu, 'The Scope of Application of Fundamental Rights Guaranteed by European Union Law on Member States' Action: Some Jurisprudential Landmarks' (2017) *Union of Jurists of Romanian Law Review* 22. M Tecqmenne, 'Minimum Harmonisation and Fundamental Rights: A Test Case for the Identification of the Scope of EU Law in Situations Involving National Discretion' (2020) 16 *European Constitutional Law Review* 493. I Gambardella, 'L'application de la Chartre des droits fondamenteux de l'Union européenne aux Etats members: le critère de mis en oeuvre du droit de l'Union comme obstacle à son effectivité' (2021) *Cahiers de droit européen* 241; H Král and P Mádr, 'On the (in)applicability of the EU Charter of Fundamental Rights to National Measures Exceeding the Requirements of Minimum Harmonisation Directives' (2021) *European Law Review* 81.

[2] C-5/88 *Wachauf* EU:C:1989:321 and C-617/10 *Åkerberg Fransson* EU:C:2013:105 might be viewed as the foundational rulings on this issue. Broadly speaking, the Charter is applicable in all situations governed by European Union law, but not outside such situations. See generally Joined Cases C-585/18, C-624/18, and C-625/18, *AK (Independence of the Disciplinary Chamber of the Supreme Court)* EU:C:2019:982, paras 80 and 81; Joined Cases C-245/19 and C-246/19 *Etat Luxembourgeois* EU:C:2020:795, para 46; C-223/19 *YS v NK*, EU:C:2020:753, paras 79 to 80; Joined Cases C-411/10 and C-493/10 *NS v Secretary of State from the Home Department* EU:C:2011:865, para 68; C-66/18 *Commission v Hungary (Enseignement supérieur)*

As is well known, the central preoccupation underpinning Article 51 was prevention of recourse to the Charter to disturb the sensitive balance between EU and Member State competence, so that the latter was not incrementally diminished by recourse to Union action aimed exclusively at protection and promotion of fundamental rights.[3] After all, Article 6 TEU vested, for the first time, the Charter with the force of law, by providing that it 'shall have the same legal value as the Treaties' with the TEU additionally featuring provisions of the ilk of Article 21 (2) (b) TEU, which assigned to the Union the task of pursuing common policies and actions, on the international scene, to consolidate and support, inter alia democracy, the rule of law and human rights.

Thus, if an unequivocal restriction on the exercise of power was not welded into the text of Article 51 itself, there was a perception of inevitability of the emergence of Commission proposals for measures disconnected from any authority of the EU to act, aside from guaranteeing fundamental rights protection. The concern was a drift toward federalism.[4]

Article 51(2) of the Charter states, in terms similar to those of the second paragraph of Article 6(1) TEU, that the 'Charter does not extend the field of application of Union law beyond the powers of the Union or establish any new power or task for the Union, or modify powers and tasks as defined in the Treaties.' Indeed, it might be viewed as unfortunate that Article 51(2), another structural/constitutional provision, was not located in a separate article of its own, given that it deals with a subject matter that is entirely different from that addressed in Article 51(1). Further, unlike Article 51(1), there have been only a small number of CJEU rulings interpreting Article 51 (2)'s relatively lucid terms.[5]

In contrast, as at the date of writing this chapter, there are around 100 judgments and Advocates General's Opinions featuring the phrase 'Member States only when they are implementing Union law' under Article 51(1) of the Charter, and even a search of these key words does not scoop up all of the judgments and Advocate General's Opinions on the circumstances in which the Charter applies at Member State level.[6]

EU:C:2020:792, para 213; C-309/96 *Annibaldi* EU:C:1997:631; C-206/13 *Siragusa* EU:C:2014:126; C-333/13 *Dano* EU:C:2014: 2358; C-638/16 PPU *X and X v Etat belge* EU:C:2017:173; C-609 and 610/17 *TSN and AKT* EU:C:2019:981; C-686/18 *Abdusef and Others* EU:C:2020:567.

[3] For accounts on the difficulties in the drafting process of Article 51 see eg H Kaila, 'The Scope of Application of the Charter of Fundamental Rights of the European Union in the Member States' in P Cardonnel, A Rosas and N Wahl, (eds) *Constitutionalizing the EU Judicial System: Essays in Honour of Pernilla Lindh* (Oxford, Hart Publishing, 2012); T von Danwitz and K Paraschas, 'A Fresh Start for the Charter: Fundamental Questions on the Application of the European Charter of Fundamental Rights' (2017) 35 *Fordham International Law Review* 1396. The draft Charter of fundamental rights was adopted in October of 2000 by the Convention entrusted with this task by Cologne European Council of 3 and 4 June 1999.

[4] Gambardella, above note 1 at 273 and sources referred to therein.

[5] See notably C-370/12 *Thomas Pringle v Government of Ireland* EU:C:2012: 756; C-40/11 *Yoshikazu Iida v Stadt Ulm* EU:C:2012:691, para 78; C-400/10 *J McB* EU:C:2010:582, para 59. It is to be noted that, irrespective of competence issues, the European Commission is liable for damages under Article 340 TFEU whenever it acts inconsistently with its role as guardian of the Treaties. See Case C-597/18 *Council v K. Chrysostomides* EU:C:2020:1028, para 96.

[6] Eg C-27/11 *Vinkov* EU:C:2012:326; C-279/09 *DEB* EU:C:2010:811. Notably, none of the CJEU rulings on the horizontal application of the Charter are generated by such a search. Eg C-414/16 *Egenberger* EU:C:2018:257.

What is more, in 2019 the Grand Chamber of the CJEU confirmed in C-609 & 610/17 *TSN and AKT* that the test of a situation having to be 'governed' by EU law is supplemented by the requirement that 'the provisions of EU law in the area concerned' had to impose a 'specific obligation' on a Member State before the latter could be said to be 'implementing' EU law.[7] However, this has fallen short of transforming Article 51(1) into a workable structural provision. This is evidenced by the fact that, already, this addition to the case-law has generated divergence in views between Advocates General and the ruling of the CJEU on whether the Charter applied to the matter at hand.[8] Indeed, such divergence has occurred in almost all the leading cases concerning Article 51(1);[9] an unfortunate state of affairs given that structural rules of EU law should, ideally, facilitate predictable outcomes and be easy for Member State judges to apply.[10] Moreover, as will be here illustrated, the 'obligation' requirement seems difficult to square with all established pillars of the case-law on Article 51(1) of the Charter. Yet it remains unclear whether the established rules so affected have been overridden or simply modified.[11]

The question might be asked; if other constitutional principles, such as those on free movement, were as difficult for Member State judges to apply as the rule imposed by Article 51(1) of the Charter, would the process of embedding the free movement rules into the corpus of core principles of EU law have proceeded as smoothly as it did? Further, the complexity of Article 51(1) compares unfavourably with Article 1 of the European Convention of Human Rights, which provides, succinctly, that the Convention applies to everyone within the 'jurisdiction' of the High Contracting Parties.[12]

In the light of the scale of the jurisprudential resources expended on a point of law which is structural rather than substantive, and the supposedly primary objective of Article 51 of binding institutions, bodies, offices and agencies of the EU to the Charter's standards, as opposed to the Member States, is it not appropriate to begin reflecting on how Article 51(1) might, eventually, be re-cast into a more user-friendly text?[13] Is not the need for this exemplified by the very existence of a portal on

[7] C-609 and 610/17 *TSN and AKT* EU:C:2019:981, para 53. The same had already been added by various chambers of the CJEU. See eg Case C144/95 *Maurin* EU:C:1996:235, paras 11 and 12; C-206/13 *Siragusa* EU:C:2014:126, paras 26 and 27; C198/13 *Julián Hernández and Others*, EU:C:2014:2055, para 35; C243/16 *Miravitlles Ciurana and Others* EU:C:2017:969, para 34; and C152/17 *Consorzio Italian Management and Catania Multiservizi* EU:C:2018:264, paras 34 and 35).

[8] Case C-238/20 *Sātini S* EU:C:2022:57. Cf the Opinion of AG Rantos at EU:C:2021:735, paras 28 to 32. For an example of a relatively recent ruling in which the CJEU held that no EU rule imposed a specific obligation, so that the Member State was not 'implementing' Union law, see C-94/20 *Land Oberösterreich (Aide au logement)* EU:C:2021:477, para 61.

[9] See further below s IV below.

[10] See further below s V.

[11] See further s III below.

[12] Granted, the circumstances in which the ECHR has extraterritorial effect has generated vibrant jurisprudence. Of the many studies see, for example, M Milanovic, *Extraterritorial Application of Human Rights Treaties: Law, Principles and Policies* (Oxford, OUP, 2011). However, outside of these narrow factual circumstances, Article 1 ECHR has been unproblematic, in terms of legal certainty, at least in comparison with Article 51 (1) of the Charter.

[13] An opportunity, perhaps to do so was lost in the 2021–2022 Conference on the Future of Europe, with the Council setting out a stall early that the conference would entail no amendment to the treaties. The Conference ran from 9 May 2021 for a year. The Council excluded amending the treaties in its position on the

the Commission's website, to help those charged with responsibility for applying the Charter to ascertain when that duty arises?[14]

What will be here proposed is pairing down, and significantly, the text of Article 51(1), and splitting 51(1) and 51(2) so that the former, as re-cast, would appear at the beginning of the Charter. In order to avoid renumbering the whole of the Charter, the revised text of Article 51(1) would be placed under a new heading 'Part II Jurisdiction' which would appear just before the Charter itself ('Part III The European Union Charter of Fundamental Rights') and after the preamble ('Part I Preamble'). As for Article 51(2), it would remain where it is and simply become Article 51.

The new text for ex-Article 51, when read in combination with revised explanations, would focus on setting out, in practical terms, when the Charter applies, to the exclusion of all concerns connected to protecting the division of competence between the EU and the Member States, but via a text that is sufficiently open-ended to accommodate evolution in the case-law. Identification by the Member State court seized of a fundamental rights dispute of a provision of EU law, aside from the Charter, that is pertinent to the dispute's resolution, has long been mooted as the touchstone for determining when a Member State is implementing EU law,[15] and isolating the precise provisions of EU law in issue is central to establishing the jurisdiction of the CJEU.[16] With appropriately modified and expanded explanations accompanying ex-Article 51(1), would such an 'identification' process not become the guiding light for Member State judges if that text referred to questions of 'interpretation or validity' of EU law in the same way as Article 267 TFEU? Moreover, this solution better reflects the constitutional status of the Charter as an instrument that is woven through the established constitutional fabric of the European Union,[17] as opposed to one that is imposed on it from above as a *Grundnorm*; the

---

Conference on the Future of Europe, 24 June 2020, www.consilium.europa.eu/media/44679/st09102-en20.pdf. Referred to at footnote 269 of Gambardella, above note 1 who notes, the regrettable absence of debate in the process on the text of Article 51. See Commission Communication on the Conference on the Future of Europe COM (2022) 404 final. See further on the viability of amending Article 51(1) A Jakab and L Kirchmair, 'Two Ways of Completing the European Fundamental Rights Union: Amendment to vs. Reinterpretation of Article 51 of the EU Charter of Fundamental Rights' (2022) 24 *Cambridge Yearbook of European Legal Studies* 239, at 248 and 249.

[14] https://beta.ejustice.europa.eu/charterclick_start_action.do?init=true&idTaxonomy=583&plang=en. Referred to at footnote 8 of Gambardella, above note 1. The, admittedly, formidable political difficulty entailed in amending the Treaties will be here put to one side. For a recent and comprehensive analysis of the law and practice of amending treaties see eg C Binder, 'Change and the Law of Treaties' (2024) 13 *ESIL Reflections*. It might be tentatively suggested that altering the text of Article 51(1), and moving it to the beginning of the Charter, is a mere technical rather than substantive change to the Treaties.

[15] Rosas, above note 1.

[16] See recently eg Joined Cases C-357/19, C-379/19, C-547/19, C-811/19, and C-840/19 *Euro Box Promotion and Others* EU:C:2021:1034, para 132.

[17] See eg K Lenaerts and JA Gutiérrez-Fons, 'The Place of the Charter in the EU Constitutional Edifice', in S Peers, T Hervey, J Kenner and A Ward (eds), *The EU Charter of Fundamental Rights: A Commentary* (Oxford, C.H. Beck, Hart, Nomos, 2014). As the CJEU recently observed in Joined Cases C-357/19, C-379/19, C-547/19, C-811/19, and C-840/19 *Euro Box Promotion and Others* EU:C:2021:1034, para 245, 'unlike standard international treaties, the Community Treaties establish a new legal order, which is integrated into the legal systems of the Member States on the entry into force of the Treaties and which are binding on their courts'.

legal paradigm of conventional international human rights instruments. This question will be explored in the pages that follow.

It is beyond contention that the Charter has been a resounding success. The complex yet delicate body of case-law developed by the CJEU has transformed the Charter into one of the world's leading human rights instruments. Moreover, this case-law has passed almost without objection from the superior courts of the Member States;[18] a testament in itself to its jurisprudential quality. At the same time, fundamental rights protection has been enhanced in a myriad of fields.[19]

Yet, the very success of the Charter renders a rethink of the text of Article 51(1) timely, to the end of enhancing the coherency of the pivotal rule governing when it applies to Member States and private legal entities, the latter to date only having been added to the scope *ratione personae* of the Charter via the case-law of the CJEU, being absent entirely from the text of Article 51(1).[20] Any lack of clarity over the meaning of Member State 'implementing' EU law, and the volume of CJEU case-law which a national judge needs to consider in deciding whether implementation is occurring at all, can only serve to discourage Member State judges from relying on the Charter, particularly when instruments such as the ECHR are equally at their disposal, along with national human rights laws and constitutional protections.[21] It is to be recalled that:

> when a court of a Member State is called upon to review the compatibility with fundamental rights of a national provision or measure which, in a situation in which the action of the Member States is not entirely determined by EU law, implements EU law for the purposes of Article 51(1) of the Charter, Article 53 of the Charter confirms that national authorities

[18] Horizontal application of the Charter has met some resistance in the Danish courts. For an account see D Elkan, R Holdgaard and G Krohn Schaldemose 'From Cooperation to Collision: The ECJ's *Ajos* Ruling and the Danish Supreme Court's Refusal to Comply' (2018) 55 *Common Market Law Review* 17. It is also noteworthy that in the light of the ruling in C-673/16 *Coman* EU:C:2018:385, the Romanian authorities still refused to issue a residence permit to the Romanian applicant's same sex husband in that case. In consequence, an application has been brought before the European Court of Human Rights, see *Coman and Others v Romania (coe.int)*. There has also been some discord over the operation of the primacy of EU law in Romanian law. For a discussion see eg M Vrabie, 'The Relationship between EU law and Romanian Constitution. Recent Developments in the Case-Law of the Romanian Constitutional Court', NISPAcee Annual Conference, 202206291626350, Final Paper_Mihaela Vrabie_30.05.2022.pdf (nispa.org). See further recently Joined Cases C-357/19, C-379/19, C-547/19, C-811/19, and C-840/19 *EuroBox Promotion and Others* EU:C:2021:1034, and C-107/23 PPU *Lin* EU:C:2023:606.

[19] To name only three examples, data protection (for a foundational ruling see eg C-311/18 *Facebook Ireland and Schrems* EU:C:2020:559), the prohibition of discrimination on the basis of sexual orientation (eg C-673/16 *Coman* EU:C:2018:385); and freedom to conduct a business, which now extends to freedom to exercise an economic or commercial activity, freedom of contract and free competition and the freedom to choose with whom to do business (eg Case C-356/21 *TP (Monteur audiovisual pour la télévision publique)* EU:C:2023:9, para 74).

[20] Eg C-414/16 *Egenberger* EU :C:2018:257. See further eg on the horizontal applicability of Article 47 of the Charter, Case C-582/21 *Profi Credito Polska* EU:C:2024:282, C-715/20 *X (Absence de motifs de résilation)* EU:C:2024:139, and C-30/19 *Braathens Regional Aviation* EU:C:2021:269. For subsequent rulings concerning the horizontal applicability of other Charter provisions see eg C-68/17 *IR* EU:C:2018:696, para 69 (Article 21 in so far as it prohibits all discrimination on grounds of religion or belief); C-569/16 and C-570/16, *Bauer and Willmeroth* EU:C:2018:871; C-684/16 *Max Planck-Gesellschaft* EU:C:2018:874 (Article 31 (2) and the right to paid annual leave). On the latter see further eg L Cecchetti, 'Unravelling Horizontal Direct Effect in EU Law: The Case of the Fundamental Right to Paid Annual Leave between "Myth" and "Practice"' (2023) 42 *Yearbook of European Law* 42.

[21] See Articles 52 (4) and 53 of the Charter.

> and courts are free to apply national standards of protection of fundamental rights, provided that the level of protection provided for by the Charter, as interpreted by the Court, and the primacy, unity and effectiveness of EU law are not thereby compromised.[22]

Against this backdrop, it is now being suggested that the difficulty of determining when the Charter applies is the most pressing challenge to its effectiveness.[23]

Further, there are elements of the constitutional edifice that provide further support for simplifying the text of Article 51(1) of the Charter. Provided that a litigant did not 'unquestionably' have the right under Article 263 TFEU to bring an action before the General Court of the European Union seeking annulment of an EU measure for breach of fundamental rights guaranteed by the Charter, and failed to exercise that right within the time period prescribed by Article 263 TFEU,[24] they remain entitled to bring an action before a Member State court questioning the validity of the pertinent EU rules, and request a reference for a preliminary ruling to the CJEU.

But in such disputes, there is no 'threshold' question requiring the Member State court concerned to consider whether the Member State is 'implementing' EU law, because the challenge is not to Member State law, but an EU law.[25] Similarly, when no rule of Member State law is identified as being the subject of the challenge, but the dispute instead concerns interpretation of a provision of EU law in conformity with fundamental rights, the threshold question of whether a Member State is 'implementing' EU law is equally irrelevant, even in cases arising before the

[22] C-357/19 *Euro Box Promotion and Others* EU:C:2021:1034, para 211, referring to C617/10 *Åkerberg Fransson* EU:C:2013:105, para 29; C399/11 *Melloni* EU:C:2013:107, para 60; and C476/17 *Pelham and Others* EU:C:2019:624, para 80. See also eg C-107/23 PPU *Lin* EU:C:2023:606. For recent guidance on the limits of the application of Member State fundamental rights standards under Article 53 of the Charter see eg Advocate General Medina, Joined Cases C-258/23 and to C-260/23 *Imagens Médicas Integradas* EU:C:2025 814, paras 50 to 54. There the Advocate General states that there are in fact three limitations to the application of Member State fundamental rights standards. She notes (i) the application of such standards presupposes that the situation in question is not entirely governed by EU law, such as, for example, when a Directive is not one entailing full harmonisation (see eg C-469/17 *Funke Medien* NRW EU:C:2019:623, paragraph 33); (ii) the application of a national standard of protection of fundamental rights must not compromise the level of protection afforded by the Charter by providing lower standards than those guaranteed under the Charter; (iii) the application of national standards of protection of fundamental rights must not compromise the primacy, unity and effectiveness of EU law (see, to that effect C399/11 *Melloni* EU:C:2013:107, para 60). The CJEU has rejected any interpretation of Article 53 of the Charter according to which the Charter gives general authorisation to a Member State to apply the higher level of protection of fundamental rights guaranteed by its Constitution and, where necessary, give it priority over the application of provisions of EU law (*Melloni* para 56).

[23] See eg Gambardella above note 1.

[24] See recently C-330/22 *Friends of the Irish Environment* EU:C:2024:19, para 50. The terminology of the CJEU has not been entirely consistent. It has also held that an action for validity can be brought before a Member State court when 'it is not obvious that an action for annulment brought by the defendant in the main proceedings would have been admissible'. See C-212/19, *Compagnie des pêches de Saint Malo* EU:C:2020:726, para 35.

[25] See notably eg C-400/10 PPU *JMcB* EU:C:2010:582; Joined Cases C-293/12 and C-594/12 *Digital Rights Ireland and Seitlinger and Others* EU:C:2014:238; C-362/14 *Schrems* EU:C:2015:650; C-601/15 PPU *N* EU:C:2016:84; C-477/14 *Pillbox* 38 EU:C:2016:324; C-543/14 *Ordre des barreaux francophones and Germanophones and Others* EU:C:2016:605; C-426/16 *Liga van Moskeen en Islamitische Organisaties Provincie Antwerpen and Others* EU:C:2018:335; C-13/23 *cdVet Naturprodukte* EU:C:2024:175; C-716/22 *Préfet du Gers and Institut national de la statistique and des études économiques II* EU:C:2024:339.

Member State courts.[26] In addition, this approach has been notably present also in disputes between private parties concerning EU Directives. For example, in the field of EU copyright law, the Directives in and of themselves fall to be interpreted in conformity with the Charter, there being no pre-requisite to create a link with Member State law.[27]

That being so, is the authority of Member State judge to rule sometimes dependent on the accident as to whether a litigant's legal team has elected to base their challenge directly on an EU rule which is pertinent to the resolution of the dispute, rather than the Member State rule purportedly implementing it? If so, is such a system of judicial remedies coherent?[28]

Therefore, and as already foreshadowed, the case will here be made to alleviate the complexity of the system of judicial remedies in place by linking the new text of Article 51(1) to Article 267 TFEU and the authority of the CJEU to issue rulings on the 'interpretation and validity' of EU law, rather than focusing on the somewhat more slippery concept of Member State implementation of EU law, or the even more enigmatic notion of 'situations'[29] governed by EU law, and now supplemented by imposition of an EU 'obligation'?[30] Once provisions of EU law are identified that are pertinent to the resolution of the dispute, and interpreted in conformity with the Charter, the fate of Member State rules that are obstructing the enforcement of these EU rules, and therefore the Charter, will be determined by long established rules on primacy, direct effect and other principles determining the relationship between EU law and Member State law. These principles will be set out in Section III.F below.

Further, as will be explained below, the established and clear demarcation of authority between the General Court and the courts of the Member States when it comes to the protection of fundamental rights, militate in favour of a new text of, new, Article 51(1) which expressly refers to the court to be seized.

It is perhaps the case that the practical need for a rule guaranteeing easy identification of the circumstances in which the Charter is applicable at Member State level was overlooked when the Charter attained legally binding force due to the intensity of the, now, historic, concern of ensuring that it would not result in expansion of EU competence, as discussed above. If this is so, can this situation now be remedied by amendment to Article 51(1) so that it supplies a more user-friendly rule, the users

[26] C-333/22 *Ligue des droits humains (vérification du traitement des données par l'autorité de contrôle)* EU:C:2023:874, para 57, 'it should be noted in this respect that, in accordance with a general principle of interpretation, an EU act must be interpreted, as far as possible, in such a way as not to affect its validity and in conformity with primary law as a whole and, in particular, with the provisions of the Charter. Thus, if the wording of secondary EU legislation is open to more than one interpretation, preference should be given to the interpretation which renders the provision consistent with primary law rather than to the interpretation which leads to its being incompatible with primary law (judgment of 21 June 2022, *Ligue des droits humains*, C817/19, EU:C:2022:491, paragraph 86 and the case-law cited).'

[27] See eg C-392/19 *Bild Kunst* EU:C:2021:181, para 54; C-265/19 *Recorded Artists Actors Performers Ltd* EU:C:2020:677, paras 85 to 91; C-260/22 *Seven.One* EU:C:2023:900, paras 40 and 44.

[28] On the coherence necessary and inherent in any system of effective judicial protection, see the Opinion of Advocate General Hogan in Case C-134/19 P *Bank Refah Kargaran* EU:C:2020:396, para 61, referring to the ruling of the Court in C-72/15 *Rosneft* ECLI:EU:C:2017:236, para 78.

[29] See notably C-617/10 *Akerberg Fransson* EU:C:2013:105, para 19.

[30] Above note 7.

being Member State judges, and which provides a rule on when the Charter applies which is expressed in more straightforward terms?

Finally, by way of preliminary remarks, this study proposes no specific amendment to the jurisdiction of the CJEU, under the combined effects of Articles 2 and 19(1) TEU, to guarantee effective judicial protection[31] with respect to all 'courts and tribunals', within the meaning of EU law, called upon to rule upon the application and interpretation of EU law, and thus which come within the judicial system of the EU, given that this jurisdiction is operative 'irrespective of the circumstances in which Member States are implementing EU law'.[32] Put otherwise, orders for reference concerning Article 19(1) and 2 TEU are admissible, under the now established case-law of the CJEU, irrespective of whether or not Member States are 'implementing' EU law.[33]

Section II addresses, in outline, the term 'institutions, bodies, offices and agencies of the Union' and shows the importance of identifying whether a fundamental rights dispute should be determined by direct application to the General Court, or instead challenge before Member State courts under the Article 267 validity mechanism. This supports the argument that identification of the court to be seized should be the starting point in any re-draft of Article 51(1) of the Charter, given that this is a core preoccupation of Member State judges.

Section III will identify the central elements of the jurisprudence on the phrase 'Member States only when they are implementing Union law' and demonstrate that a dominant feature of this case-law already lies in identifying the provisions of EU law that are pertinent to the resolution of the dispute. Section III will also address the case-law of the CJEU on horizontal application of that Charter, leaving private parties, in effect, bound by its terms in certain defined circumstances, irrespective of Member State laws that would otherwise obstruct this obligation. This is more potent than the aforementioned established practice of the CJEU of interpreting Directives in conformity with the Charter in horizontal disputes.

Section IV will make some tentative proposals for amendment to Article 51, to be suggested in the light of the developments canvassed in Sections II and III. It will also provide an outline of how the explanations to the new text of Article 51(1) might be amended to furnish Member State judges with a useful guideline document to the Charter's applicability. Section V will contain concluding remarks.

[31] A general principle of law enshrined in Articles 6 and 13 ECHR, along with Article 47 of the Charter. See recently eg Joined Cases C-357/19, C-379/19, C-547/19, C-811/19, and C-840/19 *Euro Box Promotion and Others* EU:C:2021:1034 para 219.

[32] Joined Cases C-357/19, C-379/19, C-547/19, C-811/19, and C-840/19 *Euro Box Promotion and Others*, EU:C:2021:1034, para 220. Cf Jakab and Kirchmair above note 13. For commentaries on this development see, eg A Bakardjieva Engelbrekt, A Moberg and J Nergelius, 'The Rule of Law in the EU 30 Years After the Fall of the Berlin Wall: Taking Stock and Looking Ahead' in A Bakardjieva Engelbrekt et al (eds), *The Rule of Law in the EU 30 Years After the Fall of the Berlin Wall* (Oxford, Hart Publishing, 2021). See more particularly on the evolution of the rule of law as a fundamental tenant of EU constitutional law, and the role of conditionality in its extension to central European accession states see, in the same volume, A Bakardjieva Engelbrekt, 'The Eastward Enlargement as a Driving Force and Testbed for the Rule of Law Policy in the EU', in ibid, 3–35. See further A Bakardjieva Engelbrekt, 'Rule of Law and Judicial Independence in the EU: Lessons from the Union's Eastward Enlargement and Ways Forward' (2023) 69 *Scandinavian Studies in Law* 178.

[33] Above note 2.

II. INSTITUTIONS, BODIES, OFFICES AND AGENCIES OF THE EU

As mentioned in the introduction to this chapter, these entities are the primary targets of the Charter. It is they that are bound by its terms, and Member States only enter the frame when they are 'implementing' EU law.

Thus, it is important to underscore that, unlike the situation with respect to Member States, the Charter applies to institutions, bodies, offices and agencies of the EU with respect to *everything they do*,[34] so that any court, whether it be EU or Member State, seized of a complaint concerning non-observance of the Charter by one of these entities need make no investigation as to whether, on the basis of the pertinent factual circumstances, any Member State authority has entered the frame who might be implementing EU law. This is so because the Charter is applicable upon identification of the defendant as an institution, body, office or agency of the EU as an entity alleged to have behaved inconsistently with the Charter. For example, it follows from the rulings in C584/17 P *ADR Center v Commission*[35] and C378/16 P *Inclusion Alliance for Europe v Commission*,[36] that the institutions, bodies, offices or agencies of the European Union remain, when performing a contract, subject to their obligations under the Charter.

The Institutions of the Union are designated in Article 13 TEU as the European Parliament, the European Council, the Council, the European Commission, the Court of Justice of the European Union, the European Central Bank and the Court of Auditors. Self-evidently, all measures promulgated by all of these are to comply with fundamental rights as reflected in the Charter. The CJEU has further held, however, that the term 'institution' within the meaning of Article 340 TFEU (on non-contractual liability for damages) encompasses not only the EU institutions listed in Article 13 TEU but also all the EU bodies, offices and agencies that have been established by or under the Treaties and which are intended to contribute to the achievement of the European Union's objectives.[37]

Their existence is, therefore, generally discernible by unpicking the EU legislative regime that led to their establishment. With the exception of complex scenarios, such as whether public–private partnerships can be agencies of the EU,[38] in most cases, this exercise will readily identify a body, office or agency which is obliged in all its activities to comply with the Charter. As pointed out in the explanations to Article 51, the expression 'bodies, offices and agencies' refers to all the bodies set up by the Treaties or by secondary legislation. Generally, the 'parent' EU measure itself will expressly designate the new entity so formed as an EU 'agency'.[39]

[34] C-234/21 *Défense Active des Amateurs d'Armes and Others* EU:C:2023:644, para 27 of the Opinion of Advocate General Sanchez Bordona. The Advocate General here mentions that the Charter applies to institutions, bodies, offices and agencies of the EU 'in any circumstances'.

[35] EU:C:2020:576.

[36] EU:C:2020:575.

[37] C-597/18 P *Council v K. Chrysostomides and Co and Others* EU:C:2020:1028, para 80.

[38] See for example the discussion in H Hofmann and A Morini, 'The Pluralisation of EU Executive-Constitutional Aspects of Agencification' (2012) 37 *European Law Review* 419.

[39] See for example, the Opinion of Advocate General Capeta in C-551/22 P *Commission v SRB* EU:C:2023:846, para 33, where the Advocate General points out that the status of the Single Resolution Board as an EU agency is established in the EU measure founding it.

As already mentioned, if an applicant seeking to enforce fundamental rights against an institution, body, office or agency satisfies the test for *locus standi* under Article 263 TFEU, such challenge is to be brought before the General Court of the EU within the two-month time limit set by that provision, rather than before the courts of the Member States.[40] If a litigant 'unquestionably had the right to bring an action . . . on the basis of Article 263 TFEU' they will be precluded from bringing suit questioning the validity of the measure before a Member State court, and therefore will be equally precluded from seeking referral of a question on its validity to the CJEU under Article 267 TFEU.[41] While there is no settled case-law on the precise point on the circumstances in which damages liability will be made out for breach of the Charter by the EU under the procedure set down in Articles 268 and 340 TFEU,[42] this route remains open when a complaint concerning the non-contractual liability of the EU encapsulates the Charter.[43]

Another core 'shadow' area of the topic of 'institutions, bodies, offices, and agencies' of the EU and their duties under the Charter, lies in the field composite decision making, and which court, the General Court or the administrative courts of the Member States, should be petitioned, when breach of fundamental rights is alleged in the context of such decision making. This conundrum came to the fore in C-562/12, *Liivimaa Lihaveis*.[44] But at the same time, this ruling potentially set out the road ahead for amending Article 51(1), by altering the focus to the court to be seized as the foundation stone on which to build a more coherent rule on the applicability of the Charter when Member State action is in the frame.

On 19 February 2010, Liivimaa Lihaveis submitted an application under the Estonia-Latvia operational programme for financing of a project aimed at creating a new product and brand to be produced from quality beef animals raised on the most diversified grasslands of Estonia and Latvia. Under Article 32(5) of Regulation No 1083/2006 of 11 July 2006 laying down general provisions on the European Regional Development Fund, the European Social Fund and the Cohesion Fund and repealing Regulation (EC) No 1260/1999,[45] that programme was adopted as an EU measure by Article 1 of European Commission Decision C (2007) 6603 final of 21 December 2007. By letter of 7 July 2010, Liivimaa Lihaveis was informed by a body called the Seirekomitee that this application was rejected.

[40] For a recent and detailed analysis of when a decision can be considered adopted by an institution, body, office or agency of the Union and therefore susceptible to an action for annulment under Article 263 TFEU see C-743/19 *Parliament v Council* EU:C:2022:569.

[41] C-330/22 *Friends of the Irish Environment* EU:C:2024:19, para 50, re-stating the rule in C-188/92 *TWD* EU:C:1994:90, as re-stated in C72/15 *Rosneft* EU:C:2017:236, paras 66 and 67.

[42] For a discussion see eg the text by C Rauchegger in S Peers, T Hervey, J Kenner and A Ward (eds), *The EU Charter of Fundamental Rights: A Commentary* (Oxford, Hart Publishing, 2021) paras 47.236 to 47.261.

[43] This is clear, for example, from the ruling of the General Court in T-371/22 *Montanari* EU:7:2024:494, particularly at para 129.

[44] EU:C:2014:2229. See also eg C-219/17 *Berlusconi (Fininvest)* EU:C:2018:1023. Among the many commentaries on this problem see eg M Safjan and D Dusterhaus, 'A Union of Effective Judicial Protection; Addressing a Multi-level Challenge through the Lens of Article 47 CFREU' (2014) 33 *Yearbook of European Law* 3.

[45] OJ 2006 L 210, p 25.

The Seirekomitee was established by agreement between the Republic of Estonia and the Republic of Latvia on the basis of, inter alia, Article 63(1) of Regulation No 1083/2006. Article 63 (1) provides for the establishment of a Monitoring Committee and, importantly, Article 63 (2) additionally obliges the Monitoring Committee to establish rules of procedure. The Seirekomitee was that Monitoring Committee.

Liivimaa Lihaveis brought legal proceedings before the Tartu Halduskohus (Administrative Court, Tartu) seeking the annulment of the Seirekomitee's decision rejecting its application for aid and an order requiring the Seirekomitee to re-examine the application and to adopt an administrative decision consistent with the law. They alleged breach of Article 47 of the Charter, since the decision of the Seirekomitee was not appealable. The prohibition on appeal was set out in Article 6.6.4 of a document called a 'Programme Manual' which had been adopted by the Monitoring Committee pursuant to its obligations to adopt procedural rules, as provided in Article 63 (2) of Regulation No 1083/2006.

By order of 21 September 2011, the Administrative Court, Tartu dismissed the action. On 3 October 2011, Liivimaa Lihaveis appealed against that order before the Tartu ringkonnakohus (Court of Appeal, Tartu), which sent a series of questions to the CJEU under Article 267 TFEU.

The referring court was unsure whether an action against the Seirekomitee should be brought before the Administrative courts of Estonia, or the General Court of the EU. Thus, the questions sent were as follows:

> 1. Are the rules of procedure of a monitoring committee jointly set up by two Member States, such as the programme manual adopted by the [Seirekomitee], which provide that 'The decisions of the Monitoring Committee are not appealable at any place of jurisdiction' (Chapter 6.6.4 of the programme manual) compatible with Article 63(2) of Council Regulation No 1083/2006 in conjunction with Article 47 of the [Charter]?
>
> 2. If Question 1 is to be answered in the negative, must point (b) of the first paragraph of Article 267 [TFEU] be interpreted as meaning that Chapter 6.6.4 of [that programme manual] is an act of an institution, body, office or agency of the European Union which must be declared invalid?
>
> 3. If Question 1 is to be answered in the negative, must the second sentence of the first paragraph of Article 263 [TFEU] in conjunction with Article 256(1) [TFEU] and Article 274 [TFEU] be interpreted as meaning that the General Court of the European Union or the competent court under national law has jurisdiction to hear and determine actions against decisions of the [Seirekomitee]?

The dispute in *Liivimaa Lihaveis* is perhaps most valuable because it highlights one of the core problems with Article 51 (1) which had hitherto been in the background. Since the Charter is primarily directed at the institutions, bodies, offices and agencies of the EU, a key purpose underpinning the phrase 'Member States only when they are implementing EU law' is the determination of which court, the General Court of the EU, or the courts of the Member States, are authorised to rule on the fundamental rights issues which have been raised. This theme will be revisited in Section IV below.

The CJEU noted that under the second sentence of the first paragraph of Article 263 TFEU, it had authority to review the legality of acts of bodies, offices or agencies of the Union intended to produce legal effects vis-à-vis third parties.[46] It was further established in the case-law that the judicial review mechanisms laid down in Article 263 TFEU apply to the bodies, offices and agencies established by the EU legislature which were given powers to adopt measures that are legally binding on natural or legal persons in specific areas, such as the European Aviation Safety Agency (EASA), the European Medicines Agency (EMA), the European Chemicals Agency (ECHA), the Community Plant Variety Office (CPVO) and the Office for Harmonization in the Internal Market (Trade Marks and Designs) (OHIM).[47] However, a Monitoring Committee instituted as part of an operational programme to promote European territorial cooperation was not an institution or a body, office or agency of the European Union[48] because, in an action brought under Article 263 TFEU, the European Union Court has no jurisdiction to rule on the lawfulness of a measure adopted by a national authority.[49] In reaching this conclusion, the CJEU relied on the legal structure underpinning the establishment of the Seirekomitee. It held as follows at paragraphs 49 to 51.

> 49 In the present case, under Article 63(1) and (2) of Regulation No 1083/2006, a monitoring committee is to be set up for each operational programme by the 'Member State' and each monitoring committee is to draw up its rules of procedure within the institutional, legal and financial framework of the Member State concerned.
>
> 50 Since Regulations Nos 1083/2006 and 1080/2006 provide for the possibility of establishing operational programmes to promote European territorial cooperation, the Seirekomitee was instituted jointly by the Republic of Estonia and the Republic of Latvia, as expressly stated in the second subparagraph of Chapter 7.1 of the programme document.
>
> 51 Accordingly, the General Court of the European Union does not have jurisdiction, under Article 256 TFEU, to hear an action against a decision of a monitoring committee, such as the Seirekomitee, rejecting an application for aid.

The CJEU went on to hold that, in consequence of this, point (b) of the first paragraph of Article 267 TFEU had to be interpreted as meaning that a programme manual adopted by a monitoring committee in the context of an operational programme under Regulations Nos 1083/2006 and 1080/2006 to promote European territorial cooperation between two Member States, such as that at issue, was not an act of an institution, body, office or agency of the European Union. Thus, the Court of Justice did not have jurisdiction to review the validity of the provisions of the programme manual on that basis.[50] However, with regard to the applicability of Article 47, the CJEU held as follows at paragraphs 60 to 65.

[46] EU:C:2014:2229, para 45.
[47] ibid para 46.
[48] ibid para 47.
[49] ibid para 48. The CJEU referred to C97/91 *Oleificio Borelli v Commission* EU:C:1992:491, para 9, and C64/05 P *Sweden v Commission* EU:C:2007:802, para 91.To this could be added other rulings, such as C-785/18 *GAEC Jeanningros* EU:C:2020:46, para 27 and C-743/19 *Parliament v Council* EU:C:2022:569.
[50] EU:C:2014:2229, paras 53 to 56.

60 The fact that the Seirekomitee is not an institution, body, office or agency of the European Union, as follows from the answer to the third question asked by the referring court, does not prevent Article 47 of the Charter from applying if the adoption by that committee of the programme manual is an act falling within the scope of EU law.

61 In consequence, it is necessary to ascertain whether the programme manual implements EU law, within the meaning of Article 51(1) of the Charter.

62 In accordance with the settled case-law of the Court, the concept of 'implementing Union law', as referred to in that provision of the Charter, requires a certain degree of connection above and beyond the matters covered being closely related or one of those matters having an indirect impact on the other (see, inter alia, judgment in *Kremzow*, C299/95, EU:C:1997:254, paragraph 16).

63 In the present case, it is sufficient to note that EU law required the two Member States involved in the Estonia-Latvia operational programme to implement that programme.

64 In particular, firstly, those Member States were required to institute a monitoring committee, pursuant to Article 63(1) and (2) of Regulation No 1083/2006. Secondly, all the measures intended to apply that operational programme, which include the programme manual, had to comply with the provisions of Regulations Nos 1083/2006 and 1080/2006.

65 Accordingly, it must be held that the adoption of the programme manual by the monitoring committee implements EU law within the meaning of Article 51(1) of the Charter.

On the substantive question as to whether Article 47 of the Charter had been breached, the CJEU held at paragraph 71 that 'the lack of any remedy against such a rejection decision deprives the applicant of its right to an effective remedy, in breach of Article 47 of the Charter'.

Aside, therefore, from illuminating the importance of determining the court to which a fundamental rights claim should be made, *Liivimaa Lihaeis* highlights a further crucial fact about the process of deciding whether a Member State is 'implementing' EU law and brings to the fore the pre-occupations of the Member State judge. That is, the 'certain degree of connection above and beyond the matters covered being closely related or one of those matters having an indirect impact on the other' necessary before a Member State can be held to be implementing Union law entails identification of EU measures binding that Member State, and which themselves, by definition, require interpretation in the resolution of the dispute.[51] As noted above, the first question sent by the referring court rightly asked about interpretation of Article 63 (2) of Regulation No 1083/2006 in conformity with Article 47 of the Charter.

In *Liivimaa Lihaveis* the CJEU also identified Article 63(1) and (2) of Regulation No 1083/2006, along with Regulations Nos 1083/2006 and 1080/2006 as the provisions of EU law relevant to the resolution of the dispute. Indeed, these were the only connecting factors mentioned by the CJEU. Article 63 (1) and (2) of Regulation 1083/2006 state as follows:

[51] As mentioned in the text to note 15, identification of a provision of EU law pertinent to the resolution of a dispute aside from the Charter has long since been advocated by Rosas, above note 1, as a touchstone for determining the applicability of the Charter.

> 1. The Member State shall set up a Monitoring Committee for each operational programme, in agreement with the Managing Authority, within three months from the date of the notification to the Member State of the decision approving the operational programme. A single Monitoring Committee may be set up for several operational programmes.
>
> 2. Each Monitoring Committee shall draw up its rules of procedure within the institutional, legal and financial framework of the Member State concerned and adopt them in agreement with the Managing Authority in order to exercise its missions in accordance with this Regulation.

When the legal structure at issue in *Liivimaa Lihaveis* is unpicked, the prohibition on the appeal of decisions was located in Chapter 6.6.4 of a document called the 'Programme Manual' which had been adopted by the Monitoring Committee at its first meeting. Thus, whether the ban on appeals was lawful under EU law necessarily required interpretation of Article 63(2) of Regulation 1083/2006; the provision imposing an obligation on Management Committees to adopt rules of procedure.

What impediment is there, therefore, to reducing the legal test for 'implementing' EU law to legal disputes in which the interpretation or validity of a provision of EU law is in question, or in other words, is pertinent to the resolution of the dispute?[52] After all, as the CJEU routinely observes in disputes concerning fundamental rights, under Article 94 of the Rules of Procedure of the Court of Justice, the referring court is called on to explain the relationship between the provisions of EU law of which it seeks interpretation and the national legislation applicable to the dispute brought before it. Orders for reference must therefore contain an element permitting a finding that the dispute in issue concerns the interpretation or the application of provisions of EU law other than the Charter.[53]

So why not re-draft Article 51(1) with an umbrella term flagging this, and flesh out the operation of the 'identification' process in the explanations to accompany the new provision?

III. MEMBER STATES ONLY WHEN THEY ARE IMPLEMENTING EU LAW

A. Introduction

Prior to C-609 and 610/17 *TSN and AKT*,[54] broadly speaking, the circumstances in which Member States had been held to be implementing EU law fell into four categories. The Charter was applicable (i) in all situations 'governed' by European Union law;[55] (ii) whenever Member States exercised discretionary powers, the authority for which is sourced in an EU measure;[56] (iii) when Member States derogated from the four freedoms,[57] or relied on exceptions contained in EU legislation;[58] (iv) and in the

[52] See notably Rosas above note 1.
[53] Eg C-609/17 and C-610/17 *TSN v AKT* EU:C:2019:981, para 44.
[54] EU:C:2019:981.
[55] C-617/10 *Akerberg Fransson* EU:C:2013:105, para 19.
[56] C-411/10 and C-493/10 *NS* EU:C:2011:865.
[57] C-390/12 *Pfleger and Others* EU:C:2014:281.
[58] See e. C-411/10 and C-493/10 *NS* EU:C:2011:865, para 67.

context of remedies provided by Member State law to enforce Charter rights. This is so particularly, although not exclusively,[59] with respect to Article 47 of the Charter.[60]

Of the four of these, it is submitted that it is the first which remains the most problematic in terms of legal certainty. This is partly because the requirement for EU law to impose an 'obligation' before it can be viewed as 'implementing' EU law has not been applied in all cases post *TSN v AKT*, and more specifically not even in all Grand Chamber cases.[61] Further, the assent of the 'obligation' requirement has additionally called into doubt the scope of category (ii), and the imposition of the Charter on Member State bodies when they exercise discretionary authority sourced in an EU measure, and the rule that Member State are bound by the Charter when they exercise their, discretionary, authority over remedies (point iv above).

And, hanging somewhat uncomfortably beneath all of this, is the *Egenberger* jurisprudence.[62] It establishes that there are some provisions of the Charter which, in and of themselves, vest rights which individuals can enforce, even in the absence of EU or Member State measures elaborating their content, and even in disputes in which EU law is being enforced by one private party against another and it is not possible to interpret any pertinent national legislation in conformity with an EU directive because the national legislation is *contra legem* the text of the Directive.[63] The *Egenberger* line of case-law reflects the most well-known instance of the 'horizontal' enforcement of the Charter.[64] This development will be canvassed, briefly, at the end of Section III, to demonstrate that it too would fall within a re-draft of Article 51(1) grounded on the twin pillars of the court to be seized and the interpretation and validity of EU law, with the suggested new Explanations clarifying why the *Egenberger* rule falls within it.

B. Situations 'Governed' by EU Law

As mentioned in the explanations to the Charter, one of the foundational rulings underpinning the text of Article 51, and the rule that 'the requirement to respect fundamental rights defined in the context of the Union is only binding on the Member

[59] See the Opinion of Advocate General Tanchev C-282/19 *MIUR and Ufficio Scolastico Regionale per la Campania* EU:C:2021:217, para 76 and the interesting discussion on the extent to which rights protected in the Charter, such as the Article 21 prohibition of discrimination based on religion applies to the context of remedies. The Article 17 right to property is applicable to compensation schemes set up to implement EU law. See C-238/20 *Sātini S* EU:C:2022:57.

[60] As established in C-279/09 *DEB* EU:C:2010:811. Of the many subsequent rulings see eg Joined Cases C-585/18, C-624/18, and C-625/18 *AK (Independence of the Disciplinary Chamber of the Supreme Court)* EU:C:2019:982, paras 80 and 81.

[61] Joined Cases C-245/19 and C-246/19 *Etat Luxembourgeois* EU:C:2020:795, para 46. 'The adoption, by a Member State, of legislation specifying the details of the procedure for exchange of information on request established by Directive 2011/16 constitutes such an implementation (see, to that effect, judgment of 16 May 2017, *Berlioz Investment Fund*, C682/15, EU:C:2017:373, paras 34 to 37), in particular where that legislation provides for the *possibility*, for the competent authority, of taking a decision that obliges a person holding information to provide it with that information' (my emphasis).

[62] C-414/16 *Egenberger* EU:C:2018:257.

[63] C-106/89 *Marleasing* EU:C:1990:395.

[64] See cases referred to above note 20.

States when they act in the scope of Union law' lies in the judgment of the CJEU in C-5/88 *Wachauf*.[65] There, Mr Wachauf requested compensation for the definitive discontinuance of milk production pursuant to a German law. That legislation was based on a power contained in Article 4(1) (a) of Regulation No 857/84 adopting general rules for the application of the levy referred to in Article 5c of Regulation (EEC) No 804/68 in the milk and milk products sector.[66] The German authorities refused compensation since the landlord of the farm had withdrawn his consent to the tenancy.

The CJEU held at paragraph 22 that the

> Community regulations in question . . . leave the competent national authorities a sufficiently wide margin of appreciation to enable them to apply those rules in a manner consistent with the requirements of the protection of fundamental rights, either by giving the lessee the opportunity of keeping all or part of the reference quantity if he intends to continue milk production, or by compensating him if he undertakes to abandon such production definitively.

The CJEU further held at paragraph 19 that

> Community rules which, upon the expiry of the lease, had the effect of depriving the lessee, without compensation, of the fruits of his labour and of his investments in the tenanted holding would be incompatible with the requirements of the protection of fundamental rights in the Community legal order. Since those requirements are also binding on the Member States when they implement Community rules, the Member States must, as far as possible, apply those rules in accordance with those requirements.

In other words, the *Wachauf* case itself was about whether specific provisions of an EU Regulation could be interpreted in conformity with fundamental rights, rather than being concerned with the text of a Member State measure. It was not a ruling which, in fact, elaborated upon the meaning of 'implementing' at all. Thus, the trigger for the application of fundamental rights in that case was the identification of EU legislative measures, namely Article 4(1) (a) of Regulation No 857/84, read in combination with Article 4(2) which required interpretation in conformity with EU law. Thus, as was the case in *Liivimaa Lihaveis*, the *Wachauf* ruling itself boiled down to identification of an EU rule that was pertinent to the resolution of the dispute and which required interpretation in conformity with fundamental rights. Article 4(1)(a) of Regulation 857/84 provided that 'in order to complete the restructuring of milk production at national or regional level or at the level of the collecting areas, the Member States may, in connection with the application of formulas A and B (A) grant to producers undertaking to discontinue milk production definitively compensation paid in one or more annual payments', but to be read subject to fundamental rights. It is in this context that the seminal finding of the CJEU at paragraph 19 needs to be read.

The same applies to the core jurisprudential guidance on the meaning of 'implementing' which came in the ruling of the CJEU in C-617/10 *Åkerberg Fransson*,[67]

[65] EU:C:1989:321.
[66] Official Journal 1984 L90, p 13.
[67] EU:C:2013:105.

perhaps best known in the literature for confirming that there would be no rupture with pre-Charter case-law, in the sense that a Member State measure need not have been passed for the express purpose of implementing an EU measure in order to be considered as 'implementing' EU law for the purposes of Article 51(1) of the Charter.[68] There, the applicant sought to rely on the principle of ne bis in idem, enshrined in Article 50 of the Charter, to combat what he argued to be double punishment for VAT fraud. But the preliminary question arose as to whether the proceeding brought against the applicant amounted to an 'implementation' of EU law at all. The CJEU held as follows:

> 19 The Court's settled case-law indeed states, in essence, that the fundamental rights guaranteed in the legal order of the European Union are applicable in all situations governed by European Union law, but not outside such situations. In this respect the Court has already observed that it has no power to examine the compatibility with the Charter of national legislation lying outside the scope of European Union law. On the other hand, if such legislation falls within the scope of European Union law, the Court, when requested to give a preliminary ruling, must provide all the guidance as to interpretation needed in order for the national court to determine whether that legislation is compatible with the fundamental rights the observance of which the Court ensures . . .
>
> . . .
>
> 21 Since the fundamental rights guaranteed by the Charter must therefore be complied with where national legislation falls within the scope of European Union law, situations cannot exist which are covered in that way by European Union law without those fundamental rights being applicable. The applicability of European Union law entails applicability of the fundamental rights guaranteed by the Charter.
>
> 22 Where, on the other hand, a legal situation does not come within the scope of European Union law, the Court does not have jurisdiction to rule on it and any provisions of the Charter relied upon cannot, of themselves, form the basis for such jurisdiction . . .

While the ruling in *Åkerberg* is an improvement on the guidance provided in rulings such as C-256/11 *Dereci*[69] and in which the CJEU appeared to adopt the wording of a Member State referring court, and the suggestion that the Charter applies to situations 'covered' by Union law, no express guidance was provided in *Åkerberg Fransson* on how to determine if national legislation lies outside of the scope of European Union law.

However, the *Åkerberg* ruling might also be read as anointing the identification process here advocated as the *primary* means for determining the applicability of the

[68] See for example Gambardella, above note 1 at 246. See also on this point C-682/15 *Berlioz* EU:C:2017:373, para 40. It of course remains the case that Member State measures actively taken to implement EU law fall within 'implementing Union law' under Article 51(1). Eg C-58/22 *Parchetul de pelângă Curtea de Apel Craiova* EU:C:2024:70. Interestingly, at para 27 of the Opinion of Advocate General Emilou, EU:C:2023:464, while not disagreeing that the matter concerned was an incidence of Member State implementation of EU law, the Advocate General observed that he had 'some sympathy for certain arguments put forward by the Romanian Government' to the contrary.

[69] EU:C:2011:734, para 72. For other examples where the term 'covered' is used see eg C-206/13 *Siragusa* EU:C:2014:126, para 22.

Charter, and by implication whether Member State rules fall within the scope of EU law, because the identification exercise was the primary focus of the judgment. The CJEU analysed the pertinent legal framework as follows:

> 24 In the case in point, it is to be noted at the outset that the tax penalties and criminal proceedings to which Mr Åkerberg Fransson has been or is subject are connected in part to breaches of his obligations to declare VAT.
>
> 25 In relation to VAT, it follows, first, from Articles 2, 250(1) and 273 of Council Directive 2006/112/EC of 28 November 2006 on the common system of value added tax (OJ 2006 L 347, p. 1), which reproduce inter alia the provisions of Article 2 of the Sixth Directive and of Article 22(4) and (8) of that directive in the version resulting from Article 28h thereof, and second, from Article 4(3) TEU that every Member State is under an obligation to take all legislative and administrative measures appropriate for ensuring collection of all the VAT due on its territory and for preventing evasion (see Case C132/06 *Commission* v *Italy* [2008] ECR I5457, paragraphs 37 and 46).
>
> 26 Furthermore, Article 325 TFEU obliges the Member States to counter illegal activities affecting the financial interests of the European Union through effective deterrent measures and, in particular, obliges them to take the same measures to counter fraud affecting the financial interests of the European Union as they take to counter fraud affecting their own interests (see, to this effect, Case C367/09 *SGS Belgium and Others* [2010] ECR I10761, paragraphs 40 to 42). Given that the European Union's own resources include, as provided in Article 2(1) of Council Decision 2007/436/EC, Euratom of 7 June 2007 on the system of the European Communities' own resources (OJ 2007 L 163, p. 17), revenue from application of a uniform rate to the harmonised VAT assessment bases determined according to European Union rules, there is thus *a direct link* between the collection of VAT revenue in compliance with the European Union law applicable and the availability to the European Union budget of the corresponding VAT resources, since any lacuna in the collection of the first potentially causes a reduction in the second (see, to this effect, Case C539/09 *Commission* v *Germany* [2011] ECR I11235, paragraph 72). [My emphasis]
>
> 27 It follows that tax penalties and criminal proceedings for tax evasion, such as those to which the defendant in the main proceedings has been or is subject because the information concerning VAT that was provided was false, constitute implementation of Articles 2, 250(1) and 273 of Directive 2006/112 (previously Articles 2 and 22 of the Sixth Directive) and of Article 325 TFEU and, therefore, of European Union law, for the purposes of Article 51(1) of the Charter.
>
> 28 The fact that the national legislation upon which those tax penalties and criminal proceedings are founded has not been adopted to transpose Directive 2006/112 cannot call that conclusion into question, since its application is designed to penalise an infringement of that directive and is therefore intended to implement the obligation imposed on the Member States by the Treaty to impose effective penalties for conduct prejudicial to the financial interests of the European Union.[70]

[70] See subsequently, however, the ruling in C-363/20 *MARCAS MC* EU:C:2022:21, paras 32 to 39 where the CJEU distinguished *Akerberg Fransson*, and concluded, particularly at para 38, that since Member

The salient paragraphs of *Åkerberg Fransson* have been reproduced at length because they illustrate that identifying rules of EU law that were pertinent to the resolution of the dispute was central to determining if Sweden was 'implementing' EU law. Indeed, no reference was made at all to any particular provisions of Swedish law that might be inconsistent with Article 50 of the Charter, and nor was a search made for any other connecting factors.

Indeed, and somewhat oddly, the CJEU in *Åkerberg Fransson* made no reference to the rule referred to in the year preceding in Case C-40/11 *Iida*[71] and which had been established in pre-Charter case-law,[72] to the effect that, in order to determine whether a Member State is implementing EU law,

> it must be ascertained among other things whether the national legislation at issue is intended to implement a provision of European Union law, what the character of that legislation is, and whether it pursues objectives other than those covered by European Union law, even if it is capable of indirectly affecting that law, and also whether there are specific rules of European Union law on the matter or capable of affecting it.[73]

Such factors were, in fact, described in Case C-206/13 *Siragusa*,[74] a judgment issued only a little over a year after *Åkerberg Fransson*, as being reflective of 'a certain degree of connection above and beyond the matters covered being closely related or one of those matters having an indirect impact on the other'.[75] That 'certain degree of connection', which was referred to equally in *Liivimaa Lihaveis* above,[76] has been viewed by some commentators as the foundation stone on which to test whether a Member State is 'implementing' EU law.[77] However, the CJEU in *Åkerberg Fransson* was, in practical terms, more concerned with establishing whether the legal framework underpinning the punishment afforded to the applicant for defrauding the VAT system was grounded in express provisions of EU law. As already noted, this was equally the core preoccupation of the CJEU in *Wachauf* and *Liivimaa Lihaveis*.[78]

It is beyond the scope of the present study to analyse all CJEU rulings in which the Court has ruled on the meaning of Member States 'only when they are implementing Union law'. However, the model here proposed seems to work with respect to leading rulings in which the CJEU held that a Member State was not implementing EU law.

State tax penalties and procedures related to corporation tax are not part of the European Union's own resources system, there had been no implementation of EU law for the purposes of Article 51 of the Charter.

[71] EU:C:2012:691.

[72] Case C309/96 *Annibaldi* EU:C:1997:631. See also, among other rulings, Case C87/12 *Ymeraga and Others* EU:C:2013:291, para 41.

[73] C-40/11 *Iida* EU:C:2012:691, para 79.

[74] EU:C:2014:126.

[75] ibid para 24. See also, among others, the judgment in *Kremzow*, C299/95, EU:C:1997:254, para 16.

[76] Above note 44, para 62.

[77] Eg Gambradella, above note 1.

[78] It is equally worth noting that recent CJEU rulings concerned with determining whether a Member State was 'implementing' EU law have been preoccupied with identifying the pertinent provisions of EU law and then interpreting them as the sole basis on which this question is to be determined. See eg C-352/23 *Changu* EU:C:2024:78, paras 65 to 79 and C- 265/23 *Volieva* EU:C:2024:602, paras 38 to 43. Compare, however, C-398/23 *PT II () and 'auteur d'une infraction'* EU:C:2024 :996, para 43, where an analysis is made of the existence of any other 'connecting factors' between the challenged Member State rule and the EU measure in issue. However, such analyses are becoming, apparently, relatively uncommon. No Advocates General Opinion was issued with any of these three judgments.

This is so because it is particularly evident in these rulings that the CJEU, rather than focusing on any particular Member State law, and the extent to which it is 'connected' to EU law, searches for an element of EU law alleged by one of the parties to the dispute to be relevant, and then examines its content in the light of the facts. Or to put it more directly, the content of Member State law, and whether there is a particular 'connection' is largely irrelevant.

Thus, in Case C-309/96 *Annibaldi*, [79] the CJEU while identifying the regional law in issue which had to be tested for falling withing the 'scope' of EU law, referred at paragraph 23 to 'the absence of specific Community rules on expropriation' in ruling that a dispute in which the applicant was refused under Member State law a licence to plant an orchard in a regional park fell within the exclusive competence of the Member State. In other words, the bulk of the analysis of the CJEU concerned determining whether there were identifiable provisions of EU law that might have been relevant for deciding the dispute, with the court ultimately concluding that there were not. Similarly, in case C-206/13 *Siragusa*[80] the CJEU held at paragraph 27 that

> no specific obligations to protect the landscape, akin to those laid down by Italian law, are imposed on the Member States by the TEU and TFEU provisions referred to by the referring court; nor are such obligations imposed by the legislation relating to the Aarhus Convention, nor by Directives 2003/4 and 2011/92.

It was this analysis which led the CJEU to conclude at paragraph 30 that 'there is nothing to suggest that the provisions of Legislative Decree No 42/04 which are relevant to the case before the referring court fall within the scope of EU law. Those provisions do not implement rules of EU law'.

In C-333/13 *Dano*,[81] on the other hand, the CJEU, rather than focusing on whether the EU measure in issue imposed an obligation, interpreted that provision to determine if it was pertinent to the dispute. The CJEU held as follows at paragraphs 89 to 91:

> 89 In paragraph 41 of the judgment in *Brey* (EU:C:2013:565), the Court confirmed that Article 70 of Regulation No 883/2004, which defines the term 'special non-contributory cash benefits', is not intended to lay down the conditions creating the right to those benefits. It is thus for the legislature of each Member State to lay down those conditions.
>
> 90 Accordingly, since those conditions result neither from Regulation No 883/2004 nor from Directive 2004/38 or other secondary EU legislation, and the Member States thus have competence to determine the conditions for the grant of such benefits, they also have competence, as the Advocate General has observed in point 146 of his Opinion, to define the extent of the social cover provided by that type of benefit.
>
> 91 Consequently, when the Member States lay down the conditions for the grant of special non-contributory cash benefits and the extent of such benefits, they are not implementing EU law.

[79] EU:C:1997:631.
[80] EU:C:2014:126.
[81] EU:C:2014 :2358.

In case C-638/16 PPU *X and X v Etat belge*,[82] the CJEU equally set about identifying a provision of EU law that was pertinent to the resolution of the dispute, and ruled at paragraph 44, and contrary to the Opinion of the Advocate General, that because

> no measure has been adopted, to date, by the EU legislature on the basis of Article 79(2)(a) TFEU, with regard to the conditions governing the issue by Member States of long-term visas and residence permits to third-country nationals on humanitarian grounds, the applications at issue in the main proceedings fall solely within the scope of national law.

Finally, in C-609/17 *TSN and AKT*,[83] the findings of the CJEU were also predicated on identification of an EU measure imposing an obligation on a Member State, rather than analysing the 'connection' between Member State law and EU law. When such a provision could not be identified, because the Member State had exceeded the minimum standards imposed by an EU Directive, the Charter did not apply.

In that case the CJEU was asked to rule on whether Article 7(1) of Directive 2003/88 concerning certain aspects of the organisation of working time[84] and Article 31(2) of the Charter precluded national legislation or collective agreements pursuant to which days of paid annual leave in excess of four weeks could not be carried over when they overlapped with days of sick leave. The employer argued that there was no right to carry over leave in Directive 2003/88, when that leave exceeded the four-week minimum imposed by Article 7(1) of Directive 2003/88. Article 15 of Directive 2003/88 states that Member States are allowed to 'introduce laws, regulations or administrative provisions more favourable to the protection of the health and safety of workers'. Finland had exercised this right, with one worker in *TSN and AKT* having an entitlement to seven weeks annual leave, and another to five weeks.

The CJEU observed that, inconsistently with Article 94 of its rules of procedure, the referring court had not explained the relationship between the provisions of EU law of which it sought interpretation and the national legislation applicable to the dispute brought before it.[85] It was therefore necessary to verify whether the national rules questioned for compliance with the Charter, namely those granting of days of paid annual leave which exceed the minimum period of 4 weeks laid down in Article 7(1) of Directive 2003/88 and which exclude the carrying over of those days of leave on the grounds of illness, were to be regarded as implementing that directive for the purposes of Article 51(1) of the Charter.[86]

[82] EU:C:2017:173.
[83] EU:C:2019:981. See similarly C-257/21 *Coca-Cola European Partners Deutschland* EU:C:2022 529, para 49.'In the second place, it should be noted that Article 3(1) and Article 8 of the ILO Night Work Convention, readin conjunction with recital 6 of Directive 2003/88, likewise do not impose, under EU law, specific obligations onMember States concerning the supplementing of workers' pay for night work.' See also eg C-686/18 *Adusbef* EU:C:2020:567 at para 54: 'As is clear from the foregoing, none of the provisions of EU law referred to by thereferring court in the first part of its first question require the Member States to set an asset threshold, such as theone at issue in the main proceedings, above which people's banks established as limited liability cooperativesocieties must be converted into companies limited by shares, reduce their assets or be liquidated.'
[84] [2003] OJ L 299/9.
[85] EU:C:2019:981, para 44.
[86] ibid para 45.

The CJEU recalled that the mere fact that domestic measures come within an area in which the European Union has powers cannot bring those measures within the scope of EU law, and, therefore, cannot render the Charter applicable.[87] However, the CJEU then resolved the question of determining 'implementing' EU law within the meaning of Article 51(1) of the Charter by interpreting Directive 2003/88!

The CJEU ruled, inter alia, that Article 15 was not a measure granting the Member States an option to legislate by virtue of EU law, but merely recognised the power which they have to provide for such more favourable provisions in national law, outside of the framework for the regime established by that directive.[88] Further, Finland, when providing for more than four weeks leave and adjusting their 'carry over' rule in consequence of this was not acting out of any specific 'obligation' imposed by EU law.[89]

The ruling in C-609/17 *TSN and AKT* is problematic for several reasons, not least of which is the fact that the notion of 'obligation' has not been imposed, in determining whether a Member State is 'implementing' Union law, in all subsequent Grand Chamber CJEU cases concerning this issue. Notably, Joined Cases C-245/19 and C-246/19 *Etat Luxembourgeois*[90] concerned a Member State law which fleshed out the details of a procedure established under a Directive, and a challenge to that Member State law, namely a Luxembourgish law, for compliance with Article 47 of the Charter. The CJEU gave scant consideration as to whether Luxembourg was 'implementing' EU law. At paragraph 46, the CJEU ruled that the

> adoption, by a Member State, of legislation specifying the details of the procedure for exchange of information on request established by Directive 2011/16 [on administrative cooperation in the field of taxation] constitutes such an implementation, meaning that the Charter is applicable.[91]

This in and of itself casts a shadow over whether the 'obligation' rule applies in all circumstances. Similarly, what precisely 'obligation' means, and where that obligation is to be sourced, will inevitably be subject to evolution in the case-law. In *Åkerberg Fransson*, the 'obligation' imposed on the Member State was not found in the VAT directive in issue, the interpretation of which was required in order to resolve the dispute, but rather in the primary treaties (Article 325 TFEU).[92] If *TSN and AKT* is to be squared with the established case-law, a broad view will need to be taken of where the 'obligation' imposed on the Member State is identifiable. It need not necessarily be in the provision of EU (secondary) law which falls for interpretation.

[87] ibid para 46, referring to C198/13 *Julián Hernández and Others* EU:C:2014:2055, para 36.
[88] EU:C:2019:981, para 49.
[89] ibid paras 53 and 54.
[90] EU:C:2020:795.
[91] In so doing the CJEU referred to C682/15 *Berlioz Investment Fund* EU:C:2017:373, paras 34 to 37. For a further example of a ruling in which there is scant consideration as to whether EU law imposed a 'specific obligation' but the Member State was considered to be 'implementing' EU law see eg C-540/16 *Spika and Others* EU:C:2018:565. At para 23 exercise of an EU competence by a Member State was held to be enough to satisfy the requirement of implementation of EU law.
[92] See more recently on the obligations imposed by this provision, Joined Cases C-357/19, C-379/19, C-547/19, C-811/19, and C-840/19 *Euro Box Promotion and Others*, EU:C:2021:1034 paras 181 and 182 and C-107/23 PPU *Lin* EU:C:2023:606, paras 80 to 82.

Similarly, the established case-law also suggests a broad view of what amounts to an 'obligation' imposed by EU law on a Member State. For example, in C-223/19 *YS v NK*[93] the CJEU concluded that the 'specific requirements' of EU law were enough to amount to an instance of Member State implementation of EU law under Article 51(1) of the Charter,[94] the 'requirement' of EU law in that case being the principle of equal treatment. Thus, there is some case-law supporting that an 'indirect' or tangential connection with EU law can be enough to establish Member State implementation of EU law under Article 51(1).[95] Yet *TSN v AKT* suggests that an 'indirect' connection is no longer enough but falls short of expressly over-ruling the case-law on this point.

C. Exercise by Member States of Discretionary Powers

Further, it is difficult to square the *TSN and AKT* requirement of identification of a provision of EU imposing a specific obligation on a Member State with rulings concerning areas of EU law in which a Member State has exercised a discretion. As can be seen from the discussion of *Wachauf* above, this case concerned an *option* in the hands of Member States to provide compensation in the event of cancellation of milk quotas. On what view could *Wachauf* be viewed as imposing on Member States an obligation? Whether the rule in *Wachauf* still stands will be considered further below in Section III.E.

It was established in C-411/10 and C-493/10 *NS*[96] that exercise by Member States of discretionary powers vested in them by EU legislation constituted an incidence of 'implementation' of EU law. It is difficult to discern, however, how exercise of such powers could be viewed as resulting from imposition of a precise obligation under EU law. The CJEU held as follows in *NS*.

> 64 Article 51(1) of the Charter states that the provisions thereof are addressed to the Member States only when they are implementing European Union law.
>
> 65 Scrutiny of Article 3(2) of Regulation No 343/2003 shows that it grants Member States a discretionary power which forms an integral part of the Common European Asylum System provided for by the FEU Treaty and developed by the European Union legislature.
>
> 66 As stated by the Commission, that discretionary power must be exercised in accordance with the other provisions of that regulation.
>
> 67 In addition, Article 3(2) of Regulation No 343/2003 states that the derogation from the principle laid down in Article 3(1) of that regulation gives rise to the specific consequences provided for by that regulation. Thus, a Member State which decides to examine an asylum application itself becomes the Member State responsible within the meaning of Regulation No 343/2003 and must, where appropriate, inform the other Member State or Member States concerned by the asylum application.

[93] EU:C:2020:356, paras 79 to 81.
[94] ibid paras 79 to 81.
[95] ibid.
[96] EU:C:2011:865.

> 68 Those factors reinforce the interpretation according to which the discretionary power conferred on the Member States by Article 3(2) of Regulation No 343/2003 forms part of the mechanisms for determining the Member State responsible for an asylum application provided for under that regulation and, therefore, merely an element of the Common European Asylum System. Thus, a Member State which exercises that discretionary power must be considered as implementing European Union law within the meaning of Article 51(1) of the Charter.

This ruling has always stood, therefore, for the proposition that, at minimum, a discretionary power which forms an integral part of a common EU policy, and conferred on the Member States by EU measures, must be exercised in conformity with the Charter. Advocate General Bot in his Opinion in *TSN v AKT*, and contrary to the ruling of the CJEU, took the view that Finland *was* implementing EU law under Article 51(1) of the Charter. In reaching this conclusion, the Advocate General was persuaded by the volume of CJEU case-law binding the Member States to protect fundamental rights when they exercise discretionary powers.[97]

Granted, the CJEU in *TSN v AKT* expressly held that the dispute in that case did not entail conferral on a Member State of a discretionary power, but rather exercise of a residual Member State power that remained untouched by EU law because the Member State was acting outside of the scope of the directive in issue.[98] However, it seems self-evident that another fissure has been opened in the case-law that will require clarification through even more case-law. This leaves even Member State judges well versed in Charter jurisprudence with a further difficult conceptual question to come to grips with when deciding, in the individual case, whether a Member State is implementing EU law. Namely, does a dispute entail exercise of discretionary powers conferred by EU law, or exercise of a residual power falling outside of EU law?

[97] EU:C:2019:459, footnote 60, the Advocate General noted as follows: 'See, in particular, judgment of 9 March 2017, *Milkova* (C406/15, EU:C:2017:198), concerning Article 7(2) of Council Directive 2000/78/EC of 27 November 2000 establishing a general framework for equal treatment in employment and occupation (OJ 2000 L 303, p. 16), which provides that, "with regard to disabled persons, the principle of equal treatment shall be without prejudice to the right of Member States to maintain or adopt provisions on the protection of health and safety at work or to measures aimed at creating or maintaining provisions or facilities for safeguarding or promoting their integration into the working environment". According to the Court, "the fact that, as is apparent from Article 7(2) of Directive 2000/78, Member States are not required to maintain or adopt measures such as those provided for under that provision, but have discretion in that regard, does not permit the conclusion that rules adopted by Member States, such as those at issue in the main proceedings, fall outside the scope of EU law" (paragraph 52 and the case-law cited). In that regard, "it must also be recalled that where EU legislation allows Member States a choice between various methods of implementation, the Member States must exercise their discretion in accordance with general principles of EU law, including the principle of equal treatment" (paragraph 53 and the case-law cited). It follows that "the national legislation applicable to the main proceedings falls within the implementation of EU law, which means that, in the present case, the general principles of EU law, including the principle of equal treatment, and of the Charter are applicable" (paragraph 54). See also, concerning a "discretionary clause" when determining the Member State responsible for examining an application for international protection, judgment of 16 February 2017, *C. K. and Others* (C578/16 PPU, EU:C:2017:127, paragraph 53 and the case-law cited, and also paragraph 54). More generally, it follows from the Court's settled case-law that "where a Member State adopts measures in the exercise of the discretion conferred upon it by an act of EU law, it must be regarded as implementing that law, within the meaning of Article 51(1) of the Charter" (see, in particular, judgment of 13 June 2017, *Florescu and Others* (C258/14, EU:C:2017:448, paragraph 48 and the case-law cited)).'

[98] EU:C:2019:981, paras 49 and 50.

D. Member State Remedies and Procedural Rules

Uncertainty now also clouds the applicability of the Charter to the Member States with respect to the remedies and procedural rules available to enforce EU law. The relevance of Article 47 of the Charter in this scenario was established relatively early in the case-law,[99] and which now amounts to a vast corpus of case-law.[100] At least one Advocate General has queried whether other provisions of the Charter, in addition to Article 47, apply to Member State remedies and procedural rules,[101] but until *TSN and KST*, it had never been the case that a specific obligation imposed by EU law was relevant to determining whether Member State remedies and procedural rules available to enforce EU law comply with the Charter. Rather the Member States have always enjoyed, under the division of competence between them and the EU, discretion in the availability of Member State remedies and procedural rules, subject to the principles of effectiveness and equivalence, and now Article 47 of the Charter.

E. Clarification by the Ruling in *Sātini S*?

The beginning of clarification of at least some of these issues was, perhaps, afforded, by the ruling of the CJEU in C-238/20 *Sātini S*.[102] However, the complexities generated by the 'imposition of an obligation' rule is reflected in the fact that, in this case too the Advocate General, Mr Rantos, came to conclusions differing from the judgment of the CJEU on whether a Member State law setting up a compensation scheme, in the enforcement of two provisions of EU environmental law, was an instance of Member State implementation of EU law, so that the Member State was bound by Article 17 of the Charter on the right to property. Contrary to the conclusions reached by the Advocate Geneal, the CJEU held as follows:

> 23 The Member States are implementing EU law, within the meaning of Article 51(1) of the Charter, where, in accordance with the requirements of the 'Birds' Directive and the 'Habitats' Directive, they take appropriate steps to avoid, in the special areas of conservation, the deterioration of natural habitats and the requisite measures to establish a general system of protection for the species of birds covered by the former directive.
>
> 24 First, Article 5 of the 'Birds' Directive requires the Member States to take the requisite measures to establish a general system of protection for all the bird species referred to in Article 1 of that directive.

[99] C-279/09 *DEB* EU:C:2010:811.

[100] One leading authority is Joined Cases C-245/19 and C-246/19 *Etat Luxembourgeois* EU:C:2020:795. For a full analysis of the provision see the chapter on Article 47 in S Peers, T Hervey, J Kenner and A Ward (eds) *The EU Charter of Fundamental Rights: A Commentary* (Oxford, Hart Publishing, 2021).

[101] See the Opinion of Advocate General Tanchev, C-282/19 *MIUR and Ufficio Scolastico Regionale per la Campania* EU:C:2021:217, especially at para 76 and Article 17 of the Charter as discussed above note 53. See also Article 49(1) of the Charter, and the principle of retroactive application of the more lenient criminal law, and the principle of foreseeability, precision and non-retroactivity of offences of penalties, and the ruling in C-107/23 PPU *Lin* EU:C:2023:606, para 109; C-218/15 *Paoletti* EU:C:2016:748.

[102] EU:C:2022:57.

25 Second, Article 6(2) of the 'Habitats' Directive provides that Member States are to take appropriate steps to avoid, in the special areas of conservation, the deterioration of natural habitats and the habitats of species as well as disturbance of the species for which the areas have been designated, in so far as such disturbance could be significant in relation to the objectives of that directive.

26 Furthermore, the transposition and implementation by the Member States of those measures, the objective of which is to protect birds and their habitats, inevitably have repercussions on the right to property of persons to whom immovable property situated in the areas in question belongs, since, at the very least, they are subject to restrictions on the use of that property.

27 The Member States also implement EU law, within the meaning of Article 51(1) of the Charter, when they establish schemes granting payments under the 'Birds' Directive and the 'Habitats' Directive.

28 In that regard, the mere fact that those directives do not provide for a compensation scheme themselves or that they do not impose an obligation on Member States to provide for such a scheme cannot be interpreted as meaning that Article 17 of the Charter is not applicable (see, by analogy, judgment of 9 June 2016, *Pesce and Others*, C78/16 and C79/16, EU:C:2016:428, paragraph 86).

29 In those circumstances, the Court has jurisdiction to rule on the first question.

Advocate General Rantos, at paragraphs 29 to 30 of his Opinion, took the view that there was no obligation under either the Birds or Habitats Directive to either establish a scheme of compensation or pay compensation.[103] There had therefore been no implementation of EU law, as required by Article 51 (1) of the Charter, so that the CJEU had no jurisdiction to rule on the first question, which concerned compliance of Member State implementation of the Birds Directive with Article 17 of the Charter and the right to property.[104]

On the one hand, *Satini S* contributes to coherency in the case-law, in that it seems to imply, and consistently with the early, and seminal, CJEU ruling in *Wachauf* (discussed at the beginning of this chapter) that the 'obligation' requirement does not extend to compensation schemes established at the discretion of the Member States when they are linked to some kind of substantive obligation imposed on the Member State by EU law. On the other hand, the ruling affords little faith that the task of determining whether Member State are implementing EU law has become any simpler by fiat of evolution in the jurisprudence reflected in *TSN v AKT*. The question might be posed, aside from compensation schemes, what are the other exceptions to the 'obligation' rule?

In all events, what is here proposed is an approach reminiscent of the reflections of Advocate General Cruz Villalon in *Åkerberg Fransson*. The Advocate General contended that a common feature of the different formulations 'scope', 'field of application' and 'implementation', was a requirement that Union law have a 'presence in the origin of the exercise of public authority'. That presence had to be 'as law; that is with the capacity to determine or influence to some extent the subject matter of

[103] EU:C:2021:735, paras 29 and 30.
[104] ibid paras 31 and 32.

that exercise of public authority in the Member State'.[105] By prioritising identification of a provision of EU law either requiring interpretation, or the validity of which may be questioned, and which is pertinent to the resolution of the dispute, in the way in which the CJEU proceeded in *Åkerberg Franssson*, is not such a 'presence' thereby identified? If that is so, why did it become necessary to replace the process of identification of EU *presence* that was inherent in all preceding case-law, with a far narrower test requiring the existence of specific *obligations* imposed on Member States before they can be said to be 'implementing' EU law?

F. Horizontal Application of the Charter

As already mentioned, the scope of the Charter follows the scope of EU law, and not vice versa.[106] This means that, once a provision of an EU measure, or measures, is identified that is pertinent to the resolution of a dispute, and then interpreted in conformity with the Charter, Member State judges are bound to treat any Member State rules that are inconsistent with that provision in conformity with the established rules of EU constitutional law.

Thus, if a Member State is derogating from a directly effective treaty article of the TEU or TFEU, and a Member State measure executing that derogation is inconsistent with fundamental rights as protected by the Charter, that measure is to be disapplied.[107] This further means that if the pertinent EU measure to be interpreted in conformity with the Charter is housed in an EU Regulation, it is directly applicable and has an immediate effect in the national legal system, so that all inconsistent Member State measures are to be disapplied,[108] whether the Regulation is being invoked against an emanation of the state or a private sector actor.

If the pertinent EU measure, as interpreted in conformity with the Charter, is a directly effective provision of a directive, or a decision for that matter, and it is being enforced against an emanation of the state, a Member State court is

> under a duty, where it is unable to interpret national law in compliance with the requirements of EU law, to give full effect to the requirements of EU law in the dispute brought before it, by disapplying, as required, of its own motion, any national rule or practice, even if adopted subsequently, that is contrary to a provision of EU law with direct effect.[109]

[105] EU:C:2012:340, para 33.

[106] See the Opinion of Advocate General Szpunar in C-18/18 *Glawischnig-Pieszeck* EU:C:2019:458, para 89.

[107] As established in C-390/12 *Pfleger and Others* EU:C:2014:281. It was confirmed that the Charter only applies to derogation from free movement rules, as opposed to the free movement rules themselves, in C-235/17 *Commission v Hungary (Usufruct over Agricultural Land)* EU:C:2019:432.

[108] Eg C-740/22 *Endomol Shine Finland* EU:C:2024:216 EU:C:2024:216, para 42. 'In that regard, it should be recalled that, under the second paragraph of Article 288 TFEU, a regulation is of general application and directly applicable in all Member States. Accordingly, by virtue of the very nature of regulations and of their function in the system of sources of EU law, the provisions of regulations generally have immediate effect in the national legal systems without it being necessary for the national authorities to adopt implementing measures (judgments of 16 June 2022, *Port de Bruxelles and Région de Bruxelles-Capitale*, C229/21, EU:C:2022:471, para 47, and of 30 March 2023, *Hauptpersonalrat der Lehrerinnen und Lehrer*, C34/21, EU:C:2023:270, para 77).'

[109] C-107/23 PPU *Lin* EU :C :2023 :606, para 95. See also eg C-316/22 *Gabel Industria Tessile and Canavesi,* EU:C:2024:301, paras 26 and 27.

However, if the provision of a Directive to be interpreted in conformity with the Charter is not directly effective, or that provision is being enforced horizontally by one private party against another, there is still scope for inconsistent Member State measures to stand, even though, under the established case-law, there is no 'disapplication' duty imposed on Member State judges in such circumstances.

Rather, if Member State law is inconsistent with the provision of a non-directly effective directive, or a Framework Decision for that matter, as interpreted in the light of the Charter, the obligation on the Member State judge is limited to interpreting, where possible (which means doing whatever lies within their jurisdiction) Member State law in conformity with the relevant provisions of the relevant directive. In these circumstances, Member State judges are bound to rule inconsistently with established Member State case-law, if necessary, but they are not to render an interpretation of Member State law that is *contra legem* its text.[110] or otherwise rule inconsistently with general principles of law such as legal certainty and the principle of non-retroactivity. Under settled case-law, a directive cannot of itself create obligations on the part of an individual and cannot therefore be invoked as such against him or her. If the possibility of relying on a provision of a directive that has not been transposed, or has been incorrectly transposed, were to be extended to the sphere of relations between individuals, that would amount to recognising a power in the European Union to enact obligations for individuals with immediate effect, whereas it has competence to do so only where it is empowered to adopt regulations.[111]

Once the Charter attained legally binding force, this last aspect of the established constitutional matrix represented a significant challenge for the efficacy and indeed enforceability of the Charter. Absent fresh developments in the case-law, there would be circumstances in which the Charter was, in practice, inapplicable, and notably when a dispute concerned the horizontal enforcement of directives by one private party against another, a domain in which the doctrine of direct effect is inoperative.

The CJEU responded by building on established case-law concerning discrimination on the basis of age,[112] by issuing its ruling in *Egenberger*.[113] This was a case in which one private party sought to enforce the prohibition on discrimination on the basis of religious belief, as protected by Article 21(1) of the Charter, and the right to effective judicial protection, under Article 47 of the Charter, against another private party, in the context of horizontal enforcement of an EU Directive. The CJEU held as follows at paragraphs 76 and 78 to 79:

> 76 The prohibition of all discrimination on grounds of religion or belief is mandatory as a general principle of EU law. That prohibition, which is laid down in Article 21(1) of the Charter, is sufficient in itself to confer on individuals a right which they may rely on as such in disputes between them in a field covered by EU law (see, with respect to the principle of non-discrimination on grounds of age, judgment of 15 January 2014, *Association de médiation sociale*, C176/12, EU:C:2014:2, paragraph 47).
>
> . . .

[110] See eg C-579/15 *Poplawski* EU:C:2017:503, paras 31 to 37. See also eg C-279/23 *Skarb Państwa (Retard de paiement non significatif ou de créance faible)* EU:C:2024:605.
[111] C-196/23 *Plamaro* EU:C:2024:596, para 46.
[112] See notably C-555/07 *Kücükdeveci* EU:C:2010:21 and C-144/04 *Mangold* EU:C:2005:709.
[113] C-414/16 EU:C:2018:257.

> 78 Secondly, it must be pointed out that, like Article 21 of the Charter, Article 47 of the Charter on the right to effective judicial protection is sufficient in itself and does not need to be made more specific by provisions of EU or national law to confer on individuals a right which they may rely on as such.
>
> 79 Consequently, . . ., the national court would be required to ensure within its jurisdiction the judicial protection for individuals flowing from Articles 21 and 47 of the Charter, and to guarantee the full effectiveness of those articles by disapplying if need be any contrary provision of national law.[114]

Since *Egenberger*, the CJEU has held that the right of workers to paid annual leave, as protected by Article 31(2) of the Charter, is a provision which requires no further elaboration, and is therefore enforceable in and of itself when one private party is in dispute against another over the meaning of a directive,[115] but that neither Article 27 on the right of workers to information and consultation within their undertaking, or the Article 30 guarantee against unjustified dismissal have this quality.[116]

How then to integrate this development into any re-draft of Article 51(1)? As will be explained below, the re-draft here proposed will refer only to 'interpretation and/or validity' of EU law, so that the *Egenberger* rule, along with all the core structural principles of EU law governing when Member States are implementing EU law, can be expressed in user-friendly terms in the explanations. This solution is additionally advantageous because the explanations, depending on the constitutional basis accorded to them, can be redrafted to take account of fresh developments in the case-law, when provisions of primary EU law cannot.

IV. TEMPLATE FOR A REDRAFT?

To consolidate a point already alluded to, of the six seminal rulings here discussed in detail concerning the applicability of the Charter at Member State level, that is C-562/12 *Liivimaa Lihaveis*,[117] C-617/10 *Åkerberg Fransson*,[118] C-411/10 and C-493/10 *NS*,[119] C-414/16 *Egenberger*,[120] C-609 and 610/17 *TSN v AKT*[121] and C-238/20 *Sātini S*,[122] there was agreement between the Advocate General and the CJEU on this question in only two of them, namely *Liivimaa Lihaveis* and *NS*. To this can be added the

[114] Subsequent rulings concerning the horizontal application of Article 47 include C-582/21 *Profi Credito Polska* EU:C:2024:282, para 76, C-715/20 *X (Absence de motifs de résilation)* EU:C:2024:139, C-30/19 *Braathens Regional Aviation* EU:C:2021:269. Subsequent rulings concerning the horizontal applicability of discrimination on the basis of religion include C-243/19 *Veselibas ministrija* EU:C:2020:872.

[115] C-569/16 and C-570/16, *Bauer and Willmeroth* EU:C:2018:871; C-684/16 *Max Planck-Gesellschaft* EU:C:2018:874.

[116] C-196/23, EU:C:2024:596.

[117] EU:C:2014:2229.

[118] EU:C:2013:105.

[119] EU:C:2011:865.

[120] EU:C:2018:257.

[121] EU:C:2019 :981.

[122] EU:C:2022:57.

important cases of C-638/16 PPU, *X and X v Etat Belge*[123] and C-34/09 *Zambrano*,[124] in which, again, the Advocates General concerned and the CJEU reached different conclusions from the CJEU on whether or not the relevant Member State was, in all the circumstances, 'implementing' EU law.[125]

While one view might be that all this is simply an accolade, by way of example, to the independence of the Advocates General, from another perspective it might be a reflection of the tenacity of the uncertainty that still manages to prevail with each attempt by the CJEU to settle the meaning, under Article 51(1) of the Charter, of Member States 'only when they are implementing Union law'. Demarcating the jurisdictional boundary between Member State and ECHR protection, on the one hand, and Charter guarantees on the other, is still fraught with difficulty. In all events, subsisting unpredictability of outcomes, when the Charter is well and truly embedded in its third decade as a legally binding instrument, is not ideal, because it concerns a structural rule that is essential to the Charter's proper functioning as a legal instrument. This situation falls short of encouraging Member State judges to grapple with the Charter's substance.

The solution here advocated entails removing the focus on Member State legal provisions in determining whether a Member State is 'implementing' EU law, towards identification of the provision of EU law that is relevant to resolving the dispute. Once this occurs, the fate of any Member State measure that is inconsistent with that provision of EU law, as interpreted in conformity with the Charter, will be determined in conformity with the established principle of EU constitutional law detailed in Section III.F above (eg disapplication in the event of direct effect, sympathetic interpretation, or disapplication if the *Egenberger* rule is activated). Thus, if a Member State judge has focused their analysis on whether or not a Member State law, as opposed to an EU law, conforms with the Charter, in the interests of clarity the question referred might be reformulated by the CJEU toward determining whether the, identified, provision of EU law complies with the Charter. This is consistent with the principle that the Charter is directed 'primarily' at the institutions, bodies, offices and agencies of the EU. If Member State law is obstructing the enforcement of the relevant EU rule, as interpreted in conformity with the Charter, then the CJEU need simply apply the relevant EU constitutional rule, which will depend on whether interpretation of a Regulation is in issue, a Directive, and whether or not the doctrine of direct effect applies.

This approach is also consistent with other core principles of the EU constitutional paradigm. Member State laws governing matters falling within the scope of

[123] EU:C:2017:173. For the Opinion of the Advocate General see EU:C:2017:93.

[124] EU:C:2011:124. For the Opinion of the Advocate General see EU:C:2010:560.

[125] For a recent example of a complex case in which the Advocate General and the CJEU reached the same conclusion on whether or not a Member State had been 'implementing' EU law under Article 51(1) see the ruling in C-185/23 *protectus* EU:C:2024:657, and the Opinion of Advocate General de la Tour, EU:C:2024:409. The case illustrates, however, how complex facts render even more challenging the application of the jurisprudence on 'implementing' EU law, and the primary role of identification and interpretation of a pertinent provision of EU law in deciding whether 'a degree of connection' exists 'between an act of EU law and the national measure at issue above and beyond the matters covered being closely related or one of those matters having an indirect impact on the other' (see para 42 of the judgment and the case-law referred to therein).

a directive must be examined in the light of that directive,[126] and, as far as possible, be interpreted in conformity with it. Those governing matters not falling within that scope must be examined in the light of any relevant primary law.[127]

Is it helpful, therefore, or even logical, to focus on the existence of 'connecting factors' between the Member State law in issue and the EU law which must respect fundamental rights, when, once a provision of EU law is identified as being pertinent to its dispute, all relevant Member State laws are in turn to be interpreted in the light of that EU measure, as itself interpreted in conformity with the Charter? The preliminary answer offered here is 'no'.

It is perhaps noteworthy that the various Human Rights Acts in Commonwealth jurisdictions feature a rule pursuant to which (pertinent) legislation is to be interpreted, as far as possible, in conformity with the human rights protected by those instruments.[128] This guiding principle for the application of the Human Rights Acts finds its genesis in the *Marleasing* ruling of the CJEU,[129] and is directed not at whether a rule challenged for compliance with the Human Rights Act features 'connecting factors' with a higher source of law. Rather, any rule that is pertinent to the resolution of a dispute is to be interpreted in conformity with the rights protected under the Human Rights Act. Is there any reason particular to the EU that precludes such an approach to jurisdiction under the Charter?

In the light of all the arguments canvassed in this contribution, it is therefore suggested that Article 51(1) be amended as follows. To begin with, and in order to tidy the provision, reference to the principle of subsidiarity might be removed from Article 51(1), given that it is already reflected in Article 5(3) TEU and relates in any event to Article 51(2) of the Charter. The new text of Article 51(1) might be placed under the heading 'Part II Jurisdiction' and redrafted as follows.

Part II
Jurisdiction

1. The General Court shall have jurisdiction to hear annulment proceedings brought by natural or legal persons meeting the conditions provided for under the third paragraph of Article 263 TFEU concerning alleged breach of the fundamental rights guaranteed by the Charter by acts of institutions, bodies, offices and agencies of the Union, along with jurisdiction to hear actions for damages under Articles 268 and 340 TFEU entailing breach of the fundamental rights guaranteed by the Charter. The remedies available in Article 263 nullity proceedings are a declaration that an act is void under Article 264 TFEU and interim relief under Article 279 TFEU.

2. The courts and tribunals of the Member States shall have jurisdiction to hear proceedings concerning alleged breach of fundamental rights guaranteed by the Charter with respect to all questions concerning the interpretation and/or validity of acts of the institutions,

[126] See eg AG Szpunar C-469/19 *All in One Star* EU:C:2020:822, para 27, referring to C-167/01 *Inspire Art*, EU:C:2003:512, para 73.

[127] ibid.

[128] See for example, in Australia section 32 of the Charter of Human Rights and Responsibilities Act (2006) (Vic); section 48 of the Human Rights Act (2019) (QLD); see similarly section 6 of the Human Rights Act (1990) (New Zealand).

[129] C-106/89 *Marleasing* EU:C:1990:395.

bodies, offices or agencies of the Union. A preliminary ruling may be made to the Court of Justice of the European Union pursuant to rules elaborated under Article 267 TFEU.

A 'working draft' of the explanations might read as follows:

Explanation to Part II: general remarks

The text of this provision borrows from the wording of Article 263 TFEU, Article 267 TFEU, and Article 19 TEU, and reflects the Charter's status as an instrument which has the 'same legal value' as the Treaties (Article 6 TEU). Unlike standard international treaties, the Community Treaties establish a new legal order, which is integrated into the legal systems of the Member States on the entry into force of the Treaties and which are binding on their courts. Joined Cases C-357/19, C-379/19, C-547/19, C-811/19, and C-840/19 Euro Box Promotion and Others, *EU:C:2021:1034, paragraph 245. The Charter is equally so integrated.*

Explanation to Part II (1)

The institutions of the EU are named in Article 13 TEU. They are European Parliament, the European Council, the Council, the European Commission, the Court of Justice of the European Union ('the CJEU'), the European Central Bank, and the Court of Auditors.

The bodies, offices and agencies of the EU are established by or under the Treaties and are intended to contribute to the achievement of the Union's objectives (see e.g. C-597/18 P Council v K. Chrysostomides and Co and Others *EU:C:2020:1028, paragraph 80.) Bodies, offices and agencies of the Union are generally discernible from the text of the EU legislation establishing them.*

The institutions, bodies, offices and agencies of the Union are the primary addressees of the Charter. They are bound by the Charter with respect to everything they do, whether they are challenged for failing to comply with the Charter in the context of an action for annulment (Article 263 TFEU), damages (Articles 268 and 340 TFEU), or in pursuit of interim relief (Article 279 TFEU), before the General Court of the CJEU ('the General Court'), or by way of a claim brought before the Member State courts or tribunals entailing the interpretation of EU law or challenge to its validity (e.g. C-477/14 Pillbox 38 *EU:C:2016:324; C-311/18* Facebook Ireland and Schrems *EU:C:2020:559; C-333/22* Ligue des droits humains *(vérification du traitement des données par l'autorité de contrôle 2023:874). In other words, the mere identification of an institution, body, office or agency of the Union as the entity alleged to have acted inconsistently with the Charter triggers the Charter's application.*

Nevertheless, in accordance with the rule established in C-188/92 TWD *EU:C:1994:90, if a litigant 'without any doubt' had the right under Article 263 TFEU to bring an action before the General Court seeking annulment of an act of an institution, body, office or agency of the Union for breach of fundamental rights guaranteed by the Charter (or on any other basis) and failed to exercise that right within the time period prescribed by Article 263 TFEU (two months), EU law precludes such a litigant from evading that time limit by bringing an action before a Member State court challenging the validity of the EU measure and seeking an order for reference on validity to the CJEU under Article 267 TFEU, even if Member State time limits permit such a challenge (C-330/22* Friends of the Irish Environment *EU:C:2024:19, paragraph 50).*

Only the CJEU, to the exclusion of the Member State courts, can declare an EU measure invalid (C-314/85 Foto-Frost EU:C:1987:452).

The judgment of the CJEU in C-562/12 Liivimaa Lihaveis *EU:C:2014:2229 supplies guiding principles on the application of Part II (1) when both EU bodies offices or agencies and Member State authorities are involved in acts alleged to be inconsistent with the Charter. There it was confirmed that the General Court has no jurisdiction under Article 263 TFEU to rule on the lawfulness of an act adopted by a national authority, but the Member State courts do when a national authority 'implements' EU law under the case-law of the CJEU under ex-Article 51(1) of the Charter. When a Member State is 'implementing' EU law is now subsumed by Part II (2), and its reference to 'interpretation' of acts of EU institutions, offices, bodies and agencies.*

The authority of the General Court to enforce the Charter in the context of the non-contractual liability of the EU under Articles 268 and 340 TFEU and the action for damages is evident from the ruling of the General Court in T-371/22 Montanari *EU:7:2024:494, particularly at paragraph 129.*

Explanations to Part II (2)

Part II (2) adopts the language of Article 267 (b), which provides that the 'Court of Justice of the European Union shall have jurisdiction to give preliminary rulings concerning. . .(b) the validity and interpretation of the acts of the institutions, bodies, offices or agencies of the Union'.

Under the established case-law of the CJEU, the Charter is only applicable to the acts of national authorities of the Member States when they are 'implementing' EU law. In other words, the Charter is not *applicable to everything national authorities do. The primary addressees of the Charter are the institutions, bodies, offices and agencies of the Union. Member state authorities can only become bound by the Charter by virtue of such EU acts.*

The primary route for determining whether a Member State is 'implementing' EU law, a question that only ever arises when acts of national authorities are challenged for compliance with the Charter, as opposed to an EU act itself, is to identify a provision of EU law, other than the Charter, that is pertinent to the resolution of the dispute. In this regard, see e.g. the ruling of the CJEU in Case C-206/13 Siragusa *EU:C:2014:126, paragraph 19.*

Once that provision is identified, and interpreted in conformity with the Charter, any act of a national authority impeding the application of the EU measure is subject to the Charter because the Member State is 'implementing' EU law.

This 'identification' exercise runs through all of the seminal rulings of the CJEU on the meaning of 'implementing' EU law (e.g. C-5/88 Wauchauf *EU:C:1989:321, paragraphs 19 to 22; C-309/96* Annibaldi *EU:C:1997:631, see especially paragraphs 20 to 21; C-617/10* Åkerberg Fransson *EU:C:2013:105, paragraphs 24 to 28; C-206/13* Siragusa *EU:C:2014:126, paragraph 27; C-333/13* Dano *EU:C:2014:2358, paras 89 to 90; C-638/16 PPU* X and X v Etat belge *EU:C:2017:173, paras 42 to 50;C-609 and C-610/17* TSN and AKT *EU:C:2019:981, paragraph 49; C-411/10 and C-493/10* NS *EU:C:2011:865, paragraphs 64 to 69; C-238/20* Sātini S *EU:C:2022:57, paragraphs 24 to 29; C-265/23* Volieva EU:C:2024:602, *paragraphs 46 to 47.*

It has further been held in the case-law of the CJEU that Member States are 'implementing' EU law when they derogate from the rules on free movement (e.g. Case C-390/12 Pfleger *EU:C:2014:281, paras 35 and 36*; *C- 673/16* Coman *EU:C:2018:385, paragraph 47) and when they exercise discretionary authority the source of which is grounded in an EU measure (e.g.* C-411/10 NS *EU:C:2011:865, paras 64 to 69), and when they exercise their authority to supply remedies and procedures to enforce rights grounded in EU law, subject to the principles of effectiveness, equivalence, and Article 47 of the Charter (e.g.* C-279/09 DEB *EU:C:2010:811, paras 30 to 33) sometimes termed, collectively, as the right to 'effective judicial protection', C-284/23* Haus Jacobus *EU:C:2024:558, para 32; C-673/23* Artemis Security *EU:C:2024:529, paragraph 31).These are examples of identification of pertinent provisions of EU law which trigger an instance of Member State implementation of EU law.*

These rules, however, have to be read in the light of the Grand Chamber ruling in C-609 and C-610/17 TSN and AKT *EU:C:2019:981, para 53 in which the CJEU confirmed that Member State are only 'implementing' EU law when EU law imposes a precise obligation on them. Although this requirement was absent in the contemporaneous Grand Chamber ruling in Joined Cases C-245/19 and C-246/19* Etat Luxembourgeois *EU:C:2020:795, it has been applied in subsequent rulings (e.g. Joined Cases C-257/21 and C-258/21* Coca-Cola European Partners Deutschland *EU:C:2022 529, paragraph 49).*

It is to be noted, however, that the 'obligation' can be housed in a primary provision of the Treaty, rather than the provision of EU law secondary law the interpretation of which is sought. One such Treaty provision is 325(1) TFEU on protection of the EU's financial interests (C-617/10 Akerberg Fransson *EU:C:2013:105, paragraphs 24 to 29; see more recently e.g. Joined Cases C-357/19, C-379/19, C-547/19, C-811/19, and C-840/19* Euro Box Promotion and Others, *EU:C:2021:1034 and C-107/23 PPU* Lin *EU:C:2023:606).*

Further, discretionary compensation schemes established by Member States to enforce obligations imposed by EU law amount to an instance of 'implementing' EU law (C-238/20 Sātini S *EU:C:2022:57 and C-5/88* Wachauf *EU:C:1989:321).*

Liberal interpretation of the 'obligation' requirement affirmed in C-609 and C-610/17 TSN and AKT *EU:C:2019:981 is also indicated by the ruling of the CJEU in C-223/19* YS v NK *EU:C:2020:356, 753. There the CJEU concluded that the 'specific requirements' of EU law were enough to amount to an instance of Member State implementation of EU law under Article 51 (1) of the Charter, the need to establish an 'obligation' notwithstanding. The 'requirement' of EU law in that case, and which rendered the Member State concerned to be 'implementing' EU law was the principle of equal treatment, as reflected in a Directive. (C-223/19* YS v NK *EU:C:2020:753, paras 79 to 81).*

Finally, although not an instance of Member State implementation of EU law, the horizontal application of the Charter between private parties under the circumstances established in C-414/16 Egenberger *EU:C:2018:257, falls within the parameters of Part II (2), given that this entails 'interpretation' of EU law.*

Once the rules elaborated in the explanations are applied, the only thing left, then, for a Member State judge to do, is to decide, on the basis of established principles of EU constitutional law, the fate of Member State laws that are inconsistent with the pertinent provision of EU law, as interpreted in conformity with the Charter, and which impede its application in national law. Thus, if a Member State is derogating from a directly effective treaty article of the TEU or TFEU, the Member State measure executing that derogation is to be disapplied if it is inconsistent with the Charter.[130]

If the pertinent EU act to be interpreted in conformity with the Charter is an EU Regulation, it is directly applicable and has an immediate effect in the national legal system, so that all acts of Member State authorities inconsistent with the Regulation, as interpreted in conformity with the Charter, are to be disapplied, whether the Regulation is being invoked against an emanation of the state or a private sector actor. [131]

If the pertinent EU act, as interpreted in conformity with the Charter, is a directly effective provision of a directive, or a decision for that matter [132], and it is being enforced against an emanation of the state, a Member State court, in accordance with the principle of primacy, is 'under a duty, where it is unable to interpret national law in compliance with the requirements of EU law, to give full effect to the requirements of EU law in the dispute brought before it, by disapplying, as required, of its own motion, any national rule or practice, even if adopted subsequently, that is contrary to a provision of EU law with direct effect,[133] without it having to request or await the prior setting side of the national rule or practice by legislative or other constitutional means.[134]

That said, when a natural or legal person seeks, before a Member State Tribunal, interpretation of an act of an EU institution, office, body or agency, there are some provisions of the Charter that are sufficient in themselves to confer on individuals a right which they may rely on as such in disputes between them in a field covered by EU.[135] This means that, even in horizontal disputes between private parties, these fundamental rights are to be applied by Member State courts and tribunals over inconsistent Member State measures. To date, the CJEU has ruled that those provisions are the prohibition on discrimination on the basis of religion or belief in Article 21 (1) of the Charter, Article 47 of the Charter[136] and the right to paid annual leave as protected by Article 31 (2) of the Charter.[137]

V. CONCLUDING REMARKS

One ex-Vice President of the European Commission long ago argued for the suppression *in toto* of Article 51 of the Charter, since the 'Charter should be Europe's very own bill of rights';[138] a suggestion endorsed at the time by the European Parliament.[139] What is here proposed is something more nuanced.

[130] C-390/12 *Pfleger and Others* EU:C:2014:281.

[131] Eg, C-740/22 *Endomol Shine Finland* EU:C:2024:216 EU:C:2024:216, para 23.

[132] See eg Joined Cases C-357/19, C-379/19, C-547/19, C-811/19, and C-840/19 *Euro Box Promotion and Others*, EU:C:2021:1034, para 253.

[133] See C-107/23 PPU *Lin* EU:C:2023:606, para 95.

[134] C-107/23 Lin EU:C:2023:606, para 55.

[135] C-414/16 *Egenberger* EU:C:2018:257, para 76.

[136] ibid paras 76 to 79.

[137] C-569/16 and C-570/16 *Bauer and Willmeroth* EU:C:2018:871; C-684/16 *Max Planck-Gesellschaft* EU:C:2018:874.

[138] Gambardella, above note 1, referring at footnote 6 to https://ec.europa. eu/commission/presscorner/detail/fr/SPEECH_14_327.

[139] ibid footnote 7.

As difficult as it might be, in political terms, to amend primary EU law, would not this elevated status for the Charter be more achievable if the present rule on when the Charter applies at Member State level were not burdened with the intellectual divisions that presently beset Article 51(1)? Moreover, if all that is proposed in any such amendment is the provision of a structural rule which is more user-friendly, from the perspective of Member State courts and tribunals, than the text of current Article 51 (1), and its somewhat enigmatic explanations, would that proposal for amendment necessarily meet with political resistance?

Further, Article 51(1) as it stands invites practitioners to avoid the vagaries of Member States 'only when they are implementing Union law' by identifying themselves, for the benefit of the court, which provision of EU law requires, on all the facts and circumstances, interpretation, thereby focusing their challenge on that EU rule rather than Member State laws falling within its ambit; an approach which cannot be faulted since it is consistent with the CJEU's rules of procedure. So why not elevate this route to enforcing the Charter to 'the norm'?

What is here suggested consists, in essence, of reassertion of the essence of the Charter; its primary addressees are the institutions, bodies, offices and agencies of the EU. Identification of an act of EU law other than the Charter, interpretation of which is, in all the factual circumstances, relevant to the resolution of a dispute, as the touchstone for determining when the Charter binds Member State authorities, is consistent with the Charter's core aim.

If any re-drafting proposal were to be launched, the group of people whose counsel would be essential to its deliberations would be Member State judges. It is they who are charged with untangling the spaghetti bowl of EU law, Member State law and ECHR law, when it comes to the protection of fundamental rights in Europe. It is their counsel that should guide the transformation of Article 51 from a measure primarily concerned with reinforcing the division of competence between the EU and its constituent Member States to one providing a clear workable and straightforward rule on when the Charter applies. The present writer has enjoyed, as much as any scholar, analysing the judgments of the CJEU on the meaning of 'Member State only when they are implementing Union law', and postulating on its meaning. But such exercises are of less concern to busy Member State judges, whose fidelity and support have always been central to the success of the European project.

6

Primacy of European Law and Equality of Member States (and Citizens!) Vis-à-Vis the EU/EEA Treaties

MARIA ELVIRA MÉNDEZ-PINEDO

I. INTRODUCTION

THE RELATIONSHIP BETWEEN EUROPEAN Union (EU) law and national constitutional law is a classic question still imperfectly unresolved in the field of European law. The same can be said regarding the question under the European Economic Area Agreement (EEA). The President of the Court of Justice of the European Union (hereinafter CJEU), Justice Koen Lenaerts, has written on the topic on several recent occasions, pointing out that academic criticisms of the principle of primacy of Community law 'disregard its transnational dimension, according to which that principle guarantees the equality of the Member States before the Treaties'.[1] In his view, the principle of primacy is not simply a mechanism for resolving bilateral disputes between two different but interacting legal systems but, above all, a fundamental principle which ensures that all the Member States of the Union (as well as its citizens) are equal before the law. He posits that the equality argument must form part of the general principle of the primacy of Community law over national (and thus constitutional) law in the event of conflicts.

[1] Koen Lenaerts, 'L'égalité des États membres devant les traités: la dimensión transnationale du príncipe de primauté' (2020) 4 *Revue du Droit de l'Union Européenne* 7–10 and Koen Lenaerts, 'No Member State Is More Equal Than Others: The Primacy of European Union law and the Principle of the Equality of the Member States before the Treaties' (2020) *VerfBlog* (8 October 2020) at <https://verfassungsblog.de/no-member-state-is-more-equal-than-others/verfassungsblog> and <https://tinyurl.com/23bkk9ap>. See also Koen Lenaerts, José Gutiérrez-Fons and Stanislas Adam, 'Exploring the Autonomy of the European Union Legal Order' (2021) 81 *ZaöRV* 47 and Koen Lenaerts and Stanislas Adam, 'La solidarité, valeur commune aux états membres et principe fédératif de l'Union européenne' (2021) 307 CDE 374–75. Last but not least, Justice Lenaerts has also talked about this problem in Spain. See José Carlos Fernández Rojas, 'Interview with the President of the CJEU Justice Koen Lenaerts' (2022) *Diario La Ley* (7 September 2022) at <https://tinyurl.com/9jhzmak8>.

This new narrative leads us to examine whether the CJEU has followed this line of argumentation on the equality/primacy of European law in the most recent conflicts that show the interaction of Community/EU law with the constitutional courts of Hungary,[2] Romania[3] and Poland.[4] For reasons of space, it is not possible to examine and analyse in depth and in detail the implications of these recent and interesting judgments which have already been briefly commented by recent doctrine in Spain[5] and in Germany.[6] However, it is interesting to briefly refer to the legal arguments put forward on the question of primacy/equality in these three occasions.

The findings show that the CJEU has now adopted a new strategy and line of argumentation, as a reply to increasingly critical decisions by the constitutional courts of some EU Member States (and criticism coming from the different strands of the school of the constitutional pluralism). In three new important cases, it has grounded its construction of an absolute primacy of EU law (over national constitutional law) on a new basis: the equality of the EU Member States before the Treaties and Article 4(2) of the Treaty on European Union. This construction does not include directly the reference to the equality of citizens before the law which is usually treated by the Court separately, when referring to its classic case *Costa/Enel*[7] on the primacy of Community law.

Although more research is needed to assess all the case-law of the European Free Trade Association (EFTA) Court regarding the authority and effect of EEA law and the equality argument in the last 30 years; it seems that this new trend has not travelled to the parallel field of EEA law. One of the reasons could be that the EEA Agreement excludes the primacy and direct effect of EEA law over constitutional law.[8] The President of the EFTA Court has not written either on this topic recently (to the best of the authors' knowledge).[9] This does not mean that the question is alien to EEA law or even resolved, quite the contrary. At the time of writing, there is a

[2] The Hungarian case concerns the judgment of 7 December 2021 of its Constitutional Court, case X/00477/2021 (*Alkotmánybíróság*), delivered on a request for interpretation of certain provisions of the Hungarian Basic Law, made by the government following the judgment of the CJEU of 17 December 2020 in the context of an infringement action brought by the Commission on 21 December 2018 due to the incompatibility of Hungarian asylum law with EU law. See judgment of 17 December 2020 CJEU, Case C-808/18 *Commission v Hungary* ECLI: EU:C:2020:1029.

[3] The Romanian case called *Euro Box Promotion* refers to a judgment of the CJEU of 21 December 2021 on the case-law of the Constitutional Court (*Constitutional Court*) and the Romanian law on panels specialised in anti-corruption cases. See CJEU, Cases C-357/19, C-379/19, C-547/19, C-811/19 and C-840/19 *PM and Others* ECLI: EU:C:2021:1034. See also judgment of 22 February 2022 from CJEU, Case C-430/21, *RS* ECLI: EU:C:2022:99, paragraphs 49 and 50 (effects of judgments of a constitutional court).

[4] Judgment of 5 June 2023 CJEU, Case C-204/21 *Commission v Poland* ECLI: EU:C:2023:442 (Independence and private life of judges).

[5] Manuel López Escudero, 'Desafíos y límites a la primacía del Derecho de la Unión Europea: jurisprudencia reciente del Tribunal de Justicia de la Unión Europea y de los Tribunales Constitucionales nacionales' (2022) 58 *Revista General de Derecho Europeo* 86 at <https://tinyurl.com/48y4nzy3>. See also Juan Santos Vara, 'La evolución del Derecho de la Unión Europea en tiempos de crisis' (2023) 40 *Anales de Derecho* 223–68 at <https://tinyurl.com/yc87ch9f>.

[6] David Presslein, 'Equality Equals Primacy? Or: Why the Principle of EU Member State Equality Cannot Explain the Absolute Primacy of EU Law' (2023) SSRN at <https://ssrn.com/abstract=4527954> or <http://dx.doi.org/10.2139/ssrn.4527954>.

[7] Judgment of 15 July 1964 from CJEU, Case 6/64 *Costa/ENEL* ECLI: EU:C:1964:66.

[8] Maria Elvira Méndez-Pinedo, *EC and EEA law* (Groningen, Europa Law Publishing, 2009).

[9] The latest editorial of Justice Páll Hreinsson does not refer to the authority, effect or quasi primacy of EEA law. Páll Hreinsson, 'The EFTA Court – Past, Present and Future' (2023) 62(2) *Lov og Rett* 77–78 at <www.idunn.no/doi/10.18261/lor.62.2.2>.

legislative proposal presented at the Icelandic Parliament (*Althingi*) in order to better guarantee the authority (sometimes called 'quasi' primacy) of EEA (implemented) rules over other national conflicting rules promised 30 years ago with the Protocol 35 annexed to the EEA Agreement.

The structure of the study is as follows. In the first place, and following this introduction (Section I), this study briefly summarises and comments on the three most recent cases where the CJEU has used the argument of equality of Member States before the Treaties to anchor the primacy of EU law vis-à-vis national constitutional law (Section II). Second, it explains the current status quo of the parallel question in the field of EEA law and, more specifically, focuses on the legal reform pending in Iceland (Section III). Some findings and conclusions follow at the end (Section IV).

II. THE EQUALITY OF MEMBER STATES (AND CITIZENS) BEFORE THE TREATIES AND THE PRIMACY OF EU LAW: RECENT CASES OF THE CJEU

The trend of pairing primacy with equality of Member States in EU law seems to start formally in 2021 although it was announced in 2020 with a press release from the Court.[10] Two cases from Romania (*Euro box and others*[11] from 2021 and *RS*[12] from 2022) and one from Poland (*Commission v Poland*[13] from 2023) show the new argument used by the CJEU. The link between equality of Member States/primacy of EU law is missing in an earlier case in Hungary where the relationship between European law and national constitutional law is also discussed and ruled on (*Commission v Hungary* from 2020[14]) and in another recent case in Romania of constitutional relevance (*Criminal Procedure v C.I. and Others*[15] from 2023).

A. Romania: Cases *Euro box and Others* (2021) and *RS* (2022)

In these two judgments of the CJEU addressing the primacy of Community law vis-à-vis Romanian constitutional law, the European Court concludes that the general principle of primacy gives national judges both the right and duty not to apply judgments of their constitutional/supreme higher court in the hierarchy if they are incompatible with EU law and without running the risk of disciplinary sanctions.

[10] The Press Release from the CJEU following the so-called *PSPP* Judgment (Public Sector Purchase Program) in 2020 states: 'Like other authorities of the Member States, national courts are required to ensure that EU law takes full effect. That is the only way of ensuring the equality of Member States in the Union they created'. See CJEU, Press Release No 58/20 from 8 May 2020 available at <https://tinyurl.com/4d5sbbxc>.

[11] Judgment of 21 June 2021 CJEU, Joined Cases C-357/19, C-379/19, C-547/19, C-811/19 and C-840/19 *Euro Box and Others* ECLI:EU:C:2021:1034.

[12] Judgment of 22 February 2022 CJEU, Case C-430/21 *RS* ECLI:EU:C:2022:99.

[13] Judgment of 5 June 2023 CJEU, Case C204/21 *European Commission v Poland* ECLI: EU:C:2023:442.

[14] Judgment of 17 December 2020 CJEU, Case C-808/18 *Commission v Hungary* ECLI:EU:C:2020:1029. Regarding this case, it is advisable to wait before entering into a more in-depth analysis or comment. The country's doctrine seems to offer different interpretations of the judgment and its possible political consequences.

[15] Judgment of 24 July 2023 CJEU, Case C-107/23 *Criminal Procedure v C.I. and Others* PPU ECLI:EU:C:2023:606.

National judges also have the right to examine the conformity with European law of national legislation already judged by the constitutional court.

i. Case Euro box and Others *(2021)*

In the judgment of 21 June 2021, Joined Cases *Euro Box and Others*,[16] the equality of Member States before the Treaties is mentioned in paragraph 249 which reads:

> It must be added that Article 4(2) TEU provides that the Union is to respect the equality of Member States before the Treaties. However, the Union can respect such equality only if the Member States are unable, under the principle of the primacy of EU law, to rely on, as against the EU legal order, a unilateral measure, whatever its nature.

The Court concludes its reasoning on the principle of primacy in paragraphs 262 and 263 which state:

> It follows that the principle of the primacy of EU law is to be interpreted as precluding national rules or a national practice under which national ordinary courts are bound by the decisions of the national constitutional court and cannot, by virtue of that fact and without committing a disciplinary offence, disapply, on their own authority, the case-law established in those decisions, even though they are of the view, in the light of a judgment of the Court of Justice, that that case-law is contrary to the second subparagraph of Article 19(1) TEU, Article 325(1) TFEU or Decision 2006/928.

ii. Case RS *(2022)*

In the later judgment of 22 February 2022 (Case *RS*) the Court refers again to the equality of Member States and Article 4(3) TEU in paragraphs 55 and 88 and case-law cited (effects of judgments of a constitutional court. [17]

More specifically, paragraph 55 of that judgment emphasises that compliance with the principle of primacy is necessary to ensure respect for the equality of Member States before the Treaties, which precludes the possibility of relying on a unilateral measure as against the EU legal order. For the Court, it is also an expression of the principle of sincere cooperation in Article 4(3) TEU, which requires the disapplication of any provision of national law that may be contrary to EU law, irrespective as to when that provision was adopted.

And, in paragraph 88, the Court emphasises once again the importance of the argument:

> In view of the answer given to the first question referred, the impairment of the independence of national judges resulting from such national legislation or practice is also incompatible with the principles of equality between the Member States and of loyal cooperation between the Union and the Member States, recognized by Article 4(2) and (3) TEU, with Article 267 TFEU and with the principle of primacy of Union law.[18]

[16] Judgment of 21 June 2021 CJEU, Joined Cases C-357/19, C-379/19, C-547/19, C-811/19 and C-840/19 *Euro Box and Others* ECLI:EU:C:2021:1034.

[17] Judgment of 22 February 2022 CJEU, Case C-430/21 *RS* ECLI:EU:C:2022:99.

[18] ibid.

B. Poland: Case *European Commission v Poland* (2023)

The most recent case where the argument of equality supports the primacy of EU law is the case *European Commission v Poland*[19] from 2023. The Court summarises its whole doctrine of absolute primacy of EU law vis-à-vis national constitutional law in paragraph 77 which reads:

> It follows from that settled case-law that, by virtue of the principle of the primacy of EU law, a Member State's reliance on rules of national law, even of a constitutional order, cannot be allowed to undermine the unity and effectiveness of EU law. In accordance with settled case-law, the effects of the principle of the primacy of EU law are binding on all the bodies of a Member State, without, inter alia, provisions of domestic law, including constitutional provisions, being able to prevent that (judgments of 17 December 1970, *Internationale Handelsgesellschaft*, 11/70, EU:C:1970:114, paragraph 3, and of 22 February 2022, *RS (Effect of the decisions of a constitutional court)*, C-430/21, EU:C:2022:99, paragraph 51 and the case-law cited). Compliance with that obligation is necessary in particular in order to ensure respect for the equality of Member States before the Treaties and constitutes an expression of the principle of sincere cooperation set out in Article 4(3) TEU (see, to that effect, judgment of 22 February 2022, *RS (Effect of the decisions of a constitutional court)*, C-430/21, EU:C:2022:99, paragraph 55 and the case-law cited).

C. A Brief Comment on the Cases by Academic Doctrine and the Role of the European Parliament

Much has been written on the principle of primacy in EU law, a question always covered in classical textbooks.[20] For a quick reference, it is useful to cite the most recent and relevant works in the field published in journals/edited volumes.[21]

[19] Judgment of 5 June 2023 CJEU, Case C204/21 *European Commission v Poland* ECLI: EU:C:2023:442.

[20] Damian Chalmers, Gareth Davies and Giorgio Monti, 'The Authority of European Union Law' in David Chalmers et al (eds), *European Union Law: Text and Materials* (Cambridge, Cambridge University Press, 2019) 202–48 at: <https:// doi.org/10.1017/9781108654173>; Paul Craig and Grainne De Búrca, *European Union Law. Text, Cases and Materials* 7th edn (Oxford, Oxford University Press, 2020) 303–52.

[21] Some recent relevant literature on the principle of primacy follows here: Tomi Tuominen, 'Reconceptualizing the Primacy-Supremacy debate in European Union Law'(2020) 47 (3) *Legal Issues of Economic Integration* 245–65 at: <https://doi.org/10.54648/LEIE2020015>; Clara Rauchegger, 'Four Functions of the Principle of Primacy in the ECJ's Post-Lisbon Case Law' in Katja Ziegler, Päivi Neuvonen and Violeta Moreno-Lax (eds), *Research Handbook: The General Principles of EU Law* (Cheltenham, Edward Elgar, 2021) also at SSRN: <https://ssrn.com/abstract=3724541>; Juan Ignacio Ugartemendía Eceizabarrena, 'Turbulencias sobre la primacía del Derecho de la Unión Europea: últimos desafíos, respuestas y aportaciones' (2021) 78–79 *Revista Española de Derecho Europeo* 13–52 at: https://doi.org/10.37417/REDE/num78-79_2021_678; Constitutional Court of the Italian Republic and Court of Justice of the European Union, Study meeting on Member States National Identity, Primacy of European Union Law, Rule of Law and Independence of National Judges (70th Anniversary of the CJEU, Rome 5 September 2022) at: <https://cortecostituzionale.it/jsp/consulta/convegni/5_sett_2022 /Giornata-Studio-Lenaerts.pdf>; Hafsteinn Dan Kristjánsson, 'Is the Primacy of European Union Law Absolute or Relative? Explaining Primacy in Interlocking Legal Systems' (2023) 2 *Europarättslig Tidskrift* 233–54.

However, it is out of the scope of this study to make a survey of literature on the question since other authors have already done it recently.[22] What follows is a selection of the most relevant works that deal with the abovementioned cases of the CJEU and the role of the European Parliament, publishing studies, reports and adopting a resolution in November 2023 on the implementation of the principle of primacy of EU law.[23]

i. On the Equality of Member States: Romania, Poland and General Comments by Scholarship

The political and legal context in Romania illustrates a classic situation: recognition of primacy by ordinary courts, on the one hand; and the resistance of its constitutional court,[24] on the other. On the basis of this different context, Ziller has noted (in his study for the European Parliament) that it would be unwise to compare the position of the Romanian Constitutional Court with that of the German Constitutional Court, which carried out an *ultra vires* review of European law.[25]

Commenting on the first *Euro Box and Others* case, Justice Koen Lenaerts has pointed out that the Court of Justice strongly stated

> that EU law does not impose a particular constitutional model, but that it is for each Member State to choose the model that its citizens like most, provided that such a model respects the basic values of the Union, and in particular judicial independence.[26]

In those circumstances, Santos Vara agrees with the strength of the court's ruling. In his view, paragraphs 245–50 of the *Euro Box and Others* judgment show that 'the scope of primacy is linked to judicial independence as a basic element of the rule of law and extends even to constitutional courts that are reluctant to accept the primacy of EU rules'. In his view, the CJEU has no doubts about replying forcefully to the defiance of the Romanian Constitutional Court and reconfirms its case-law on the primacy of EU law and its exclusive competence in its interpretation and application.[27]

[22] Jacques Ziller, *The Primacy of European Law* (European Parliament, Directorate-General for Internal Policies of the Union, Policy Department C – Citizens' Rights and Constitutional Affairs, 2022) at <www.europarl.europa.eu/RegData/etudes/STUD/2022/732474/IPOL_STU(2022)732474_EN.pdf>. See also Elvira Méndez-Pinedo, 'La primacía absoluta o relativa del derecho de la Unión Europea: recensión de doctrina académica sobre la jurisprudencia reciente de tribunales constitucionales' (2023) 76 *Revista de Derecho Comunitario Europeo* 113–54 at <https://doi.org/10.18042/cepc/rdce.76.04>.

[23] European Parliament, Committee on Legal Affairs and Committee on Constitutional Affairs, *Report on the implementation of the principle of primacy* (7 November 2023) section or consideration c) and conclusion 1) at www.europarl.europa.eu/doceo/document/A-9-2023-0341_EN.html>; European Parliament, Resolution on the implementation of the principle of primacy (23 November 2023), at www.europarl.europa.eu/doceo/document/TA-9-2023-0406_EN.pdf.

[24] In its judgment of 8 June 2021, 390/2021, the Romanian Constitutional Court held that a court does not have jurisdiction to examine the conformity with EU law of a national provision which that constitutional court itself has declared to be in conformity with Article 148 of the Romanian Constitution. In the light of this case-law of the Romanian Constitutional Court, ordinary judges referred the matter again to the CJEU for a preliminary ruling as to whether they should follow the case-law of their Constitutional Court or the CJEU.

[25] Ziller, above note 22, 38.

[26] Fernández Rojas, above note 1.

[27] Juan Santos Vara, above note 5, 255.

This case has also been commented on by Parashu[28] and a very critical study of the legal argumentation is offered by Weber.[29]

As for the case *RS*,[30] it is important to note that the Court recalls in paragraph 72 its exclusive competence on the interpretation of EU law and the obligations of a constitutional court vis-à-vis a preliminary ruling of the CJEU:

> The Court of Justice has exclusive jurisdiction to give a definitive interpretation of EU law, (and) the constitutional court of a Member State cannot, on the basis of its own interpretation of provisions of EU law, including Article 267 TFEU, validly declare that the Court of Justice has delivered a judgment which exceeds the limits of its jurisdiction and thus refuse to comply with a judgment delivered by the Court of Justice in preliminary ruling proceedings.[31]

The most relevant general comment on these recent cases and their context has been made recently by Presslein[32] who also has a critical view on the equality argument as a constitutional doctrine intended to construct and secure the absolute primacy of EU law. The case *RS* has also been commented on by Wahl.[33]

In a parallel way, Presslein has noted that:

> the CJEU also establishes a link between primacy and Article 19(1) TEU: by ordering national courts to effectively apply EU law and obliging them to disregard conflicting national law, it also declares primacy to be a component of judicial independence and 'upgrades' it to an independent norm.[34]

As regards the most recent case, *Commission v Poland*,[35] it is important to place it in a prior context of confrontation and absentia by its constitutional court as already

[28] Dimitrios Parashu, 'Developing Billiard Skills: The CJEU Judgment in Euro Box Promotion, a Reaction to Recent Romanian Constitutional Case Law' (European Law Blog, 21 February 2022) <https://europeanlawblog.eu/2022/02/21/developing-billiard-skills-the-cjeu-judgment-in-euro-box-promotion-a-reaction-to-recent-romanian-constitutional-case-law/>.

[29] Ferdinand Weber, 'The Identity of Union Law in Primacy: Piercing Through Euro Box Promotion and Others' (2022) 7(2) *European Papers* 749–71.

[30] Judgment of 22 February 2022 CJEU, Case C-430/21 *RS* ECLI: EU:C:2022:99, paragraphs 49 and 50 (effects of judgments of a constitutional court).

[31] ibid.

[32] Presslein, above note 6, 8–9 and 30. In this article, the author acknowledges that the question of primacy of EU law over constitutional law still awaits its final answer. More importantly, he critically examines the new line of argument by the CJEU and explains why, in his view, it cannot sufficiently establish an absolute primacy of EU law. Instead, he proposes to use the equality of the EU Member States for national constitutional control mechanisms on European integration and a new test criterion for the CJEU to challenge potential abuses of such mechanisms. As he states himself, he pleads 'for more comparative judicial dialogue in the European judicial network ("Verfassungsgerichtsverbund")'.

[33] Thomas Wahl, 'CJEU again Finds Romanian Judicial System Flawed' (EUCrim, 10 March 2022) <https://eucrim.eu/news/cjeu-again-finds-romanian-judicial-system-flawed/>.

[34] Presslein, above note 6, 8.

[35] CJEU, Judgment of 5 June 2023, *Commission v Poland*, C-204/21, EU:C:2023:442 (Independence and private life of judges). The Commission took the view that Poland had failed to fulfil its obligations under the second subparagraph of Article 19 (1) TEU, which provides for the obligation of Member States to provide remedies sufficient to ensure effective judicial protection in the fields covered by EU law, under Article 47 of the Charter, relating to the right to an effective remedy and to an independent and impartial tribunal previously established by the law, under the second and third paragraphs of Article 267 TFEU, which contains the power (second paragraph), for certain national courts, and the obligation (third paragraph) for others to make a reference for a preliminary ruling, in accordance with the principle of the primacy of EU law and under Articles 7 and 8 of the Charter.

described and studied by some authors.[36] In its judgment, the Court upholds the Commission's action and recalls the close link between the primacy of European law and the effective judicial protection of citizens' rights which is a matter for all national courts. This case has been commented on by Coli[37] and Leichsenring.[38]

It is also interesting to note, as Santos Vara rightly points out, that

> [t]he examination of the judicial saga of the CJEU on judicial independence in Poland shows that infringement actions accompanied by interim suspension measures on pain of heavy fines have proved to be more effective in practice than the questions referred for a preliminary ruling to reverse the situation.[39]

ii. On the Equality of Member States and Article 4(2) TEU

In his study, Presslein starts by clarifying that the equality argument is not that novel, since it was proposed earlier by Fabrini in 2015.[40] Five years later, this approach was taken up by the CJEU's President Koen Lenaerts after the *PSPP* judgment.[41] Furthermore, in Presslein′s view, 'it does not wield the power it initially promised and that it cannot support the concept of an absolute primacy of EU law'.[42]

Vosa refers instead to a new principle of 'essentiality in the European legal order',[43] a legal principle that can be regarded as a general principle of Union law and has potential to promote equality among States and citizens as laid down in Articles 4(2) and 9 TEU.[44] He conceptualises the principle in the following way:

> Conclusively, thanks to the essentiality argument, all Member States can claim that an equal treatment be reserved to all: no EU law measure should be applied if it hits sensitive national interests as settled by democratic self-government, particularly if fundamental

[36] Niels Petersen and Patrick Wasilczyk, The Primacy of EU Law and the Polish Constitutional Law Judgment; Luxembourg: Study for the European Parliament (2022) available at www.europarl.europa.eu/RegData/etudes/STUD/2022/734568/IPOL_STU(2022)734568_EN.pdf>.

[37] Martina Coli, 'Don't try to discipline your judges (and prevent them from applying EU law): the Court of Justice's judgment in Commission v. Poland (C-204/21)' (Diritti Comparati, 12 July 2023). <www.diritticomparati.it/dont-try-to-discipline-your-judges-and-prevent-them-from-applying-eu-law-the-court-of-justices-judgment-in-commission-v-poland-c-204-21/>.

[38] Til Leichsenring, 'Poland's Extended Disciplinary System' (VerfBlog, 2 July 2023) <https://verfassungsblog.de/polands-extended-disciplinary-system/>.

[39] Santos Vara, above note 5, 242.

[40] Presslein, above note 6, 10 refers to Fabrini as the origin of the equality argument based on Article 4(2) TEU as a tool to resolve the so-called 'Gauweiler Saga' concerning the legality of the European Central Bank's OMT programme. See Federico Fabbrini, 'After the OMT Case: The Supremacy of EU Law as the Guarantee of the Equality of the Member States' (2015) 16 *GLJ* 1004, 1012–21.

[41] Lenaerts, *VerfBlog* (8 October 2020), above note 1.

[42] Presslein, above note 6, 29.

[43] Giuliano Vosa, 'Rasgos tempranos del principio de esencialidad ¿Una lección europea (por cierto, contraintuitiva) desde Karlsruhe?' (2021) 68 *Revista de Derecho Comunitario Europeo* 113–55 at <https://doi.org/10.18042/cepc/rdce.68.04>.

[44] Art 9 EU Treaty reads: 'In all its activities, the Union shall observe the principle of the equality of its citizens, who shall receive equal attention from its institutions, bodies, offices and agencies. Every national of a Member State shall be a citizen of the Union. Citizenship of the Union shall be additional to and not replace national citizenship'.

> rights are at stake. This argument would give a reinforced legal substance to the duty of loyal cooperation; it would be addressed to all Member States and to the EU institutions, too, which are bound to respect fundamental rights as associated with their essential character whether they act within or outside the EU's legal framework.[45]

Presslein concurs with Lindeboom on the reasons why the CJEU has now invoked it nevertheless.[46]

> The CJEU needs new argumentative *topoi*. The arguments used previously, namely the notion of the EU being an independent legal order and the autonomy of EU law, are currently losing their clout. Making recourse to the equality of the EU Member States is thus useful as it is a hitherto 'unused' concept.[47]

Then Presslein makes a good summary of the legal reasoning of the Court. In the first place, in a classic line of argumentation, the Court refers to its established case-law according to which a new independent legal order has been created by all Member States with the EU Treaties. As is usual in public international law, the 'pacta sunt servanda' customary rule applies, that is to say, subsequent unilateral measures contrary to this legal order are excluded and inacceptable. If the opposite was possible, the unique nature of supranational EU law would be lost, which would affect European integration and the achieving of its goals.

In the second place, the CJEU also emphasises that this independent legal order had been repeatedly confirmed by the Member States. In particular, the Member States accepted the primacy of EU law by ratifying the Treaty of Lisbon and Declaration No 17 on the primacy of EU law.[48]

And, in the third place, Presslein looks at how the CJEU relies on the equality of the Member States before the Treaties, enshrined in Article 4(2) TEU to construct a 'new' doctrine on the primacy of EU law:

> According to the Court's, the only way to ensure respect for the Treaties is by preventing individual Member States from taking unilateral measures against EU law. Furthermore, the CJEU reiterates that it is the sole interpreter of EU law and its primacy, since such a task could not be exercised by the many different national (constitutional) courts of the individual Member States.[49]

He concludes with the following finding:

> In sum, both judgments, Euro Box Promotion et al. and RS, allowed the CJEU to clarify the meaning of judicial independence as mentioned in Article 19(1) Sub-section 2 TEU. Moreover, they granted the Court the opportunity to elaborate further on the relationship

[45] Vosa, above note 43, refers in his conclusions to the essentiality principle as 'an universalisable apology of the right to resistance' as defined by Juan Ignacio Ugartemendía Eceizabarrena, 'El derecho de resistencia y su "constitucionalización"' (1999) 103 *Revista de Estudios Políticos* 213–45.

[46] Justin Lindeboom, 'Is the Primacy of EU Law Based on the Equality of the Member States? A Comment on the CJEU's Press Release Following the PSPP Judgment' (2020) 21 *GLJ* 1032, 1035–36.

[47] Presslein, above note 6, 28.

[48] See also European Parliament, *Report on the implementation of the principle of primacy* (7 November 2023) at <www.europarl.europa.eu/doceo/document/A-9-2023-0341_EN.html>.

[49] Presslein, above note 6, 9.

between EU law and national constitutions. For the first time, the Court invoked the equality among the EU Member States to justify an absolute primacy of EU law over national law.[50]

iii. On the Equality of the Citizens

Presslein also notes that the Court infers that unilateral measures adopted by Member States and challenging the primacy doctrine could lead to inadmissible discrimination on the basis of nationality.[51] Other doctrinal studies place, however, more emphasis on the equality of citizens. For instance, Klamert attaches significance to Article 4(2) TEU only to the extent that it reinforces the equality of citizens by means of the equality of States.[52]

In reality, the equality of citizens argument (in relation with primacy) is treated by the Court separately in the case *Euro box and others*.[53] The Court constructs it as a seminal principle of EU law together with the *Costa/Enel* ruling from 1964, stating in paragraph 246:

> Thus, in the judgment of 15 July 1964, *Costa* (6/64, EU:C:1964:66, pp. 593 to 594), the Court laid down the principle of the primacy of Community law, which is understood to enshrine the precedence of Community law over the law of the Member States. In that regard, it found that the establishment by the EEC Treaty of the Community's own legal system, accepted by the Member States on a basis of reciprocity, means, as a corollary, that they cannot accord precedence to a unilateral and subsequent measure over that legal system or rely on rules of national law of any kind against the law stemming from the EEC Treaty, without depriving the latter law of its character as Community law and without the legal basis of the Community itself being called into question. In addition, the executive force of Community law cannot vary from one Member State to another in deference to subsequent domestic laws, without jeopardising the attainment of the objectives of the EEC Treaty or giving rise to discrimination on grounds of nationality prohibited by that treaty.[54]

The same argument is repeated by the CJEU in the second case examined, *RS*,[55] at paragraph 48 which refers to the previous case *Euro box and others* (paragraph 246) and is almost identical in its drafting.

In a more recent commentary, O'Neill, on the other hand, specifically studies the recent jurisprudence of the CJEU on the necessary judicial independence and Article 19 TEU (respect for the law in the application and interpretation of the Treaties and effective judicial protection of citizens) and concludes that it is based on the previous doctrines of primacy and the useful effect or the obligation to guarantee the

[50] ibid.
[51] ibid, 8.
[52] Marcus Klamert, 'Supremacy, the Uniformity of EU Law, and the Principle of Equality' (2021) 18 *Graz Law Working Paper* (8 November 2021) at <https://ssrn.com/abstract=3958290>.
[53] See CJEU, Cases C-357/19 *Euro Box Promotion and others* ECLI: EU:C:2021:1034 at para 246.
[54] ibid.
[55] CJEU, Case C-430/21 *RS* ECLI: EU:C:2022:99, para 48.

effectiveness of EU law.[56] Last but not least, CJEU judge Von Danwitz recalls the need to ensure the uniform interpretation of law in relation to primacy and European judicial dialogue and offers a series of theoretical premises (or seven theses) in this regard.[57]

iv. The Role of the European Parliament: Studies and Resolution on the Primacy of EU Law

It is also very interesting to note the publication of some studies done for the European Parliament on the principle of primacy in 2021 and 2022.[58] Even more interestingly, the newest joint report of the Committee on Legal Affairs and the Committee on Constitutional Affairs of the European Parliament on the principle of primacy from 7 November 2023 puts stronger emphasis on the equality of the citizens than the equality of Member States on the basis of the fundamental values and principles of the Union (Article 2). The report states:

> The justification of the principle of primacy by the CJEU is thus essentially based on the need for an effective and uniform application of EU law, which are the basis for the equality of citizens under the law. In turn, the effectiveness and uniformity of the application of EU law, without which the system envisaged by the Treaty – with institutions empowered to adopt acts – cannot function, can only be ensured if it takes precedence over national law.[59]

The joint report has been followed by a Resolution of the European Parliament from 21 November 2023 on implementation of the principle of primacy, which likewise underscores the link between the principle of primacy and the equality of EU citizens.[60] The legal arguments advanced in the Resolution are extremely relevant (especially paragraphs B and C and conclusion number 1). For the Parliament, the EU is a community based on the rule of law and therefore dependent on the effective and uniform application and enforcement of its law by the CJEU and Member States' courts. Such necessary effectiveness and uniformity can only be secured if EU law takes precedence over diverging national law in areas where EU law is applicable (in cases of conflict). For these reasons, the principle of primacy is a fundamental

[56] Ruairi O'Neill, 'Effet Utile and the Re-organisation of National Judiciaries: A Not So Unique Institutional Response to a Uniquely Important Challenge?' (2022) 27 *European Law Journal* 240–61 at <https://doi.org/10.1111/eulj.12437>. In this article, O'Neill points out that, although the jurisprudence on judicial independence is unprecedented, the Court of Justice has done everything possible to ensure that the evolution of EU law supported by its rulings is based on previously established doctrines (principle of primacy of EU law and the obligation to ensure the effectiveness of EU law in the domestic legal order).

[57] Thomas von Danwitz, 'Uniform Interpretation and Primacy of Union Law in the Dialogue of the Courts', *Verfassungsblog*, 4 November 2022, <https://verfassungsblog.de/uniform-interpretation-and-primacy-of-union-law-in-the-dialogue-of-the-courts/>.

[58] Ziller, above note 22, 38. See also study by Petersen and Wasilczyk, above note 36. See also European Parliament, 'Primacy's Twilight? On the Legal Consequences of the Ruling of the Federal Constitutional Court of 5 May 2020 for the Primacy of EU Law' (Directorate-General for Internal Policies of the Union, Policy Department C – Citizens' Rights and Constitutional Affairs, 2021) at <www.europarl.europa.eu/RegData/etudes/STUD/2021/692276/IPOL_STU(2021)692276_EN.pdf>.

[59] European Parliament, above note 23.

[60] ibid.

cornerstone of the European legal order and essential for its correct functioning.[61] Furthermore, the principle of primacy of EU law is not just a legal doctrine but also a reflection of the political and economic integration of the EU.[62] Following the same spirit, the principle of primacy contributes to the creation of an 'ever closer union among the peoples of Europe', as envisaged by the Treaties.[63] Last but not least, the Parliament states that 'the primacy of EU law is also intrinsically linked to the principle of equality before the law, as it guarantees equal protection of the rights conferred by EU law to all EU citizens'.[64] As the guardian of the Treaties, the Commission is called on to fully exercise its powers in this regard.[65]

As a final recommendation, the Parliament recalls that the precedence of EU law was explicitly laid down as a clause in the Treaty establishing a constitution for Europe and therefore favours that the principle of primacy be included as an explicit Treaty provision in the future.[66]

v. Summing It All Up: A Reply to the School of Constitutional Pluralism

In short, in all the cases referred to above, the Court of Justice and the European Parliament construct the principle of primacy by directly reaffirming the values on which the EU is founded (Article 2 TEU) and the necessary link between the primacy, uniformity and equality of the Member States (and their citizens) before the Treaties (Article 4(2) TEU).[67] The effective and uniform application and enforcement of EU law by national courts and the exclusive monopoly of the CJEU on the interpretation and validity of EU law justify this principle. The European Parliament, furthermore, prefers to recall that the primacy of EU law is not only about Member States but guarantees equal protection of the European rights conferred by the Treaties to all EU citizens.

Regarding the trend of judicial resistance to the primacy of EU law by some constitutional courts, it is important to note that some scholars are already discussing the creation of a separate appeal chamber of the Court of Justice that would exclusively dedicate to reviewing the constitutional issue of the delimitation of competences between the EU and the Member States.[68] In their view, that would help to avoid future clashes/confrontation between the Court of Justice and some highest, supreme or constitutional courts in Europe. However, this question is far from being simple to

[61] ibid, B.
[62] ibid, C.
[63] ibid, C.
[64] ibid, C.
[65] ibid, conclusions n 16–18, and recommendations 21–23.
[66] ibid, conclusion n 1. See also European Parliament, Committee on Legal Affairs and Committee on Constitutional Affairs, Report, above note 23.
[67] Presslein, above note 6, 8–9. See also Santos Vara, above note 5, 256 who refers only to the CJEU; and Fernández Rojas, above note 1.
[68] This chamber should be composed in equal parts of judges of the Court of Justice and judges of highest courts of the Member States. That way it would be absolutely impartial and not biased towards EU institutions. See Daniel Sarmiento and Joseph HH Weiler, 'The EU Judiciary after Weiss: Proposing a New Mixed Chamber of the Court of Justice' Verfassungsblog, (2 June 2020) at <https://verfas sungsblog .de/the-eu-judiciary-after-weiss>.

solve, since it is not always easy to distinguish questions of competence from questions of mere legality in the EU legal order.[69]

The relationship between the legal system of the European Union and those of its Member States is a difficult topic that the so-called trend of 'constitutional pluralism' has studied in depth. Since the 1990s, the pluralist movement has offered a different normative account on the relations between European law and the national legal orders.[70] Different authors have contributed with their publications to a school of constitutional pluralism that defends the relativity of the primacy of the law of the Union and the constitutional/domestic perspective of EU Member States (almost all of them dualistic vis-à-vis international law). Although it is not possible here to offer a complete summary of the diverse doctrinal works and different strands of this school of thought, most authors share the following premise. They leave behind the concept and the unitary nature of EU law from a theoretical point of view and call for a broader interpretation that would take into account the empirical jurisprudence of supreme national courts in practice.[71] However, this specific line of scholarship has also been strongly questioned by its peers and it is now clear that the challenges that constitutional pluralism and recent judicial (constitutional) resistance to the authority and primacy of EU law have become systemic and unsustainable.[72]

In fact, the 2023 Resolution from the European Parliament constitutes a formal reply to the most important thesis advanced by constitutional pluralism and different constitutional rulings in some EU Member States, as its conclusions (points 7 to 9) state that those claims are incompatible with EU legal integration[73] and that the judicial dialogue between national constitutional or supreme courts and the CJEU should be constructive and not legitimise any disregard for the decisions of the CJEU (point 10).[74]

[69] Some authors have argued that the proportionality test required by the Federal Constitutional Court was merely a requirement of legality. In fact, Art 5 TEU distinguishes between the existence of a competence and its exercise; and proportionality only concerned the latter. See Editorial Comments, 'Not Mastering the Treaties: The German Federal Constitutional Court's PSPP Judgment' (2020) 57 *Common Market Law Review* 965; and Mattias Wendel, 'Paradoxes of Ultra-Vires Review: A Critical Review of the PSPP Decision and Its Initial Reception' (2020) 21 *German Law Journal* 979.

[70] For a recent survey of literature of the most important authors contributing to the different strands of the school of constitutional pluralism, see Maria Elvira Méndez-Pinedo, 'Constitutional Pluralism and Legal Perspectivism in European Union Law' (2020) 10(1) *Juridical Tribune* 5 at: <https://heinonline.org /HOL/P?h=hein.journals/juridtrib10&i=5.

[71] For further reference on the school of constitutional pluralism see also Matej Avbelj and Jan Komarek (eds), *Constitutional Pluralism in the EU and Beyond* (Oxford, Hart Publishing, 2012); Matej Avbelj, *The European Union under Transnational law. A Pluralist Appraisa*l (Oxford, Hart Publishing, 2018) and Matej Avbelj and George Davies (eds), *Research Handbook on Legal Pluralism and EU Law* (Cheltenham, Edward Elgar, 2018).

[72] Arthur Dyevre, 'Domestic Judicial Defiance in the European Union: A Systematic Threat to the Authority of EU Law?' (2016) 35 *Yearbook of European Law* 106. See also R Daniel Kelemen, 'On the Unsustainability of Constitutional Pluralism: European Supremacy and the Survival of the Eurozone' (2016) 23 *Maastricht Journal of European and Comparative Law* 136. For an earlier critique of the constitutional pluralist movement, see Julio Baquero Cruz, 'The Legacy of the Maastricht-Urteil and the Pluralist Movement' *EUI Working Paper RSCAS* (2007/13) and (2008) 14(4) *European Law Journal* 389–422. More recently, from same author 'Another Look at Constitutional Pluralism in the European Union' (2016) 22(3) *European Law Journal* 356–74 at: <https://doi.org/10.1111/eulj.12178>.

[73] European Parliament, Resolution, above note 23.

[74] ibid.

III. THE AUTHORITY OF EEA LAW IN THE EEA AGREEMENT (QUASI-PRIMACY)

I now move on to the parallel question of the authority of EEA law and to explore whether the new legal reasoning of primacy/equality constructed by the CJEU has had an influence on the EEA Agreement. The scope and nature of the EEA legal order have been perfectly summarised by Justice Páll Hreinsson in 2023:

> This January marks the 30th anniversary of the internal market, one of the EU's most significant achievements. The EEA brings the participating EFTA States under the internal market umbrella, without subjecting them to, in the words of *van Gend en Loos*, the 'new legal order of international law' represented by the European Union, to which they had voiced resistance. The resultant tension built into the Agreement was, by and large, left to the EFTA Court to resolve. In *Sveinbjörnsdóttir* (E-9/97), the Court developed its vision of the EEA, holding that it constitutes an 'international treaty *sui generis* which contains a distinct legal order of its own' with an unwritten principle of State liability equalling that found in EU law. Another example of the EFTA Court shaping the EEA legal order to ensure homogeneity with EU law is the recognition of fundamental rights as general principles of EEA law.[75]

A comparative analysis could therefore be done regarding the equality argument before the EEA Agreement since this international treaty (even more sui generis than the supranational EU law) is based on reciprocity and homogeneity and must provide 'similar' rights for European citizens (but not identical). However, this exercise should take into account, as it was clear from the first Opinion of the CJEU on the EEA Agreement from 1991 that primacy and direct effect are distinct features of the EU Treaties but not of the EEA legal order.[76]

A. Some Important Legal Provisions

The authority and effect of EEA law are classic topics studied in the field.[77] To make the arguments short, they are primarily covered by the preamble, Articles 3, 119 and the Protocol 35 of the EEA Agreement on the implementation of EEA Rules.

The Preamble to the EEA Agreement states that:

> CONSIDERING the objective of establishing a dynamic and homogeneous European Economic Area, based on common rules and equal conditions of competition and providing for the adequate means of enforcement including at the judicial level, and achieved on

[75] Hreinsson, above note 9.

[76] In paragraph 21 of its Opinion 1/91 (First Opinion of the EEA Agreement) of 14 December 1991 (ECLI:EU:C:1991:490), the Court thus found that the EEC Treaty, albeit concluded in the form of an international agreement, nonetheless constitutes the constitutional charter of a Community based on the rule of law, and that the essential characteristics of the Community legal order thus established are in particular its primacy over the law of the Member States and the direct effect of a whole series of provisions which are applicable to their nationals and to the Member States themselves.

[77] Maria Elvira Méndez-Pinedo and Ólafur Ísberg Ólafsson, *The Primacy and Authority of European Law (EU and EEA Law)* (Law Institute, University of Iceland, 2012).

> the basis of equality and reciprocity and of an overall balance of benefits, rights and obligations for the Contracting Parties.

Article 3:

> The Contracting Parties shall take all appropriate measures, whether general or particular, to ensure fulfilment of the obligations arising out of this Agreement.
>
> They shall abstain from any measure which could jeopardize the attainment of the objectives of this Agreement.
>
> Moreover, they shall facilitate cooperation within the framework of this Agreement.

Article 119:

> The Annexes and the acts referred to therein as adapted for the purposes of this Agreement as well as the Protocols shall form an integral part of this Agreement.

Protocol 35:

> Whereas this Agreement aims at achieving a homogeneous European Economic Area, based on common rules, without requiring any Contracting Party to transfer legislative powers to any institution of the European Economic Area; and. . . . Whereas this consequently will have to be achieved through national procedures; . . . . . . Sole Article. . . . . . For cases of possible conflicts between implemented EEA rules and other statutory provisions, the EFTA States undertake to introduce, if necessary, a statutory provision to the effect that EEA rules prevail in these cases.

B. The Difficult Question of the 'Quasi-primacy' of EEA Law in Norway and Iceland

As it is obvious from the reading of the very few provisions quoted above, the question of the 'quasi' primacy of EEA law vis-à-vis national constitutional law is also extremely delicate and unresolved. Norway and Iceland adopted national provisions to this effect.

Norway implemented Protocol 35 EEA Agreement with Section 2 of EEA Act which reads:

> Provisions of law that serve to fulfil Norway's obligations under the [EEA] Agreement shall, in the event of conflict, take precedence over other provisions regulating the same conditions. The same applies if a statutory instrument that serves to fulfil Norway's obligations under the [EEA] Agreement is in conflict with another statutory instrument, or conflicts with a later law.[78]

Although the situation in Norway offers more legal certainty *prima facie*; a very serious problem of interpretation and application of national law overruling EEA law

[78] Norway, Act no 109/1992 on the implementation in Norwegian law of the main part of the agreement on the European Economic Area (EEA). Lov 27. nov 1992 nr. 109 *Det europeiske økonomiske samarbeidsområde* (EØS) available at: <https://lovdata.no/dokument/NL/lov/1992-11-27-109> (author's translation).

took place some years ago in the so-called NAV scandal which led to the re-opening of many criminal cases and State liability for breach of EEA law.[79]

Iceland implemented Protocol 35 EEA Agreement with the Article 3 of EEA Act which is constructed as a rule of interpretation and provides:

> [S]tatutes and regulations shall be interpreted, in so far as appropriate, in conformity with the EEA Agreement and the rules laid down therein.[80]

In 2023, 2024 and 2025 a legislative proposal was presented before the Icelandic Parliament (*Alþingi*) in order to reform the original Icelandic EEA Act no 2 from 1993. The proposal, if approved, would have secured the proper application and interpretation of Protocol 35 of the EEA Agreement into national law (precedence/quasi-primacy as a rule of conflict and not only as a rule of friendly interpretation).[81]

The legislative proposal introduced a totally new Article 4 which reads:

> [new] Article 4:
>
> If a clear and unconditional legal provision that correctly implements an obligation under the EEA Agreement is incompatible with another general legal provision, the former shall take precedence, unless Alþingi has prescribed otherwise. The same applies to obligations that are implemented by government orders.

At the time of writing, the proposal has not been discussed again by the Parliament during 2024, nor 2025 since it is somehow controversial for some politicians of the majority in government. On the other hand, important figures in the EEA legal world have expressed support for this reform. In their view, the new wording means simply fulfilling a 30-year-old promise and could be a response to put an end to the infringement action started by the EFTA Surveillance Authority (ESA) in 2020.[82] The Supreme Court of Iceland, in the recent case Anna Bryndís from 2024 has once more ruled that the principle of judicial interpretation of national law in light of EEA law (Article 3 EEA Act 2/1993) has clear limits and cannot secure the due application of European law in all circumstances.[83]

C. The Role of the EFTA Court

The EFTA Court has not directly relied on the principles of equality and reciprocity of EEA Member States in order to interpret the legal framework of the EEA

[79] See Report of Investigation by Finn Arnessen and other experts, NOU 2020: 9. *Blindsonen – Gransking av feilpraktiseringen av folketrygdlovens oppholdskrav ved reiser i EØS-området* available at www.regjeringen.no/no/dokumenter/nou-2020-9/id2723776/?ch=2.

[80] Iceland, Act No 2/1993 on the European Economic Area ('the EEA Act') (*Lög nr. 2/1993 um Evrópska efnahagssvæðið*) at: <www.althingi.is/lagas/153a/1993002.html>.

[81] See EFTA Surveillance Authority, Reasoned Opinion of 30 September 2020 on Iceland breaching Article 3 and Protocol 35 EEA Agreement and amendment to the European Economic Act, no 2/1993 (Protocol 35) pending before the Icelandic Parliament (*Althingi*) at <www.althingi.is/altext/153/s/1392.html>.

[82] Most comments are in Icelandic. On the authority of EEA law and constitutional sovereignty in Iceland, see Davið Þór Björgvinsson, 'Fullveldi og forgangur EES-reglna' (4 April 2023) <https://uni.hi.is/davidth/2023/04/04/fullveldi-og-forgangur-ees-reglna/>.

[83] Supreme Court of Iceland, Ruling in case 24/2023 *A v Iceland* of 28 February 2024 following the advisory opinion of the EFTA Court in case C-5/22 *Anna Bryndís Einarsdóttir v the Icelandic Treasury* from 29 July 2022, not yet reported. A legal summary of the Icelandic ruling in English will be available later this year.

Agreement.[84] However, it does not mean that these values/goals/outcomes are not there since some seminal and recent cases adjudicated by this court deal with the principles in a more elliptical or implicit way, mostly through the principle of homogeneity (a key principle of the EEA Agreement).

For instance, in the recent case *RS*[85] 'the EFTA Court recalls that an important objective of the EEA Agreement is to ensure the equal treatment of individuals and economic operators and equal conditions of competition, as well as adequate means of enforcement' (referring to seminal case *Erla Maria*).[86] This judgment prevents a highest court of an EEA State (Liechtenstein) to refuse to apply implemented EEA law in a concrete case even during a short and temporary period. Such a result would not only undermine the homogeneous and uniform application of EEA law but also the equality among EEA States. Here we see an outcome similar to the one required by reciprocity/equality of States in EU law.

As for the equality of citizens before the EEA Agreement, more research is needed to explore how it has been constructed in depth. To the best of the author's knowledge, the EFTA Court has never used the term 'equality' in its 30 years of case-law. However, Justice and President Páll Hreinsson has referred to the challenge of ensuring equal treatment of EFTA and EU citizens in a common area of freedom, security and justice without internal frontiers (since the EFTA Court has no jurisdiction over the Schengen Agreement, the Agreement on the European Arrest Warrant and other related agreements which the EFTA States have concluded with the EU).[87]

The cases from the EFTA Court which most highlight the need to secure the equality (understood mostly as equal treatment (of citizens)) are the ones which deal with the risk of a gap emerging between the EU legal order and the EEA legal order (two pillars) following developments in European legal (and political) integration not exactly symmetrical in the EEA system based on cooperation.

Here it could be relevant to refer to cases *Gunnarsson*,[88] *Jabbi*[89] and *Campbell*[90] where the EFTA Court develops the scope of Directive 2004/38 in EEA law more extensively than the European Court of Justice (ECJ) had been prepared to, in order to include rights against the home State when a cross-border element has been generated (compensating for the absence of a similar right of EEA citizenship in the EEA Agreement).

A parallel development in the field of free movement and rights for economically inactive persons for EEA nationals followed after the *NAV* judgment,[91] which

[84] When searching in the EFTA Court's database for decided cases using the keyword 'equality' there are no results. The same happens if the search is done with 'reciprocity' as keyword.

[85] EFTA Court, case E-11/22 *RS*, para 43 (judgment of 4 July 2023 not yet reported).

[86] EFTA Court, case E-9/97 *Erla Maria Sveinbjörnsdóttir* [1998] EFTA Ct Rep 95, para 57.

[87] Hreinsson, above note 9.

[88] EFTA Court, case E-26/13 *Gunnarsson* [2014] EFTA Ct Rep 254.

[89] EFTA Court, case E-28/15 *Jabbi* [2016] EFTA Ct Rep 575.

[90] EFTA Court, case E-4/19 *Campbell* [2020] not yet reported paras 55–59.

[91] EFTA Court, case E-8/20 *NAV* [2021] judgment of 5 May 2021 not yet reported. The *NAV* case deals with a prior authorisation system, making the right to a sickness benefit subject to a condition of presence in Norway. Similar cases in the EU fell under Article 21 TFEU. However, the EFTA Court adopted a similar expansive interpretation to Article 36 EEA as that adopted in the ECJ's judgment in *I.N.*, in order to bridge possible gaps between the EU and EEA legal orders, as regards the status of economically inactive persons, To this effect, the EFTA Court referred to the case *I.N.*, finding out that the freedom conferred by Article 36 EEA also includes the freedom for recipients of services to go to another EEA state to receive a service there, without being hindered by restrictions.

strongly relied on the case *Ruska Federacija v I.N.* from the CJEU where the nature of EEA law and the EEA Agreement were put in context and reset or updated to the current date.[92]

Commenting on this important case from the CJEU, Justice Páll Hreinsson has written that:

> Recent examples demonstrate that the EFTA Court and the CJEU take their role in protecting individual rights, and in particular, human rights, seriously in the EEA's multi-layered system of governance. In *Ruska Federacija* (C-897/19), the CJEU presented a most welcome vision of the EEA order, not least in terms of fundamental rights protection. This judgment, in which the CJEU emphasised the «special relationship» between the EU, its Member States and the EFTA States, represents an updated assessment of the EEA Agreement's place within – and alongside – the EU legal order. The CJEU remarked that the combination of the EEA Agreement and the Schengen Agreement renders the situation of a national of an EFTA State objectively comparable with that of an EU citizen to whom, in accordance with Article 3(2) TEU, the EU offers an area of freedom, security and justice without internal frontiers, in which the free movement of persons is ensured.[93]

We can therefore conclude this section with the assessment that the principles of equality of Member States (and citizens) in EU law are implicitly acknowledged in the EEA legal system and in the case-law of the EFTA Court through the EEA principles of reciprocity, legislative and judicial homogeneity and similar rights for citizens and economic operators.[94]

III. CONCLUSIONS

There is a new line of argumentation by the CJEU which uses the 'equality' argument to support the (absolute) primacy of EU law. It started with a Press Release (8 May 2020) after the *PSPP* judgment in Germany ('Gauweiler Saga' and the legality of the ECB's action) but has led to three judgments so far: 1) Case *Euro box and Others* (21 June 2021) (Romania); 2) Case *RS* (22 February 2022) (Romania); and 3) Case *European Commission v Poland* (5 June 2023) (Poland).

The claims of the CJEU on the primacy of European law in the most recent constitutional cases have not changed. The Court has reaffirmed its doctrine in an express, unequivocal and clear-cut manner. In all three cases studied, the CJEU has rejected

[92] CJEU, case C 897/19 *PPU*, ruling of 2 April 2020. EU:C:2020:262. The case *Ruska Federacija v I.N.* is probably the most recent example where we see an updated assessment of the EEA Agreement's place within – and alongside – the EU legal order. It is a good example of systemic integration or putting EEA law in its unique and proper context. The Court's logic in extending the mutual trust principle to Iceland is partly based upon the high level of trust involved in the areas of overlapping agreements (particularly Schengen, the Surrender Agreement, and indeed the EEA Agreement itself). For the Court, these multiple agreements entailed that Iceland – an EFTA State with what the Court termed a 'special relationship' to the Union – was to be 'trusted' as a partner to protect individual rights in an equivalent manner to an EU Member State.

[93] Hreinsson, above note 9.

[94] On the principles of EEA law see Páll Hreinsson, 'General Principles', in Carl Baudenbacher (ed), *The Handbook of EEA Law* (New York, Springer, 2016) 349 ff.

the arguments based on the constitutional identity of the Member States, as well as various interpretations of the primacy that would undoubtedly compromise the unity and effectiveness of EU law. The Court has mostly referred to the necessary equality of Member States (while the equality of citizens is treated separately).

The academic doctrine has already studied this new line of argumentation. Fabrini proposed the 'equality' argument in 2015 based on Article 4(2) TEU. More recently, other authors have commented on the rulings. Some scholars are critical and sceptical regarding the new narrative (Presslein and Weber). The European Parliament, instead, prefers to put the focus on the equality of citizens vis-à-vis EU law in its most recent studies and in its resolution on primacy from 2023.

On the other hand, 'equality' is a word that seems to be missing as such in the case-law of the EFTA Court. Its President Justice Páll Hreinsson has not written about it either in connection with the authority of EEA law. However, since it is in the Preamble of the EEA Agreement, it is implicitly treated in some rulings of the EFTA Court via other principles that deal with reciprocity (equality of States) and legal/judicial homogeneity between EU and EEA law (equality of citizens before the law). The goal of providing similar rights and equal treatment for citizens and economic operators in the EU and EEA and the need to secure effectiveness to EEA law lie behind the case-law of the EFTA Court.

The authority and effect of EEA law vis-à-vis national (constitutional) law derive mostly from Protocol 35 to the EEA Agreement. Norway introduced a rule of conflict to give precedence to national-compliant EEA law over other legislation (Section 2 EEA Act no 109/1992) but Iceland introduced a rule of friendly interpretation (Article 3 EEA Act no 2/1993). The status of the relationship between EEA law and national constitutions remains a grey area, politically sensitive, constitutionally problematic and still unresolved. There is a pending legislative proposal in Iceland to introduce a rule of conflict giving precedence to duly EEA implemented rules over other conflicting domestic rules, a legal provision that was promised 30 years ago but not properly executed. However, in both countries, a national trend of 'strict application of dualism doctrine for incorporation of international law' (understood as strict and black letter understanding of the concept of sovereignty) may lead to the overruling of EEA individual rights in some unfortunate cases (in spite of the principles of homogeneity and reciprocity with EU law).

Part III

The EU Internal Market as a Transformative Legal and Economic Order

7

The New Legal Order and the Ecosystem: How the EU's Internal Market Was Shaped, and How It Is Changing

STEPHEN WEATHERILL

I. INTRODUCTION

DURING HIS TIME AS the EU's chief negotiator in the Brexit talks, a job that would have driven a saint to distraction, Michel Barnier became fond of referring to the importance of the EU as an 'ecosystem'. In October 2018 he described the EU's main asset as 'our single market, that ecosystem of standards, certifications, rights, regulations, supervision and jurisdiction that we have constructed together'.[1] In February 2020 he noted that the UK had chosen no longer to 'participate to our common ecosystem of rules, supervision and enforcement mechanisms'.[2]

The immediate context surrounding his use of the term 'ecosystem' was a determination to reject the fanciful demands of some Brexiters that the EU should allow the dismantling of its interlocking project by permitting the UK, after Brexit, to select which rules it was willing to follow (those promoting unrestricted free trade, mainly) while setting aside not only substantive measures it disliked (social policy, labour market regulation, consumer and environmental protection) but also the constitutional and institutional disciplines underpinning the creation and enforcement of EU law. No! This is not an à la carte menu – it is an ecosystem!

Creating a form of association with the EU is possible without membership, and Barnier's famous 'staircase' offers a simple glimpse of what is on offer,[3] but from the EU perspective non-membership must be qualitatively and quantitatively different from membership. The higher the level of alignment and associated discipline a state is willing to accept, the greater the benefits the deal with the EU will deliver, but the ecosystem must be protected. Although there is great intellectual interest in

[1] https://ec.europa.eu/commission/presscorner/detail/en/SPEECH_18_6089.
[2] https://ec.europa.eu/commission/presscorner/detail/en/SPEECH_20_340.
[3] fingfx.thomsonreuters.com/gfx/rngs/BRITAIN-EU/01006039065/brexit.jpg.

understanding what models of association with the EU are available and why,[4] there was no intellectual sheen to the Brexiters' approach, both before and after the fateful referendum in 2016. There was only petulant resentment, sullen obstinacy and shameless dishonesty. Barnier knew this, and Ulf Bernitz did too. He was dismayed by Brexit but, even more so, he was shocked by the wanton ignorance and casual arrogance which it unleashed in a country for which he had respect and admiration.

The notion of an 'ecosystem' is helpfully suggestive, and it deserves to live on, beyond the trauma of Brexit. I wish to combine it with the discourse of novelty. In its earliest judgments on the nature of (what is today) EU law the Court embraced a vision of EU law as new – that is, something that is international law but which is, by virtue of certain distinctive features identified by the Court as necessarily flowing from the objectives pursued by the Treaty, a new kind of international law. This was a matter with constitutional dimensions, but it has institutional aspects too, and substantive law has a role to play too. That is my ambition here in this chapter – to consider the whole new package of an ecosystem, but to focus on the internal market in particular as a new legal and economic order. I do this because Ulf always impressed on me his understanding of the integrated EU system – the ecosystem! – as more than the sum of its detailed parts.

II. SITES OF THE NEW LEGAL ORDER AND THE ECOSYSTEM

The Court's nurturing of a 'new legal order' is well-known in its *constitutionalised* manifestations. In the landmark ruling in *Van Gend en Loos* in 1963 it hailed the system established by the Treaties as a 'a new legal order of international law for the benefit of which the states have limited their sovereign rights, albeit within limited fields, and the subjects of which comprise not only Member States but also their nationals'.[5] In concrete terms this entailed that individuals could rely on sufficiently precise and unconditional provisions of EU law in proceedings before national courts in the Member States – the notion of direct effect. Moreover the Court long ago, in the 1964 ruling in *Costa v ENEL*, insisted that EU law enjoys the attribute of primacy.[6] It shall be applied in preference to national law in the event of conflict, so the national judge's job is to 'disapply' the offending national rule.[7]

The orthodox approach to international treaties holds that their effects within national legal orders, if any, derive from the choices made by *national* constitutional law. But the Court from the early days has insisted that by contrast the way in which EU law should be handled at national level is the subjection of direction pursuant to EU law. The Court has over time provided ever more intricate such directions. For example, the duty of consistent interpretation requires a national court called on to interpret national law operating in an area within the scope of an EU Directive 'to do

[4] See eg M-L Öberg, 'Friend Zone Forever? The Essence of and Justifications for the EU's Decision-Making Autonomy' (2023) 61 *Journal of Common Market Studies* 1622; M Cremona and N Nic Shuibhne, 'Integration, Membership, and the EU Neighbourhood' (2022) 59 *Common Market Law Review* 155.

[5] Case 26/62 *Van Gend en Loos* ECLI:EU:C:1963:1.

[6] Case 6/64 ECLI:EU:C:1964:66.

[7] Eg Case C-314/08 *Krzysztof Filipciak* ECLI:EU:C:2009:719.

so, as far as possible, in the light of the wording and the purpose of the Directive in order to achieve the result pursued by the latter'.[8] The insistence that remedies available at national level shall be effective, now codified in Article 19(1) TEU and Article 47 of the Charter but the subject of development by the Court in case law beginning as far back as 1976,[9] deprives national systems of autonomy in matters of procedure and remedies. The most audacious instance of this promotion of remedial effectiveness is found in the doctrine that EU law creates a responsibility for national courts to order compensation in favour of those suffering loss caused by a sufficiently serious violation of EU law committed by public authorities[10] and even in some circumstances by private parties.[11] Where does all this come from? The Court has airily declared these legal duties imposed on national courts to be 'inherent in the system of the Treaty'.[12]

All of this involves reliance on *EU law* to make – increasingly specific and concrete – demands of *national* judiciaries. The result is the protection of individuals in a manner that is denser and more intricate than would ordinarily be demanded under international law and also, instrumentally, it leads to more effective policing of EU law by those empowered individuals.

Institutionally too the EU has strong claims to require the language of novelty. The long-standing model attributes to the Commission the exclusive right of legislative initiative (in most areas of Union activity) while granting decision-making authority to the Council and the Parliament acting (in most areas of Union activity) by co-decision. In this way the need to release some degree of scope for autonomous action at EU level, necessary to achieve effective problem-solving, is married to legitimation through the approval of both the Member States and the peoples of Europe, necessary to equip the system with standards of representation and accountability.

But the narrative of novelty is not confined to constitutional and institutional matters. In trade law too the Court has made distinctive and bold choices, with the consequence that it has shaped an internal market which is itself a new design, with no direct comparator anywhere on the planet. Its contours are drawn loosely by the Treaty and it has been for the Court to make crucial interpretative choices which have resulted in an EU internal market which is characterised by a high level of control over national regulatory initiatives which impede cross-border trade. The Court's landmark rulings on free movement have helped to develop a specifically *EU* understanding of trade integration in a way that resembles the construction of a distinctively *EU* constitutional and institutional law, distanced from and denser than orthodox international law.

There is an 'economic ecosystem'; there is a new legal order. The breadth and depth of the project should never be underestimated. It is, however, also a project which can and does change in shape. That is the story told in this chapter.

[8] Eg Case C-106/89 *Marleasing SA v CIA* ECLI:EU:C:1990:395; Cases C-397/01 to C-403/01 *Pfeiffer* ECLI:EU:C:2004:584.

[9] Case 45/76 *Comet* ECLI:EU:C:1976:191.

[10] Cases C-6/90 and C-9/90 *Francovich and Others v Italian State* ECLI:EU:C:1991:428; Joined Cases C-46/93 and C-48/93 *Brasserie du Pêcheur v Germany* and *R v Secretary of State for Transport, ex parte Factortame Ltd* ECLI:EU:C:1996:79; Case C-224/01 *Köbler* ECLI:EU:C:2003:513.

[11] Case C-453/99 *Courage v Crehan* ECLI:EU:C:2001:465.

[12] Cases C-397/01 to C-403/01 note 8 above para 114; Cases C-6/90 & C-9/90 note 10 above para 35.

III. *CASSIS DE DIJON* AS AN INTERPRETATIVE CHOICE

It is well over 40 years since the Court of Justice decided *Cassis de Dijon* – more properly *Rewe-Zentrale AG* v *Bundesmonopolverwaltung für Branntwein* – but it is anything but old news.[13] *Cassis de Dijon* was truly a landmark. Most of all it insisted on an interpretation of free movement law which had radical implications for the shape of the internal market in general, and for the regulatory autonomy of the Member States and the place of legislative harmonisation pursued at EU level in particular.

We all know what happened. French-made blackcurrant liqueur could not be sold in Germany because it did not comply with German rules governing composition. The liqueur was not excluded from the German market because it was French. The liqueur was excluded from the German market because it failed to conform to German standards, specifically it lacked sufficient alcoholic strength. The problem was not discrimination on the basis of origin. The problem was that German technical standards happened to differ from French technical standards.

The Court's job was to consider how what is today Article 34 TFEU applied in these circumstances where the EU internal market was fragmented along national lines as a result of regulatory diversity. The matter was not entirely new, and already in a case concerning the services sector the Court had offered hints of its preference,[14] but in *Cassis de Dijon* the Court crafted a new formula apt to address the problem of disparity between national technical standards on product composition. In its eighth paragraph, the ruling explains that in the absence of common EU rules:

> Obstacles to movement within the Community resulting from disparities between the national laws relating to the marketing of the products in question must be accepted in so far as those provisions may be recognized as being necessary in order to satisfy mandatory requirements relating in particular to the effectiveness of fiscal supervision, the protection of public health, the fairness of commercial transactions and the defence of the consumer.

Measures of the type applied to product composition in the case by Germany are trade barriers. That does not make them automatically inapplicable but it does require the rule-maker to show a justification for their continued application to imports. In *Cassis* itself there was none. The rules were not 'necessary'. Germany could show no good reason why German consumers should not be allowed the opportunity to try a different type of liqueur from that normally available on the German market. In the absence of justification the host State, here Germany, is denied the competence to apply its rules to impede imports, and in consequence the trader is allowed to penetrate the market of the host State merely by virtue of having complied with the rules of the home State, here France. So the free movement provisions create a non-absolute principle of home country control. The result: German consumers, not the German public authorities, should decide whether French-style Cassis shall thrive in the German market.

[13] Case 120/78 *Rewe-Zentrale AG v Bundesmonopolverwaltung für Branntwein* ECLI:EU:C:1979:42.

[14] Case 334/74 *Van Binsbergen* ECLI:EU:C:1974:131.

This interpretation of (what is today) Article 34 ensured that EU free movement law would reach into national regulatory autonomy even in circumstances where no origin-based discrimination was involved. So too it ensured that judicially driven integration would be capable of biting such rules which lacked justification, requiring their disapplication in so far as they impeded imports. This caused a correspondingly diminished role needed for legislative action at EU level.

The internal market is founded on a mix between the application of the free movement rules to obstructive national rules and EU legislative initiatives. *Cassis* extended use of the former at the expense of the latter. This is its key and enduring structural significance.

Cassis was thus a judgment which reveals choices about both the vertical distribution of competences and the horizontal allocation of powers in the EU, and it counts as an important choice about the shape of the new legal order which underpins the EU internal market – an economic ecosystem.

IV. *CASSIS DE DIJON*: THE VERTICAL IMPLICATIONS

Cassis addressed the vertical distribution of competences in the EU. EU law controls State choices: national measures which restrict inter-State trade must be set aside unless shown to be justified by the regulator.

It has been cleverly put that the host State must show 'legal empathy' towards the regulatory practices of the home State.[15] Difference is not a sufficient reason to refuse market access to a non-complying product or service. EU law demands more of the regulating host state. It must engage with the substance and motivation of different practices preferred in other Member States and it may enforce its own local standards only where it is able to demonstrate that those of the home State are in some way inadequate.

Article 36 TFEU allows room to justify national measures 'on grounds of public morality, public policy or public security; the protection of health and life of humans, animals or plants; the protection of national treasures possessing artistic, historic or archaeological value; or the protection of industrial and commercial property'. It supplements this list with a second sentence which admonishes that such national action shall not 'constitute a means of arbitrary discrimination or a disguised restriction on trade between Member States'. But the Court has gone further. Where is consumer protection, social welfare and environmental protection in Article 36? In *Cassis de Dijon* the Court was doubly creative. It not only decided that variation between technical standards fell within the discipline asserted by Article 34, thereby pushing EU free movement law beyond a discrimination-based focus, it also accepted that a wide range of justifications in the public interest may be advanced by a regulating authority, stretching far beyond the specific and limited list contained in Article 36 TFEU. This is the importance of paragraph 14 of the ruling. In cases where justification is under review the question is whether the purposes pursued by the national measure that restricts inter-State trade 'serve a purpose which is in the general interest and such as to take precedence over

[15] K Nicolaïdis, 'Mutual Recognition: Promise and Denial, From Sapiens to Brexit' (2017) 70 *Current Legal Problems* 227, 244.

the requirements of the free movement of goods'. This is to announce a general public interest test, and it gives room for a vast range of concerns to be advanced as potential justifications – even if they are not listed explicitly in the Treaty provisions.

An exhaustive list of justifications recognised by the Court in its case law over the years is not called for. In fact it could not be drawn up – the point is that the Court has an open-ended understanding of what type of value pursued by national market regulation might prevail against the imperative of trade integration. Consider only that claims founded on EU free movement law have been pitched against justifications as diverse as the protection of the environment[16] and of the consumer,[17] the conservation of biodiversity,[18] the defence and promotion of culture and artistic property,[19] the preservation of press diversity,[20] respect for human dignity,[21] concern for animal welfare,[22] regulation of particular features of sport,[23] and to ensure the survival of small and medium-sized businesses.[24] Etcetera! Some of these values have subsequently been written into the Treaty superstructure and/or into the Charter of Fundamental Rights as concerns to be taken into account in the definition and implementation of all other EU policies, including that of pursuit of an internal market, but some have not. In any event the Court's approach in this area in the main pre-dates the patterns of Treaty revision. So it is correct to focus on the Court's innovative vigour.

Sometimes the justification is in its particular context sufficiently compelling to be treated as apt to restrain the deregulatory dynamic of free movement law. Sometimes, as in *Cassis* itself, it is not. But the structural point is that the Court pursues the examination even though the Treaty provisions on free movement themselves do not accommodate any explicit direction to take account of such broad regulatory concerns and even though in some cases the Treaty equips the EU with little or no legislative competence to address the matters motivating the national measures.

This is a new legal order – of substantive economic law. Call it an economic ecosystem. The key theme is the vertical distribution of competence, whereby EU law asserts a power of review over national measures of market regulation which have the effect (even if not the intent) to obstruct inter-State trade.

V. *CASSIS DE DIJON*: THE HORIZONTAL IMPLICATIONS

The Court in *Cassis* chose to interpret Article 34 as more vigorous than a mere anti-discrimination norm, with consequences for the vertical distribution of

[16] Eg Case 302/86 *Commission v Denmark* ECLI:EU:C:1988:421; Case C-379/98 *Preussen Elektra* ECLI:EU:C:2001:160; Case C-573/12 *Ålands Vindkraft AB* ECLI:EU:C:2014:2037.

[17] Eg Case C-441/04 *A-Punkt Schmuckhandels* ECLI:EU:C:2006:141; Case C-265/12 *Citroen Belux* ECLI:EU:C:2013:498.

[18] Eg Case C-67/97 *Ditlev Bluhme* ECLI:EU:C:1998:584.

[19] Eg Case C-531/07 *Fachverband/LIBRO* ECLI:EU:C:2009:276.

[20] Eg Case C-368/95 *Vereinigte Familiapress Zeitungsverlags- und vertriebs GmbH v Heinrich Bauer Verlag* ECLI:EU:C:1997:325.

[21] Eg Case C-36/02 *Omega Spielhallen* ECLI:EU:C:2004:614.

[22] Eg Case C-219/07 *Nationale Raad van Dierenkwekers en Liefhebbers* ECLI:EU:C:2008:353.

[23] Eg Case C-415/93 *Bosman* ECLI:EU:C:1995:463; Case C-680/21 *Royal Antwerp* ECLI:EU:C:2023:1010.

[24] Eg Case C-464/05 *Maria Geurts* ECLI:EU:C:2007:631.

competences. Article 34 asserts a relatively tight grip over Member State regulatory practice. But consider also the horizontal institutional implications of the ruling. The Court's approach had important consequences for the division of labour between the Court and the EU's legislative institutions in the development of the internal market.

Had the Court chosen to limit the scope of Article 34 to control of physical barriers to trade and overtly discriminatory practices it would have left in place the challenged German technical standards as obstacles to the marketing of French-made Cassis. But the Treaty envisaged – the Treaty still envisages – a means to address that problem, namely legislative harmonisation. The Bundesmonopolverwaltung in *Cassis* argued before the Court for a legislative not judicial solution, meaning that the German product standards should not be set aside as incompatible with free movement law but rather should remain in place until such time as the EU had got round to adopting common standards through the political process. This is discussed in the Opinion of Advocate General Capotorti in the case. The Court, in rejecting this approach, emphasised instead the reach of free movement law into national practices which lacked any discriminatory intent or effect but at the same time, in doing so, it emphasised its own role and that of national judges in adjudication. It removed the need for legislative action. In fact in principle legislative action at EU level would be needed *only* where national rules were justified, for only then would trade barriers survive the review pursued under free movement law.

The Commission leapt on this institutional consequence. It published a Notice in 1980 which embraced with glee and gusto this feature of *Cassis*.[25] Having drawn attention to the vertical implications of the ruling by noting that 'Member States, when drawing up commercial or technical rules liable to affect the free movement of goods, may not take an exclusively national viewpoint and take account only of requirements confined to domestic products', it moved then to the horizontal plane. It added that

> The Commission's work of harmonization will henceforth have to be directed mainly at national laws having an impact on the functioning of the common market where barriers to trade to be removed arise from national provisions which are admissible under the criteria set by the Court.

This 'artful interpretation of the ruling and . . . bold assertion of new policy'[26] set the tone for the Commission's work programme but also more generally for the regulatory shape of the internal market that was being created, and in particular for the relationship between (deregulatory) free movement law and (re-regulatory) legislative harmonisation. The Commission proceeded to locate this thematic readiness to reduce the intensity of the programme of legislative harmonisation and instead to place heavier reliance on judge-driven free movement law at the very heart of the

[25] [1980] OJ C256/2.

[26] K Alter and S Meunier-Aitsahalia, 'Judicial Politics in the European Community: European Integration and the Pathbreaking Cassis de Dijon Decision' (1994) 26 *Comparative Political Studies* 535, 542. See also B Leucht, 'The *Cassis de Dijon* judgment and the European Commission' in A Albors-Llorens, C Barnard and B Leucht (eds), *Cassis de Dijon: 40 Years On* (Oxford, Hart, 2021).

agenda set by the hugely influential 1985 White Paper on *Completion of the Internal Market*.[27]

This is central to the novelty of the type of internal market that is being created. The Court's approach was bold and transformative. Had it been more cautious, and had it chosen not to apply Article 34 TFEU to diverse but non-discriminatory technical standards, then a vast amount of harmonisation would have been required to tackle such endemic market-fragmenting regulatory diversity. This would have led in turn to centralisation and homogeneity, as EU rules suppressed national variation. This, as the Commission put it in 1985, would have been 'over-regulatory . . . inflexible and could stifle innovation'.[28] The Court in *Cassis* protected the EU's internal market from this outcome by its willingness to let directly effective free movement law bite even where legislative intervention has not.

VI. THE SHAPE OF THE INTERNAL MARKET

The Court's interpretation of free movement law demonstrably affects the allocation of constitutional and institutional power within the EU. It does so in a way which is not the subject of explicit direction in the Treaty. Article 26 TFEU's definition of the internal market holds that it 'shall comprise an area without internal frontiers in which the free movement of goods, persons, services and capital is ensured in accordance with the provisions of the Treaties', but nothing in those Treaties spells out what shall be the precise relationship between the free movement rules and legislative harmonisation – between courts and the political process – in achieving that aim. The shape of the internal market is not constitutionally pre-ordained, but instead has been determined over time by the Court's choices of interpretation and the readiness of the legislative institutions to respond.[29]

So in *Cassis* the Court decided that diversity of the type revealed by the national technical standards at stake in the case needs to be addressed by EU internal market law because the application of such standards has the effect of partitioning the EU internal market along national lines. As foreseen by the Treaty, the EU's internal market is a more ambitious project than a simple elimination of tariffs and border controls: it reaches behind the border to address regulatory or non-tariff barriers to trade. But the Court in *Cassis* also made a choice about *how* those barriers would be addressed. The Treaty is silent on the relationship between the reach of free movement law and legislative harmonisation. The Court in *Cassis* made a choice that privileged the application of the former over the latter. And this has an impact on the substance of the market being created. Preferring free movement law over legislative harmonisation is to prefer diversity of products and services and of production standards within the internal market – it is to champion consumer choice rather than the rise of legislatively mandated 'Europroducts'.

[27] COM (85) 310, https://eur-lex.europa.eu/legal-content/EN/ALL/?uri=CELEX:51985DC0310.
[28] ibid, para 64.
[29] See generally S Weatherill, *The Internal Market as a Legal Concept* (Oxford, OUP, 2017).

The internal market is a patchwork mix of non-harmonised and harmonised sectors. *Cassis* is important for widening the scope for disciplining non-harmonised sectors according to the demands of the free movement rules applied by courts and for consequently narrowing the required breadth of harmonisation pursued through the political process. A new legal order, an economic ecosystem!

VII. THE CHANGING SHAPE OF THE INTERNAL MARKET

Cassis de Dijon asserts a preference for judge-led integration ahead of legislative harmonisation as a means to discipline technical standards in the EU internal market. This is the reason for its iconic status in EU law. And yet there is ample evidence that things are changing.

The EU's internal market is founded on a combination of deregulatory free movement law and re-regulatory legislative harmonisation – on non-harmonised and harmonised sectors. *Cassis* insisted on the application of free movement rules to national technical standards which caused fragmentation of the internal market and eliminated the need to await legislative intervention at EU level. However, legislative harmonisation increasingly proliferates in today's internal market.

Let us take blackcurrant liqueur itself as a perfect illustration. *Cassis de Dijon* was decided in 1979 on the basis that French-made liqueur could be sold in Germany because obstruction caused by German technical rules could not be justified under EU primary law, Article 34 TFEU as it is today. The result of the dispute would be the same today – but for a different reason. Today the reason why French-made liqueur cannot be excluded from the German market is that EU secondary legislation provides a common foundation for the definition of such liqueurs applicable across the whole internal market.[30] The story of how Cassis de Dijon came to acquire an EU legislative definition is of general relevance in the shaping of the internal market. It tells us that there are incentives to prefer the security and clarity of harmonisation as a more reliable basis for managing the internal market than is supplied by the principle of conditional mutual recognition applicable in non-harmonised sectors. There was a strong demand for clear legislative rules set at EU level which would govern the sector in a more predictable and reliable manner than can be delivered by ad hoc reliance on the free movement rules to tackle obstructive national standards met from time to time in economic activity. And that demand was met by the EU political process. This is why there is today an EU definition of the type of liqueurs which are permitted in the EU's internal market.[31] In this sense the *Cassis* judgment ultimately focused attention on the need for EU harmonised rules, not the absence. This is true across many sectors.

The Commission's enthusiasm for *Cassis de Dijon* as the foundation stone of the internal market which was so prominent in 1980 and 1985 has waned over time,

[30] Reg 2019/787 [2019] OJ L130/1.

[31] The story is told in S Weatherill, 'Did *Cassis de Dijon* Make a Difference?' in A Albors-Llorens, C Barnard and B Leucht (eds), *Cassis de Dijon: 40 Years On* (Oxford, Hart, 2021).

although one must examine documentation relevant to the management of the internal market with great care to discover this.

In 2003 the Commission confessed that:

> The principle [applicable to the management of non-harmonized sectors] is that there are no specific procedural rules and no extra paperwork. This is its strength, but at the same time its weakness. When problems occur, there is little or no transparency, there is no commonly agreed approach to evaluating whether levels of protection are equivalent and there is no clear procedure for a company to challenge a negative decision.[32]

The scheme envisaged by *Cassis* is 'invisible' in day-to-day practice[33] – which is a strength but also a weakness. Understanding the benefits of reliance on the Cassis model must be accompanied by shrewd appreciation of its costs. It is a real benefit that applying free movement law rather than rushing to harmonise exerts a relatively light touch deregulatory impact and, moreover, helps to preserve diversity at national level. It also reduces costs by diminishing the need to prepare and agree top-down homogenising measures of legislative harmonisation. However, costs of a different type emerge. They are incurred at a later stage, and most of all they arise because of the difficulties of being confident whether a national rule which obstructs trade will be treated as justified or not. Litigation may be needed, which is slow and expensive and, even if successful in removing the obstacle to trade, economic harm will already have been inflicted. Legislative harmonisation, which sets the rules in advance, offers a more stable and predictable basis for trade within the internal market.

In 2005 the Commission noted that 'neither producers nor market surveillance authorities are sure to what extent products from one Member State can enter another Member State's market without modification' and added that according to the European Business Test Panel, 53 per cent of businesses were not even familiar with the principle of (conditional) mutual recognition.[34] The heroic tone of 1980 and 1985 is long gone! The internal market has a tension at its core. It wants to assume that national borders are economically irrelevant but it functions on the basis of highly diverse national administrative and bureaucratic capacities and infrastructure. EU rules are implemented in a decentralised manner through diverse national cultures, and blockages and unevenness is simply inevitable. But this bites especially hard in non-harmonised sectors, where even on paper there are no common EU standards on which to rely in the event that an obstacle to inter-State trade caused by a national measure is met. Harmonisation offers itself as a more reliable basis for managing the internal market than non-harmonisation based on conditional mutual recognition of the type devised in Cassis. And, as explained, in the case of blackcurrant liqueur exactly that shift to harmonisation has occurred.

[32] COM (2003) 238 page 7.

[33] J Pelkmans, 'Mutual Recognition in Goods: On Promises and Disillusions' (2007) 14 *Journal of European Public Policy* 699, at 703, 708.

[34] Commission Second Implementation Report of the Internal Market Strategy 2003–2006, COM (2005) 11 page 8.

It would be a long, tough and frankly mind-numbingly dull job to concoct a comprehensive list of sectors which are today regulated (in whole or in part) by common EU rules rather than being left to the more ad hoc discipline of free movement law. However, one can gain some insight into the shift that has occurred by coming at the matter from the other direction – by looking at patterns of litigation over time. Jan Zglinski has done this. His empirical survey of the Court's free movement case law shows the number of occasions on which the Court is asked to tackle questions associated with the Treaty provisions on the free movement of goods has declined dramatically.[35] They are, he demonstrates, disappearing from the Court's docket. He argues convincingly that the rise of EU legislation is a major reason for the decline.

Another empirically driven study reaches similar conclusions via a different route. Šadl, López Zurita and Piccolo have categorised the case law on the internal market and show that there has been over time a marked shift away from litigation promoting liberalisation towards litigation involving disputes about the nature of the EU's rules regulating particular sectors.[36] The decisive shift, they argue, came between 2007 and 2010 and since then it has been harmonisation, not free movement, which has predominated. They draw the entirely fair conclusion that this trend in the case law is an accurate mirror of the true balance between non-harmonised and harmonised sectors in the internal market.

Less emphasis on free movement, more emphasis on legislation! The picture of the internal market's legal infrastructure painted by these scholars feels correct to me. Let one example suffice. An area that generated many free movement cases in the past was the regulation at national level of unfair commercial practices, in which the Court was invited to decide when the national intervention was justified even where it obstructed cross-border trade.[37] But since 2005 the EU has a harmonised regime governing such practices, contained in Directive 2005/29.[38] Litigation is still plentiful in this area, but it typically concerns the intricacies of the Directive, not the Treaty free movement rules.[39]

This is truly intriguing. The sternest criticism of the Court's choice in *Cassis de Dijon* holds that it went too far in asserting a review of national practices in order to promote the EU's ambition to create its internal market. As Fritz Scharpf, perhaps the most prominent and sophisticated such critic, put it, the Court's push beyond a mere anti-discrimination norm transformed the rules on free movement into individual rights enforceable directly against Member State public authorities by virtue of the constitutional character of EU law. It was, he alleges, 'a revolutionary act of judicial

[35] J Zglinski, 'The End of Negative Market Integration: 60 Years of Free Movement of Goods Litigation in the EU (1961–2020)' (2024) 31 *Journal of European Public Policy* 633.

[36] U Šadl, L López Zurita and S Picccolo, 'Route 66: Mutations of the Internal Market Explored Through the Prism of Citation Networks' (2023) 21 *International Journal of Constitutional Law* 826.

[37] Eg Case 382/87 *Buet v Ministère Public* ECLI:EU:C:1989:198; Case C-470/93 *Verein gegen Unwesen in Handel v Mars* ECLI:EU:C:1995:224; Case C-441/04 note 17 above; Case C-368/95 note 20 above.

[38] [2005] OJ L149/22.

[39] Eg Case C-122/10 *Ving Sverige AB* ECLI:EU:C:2011:299; Case C-428/11 *Purely Creative Ltd and others v OFT* ECLI:EU:C:651; Case C-435/11 *CHS Tour Services* ECLI:EU:C:2013:574.

self-empowerment'.[40] *Cassis*, he believes, generated an excessive 'constitutionalisation' of the EU's treaties which, as a result of the Court's choices, place rules and policy beyond political determination, whether at EU level or at national level. Whether (non-discriminatory) national policies survive review depends on judicial adjudication. So, for Scharpf, the operation of treaty-based economic liberties 'reduces the domain of political legislation and it enlarges the space for authoritative judicial interpretation'.[41]

There is room to doubt whether the problem is as large as Scharpf's account portrays, without in any way denying the serious intent behind his powerful scholarship.[42] The recent work of Zglinski and Šadl, López Zurita and Piccolo does not refute the anxieties of Scharpf and others about the aggressively deregulated market towards which the Court's choice in *Cassis* pushed, but it does show that one must not under-estimate just how much politically driven market regulation at EU level has accompanied judge-led deregulation of national markets in the name of free movement. As a minimum an empirically driven understanding of how non-harmonised sectors are steadily converted by legislative intervention into harmonised sectors acts as a caution that discussion of the balance between deregulation and re-regulation in the EU internal market needs to be sensitive to the particular sector under examination. Technical product standards are not the same as the regulation of, say, public services, where not simply EU rule-making but EU rule-making with distributional consequences is in question. There is no single 'one size fits all' narrative which does justice to the complex and varying balance between non-harmonised and harmonised sectors.

Today the everyday reality of the EU internal market is that in many sectors it operates primarily on a dense legislative foundation, not on litigation before the Court concerning free movement law. This does not mean that understanding *Cassis* to have embraced Treaty-based free movement as the starting-point in the control of the trade-restrictive effect of diverse national technical standards in preference to emphasising the place of legislative harmonisation is wrong. It is not wrong. It is exactly what *Cassis* did. But it suggests that *Cassis* unleashed a dynamic. Over time its limitations as a model have become more widely appreciated, and the internal market has gradually changed its regulatory shape. Politically driven market regulation at EU level increasingly supplements judge-led deregulation of national markets, and it appears that the point is that the latter provokes the former by highlighting that predictable rules set at EU level facilitate the development of the development of the internal market more successfully than ad hoc resort to free movement law. *Cassis* suggested a project of deregulation supplemented by pockets of (re-)regulation. Today the internal market is predominantly a project of (re-)regulation.

[40] F Scharpf, 'De-constitutionalisation of European Law: The Re-empowerment of Democratic Political Choice' in S Garben and I Govaere (eds), *The Division of Competences between the EU and the Member States: Reflections on the Past, the Present and the Future* (Oxford, Hart, 2017) at 289. See also D Grimm, 'The Democratic Costs of Constitutionalisation: the European Case' (2015) 21 *European Law Journal* 460.

[41] ibid, 287.

[42] See more fully S Weatherill, 'The Beauty and the Beast: Is European Union Internal Market Law "Over-constitutionalised"?' in T Ćapeta, I Goldner Lang and T Perišin (eds), *The Changing European Union: A Critical View on the Role of Law and the Courts* (Oxford, Hart, 2022).

VIII. CONCLUSION

The EU internal market is new. It is different. The EU internal market experience is not that of Canada,[43] nor is it that of Australia[44] or that of the USA.[45] Arrangements in these internal markets vary according to the extent to which constituent units are permitted to pursue different regulatory policies; they vary according to the scope of law-making competence and powers allocated to the central authority; they vary according to the governing institutional (judicial and political) arrangements. There is no single concept of an internal market.[46] In the EU the relationship between free movement and legislative harmonisation is undefined by primary law. This is the space in which the Court has been asked to make vital decisions which engage vertical (EU/ Member State) and horizontal (judicial/ political) implications.

Cassis de Dijon was of major significance in shaping the EU's own particular version of an internal market. The Court chose to widen the scope for disciplining non-harmonised sectors according to the demands of the free movement rules beyond a mere non-discrimination standard. This meant in turn that the breadth of harmonisation pursued through the political process would be reduced. The consequence was to reduce the workload of the Commission (and of the other political institutions), but its more profound significance is felt in the nature of the internal market created. The Court's approach champions diversity of products and services in the market, preserves consumer choice and limits the rise of legislatively mandated 'Europroducts'. Only where free movement law fails to set aside national rules which obstruct inter-State trade, most obviously where they are shown to be justified as serving a general interest ranking above trade integration, is there a shift to EU-level regulation achieved by legislative harmonisation. The internal market is therefore a mix of non-harmonised sectors regulated at national level but disciplined by the EU's free movement rules and harmonised sectors governed in whole or in part by common EU standards.

Truly, it is a new legal order and an economic ecosystem. But things have changed, and things are changing. *Cassis* stands in principle for a mix of non-harmonised and harmonised sectors in which the former are prioritised. Today the strong impression is that in practice the priorities have been reversed. Take care to conduct a sector by sector assessment, but much of the EU internal market is today densely regulated by common EU rules. It appears that this has occurred because of demand for a more stable regulatory environment than can be delivered by reliance on the *Cassis* model of free movement. The lesson is a familiar one. Markets need rules.

[43] See eg A Hinarejos, 'Free Movement, Federalism and Institutional Choice: A Canada/ EU Comparison' (2012) 71 *Cambridge Law Journal* 537.

[44] See eg C Staker, 'Free Movement of Goods in the EEC and Australia: A Comparative Study' (1990) 10 *Yearbook of European Law* 209.

[45] See eg E Knook, 'Guns and Tobacco: The Effect of Interstate Trade Case Law on the Vertical Division of Powers' (2004) 11 *Maastricht Journal of European and Comparative Law* 347; JA Gutierrez Fons, 'Transatlantic Adjudication Techniques: The Commerce Clause and the EU's Internal Market Harmonization Clause in Perspective' in E Fahey and D Curtin (eds), *A Transatlantic Community of Law* (Cambridge, CUP, 2014); and more generally M Egan, *Single Markets: Economic Integration in Europe and the United States* (Oxford, OUP, 2015).

[46] See S Weatherill, *The Internal Market as a Legal Concept* (Oxford, OUP, 2017).

8

Revisiting the Foundations of EU Free Movement Law in Light of New Developments and Challenges

ULLA NEERGAARD AND SYBE DE VRIES[1]

I. INTRODUCTION

THROUGHOUT HIS ACADEMIC CAREER, Ulf Bernitz was occupied by what he referred to as 'market law', about which he has explained:

> The foundation of legal rules for the market place consists partly of legislation but also, to a great extent, of unwritten legal rules which form the basis for special regulations. Together, these rules make up the legal area which I have chosen to call market law. Market law has as its purpose to draw up *the legal framework/or the activity of undertakings in the market place by means of rules concerning primarily their establishment, marketing, competition, and production.* To a large extent these rules aim at consumer protection. What is characteristic of the market-law rules is thus that they function as a *framework type of rules* which on a more general level guarantee, but also draw up the boundaries for, the freedom of action of firms in the market place. From these market-law rules one must distinguish all those private law rules of a contract- and property-law character that are directly tied to the *individual* commercial transactions which within this framework take place continuously in the market place, primarily in the form of sales, rentals and contracts for the provision of services.[2]

[1] The chapter to some degree builds on discussions in relation to our presentation 'Recalibration of EU Internal Market Law Paradigms in Light of the EU Green Deal' at the workshop on 'Navigating the Environmental Transition: The European Green Deal and the Rule of Law', University of Maastricht, 1–2 June 2024.

[2] U Bernitz, 'Market Law as a Legal Discipline', in *Scandinavian Studies in Law*, vol 23 (Uppsala, Almqvist & Wiksell International, 1979) 56, 61–62. Here, it is explained at 55 that the ideas contained therein go back to 1969. Following this, many other works on 'market law' have been published (see further eg <bernitz.se/bocker-och-artiklar>).

In his conceptual map of market law, Ulf Bernitz also included what today mainly is referred to as EU Internal Market law, and thereby free movement law.[3] Indeed, the EU's economic order is, first and foremost, characterised by the creation of an Internal Market, which is legally brought about by the application and enforcement of the Treaty provisions on free movement and competition, and by the adoption of legislative harmonisation measures by the EU legislator. According to Advocate General Szpunar, the Internal Market, which

> constitutes – depending on one's perspective – the means or the end of the process of European integration, is so fundamental to the Union's legal order that it is taken as a given and constitutes no less than the central organisational principle of the Treaties.[4]

So far, this has appeared as sufficiently flexible to grasp changes of societies. However, with regard to free movement law, it might be that the ways in which the foundations of this area have manifested themselves, are too frozen in a pre-Lisbon orthodoxy, and thus not sufficiently capturing newer developments including the many new challenges Europe is currently facing, such as the green, digital, security and 'human rights' transition in the EU, combined also with worries essentially having an economic character.

The year 2023 marked the thirtieth anniversary of the Internal Market, which has served as an occasion for different actors to evaluate the process so far and to present new ideas for the future of European integration. Strikingly, it has for instance been emphasised that – in the words of Vandermeeren – there is a need for a new momentum and a stronger ambition.[5] Also, it has been stressed by Letta that: 'the international scenario has profoundly changed, highlighting the need to develop a new Single Market', and that:

> The Single Market framework, rooted in the definition of the four freedoms, – the free movement of people, goods, services and capital – is fundamentally based on 20th-century theoretical principles. This becomes evident when considering how this categorization now seems outdated, failing to reflect the evolving dynamics of a market increasingly shaped by digitalization, innovation and uncertainties related to climate change and its impact on society.[6]

Furthermore, the Commission itself has expressed that:

> The Single Market has benefitted citizens, businesses and the EU as a whole in economic, social and geopolitical terms. While these benefits are undisputed, further joint efforts remain to be continued in order to explore and find solutions in order to benefit further from the potential which is still untapped. The Single Market will also have to continue to

[3] U Bernitz, *Market Law as a Legal Discipline* (Uppsala, Almqvist & Wiksell International, 1979) 66–68.

[4] Case C-16/18 *Dobersberger* [2019], Opinion of AG Szpunar, para 21. Also see M Bobek who emphasises the need to still apply Internal Market law as the solid and reliable core of EU law, in: J Adams-Prassl, A Ezrachi, S Bogojevic and D Leczykiewicz, *The Internal Market Ideal; Essays in Honour of Stephen Weatherill* (Oxford, Oxford University Press, 2024) 37–38.

[5] F Vandermeeren, '30 Years of Single Market – Taking Stock and Looking Ahead' (Report, European Commission, 2022) 7.

[6] E Letta, Much more than a market. Speed, security, solidarity. Empowering the Single Market to deliver a sustainable future and prosperity for all EU Citizens, 2024, 7, www.consilium.europa.eu/media/ny3j24sm/much-more-than-a-market-report-by-enrico-letta.pdf (emphasis omitted).

adapt to the new realities of the geopolitical environment, technological developments, the green and digital transitions and the need to boost the EU's long-term competitiveness and productivity.[7]

Against that background, we wish here to honour Ulf Bernitz and his lifelong interest in and contributions to market law as a legal discipline by providing reflections of value to the overall theme of the present book, namely the EU as a transformative legal and economic order. Thus, the chapter intends – at a general level – to critically revisit the very foundations of the free movement law regime, however mainly limited to primary law and negative integration. Also, it is not our intention to come up with definite solutions, but rather to raise questions and thought directions for further discussion.

Accordingly, we will first outline the overall nature of the Internal Market (Section II). Then, we will present the free movement law framework in general terms (Section III). This is followed by an analysis of the rationale and objectives thereof, combined with a discussion of whether these findings call for a recalibration of the current foundations (Sections IV and V). The final section draws some overall conclusions about the key issues examined in the chapter (Section VI).

II. THE NATURE OF THE INTERNAL MARKET

In the period from the establishment of the EEC in 1958 to the entry into force of the Maastricht Treaty and the establishment of the EU in 1993, the Internal Market was undoubtedly the most dominant 'project'. Today, it is still very important, but it no longer stands alone as witnessed already by, for instance, the green transition manifested prominently in the 'Green Deal'.[8] In other words, 'the law of the internal market, while it was indeed the first one, is evolving in splendid isolation from other, newer areas of EU law'.[9] According to Article 26(2) TFEU, it is 'simply' defined as comprising an area without internal frontiers in which the free movement of goods, persons, services and capital is ensured in accordance with the provisions of the Treaties. It is hereby emphasised that the Internal Market is intended to be a single space, which is unfragmented.[10]

As already understood from Article 26(2) TFEU, the Internal Market seems intrinsically linked to 'free movement'. This term is only mentioned a few times in the Treaty of European Union (TEU).[11] In the Charter of Fundamental Rights of

[7] European Commission, Communication from the Commission to the European Parliament, the Council, the European Economic and Social Committee and the Committee of the Regions. The Single Market at 30, COM(2023) 162 final, p. 21. As an example from literature, see eg J Zglinski, 'The Internal Market as a Dynamic Process: Five Scenarios for the Future' in J Adams-Prassl, A Ezrachi, S Bogojevic and D Leczykiewicz (eds), *The Internal Market Ideal: Essays in Honour of Stephen Weatherill* (Oxford, Oxford University Press, 2024) ss 77–98.

[8] Re 'the European Green Deal' (*The European Commission*), see <commission.europa.eu/strategy-and-policy/priorities-2019-2024/european-green-deal_en>.

[9] Bobek, above note 4, 36.

[10] S Weatherill, *The Internal Market as a Legal Concept* (Oxford, Oxford University Press, 2017) 3.

[11] See its preamble and Article 3(2) TEU.

the European Union (CFREU), reference is made to free movement in the preamble and in Article 45 CFREU. In the Treaty on the Functioning of the EU (TFEU), free movement is much more closely linked to the construction of the Internal Market. In that context it is constructed as a means of ensuring free market access across national borders and the dismantling of trade barriers. The core of these rules is more specifically concerned with the free movement of goods, services, capital and persons. The rules are constructed as general Treaty provisions that have the character of rules prohibiting restrictions and discrimination. The provisions of particular relevance are Articles 34 (goods), 45 (workers), 49 (freedom of establishment), 56 (services) and 63 (capital) TFEU. These central, primary law rules have largely been left unaltered since the very foundation of the EEC, but their interpretation has not. In addition, since the Treaty of Maastricht, also Union citizenship, especially as regulated in Article 21 TFEU, has had an important role also in relation to the Internal Market. Generally speaking, these provisions are typically concerned with prohibitions of discrimination on grounds of nationality and of more generally constructed restrictions. Thus, also Articles 18 TFEU and 21 CFREU are of some interest in this context.

Viewed historically, free movement can be seen as having arisen in a context of market law, and it is in this context that the Internal Market is primarily understood. However, free movement in the EU Treaty and the CFREU has evolved and can now be understood just as well into a fundamental/human rights context. These two 'contexts' are thus closely interlinked and cannot be kept completely separate, and to complicate matters further, fundamental rights are commonly viewed as originally having been introduced in EU law and developed by the CJEU, mainly in the context of free movement as general principles of EU law. Similarly, free movement may simultaneously be viewed as a general principle and a fundamental right or freedom in its own right. Thus, the four freedoms can today be seen as a specific amplification of some of the fundamental rights enshrined in the CFREU.[12] Indeed, the CJEU has frequently referred to free movement rules as having a 'fundamental character'.[13]

As the creation of the Internal Market is an inherently 'dynamic process',[14] it needs constant 'effort, vigilance and updating'.[15] As a legal concept, the Internal Market may be seen as complex and heterogeneous.[16] Indeed, as pointed out by Dawson and de Witte, the Internal Market to a large degree constitutes a puzzle: 'Analysing the law and governance of the internal market is like trying to solve a Rubik's cube. Where things might appear in order on one side; they are in complete disarray on the other sides'.[17] It has also been labelled as ambiguous, which leaves considerable space for

[12] See eg Case C-390/12 *Pfleger*, ECLI:EU:C:2014:281.

[13] See eg Case C-265/95 *Spanish Strawberries*, ECLI:EU:C:1997:595.

[14] K Mortelmans, 'The Common Market, the Internal Market and the Single Market, What's in a Market?' (1998) 35 *Common Market Law Review* 101, 102.

[15] C Barnard, *The Substantive Law of the EU* (Oxford, Oxford University Press, 2022) 18.

[16] Weatherill, above note 10, 223.

[17] M Dawson and F de Witte, *EU Law and Governance* (Cambridge, Cambridge University Press, 2022) 130.

political and economic choices on the EU's legislative strategies and the level of intensity of the regulation of its space, as here expressed by Weatherill:

> The EU is committed to its internal market. Article 3(3) TEU declares that the Union 'shall establish an internal market'. It is defined by Article 26 TFEU as 'an area without internal frontiers in which the free movement of goods, persons, services and capital is ensured'. This reflects the aspiration to convert markets historically fragmented along national lines into a single economic space spanning the entire territory of the EU. Article 26's formula is elegant but at the same time ambiguous. It reveals nothing about the intended relationship between EU-level market regulation, on the one hand, and, on the other, market deregulation promoted by the subjection of national regulatory choices to the discipline of the free movement rules.[18]

III. THE FREE MOVEMENT PRIMARY LAW FRAMEWORK

Although the central, primary law rules have largely been left unaltered since the very foundation of the EEC and are very sparse in substantive detail, the CJEU has taken important choices as to shaping their content. This has led Weatherill to emphasise that:

> It would exaggerate to describe the internal market as consequently a judge-made enterprise, but it would not exaggerate at all to insist that the Court has been delegated a power and responsibility to make key choices about the shape of the internal market. It has not always made those choices with perfect clarity, and it has sometimes changed its mind.[19]

In general, the core free movement rules as presented above can be seen as stipulated to exercise control over measures adopted at the national level that are apt to jeopardise the aim of establishing the Internal Market. However, the four economic freedoms have developed from ostensibly political and economic obligations for the Member States into economic principles and subjective rights for citizens and businesses. This development was initiated by the CJEU, which postulated the principles of direct effect and primacy in the *Van Gend & Loos* and *Costa/Enel* cases of 1963 and 1964.[20] This fundamental rights' character of the four freedoms reinforces their strength and the breadth vis-à-vis other Treaty provisions and policies. As pointed out by Garben, the CJEU has taken an extremely inclusive approach, continuously 'emphasising that practices, goods, and services are not excluded from the scope of the Treaty simply because they fall in areas of Member State competence or because they are politically sensitive'.[21] Thus, the free movement rules are undoubtedly tremendously powerful tools.

[18] S Weatherill, 'Comparative Internal Market Law: The UK and the EU' (2021) *Yearbook of European Law* 432.

[19] S Weatherill, 'The Several Internal Markets' (2017) *Yearbook of European Law* 3.

[20] Case 26/62 *Van Gend & Loos*, ECLI:EU:C:1963:1; and Case 6/64 *Costa v Enel*, ECLI:EU:C:1964:66. See also SA de Vries, *Grondrechten binnen de Europese interne markt: een tragikomisch conflict tussen waarden in de 'Domus Europaea'* (Zutphen, Uitgeverij Paris, 2016) 9.

[21] S Garben, 'Confronting the Competence Conundrum: Democratising the European Union through an Expansion of its Legislative Powers' (2015) 35 *Oxford Journal of Legal Studies* 55, 60.

However, just like 'other' fundamental rights, the Treaty provisions on free movement do after all not have an absolute character. The CJEU has for instance formulated this as follows in the *Schmidberger* case:

> [W]hilst the free movement of goods constitutes one of the fundamental principles in the scheme of the Treaty, it may, in certain circumstances, be subject to restrictions for the reasons laid down in Article 36 of that Treaty or for overriding requirements relating to the public interest, in accordance with the Court's consistent case-law since the judgement in Case 120/78 *Rewe-Zentral* (*Cassis de Dijon*) [1979] ECR 649.[22]

Common to the CJEU's scheme of thinking applied in the majority of the classic free movement judgments is therefore also today – simply expressed and on the condition that the provisions are considered applicable in the case at hand – a two-pronged test. The first prong of the test contains an assessment as to whether a given national measure involves discrimination on the grounds of nationality and/or in a very wide sense constitutes a hindrance for (and/or restriction of) the free movement.[23] The other prong of the test includes an assessment of whether a given national measure can be 'justified'. Hereby a given measure can be upheld by reference to either: a) the Treaty-based exceptions (also called 'express derogations'); b) overriding interests of public interest (also called 'rule of reason' exceptions or 'court-induced' justifications); or c) fundamental rights, where the latter two categories have in principle been introduced in the CJEU's case-law.[24] A successful application of these exceptions would then cause the measure in question, despite otherwise being in conflict with one or more of the free movement rules, to be considered as justified. The applicable scrutiny in that regard may vary according to which category of exception is at stake, where it especially may be of importance whether the nature of the measure in question is discriminatory or not.[25] If justified, in particular, the principle of proportionality may have to be assessed, too. All in all, an otherwise unlawful measure can, after all, stand as being in conformity with the Treaty of Lisbon.

IV. THE ECONOMIC RATIONALE OF THE INTERNAL MARKET

The Spaak Plan from 1956, which formed the basis for the EEC Treaty, described the predecessor of the Internal Market, namely the Common Market, in the following terms:

> The objective of a common European market must be to create a vast zone of common economic policy, constituting a powerful unit of production, and making possible continuous growth, an increase in stability, an accelerated raising of the standard of living and the development of harmonious relations between the States which it unites . . . However, these

[22] Case C-112/00 *Schmidberger*, ECLI:EU:C:2003:33, para 78.

[23] See in particular the judgments in Case C-142/05 *Mickelsson & Roos*, ECLI:EU:C:2009:336 and Case C-110/05 *Commission v Italy*, ECLI:EU:C:2009:66.

[24] As to the role of fundamental rights, see further U Neergaard and SA de Vries, 'The (Digital) Internal Market and the Interaction between Free Movement and Fundamental Rights', in A Engel, X Groussot and GT Petursson (eds), *New Directions in Digitalisation: Perspectives from EU Competition Law and the Charter of Fundamental Rights* (Cham, Springer Nature, 2024).

[25] See further U Neergaard and R Nielsen, *EU-ret* (Copenhagen, Karnov Group, 2024) 324 et seq.

> advantages of a common market can only be achieved if time is granted and means are collectively made available to permit necessary adaptations to be made, if practices which distort competition between producers are ended and if co-operation between the States is established in order to ensure monetary stability, economic growth and social progress.[26]

It is already from here clear, also in consideration of the significance continuously given to this plan, that the theory at the time was completely permeated by economic thinking and aims. This was to become the dominant rationale of Internal Market and free movement law.[27] Combined with the power of the CJEU as described above, being an interpreter laying a huge emphasis on the *telos* of the Treaties, this rationale has continuously been of enormous importance.

Moving quickly ahead of time, the importance of this rationale has not lessened. Attention in that regard may for instance be paid to an opinion by Advocate General Szpunar, who also has emphasised the importance of the economic dimension, by his reference to 'the economic concept of comparative advantage' as being of essence:

> The internal market with its fundamental freedoms not only constitutes the historical legal cornerstone of the Treaties and their central organisational principle, but has also, since the outset of the integration process, been characterised by its dynamism. It is one of the stated aims of the Union . . . and stands prominently in the FEU Treaty in Title I of Part Three. Legally defined since the Single European Act as 'an area in which the free movement of goods, persons, services and capital is ensured in accordance with the provisions of the Treaties' . . . it aims to provide for a free flow of products and factors of production within the Union, against the background of the economic concept of comparative advantage.[28]

According to dominant, long-lasting narratives, the rationale of Internal Market law is, first and foremost, economic with a focus of enabling continuous growth and wealth.[29] In a targeted application of the fundamental freedoms, the CJEU has functioned and still functions as an 'engine of integration' and sometimes as an engine of liberalisation.[30]

Likewise, it is clear from, for instance, the following statement of the Commission that this institution also nowadays takes a major pride in the economic benefits of the Internal Market:

> The Single Market is one of the greatest achievements of the European project. It has made Europe one of the most attractive places in the world to live and do business. Over the last 25 years, it has been instrumental in increasing the prosperity and wealth of the citizens of the European Union . . . By virtue of its diversification, the Single Market has helped to improve the resilience of the European economy and the Economic and Monetary

[26] 'Rapport des Chefs de délégation aux ministres des affaires étrangères', quoted from K Mortelmans, 'The Common Market, the Internal Market and the Single Market, What's in a Market?' (1998) 35 *CML Rev* 101. Author's own Translation from Mae 120 f/56, corrigé, pp 13–14.

[27] See generally R Baldwin and C Wyplosz, *The Economics of European Integration* (Maidenhead, McGrawHill, 2022).

[28] Opinion in Joined Cases C-360/15 and C-31/16 *X and Visser*, ECLI:EU:C:2017:397 para 1.

[29] See eg Barnard, above note 15, 4, where it is explained that 'the benefits of free trade can be summarized briefly – free trade allows for specialization, specialization leads to comparative advantage, and comparative advantage leads to economies of scale, which maximize consumer welfare and ensure the most efficient use of worldwide resources'.

[30] N Dunne, 'Liberalisation and the Pursuit of the Internal Market' (2018) 43 *European Law Review* 803, 809.

> Union . . . By virtue of its scale, it has boosted the standing and influence of the European Union in the world.[31]

From the conclusions of the European Council meeting in June 2024, it is equally evident that the Internal Market still politically is seen as playing a crucial role:

> Our greatest asset in that endeavour is the Single Market, the long-term engine of prosperity and convergence that enables economies of scale. We will therefore deepen it further, notably in the areas of energy, finance and telecommunications. We will remove remaining barriers, particularly in relation to services and essential goods, and ensure equal access to the Single Market through improved connectivity.[32]

Throughout the document, there are continuous references to 'growth', 'economic growth' and 'sustainable growth'.[33] It is not clear what the different choice of wording may be grounded in, if anything. However, it under all circumstances shows that the growth paradigm is still more than highly prioritised and thereby confirms a long-held view that '[t]he link between European integration and growth rests on the logic of growth'.[34]

In general, the core of the Internal Market/free movement law has, in other words, for long by many been viewed as based on a predominantly market-based, at times neo-liberal, vision, premised on deregulation, efficiency and the assumption of formal equality between individuals. However, despite this overall impression of Internal Market law as primarily focusing on the elimination of barriers to trade and the creation of a level playing field for competition, the picture is at the same time a bit more multifaceted. This is particularly so where the CJEU recognises public interest justifications for restrictions on free movement, and where the EU legislator steps in using its broad mandate under the Internal Market legal basis of Article 114 TFEU to also protect public, non-economic interests.

V. THREE REASONS FOR RECALIBRATING THE FOUNDATIONS OF INTERNAL MARKET LAW

In the following we discuss three reasons why in our view there might be a need to adjust the predominantly market-based, economic growth rationale of Internal

[31] European Commission: Communication from the Commission to the European Parliament, the European Council, the Council, the European Economic and Social Committee and the Committee of the Regions, The Single Market in a changing world. A unique asset in need of renewed political commitment, COM(2018) 772 final, at 1.

[32] European Council, European Council meeting - Conclusions, Brussels, 27 June 2024, EUCO 15/24, p 19. Also see eg p 8, where it is stated: 'Following its conclusions of April 2024 and the Presidency report on work towards a new European competitiveness deal, the European Council reviewed progress on initiatives to enhance the Union's competitiveness, secure its economic resilience and achieve the full potential of the Single Market.'

[33] These terms are similarly present in European Commission, Communication from the Commission to the European Parliament, the Council, the European Economic and Social Committee and the Committee of the Regions. The Single Market at 30, COM(2023) 162 final.

[34] R Baldwin and C Wyplosz: *The Economics of European Integration* (Maidenhead, McGrawHill, 2022) 165.

Market law with a view to address the many challenges that Europe currently is facing. This would not necessarily entail that the market as such, as an organising principle, should be abandoned. Rather, it might require us to revisit and rethink the economic activities that take place within the market and thus also the legal rules and principles which, after all also according to Ulf Bernitz himself, draw up the basic framework for these activities.[35]

A. Newer Economic Thinking

Economic theory has not only in EU law, but in reality, in every aspect of public life, a tremendous authority.[36] However, that should so much more be a reason for questioning its impact and recommendations. Today it appears as recalibrating itself to embrace new realities, the relevance of which should self-evidently be taken into consideration also in the sphere of interpreting the Treaties. As just one example of newer, influential thoughts within the discipline of economics, attention may be brought to Raworth who has put forward a radically new compass, designated as 'doughnut economics', for guiding humanity.[37] She introduces it in the following terms:

> What if we started economics not with its long-established theories but with humanity's long-term goals, and then sought out the economic thinking that would enable us to achieve them? I tried to draw a picture of those goals and, ridiculous though it sounds, it came out looking like a doughnut – yes the American kind with a hole in the middle . . . [I]n essence it is a pair of concentric rings. Below the inner ring – the social foundation – lie critical human deprivations such as hunger and illiteracy. Beyond the outer ring – the ecological ceiling – lies critical planetary degradation such as climate change and biodiversity loss. Between those two rings is the doughnut itself, the space in which we can meet the needs of all within the means of the planet.[38]

Raworth furthermore explains:

> [The Doughnut] points towards a future that can provide for every person's needs while safeguarding the living world on which we all depend. Below the Doughnut's social foundation lie shortfalls in human well-being, faced by those who lack life's essentials such as food, education and housing. Beyond the ecological ceiling lies an overshoot of pressure on Earth's life-giving systems, such as through climate change, ocean acidification and chemical pollution. But between these two sets of boundaries lies a sweet pot – shaped unmistakably like a doughnut – that is both an ecologically and socially just space for humanity. The twenty-first century task is an unprecedented one: to bring all of humanity into that safe and just space.[39]

[35] U Bernitz, *Market Law as a Legal Discipline* (Uppsala, Almqvist & Wiksell International, 1979) 55.

[36] See eg K Raworth, *Doughnut Economics – Seven Ways to Think Like a 21st Century Economist* (White River Junction, Vermont,London, Chelsea Green Publishing, 2017) 5, who states: 'Economics is the mother tongue of public policy, the language of public life and the mindset that shapes society.'

[37] See eg ibid 39.

[38] See eg ibid 8–9.

[39] See eg ibid 39.

In particular, Raworth is strongly critical of what we above explained as a dominant goal pursued by the EU, namely (endless) growth (as well as the connected GDP).[40] Indeed, mainly focusing on growth brought to the extreme would be counterproductive for many other aims of importance today, even though it may also be recalled that growth to some degree may at the same time be important in enabling the financing of, for example, a green transition and that Europe also currently faces worries as to competitiveness, etc.

With reference to 'the ideology of growthism', this focus on growth is from a different perspective also deeply criticised by de Schutter, who is a lawyer specialised in economic and social rights. He has in a recent United Nations report explained (and on the basis thereof criticised the underlying assumptions):

> Defined as the increase in gross domestic product (GDP), economic growth has long been seen as desirable for its own sake. Economists have debated how it can be achieved and politicians how its benefits could be shared. Human rights bodies have seen growth as an indispensable condition for the realization of economic and social rights, based on the assumption that without growth, there would be no resources to mobilize for the progressive realization of such rights – for investments to be made in the provision of health care, social housing or education, or for the creation of jobs . . . Governments still act as if infinite growth were possible. Ignoring the warnings of scientists, . . . they seem to believe that economic activity can expand endlessly, as if the Earth will forever provide limitless resources and absorb the waste resulting from our apparently endless quest for more.[41]

As a third example of new thinking, attention may be brought to the fact that the influential, Nobel-prize winning economist Joseph Stiglitz, recently has claimed that neoliberalism has failed.[42] Inter alia, Stiglitz thought-provokingly states that: 'The current neoliberal economic system is not environmentally, socially, politically, or economically sustainable'.[43] This, thus, may fundamentally be of relevance to the Internal Market rationale revisited here, too, as it by many is viewed as neoliberal in nature.

The debate as to how newer economic thinking might become reflected in the law in general,[44] and EU free movement law in particular is still in its infancy, and further research is necessary. Ulf Bernitz' systematisation of the legal framework that constitutes market law could serve as an important source of inspiration and starting point for rethinking Internal Market law. He identified five freedoms, which support the market economy, of which EU free movement law is a specific amplification: the

[40] See eg ibid at 26 and 22 as well as in particular chapter 7.

[41] O de Schutter, *Eradicating poverty beyond growth. Report of the Special Rapporteur on extreme poverty and human rights, Olivier De Schutter,* United Nations, General Assembly, Human Rights Council, Fifty-sixth session, 18 June–12 July 2024, A/HRC/56/61, p. 2. Also see O de Schutter, *The Poverty of Growth* (London, Pluto Press, 2024).

[42] JE Stiglitz, *The Road to Freedom. Economics and the Good Society* (London, Allen Lane, 2024) ch 11.

[43] ibid 235.

[44] There are examples of legal scholars, who have sought to assess the implications of degrowth or post-growth theories for the law, see eg J Bétaille, 'La science juridique face à l'hypothèse de la post-croissance: méthodologie, critique et analyse écosystémique du droit', in A Bailleux (ed), *Le droit en transition: Les clés juridiques d'une prospérité sans croissance* (Brussels, Presses de l'Université Saint-Louis, 2020).

freedom of establishment, the freedom of competition, the freedom of contract, the freedom of consumption and the freedom of association.[45] According to him, what is relevant is the fundamental function of the freedoms as they set norms for the market place; but market law as such 'has the advantage of not being tied to a particular economic or political programme'.[46] In a similar vein and at approximately the same time, legal scholars in Belgium and the Netherlands developed the fundamental legal principles of freedom, equality and solidarity as principles of public economic law in general and European economic law in particular. These principles have been seen as central in guiding and supporting the development of the market economy.[47] Hence, important questions that newer economic thinking would trigger are inter alia: a) could, and if so, how should the freedoms be recalibrated and reframed in relation to eg sustainability, justice and responsibility; b) what would this mean for the important principle of free movement and the balancing exercise as currently conducted by the CJEU as well as for EU legislative harmonisation within the framework of the Internal Market; and c) do we need to develop and accept new, additional guiding principles for the EU economic order, such as ecological responsibility, justice, propriety and honesty?[48]

B. The Changed Treaty Context with a Stronger Focus on Public Interests

The current economic rationale is to some degree understandable from a historical point of view with respect to the objectives of the EEC/EC/EU over time. Indeed, Article 2 of the 1957 Rome Treaty stated the objectives as follows:

> It shall be the aim of the Community, by establishing a Common Market and progressively approximating the economic policies of Member States, to promote throughout the Community a harmonious development of economic activities, a continuous and balanced expansion, an increased stability, an accelerated raising of the standard of living and closer relations between its Member States.

As explained by Govaere:

> From 1957 until 2009, the Treaties continued to express, albeit with slight modifications over time, the original vision of a common/internal market which is inherently and necessarily 'instrumental' and 'reactive'. Instrumental, in the sense that the establishment of the internal market was initially not conceived as an objective as such. Creating economic interdependence by merging the national markets as much as possible into one common market was rather considered to be a necessary instrument to achieve the higher political

[45] U Bernitz, *Market Law as a Legal Discipline* (Uppsala, Almqvist & Wiksell International, 1979).

[46] ibid 74.

[47] See P VerLoren van Themaat, *Rechtsgrondslagen van een nieuwe internationale economische orde* (Groningen, Wolters Noordhoff, TMC Asser Instituut, 1979); W van Gerven, 'De ontwikkeling van de sociaal-economische rechtsorde in EG-verband', in *Waarheen gaat onze sociaal-economische orde?* Annalen van het Thijmgenootschap, jrg. 64 (Amboboeken, Baarn, 1976). K Hellingman and KJM Mortelmans, *Economisch Publiekrecht – Rechtswaarborgen en rechtsinstrumenten* (Deventer, Kluwer, 1989).

[48] P Phoa, 'Narratives in Flux – Legal Language, Digital Technologies and the Climate Crisis' (2023) 2(2) *Comparative Law and Language* 9.

> objectives of the European integration process, in particular maintaining peace and stability on the European continent.[49]

It is in this connection of relevance that Article 3 TEC lists the activities, which are necessary to achieve the objectives of Article 2 TEC, namely inter alia:

> For the purposes set out in the preceding Article, the activities of the Community shall include, under the conditions and with the timing provided for in this Treaty:
>
> (a) the elimination, as between Member States, of customs duties and of quantitative restrictions in regard to the importation and exportation of goods, as well as of all other measures with equivalent effect;
>
> (b) the establishment of a common customs tariff and a common commercial policy towards third countries;
>
> (c) the abolition, as between Member States, of the obstacles to the free movement of persons, services and capital.

Nevertheless, the Internal Market is now embedded in a significantly changed Treaty framework, where especially the Treaty of Lisbon's introduction of Article 3(3) TEU is important. The provision stipulates:

> The Union shall establish an internal market. It shall work for the sustainable development of Europe based on balanced economic growth and price stability, a highly competitive social market economy, aiming at full employment and social progress, and a high level of protection and improvement of the quality of the environment. It shall promote scientific and technological advance.
>
> It shall combat social exclusion and discrimination, and shall promote social justice and protection, equality between women and men, solidarity between generations and protection of the rights of the child.
>
> It shall promote economic, social and territorial cohesion, and solidarity among Member States.
>
> It shall respect its rich cultural and linguistic diversity, and shall ensure that Europe's cultural heritage is safeguarded and enhanced.

Hereby, especially the aim of creating a highly competitive social market economy may be highlighted, as it may be understood as reinforcing the importance of other, non-economic values and fundamental rights. This, in principle, marks an important 'shift in emphasis – from a pure market-based, neo-liberal vision premised on deregulation, efficiency, and the assumption of formal equality between individuals – to one which recognizes the need to accommodate and indeed values a wider range of interests'.[50]

However, as pointed out by Govaere, 'little or no attention has been devoted in case-law or doctrine to the single most visible change introduced by the Lisbon

[49] I Govaere, 'Internal Market Dynamics: On Moving Targets, Shifting Contextual Factors and the Untapped Potential of Article 3(3) TEU', in S Garben and I Govaere (eds), *The Internal Market 2.0* (Oxford, Hart Publishing, 2020) 81–82.

[50] Barnard, above note 15, 34.

Treaty'.[51] As also pointed out by Govaere, the CJEU simply points back to pre-Lisbon rulings as the basis for a consistent line of case-law, which still remains valid post-Lisbon, but which nonetheless seems highly problematic for the CJEU, as it bluntly does so without explaining the underlying rationale, and how this squares with the reformulation of the Internal Market objective, but also with the above-mentioned repeal of former Article 3 TEC, which was very much the anchorage of the pre-Lisbon case-law.[52] In that regard, it is of interest that the EU's commitment to realising a social market economy has also prompted Advocate General Cruz Villalón in the case *Santos Palhota* to suggest that the pre-Lisbon orthodoxy needs to be reconsidered.[53]

The extent to which the Treaty context should be exactly reflected in Internal Market law is unclear, as long as the Treaty itself contains a range of often contradictory objectives and tasks. These can at times for instance contribute to a fair, 'green' and inclusive Internal Market, and at other times quite the opposite. Of importance to that example, it may be emphasised that Article 3(3) TEU speaks of sustainable development and the establishment of a social market economy, but also of balanced economic growth and price stability, and high competitiveness. Article 39 TFEU on agriculture sets out the objectives of the EU agricultural policy relating to increasing agricultural productivity, stabilising markets and reasonable prices for consumers. The words sustainability or environment do not appear in this provision. At the same time, we have the aforementioned Article 11 TFEU, which states that: 'Environmental protection requirements shall be integrated into the definition and implementation of Union policies and actions, in particular with a view to promoting sustainable development.'

C. The Manifold Current Challenges for Europe

The third and last reason relates to the several crises mentioned above, including for example the green and digital transition of our societies, the rapidly deteriorating geopolitical circumstances with the consequential focus on strategic autonomy,[54] social resilience and finally economic resilience. As to the latter, Baldwin and Wyplosz have explained that:

> EU growth has been abysmal since the Global financial Crisis exploded in 2008 followed soon by the Eurozone Crisis that started in 2010. Ten years after these shocks, the moderate recovery in growth rates was again demolished by the pandemic. At the time of writing in

[51] Govaere, above note 44, 77.

[52] ibid 89.

[53] Case C–515/08 *dos Santos Palhota and Others*, ECLI:EU:C:2010:589, paras 51–53; C Barnard and S de Vries, 'The "Social Market Economy" in a (Heterogeneous) Social Europe: Does it Make a Difference?' (2019) 15(2) *Utrecht Law Review* 47.

[54] Ie the ability to act autonomously without being dependent on other countries in strategically important policy areas. See further eg '"European Sovereignty" in Times of Poly-Crises: From *Original Manifestations to Points of Concern'*, in Gavin Barrett, Peter-Christian Müller-Graff, Viktor Vadász and Jean-Philippe Rageade (eds), *European Sovereignty: The Legal Dimension* (Cham, Springer Nature, 2024).

> early 2022, recurrent waves of infection continue to hold down income growth in Europe and in most economies around the world.[55]

To this diagnostic the Russian invasion of Ukraine should be added, which has also had a huge impact in this regard. Under all circumstances, these challenges are now all crucial drivers of change for Internal Market law.[56] The EU's legislative agenda is indeed increasingly focused on these matters. These can for example range from health, defence, the economy and inequality, biodiversity, climate change, food systems and digitalisation to the ability to uphold democratic values.

The Internal Market thus plays an increasingly pivotal role in proactively contributing to other, non-economic goals and in increasing strategic autonomy.[57] Thereby, the EU legislature has cumulatively managed to become 'a law- and policymaker in (partial or total) replacement for its Member States in an extravagantly wide range of areas', exploiting the 'broad and fuzzy contours' of the internal market legal basis of Article 114 TFEU.[58]

From the need to accommodate much more multifold objectives through Internal Market legislation, a picture of a more mission-oriented Internal Market has emerged, an idea that can be even traced back to the above-mentioned Spaak report of 1956, which after all refers to the Internal Market as 'a powerful unit of production and making possible continuous growth, an increase in stability, an accelerated raising of the standard of living'.[59] This equally underscores the development of a more pluralist narrative of Internal Market law, possibly rendering the predominantly market-based, neo-liberal vision of the Internal Market of the 1990s outdated as essentially being too one-eyed.

The fact that Internal Market law is important in achieving the EU's current political priorities, may, however, come at a price. As Vandermeeren states, certain obstacles to trade and free movement 'that have a more direct impact on the EU's strategic autonomy objectives could be considered and addressed as a priority', whereas other obstacles will have to be accepted.[60] Looking at more recent legislative strategies to regulate the Internal Market, it seems indeed that the removal of trade barriers and the focus on free movement are mostly not the core anymore of Internal Market legislation.[61]

[55] R Baldwin and C Wyplosz, *The Economics of European Integration* (Maidenhead, McGrawHill, 2022) 162.

[56] See eg the European Commission's Communication 'Towards a green, digital and resilient economy – our European growth model', COM(2022) 83 final.

[57] Govaere, above note 44, 75–91.

[58] Weatherill, above note 10, 153.

[59] K Mortelmans, 'The Common Market, the Internal Market and the Single Market, What's in a Market' (1998) 35 *Common Market Law Review* 102–03: 'The objective of a common European market must be to create a vast zone of common economic policy, constituting a powerful unit of production, and making possible continuous growth, an increase in stability, an accelerated raising of the standard of living and the development of harmonious relations between the States which it unites. [. . .] [W]here in theory liberalization of trade at a world-wide level appears to be desirable, a true common market can in the end only be realized between a limited group of States, which one would wish to be as broad as possible.'

[60] Vandermeeren, above note 5, 31.

[61] SA de Vries, 'Recent Trends in EU Internal Market Legislation – Bringing Back the Old Concept?', in T van den Brink and V Passalacqua (eds), *Balancing Unity and Diversity in EU Legislation* (Cheltenham, Edward Elgar Publishing, 2024) 17–42.

However, if this view corresponds to an Internal Market that is 'green', creates wealth, promotes social and non-market interests, and diminishes inequalities, legislative harmonisation within the context of the Internal Market should support that. This is also in line with the above-mentioned report by Letta, which focuses on a more instrumental, strategic Internal Market to achieve a sustainable and prosperous society for European citizens.[62]

VI. CONCLUSIONS

Above, we have critically revisited the foundations of free movement law, and much has indeed occurred within the area of market law as a legal discipline since the early writings of Ulf Bernitz. In particular, we have – in light of newer challenges – focused on certain contributions to newer economic theoretical thinking, the new and fundamentally changed overall objective of a social market economy in the Lisbon Treaty, and the ambiguous interrelationship between the many new objectives today. On the basis thereof, we suggest that there may be a need for reconsideration of present foundations of free movement law in the primary law interpretations of the CJEU.

Within the free movement regime, the CJEU has continuously been balancing market and non-market interests against one another, and has generally done so successfully. However, the consequences of a reconsideration as suggested may be that it could be discussed whether the strict ranking of the first and second prong is still viable given the above considerations. The inherent priority of the test is always free movement, that is, economic aims, as coming alive in the first prong; only if duly argued can non-market interests be given priority as it is expressed with the second prong.[63] This implies that other aims *always* in principle are only secondary in nature.

[62] E Letta, 'Much more than a market – speed, security and solidarity', <consilium.europa.eu/media/ny3j24sm/much-more-than-a-market-report-by-enrico-letta.pdf>.

[63] See eg J Zglinski, 'The Internal Market as a Dynamic Process: Five Scenarios for the Future', in J Adams-Prassl, A Ezrachi, S Bogojevic and D Leczykiewicz (eds), *The Internal Market Ideal: Essays in Honour of Stephen Weatherill* (Oxford, Oxford University Press, 2024) 88–89, who of some relevance here argues: 'Against this backdrop, another way forward for the EU internal market could lie in doing the polar opposite: curbing negative integration. This would entail limiting the role of (primary) free movement law and, relatedly, of the Court of Justice in market regulation. There are several ways in which this objective could be achieved, but two proposals have gained momentum in the literature . . . The first involves a re- interpretation of the four freedoms. Instead of applying to most, or as some would argue, virtually all restrictions on cross- border trade and economic activity, their scope could be narrowed down to a principle of non- discrimination. The second proposal goes further and involves their de-constitutionalization. The formal status of the four freedoms within the legal hierarchy of European law would be "downgraded" from primary to secondary law, meaning that they would no longer occupy the elevated position of constitutional provisions but be on a par with ordinary legislation and, as such, open to the influence of ordinary politics . . . These suggestions might feel counterintuitive at first: how would curtailing free movement rights help advance the internal market? Answering this question requires an understanding of the ideational origins of these proposals. They do not come from a dissatisfaction with insufficient levels of trade between the Member States or a longing for greater economic freedom in Europe. Au contraire, they are rooted in a critique of the status quo which holds that the EU internal market in general, and the Court of Justice's free movement case-law specifically, have gone too far, unduly prioritizing deregulation over regulation, and economic interests over democratic and social concerns. In other words, the proposals do not aim at advancing the internal market in the traditional sense of "more trade, closer economic integration". They seek to create a more democratic, socially responsive, and, ultimately, legitimate internal market, . . . even if this should come at some economic cost in the form of reducing cross-border exchanges.'

Such a hierarchy, although *once* in conformity with the rationale of, the objectives of and the economic thinking behind the Internal Market, might no longer be so.

The above analysis has intended to open a debate as to whether a much more significant paradigm shift might be necessary, even if this does not necessarily imply an abandonment of the market as an organising principle. This claim especially appears as supported by the fact that the theoretical foundation thereof currently is crucially under redefinition, already because many economists in their search for solutions to for example the ecological crisis within planetary boundaries, now discuss and develop ideas about for example degrowth, post-growth or doughnut economics.[64] Thus, to us, the Internal Market paradigms may be in need of rethinking to ensure that they can better serve as a compass for achieving current and future challenges, thereby ensuring that they are sufficiently capable, resilient and future-proof to contribute to the transition of our current societies into the new needs. It should be ensured that the Internal Market becomes part of the solution and not part of the problem; thus, it is not necessarily the fundamental law that needs to change, but the approach to it.[65] We hope thereby to have opened the discussion and encouraged further reflection.

[64] See for instance Raworth, above note 36; Bétaille, above note 44.

[65] Similarly, see S Holmes, 'Climate Change, Sustainability, and Competition Law' (2020) *Journal of Antitrust Enforcement* 355.

Part IV

A New EU Market Law for the Data-Driven Economy

9

The EU Data Act's Rules on Access to and Use of Data and the Rules of the Market

HANNS ULLRICH*

I. INTRODUCTION

THIS CONTRIBUTION ON THE EU Data Act's rules on access to and use of data must begin on a note of amazement. In the eyes of a student of the old market law of the hand-driven economy the EU legislature, faced with the threat of its market becoming ever more dominated by a few giants of a foreign digital industry, seems to have built the new market law of a data-driven economy by establishing some walls before laying the fundament. Reacting to the pressing problem of losing control over the technological direction of its economy and seizing the political opportunities for effective legislation, its focus was on subjecting the major new actors on its 'digital market' to particular rules: digital service providers to a specific regime of liability for unlawful content,[1] intermediaries to an administrative registration system ensuring some minimum transparency of their business presence[2] and central platforms to an ex ante control of the compatibility of their gatekeeping activities with the requirements of competitively fair functioning markets.[3] The latter rules even supersede in part the still applicable rules of competition of primary

* At the time of submitting the contribution the Data Act had entered into force, but not yet into application; see below note 7. It was not possible any more to add the literature accompanying the gradual application of the Data Act.

[1] Reg (EU) 2022/2065 of the European Parliament and of the Council of 1 October 2022 on a Single Market for Digital Services (Digital Services Act), OJEU 2022 L 277, 1 (DSA).

[2] Reg (EU) 2022/868 of the European Parliament and of the Council of 30 May 2022 on European Data Governance (Data Governance Act), OJEU 2022 L 152, 1 (DGA) with in particular Chapter III on Requirements applicable to data intermediation services (Arts 10–15), Chapter IV on Data altruism (Arts 16–28).

[3] Reg (EU) 2022/1925 of the European Parliament and of the Council of 14 September 2022 on contestable and fair markets in the digital sector (Digital Markets Act), OJEU 2022 L 265, 1 (DMA).

Union law (Articles 101, 102 TFEU)[4] and/or of – possibly revised – national competition laws.[5] However important these particular rules actually are for containing the influence and power of some selectively identified market actors within the limits of a framework regulation of digital markets, they are peripheral to the regulation of the core of these markets which is access to and use of their essential resources, namely data. It has long been the case that such data may be held and are offered for business re-use by the public sector,[6] but the bulk of economically relevant data originates from within and is controlled by the private sector. Therefore, 'harmonised rules on fair access to and use of data'[7] could serve as a solid fundament for the well-functioning of an innovative data-driven economy. This, indeed, is what the EU legislature expects the Data Act to do, but it did not design the rules of the Act accordingly. Therefore, rather than presenting the Data Act's rules on access to and use of data of the private sector in detail, this contribution focuses on their conceptual underpinnings and systemic deficits.[8]

II. ACCESS TO AND USE OF DATA HELD UNDER DE FACTO CONTROL

A. The Structure of the Data Act's Access Regime

The introductory recitals of the Data Act note that, due to the transformative effects that data-driven technologies have on all sectors of the economy, the proliferation of

[4] See inter alia, N Moreno Belloso and N Petit, 'The EU Digital Markets Act (DMA): A Competition Hand in a Regulatory Glove' (2023) 48 *EL Rev* 391; J Cremers et al, 'Enforcing the Digital Markets Act: Institutional Choices, Compliance, and Antitrust' Yale Tobin Center for Economic Policy, Policy Discussion Paper 7, 1 December 2022, throughout; H Schweitzer et al, 'Data Access and Sharing in the EU: Towards a Coherent Legal Framework for the Emerging Data Economy', Report of 8 July 2022 to the German Bundesminister für Wirtschaft und Klimaschutz (accessible at ssrn.com/abstract=4270272), sub E.III. (133 and throughout); for a critical illustration of the current enforcement focus of competition policy on practices covered by the DMA (Art 6(5)) see G Colangelo, 'Antitrust Unchained: The EU's Case Against Self-Preferencing' (2023) *GRURInt* 538.

[5] See J Drexl, B Conde Gallego et al, 'Position Statement of the Max Planck Institute for Innovation and Competition of 2 May 2023 on the Implementation of the Digital Markets Act (DMA)', Max Planck Institute for Innovation and Competition Research Paper 23-11, ssrn.com/abstract=4437220; J van den Boom, 'What Does the Digital Markets Act Harmonise? Exploring Interactions Between the DMA and National Competition Laws' (2023) 19 *Eur Comp J* 57; F Bien, 'Regulierung von Online-Plattformen' (2022) *JZ* 830; J-U Franck and M Peitz, 'Digital Platforms and the New 19a Tool of the German Competition Act' (2021) 12 J *Eur Comp L & Pract* 513.

[6] DGA, above note 2, Chapter II on re-use of certain categories of protected data held by public sector bodies (Arts 3 to 9) and recitals 6 et seq.

[7] Reg (EU) 2023/2854 of the European Parliament and the Council of 13 December 2023 on harmonized rules on fair access to and use of data (Data Act), OJEU (L series) of 22.12.2023; as far as relevant here the Act will apply from 12 September 2025 onwards, see Art 50(2), (4), (5). For preparatory documents see Proposal for a Regulation of the European Parliament and of the Council on harmonized rules on fair access to and use of data (Data Act), Council, interinstitutional file: 2022/0047 (COD)), Analysis of final compromise text in view to agreement, Brussels 7 July 2023, Council Doc. 11284/23 with annex (to the clean Trilogue compromise text of 26/27 June 2023); for the original proposal of the Commission see COM (2022) 68 final of 23 February 2022.

[8] Chapters V (Arts 14 to 22) on 'Making Data available to public sector bodies' and Chapter VII (Art 32) on 'Unlawful international governmental access and transfer of non-personal data' will not be considered here.

products connected in particular to the internet has increased the volume and potential value of data for consumers, business and society.[9] And yet the Act addresses the legal and practical problems resulting therefrom only selectively.[10] As indicated by the full title of the Data Act and its recital 2, the main concern of the legislature is about promoting access to and use of data by data sharing. To this effect, Chapter II of the Data Act on 'business to consumer and business to business data sharing' provides for general rules on mandatory accessibility by users of data generated by the use of connected products and by related services (Articles 3 to 7). Chapter III on 'obligations for data holders obliged to make data available pursuant to Union law' complements these rules by Articles 8 to 12, which apply in case a data holder's duty to make data accessible arises in business-to-business relations. In addition, Article 13 of Chapter IV on 'unfair contractual terms related to data access and use between enterprises' outlaws 'unfair contractual terms' that are 'unilaterally imposed on another enterprise' when entering into a voluntary data sharing agreement.[11]

Thus, a distinct dividing line runs across the access regime. While Chapter II on mandatory access applies equally to both end-consumers and enterprises as users of connected products, Chapter III covers only the rights and obligations that may arise in business-to-business relations. Put differently, whereas Chapter II establishes a self-contained regime, Chapter III adds complementary rules that apply only in the context of mandatory inter-enterprise data sharing. Less visible is a different, but similar distinction between the law that applies to voluntary data sharing between enterprises on the one hand, and, on the other, voluntary data sharing between enterprises and end-consumers. As mentioned, as regards the former, Article 13 Data Act introduces a particular set of rules outlawing unilaterally imposed unfair contractual terms; as regards the latter, Article 1(9) Data Act expressly retains the applicability of the Union's general law on consumer protection.[12] However, both regimes rest on a principle that is implicit to the ratio legis and the operation of the Data Act, which is its preference for voluntary data sharing. Articles 7(2) and 12(2) Data Act indirectly confirm this implied principle by providing that the terms of contracts that parties conclude within the framework of the mandatory access regime may not to the detriment of the user or of a party deviate from or change its rules, that is, these rules only serve to protect the individual interests of the users or of a party but are without prejudice to the general freedom of contracting. In short, contrary to first impression, the basic principle of the Data Act is voluntary data sharing by mutual agreement; mandatory accessibility of product data constitutes

[9] Recital 1 Data Act.

[10] An important problem relates to the freedom of customers to switch between providers of data processing services, which Chapter VI seeks to ensure as a matter of principle (Arts 23, 24)) on both the contractual (Art 25 to 29) and the technical level (Art 30). Another one concerns interoperability, which Chapter VIII seeks to support in respect of data spaces (Art 33) and data processing services in general (Art 35) by providing for essential requirements of transparency and functionality of the service offered and for rules on standardisation of the subject matter and modes and means of data sharing. Although these rules are at least indirectly supportive of data sharing, they cannot be presented here.

[11] Art 8(2) Data Act provides that Art 13 applies (a fortiori) also within the framework of the mandatory access regime of Art 5 Data Act or of otherwise applicable Union law or national law.

[12] Art 1(9) Data Act states that the Act 'complements and is without prejudice to Union law which aims to protect the interests of consumers and ensure a high level of protection'; see also recitals 9, 28.

but a particular part or one cornerstone of this principle. Recital 5 expresses this complementary relationship quite clearly by stating: 'Private law rules are key in the overall framework for data sharing. Therefore, this Regulation adapts rules of contract law and prevents the exploitation of contractual imbalances that hinder fair access to and use of data'.

It is in this way that the legislature pursues the main objective of the Data Act, which is to eliminate barriers to data sharing that prevent an optimal allocation of data for the benefit of society and the well-functioning of the Internal Market for data.[13] While recital 2 lists quite a number of barriers, such as a lack of incentives to enter voluntarily into data-sharing agreements, uncertainty about rights and obligations in relation to data, a lack of common data sharing practices, the high fragmentation of information in data silos, bottlenecks impeding data access and some technical obstacles, other recitals stress that the main and almost common cause of their existence is the unequal distribution of market power, that is, a structural asymmetry or distortion of competition in the markets for data and data-based products and services.[14]

B. Voluntary Data Sharing between Enterprises

i. The Problem of Unequal Bargaining Power

The Data Act expresses the legislature's concern about unequal power of market actors most clearly in Chapter IV on voluntary data sharing between business firms.[15] Article 13 on 'unfair contractual terms unilaterally imposed on another enterprise' provides that 'a contractual term concerning access to and use of data or liability and remedies for the breach or the termination of data-related obligations, which has been unilaterally imposed on another enterprise, shall not be binding on the latter enterprise if it is unfair', that is, 'if it is of such nature that its use grossly deviates from good commercial practice in data access and use, contrary to good faith and fair dealing'. Recitals 58 and 61 make it clear that the provision aims at controlling excessive contractual terms where a stronger market position has been abused by the exercise of leverage power.

To this effect, Article 13 establishes a rule of control of unfair contractual terms that applies to either party and does so irrespective of its particular nature or its specific business. In particular, it addresses both the case of a data holder exercising its market power to the disadvantage of a data recipient when giving access to data and the case of a data recipient using its demand power in order to unilaterally

[13] See recitals 2, 4 Data Act and most revealing the reformulation of the objectives of the Act by its concluding recital 119: 'ensuring fairness in the allocation of value from data among actors in the data economy'. In reality, a fair allocation of value will result only from a proper operation of competition in that market. It is this that the Data Act must ensure; see also recital 26: 'foster the emergence of liquid, fair and efficient markets for non-personal data'.

[14] See again recital 5 and also recitals 27, 40, 48, 49, 61, 90.

[15] While Art 13 of the Commission's proposal for a Data Act (above note 7) covered only unfair contract terms imposed on small and medium-sized enterprises, Art 13 as enacted provides for the control of unfair terms that are unilaterally imposed on the other business party whatever its size.

impose its preferred contractual terms on the data holder when asking for access.[16] Although a pronounced data dependency of the weaker party may exist in both cases and serve as an indicium of unequal bargaining positions of the parties, it is not the decisive and not even the main consideration underlying Article 13,[17] and, therefore, may not determine, let alone limit its application. Rather, by equating the existence of unequal bargaining positions with the power of a party to unilaterally impose an unfair contractual term on the other party, Article 13(6) Data Act extends the control to the exercise of any market power irrespective of the grounds or facts upon which it rests. Practically speaking, Article 13 relies on a sort of a per se test, which is that when despite its effort to negotiate an unfair term a party has not been able to influence the content of an unfair term this term is considered to have been unilaterally imposed by virtue of the superior bargaining position of the party that supplied the term.[18] This broad understanding of the rationale underlying the control of unfair contractual terms is confirmed by the legislative history of Article 13,[19] by recitals 58 and 61, which expressly state the legislature's concern about contractual imbalances that may result in uneven access to and distorted conditions of use of data, and by the fact that the provision applies not only to data-specific transactions but to any transaction containing some data sharing elements.[20] Thus, the power of a party to unilaterally impose on the other party an unfair term regarding access to or use of data may well result from the interest the latter party has in the overall bargain.[21]

[16] See J Drexl et al, Position Statement of the Max Planck Institute for Innovation and Competition of 25 May 2022 on the Commission's Proposal of 23 February for a Regulation on harmonised rules on fair access to and use of data (Data Act), Max Planck Institute for Innovation and Competition Research Paper No. 22-05 = ssrn.com/abstract=4136484, para.127. Note that in a reciprocal data-sharing agreement one of the parties or even both parties may be data holders and data recipients at the same time.

[17] As proposed de lege ferenda by Drexl et al, above note 16 para 125; see also below note 41.

[18] Recitals 58 and 59 define the critical level of asymmetric bargaining positions as the power of a party to practice a 'take it or leave it' strategy in contract negotiations. Compared to a genuine market-power-test or the criterion of data dependency, as favoured by Drexl et al, above note 16, a take it or leave it practice is relatively easy to prove by the history and documents of the negotiation process. The downside of the criterion is that it lends itself to being circumvented by merely formalistic negotiation manoeuvres. In addition, whenever a party is not sophisticated enough or too weak to attempt negotiating an unfair contractual term, the term will remain exempt from control and become part of the contract; see for a critique Drexl et al, above note 16, paras 122 et seq; A Wiebe, 'Der Data Act – Innovation oder Illusion?' (2023) *GRUR* 1569, 1574; A Wiebe, 'Der Data Act als vertragsrechtlicher Rahmen für Datennutzungsverträge' (2023) *CR* 777, paras 17 et seq.

[19] Art 13 of the Commission's proposal for a Data Act (above note 7), which covered only unfair contractual terms that are unilaterally imposed on small and medium-sized enterprises, aimed at protecting a category of enterprises that typically are the minor parties of inter-business transactions whatever their subject matter. It thus mirrored a particular concern about the effects of an asymmetric market structure on data access whereas Article 13 as finally enacted is concerned with fairness in data sharing in general.

[20] According to recital 60 'the rules on unfair contractual terms should apply only to excessive contractual terms that are related to making data available . . . Other parts of the same contract, unrelated to making data available, should not be subject to the unfairness test laid down by the Regulation'. For the problems of applying Art 13 to such composite transactions see below text at note 44.

[21] Think of the supplier-assembler relationship in assembly industries, which often enough are characterised by the dependency of the supplier. More generally speaking, the interest in a transaction may be determined by many technical factors, such as the quality of the materials used or the uniqueness of engineering quality, rather than mainly by the added value of use data access to which may be routine commercial practice.

ii. Determining Unfairness of Non-core Contractual Terms

The broad definition of the threshold criterion for controlling unfair contractual terms of agreements involving data sharing is further confirmed by the fact that the substantive standards of control are not systematically tailored to protect the weaker party only as regards its vulnerability as a data holder or data recipient. Rather, they are normatively ambivalent, systematically incoherent and not sufficiently targeted to the barriers to data sharing they are supposed to overcome. This holds true for the basic distinction between the contractual terms defining the main subject matter of the contract, in particular the price asked for in exchange for the data supplied, the adequacy of which Article 13(8) exempts from control, on the one hand, and, on the other, all the other terms that Article 13 subjects to a control for unfairness. The general idea underlying this classic distinction between the core terms and the complementary terms of a transaction is that, irrespective of the superior bargaining position that a party may hold, the principle of contractual freedom implies its autonomy to determine the subject matter of the contract it wishes to conclude and the contract price.[22] In addition, the assumption is that protecting this fundamental autonomy of both parties even in case of unequal bargaining positions will not unduly distort an efficient operation of the market.[23] However, it is precisely these core terms of data sharing agreements that present the main hurdles to data sharing: the specification of the subject matter in terms of quality and volume of the data to be shared, the purpose, time and means of sharing them and the comparative assessment of their value.[24] Therefore, given the inherently non-transparent nature of data markets as regards the availability of data and their nature and price, which makes quality/price comparisons a difficult exercise and increases transaction costs,[25] this general assumption will hardly hold, or will hold only if the liquidity and efficiency of data markets[26] is generally improved by rules that enhance the tradability of data.[27]

[22] See recitals 59 and 61.

[23] Note that in the field of competition law it is common ground that, when it comes to controlling the borderline case of the anticompetitive exercise of market dominance within the meaning of Art 102 TFEU, the rule is that even a firm dominating the market may freely pursue its legitimate commercial interests and set prices as any competitor would; it is not the market power as such, but only the abuse of market dominance that is prohibited; see H Ullrich, 'Zur besonderen Verantwortung marktbeherrschender Unternehmen', in F Thouvenin et al (eds), *Kreation – Innovation – Märkte, Festschrift R. Hilty* (Berlin, Springer, 2024) 1095, 1098 and throughout with references.

[24] See also the barriers to data sharing that recitals 2 and 26 Data Act list, such as a general lack of incentives for voluntary data sharing, uncertainties of rights and obligations in relation to data, fragmentation of information in data silos, bottlenecks impeding access etc, and see note 32. For a more elaborate presentation of the core problems of data sharing see inter alia L von Ditfurth, *Datenmärkte, Datenintermediäre und der Data Governance Act* (Berlin, de Gruyter, 2024) 39 et seq, 70 et seq, 99 et seq; Schweitzer et al, above note 4, sub D.III (91), E.II (128 et seq.); N Schur, *Die Lizenzierung von Daten* (Tübingen, Mohr Siebeck, 2020) 181 et seq, 225 et seq.; M Scheufen, 'Datenlizenzvertäge für das Data Sharing von Unternehmen' (2023) *IW-Kurzbericht* 64.

[25] Note that the Data Act considerably contributes to this lack of market transparency by allowing the data holder to rely on technical protection measures and trade secret protection as a way of exercising a broad de facto and de iure control over the data it holds; see below II.D.i.a and b.

[26] According to its recital 26, the Data Act's objective is 'to foster the emergence of liquid, fair, and efficient markets for non-personal data'.

[27] See below II.D.ii.c.

Despite the legislature's respect for the principle of contractual freedom, Article 13 Data Act extends the control of unfair contractual terms even to those that form part of individually negotiated, customised data-sharing contracts or covenants of broader transactions. This it does, first, by subjecting any unfair contractual term to control that a party unilaterally imposes on another party, rather than only non-negotiated standard terms,[28] and, second, by providing for a list of contractual terms that are only presumed to be unfair, but may 'not (be) unfair in the specific circumstances of the case'.[29] In addition, since the criteria by which Article 13(5) Data Act defines the presumably unfair operation of a contractual term are generally vague and normatively indeterminate,[30] judicial control of the unfairness will have to be circumstance-specific. The upshot of this legislative technique is that, instead of serving as a practical illustration of how the general benchmark of unfairness is to be understood that Article 13(3) Data Act sets by the test that contractual terms may not 'grossly deviate from good commercial practice in data access and use, contrary to good faith and fair dealing',[31] Article 13(5) only adds to the legal uncertainty that is inherent in the vague terms of this principled test.[32] This uncertainty is exacerbated by the fact that in the case of data-sharing agreements, which frequently have the character of a service and/or require a close a cooperation between and investments by both parties, the distinction between the core terms and the complementary terms is not easy to make, because complementary – rather than merely ancillary – terms may co-determine the commercial scope and reliability of the transaction.[33]

This ambivalent legislative technique may well be explained by the early stage of a just developing contractual practice that has not yet produced a generally accepted normative 'Leitbild' or model-design of data-sharing agreements as a particular

[28] See above text at note 18 et seq. It is therefore potentially misleading to assimilate Art 13 Data Act to the control merely of standard terms of contract; see inter alia D Staudenmayer, 'Der Verordnungsvorschlag der Europäischen Kommission zum Datengesetz' (2022) *EuZW* 596, 597 et seq. Data-sharing agreements between business firms may, but need not be concluded on standardised terms and require control over the exploitation of unequal bargaining positions on the basis of the principles of Art 13(3) Data Act rather than only on the basis of Art 102 TFEU.

[29] See Art 13(5) and recital 62 Data Act.

[30] See eg Art 13(5), lit. a): 'inappropriately limit remedies'; lit.b): 'significantly detrimental to the legitimate interests'; lit. c): 'not entitled to use . . . the value of such data in an adequate manner'; lit. g): 'no valid reason'; and see in particular the cumulative use of indeterminate criteria in lit. f): 'enable the party . . . to terminate the contract at unreasonably short notice, taking into consideration any reasonable possibility of the other contracting party to switch to an alternative and comparable service and the financial detriment caused by such termination, except where there are serious grounds for so doing'.

[31] T Gerpott, 'Vorschlag für ein europäisches Datengesetz' (2022) *CR* 271, para 45 noted this deficit early on; see also Staudenmayer, above note 28, 598.

[32] Significantly, recital 61 Data Act states as a general guideline that 'criteria for identifying unfair contractual terms should apply only to excessive contractual terms where a stronger bargaining position has been abused', but does not inform the reader how to distinguish these excessive terms from 'the vast majority of contractual terms that are commercially more favourable to one party than to the other' but are 'the normal expression of the principle of contractual freedom', and, therefore, are valid.

[33] See Art 13(5), lit. g) Data Act, which lists examples of important elements of the agreement the terms of which a superior party may not substantially change ex post, such as the conditions related to the nature, format, quality or quantity of the data.

legal category of commercial transactions.[34] However, it reveals the futility of legislative efforts that aim at remedying the slacking development of a broad contractual practice but that, due precisely to the absence of enough experience, cannot offer workable standards of good commercial practice.[35] Thus, the emergence of legally reliable standards and predictability of their application may not be expected before the judicial implementation of Article 13(5) Data Act has matured into sufficient and sufficiently established case law, thus only years from now, when the current wave of data-driven innovation most likely will have ebbed away.[36]

iii. A Special or a General Regime?

This sceptical appraisal of Article 13 Data Act is not meant to generally deny the desirability of controlling unfair contractual terms of voluntary data sharing agreements concluded between enterprises,[37] and be it that the control becomes effective only over time. However, one wonders what the added value of the regime of Article 13 Data Act regime might be as compared with the application of existing rules on unfair contractual terms in inter-business transactions in general.[38] Undoubtedly, in the EU there is a harmonising effect that may be valuable enough in itself, particularly so in a data-driven economy that quite naturally extends beyond national borders. But if that is the desired effect, why should harmonisation remain limited to the control of 'contractual terms concerning access to and the use of data or liability and

[34] See von Ditfurth, above note 24, 68 et seq; Wiebe (*GRUR* 2023), above note 18, 1574. In Germany the current discussion on appropriate model terms for data-sharing agreements focuses on the design of contracts concluded within the framework of mandatory data access (see inter alia C Czychowski, 'Shaping the Data Economy: Ausgestaltung von Datenüberlassungsverträgen aus Herstellerperspektive' (2024) *CR* 80; T Ehlen and P Sebulke, 'Der Data Act: Zwischen Markt- und Vertragsgestaltung' (2024) *CR* 84, to which Art 13 also applies by virtue of Art 8(1), (2) Data Act).

[35] Art 41 Data Act obliges the Commission to establish and recommend model contracts before the entry into application of the Data Act on 12 September 2025 (Art 50(2) Data Act). However, the Commission cannot itself develop such model contracts but only select recommendable models that industry associations propose. This requires time and presupposes that the models, developed by associations, will be generally acceptable and accepted or else they cannot be presumed to represent good commercial practice; see A Metzger and H Schweitzer, 'Shaping Markets: A Critical Evaluation of the Draft Data Act' (2023) *ZEuP* 42, 65 et seq; for a summary of initiatives providing model contracts see European Commission (ed), *Study on Model Contract Terms and Fairness Control in Data Sharing and in Cloud Contracts and on Access Rights* (authored by Timelex, ICF, Wavestone) (Brussels, 2022) 221 et seq. Whatever the merit of these model contracts, fairness ranges along a broad spectrum, and model contracts define only a starting point for individual contract negotiation. Therefore, deviations from their terms cannot be presumed to amount to unfair terms.

[36] Art 49(1) Data Act provides that by 12 September the Commission shall carry out an evaluation and submit to the Parliament and the Council a report inter alia on the question 'whether the list of unfair contractual terms referred to in Art.13 is up-to-date in light of new business practices and the rapid pace of market innovation' (Art 49(1) lit. g)). Since Art 13 will only apply to contracts concluded after 12 September 2025 (and in the case of long-term contracts only with effect from 12 September 2027), one wonders, first, whether Art 13 will be up-to-date at all when it first becomes applicable, and, second, what importance a report might have that, due to the short reporting period, cannot possibly take account of the judicial implementation of Art 13 Data Act.

[37] Contra Metzger and Schweitzer, above note 35, 63 et seq.

[38] Note that even this beneficial effect will be limited because the vague criteria of unfairness of Art 13 Data Act need to be substantiated by reference to fairness criteria provided for in the applicable national laws; see inter alia Wiebe (CR 2023) above note 18, 782. For the relationship between Art 13 data Act and national law in general see L Beinke and I Daute, 'Der Fairnesstest des Data Act' (2024) RDi 69, 71 et seq.

remedies for the breach or the termination of data related obligations' (Article 13(1) Data Act)? Most of the contractual terms that Article 13(4) and (5) Data Act list as being either unfair per se or presumably unfair would be unfair when unilaterally imposed on another party in relation to contracts of whatever subject matter and related obligations.[39] Only Article 13(5) lit. b), lit. c) and lit. e) Data Act specify the legislature's concern about contractual terms that may affect the particular interests that the party upon which the terms have been imposed, may have in regard to data as the subject matter of the transaction.

At any rate, contrary to what the focus of Article 13 Data Act on data-related contractual terms seems to suggest, it is questionable whether the qualification of contractual terms of data sharing agreements as unfair will or should crucially depend on the fact that they relate to data and that, therefore, their control should aim at protecting a data-specific vulnerability of the interests of the other party. The problem here is that data-specific interests of a party tend to be firm-specific or business-specific; this, not the data as such create a party's data dependency.[40] Therefore, protecting a party against unfair contractual terms by which the other party unfairly exploits the former party's 'data dependency' really means protecting particular business categories or business formats. That, however, is not the aim of the Data Act, which is to stimulate innovation, not to preserve particular business positions on the market.[41]

In addition, interpreting the unfairness standard of Article 13 Data Act by reference to a party's particular data dependency would hardly be appropriate in the

[39] See Art 13 (4) lit. a) and lit. b) and Art 13(5) lit. a) and lit. d) Data Act, and see also Art 13(4) lit.c) regarding terms by which the superior party reserves itself both the exclusive right to determine whether the performance of the contract by the other party is in conformity with the contract and the exclusive right to interpret any contractual term. Likewise Art 13(5) lit. d) relating to terms excluding a party's right to terminate the contract within a reasonable period, and Art 13(5) lit. g) relating to terms that would enable the superior party to substantially change the price or other essential conditions regarding the subject matter or the performance of the contract where there is no valid reason and no right of the other party to terminate the contract, concern hypotheses that are not specific to the practice of data-sharing agreements.

[40] This difference is overlooked by authors who hold that Art 13 Data Act is to compensate for a party's data dependency, see Wiebe (GRUR 2023) above note 18, 1575; Staudenmayer, above note 28, 600 (right col). At any rate, taking data dependency as a starting point for qualifying a contractual term as unfair does not fit with the connecting factor of control, which is unequal bargaining power in general; see text following note 16.

[41] More particularly, determining the unfairness of contractual terms by reference to the weaker party's dependency on the availability and use of data implies an assessment of that party's business needs and/or business format that is akin to the analysis that is required when applying the rules of competition law to the anticompetitive exercise of relational market power, eg, §§ 19, 20 German Act Against Restraints of Competition (see Drexl et al, above note 16, para 125). It will unduly burden inter partes litigation over disputes regarding single commercial transactions and miss the objective of Art 13 Data Act. The provision aims at protecting the weaker party against exposure to contractual terms that are unfair in the context of the particular transaction, rather than at enabling it to maintain its business format or type of business, let alone at compensating for its structural disadvantage in competition. Significantly, the unfairness criteria of Art 13 Data Act were not changed when in the Commission's proposal for a Data Regulation (above note 5) Art 13 was transformed from a provision protecting micro, small and medium-sized enterprises into one protecting any business enterprise against unilaterally imposed terms that are unfair. For the difficulties and complexity of determining relational market power or dependency by reference to a market actor's business format, needs and alternatives of supply see K Markert in U Immenga and E-J Mestmäcker (T Körber et al, eds), *Wettbewerbsrecht*, Vol 2, GWB, 7th edn (Munich, CH Beck, 2024) § 20 GWB, annot. 16 et seqwith references.

context of a system of attribution of control over data the design of which purposively follows a principle of de facto acquisition and possession rather than a legal principle of attribution on the merits.[42] With respect to non-personal data, which typically are of multi-purpose use, the issue in data sharing precisely is not one of a proper attribution of 'property' or 'ownership', that is, of attributing the data or their use in accordance with their origin in the efforts of one of the parties. Rather, it is whether the 're-distribution' between the parties of the opportunities to use the data shared rests on an exercise of bargaining power of a party that abusively distorts the commercial balance of the transaction. Furthermore, implementing the standard of unfairness with a view to protecting the data-specific interests of a party implies qualifying data as sui generis contractual subject matters although the problems raised by unequal bargaining positions in data sharing deals are neither necessarily nor at least typically related to the market failures that arguably may result from the particular characteristics of data as a public good, that is, as information or as an element of information.[43] Worse, a data-specific understanding and implementation of the standard of unfairness is likely to miss the fact that in a data-driven economy data are ordinary subject matters of commercial contracts in general and are traded both separately and as part of complex transactions the commercial unity of which requires the application of uniform standards rather than of separate standards of divergent substance.[44]

Ultimately, the point is that, although Article 13 Data Act applies only to data access and use and related obligations, the rationale of its regime of control is not to enhance the tradability of data as such; at best it is to smooth the way for commercial transactions that relate to data as an important input or output of economic activities in general, that is, it is to contribute to rendering data markets as 'liquid, fair and efficient'[45] as any market should be. In that regard, however, the legislature's concern is not about market actors' alleged fears of being exposed to practices of unilaterally imposed unfair contractual terms that it needs to address by a particular regime of quasi-regulatory control because they specifically characterise data

[42] See below II.D.i.a and b; ii.b.

[43] See the definition by Art 2(1) Data Act. For the problems that, due to asymmetric knowledge distribution, information spill-over etc, data markets might fail to function optimally see inter alia Schweitzer et al, above note 4, 70 et seq; B Lundqvist, *Regulating Data Access and Transfer of Data* (Cambridge, Cambridge University Press, 2023) 26 et seq; von Ditfurth, above note 24, 27 et seq, 38 et seq, all with references. Depending on the circumstances, the information effects of data and/or data-related externalities may, but need not, exist to an extent that they necessarily result in or substantially contribute to a firm acquiring market power; typically such power rests on many and diverse grounds. As regards more specifically unequal bargaining positions, in a data-driven economy with its general need of data sharing the asymmetry of the bargaining positions of the parties, ie the fact that a party could unilaterally impose an unfair term on another party, will result mainly from the circumstances of the contract negotiations, the relative importance that a particular data sharing agreement has for the parties and/or also from factors that are unrelated to data power, such as, inter alia, from the dependency relations existing in supply chains, the demand power of buyers of large volumes of data-related goods or services or from – often sector-specific – high levels of market concentration.

[44] It is troublesome enough that composite transactions are subject to two sets of rules, namely those of Art 13, which apply to the data-related parts of the transaction, and those of national law that apply to the other parts if the applicable national law subjects the terms of inter-business transactions to a control of their unfairness, and be it a national law that follows principles similar to those of Art. 13 Data Act, as do, eg §§ 305 BGB; for details see Wiebe (CR 2023) above note 18, paras 21, 29, 31 et seq, 36, 39 et seq; Staudenmayer, above note 28, 597 et seq.

[45] See recital 26 Data Act.

markets and impair their well-functioning.[46] Many markets are structured unevenly, and unequal bargaining positions are a wide-spread phenomenon; their exploitation by means of unfair terms is frequent enough and, therefore, a general concern of civil and commercial law.[47] Likewise, commercial transactions in which enterprises in general or enterprises of particular industrial sectors have high stakes and/or on which their business depends relate to many subject matters that concern not only the individual interest of the party to the transaction, but are also of particular interest for the economy in general or for society, such as, inter alia, medicinal products and services, the supply of essential food or the provision of goods and services mitigating climate change or protecting the environment. Rather, when the legislature of Article 13 Data Act decided to rely on rules of private law as a way to control unfair contractual terms of data-sharing agreements it opted for a regime of control that by its very nature must apply equally to any commercial transaction and irrespectively of its particular subject matter. Only a general regime will not distort inter-sectoral and/or cross-market competition and fit a data-driven economy where data sharing is general practice and relates to a broad range of products and services. It would set a – minimum! – standard of fair dealing, which rather than applying only to the data-related parts of a transaction would extend to all its parts. A split regime is unfair in itself.[48]

C. Mandatory Accessibility of 'Internet of Things (IoT) Data': A Regulatory Regime

In contrast to the general rules on unfair contractual terms of data-sharing agreements between enterprises, the substance of which Chapter IV Data Act borrows

[46] Market actors' concerns about legal obstacles to data sharing relate to uncertainty about their rights and obligations regarding data in general, in particular protection of personal data, risks of uncontrolled access by third parties and the problems of designing appropriate contracts, but hardly to particular risks of becoming exposed to non-core contractual terms that might be unfair; see inter alia, Fraunhofer Institut für Software und Systemtechnik (ed), *Anreizsysteme und Ökonomie des Data Sharings* (Incentives and Economics of Data Sharing, IEDS), March 2022, sub 3.5, at 50 et seq, accessible at www.ieds-projekt.de: As compared to organisational, technical and economic obstacles to data sharing legal obstacles account for 68 per cent, out of which 52 per cent relate to uncertainty about how to design the agreement lawfully; see also the references by von Ditfurth, above note 24, 46 et seq; misleading Commission, Staff Working Document SWD(2022)34 final of 23.2.2022, Impact Assessment Report accompanying the proposal for a Data Act, above note 7, summarising at 11 the stakeholders' replies to an online consultation: 44 per cent of replies indicating 'abuse of contractual imbalance' as an obstacle to contractual access to data as compared to 42 per cent indicating unreasonable prices. European Commission, above note 35, sub 4. (Causes of the problem) does not identify unfair terms as a particular cause, but presents only a list of issues and possible imbalances that need to be dealt with in a data-sharing agreement. However, imbalances are not an indication of unfairness (see recital 61 Data Act), and unfairness of contractual terms is not an access problem. Rather, the problem is one of sub-optimal market transactions because data-sharing agreements will be concluded despite the unfairness of their non-core terms. Thus, the question is one of determining the non-acceptable degree of imbalances of market transactions, which is a general, not a data-specific question.

[47] See references above note 44.

[48] See above note 44. It is unfair because it allows the superior party to direct the unfair use of its bargaining power to the terms of other parts of the agreement or to simply hide the abuse of its bargaining power by splitting the transaction into two agreements, one on data-sharing and one on the underlying commercial deal, eg, the sale or lease of a product, a supply agreement in a vertical value chain or a cooperative specialisation agreement.

from conventional legal concepts and casts in its single Article 13, Chapters II and III of the Data Act establish a special regime for 'IoT-data' that is intended to accelerate the general acceptance of the IoT as part of the new data-driven economy.[49] It consists of a set of mandatory legal rules that provide for and govern the accessibility of data concerning the performance, use and environment of connected products and related services (Article 1(2) lit. (a) Data Act). In its simplest form, the prototypical scenario underlying these rules is the case of the user of a connected product, typically its owner, renter or lessee, who needs to obtain the data resulting from that product's use either for itself or for enabling a third party to render it a service of some kind, these 'use data' being held, however, by another person, the data holder, typically the manufacturer (or vendor, rentor or lessor) of the connected product.[50] The relevant provisions of the Data Act are Articles 3 to 7 (Chapter II) on access of the user to the data that are generated by the use of a connected product, on the position of the data holder and on that of third parties in relation to the user and the data holder on the one hand, and, on the other, Articles 8 to 12 (Chapter III) on the obligations (and rights) of data holders that according to Article 5 of Chapter II must make data available to a data recipient.[51]

i. The Principles: Self-accessibility, Alternatively Access on Demand

According to Articles 3 and 4 Data Act, the special regime applies to data that are generated by the use of connected products and that concern its use or environment and to data that result from a related service and that represent the digitisation of user actions or events related to the connected product.[52] As it applies only to connected products, meaning products that communicate the data electronically or otherwise, and to intrinsically related services, the regime is IoT-specific and limited to ensuring the data-based functioning of connected products and related services.

Article 3(1) Data Act provides for the basic rule of this regime, which is that

> connected products shall be designed and manufactured and related services shall be designed and provided in such a manner that product data and related service data . . . are,

[49] For the concept and an illustration of the operation of the Internet of Things see recital 14 Data Act.

[50] See the definitions by Art 2(12), (15) Data Act and recitals 18, 24; see also Arts 4(10) and 6(2) lit.e) Data Act that assume the identity of data holder and manufacturer. For a detailed analysis of these triangular relations, their variations and possible extension to a pentagon of relations see Metzger and Schweitzer, above note 35, 51 et seq. The complexity of the relationships increases in cases where the data holder does not form part of a supply or distribution chain, but acts as an independent data collector and provider, eg a satellite or drone operator collecting and using (transforming) data generated by the users of agricultural machinery, cars, ships or aircraft. For the sake of simplifying the line of argument, in the following text data holder always means the manufacturer of the connected product and/or the provider of a related service.

[51] Although Chapter III mainly concerns the relationships resulting from the exercise of the access right provided for by Arts 4–7 Data Act, it is of broader application because it expressly also covers the obligations and rights of data holders that may arise under mandatory access rules of other applicable Union law or national law, eg under sectoral law (so-called horizontal concept); see Art 1(2) lit. b), Art 8(1) Data Act.

[52] For the relevant statutory definitions see Art 2(5) and (6) Data Act (connected products and related services) and Art 2(15), (16) Data Act (product data and related service data); see also below note 54.

> by default, easily, securely, free of charge, in a comprehensive, structured, commonly used and machine-readable format . . . directly accessible to the user.[53]

That is, the 'product data'[54] ought to be self-accessible for the user of the connected product or related service. Although, ultimately, the rule of Article 3(1) is hardly enforceable,[55] it is of practical importance to the extent that data that by virtue of a product's design a user can easily and securely access directly in a commonly used and machine-readable format, are 'free' data in the sense that they are not under the control of a data holder.[56] Not only the user but also any third party may access them; both may operate with them or cooperate on the basis of these data, for example as regards complementary or peripheral goods or services.[57] Thus, there is no need here for ensuring access by a particular legal regime;[58] more precisely, Article 3(1) Data Act reduces the need to the extent that is technically feasible.

[53] In addition, Art 3(2) Data Act obliges the contractor of a contract for purchase, rent or lease, which can be the manufacturer, to provide the user before the conclusion of the contract with detailed information on the functionality of the product as regards data generating and storing and, in particular on 'how the user may access, retrieve . . . erase the data, including the technical means to do so' (lit. d)), ie, Art 3(2) Data Act aims at facilitating direct access. Similarly, Art 3(3) obliges the supplier of a related service to provide the user with comprehensive information on the data the supplier of the service is to obtain as a prospective data holder, on their accessibility by the user, and on whether as a prospective data holder it expects to use the data itself or to allow to third parties to use the data for purposes agreed upon with the user; see recital 24, and for details G Ebener, M Wienröder in M Hennemann et al (eds), *Data Act* (Baden-Baden, Nomos, 2024), 56.

[54] Art 2(15) Data Act defines product data as use generated data, namely as the 'data generated by the use of a connected product that the manufacturer designed to be retrievable, via an electronic communications service, physical connection or on-device access, by a user, data holder or a third party, including, where relevant, the manufacturer'. For the nature and scope of the relevant data see in more detail recital 15 Data Act; for the definition of related service data see Art 2(16) Data Act.

[55] Even if technically conceivable, it is not possible and not intended by the Data Act to sanction a manufacturer who does not comply with Art 3(1) Data Act by way of a sales prohibition or of injunctive relief obliging it to redesign and produce a connected product in such a form that its use data become self-accessible for the user. The sanction for any deficit of self-accessibility is mandatory accessibility according to Art 4 Data Act. As noted by L Antoine, 'Datenzugangsrechte im finalen Data Act – Fortschritt, Rückschritt, neue Fragen' (2024) *CR* 1, 3; a manufacturer thus retains enough leeway for designing connected products according to its preferences for either the Art 3 regime or for that of Art 4, which latter generously satisfies its interests; see below II.C.ii; iii.c; II.D.i.

[56] Still, Art 3(1) requires the user to actively seek access to the data; see L Specht-Riemenschneider, 'Der Entwurf des Data Act' (2022) 9 *MMR Beilage* 809, 815. Thus, Art 3(1) Data Act most likely will benefit industrial users rather than end-consumers.

[57] The examples are refilling, reloading, repairing or maintenance, supplying and connecting peripheral goods or services etc; they typically correspond to the purpose of the Data Act's access rules, which is to enable 'users to benefit from aftermarket, ancillary and other services' (recital 16); see also recitals 6, 14 et seq, 30. The general idea is that since the IoT allows value to be added to products by connecting them and related services digitally to other products and services the various actually or potentially adjacent markets need to be opened, ie freed from barriers resulting from control over data by data holders.

[58] On the relationship between Art 3 and Art 4 Data Act see Specht-Riemenschneider, above note 56, 815. The wording of Art 4(5), 2nd sent., Art 4(10), Art 5(3), lit. c), Art 5(4), 2nd sent. Data Act and the rules on trade secrets (Art 4(6) to (9), Art 5(9) to (12) Data Act) and on misuse of information (Art 4(13), 2nd sent., Art 5(6) Data Act) point to the non-applicability of the regime of Arts. 4 et seq. Data Act in cases where product data are directly accessible within the meaning of Art 3 Data Act. Frictions between Art 3 and Arts 4 et seq. will arise if parts of the product data are directly accessible but others are not. Besides, Art 3 Data Act may produce undesirable side effects. First, while Art 3 Data Act defines self- accessibility from the perspective of the average (non-expert) user, it may trigger mandatory access at a rather low level and, consequently, also the application of Arts 4 to 9 Data Act, which limit the data that are accessible to the user (see text following note 60) and establish a narrow framework for the services of third parties,

In introducing such a regime of mandatory accessibility of IoT data, Article 4(1) Data Act seems to present an identically designed counterpart to self-accessibility pursuant to Article 3(1) Data Act. If and to the extent that data cannot be directly accessed by the user from the connected product or related service, Article 4(1) Data Act obliges the data holder to make the 'readily available data' accessible to the user.[59] It must do so upon simple request by the user (Article 4(1), 2nd sent.), 'without undue delay, of the same quality as is available to the data holder, easily, securely, free of charge in a comprehensive, structured, commonly used and machine-readable format, and, where relevant and technically feasible, continuously and in real time' (Article 4(1), 1st sent.). Thus, by using a language similar to that of Article 3(1) Data Act Article 4(1) seems to offer an equivalent substitute to direct accessibility in case this is not feasible and a complement in case direct access does not, as it should, reveal all product data to the user.[60] However, the scope of mandatory accessibility under Article 4 Data Act is narrower than self-accessibility as required by Article 3(1) Data Act, because Article 2(17) Data Act limits 'readily available data' to those that the data holder lawfully obtains or can lawfully obtain from the connected product or related service 'without disproportionate effort going beyond a simple operation'. In practice, this narrow definition does not set a standard of access that is equivalent to self-accessibility of all product data as required by Article 3(1) Data Act or at least one that fully conforms to the needs of the user that the Data Act is supposed to protect, such as full accessibility for maintenance and repair of a connected product by a third party or its interaction with complementary or peripheral components and related services.[61] Rather, the criterion of 'readily available data' seems to correspond to the particularity of mandatory access, which precisely is its operating by virtue of strict law, including the fact that the user must be granted access free of charge. Obviously also, it corresponds to the manufacturer's freedom to design connected products according to its interests in the accessibility of the data they generate, that

---

who, when asked for expert advice, might be able to ensure self-accessibility of the product data by the user; see below II.C.ii.c; iii; II.D.ii.a. It is to be hoped that in practice a grey area will develop between the application of Arts 3 and 4 Data Act where both the user and third parties enjoy some margin of choice. Second, since the regime of mandatory access favours the data holder (see following text and below II.C.ii., the manufacturer/data holder may tend to avoid product designs that allow self-access to the product data; see note 55 and below text following note 149.

[59] Art. 2(12) Data Act defines the user as 'a natural or legal person that owns a connected product or to whom temporary rights to use that connected product have been contractually transferred, or that receives related services'. Thus, the typical user is the owner, the renter or the lessee of connected products; see recitals 18, 24.

[60] In contrast to Art 3(1) Data Act, Art 4(1) refers to 'data' in general rather than only to 'product data'. Nevertheless, the provision does not cover all product-relevant data but only 'use data' (see above note 54), because it is the use made of the product by the user that justifies its mandatory access; see recitals 15, 18. Arts 4(1), 5 (1) of the Commission's proposal for a Data Act (above note 7) referred more clearly to 'the data generated by the use of a product or related service'. There is no reason to assume that the change of wording was meant to modify the meaning of Art 4(1) Data Act. Rather, the legislature's intention precisely was to additionally limit access to those product data that are 'readily available'; see the definition by Art 2(17) Data Act.

[61] For this purpose of the Data Act see recitals 16, 30; for the problems of interpreting the criterion of 'readily available data' in accordance with the purpose of the regime of mandatory accessibility see Daria Kim and Man Wai Kwok, Data Usability as a Parameter of Rights and Obligations under the EU Data Act, Max Planck Institute for Innovation and Competition Research Paper No. 24-04 = ssrn.com/abstract=4720900, sub III.

is, the readily available data.[62] Thus, the criterion reveals the true functioning of Article 4(1) Data Act, which is to open but a small window of mandatory accessibility of some out of the bulk of data that, in principle, the data holder may control and use as it sees fit. Irrespective of the legislature's apparent 'good intentions', much of the design of the following paragraphs of Article 4 and Articles 5 to 7 Data Act also obfuscates by seemingly user-friendly rules the strength of the position the data holder retains under the Data Act vis-à-vis both the user and third parties.

ii. The Relationships User – Data Holder – Third Party: An Uneven Triangle

a. The Positions of the User . . .

Prima facie, Chapter II of the Data Act seems to assign to the user of connected products or related services a central role in the triangular relationship data holder – user – third party.[63] In practice, however, its role is more that of a person who is in charge of opening the doors, but is not in control of their key, the data. True, by virtue of a mandatory rule of law the user may obtain access to all readily available product data, not only to the data that are specific to the particular use it makes of the connected product.[64] However, even though it may obtain such access upon simple request, where feasible through electronic means rather than only upon prior contractual agreement (Article 4(1), 2nd sent. Data Act), the user has to take that initiative,[65] and it has to become active itself because the data holder needs to grant access only in situ, that is, on the connected product or on a computing instance of the manufacturer, and essentially only to raw product data.[66] It is also true that the user is free to use the data it accessed not only in ways that are determined by the functionality of

[62] See the definition of product data by Art 2(15) Data Act (above note 54), and also recital 20 Data Act: 'Readily available data does not include data . . . where the design of the connected product does not provide for such data being stored or transmitted outside the component in which they are generated or the connected product as a whole'.

[63] See Wiebe (GRUR 2023) above note 18, 1570; Antoine, above note 55, 3.

[64] See above note 54, 60. Recital 15 describes the scope of mandatory access in detail; see also Kim and Kwok (above note 61) sub III.

[65] See recital 21 Data Act. The requirement that the user must explicitly request access does not only serve a proper identification of the user including the creation of a user account. As informal as the request may be, it triggers a special relationship between the data holder and the user that comes in addition to the contract for the acquisition, rent or lease of the connected products and entails the particular rights and duties the user and the data holder have under Arts 4 to 7 Data Act in relation to the use data. In addition, the request has a clearing function. Since the data holder is under no obligation to additionally grant access to data that are directly accessible the request is inadmissible if Art 3(1) Data Act applies; see Specht-Riemenschneider, above note 56, 815.

[66] See references above note 64; Specht-Riemenschneider, above note 56, 815 et seq. Drexl et al, above note 16, paras 65 et seq; W Kerber, 'Governance of IoT Data: Why the EU Data Act Will Not Fulfill Its Objectives' (2023) *GRUR Int* 120, 124. Art 2 Data Act does not provide for a definition of 'make . . . accessible'. The German version ('stellt . . . bereit') appears to be more user-friendly than the English text. At any rate, it seems that the data holder enjoys a certain freedom as regards the technical ways of offering access, eg., in situ or otherwise; see recital 22 in fine; Th Ehlen and Ph Sibulke, 'Der Data Act: Zwischen Markt- und Vertragsgestaltung' (2024) *CR* 84, 86, para 11; M Hennemann and B Steinrötter, 'Der Data Act' (2024) *NJW* 1, 3, para 11; K Kaesling, 'B2B und B2C-Datenzugang nach dem Data Act' (2024) *GRUR* 821, 824 et seq. For the data holder the issue is also one of cost. While it may not charge the user, it may charge a third party serving the user, Art 5(1) and recital 46 Data Act. A limit to the manufacturer's freedom to design possibly results from Art 4(4) Data Act in fine.

the connected product, but for all lawful non-commercial or commercial purposes, including the improvement or development of its own – non-competing[67] – products or services and the use by third party service providers.[68] Clearly, in most of these respects it is less the end-consumers who will benefit from mandatory data accessibility than the business users who are likely to have the broader interests in the use potential of the use data of connected products and who, in a market economy, must be expected to actively explore and exploit it.

Similarly, Article 4(13), 1st sent. Data Act, pursuant to which 'a data holder shall only use any readily available data that is non-personal data on the basis of a contract with the user' confers upon the latter a more contestable position than appears at first glance.[69] For one thing, the rule needs to be interpreted narrowly. By subjecting the use of readily available product data by the data holder to the prior consent of the user Article 4(13) 1st sent. Data Act elevates non-personal data to the level of protection of personal data,[70] but why then only the readily available product data rather than all the data that the product generates when used by a particular user?[71] And why also the use of these data by the data holder for purposes of improvement of the connected product or of developing new products?[72] There is no justification for allowing the user to control and block the use of any non-personal product data for such purposes.[73] Unless strictly limited to user-specific data, that is, personal data, the application of the rule is bound to conflict with the objectives of the Data Act,

[67] E contrario Art 4(10) Data Act, which provides that 'the user shall not use the data obtained pursuant to a request . . . to develop a connected product that competes with the connected product from which the data originate'; see also below II.C.iii.c.

[68] See recitals 2, 26, 30 Data Act.

[69] See inter alia Ehlen and Sibulke, above note 66, 86, paras 10, 13; Metzger and Schweitzer, above note 35, 54; Drexl et al, above note 16, paras 46 et seq; M Leistner and L Antoine, 'IPR and the use of open data and data sharing initiatives by public and private actors', Study commissioned on request of the Committee of Legal Affairs by the European Parliament's Policy Department for Citizen's Rights and Constitutional Affairs, Brussels 2022, 92 et seq (available at www.europarl.europa.eu/supporting-analyses).

[70] The legislature seems to favour the assimilation of non-personal use data to personal data as a way of synchronising the exercise by the user of its rights in personal data with the pursuit of its interest in monetising the non-personal data; see recitals 34, 35 Data Act; for a critique see Metzger and Schweitzer, above note 35, 54/55; Leistner and Antoine, above note 69, 92.

[71] And if the reason for requiring consent by the user is a need for parallel treatment of personal and non-personal data, why require consent only for the data the use of which a particular user expressly claims under Art 4(1) Data Act rather than also for the use of data generated by other users? Recitals 15, 18 Data Act do not convincingly answer the question why the user may control the use of the product data as if they were its own; see below II.D.ii.a and b.

[72] See recital 25 Data Act. This begs the question whether by refusing access to a user that does not agree to legitimate use of the product data by the data holder that data holder violates Art 4(1) or (4) Data Act, and, if so, whether irrespective of the application of Art 102 TFEU or of national competition law a user's refusal to consent to the use of the product data by the data holder may constitute a misuse of its position under Art 4(13) Data Act; see also Leistner and Antoine, above note 69, 93, and below note 191. Whatever the answer, Art 4(13) Data Act is likely to become a source of conflicts that impede effective data sharing within due time.

[73] Drexl et al, above note 16, para 49 rightly point out that the user is in no legal position that justifies Art 4(13) Data Act, because it is the very nature of non-personal data that they be freely used by whoever is in control of them. Nevertheless, they see a need for a consent requirement protecting the user against misuse of the data of a powerful data holder as provided for by Art 4(13), 2nd sent. Data Act. However, there is no reason to assume that the user typically needs more protection against misconduct by the data holder than the latter needs against a user misusing its position.

which are to enhance competition and innovation in the digital economy.[74] Worse, in case of a business-to-business relationship between the user and the data owner it invites collusive market dividing as the tacit or implicit basis or part of a data-sharing agreement,[75] which the parties might otherwise conclude voluntarily anyway out of their own, independent interest. For the same reason, the notion of 'use' of the readily available product data by the data holder needs to be construed narrowly. By definition, the data holder has control of the data. Why should it and how could it be prevented from observing them,[76] for instance as regards the connected product's deficits of performance and potential improvement? If at all, then only those acts may need the user's consent by which the data holder actively exploits the value potential that readily available data may have on the market.

b. ... of the Data Holder ...

For another thing, in the prototypical case of the data holder being also the manufacturer of a connected product, at least the user who is an end-consumer will hardly ever be in a bargaining position that enables it to benefit from Article 4(13), 1st sent. Data Act by refusing or limiting the use of the readily available product data by the data holder. Even though the data holder may not by contractual stipulation prevent the user from using the data itself or from outsourcing their use to a third party pursuant to Article 5(1) Data Act,[77] it may always make the conclusion of the contract for the sale, rent or lease of the connected product dependent on the user's consent to the use of the data by the data holder for lawful purposes.[78] Most likely, such tying of the contract required by Article 4(13), 1st sent. Data Act to the contract on the supply of the connected product will be a matter of the standard terms of the latter contract,[79] and it may result in the data holder/manufacturer competing freely with third parties on aftermarkets and/or on adjacent or ancillary markets, always provided that when asking for consent the data holder/manufacturer abstains from directly or indirectly exercising undue pressure (Article 4(4) Data Act). As a result, Article 4(13), 1st sent.

[74] See recitals 25, 32 Data Act.

[75] Since the parties to an agreement under Art 4(13), 1st sent. Data Act may define the use the data holder may make of the product data, Art 4(13), 1st sent. potentially defeats the purpose of Art 4(5) Data Act pursuant to which the data holder may not, for the purpose of user verification, require the user to provide any information beyond what is necessary to this effect, in particular not information on the use the user will make of the product data. The purpose of this rule is to prevent a competitively relevant information exchange regarding the user's business plans; see Metzger and Schweitzer, above note 35, 55. However, Art 4(13) negotiations will result in exactly such information to the benefit of the user and, despite Art 4(13), 2nd sent. Data Act, indirectly or implicitly also to the benefit of the data holder. Contract negotiations do reveal the parties' positions. As a practical matter, the protection of the interests of the user by Art 4(13), 2nd sent. Data Act is both excessive and elusive; contra Drexl et al, above note 16, paras 50 et seq; see also below II.C.iii.b.

[76] This follows a fortiori from general concepts of copyright law, in particular software copyright law, Art 5(3) Dir 2009/24/EC on the legal protection of computer programs; see also Metzger and Schweitzer, above note 35, 54, n. 41. Despite the importance of the term 'use', the catalogue of definitions of Art 2 Data Act does not list it but only the term 'processing' (No. 7) as a general term including 'collection, recording ... use' of data.

[77] Art 7(2) Data Act; as regards outsourcing the use of use data to third parties, see below II.C.ii.c.

[78] See recital 25 Data Act.

[79] Specht-Riemenschneider, above note 56, 816 et seq (820); Wiebe (GRUR 2023), above note 18, 1571; Ehlen and Sebulke, above note 34, 87, para 15.

Data Act will hardly impair the business of manufacturers of connected mass products other than by imposing on them another bureaucratic burden and the risk of legal disputes with consumer associations should the manufacturers' lawyers draft the standard terms too one-sidedly.

In case the user of a connected product is an enterprise it may wish to take more advantage of its position under Article 4(13), 1st sent. Data Act, but the negotiating and contracting practices of the manufacturer/data holder will not differ fundamentally. Of course, it cannot limit or exclude the use of the readily available product data by the business user, except if the latter would violate the non-competition rule of Article 4(10) Data Act.[80] However, the manufacturer/data holder will make sure that the sale, rent or lease of its connected products does not negatively affect its own business interests by contractual terms that restrict the actual and potential use it needs to make itself of the readily available product data. The Data Act does not object to such conduct since it is in furtherance of its objectives, namely a broad use of data that serves inter alia to improve existing connected products or develop new connected products.[81] Rather, the problematic power relationship between the manufacturer/data holder and the business user is the reverse one, where the latter is able to exercise some demand power that results, for example, from dependency in a supplier-assembler relationship, from the volume of the connected products the user wishes to buy, rent or lease,[82] or from the particular nature of the connected product. If in such a case the bargaining positions of the parties are more or less equal, issues of mandatory accessibility of product data may not even arise as the parties may agree on a broader data-sharing agreement anyway.[83] If, however, the business user wishes to retain all or essential parts of product data for its own use, for instance because it is worried about the manufacturer/data holder becoming a competitor on one of its own markets, and if, due to its market position, it is able to exercise to this effect the power it has under Article 4(13) Data Act, the purpose of the Data Act will be put in jeopardy. The open question then is whether the control of unfair contractual terms pursuant to Article 13 Data Act and/or the control of the abuse of market power pursuant to Article 102 TFEU will suffice to overcome an over-protectionist application of Article 4(13), 1st sent. Data Act and contain the problem.

Similarly, in its relationship with a third party, the user will find itself in a less comfortable position then a literal reading of the relevant provisions of the Data Act (Articles 5 to 12)[84] suggest. It is true that when dealing with a third party, such as a

[80] See below II.C.iii.c.

[81] See recitals 25, 32 Data Act, the latter recital pointing to the need to preserve the interest of the data holder in investing in new connected products under the umbrella of the non-competition rules of Art 4(10) and 6(2) lit.e) Data Act.

[82] Think of a car rental firm or of a transportation firm that buys its fleet of cars from a car manufacturer or leases it from a financing subsidiary of the car manufacturer and needs the data not only for doing maintenance and repair itself (rather than having it done by the car manufacturer), but also for the management of the operation of its fleet. It may, therefore, wish to keep some control over 'its' data rather than share them with the manufacturer or with the lessor even though they also have a legitimate interest in using these data. The aircraft and shipbuilding industries may offer similar examples.

[83] See recital 26 Data Act.

[84] Despite the structure of the Data Act, Arts 8 to 12 really do not constitute a separate chapter, but a complement of Chapter II in that they define the rights and obligation that the data holder and third parties have under Arts 5 and 6 Data Act.

provider of repair or maintenance services or a supplier of peripheral components or services the connected product is designed to communicate with,[85] it is the user who determines the purpose and the conditions of the use of data by the third party (Article 6(1) Data Act). It is also in the interest of the user – and in its own interest! – that the data holder may not make data available to third parties for purposes other than the fulfilment of their contract with the user (Article 6(14) Data Act). However, except for this basic autonomy regarding the scope of use of the data, the Data Act provides for a surprising limit of the user's freedom of contracting with third parties, namely its free choice of the contract partner. By an abstract per se-rule of interventionist nature that is entirely misplaced in a general framework regulation of the data market, Articles 5(3), 6(2) lit. d) Data Act exclude a priori and with per se effect designated 'gatekeepers' within the meaning of Article 3 Regulation (EU) 2022/1925 (Digital Markets Act, DMA) from eligibility as third parties as if their position and conduct on the market were inherently anticompetitive and disadvantageous to users.[86] However, the opposite may be true as well, and there is also an issue of the freedom of contracting in general and of the user's freedom of choice, in particular.[87]

c) . . . and of the Third Party

Surprisingly also, although Article 4(1) Data Act aims at putting the user in a position that is equivalent to self-accessibility of product data, it apparently is not generally expected to itself make the 'readily available data' available to a third party. It is true that if a user 'receives' the data in an appropriate form and is willing and expert enough to make them directly available to a third party, it may do so.[88] However, it

[85] See above note 57.

[86] Compare the catalogue of practices by gatekeepers that Arts 5 and 6 DMA qualify as unlawful.

[87] See the critique by Drexl et al, above note 16, paras 90 et seq; Metzger and Schweitzer, above note 35, 59; T Gerpott, 'Vorschlag für ein europäisches Datengesetz' (2022) *CR* 271, 276, para 24. The strict non-eligibility of gatekeepers as third parties may go at the expense of the user and even of the data holder/manufacturer, in particular if a gatekeeper is the single source for the optimal use of the product data.

[88] See recital 30 Data Act which states that the user may provide 'the data the user has received while exercising its rights under this Regulation . . . to a third party . . . or . . . instruct the data holder to do so. The request should be submitted by the user'. The first alternative clearly points to the user being permitted to make the data it has received directly available to a third party with the result that Arts 5, 8 and 9 Data Act are not applicable see Metzger and Schweitzer, above note 35, 58: Antoine, above note 55, 5, para 24 in fine; Wiebe (GRUR 2023), above note 18, 1572, left col. Permitting the user to directly make the data available to a third party is not without problems. The logic of the triangular contractual relationship rests on the idea of the co-generation of the product data in the sense that, on the manufacturers/data holder's side, they are determined by the functionality of the product design, and, on the user's side, by the use made of the product. The idea then is that the manufacturer/data holder and the user should be allowed to 'share' the value potential of the data by putting them to use independently either themselves or by making them directly accessible to a third party (see Specht-Riemenschneider, above note 56, 816, 819 et seq, 823; Antoine, above note 55, 2, paras 3, 26 et seq, Leistner and Antoine, above note 69, 92 et seq. If, however, for fear of the third party's uncontrolled intervention and competition with the data holder that idea appears to be not acceptable, then the triangular relationship may not be understood as allowing the – often enough less expert and/or less invested – user to bypass the manufacturer/data holder, who is legally obliged to make the data available to it and to do so at no charge, by directly 'selling' the data to a third party that is an industrial firm and most likely a competitor of the manufacturer/data holder on aftermarkets. Nor should such third party have a way of directly obtaining Art 4(1) data at no or little cost from a generous user.

may not to this effect use the service – and not even the advice? – of a third party.[89] Instead, pursuant to Article 5(1) Data Act, the user must request the data holder to 'make the readily available data available . . . to a third party' whereupon the data holder must make them available to the third party in accordance with Articles 8 and 9 Data Act, that is by way of a separate agreement with the third party regarding 'the arrangements for making the data available' (Article 8(1) Data Act). Depending on the circumstances, such direct communication between the third party and the data holder may serve the interests of the user, because often enough and in particular if the user is the end-consumer it is the third party that, due to its expertise, is best placed to assess which product data are needed and in which form. In addition, the true need may become apparent only over time during the performance of the contract with the user. However, due to the necessity of involving the data holder, the user may become exposed to frictions occurring in the relationship between the data holder and the third party.[90] Instead of being the sovereign consumer as which the Data Act seems to see it, the user becomes involved in the conflicts between the data holder and the third party, as their interests are bound to collide whenever the data holder and the third party are competitors, which they are likely to be on aftermarkets and ancillary or otherwise adjacent markets.[91] The problem is evidenced, but obviously not solved by Articles 4(4) and 6(2) lit. a) Data Act, which oblige the data holder and the third party, respectively, to abstain from unduly impairing the exercise of the rights and choices the user has under Chapter II. At any rate, whatever its terms, ultimately the contractual arrangement between the data holder and the third party is likely to be at the expense of the user because the latter has to pay for the costs that the third party has incurred in order to provide its supplies and/or services for the user.[92]

Clearly, in this respect, much will depend on the third party's market position. However, although the Data Act aims at strengthening third parties as competitors of data holders on aftermarkets and ancillary markets, it does little to make them active market participants. Thus, while it is supposed to take a strong interest in broad access to product data,[93] a third party must get along with an access claim that is derived from and possibly limited by the claim the user raises under Article 5(1) Data Act. By providing that 'a data holder shall not make data available to a data recipient . . . unless requested to do so by the user under Chapter II',[94] Article 8(4) Data Act expressly confirms that a third party has no way of directly approaching a data holder. It is apparently because of this squeezed-in position of the third party rather than

[89] Again, the access regime appears to be too rigid; see above note 58. In addition, if at all, then it will be the business user rather than the end-consumer that most will benefit from the option to make the data it accessed according to Art 4(1) Data Act directly available to a third party.

[90] See Drexl et al, above note 16, para 71.

[91] See recitals 16, 20, 32 Data Act.

[92] See Drexl et al, above note 16, para 72.

[93] See recitals 16, 26, 30, 32 Data Act. Obviously, providing third parties merely with a derived claim to access constitutes an inefficient incentive for them to enter into innovative competition on aftermarkets or ancillary markets; see also above note 58 and below text at note 102 and sub II.D.ii.a, in particular text at note 192 et seq.

[94] Art 2(14) Data Act defines data recipient as 'a . . . person, acting for purposes which are related to that person's trade, business, craft or profession, other than the user . . . to whom the data holder makes data available, including a third party following a request by the user to the data holder'.

because of a data holder's presumed market power alone[95] that Article 8(1) Data Act subjects the 'arrangement' between the data holder and a third party to a requirement of compatibility with fair, reasonable and non-discriminatory terms and conditions (so-called FRAND terms) and, in this way, seeks to protect the latter against the data holder abusively exploiting its statutorily reinforced bargaining position. However, here as in other contexts of regulatory market intervention, FRAND terms are poor substitutes for freely negotiated, market-determined contractual terms. They merely simulate adequate market conditions and equal bargaining positions of the parties. Due to their vagueness, FRAND terms become workable only when specified according to the circumstances of a particular case. Thus, Article 8(1) Data Act is likely to be more a source of litigation than a support of the third party,[96] particularly so in the critical, but typical case of the data holder and the third party being competitors on aftermarkets or ancillary or neighbouring markets. In addition, Article 8(3) Data Act, pursuant to which a third party may request the data holder to provide information explaining the non-discriminatory character of the conditions of their arrangement, while well-intended and cautious in distributing the burden of proof, introduces an adversarial rather than a cooperative element into the negotiation and the relation between the data holder and the third party that will not necessarily improve the latter's position.

As it constitutes the core of FRAND terms, the compensation that the third party has to pay the data holder for making data available (Article 9 Data Act) may entail similar problems. However, it is not these problems but the compensation itself which makes the third party remain on the short side of the triangle user – data holder – third party. Even though the compensation may cover only 'the costs incurred . . . in making the data available',[97] and 'should not be understood to constitute payment for the data itself',[98] that is, may not be equated with royalties for the use of the data,[99] it constitutes a burden for the third party that is not to be easily justified, in particular not as regards its including a margin (Article 9(1) Data Act). According to recital 46, Article 9 Data Act aims at promoting 'continued investment in generating and making

[95] Contra Metzger and Schweitzer, above note 35, 64. It is the privileged position that Arts 4(1), (14), 5(1), 6((2) lit. c), and 8(4) Data Act confer on the user and the data holder, respectively, that renders third parties dependent on their joint consent.

[96] More optimistic are Metzger and Schweitzer, above note 35, 66 et seq. It is true that, whereas in the context of litigation on standard essential patents (SEP) issues of determining FRAND licensing terms typically are raised by a defendant being sued for infringement, in the context of Arts 8 and 9 Data Act FRAND conditions are likely to be asked for as part of an access claim of the third party. However, the difficulties of a proper interpretation and application of FRAND conditions are essentially the same. In both hypotheses they exacerbate dependency and burden effective and timely access. For a conceptual analysis see C Ducuing and L Schirru, 'Making Data Available under FRAND Terms' in C Ducuing, T Margoni and L Schirru (eds), White Paper on the Data Act Proposal, CITIP Working Paper 2022, KU Leuven Centre for IT & IP Law; N Gajek and J Hegener, 'Datenzugang nach FRAND-Kriterien' (2024) *GRUR* 1068.

[97] Art 9(2) lit. a) Data Act, which expressly includes 'the costs necessary for the formatting of data, dissemination via electronic means' and 'storage'. Recital 47 Data Act makes clear that the cost of collecting or producing data are not covered, whereas the costs of 'facilitating concrete data requests' may be included. Art 9(2) lit. (b) Data Act does not apply in Art 5(1) cases.

[98] Recital 46, penultimate sent. Data Act.

[99] At least in the context of Arts 5(1), 9(2) lit. (a) Data Act, it is, therefore, misleading to refer to the term 'royalty' as used in the context of licensing intellectual property; but see Metzger and Schweitzer, above note 35, 69 et seq.

available valuable data' by the data holder. This aim is in conflict with the Data Act's very concept of mandatory access. The majority of the data in question are 'use' data, which the user generated and may receive free of charge directly from the data holder (Article 4(1) Data Act). If for whatever reason, such as its lack of expertise, the user wishes to have a third party intervening on its behalf, Article 5(1) Data Act provides that upon its request the data holder must make these data available to that third party in the same form as if the user claimed access for itself. Therefore, both provisions stand in a complementary relationship and, in that relationship, are intended to serve as a substitute to self-accessibility of the data, that is, they purport to make the data as perfectly available to the user as are self-accessible data. Article 9(1) lit. a) Data Act undercuts this concept,[100] and it so does without sufficient justification. To the extent that Article 5(1) Data Act aims at enabling third parties to render services concerning existing connected products, such as repair and maintenance and the like, the incentive rationale of promoting investment by the data holder in generating valuable data is irrelevant. To the extent that the incentive is meant to promote continued investment by the data holder in generating valuable data in the future, a system of compensating only for the costs of making data available will hardly be effective, except if the profit margin is blown up. At any rate, incentivising only investments by the data holder conflicts with the Data Act's goal of also furthering innovation by third parties competing on aftermarkets and ancillary or adjacent markets.[101]

Admittedly, in a data-driven economy use data of products generally are not as directly accessible as they used to be at least for expert third parties, in particular the craftspeople, in the old analogue economy. Arguably, this basic factual difference would justify granting third parties a direct claim to access to product data, and be it only for specified purposes.[102] This would enable them to compete with the manufacturers for the corresponding services independently of a prior consent by users. Such a claim would reduce their double handicaps, which are, first, that they need to wait for individual users to ask for their service, whereas use data are useful only if collected from a multitude of users.[103] Second, given that they have to wait for

[100] See Metzger and Schweitzer, above note 35, 69; also Specht-Riemenschneider, above note 56, 823 left col. According to recital 46 Data Act, the legislature was well aware of the conflict, but struck a compromise that does not satisfy any of the Data Act's objectives. Its suggestion that the profit margin may be reduced because and to the extent that the data are co-generated by the user (recital 47) only shifts the conflict to the parties.

[101] See recital 32 Data Act.

[102] See also text at note 93. For a general critique of third parties being refused the right to obtain direct access to the data held by the data holder see inter alia R Podszun, *Der EU Data Act und der Zugang zu Sekundärmärkten am Beispiel des Handwerks* (Baden-Baden, Nomos, 2022) 62 and throughout.

[103] This means that third parties will find it difficult to obtain sufficient access to data resulting from the use of end-consumer products. Recital 47 Data Acts suggests 'long-term arrangements between data holders and data recipients, for instance via a subscription model or the use of smart contracts', but does so in respect of business relationships only. At any rate, this suggestion does not alleviate the problem of complying with the requirement of user-per-user consent. Framework agreements may help, but often enough are not in the interest of the manufacturer; see E Macher and J Graf Ballestrem, 'Der neue EU Data Act: Zugang zu Daten – und Geschäftsgeheimnissen?' (2023) *GRUR Prax* 661, paras 25 et seq. At any rate, such framework agreements pre-suppose a cooperative relationship between the manufacturer and a third party rather than a competitive one. Concomitantly, third-party providers of repair or maintenance services and the like may try to reach framework agreements providing for opt-in consent mechanisms with the users, at least with large users or groups of users. All of this is evidence of the bureaucratic transaction processes the Data Act entails; see also below note 147.

such consent, third parties suffer from a time lag. By contrast, manufacturers, which quite naturally are familiar with the functionality and functioning of their products, benefit from a head start for offering the necessary and/or complementary services to users.[104] All these factual disadvantages will be compounded by the probability that, due to the difficulties of verifying the costs and the adequacy of the margin included in the compensation for making data available, that compensation will be nothing else and nothing less than the price the data holder sets and is likely to obtain from the third party as a matter of efficient negotiation practice.[105]

iii. A Triangle within a Protective Frame

The data holder's disclosure obligations regarding non-discrimination (Article 8(4) Data Act) and cost calculation (Article 9(7) Data Act) relate to fairness in contracting. As such they form part of a protective frame that the Data Act establishes for the triangular relationship between the user, the data holder and the third party. It reveals how the legislature perceives the power relations between these actors. These run along four lines: preserving the individual's autonomy, delimiting established businesses, maintaining control of product data, and providing for dispute settlement and adjudication.[106]

a. Preserving Individual Autonomy

In the first regard, the legislature sees mainly the user to be in need of protection against an unfair exploitation by the data holder or the third party of the superior position they may hold on the market. Article 4(4) Data Act provides that

> data holders shall not make the exercise of choices or rights under this Article by the user unduly difficult, including by offering choices to the user in a non-neutral manner or by subverting or impairing the autonomy, decision making or choices of the user via the structure, design, function or manner of operation of a user digital interface or a part thereof.

Article 6(2) lit. a) Data Act subjects the third party to a similarly worded prohibition. The question is which function these provisions are to fulfil. Clearly, as far as the prohibition relates to practices using the structure, design, function or manner of operation of a user digital interface in order to influence a user's choice, it covers a

[104] The more so as the manufacturer/data holder may secure itself the possibility to use the product data already when selling or letting the connected product; see above II.C.ii.b, text at note 79.

[105] Art 9(7) Data Act will not help. It provides that 'The data holder shall provide the data recipient with information setting out the basis for the calculation of the compensation in sufficient detail that the data recipient can assess whether the requirements of paragraphs 1 to 4 are met'. Although, unlike the information the data holder has to provide in case the data recipient suspects contractual conditions to be discriminatory (Art 8(4), 2nd sent. Data Act), the cost-calculation sheet seems to be a formal requirement that the data holder always has to submit during contract negotiations rather than only upon request by the data recipient, challenging it will be an option only if the data recipient is prepared for a dispute.

[106] Art 10 Data Act provides for the settlement by certified dispute bodies of disputes between enterprises that relate to Arts 8, 9 and 13 Data Act. The matter cannot be dealt with here. Adjudication of disputes comes within the jurisdiction of Member States' courts. However, a data holder's refusal to grant access to data on grounds of trade secret protection may be brought before administrative bodies of Member States (so-called 'competent authorities', Art 37 Data Act); see Arts 4(9), 5(12) Data Act, and below II.D.i.a.

data-specific technical aspect that is a concern of competition law anyway. Therefore, the first question to answer is why and, if so, how the prohibition should apply irrespective of the conditions and criteria to which it would be subject as a rule of competition law.[107] Second, both this data-specific aspect of the prohibition and its broader focus on the data holder or a third party unduly interfering with the user's rights and choices ultimately relate to the same concern of the legislature, namely that of preserving the individual's autonomy. Since this is a general concern, the question is why the Data Act restates it as a matter of principle, a question that is the more troubling as it restates this general concern in the broadest, normatively elusive terms. The examples that come to mind in addition to those known from competition law, such as requests by the data holder or the third party for an unduly broad scope of the user's consent to their use of the product data, obviously ask for at least some legislative guidance as to when a request is 'unduly' broad. Such guidance is the more needed as Member States' courts will tend to interpret Articles 4(4) and 6(2) lit. a) Data Act by reference to the general good faith principles of the national laws that they have to apply to the contracts for the sale, rent or lease of the connected product. As a result, Articles 4(4) and 6(2) lit. a) Data Act will produce effects that in the Internal Market will differ from Member State to Member State, a development that will be reinforced by the fact that the Data Act largely leaves the sanctions for the violation and the enforcement of the prohibition to implementation by national law.[108] As worded, Articles 4(4) and 6(2) lit. a) Data Act seem to aim at more than merely preventing practices that are commonly held to be unlawful, such as misuse of the law or circumvention of the user's rights and choices. But what in addition to full compliance with their obligations does the legislature expect from the data holder and the third party, respectively?[109] Whose user's rights and choices does it have in mind, those of any user, of the business user or, more particularly, those of the end-consumer?

[107] Among the many examples, the most prominent one is self-preferencing by data holders that may not only run afoul of Art 6(5) DMA, but also of Art 102 TFEU or of national competition law, eg, § 19a(2) German Act Against Restraints of Competition (GWB); see CJEU of 10 September 2024, case C-48/22 P, *Google et al v Commission*, ECLI:EU:C:2024:726; for the literature inter alia G Colangelo, 'Antitrust Unchained: The EU's Case Against Self-Preferencing' (2023) *GRUR Int* 538; Lundqvist, above note 43, 76 et seq; J Bodenstein and S Zinndorf, 'Digitales Selbstbevorzugungsverbot im Missbrauchssrecht: Müssen Plattformen den Wettbewerber doch zum eigenen Nachteil fördern?' (2024) *ZWeR* 1; for a systematic analysis of the relationship between the Data Act, the DMA and general competition law see H Schweitzer and A Metzger, 'Data Access under the Draft Data Act, Competition Law and the DMA. Opening Data Treasures for Competition and Innovation?' (2023) *GRUR Int* 337.

[108] Art 11(5) Data Act covers only violations of Art 6(2) lit. a), b) Data Act by a third party, but not violations of Art 4(4) Data Act by the data holder. In addition, the sanctions provided for by Art 11(2) Data Act do not fit violations of Art 6(2), lit. a), b) Data Act, see below II.D.i.c.

[109] Recital 38 Data Act suggests that Arts 4(4) and 6(2) lit. a) Data Act also aim at preventing unfair practices, such as the use of 'dark patterns' or similar manipulative techniques.
Note that the provisions only oblige the data holder or the third party to abstain from impairing the user's freedom, but do not oblige them to take affirmative action. More particularly, the data holder need not facilitate access to the data beyond what is required by Art 4(1) Data Act or store data, at least not if it has no reason to expect a request for access; see D Bomhard and M Merkle, 'Der Entwurf eines Data Act' (2022) *RDi* 168, paras 41 et seq, Specht-Riemenschneider, above note 56, 815. Therefore, Art 4(4) Data Act may not be relied upon to improve access by end-consumers, as once recommended by commentators of the Commission's Proposal for a Data Act (above note 7); see Specht-Riemenschneider, ibid at 816 et seq.

As apparently required by the regulatory nature and purpose of its access regime, the Data Act is less concerned with the rights and choices that the data holder or the third party may have vis-à-vis the user. The Act subjects the data holder to the rules on data access (Article 4 Data Act) simply because it is in control of the data. Yet, neither before nor upon making the data available may it use those data without contractual permission by the user (Article 4(13) Data Act), that is, it seems to have no right in or to the data.[110] As mentioned, the Data Act does not allow the third party to independently obtain product data from the data holder (Article 8(4) Data Act), but instead makes their use by a third party entirely dependent on consent by the user (Article 6(1) Data Act). In either relationship, the grant of the consent by the user or its refusal or limitation is not subject to any control. The general rules apply, and do so mainly to the advantage of the data holder,[111] but hardly to that of the third party, who typically comes in only after the data holder.[112] It is only exceptionally that they may come in for controlling the user, namely only in case it dominates the market and abuses its position in ways competition laws forbid. Thus, the concept of the Act remains intact, which is that the data holder is presumed to be in a superior position and the user in need of protection. The Data Act generously affords the user that protection as a matter of law, but it does not modify the power relations between the user and the data holder or between the user and third parties. The fact that the third party has no direct access to the data held by the data holder but needs the consent of the user does not reduce the latter's dependency on an adequate offer by an expert third party or improve its position otherwise. To the contrary, it only frustrates the autonomy of the third party and impairs its ability to offer a broad spectrum of innovative goods or services.

As regards, the relationship between the data holder and a third party, the Act is not concerned with their contracting freedom at all. It subjects the contractual arrangement on the use of the product data by the third party to a regulatory regime, namely to FRAND terms, thus to conditions as if perfect competition existed on the relevant market (Articles 8 and 9 Data Act). The aim seemingly is to protect the third party, but again, the power relations are not fundamentally modified. The Data Act recognises the existence of unequal bargaining positions and subjects the exploitation of a superior position only to marginal control (Articles 8(2), 13 Data Act).[113] In addition, it accepts tel quel the costs that the data holder incurs when making data available (Article 9)2) lit. a) Data Act), and it does only little to make the non-discrimination rule of Article 8(3) Data Act more effective than the prohibition of discrimination provided for by European and national competition law.[114] Ultimately, the FRAND regime of Articles 8 and 9 Data Act seems to be not so much conceived of as a – minimum – protection of the third party's autonomy regarding its relations

[110] But see below II.D.i.b and c. At any rate, the data holder may observe and analyse the data, see above note 76.

[111] See text above text at note 78 et seq.

[112] See text above, text following note 103 et seq.

[113] See above II.B.

[114] Since discriminatory practices by a data holder will be effective and harm competition only if the data holder has at least relational market power, competition law may generally protect third parties sufficiently. See in addition to Arts 101(1) lit. d), 102 lit. c) TFEU inter alia § 20 GWB or art 442-1(4) French code de commerce. Besides, if the legislature intended to establish a general non-discrimination rule, the user also should be subject to it.

with the data holder than as a regulatory mechanism that, however imperfectly, helps contain the costs within reasonable limits that a third party is likely to pass on to the user.[115] In this respect, Article 8 and in particular Article 9 Data Act only confirm the supporting role Articles 5(1), 6(1) and 8(4) Data Act assign to the third party.

b. Delimiting Business Spheres

Another part of the protective frame in which the legislature cast the triangular relations between the user, the data holder and third parties relates to the delimitation of the business interests of the parties. For one thing, Article 4(13), 2nd sent. and Article 5(6) Data Act provide that

> A data holder shall not use any readily available data to derive insights about the economic situation, assets and production methods of or the use by the user (the third party) in any other manner that could undermine the commercial position of that user (third party) on the markets on which the user (the third party) is active.[116]

By their broad wording both provisions reach beyond the protection of trade secrets and beyond preventing direct industrial espionage. Rather, they seem to be motivated by the legislature's concern for the particular risks that, due to its sensitive subject matter and to the technical interaction during data access, a mandatory regime of access to data may imply.[117] However, they also read like a *protestatio facta contraria* because the data holder does have the readily available data, and it does have them as part of all the data it collects. Therefore, it more or less has the 'insights' already. Even if Article 4(13), 2nd sent. and Article 5(6) Data Act mean insights resulting from data that are derived from the readily available raw data, gaining such insights need not require a particular analytic effort.[118] Besides, insights do not as such 'undermine' the commercial position of the user or the third party, but will do so only if used for this purpose or to this effect. Therefore, in order to make the provisions practically applicable, the legislature ought to have specified the criteria that render acts of 'deriving insights' or of 'undermining' the user's or third party's commercial position unlawful. It should also clarify in relation to whom the commercial position of the user or of the third party may not be undermined: in relation to their competitors, in respect of the relationship between the user and the third party, or only in relation to the data holder? Arguably, one of the objectives of Article 4(13) 2nd sent. and

[115] See above text at note 92.

[116] The wording of Art 4(13), 2nd sent. and Art 5(6) Data Act differ in that the latter provision adds 'unless the third party has given permission to such use and has the technical possibility to easily withdraw that permission at any time'. At least when the user is an enterprise, Art 4(13), 2nd sent. Data Act needs to be complemented by the same rule of exception.

[117] See on the ambiguous rationale of the provisions P Picht, 'Caught in the Acts: Framing Mandatory Data Access Transactions under the Data Act, further EU Digital Regulation Acts, and Competition Law', Max Planck Institute for Innovation and Competition Research Paper No 22-12, 20: Drexl et al, above note 16, para 50 assume that Art 4(13), 2nd sent. Data Act is inspired by both trade secret law and data protection law, but that rationale does not explain the broad terms of the provision and it does not really fit Art 5(6) Data Act.

[118] The access request may by itself provide insights into the user's or the third party's needs and business practice, production methods or use of the connected product, and the data may yield insights into the ways in which the connected product is used.

Article 5(6) Data Act is to prevent a data holder from misusing its position in order to increase the dependency of the user and/or the third party as part of an ecosystem it leads. More generally, the provision may be understood as rules shielding the business spheres of the user and the third party against a data holder's attempt to undermine their independence.

The legislature's concern about keeping the parties separate inside the triangle by protecting the integrity of their business spheres relates to each of them. Thus, the user 'shall not use such data (i.e. the data obtained pursuant to Art. 4(1) Data Act) to derive insights about the economic situation, assets, and production methods of the manufacturer or, where applicable the data holder' (Article 4(10), 3rd alt. Data Act).[119] Article 6(2) lit. e) Data Act subjects the third party to the same obligation of non-interference with the business sphere of the data holder. However, unlike Article 4(13), 2nd sent. and Article 5(6) Data Act, neither Article 4(10) nor Article 6(2) Data Act qualify their non-interference rules by requiring that the insights the user or the third party derive from the data 'could undermine the commercial position' of the manufacturer or the data holder. Still, for the reasons given above and as a matter of ensuring the consistent operation of the law the qualifying criterion needs to read into Article 4(10), 3rd alt. and Article 6(2), lit. (e) Data Act. At any rate, the non-interference rule to which the user and the third party are subject may not be understood as a complement or an extension of the non-competition rules that the same Articles 4(10) and 6(2) lit. e) Data Act provide for. These rules are broad enough anyway.

c. Exclusivity on Product Markets

According to Article 4(10), 1st alt. and Article 6(2) lit. e), 1st alt. Data Act the user and the third party shall not use data they obtain or receive pursuant to Articles 4(1) or 5(1) Data Act, respectively, to develop a connected product that competes with the connected product from which the data originate.[120] In accordance with the Data Act's focus on competition on aftermarkets and ancillary markets, these non-competition rules do not cover the development of related services.[121] The aim of the rules is 'to avoid undermining the investment incentives for the type of connected product from which the data are obtained' by the user or the third party developing interchangeable or substitute products.[122] The rules thus exclude horizontal competition by the user or a third party on the same market on which the data

[119] Despite its concern about the third party unduly exploiting the position it enjoys in its relationship with the user (see Art 6(2) lit. a), b), h) Data Act), the Data Act does not provide for a rule preventing a third party from interfering with the business sphere of the user, nor, a fortiori, for a rule preventing the user from interfering with that of the third party. Whereas in the latter case the risk of interference appears to be negligible, in the former it may not be that negligible. The Data Act's focus is only on the data holder, its aggressiveness and vulnerability.

[120] Although the wording of the provisions varies slightly, they must be read in the same way. Art 6(2) lit. e) Data Act does not expressly refer to Art 5(1) Data Act, but it applies only to Art 5(1) cases; see Art 5(1) and the heading of Art 6 Data Act. Given this context, Art 6(2) lit. e) Data Act may cover only the development of connected products by the third party, not any product that competes with the connected product from which the data originate; see Art 4(10) Data Act and recital 32.

[121] Recitals 6, 16, 32.

[122] Recital 32.

holder competes for its connected products, the 'same market' being defined as it is generally understood by competition law.[123] It is precisely for this reason that the rules on non-competition were criticised early on.[124] Not only are substitutability of products and the level of its relevance under competition law notoriously difficult to determine by reference to such fluid factors as (sufficient) differences of price, product characteristics, intended use[125] and – not mentioned by the legislature – relevant geographic markets or sales periods. Rather, by its very nature the data-driven economy draws its impulses precisely from the availability and use of data, including in particular use data.[126] Therefore, contrary to the legislature's intentions to abstain from granting exclusive rights to the data holder,[127] the rules on non-competition confer upon the data holder a position of exclusivity where exclusivity really matters, on the principal market for connected products. It does so on exactly the ground on which the protection of intellectual property rests – the disincentive effect of easy, too early imitation[128] – and at the expense of the best qualified competitors: The user, who typically is familiar with the functionalities of the connected product and, when acquiring or renting the connected product, most likely will readily allow the data holder to also use the data,[129] but may not compete with the data holder on the basis of the data its product generate when in use; the third party, typically an expert in the field, also may not compete with the data holder on the product market, but, in addition to the obligation to pay the data holder a compensation,[130] must accept that the data holder competes with it on the aftermarket and ancillary markets. In terms of innovation foregone, the opportunity costs of the non-competition rules are likely to outweigh their 'incentive effect',[131] the more so as the data holder appears

[123] Recital 32.

[124] See inter alia Metzger and Schweitzer, above note 35, 61 et seq; Schweitzer and Metzger, above note 107, 346 et seq; Podszun, note 102, 82 et seq; Leistner and Antoine, above note 69, 88 et seq; I Graef and M Husovec, 'Seven Things to Improve in the Data Act', ssrn.com/abstract=4051793, sub 2; less critical Drexl et al, above note 16, para 87; Picht, above note 117, 19, 21.

[125] As listed by recital 32 Data Act; see also below notes 131, 177.

[126] See Metzger and Schweitzer, above note 35, and Schweitzer and Metzger, above note 107, pointing in particular to innovation by personalised connected products. Arguably, another example of the counterproductive effects of Art 4(10) Data Act would be that it may prevent the user from developing on the basis of its own use data a more or less improved version of the connected product that serves as a tool for its own manufacturing process or forms part of its own goods, ie, from switching from outsourcing to in-house supply.

[127] See recitals 6, 25 Data Act, and see text at note 209 et seq.

[128] Innovation incentives result from dynamic competition on open markets, which in conjunction with demand-side competition also determines the return on investment. Intellectual property rights, such as patents, only permit the innovator to capture the market opportunities and to defend the innovation against – too early! – imitation; for the market rationale of technological intellectual property see H Ullrich, 'Legal Protection of Innovative Technologies: Property or Policy' in O Granstand (ed), *Economics, Law and Intellectual Property* (Boston, KAP, 2003) 439, 447 et seq; H Ullrich, 'Patent Dependency Under European and European Union Patent Law' (2023) *GRUR Int* 1107, 1114, 1116 with references.

[129] See text above at note 78 et seq.

[130] See Art 9(2) lit. a) Data Act and above text following note 99.

[131] A more proportionate rule of non-competition would provide for a time limit and protect the data holder only against misuse of the data for purposes of imitation of the connected product rather than protect it against any substitute products that in some way rest on the use of data generated by the connected product, ie it would cover only identical or quasi-identical products. As they stand, the non-compete rules may have a broader scope than patent protection, which precisely does not exclude substitute competition by products the design of which learned from the patented technical teaching, but does not use it (see also

to be sufficiently shielded against direct competition by the rules on trade secrets and technical protection measures that also cover its data know-how concerning the connected product and the manufacturing methods.

D. Mandatory Accessibility of IoT Data: A Transformative Regime?

i. De Facto Control and Legal Protection of IoT Data

According to the view commonly held by legal literature, the data holder owes its power over IoT data to the fact of having them under techno-practical control. It is this position of mere de facto control which allowed the legislature to subject it without hesitation to a regime of mandatory accessibility, but which as a position of power also made it resist the pressure of that regime. As shown, although the Data Act attributes to the user the role of sort of a legal 'comptroller' of the triangular relationship between the user, the data holder and the third party, it is the data holder who remains largely in economic command.[132]

a. Mandatory Access to Trade Secrets

This economic command appears to be even reinforced in case the data held by the data holder constitute or form part of its trade secrets, because these enjoy protection by law and, thus, limit the legislature's political discretion. The attempt to maintain both the confidentiality of data and open mandatory access to them necessarily leads into a dilemma choice between mutually exclusive legislative approaches.[133] Article 4(6) Data Acts seeks to reconcile these contradictory regimes by pretending that 'trade secrets shall be preserved' through forcing the data holder to identify the confidential data and to share them with the user by way of an agreement on the 'proportionate technical and organisational measures necessary to preserve the confidentiality of the shared data, in particular in relation to third parties'.[134] Only if the parties cannot reach such an agreement may the data holder withhold the identified data. However, it must duly substantiate its decision, provide it in writing to the user and notify

below note 177). Even if the patented teaching is used, patent law would not allow the data holder to block major improvements over or alternatives to the connected product; see the limits to the patent exclusivity set by national laws implementing Art 31, lit. l) TRIPS Agreement; for details Ullrich, above note 128, 1110 and throughout. Contrary to the Data Act's objective and to the process of innovation typically advancing by incremental steps, the non-compete rules impede follow-on innovation.

[132] See above II.C.ii.

[133] The legislature acknowledges this dilemma in recital 31 Data Act only to refrain from resolving it by giving full priority to the accessibility of data as would allow Art 3(2) Directive (EU) 2016/93 of 8 June 2016 on the protection of undisclosed know-how and business information (trade secrets), OJ EU 2016 L 157, 1; see A Wiebe, 'The Data Act Proposal – Access Rights at the Intersection with Database Rights and Trade Secret Protection' (2023) *GRUR* 227, 234.

[134] As to such measures, Art 4(6) Data Act lists 'model contractual terms, confidentiality agreements, strict access protocols, technical standards and the application of codes of conduct', thus consensus-based measures rather than measures the data holder may define unilaterally in accordance with its understanding of the vulnerability of the trade secret and its interest in a sufficient confidentiality of the data.

the competent authority of it (Article 4(7) Data Act).[135] The data holder may also suspend data sharing in case the user fails to implement the measures agreed upon with the user or in case the user undermines the confidentiality of the trade secret. Again it must substantiate its decision in writing, provide it to the user and notify the competent authority (Article 4(7) Data Act). In all these cases, the substance of the user's claim to access by way of data sharing remains unaffected; it is only as a matter of procedure that the data holder's duty to comply with the claim is suspended as long as the user does not take and observe the necessary and proportionate measures for maintaining confidentiality, and the choice of the procedural mechanism is not with the data holder,[136] but with the user: It may seek redress before a national court (Article 4(9), 1at alt. Data Act), lodge a complaint with the competent authority (Article 4(9) lit.a) Data Act)[137] or agree with the data holder on dispute settlement (Article 4(9) lit.b) Data Act).[138]

By contrast, according to Article 4(8) 1st sent. Data Act it is only

> in exceptional circumstances, where the data holder who is a trade secret holder is able to demonstrate that it is highly likely to suffer serious economic damage from the disclosure of trade secrets, despite the technical and organizational measures taken by the user . . . that a data holder may refuse on a case-by-case basis a request for access to the specific data in question.

It must substantiate the high likelihood of serious economic damage on the basis of objective elements, such as in particular the (insufficient) 'enforceability of trade secrets protection in third countries, the nature and level of confidentiality of the data, and the uniqueness and novelty of the connected product', and it must do so in writing without undue delay and notify the competent authority of its refusal (Article 4(8)

[135] Art 37(1) Data Act obliges Member States to 'designate one or more competent authorities to be responsible for the application and enforcement of this Regulation'. Art 37(8), (9) Data Act provide for the institutional independence and the human and technical resources of these authorities. Art 37(5) defines the tasks and powers of the competent authorities; these are essentially of supervisory nature but include investigative powers (Art 37(5) lit. c) and Art 37(14) Data Act) and the power to impose effective, proportionate and dissuasive financial penalties (Art 37(5) lit. (d) with Art 40 Data Act); see also below note 137.

[136] However, if the user actually violated the trade secret or is about to violate it, the data holder may bring an action for provisional or precautionary measures or for injunctive and corrective relief under national law implementing Arts 10 et seq, 12 et seq Trade Secrets Dir. In that case, the user may rely on Art 4(1), (6) Data Act only as a defence.

[137] Pursuant to Art 4(9) lit.(a) Data Act upon a complaint the competent authority 'shall, without undue delay, decide whether and under which conditions the data sharing is to start or resume'. According to Art 37(5), lit.(b) Data Act, Member States must ensure that the tasks of the competent authorities (see above note 135) include 'handling complaints arising from alleged infringements of this regulation, including in relation to trade secrets, and investigating to the extent appropriate, the subject matter of complaints and regularly informing complainants . . . of the progress and outcome of the investigation within a reasonable period'. Given that the dispute between the data holder and the user is an inter partes dispute that essentially relates to their individual interests rather than to a public interest, the competence of an administrative body enjoying ex officio investigative power presents another questionable regulatory aspect of the Data Act. It invites forum shopping and may easily lead to conflicting lines of adjudicature regarding not only the trade secret exception but also the scope of the underlying access claim.

[138] Art 4(9) lit. b) Data Act refers to the dispute settlement mechanism by certified dispute settlement bodies that Art 10(1)–(3) Data Act provides for disputes pursuant to Art 4(3) and (9), Art 5(12) and Chapters III and IV of the Data Act. For the dispute settlement procedure see Art 10(7)–(9), (12), (13) Data Act.

2nd sent. Data Act).[139] The user may then challenge the refusal by seeking redress before a national court,[140] by lodging a complaint with the competent authority or by agreeing with the data holder on dispute settlement (Article 4(9) Data Act).

In case the user requests the data holder to grant a third party access to data that constitute or form part of a trade secret held by the data holder, the latter must share the trade secret with the third party, but 'only to the extent that such disclosure is strictly necessary to fulfil the purpose agreed between the user and the third party' (Article 5(9) 1st sent. Data Act).[141] The obligations of the third party equal those of the user: The data holder and the third party must agree on the safety conditions of such sharing of confidential data; the data holder may withhold or suspend data sharing in case the third party does not sufficiently respect confidentiality, but again it may not refuse access except in exceptional circumstances where there is a high likelihood of serious economic damage (Article 5(9)–(11) Data Act). In case the data holder suspends data sharing or even refuses access, the third party may challenge the data holder's decision before national courts or a competent authority or agree with the data holder on dispute settlement (Article 5(12) Data Act).

Given the narrow grounds on which the data holder/secrets holder may refuse to share confidential data with the user and/or a third party, the scope of confidential data that it is obliged to share under Articles 4(6) and 5(9) Data Act seems to be rather large. However, it is difficult to realistically estimate the magnitude of the conflict between opening access to data that, by definition, are virtually secret[142] and preserving confidentiality of data that qualify for protection under trade secret law. On the one hand, although Article 2(1) lit. a) and lit. (b) Trade Secrets Directive define the protectable subject matter quite broadly,[143] it appears plausible to assume that

[139] For the powers of the competent authority see above notes 135, 137.

[140] In addition to its claim under Art 4(1), (8) Data Act the user may rely on Art 102 TFEU or national competition rules as they apply to refusals to deal by market dominating enterprises.

[141] Since the scope of the data the third party may access is determined by its agreement with the user (Art 6(1) Data Act), Art 5(9) Data Act hardly puts an additional limit to the third party's access to the data holder's trade secret; see M Grützmacher, 'Data Act: Datenzugang und Geschäftsgeheimnisschutz' (2024) *CR* 281, 287, para 36 with references; Wiebe (GRUR 2023), above note 18, 235; D Pauly, F Wichert and J Baumann, 'Schutz von Geschäftsgeheimnissen nach dem Data Act' (2024) *MMR* 211, 214. At any rate, Art 5(9) Data Act may not be read as allowing third parties only a purpose-bound access to the confidential data, such as only for repair or maintenance services or else it could become the Trojan horse enabling trade secret holders to 'monopolise' the innovation potential inherent in the multi-functionality of data that the Data Act precisely wishes to keep accessible for innovative competition.

[142] In the sense that they are not 'readily accessible' (Art 2(1) lit. (a) Trade Secrets Dir) because not directly accessible (Art 4(1) Data Act), see B Lorenzen, 'Geschäftsgeheimnisschutz und Data Act' (2023) 14 *ZGE/IPJ* 250, 253. However, although data represent information only digitally (Art 2(1) Data Act), that information may be inferred from them more or less easily and, as such, may be confidential or generally known or otherwise readily accessible; see Wiebe (GRUR 2023), above note 18, 232 with references; U-M Mylly, 'Trade Secrets and the Data Act' (2024) 55 *IIC* 368, 371 et seq.

[143] Art 2(1) lit. a), b) Trade Secrets Dir define trade secrets as any information that is 'secret in the sense that it is not, as a body or in the precise configuration and assembly of its components, generally known among or readily accessible to persons within the circles that normally deal with the kind of information in question' and that 'has commercial value because it is secret'. It is hard to think of a broader definition, but it is derived from Art 39 TRIPS Agreement. Compare also the definition of know-how in Art 1(1) lit. i) Commission Reg. (EU) 316/2014 of 21 March 2014 on the application of Art 101(3) TFEU to categories of technology transfer agreements (OJEU 2012 L 93,17), which require that the know-how be substantial, ie significant and useful for the production of the licence products.

readily available data of connected (end-) consumer products generally will not or no longer qualify for trade secret protection.[144] It may also be that raw data that are readily available within the meaning of Articles 2(17), 4(1), 5(1) Data Act will only exceptionally represent information that is commercially valuable enough to merit protection as a trade secret.[145] If so, the risk that mandatory accessibility of IoT data will by its broad scope of application result in numerous data sharing agreements and, therefore, undermine trade secret protection appears to be limited.

On the other hand, in case the data the holder/trade secret holder must share with the user and/or a third party do constitute a trade secret within the meaning of Article 2(1) Trade Secrets Directive, Articles 4(6) and 5(9) Data Act undercut a fundamental principle of trade secret protection, which is that it is the trade secret holder alone who determines with whom to share the trade secret, for example, by way of a know-how licence. This is not only a matter of the data holder's/trade secret holder's autonomy, but also one of preserving the very essence of trade secret protection: The confidentiality of the information primarily rests on its sharing with only a few carefully selected trustworthy parties.[146] The mandatory character of Article 4(1) and 5(1) Data Act means that the trade secret holder may not itself select its data-sharing partner or, if it wishes to select such partner, must do so when selling or letting the connected product, that is, it must subject the sale to preselection of a trustworthy trade secret partner. Worse, due to Article 5(1) Data Act, the data holder has no control whatsoever over the third party or parties that the buyer or renter may choose

[144] Think of household appliances and the like. In case such data qualify for trade secret protection, the manufacturer/data holder must be presumed to have abandoned its claim when selling or letting connected mass products because it necessarily will anticipate that such products will and need to be repaired, maintained or become subject to other services by an unlimited number of third party service providers. Besides, the data generated by the use of a single connected product rarely have a commercial value for the manufacturer/data holder or, if they do, it is precisely the opportunity value for attracting services by third parties that the Data Act attributes to the user, not to the trade secret holder (but see below II.D.ii.b). In addition, it does not make sense to burden trade with the transaction costs of formal and ultimately fictitious confidentiality arrangements. The teachings of the doctrine of exhaustion of intellectual property rights upon the first sale of the embodiments of a patented technological invention or of a copyright-protected work come to mind, but the analogy, if applicable, has its limits. Arguably, one is that the aggregation of the data of connected mass products by systematic collection has a value of its own, not the least being its potential for innovation. Again, however, the access rules of the Data Act aim at opening this potential for dynamic competition.

[145] Literature mostly discusses the question whether in general raw data may qualify for protection as trade secrets rather than the question whether the data that are to be made available pursuant to Arts 4(1) and 5(1) Data Act so qualify, or it focuses on the grey area that exists between pure raw data and informative raw data; see Mylly, above note 142, 372 et seq; Grützmacher, above note 141, 283 et seq, paras 14 et seq. (19); but see E De Noyette and T Margoni, 'The Data Act and the 2016 Trade Secrets Directive' in Ducuing, Magoni and Schirru (eds), above note 96, 79, 80; T Aplin, A Radenauer et al, 'The Role of EU Trade Secrets Law in the Data Economy: An Empirical Analysis' (2023) 54 *IIC* 826, 843. However, given that the concept of readily available data refers to the practical efforts necessary to make the data available (Art 2(17) Data Act), a preliminary issue is how this test relates to that of Art 2(1), lit. c) Trade Secrets Dir, which requires the holder of a trade secret to take reasonable steps to keep the information secret. May the trade secret holder oppose claims to access on the ground that because of the measures that are necessary to maintain confidentiality of the information the data are not readily available, ie, that making them available requires a 'disproportionate effort going beyond a simple operation' (Art 2(17) Data Act), and that, therefore, it is under no duty to grant access in the first place?

[146] See Mylly, above note 142, 384 with references; for know-how licensing see C Osterrieth and M Weinert, 'Patent- und Knowhow Lizenzvertrag' in D Pfaff and C Osterrieth (eds), *Lizenzverträge*, 4th edn (Munich, CH Beck, 2018) 192, paras 3 et seq.

for expert advice, cooperation or services of repair, maintenance and the like,[147] and with whom the data holder then must share the confidential data.

As said, conflicts between mandatory accessibility of product data and trade secret protection may not arise too frequently, but where they do arise they constitute a real threat to the trade secret. Unless the connected product is a singular good that is sold only once, the data holder must share its confidential data with the multitude of users to which it sold or let the connected product. These users may request access to the data by different third parties at the same time or over the product's life time, and they may resell the product to other users, in which case they remain bound by the confidentiality agreement while the new user must, in is turn, enter into such agreement with the data holder/trade secret holder.[148] Ultimately, whatever measures of control of confidentiality the parties originally agree upon pursuant to Articles 4(6) and 5(9) Data Act, there is a risk of leakage of the data that is likely to get out of control, at least over time. Worse, the assumption that the data are not generally known among or readily accessible to persons within the relevant expert circles may become a fiction.[149] Depending on the nature of the connected product and of the data, the problem may be mitigated to some extent by the obsolescence of the data, but it remains a systemic one. It confronts the data holder/trade secret owner, typically the manufacturer of the connected product, with the alternative to either abstain from seeking trade secret protection for the non-core parts of its data-based know-how or, if technically feasible, to design the connected product in such a way that its use does not generate confidential data in readily available form.[150] The former option will appear acceptable to those who think that trade secret protection extends too far anyway; the latter option defeats the Data Act's purpose, but is more likely to be preferred by at least some industries.[151]

b. Technical Protection Measures Legalizing De Facto Control

In practice, the choice of approach will be influenced by the powers of de facto control over IoT data that Article 11 Data Act confers upon the data holder. According to the first paragraph of that provision 'A data holder may apply appropriate technical

[147] This practical difficulty may invite manufacturers of connected products and third parties, such as major service providers, to enter into framework agreements providing for rules on both users' consent and confidentiality (see above note 103), the result being a limitation of the users' freedom of choice. Major users or groups of users may in their turn join the club or even establish it with the result of markets becoming privately administered rather than remaining open for innovative competition.

[148] There is a risk of a double mismatch here between, first, the user's consent to the use of the product data, which is bound to the time of possession of the connected product, and the unlimited duration of the confidentiality agreement, and, second, the interest of the trade secret holder in preserving confidentiality and the user's awareness of the confidentiality once it no longer owns or possesses the connected product. In short, the moral hazard increases.

[149] See Art 2(1) lit. c) Trade Secrets Dir; Mylly, above note 142, 374.

[150] Another concern may be an over-claiming of trade secret protection that results in impairing the free flow of data; see Mylly, above note 142, 290; see also Drexl et al, above note 16, para 281. More particularly, over-claiming leads to unjustified requests for confidentiality agreements under Arts 4(6) and 5(9) Data Act that in turn may help the data holder integrate users and third parties into its ecosystem.

[151] The principle of self-accessibility (Art 3(1) Data Act) might set a limit to such a design strategy of industry, which is why the principle is criticised by advocates of trade secret protection; see Grützmacher, above note 141, 287 and throughout.

protection measures, including . . . encryption, to prevent unauthorized access to data, including meta data'. While such technical protection measures (TPM) 'shall not . . . hinder a user's right to obtain a copy of, retrieve, use or access data' the user 'shall not alter or remove such technical protection measures unless agreed by the data holder' (Article 11(1) 2nd and 3rd sent. Data Act). If a user alters or removes TPM, the data holder is entitled to various forms of relief, including injunctive and/or monetary relief (Article 11(4) 1st alt. with Article 11(2) Data Act).[152] Likewise, third parties[153] and data recipients may not alter or remove TPM unless agreed by the data holder (Article 11(1), 3rd sent. Data Act); if they do the data holder may request from them relief in the forms mentioned (Article 11(3) lit. e with Art. 11(2) Data Act). These rules are not self-evident. Unlike rules of copyright law that, as an additional layer of copyright protection, shield a copyright holder's TPM against circumvention,[154] Article 11 Data Act establishes TPM as an independent, self-contained legal tool for data holders to shield data from access irrespective of the legal nature of the data in question, most of which typically are in the public domain.[155] Unlike trade secrets, the confidentiality of which may be ensured by TPM,[156] there is not even any requirement of individual merit. The mere fact of techno-practical control is elevated to a legal reason justifying the protection of the de facto power of the data holder, an elevation that is reinforced by the fact that the sanctions for altering, removing or circumventing TPM are the same as those for the violation of the substantive rules on data access (Article 11(2), (3) Data Act).[157]

[152] See below note 157 and text at sub II.D.i.c. Since Art 11(2) Data Act provides for relief that is designed to undo the effects of conduct of third parties that Art 11(3) Data Act defines as unlawful, not all the forms of relief it provides for may constitute the proper remedy to interference with TPM by the user.

[153] Art 11(1), last sent. Data Act seems to cover only conduct by third parties that the user has already designated (see also Art 2(14) Data Act) rather than any third party that interferes with the IoT data without authorisation by the data holder. This limitation may raise issues of determining whether relief is available under Art 11(1) Data Act or only under general law, eg, in case the third party is not, not yet or no longer designated by the user.

[154] See Art 7(1) lit. (c). Dir. 2009/24/EC of 23 April 2009 on the legal protection of computer programs (OJ EU 2009 L 111, 16) and in particular Art 6 Dir. 2001/29/EC of 22 May 2001 on the harmonization of certain aspects of copyright and related rights in the information society, OJEU 201 L 167/10, as amended.

[155] Art 2(1) Data Act defines data as 'any digital representation of acts, facts or information and any compilation of such acts, facts or information'. Recital 14 lists as relevant data those that concern the performance, use or environment of a connected product. As to access that may be unlawful due to copyright protection of data see L. Stähler, 'Article 11 of the Data Act – The regulation of unauthorized access to data', in Ducuing, Magoni and Schirru (eds), above note 96, sub 5.2.2; Leistner and Antoine, above note 69, sub 3.2.3. For a critique of the concurrent protection by copyright and TPM see V Moscon, 'Data Access Rules, Copyright and Technological Protection Measures', in Thouvenin et al (eds), above note 23, 1033, 1044 and throughout.

[156] See C Rehaag and P Straszewski, 'Das neue Gesetz zum Schutz von Geschäftsgeheimnissen in der Praxis' (2019) *Mitt.dt.Patanw* 249, 252 et seq; H Harte-Bavendamm in H Harte-Bavendamm (ed), *Gesetz zum Schutz von Geschäftsgeheimnissen*, 2nd edn (Munich, CH Beck, 2024) paras 55 and throughout (62, 65).

[157] For these sanctions see below II.D.i.c. The point is that according to Art 11(1) last sent., Art 11(3) lit. c) and Art 11(4), 1st alt. Data Act the mere act of a third party or of the user of altering or removing TPM without agreement by the data holder entitles the latter to request that third party or the user (a) to erase the data, (b) to end the production, offering or placing on the market or use of goods, derivative data or services produced on the basis of knowledge obtained through such data (Art 11(2) lit. (a), (b) Data Act). TPM thus become the legal means to protect IoT data independently, namely in addition to the rules that limit the scope of a third party's authorised use of the data that the data holder has to make available to it (Art 5(1) Data Act), and, thus, define the lawful use of these data by the third party; see Art 11(3) lit. b) Data Act.

This surprising elevation of TPM to the status of a legal tool for controlling access to IoT data is not mitigated by the requirements, first, that the data holder may install TPM only to prevent 'unauthorized access to data' (Article 11(1) 1st sent. Data Act) and, second, 'to ensure compliance with Arts. 4, 5, 6, 8 and 9 as well as with the agreed contractual terms for making data available' (Article 11(1) 1st sent. Data Act). The former requirement relates to the authorisation the data holder may grant or refuse in accordance with Articles 4(1), (2), (10) (13), (14) and Articles 5(1), Article 6(1), (2), Article 8(4) Data Act and the consent given by or agreed upon with the user. It thus refers back to the – possibly, if not typically – asymmetric power relations between and the interest of the data holder and the user, respectively.[158] The latter requirement confers upon the data holder the position of a supervisor of all parties concerned as regards their complying with the regime of mandatory accessibility of IoT data. This position allows it to safeguard its own interests as regards, for example, the form of making data available under Articles 4(1), 5(1), 8(1) and 9(2) lit. a) Data Act, or the effectiveness of the protection it enjoys from direct competition (Articles 4(10), 6(2) lit. (a) Data Act), on the one hand. On the other, as regards the interests of the user and of third parties, this position obviously is that of the fox set to keep the geese.[159] At any rate, neither requirement relates in any way to the legal nature of the IoT data or gives substance to elevating TPM to the status of a legal means of protecting IoT data.

c. Enhanced Individual Enforcement of Selected Rules of Protection

In addition, and independently of the protection of or an interference with TPM, Article 11 Data Act introduces a number of 'provisions on unauthorized use or disclosure of data',[160] which asymmetrically protect primarily the data holder and do so mainly against acts done by a third party. Thus, Article 11(3) lit. a) Data Act expands on Article 5(5) Data Act by providing that a third party may not for the purpose of

[158] See above text at note 79 et seq. For the conflicting interests of the data holder and the user regarding the scope of the authorisation see Stähler, in Ducuing, Magoni and Schirru (eds), above note 96, sub 5.2.1. Part of the problem here is the fact that it is the data holder who holds the data that are generated by a more or less large number of identical or similar connected products that are owned or held by different users. The data holder, thus, is at the centre of control by virtue of TPM and must coordinate authorised access to the data generated by the individual users while having an interest of its own in access not only to the individual data, but to the totality of the data.

[159] Although the data holder is sort of the custodian of the data generated by the user of a connected product, the Data Act is silent as regards its duties, apparently because it relies on the data holder's self-interest in TPM. However, TPM may be insufficient or be insufficiently controlled by the data holder. Since use data may form part of the user's technical or commercial know-how or even of its trade secrets, the question arises why the data holder is not held to the same standard of liability as the user is by Art 11(4) Data Act as regards the agreed upon technical and organisational measures for preserving confidentiality of secret know-how.

[160] In contrast to the confusing heading of Art 11 Data Act: 'Technical protection measures on the unauthorized use or disclosure of data', the heading of Art 11 of the Commission's proposal (above note 7) clearly distinguished between the two different matters, the first being covered by Art 11(1) and the second by Art 11(2). As proposed, Art 11(2) was clearly structured. It only protected the data holder against acts of third parties (data recipient) and defined the prohibited acts before setting forth the available forms of relief. It was only in the legislative process that Art 11 was unsystematically complemented by adding lit. d) and e) to its para. (3) and by introducing paras (4) and (5).

obtaining data provide false information to a data holder, deploy deceptive or coercive means or abuse gaps in the technical infrastructure of the data holder. Article 11(3) lit. b) Data Act enjoins the third party from using the data made available to it for unauthorised purposes, including the development of competing connected products as outlawed by Article 6(2) lit. e) Data Act.[161] While the latter point is rather self-evident, the former is surprising because in the system of the Data Act it is the user that defines the purposes for which the data holder or the third party may use the IoT data (Articles 4(13), 6(1) Data Act). In this respect, Article 11(3) lit. b) Data Act obviously upgrades the position of the data holder.[162] Article 11(3) lit. c) Data Act complements Article 5(9)–(11) Data Act by entitling the data holder to relief in case a third party unlawfully discloses data to another party. In addition, Article 11(3) lit. d) Data Act provides for the liability of a third party that does not maintain the technical and organisational measures as agreed upon pursuant to Article 5(9) Data Act. Thus, Article 11(3) lit. c) and d) Data Act reinforce the contractual liability of the third party and the protection of the trade secrets in general.[163]

While Article 11(4), 2nd alt. Data Act holds the user to the same liability for maintaining the confidentiality of the data holder's trade secrets as a third party is held to,[164] as regards other potentially harmful conduct the user is not subject to the same rules of enhanced enforcement of Article 11(2) Data Act. In particular, Article 11 Data Act neither provides for an equivalent to its paragraph (3) lit. a) in case the user violates the fairness rule of Article 4(11) Data Act nor for an equivalent to its paragraph (3) lit. b) in case the user violates the non-compete rule of Article 4(10) Data Act. The reasons for this differentiation are not evident. Possibly, although not very plausibly, it is due to the fact that, first, the third party potentially is a competitor of the data holder on the aftermarket or on ancillary markets of the connected product, and, second, as regards access to the IoT data, the data holder and the user are on a par as co-generators of the data. Significantly, as regards undue interference

[161] Note that Art 6(2) lit (e) Data Act contains not only the non-compete rule, but also enjoins the third party from seeking insights into the economic situation, assets and production methods of the data holder.

[162] Upon first impression, under Art 11(3) lit. b), 1st alt. Data Act only the user would appear to be entitled to relief when the third party uses the data for unauthorised purposes, since any use of the product data by a third party requires its consent (Arts 4(13), (14), 6(1), 8(4) Data Act). Accordingly, Art 11(2) 1st sent. Data Act entitles the user to relief, 'where applicable'; see also Art 11(2) lit. c) and d) Data Act. However, the data holder is not only the custodian of the data, but has an interest of its own in the data being used only upon authorisation (Arts 4(10), (13), 6(3) lit. e) and 8 (4) Data Act), because unauthorised use of data by a third party may affect its position in competition. However, since Art 11(3) Data Act expressly addresses only the particular concerns of the data holder, in particular the non-compete rule of Art 6(2) lit e) (see Art 11(3) lit. b), 2nd alt.), the provision apparently is to be read as directly protecting only the data holder's interests and merely indirectly also those of the user. The legislative history of the provision also suggests such reading; see above note 160. At any rate, Art 11(3), lit. b), 1st alt. Data Act must be read narrowly or else its application may result in transforming the requirement of user consent into a rule of property-like effect.

[163] Compare Art 4(3) lit. b), c) Trade Secrets Dir; note also that the German version of Art 11(3) lit. c) Data Act translates 'unlawfully disclosed data' by 'unrechtmäßig Daten . . . weitergegeben' instead of 'unrechtmäßig . . . offengelegt'.

[164] Art 11(4) Data Act even extends the enhanced enforcement to 'any other party that receives the data from the user by means of an infringement of the Regulation', the data in question apparently being those that are covered by TPM or by a trade secret. Art 11(3) lit. d), c) Data Act do not provide for a similar extension in case another party receives such data from a third party by means of an infringement of the Data Act, eg, by infringement of Art 6(2) lit. c) Data Act; compare also Art 4(4), (5) Trade Secrets Dir.

with the user's autonomy of choice, if committed by a third party (Article 6(2) lit. a) Data Act), Article 11(5) Data Act entitles the user to enhanced relief, but not if it is committed by the data holder (Article 4(4) Data Act). More generally, Article 11(2), (3) Data Act focuses on the conduct of the third party, and marginally also on that of the user (Article 11(4) Data Act), but – despite the likelihood of it enjoying a strong bargaining and market position – not at all on that of the data holder.

The forms of relief that the data holder and, where applicable, the user may request under Article 11(2) Data Act make clear to what extent their positions are enhanced beyond contract law: infringers must (a) erase the data made available by the data holder; (b) end the production and marketing or use of goods, derivative data or services produced on the basis of the knowledge obtained through such data;[165] (c) inform the user of the unauthorised use or disclosure of the data;[166] (d) 'compensate the party suffering from the misuse or disclosure of such unlawfully accessed or used data'.[167] Even without entering into a detailed comparative analysis it is obvious enough that these forms of relief are closely akin to those available under Article 12 et seq. Trade Secrets Directive. However, they do not only apply in case of a violation of confidentiality requirements, but also in all the other cases, such as when TPM are altered or removed by the third party or by the user,[168] when the third party provides deceptive or simply false information for obtaining data or when it uses the data for competing with the data holder on the product market or for other unauthorised purposes, and whenever data are unlawfully disclosed to other parties by the third party or the user (Article 11(3) lit. a) to c) and lit. e) Data Act). Apparently, the legislature considers these forms of misappropriation and misuse of IoT data to constitute tortious conduct, and, thus, invites thinking of the protection of data as a sub-form of quasi-(intellectual) property as was the case when it reinforced the protection of trade secrets.[169] It is true that substantial differences remain, in particular the fact

[165] Art 11(2), lit. (b) Data Act provides for the main and most comprehensive relief. It obligates infringers: '(b) to end the production, offering or placing on the market or use of goods, derivative data or services produced on the basis of knowledge obtained through such data, or the importation, export or storage of infringing goods for those purposes, and destroy any infringing goods, where there is a serious risk that the unlawful use of those data will cause significant harm to the data holder, the trade secret holder or the user or where such a measure would not be disproportionate in light of the interests of the data holder, the trade secret holder or the user'.

[166] Art 11(2) lit. c) Data Act reads: 'to inform the user of the unauthorized use or disclosure of the data and of the measures taken to put an end to the unauthorized use or disclosure of the data'.

[167] It is not clear what Art 11(2) lit. d) Data Act means by 'compensate the party suffering' from the misuse or disclosure of such unlawfully accessed or used data. If, as suggested in the text, Art 11(3) Data Act defines some particular forms of tortious conduct, then the data holder or the user ought to have a claim for damages suffered, albeit not necessarily for profits lost, rather than only a claim to compensation for its 'suffering'. Besides, both terms are indeterminate: What compensation for which suffering? The legislature's abstention from determining the legal nature of non-personal IoT data and of the individual rights that the data holder and possibly the user might have in them is evident here, see also below II.D.ii.c.

[168] See above at II.D.ii.b.

[169] For the discussion on the nature of trade secret protection see: A Ohly in Harte-Bavendamm, above note 156, Einl. A, paras 21 and throughout with references; A Glinke in F Keller, M Schönknecht and A Glinke (eds), *Geschäftsgeheimnisschutzgesetz* (Munich, C.H. Beck, 2021) Einl. B, paras 101 and throughout; T Hoeren, 'The EU Directive on the Protection of Trade Secrets and its Relation to Current Provisions in Germany' (2018) 9 *JIPITEC* 138, para 6 (minor IP right); critical J Schovsbo and T Riis, 'To Be and Not to Be an IPR: The Protection of Trade Secrets in the EU' (2019) 41 *EIPR* 401; A Wiebe and N Schur, 'Protection of Trade Secrets in a Data-driven, Networked Environment – Is the Update Already

that most of the acts in question rest on wilful or negligent conduct.[170] However, the combined effects of the relief that is available in case the third party or, where applicable, the user disregards TPM, the confidentiality of trade secrets or the mandatorily guaranteed or, if applicable, mutually agreed upon scope of consent to access and use of IoT data arguably transform the data holder's and the user's positions into that of – common, but separate and unequal[171] – beneficiaries of a multi-layered protection of IoT data that may be a first step of the development of a negative or defensive digital quasi-property.[172] As regards more particularly the data holder, an additional strength of its position results from the fact that it holds all the data that the users generate when using the product it sold, and that in respect of their use it enjoys a legally secure broad exclusivity on the relevant product market.[173]

ii. Consensus-Dependent Instead of Competition-Based Use of IoT data

This assessment of the data holder's position contradicts the EU legislature's explicit policy view that 'In order to realize the economy benefits of data . . . and the development of data-driven value creation by Union enterprises a general approach to assigning rights regarding access to and use of data is preferable to awarding exclusive right of access and use',[174] and it contradicts its warning that, therefore: 'This Regulation should not be understood to confer any new right on data holders to use product data or related service data.'[175] However, it is not the formal concept of the legislature that matters, but the legal and economic consequences of the regime of access to and use of data that it actually established, that is, the attribution of legal means or rights that enable the holder of data to alone capture and control market opportunities, and, thereby, the value potential of the data.[176] As stated, the Data Act confers upon the data holder a broad range of legally secured means for excluding others from obtaining and using product data for developing, manufacturing and marketing improved or entirely innovative products, in particular TPM, trade secret protection, tort claims against unfair access to and unauthorised use of data and an

---

Outdated?' (2019) *GRURInt* 746 precisely argue that TPM may bring data within the scope of trade secret protection.

[170] By contrast, the non-availability of injunctive relief in cases in which the violation does not produce a serious risk of causing a 'substantial harm to the data holder, the trade secret holder or the user' or in cases in which it is 'disproportionate in the light of the interests of the data holder, the trade secret holder or the user' (Art 11(2), lit. (b) in fine Data Act) does not make much of a difference. These limitations are of a general nature; see Art 3(2) Directive 2004/48/EC of 29 April 2004 on the enforcement of intellectual property rights (OJEU 2004 L 157, 45), and similar to those provided for by Art 13 Trade Secrets Dir.

[171] See below II.D.ii.a and b.

[172] For the various approaches to developing rights in data and their different functions see F Szilági, 'The Necessity of Data Allocation: A Plea for a Private Law (Property Law) Perspective' (2021) 10 *Eur Prop LJ* 180, 186, 204, and references below notes 210, 213; generally H Zech, 'Materielle und immaterielle Güter – Die Güterzuweisungsfunktion des Privatrechts' (2023) 15 *ZGE/IPJ* 53 and throughout; for defensive rights ibid 72 et seq.

[173] For an economic assessment of the effect of (de facto) data exclusivity under the Data Act see Kerber, above note 66, 120, 128 et seq.

[174] Recital 6 Data Act.

[175] Recital 25 Data Act.

[176] See references above note 128.

exclusivity of use of the data for developing substitute products.[177] Since, by definition, the data holder holds the total of the data its products generate when used, these legal tools enable it to harvest all the economic fruits of data.

a. The Function of the User's Consent I: Exclusion?

Of course, in order to achieve this result, the data holder needs the consent of the users to use the data they generate when using the connected products. In general, however, the data holder should have no problem obtaining the users' consent to the use of the product data. For one thing, a user has no reason to refuse to consent to the use of the product's data for developing improved or entirely innovative products, since it may not itself use the data for such purpose or allow a third party to so use the data (Article 4(10) Data Act). For another, as regards consent to use for other purposes the user will only exceptionally have an interest in excluding the data holder. The most important of these other purposes relates to the use of the data for connecting the product to complementary, peripheral or ancillary products or services. It is for enabling the user to optimally attain this purpose that the legislature introduced the mandatory accessibility of the product data by the user and the consent requirement, since this will allow the user to fully benefit from open competition on aftermarkets and on ancillary markets.[178] It follows that the user is not likely to refuse its consent and, thus, exclude the data holder from these markets. Irrespective of the fact that typically the bargaining relations between the data holder and the user are not favourable to such refusal,[179] it is hardly in the interest of the user to forego the benefits of competition between the data holder and a third party in respect of products or services relating to the connected product it owns or possesses.

More generally, as regards the use of the product data in a context that is unrelated to the connected product from which they originate, such as, for example, for developing products for markets other than the relevant market of the particular connected product, the user will only exceptionally have enough reason to exclude the data holder by way of a refusal of consent. Two hypotheses come to mind. First, the user may wish to use the data it generated by the use of its connected product for developing itself or with the help of a third party an innovation of its own and, accordingly, exclude or at least hinder the data holder as an actual or potential competitor on this innovation market.[180] Second, under Article 5(1) Data Act, a third party may seek the user's support for using the product data for developing its own

[177] See above II.C.iii.c. The scope of the non-compete rules of Arts 4(10) and 6(2) lit. e) Data Act appears to be broader than that of patent protection, which does not cover acts of experimental use (Art 27 lit. b) Patent Court Agreement, UPCA), and also broader than trade secrets protection; see Art 3(1) lit. b) Trade Secrets Dir. In addition, 'use of the data' to develop a competing product must be understood narrowly so as not to block the use of generally available, unprotected information. More generally, the principle of proportionality must inform the interpretation of the non-compete rules rather than only the grant of the remedies to infringement (Art 11(2) lit. b) in fine Data Act); see also above note 131.

[178] See recitals 6, 16, 30, 32 Data Act, and above text at note 91 et seq.

[179] See above text at notes 78 et seq, 80 et seq.

[180] Metzger and Schweitzer, above note 35, at 51, 56 discuss the reverse hypothesis that in order to risk high investment in innovation the data holder may need an exclusive position also on aftermarkets or ancillary markets. Art 7(2) Data Act does not allow the data holder to request such a waiver from the user.

innovation on other markets than the market of the connected product, and, to this end, ask for the exclusion of the data holder as an actual or potential competitor.[181] In the first hypothesis, the consent requirement is relied upon as sort of a reverse non-compete rule in favour of the user; in the second hypothesis, the user's role as an actor on the demand side of the market is elevated from that of the arbiter of competitive offers of supply to that of an actor allocating innovation and market opportunities by way of either refusing to request Article 5(1)-access for a third party or making such requests selectively. In other words, the user would come to distribute innovation and market opportunities among actors on markets on which it may not even be present on either the supply or the demand side.[182] The common feature is an upgrading of the function and an up-valuation of the user's consent as an independent, self-contained asset that is not supported by its justification, but rather draws on that of the exclusivity effect of an intellectual property right.[183] However, according to the legislature, the justification for requiring the consent of the user to the use of the product data rests on its ownership or possession of the connected product as a tangible good with the consent requirement serving as a complement that enables the user to enjoy the connected product's full functionality.[184] Accordingly, each time the connected product is transferred as a tangible good, the power to consent passes on to the new user. Depending on the latter's use of the product and on the kind of data, the consent requirement will cover the same, similar or different data, but the link always is the particular product. Therefore, there is no basis for extending the consent requirement to controlling the use of product data for other purposes than those that allow the user to enjoy the entire functional potential of the particular connected product.[185]

Significantly, in case the data holder uses the product data without the user's consent or violates the limits of the consent given, the Data Act does not provide

[181] While according to Art 6(2) lit. h) Data Act a third party may not prevent the user that is a consumer from making the product data it receives available to other parties, Art 8(4) Data Act allows the user to request the data holder to make the data available to a third party 'on an exclusive basis', ie, at the exclusion of other third parties. By contrast, the Data Act does not address the hypothesis of the user requesting a data holder to make the data (exclusively) available to a third party while refusing to consent to the use of the product data by the data holder. While Art 4(13) Data Act implicitly allows the user to refuse to consent to the use of the product data by the data holder, refusing consent only to confer a full exclusivity upon a third party arguably amounts to a misuse of the consent requirement. It discriminates the data holder who may not obtain such exclusivity (see above note 180), and it runs afoul of the Data Act's purpose to broaden the basis for innovation, and overstretches the function of the consent requirement; see text below at note 192 et seq.

[182] For instance, at the request of a third party or as a matter of enhancing the value potential of its consent the user may limit the consent to the use of the data for specified purposes, products, services or geographic markets only just as would the licensor of an intellectual property right. Such practices would not only be available to big users. Big service providers may as third parties seek and obtain the requests for Art 5(1) access from a large number of users of connected products, and may do so on a sole or exclusive basis, except if the users are consumers (Art 6(2) lit. h) Data Act.

[183] See the inconsistent argument by, inter al, *Specht-Riemenschneider*, above note 56, 823: A third party may have to pay 'royalties' in order to make the user request data access according to Art 5(1) Data Act, while (at 817) no intellectual property rights exit in data. The user is allowed to participate in a value potential to the creation of which it has contributed nothing of substance, see below II.D.ii.b.

[184] See recital 18 Data Act.

[185] See recitals 6, 16, 30 Data Act.

for any sanctions other than contract law-sanctions.[186] More particularly, there is no counterpart to Article 11(2), (3) Data Act that would establish an enhanced tort liability of the data holder.[187] Also it is rather questionable whether Member States may introduce any enhanced liability of the data holder. National law may implement the access regime, but not interfere with the concepts upon which it rests or otherwise jeopardise its uniform operation in the Internal Market. As regards these concepts, Article 11(2) and (3) Data Act rest on the assumption that, irrespective of the fact that the data holder has no property right in the product data, it is entitled to their protection against certain acts of 'misappropriation' and misuse by third parties. The requirement of consent by the user does not transform these product data into 'user data', which, being the user's 'own' data, would enable the user to claim redress by way of injunctive relief (Article 11(2) lit. b) Data Act) or compensation for damages (Article 11(2) lit. d) Data Act) from the data holder.[188] In short, the Data Act does not bring the user on a par with the data holder. The reason is that under Articles 4(1) and 5(1) Data Act the user has no a right to or over the data, but only a right to access them while they are under the control of the data holder. Consequently, it is only allowed to control their use by way of giving or refusing to give the data holder its consent.

Prima facie, it may appear unsatisfactory to read the consent requirement narrowly as a corollary of the right to access the product data that only serves the user's interest in benefitting from the full functional potential of the connected product. From this perspective, the purpose of the consent requirement is merely a defensive one. It enables the user to prevent the data holder from using the data that are generated by the use of the connected product for its own purposes and/or to the detriment of the user, the justification being that it is through the request for access that the data holder is informed of the relevance of the data for the user.[189] However, that purpose is justification enough. The consent requirement cannot be meant to allow the user to reciprocate the non-compete rule of Article 4(10) Data Act by a

[186] See Arts 7(2) and 12(2) Data Act. If a data holder disregards Arts 4(13), (14) or 8(4) Data Act, it violates the law and its use of the data is unlawful. However, unless the legal status of data is upgraded to that of a legally protected asset and the value of that asset attributed to the user, there is no basis for considering Arts 4(13), (14) or 8(4) Data Act as rules that in case of an infringement by the data holder trigger tort liability. Since the Data Act abstains from determining the legal nature of data, also the nature of the consent requirement and the consequences of its violation remain open. It may simply be an example of a *lex imperfecta*, see also below II.D.ii.b.

[187] As to the protection of the user against third parties that use product data without the consent of the user, it essentially rests on contract law (Art 6(1) Data Act and, arguably, on Art 11(3) lit. b) Data Act, see above note 162.

[188] See above note 167, 186.

[189] See Art 4(13), 2nd sent. Data Act. At the latest when a user requests access to the product data, a data holder is likely to learn or to be able to learn of the needs of repair or of maintenance of the connected product, of the frequency and modes of its use, of the conditions under which it is used (see Art 2(5) Data Act: 'environment'), etc, and possibly also of not expected uses. While the data do not become user-specific or personal for that reason alone, they represent 'on the spot' product testing information that may serve innovation on various markets, those of the user and/or those of the data holder (and third parties); they may also constitute a considerable information advance or be sensitive information within the meaning of Art 4(13), 2nd sent. Data Act. For the rationale of Art 4(13), 2nd sent. Data Act see above II.C.iii.b. Clearly, Art 4(13), 2nd sent. Data Act is hardly relevant for users that are end-consumers, but neither is the consent requirement; see above II.C.ii.b and below at II.D.ii.b.

refusal to consent, that is, by excluding the data holder from using the product data for innovative competition on markets that are unrelated to the connected product and on which the user wishes to enter itself by innovation based on the product data. The non-compete rule is unsound enough;[190] it should not be replicated by an equally unsound reading of the consent requirement that would allow the user to create on its own and according to its individual business strategy a property-like exclusivity over the use of the data that the Data Act does not provide for.[191] Put differently, the user may not rely on its right to access the product data in a way that perverts it into a right to exclude the data holder from also using the product data in competition.

As regards the second hypothesis, the question is whether the user, who itself may always use the product data for any lawful purpose, may rely on its access right in order to enable third parties who, like the user, may not compete with the data holder on the market for the connected product, to compete with the data holder on markets that are unrelated to the markets of that product. The question arises because, in principle and practice, Articles 4(1) and 5(1) Data Act prevent third parties from obtaining product data directly from the user,[192] while the data holder may not make them available to a third party except upon request by the user (Article 8(4) Data Act). Extending the user's right to request access to the product data for third parties for purposes of competition on other markets than aftermarkets and ancillary markets may appear particularly justified because third parties may be most competent competitors for 'the development of new, innovative connected products . . . (and) of entirely novel services making use of the data concerned'.[193] Since the data from a large number of users and/or from a variety of connected products or related services may be needed in order to develop such entirely novel services,[194] third parties that can rely on a broad customer base may be well placed as innovators. Therefore, from the perspective of general competition policy, third parties should be more than welcome that engage in innovation not only on aftermarkets or ancillary markets but at least also on product markets other than that of the connected product.[195] The Data Act, however, considers them merely the expert substitutes of the user as regards the exploitation of the connected product's

[190] See above II.C.iii.c.

[191] See below II.D.ii.b. More particularly, it may not be argued that in order to risk investment in innovation the user may need to protect itself against competition by the data holder. That exactly is the rationale underlying patent protection, but patents are granted only upon condition of merit of the invention, and their protection is subject to limitations and exceptions whereas the user's refusal to consent is not subject to any limitation except to the extreme one that the general rules on competition provide for (Art 102 TFEU); see also above note 72.

[192] See above II.C.ii.c with note 88.

[193] See recital 32 Data Act. The non-compete rule of Art 6(2), lit. (e) Data Act is evidence enough of the legislature recognising third parties as able potential competitors.

[194] See recital 32 Data Act. See also A Wiebe, C Helmschrot and O Kreutz, 'Data Governance bei Connected Cars' (2023) *CR* 484, 485, para 85, and note that it is not only the accumulation of data from a variety of (similar) connected products that may provide important technological insights, but precisely also the accumulation of data generated by a variety of users of the same connected products.

[195] For a narrow reading of the non-compete rule of Art 6(2) lit. e) Data Act that avoids shielding the data holder from any substitute competition see above text following note 124, and above note 177.

functionality and potential of use.[196] Accordingly, it seems to recognise them only as competitors of the data holder on aftermarkets and ancillary markets.[197]

However shortsighted the legislature's view may be, the access right of the user provides no basis for broadening it. As said, the access right constitutes no more than a right that secures the user access to the product data while they are under lawful control by the data holder. Its purpose is to protect the user's interest in enjoying the full functional potential of the connected product under conditions of open competition, that is, to itself exploit the product's functional potential in competition, to innovate on the basis of the product data as carriers of information that results from its use of the connected product, and to call in a third party of its choice whenever it considers this to be necessary or simply desirable for the exploitation of the product's functionalities. The consent requirement protects this autonomy of the user against the risk that, due to its holding the data, the data holder might use the product data or the access request for its own purposes and/or to the detriment of the user. Its function is to secure the user's right to access the product data, not to transform this access right into a right of control over the data as if they were the user's data, that is, a right that would allow the user to regulate competition on general markets and allocate opportunities for innovation between the data holder and third parties by way of request and consent or refusal or limitation of such request and consent. Accordingly, the data holder is under no obligation to comply with such requests.[198]

b. The Function of the User's Consent II: Participation?

Commonly, the obligation of the data holder (and, for that matter, of third parties) to abstain from using the data that the connected product generates unless the user consents to such use is not analysed from the perspective of ensuring open, dynamic competition based on the use of IoT data, but from the narrower perspective of whether and how to enable the user to participate in the benefits that may accrue to the data holder (or to a third party) when it uses the product data for its own purposes, that is, whether and how the user may 'monetise' the product data.[199] The idea underlying this

[196] See Arts 5(1), 6(1), (2) lit. c) and h) Data Act; also above notes 58, 89 and text sub II.C.ii.c.

[197] See recitals 6, 16, 30 Data Act, on the one hand, and, on the other, recital 32 Data Act.

[198] There simply is an inherent limit to the rules of Arts 4(1) and 5(1) Data Act that results from the fact that they aim at enabling the user to access the product data as a matter of satisfying its interest in enjoying the functionalities of the connected product, rather than at enabling third parties to access the product data in their own, independent interests. This limit of the consent requirement also means that the user may not prevent third parties from obtaining the data directly from the data holder for purposes that are unrelated to the use of the connected product. Again, the product data are not the user's data! Rightly or wrongly, it is the data holder to which the Data Act attributes the power to control the data, and the data holder is not likely to block their use in areas outside its business interests; see Drexl et al, above note 16, para 19. At any rate, it is also the data holder that is more likely to be subject to an obligation to grant access to the product data as a matter of complying with competition law, in particular with the special responsibility for respecting competition that Art 102 TFEU imposes on it; see Schweitzer and Metzger, above note 107, 339 et seq, 348 et seq; hesitating Lundqvist, above note 43, 73 et seq.

[199] See recitals 18, 4th sent.; 25, penult. sent. Data Act; Specht-Riemenschneider, above note 56, 818; more generally (monetisation of product data by the user) M Hennemann, in Hennemann et al (eds), above note 53, 29 et seq.

question is that when using the connected product the user 'co-generates' the product data as it unfolds the functionalities that, on its side, the manufacturer/data holder co-generates by the design of the product, on the one hand, and, on the other, that these data have particular value characteristics. First and primarily, they render the invisible functioning of the product visible in a machine-readable form that may be stored, processed and re-used; second and often enough no less important, as carriers of information the data may be of multi-functional use. This co-generated functional and multi-functional utility of product data presents a plus value in which the user allegedly should have a share. However, neither from the perspective of practice nor from the perspective of legal principle is there enough reason for raising the consent requirement to the level of an entitlement that would allow the user reasonably and effectively to refuse consent to the use of the product data by the data holder (or by a third party) in order only to make the latter pay it a share of the plus value that the data may have on the market or at least may have for the data holder.

To begin with, elevating the consent requirement to an entitlement to participation in the plus value of product data makes practical sense mainly if it not only increases the user's willingness to consent to the use of the product data but also results in their broader and more efficient use by other market actors. However, these market actors' interest in obtaining the user's consent to the use of product data is likely to be limited.[200] More particularly, due to the non-compete rule of Article 6(2) lit. e) Data Act, third parties may not use the product data on the market that is of the greatest interest, which is the market of the connected product, but only on aftermarkets and ancillary markets where they may have to face competition by the data holder. In addition, they will be reluctant to pay for the use of data that they need in order to render a service for which the user has to pay them in the first place. Therefore, third parties most likely will be interested only in the use of the data for rendering their services to other users of the same or similar connected products or for alternative purposes. Even if that is the case, a third party's willingness to pay for such further use will be limited by the fact that is has to compensate the data holder for its making the data available (Article 9 Data Act). Since, in addition, the user cannot itself fully and effectively control the use of the data by the third party, but needs at least some technical cooperation by the data holder, the user can only exceptionally expect its consent to secure it a participation in the data's plus value that is worth the effort.[201]

The limited demand for the user's consent to the exploitation of the plus value of the product data will not really be compensated for by the data holder's interest in the use of the data. Although the data holder appears to be the first to which the user should turn for monetising its consent because the data holder also holds the

[200] This is not to deny the interest players on non-product markets, such as insurance companies, may have in accessing product data of automobiles; see eg, Südd. Ztg. of 18 October 2023, 16: 'Wem gehören die Daten?'; FAZ of 23 January 2022, 22: 'Allianz: Roboterauto-Daten sollen an Treuhand gehen'. However, they will prefer and possibly need to obtain the product data of all relevant users and, therefore, turn to the data holder for accessing the data.

[201] Although the consent agreement typically will provide for accounting obligations, the user will need a technical control and, to this end, may need the cooperation of the data holder. This also means that it also needs to contractually coordinate its relations with both the data holder and the third party, a matter that may be difficult to handle in business-to-consumer relations.

product's design and operational data and, thus, is best placed to assess the value of the product data and to exploit it, its willingness to concede to the user a particular monetary participation in the plus value of the product data is likely to be limited as well. As mentioned, in general the data holder may ask for and obtain the user's consent to the use of the product data anyway early on as part of the bargain when selling or letting the connected product.[202] This means that typically a particular participation fee will neither be specified nor negotiated separately. In addition, at that early point of time, the full potential of the multi-functionality of the product data, in particular their potential for innovation, may not yet be known or be too uncertain, and so may be the prospects of their commercial exploitation. Moreover, at least as far as connected mass products are concerned, in particular end-consumer products, the data holder may not even have an interest in obtaining the individual user's consent, but only in obtaining the consent to use the product data that result from the use of the connected product by a representative number or group of users. In such case, the product data only have a random value, and they have it not because of a lack of use potential of the product data of the individual user's product, but because of the systemic use potential of product data.[203]

All in all, there are many constraints to the participation of the individual user in the plus value of product data, not the least being that, even if possible, in monetary terms the participation of the user in the product data's plus value is likely to be small or negligible in most cases, the exception possibly being a participation in the plus value of the data of more or less singular connected products of high-tech industrial use. It remains to be seen whether, notwithstanding all the constraints and the divide between the product data of connected end-consumer products, other (industrial) mass products and singular connected products of high-tech industrial use, a practice of value-sharing between the user, the data holder und third parties will develop and contribute to a broader and efficient use of product data by a relevant number of market actors.[204] Certainly, however, the liquidity of the market will not be enhanced.[205] This means that within the framework of the Data Act's mandatory access regime the IoT data will not be traded on the market at the full plus value that they would have under conditions of open workable competition.

c. Contract and Regulatory Rigidity

The welfare losses that are likely to result from the rigid consent requirement and its potential participatory function may hardly be justified on countervailing legal

[202] See above text at note 78 et seq.

[203] This systemic particularity of product data raises additional issues of equal treatment of users as regards their entitlement to participation in the plus value of product data that cannot be dealt with in this contribution.

[204] Irrespective of the impact divergent bargaining positions may have on the outcome of the negotiations on the consent of the user (see above II.C.ii.b); also text at note 202), practical considerations may overshadow the participation issue, e.g., users that are end-consumers tend to focus only on the terms of acquisition of the connected product; by contrast, industrial users may also be interested in some additional data sharing, eg, in accessing data that are not readily available (Art 4(1) Data Act) and/or in obtaining access also to the general design and operational data of the connected product.

[205] Recital 26 Data Act.

grounds relating to the respect for the legitimate interests of the user or of the data holder. More particularly, the mere fact that the product data are generated by the use that the user makes of the connected product does not sufficiently support a claim to (monetary) participation in the plus value of the product data because, in itself, such use is not meritorious enough. It will be regular and routine use, but it will also be non-expert use, inadequate, inadvertent or improper use, overuse or underuse, even passive use.[206] Obviously, although these uses may be highly relevant to the analysis of the product's operation and functionality, they do not justify participation in the potential plus value of the data. In addition, the data need not be user-specific. To the contrary, in many cases it is the average user's use of the product that matters, not that of the individual user. Nor is it plausible that because 'the user bears the risks and enjoys the benefits of the connected product . . . (it) should be entitled to derive benefit from data generated by that connected product'.[207] While the premise is correct and supports the user's claim to access, the conclusion does not logically follow from it. Since the user pays for the acquisition of a connected product, it is entitled to benefit from the product's full functionality as a connected product. By contrast, the user's interest in monetising the product data as such precisely reaches beyond the use of the connected product and also beyond the use of the data for that product, that is, it is outside the bargain for the sale, rental or lease of the product. By definition, there are two separate and different goods, the tangible and the intangible,[208] and the entire idea is to trade them separately. If the user is to separately monetise the product data it may access free of cost as a matter of obtaining the full benefit of the product's functionality, the profit resulting from their plus value will come to it as a windfall profit – and as an invitation to the data holder to revise its pricing policy!

This, indeed, is the basic dilemma. If instead of the user the data holder were allowed to independently monetise the data, much of their plus value would likewise come to it as a windfall profit. It is true that, because it designs the connected product, the data holder pre-determines or, for that matter, 'co-generates' the data that result from the use of the product. However, since the functionality of the product determines its price, the data holder may recoup the investment it made in the design and manufacture of the connected product by the aggregate sales of the product. This may be one of the reasons why the legislature decided not to create a property-like right in data of the data holder. However, it did not create such a right of the user either.[209] Instead of attributing rights in product data to the individual actors concerned, it left the distribution of the plus value of such data to the parties arranging for it by way of contract within the framework of a regime of mandatory accessibility of IoT data. While this contribution is not the place to discuss again the pros and cons of one or the other kind of rights in data in general,[210] a regrettable aspect of the legislature's

[206] Recital 15 Data Act.

[207] Recital 18 Data Act.

[208] For this classic distinction see recently J Drexl, 'Lessons from Intellectual Property Law for Designing Modern EU Data Law', in Thouvenin et al (eds), above note 23, 981, 983 et seq.

[209] See recitals 6, 25 Data Act. The Data Act defines the legal position of the user restrictively even as regards protection under tort law; see text at notes 186 et seq.

[210] See above note 172; recently Drexl, above note 208, 987 and throughout; for the earlier discussion H Ullrich, 'Technology Protection and Competition Policy for the Information Economy, in J-M Bruguière

approach is that it legalises a data holder's western-style practice of taking any data under control it can get hold of. It, thus, allows the data holder to deal with the data irrespective of the nature of their informational substance as if they were its own, that is, it allows the data holder to de facto privatise the public domain.[211] Understanding the requirement of the user consenting to the use of the product data as entitling it to participation in the plus value of the data additionally consecrates these practices.

Be this as it may, the fact that the legislature abstained from establishing explicit rules on the allocation of the plus value of IoT data but, instead, left the problem to the parties resolving it by their contracting initiatives and practices is likely to result in the Data Act's rules on access remaining a regulatory regime that will hardly contribute to competition developing more intensely on aftermarkets and ancillary markets than the competition rules ensure in the analogue world, let alone contribute to competition spreading beyond these markets. The reason for this scepticism is that the legislature did not really follow the inner logic of a concept of value allocation by free contractual arrangement either.[212] In order to ensure efficient outcomes, such a concept must allow all market forces to play, including third parties that in one way or the other contribute to or benefit from the use and/or the (multi-)functionality of product data. However, instead of introducing some general access right that would also enable third parties to independently access unprotected product data for any legitimate and fair use and, thus, implement the principle of enhanced communication by digitisation of information upon which the internet rests, or, alternatively, of adopting at least the concept of co-generation of product data by the data holder and the user that would allow both to independently use and exploit the data, the Data Act squeezes the use and exploitation of product data into a narrow regulatory framework.[213] Although this framework is intended to accommodate the conditions of access and use to the needs and interests of all of the parties concerned, it is highly asymmetric with the data holder enjoying a position of quasi-exclusivity and advantages of costs and information that in themselves are problematic enough.[214] In

---

and C Geiger (eds), *Mélanges M. Vivant Paris* (Paris, Dalloz, 2020) 457, 474 and throughout with references (= Max Planck Institute for Innovation and Competition Research Paper No. 19-12, ssrn.com/abstract = 3437177, sub C.3.b),(ii),(iii)).

[211] Ullrich, above note 210, 481. The data holder's main tool of 'privatising' the data are TPM, but these are only protected as such, not as providing rights in data; see above II.D.i.b.

[212] According to Schweitzer et al, above note 4, sub C. II. that concept grosso modo prevails in the USA. For details see American Law Institute and European Law Institute (eds), ALI-ELI Principles for a Data Economy - Data Transactions and Data Rights, ELI Final Council Draft (N Cohen and C Wendehorst, Reporters), 27 September 2021, available at www.europeanlawinstitute.eu sub projects&publications/publications.

[213] For a general analysis of the policy options for attributing the power to use and exploit product data and the choice made by the Data Act see M Eckardt and W Kerber, 'Property Rights Theory, Bundles of Rights on IoT Data and the EU Data Act' (2023) 57 *J Eur L Econ* 113 and throughout. Andrássy Working Paper Series in Economics and Business Administration No 51=ssrn.com/abstract=4376833 with references. On the co-generation concept see Eckardt and Kerber, ibid, sub 4.3; Schweitzer et al, above note 4, 213, 216; Metzger, Schweitzer, above note 35, 50 et seq. The problem with the concept is that it operates asymmetrically; see below note 214. J Drexl, Data Access and Control in the Era of Connected Devices, Brussels, BEUC, 2018, sub 5.3 early on advocated for a general access right but made third parties' access dependent on consent by the user, ibid sub 5.3.f).

[214] See above II.C.ii.b and c; II.C.iii.c. Nota bene, as regards the advantages of the data holder, it holds (or may obtain) the totality of the data of the product (design, functioning, use) of all users, while the user and the third party may only indirectly access merely the readily available data of the particular user's product. At the latest when arranging with the third party for making the data available to it, the data holder learns

addition, instead of establishing a level playing field for all market actors the Data Act provides for a system of mutual dependencies between them that require each party, before taking action, to contract with at least one, typically with both other parties of the triangular relationship user, data holder and third party. Frequently, therefore, there will be a need for a minimum of contract coordinating, and there will be considerable transaction costs and loss of time.[215] More importantly, this consensus orientation of the access regime is likely to negatively affect that autonomy and spontaneity of business conduct on the market on which the efficient operation of competition rests as a welfare-enhancing process of rivalry for consumer demand and of discovery of innovation opportunities. This inherent conflict of the regulatory access regime with the principles of open competition comes at the expense of both the public interest and the individual interests of parties that hold only a weak bargaining position[216] or that the regime relegates to the position of outsiders as it does in the case of third parties.[217]

III. CONCLUSION

The poor prospects for the Data Act's access regime attaining its objectives may be due, in part, to the over-complexity of its regulatory design and its built-in inertia.[218] It may also be that IoT data are particular enough to be dealt with separately by the legislature.[219] However, the IoT is not particular enough to permit the legislature circumventing the fundamental question of the legal status of data, quite to the contrary. When resolving the conflict between access to data and the protection of

of the purpose for which the third party – and the user in the first place – needs the data (Art 5(1), last sent.; Art 8 Data Act), and it will do so a fortiori in the typical cases of repeated or continuous access. In addition, the data holder is compensated for making the data available to a third party (Art 9 Data Act), and with all these advantages it may compete with the user and/or the third party on all markets whereas both of the latter are subject to non-compete rules regarding the product market (Arts 4(10), 6(2) lit. e) Data Act). Put popularly, the user is the underdog and the third party an outsider; see also Art 11(2), (3) Data Act and above II.D.i.c.

[215] Despite the potential of 'smart contracting' for limiting transaction costs (see G Borges, 'Smart Contracts für Datentransaktionen und der Data Act' (2024) *CR* 425), the essential costs remain: defining and adapting the substance of the contract according to the parties' needs and objectives, monitoring the operation of the contract, enforcing it in case of non-performance or of other violations; see also above notes 103, 147.

[216] See above II.C.ii.b. For one thing, the control of unfair contractual terms (Art 11(2), Art 13 Data Act) cannot compensate for the unequal bargaining relations between the parties, but can only mitigate the exercise of superior bargaining power (for the limits of Art 13 Data Act see above II.B). For another, whatever the reasons are for the development of unequal bargaining positions, it is the objective of a system of free and open competition to ensure that by its very operation competition will not only contain, but erode the existence of market power or prevent its abusive exercise; for the disempowering function of competition, see EJ Mestmäcker and H Schweitzer, *Europäisches Wettbewerbsrecht*, 3rd edn (Munich, CH Beck, 2014) §3, para 77. Put differently, while the existence of unequal bargaining positions justifies the control of unfair contractual terms, the availability of such control does not excuse a regulator abstaining from opening up competition for all or from optimising its workability.

[217] See above note 214.

[218] See also Kerber, above note 66, 121 and throughout; for critical résumés see inter alia Wiebe (GRUR 2023), above note 18, 1577 et seq; Antoine, above note 69, 7, paras 38 et seq.

[219] For the broad (horizontal) scope of application of parts of the Data Act's access regime see above note 51.

trade secrets by a compromise, it put the latter into jeopardy without enhancing the accessibility of product data for more than a limited number of market actors, that is, without ensuring the optimal exploitation of the data's potential for multi-functional use. The requirement that the user must consent to any use of the product data constitutes only a poor substitute to its independent entitlement to the use of the data, has at least a retarding effect on the use of product data by other market actors, and begs the question whether the user is really best placed to determine the economic potential and future use of product data.[220] By elevating TPM to the status of legally protected tools for establishing and maintaining a de facto control over data the legislature dissimulates the fact that TPM do not merely serve to protect investment in the digitisation of information and its communication but for all practical purposes protect the information itself.[221] Much of this information is unprotected and/or not protectable and should be independently accessible by all market actors concerned.[222] It is for this reason more than for any other that concepts of exclusivity of attribution and use do not fit data. At the same time, however, the data-driven economy of the IoT asks for some basic protection of digitised information that would enhance the tradability of data on markets,[223] and, thus, would also cater to their allocation to optimal uses of their multi-functionality.[224]

No doubt, regardless of what general legal principles and doctrinal concepts teach, at least the bigger industrial users of connected products will rely on the requirement of their consent to the use of product data by data holders and/or third parties as a lever for sharing data and/or participating in the plus value of product data. This means that not only the data holders but also the users will have an – indirect – interest in the availability and effectiveness of de facto control over data, if not even a direct one, since, in their turn, the users may hold data. Ultimately, this commonality of interests will foster the acceptance of mere de facto control by TPM and trade secrets and contribute to it extending ever more to information that is in the public domain. Therefore, it is all the more important to concomitantly enhance

[220] See above II.C.ii.a; D.iii.a and b; also Wiebe (GRUR 2023), above note 18, 1578; Antoine, above note 69, 7, para 39. The user's role may become particularly ambivalent in case the product data include personal data, which they frequently do. The principle is that the Data Act applies without prejudice to the protection of personal data by Union law (Art 1(5) and recital 7 Data Act), but the frictions are many; for details see S Richter, 'Vereinbarkeit des Entwurfs zum Data Act und der DS-GVO' (2023) MMR 163; Hennemann in Hennemann et al (eds), above note 53, 40 et seq; Specht-Riemenschneider, above note 56, 810 et seq.

[221] See Art 1(1) Data Act; Drexl in Thouvenin et al (eds), above note 23, 989 et seq.

[222] Arts 4(6)–(8), 5(9)–(11) Data Act precisely distinguish between data that are reserved to the data holder because they are both not generally known and commercially valuable (Art 2(1) Trade Secrets Dir), on the one hand, and, on the other, general use data. The latter form part of the professional expertise of the data holder, the user and the third party, respectively, and, over time, develop into their expert experience as unprotected but valuable know-how.

[223] According to the cooperative empirical study by Fraunhofer Institut für Software und Systemtechnik ISST et al, above note 46, sub 3.5, 52 et seq, 68.1 per cent of the firms questioned see legal problems as an obstacle to data sharing, and 77.2 per cent consider the risk of unauthorised access by third parties an obstacle; for similar findings see M Scheufen, 'Hemmnisse beim Data-Sharing' (2024) 54(2) *IW-Trends* 65, 73.

[224] For the allocative function and the imperfections of technology markets see inter alia, D Harhoff, 'Markets for Technology and Licensing – Empirical Evidence and Policy Options', in H Ullrich, P Drahos and G Ghidini (eds), *Kritika – Essays on Intellectual Property*, Vol 6 (Cheltenham, Edward Elgar, 2024) 1 and throughout with references.

the tradability of data and the transparency of trade in data. Instead of relying on auxiliary ways and means alone, the Data Act should have addressed squarely the dilemma that exists between general access to data and secure trade in data. Not least because of this failure will the Data Act hardly hold the promise it makes in its recital 26: to foster the emergence of liquid, fair and efficient markets for non-personal data!

10

Article 13 of the Data Act as EU Contract Law

MAGNUS STRAND*

I. INTRODUCTION

EU LAW IS RARELY directly applicable to contracts between private parties, even though Article 101(2) TFEU has always provided an exception to that main rule.[1] Other instances of contractual rules in EU law are mainly found in sector-specific directives.[2] Another example has been enacted through Article 13 of the 2023 Data Act,[3] adopted under Article 114 TFEU, which sets out a binding rule making certain unfair contractual terms non-binding on a party on whom it has been unilaterally imposed.[4] As the Data Act is a regulation, Article 13 will be directly applicable in all Member States and shall apply to contracts concluded after 12 September 2025.[5] Article 13 thus constitutes a new example of EU regulation of contractual relations.

* Thanks are due to the editors and to Dr Donal Casey, Dr Hajo Michael Holtz, Dr Andreas Kotsios and to the entire 'AI in law and business discussion group' at Uppsala University for useful comments on draft versions.

[1] As is well-known, the EU has no competence to adopt broad private law legislation. Nonetheless, limited aspects of private law have been addressed in order for other harmonising legislation to function as intended. There is no room to go in-depth into the discussion on EU competence here, neither generally nor with particular focus on the Data Act. Ulf Bernitz addresses the constitutional issue in *Europarättens genomslag* (Stockholm, Norstedts Juridik, 2012) 179–80. On art 101(2) TFEU as a contractual provision, see ibid 271–74.

[2] Such as Council Directive 93/13/EEC of 5 April 1993 on unfair terms in consumer contracts [1993] OJ L 95/29; or Directive (EU) 2015/2302 of the European Parliament and of the Council of 25 November 2015 on package travel and linked travel arrangements [2015] OJ L 326/1. The broader contract law attempt by the Commission, in Proposal for a Regulation on a Common European Sales (2011/0284 (COD)), was unsuccessful. On this initiative, see Bernitz, *Europarättens genomslag*, above note 1, 167–89.

[3] Regulation (EU) 2023/2854 of the European Parliament and of the Council of 13 December 2023 on harmonised rules on fair access to and use of data (Data Act) OJ L 2023/2854.

[4] ibid. The binding nature of the rule follows from art 13(9): Parties may not contract out of its application. Nonetheless, it should be possible for a party to waive its rights under art 13 at a point in time when those rights have become enforceable, provided that such a waiver is 'freely agreed to, with the result that it must not amount to an abuse of the creditor's freedom of contract which is attributable to the debtor'; Case C-406/21, *A Oy v B Ky and Joint heirs of C*, EU:C:2022:816, para 59.

[5] Data Act art 50(5).

The balancing of commercial freedom in the market economy, on the one hand, and regulating to counter its negative side effects, on the other hand, is arguably the overarching theme of the works of Ulf Bernitz. On the very first page of his 1969 PhD thesis, he recognised that law governing our markets 'mirrors fundamental political and economical decisions made in society', and the 'continuing wrestling match between proponents of centrally governed and ungoverned industry'.[6] Some 44 years later, the Court of Justice held in *Sky Österreich* that 'Article 16 of the Charter covers . . ., the freedom of contract . . . [which] includes, in particular, the freedom to choose with whom to do business . . . and the freedom to determine the price'.[7] However, the Court also held that this freedom 'is not absolute, but must be viewed in relation to its social function'.[8] In his textbook on the legal foundations of market economy and competition law, which is widely used in Sweden (and now kept updated by professor Lars Henriksson), Bernitz acknowledged this balancing exercise as a point of departure for understanding competition law and consumer law.[9]

The same balancing exercise is expressed in the Data Act, and in particular in its Article 13. The purpose of Article 13 is to govern business-to-business (B2B) contract terms on the sharing of data which is collected, generated and processed in relation to online products, referred to in the Act as 'connected products'.[10] While much of the Data Act focuses on business-to-consumer (B2C) relations,[11] and in particular on user rights in relation to connected products, B2B issues are closely linked to the B2C issues. The user rights protected by the Data Act are essentially rights to harness the power of users' data, including, under its Article 5, a power to transfer those data to third parties whose services can help users reap further benefits from their data. Under recital 42, this right for users should be enforceable. As a consequence, providers of connected products or 'related services' may be under an obligation to share data with third parties at the request of users (or as a consequence of obligations under the Data Act or other applicable law). The B2B parties, that is, the

[6] Ulf Bernitz, *Marknadsrätt: En komparativ studie av marknadslagstiftningens utveckling och huvudlinjer* (Jurist- och samhällsvetareförbundets Förlags AB 1969) 11. Translation by this author. This quote illustrates that his pioneering work was written in a very different global political landscape than the current, but even though the specific political situation has shifted, the wrestling match continues. Regulatory intervention is a political choice in a specific economic and political context, but to not intervene is also a political choice, and none of them is self-evidently the 'universal baseline option'.

[7] Case C-283/11, *Sky Österreich GmbH v Österreichischer Rundfunk*, EU:C:2013:28 paras 42–43.

[8] ibid para 45.

[9] Ulf Bernitz and Lars Henriksson, *Svensk och europeisk marknadsrätt 1: Konkurrensrätten och marknadsekonomins rättsliga grundvalar* 6th edn (Stockholm, Norstedts Juridik, 2023) 28; see also Bernitz, *Marknadsrätt*, above note 6, 69.

[10] The Data Act targets the Internet of Things (IoT), but under the definition of 'connected product' in art 2(5) its scope extends to any product 'that obtains, generates or collects data concerning its use or environment and that is able to communicate product data via an electronic communications service, physical connection or on-device access'. However, art 2(5) excludes from the scope of the Data Act products whose primary function is the storing, processing or transmission of data on behalf of any party other than the user.

[11] Admittedly, the Data Act only rarely uses the term 'consumer', as most rights are instead extended to a much broader category indicated by the term 'user'; a user can be a business. With this said, it remains true that much of the Data Act focuses on business-to-consumer (B2C) relations.

data holders who provide a connected product and/or related service and the data recipients to whom data should be transferred, will therefore need to contract on the necessary sharing of data. Under Article 8(1) of the Data Act those contracts must be designed so that the data is made available under 'fair, reasonable and non-discriminatory terms and conditions and in a transparent manner'. To that end, under Article 8(2), a contractual term 'shall not be binding if it constitutes an unfair contractual term within the meaning of Article 13 or if [it limits . . .] the user's rights'. Article 1(10) of the Data Act further suggests that the same rules will apply to voluntary data sharing contracts.

The more precise meaning of what is an unfair contractual term in a B2B contract, within the meaning of the Data Act, is thus further explained in Article 13. Under Article 13(1) of the Data Act:

> A contractual term concerning access to and the use of data or liability and remedies for the breach or the termination of data related obligations, which has been unilaterally imposed by an enterprise on another enterprise, shall not be binding on the latter enterprise if it is unfair.[12]

Article 13 will be discussed here against the backdrop of writings on EU law and contract law by Ulf Bernitz, to whom this author is personally indebted for both his inspiration and his concrete assistance in matters connected to academic publishing and career choices. The essential elements of the rule in Article 13 of the Data Act will be identified and analysed in light of the previous *acquis* of EU contract law. The writings of Ulf Bernitz will be used to discuss thorny issues in relation to Article 13 – of which there are several. Focus will be on the following four:

1. What is meant by 'unfair' contractual terms under Article 13?
2. When should such a contractual term be considered to have been 'unilaterally imposed' on a contracting party by its co-contractor?
3. What is meant by stipulating that an unfair contractual term 'shall not be binding' on the enterprise upon which it has been unilaterally imposed?
4. Under what circumstances should an unfair contractual term be considered 'severable' from the remaining terms of the contract?

These issues will be addressed in turn below. As Bernitz has repeatedly pointed out, EU law concepts have an autonomous meaning under EU law that may differ from those in the laws of the Member States.[13] Therefore, an inquiry into these questions should be made on the basis of EU law sources, but with an openness to national law where EU law itself has such an openness.

In the final section, there will be some reflections on Article 13 of the Data Act as an addition to (the scarce) EU law excursions into contract law.

[12] Art 13(2) then stipulates what may perhaps be self-evident; that a contractual term 'which reflects mandatory provisions of Union law, or provisions of Union law which would apply' but for the contractual term at issue, must not be regarded as unfair within the meaning of art 13. The Commission has published a 'Frequently Asked Questions' document, available at <https://digital-strategy.ec.europa.eu/en/library/commission-publishes-frequently-asked-questions-about-data-act>, but it adds nothing tangible on art 13.

[13] Bernitz, *Europarättens genomslag*, above note 1, 57; Ulf Bernitz, *Europarättens tillämpning* (Hedvig Bernitz ed, Stockholm, Norstedts Juridik, 2023) 158.

II. UNFAIR CONTRACTUAL TERMS

A. The Definition of Unfair Contractual Terms and Its Background

The definition of what is an unfair contractual term is in Article 13(3): 'A contractual term is unfair if it is of such a nature that its use grossly deviates from good commercial practice in data access and use, contrary to good faith and fair dealing.'

Before proceeding to in-depth analysis of this rule, it is noted that the Data Act sets limits on the scope of the prohibition against unfair terms. These limits follow from reading Article 13 in conjunction with Article 8(2) of the Act. First, the material scope of the prohibition against unfair terms is limited by stipulating that the contractual term targeted must concern either

1. 'access to and the use of data', which is a reference to the rights to access and use conferred by the Data Act, or
2. 'liability and remedies for the breach or the termination of data related obligations', which is a reference to enforcement issues largely governed by national law.[14]

This is similarly stated in recital 60 of the Data Act:

> [Article 13] should apply only to those elements of a contract that are related to making data available, that is contractual terms concerning access to and use of the data as well as liability or remedies for breach and termination of data related obligations. Other parts of the same contract, unrelated to making data available, should not be subject to the unfairness test.

Another limit to the material scope of Article 13(3) is set out in 13(8), from which it follows that the Article 'does not apply to contractual terms defining the main subject matter of the contract or to the adequacy of the price, as against the data supplied in exchange'. This will be examined below.

Article 13(3) also limits the personal scope of the prohibition as it covers only contractual terms imposed 'by an enterprise on another enterprise'. In other words, as was stressed above, Article 13 of the Data Act only covers B2B contracts. As pointed out by Hanns Ullrich, in his contribution to this volume, Article 13 does not presume that data holders will be the infringing party – it covers unfair terms B2B whether stipulated by data holders or data recipients.[15] As regards B2C contracts, recital 28 of the Data Act refers to the Unfair Terms Directive and to the Unfair Commercial Practices Directive.[16] The Commission had intended an even narrower scope to Article 13, limiting its application to situations where the enterprise, upon which an unfair contractual term was imposed, was an SME 'as defined in Article 2 of the Annex to Recommendation 2003/361/EC'.[17] This was taken out in legislative negotiations.

[14] Data Act ch IX.

[15] Hanns Ullrich, ch 9 in this book.

[16] Directive 2005/29/EC of the European Parliament and of the Council of 11 May 2005 concerning unfair business-to-consumer commercial practices in the internal market [2005] OJ L 149/22.

[17] Commission, Proposal for a Regulation of the European Parliament and of the Council on harmonised rules on fair access to and use of data (Data Act) 2022, art 13(1) in the proposed regulation.

The wording of Article 13(3) is inspired by Article 7(1) of the Late Payments Directive.[18] The Court of Justice has not elaborated on the interpretation of the phrase, but it is explained in recital 28 of the Late Payments Directive that the phrase used was adopted, in turn, from the Draft Common Frame of Reference (DCFR).[19] The DCFR is an academic 'model code' for European private law, funded by the Commission to serve in its legislative work.[20] It has relevance for the interpretation of EU contract law rules insofar as it is a restatement of private law principles common to the traditions of the Member States. For instance, those common principles underlie Article 340(2) TFEU and Article 41(3) of the Charter, and have inspired, when relevant and in the absence of harmonisation, the case law of the Court of Justice.[21] As the DCFR is an explicit inspiration for the wording of Article 7(1) of the Late Payments Directive, and therefore also for the wording of Article 13(3) of the Data Act, it is interesting to look more closely at the model rules of the DCFR in this context.

The DCFR sets out different tests for the unfairness of contractual terms depending on the characters of the parties, that is, whether the contracts are peer-to-peer, B2C or B2B contracts. B2B contracts are covered by DCFR Article II-9:405. The DCFR full edition also includes notes and explanations for each rule. In the explanations to this model rule[22] it is clear that the phrase, which has been transposed into the Late Payments Directive and now into the Data Act, is intended to frame unfairness as a narrowly construed exception to the general rule that the agreed terms in B2B contracts should be respected. This confirms that Article 13 of the Data Act should be used restrictively: a 'gross' deviation, as set out in Article 13(3), is evidently a high bar to unfairness. By way of comparison, the Unfair Terms Directive (only) requires that the contractual term at issue causes 'significant imbalance' between the parties for it to be regarded as unfair within the meaning of that directive.[23] Moreover, the extensive case law of the Court of Justice on the Unfair Terms Directive has, as Bernitz has argued, a tangible focus on consumer protection.[24] The interpretative perspective of consumer protection will not be relevant under Article 13 of the Data Act, however. This further underlines the exceptional character of Article 13 of the Data Act as a B2B rule. In a B2B context, any parallels to the Unfair Terms Directive, and case law under that directive, must be made with great caution.

[18] Directive 2011/7/EU of the European Parliament and of the Council of 16 February 2011 on combating late payment in commercial transactions [2011] OJ L 48/1.

[19] Christian von Bar and Eric M Clive, *Principles, Definitions and Model Rules of European Private Law Draft Common Frame of Reference (DCFR) Full Edition* (Munich, Sellier European Law Publishers, 2009). Interestingly, the DCFR (642) cites art 3(3) of the previous EU Late Payments Directive (Directive 2000/35/EC of the European Parliament and of the Council of 29 June 2000 on combating late payment in commercial transactions [2000] OJ L 200/35) as its inspiration (although this was phrased slightly differently) – full circle!

[20] Bernitz, *Europarättens genomslag*, above note 1, 164–66.

[21] See eg Case C-47/07 P, *Masdar (UK) Ltd v Commission of the European Communities*, EU:C:2008:726 para 47.

[22] Bar and Clive, above note 19, 641; Case C-575/18 P, *Czech Republic v European Commission*, EU:C:2020:530 para 82.

[23] Bernitz comments on the meaning of 'significant imbalance' in Bernitz, above *Europarättens tillämpning*, above note 13, 200–01.

[24] ibid 191.

B. Delineating the Substantive Meaning of Unfairness

Against this background, let us proceed to an analysis of the meaning of 'unfairness' under Article 13(3). The Commission has submitted that contractual terms should be seen as unfair within the meaning of the Data Act if they 'go beyond being simply disadvantageous and are abusive, putting an excessive burden on one party'.[25] This is further underlined in recital 61 to the Data Act:

> The vast majority of contractual terms that are commercially more favourable to one party than to the other, including those that are normal in business-to-business contracts, are a normal expression of the principle of contractual freedom and continue to apply. For the purposes of this Regulation, grossly deviating from good commercial practice would include, inter alia, objectively impairing the ability of the party upon whom the term has been unilaterally imposed to protect its legitimate commercial interest in the data in question.

Accordingly, the ban on unfair contractual terms in the Data Act was drafted for quite restrictive use, reserving the label of 'unfair' in B2B relations to abusive practices that undermine the contractual freedom of one of the parties.

What may constitute such abusive practices, then? While Article 13(3) is an abstract provision, Article 13(4) identifies a few narrowly defined classes of contractual terms that 'shall be unfair for the purposes of paragraph 3', and Article 13(5) identifies classes of contractual terms that 'shall be presumed to be unfair'. These will be referred to as the 'black list' and the 'grey list', respectively. There is no room here to discuss the content of the lists in detail, but they can be summarised as follows: the black list excludes contractual terms that limit liability for intentional and grossly negligent infringements of the Data Act, that limit the use of remedies by the victimised contractor and/or give one party the right to interpret the contract or determine if data is supplied in conformity with the contract. Although the black list in Article 13(4) pinpoints certain terms that are automatically classified as unfair, the list is non-exhaustive. The purpose of the black list thus seems to be twofold: it not only pinpoints certain unfair terms, it also offers guidance on what other terms may be unfair within the meaning of Article 13(3). As explained in recital 62, 'the terms listed as unfair contractual terms . . . should serve as a yardstick to interpret the general unfairness provision'. Consequently, other similarly abusive contractual terms can also be held to constitute gross deviations from good commercial practice in data access and use and therefore be unfair within the meaning of Article 13(3).

The grey list is longer and more multifaceted. It includes contractual terms affecting liability and remedies in other unreasonable ways than those in the black list, but also terms that abuse the balance of powers between the parties with regard to the access and use of data of the other party, or offer possibilities to unilaterally change core aspects of the contract. By contrast from the black list, the grey list in Article 13(5) seems to be an exhaustive list of contractual terms that should be presumed

[25] Commission, SWD(2022) 34 final, Commission Staff Working Document, Impact Assessment Report, Accompanying the document Proposal for a Regulation of the European Parliament and of the Council on harmonised rules on fair access to and use of data (Data Act) 166.

to be unfair within the meaning of Article 13(3). The presumption can be rebutted by demonstrating that the contractual term listed is not unfair in the specific case in question.[26] It could perhaps be possible for the Court of Justice to extend the grey list. In any case, it is clear that there can be other types of unfair contractual terms than those listed in Article 13(4) and (5).[27] By comparison, the Unfair Terms Directive non-exhaustive 'grey list' seems to be a whiter shade of grey than its counterpart in the Data Act, as the former only lists terms 'which may be regarded as unfair', thus providing examples, and does not stipulate a presumption of unfairness. Bernitz has nonetheless pointed out that the grey list in the Unfair Terms Directive is generally perceived as indicating a presumption of unfairness pertaining to the contractual terms listed, and that it has been interpreted as such in Swedish legislative preparatory works.[28]

Does Article 13 cover unfair prices? The short answer is no. It follows from Article 13(8) that the Article 'does not apply to contractual terms defining the main subject matter of the contract or to the adequacy of the price, as against the data supplied in exchange'. A very similar limitation is set out in Article 4(2) of the Unfair Terms Directive,[29] which concerns B2C contracts. Bernitz has explained that this limitation in the Unfair Terms Directive serves to clarify that the rule is not intended to constitute a regulation of prices on the market, neither per se nor indirectly through an evaluation of the balance between the main subject matter of the contract and the consideration.[30] It is similarly stated in the Commission Impact Assessment Report, accompanying its proposal for the Data Act, that issues pertaining to price and its relation to the main subject matter of the contract should in principle be 'left to the parties' negotiations' in the context of data sharing.[31] There are nonetheless caveats to this statement.

First, recital 58 indicates that unfairness can concretely mean 'that access to data is commercially less viable and sometimes economically prohibitive'. Moreover, the grey list in Article 13(5) includes a sub-paragraph (g), which presumes contract terms to be unfair if they enable one contractor 'to substantially change the price specified in the contract' without valid reason for such changes.[32] Consequently, Article 13(8) should not be read as to indicate that economic repercussions from unfair contractual terms are excluded from the assessment of unfairness. There are nonetheless caveats to this statement.

Second, prices exacted by data holders are indirectly regulated by Article 9 of the Data Act, which introduces a right to reasonable, non-discriminatory compensation for data holders, which 'may include a margin' and which is broader in scope than Article 13 as it has no restriction to 'gross' deviations from its standard. Article

[26] Data Act rec 62.

[27] ibid.

[28] Bernitz, *Europarättens tillämpning*, above note 13, 201. The Swedish government bill referred to is prop. 1994/95:17, where at p 48 the grey list of Council Directive 93/13/EEC (above note 2) is said to include such a presumption. See also Ulf Bernitz, *Standardavtalsrätt* 9th edn (Stockholm, Norstedts Juridik, 2018) 178–80.

[29] Council Directive 93/13/EEC, above note 3.

[30] Bernitz, *Europarättens tillämpning*, above note 13, 199. On the twentieth-century history of price regulation see Bernitz, *Marknadsrätt*, above note 6, 165–67.

[31] Commission SWD(2022) 34 final, above note 25, 166.

[32] This mirrors point 1(j) in the Annex to Council Directive 93/13/EEC (n 3).

9(2)–(3) proceeds to outline a framework for what is reasonable compensation.[33] At first glance, Article 9 seems to protect the interests of data holders to be compensated for their costs in relation to data sharing, but Article 9(4) explicitly protects data recipients who are SMEs or non-profit research organisations, and Article 9(7) orders data holders to keep data recipients informed of how their claims for compensation have been calculated, 'so that the data recipient can assess whether the requirements of paragraphs 1 to 4 are met'. There is therefore a certain tension, or at least a potential overlap, between Articles 13 and 9.

It seems from the above that Article 13 is not intended to cover pricing as such, even if economic aspects can be part of the assessment of unfairness. Instead, Article 9 covers 'compensation' which, according to recitals 46 and 47, 'should not be understood to constitute payment for the data itself' but rather for making it available to the data recipient. Under Article 9(5), the European Data Innovation Board will assist the Commission to issue guidelines on how to estimate reasonable compensation in this context. It nonetheless remains unclear what should be the legal consequence if compensation is not regarded as reasonable and non-discriminatory under Article 9. For instance, could a court review the compensation agreed? Could a claim for contractual damages be brought before the competent court? In the absence of a body of EU case law, or standards for good commercial practice, it is agreed that these issues will be governed by national law,[34] albeit subject to EU principles of effective judicial protection.[35]

In sum, the prohibition against unfair contractual terms in Article 13 of the Data Act is restricted in scope and should be expected also to be used restrictively. Contractual terms are unfair within the meaning of Article 13 only if they grossly deviate from good commercial practice, thereby constituting an abuse of the contractor upon which it is imposed. It will consequently not suffice for the contractual term at issue to simply be disadvantageous to one of the co-contractors. The imbalance between the two, in the contractual term at issue (albeit seen in context),[36] must be significantly more pronounced.

III. UNILATERAL IMPOSITION OF CONTRACTUAL TERMS

The next issue to be explored is when an allegedly unfair contractual term can be considered to have been 'unilaterally imposed' on a contracting party by its co-contractor. This is explained in Article 13(7):

> A contractual term shall be considered to be unilaterally imposed within the meaning of this Article if it has been supplied by one contracting party and the other contracting party

[33] In this context, notice also arts 15 and 20 of the Data Act, concerning requests for data by public agencies in order to respond to a crisis, and fair compensation to data holders for this sharing of data.

[34] Ullrich (note 15).

[35] On how these principles can play out in EU law on the digital market, see Magnus Strand, 'Private Enforcement under the Digital Markets Act: Rights and Remedies Revisited' (2024) 7 *Nordic Journal of European Law* 120–34.

[36] The DCFR includes a model article II-9:407 setting out contextual factors to be considered in assessing unfairness in B2B contracts; Bar and Clive, above n 19, 649.

> has not been able to influence its content despite an attempt to negotiate it. The contracting party that supplied the contractual term bears the burden of proving that that term has not been unilaterally imposed. The contracting party that supplied the contested contractual term may not argue that the term is an unfair contractual term.

As mentioned, Article 13(7) of the Data Act does neither reserve the stronger position for data holders, nor presume that data holders will be in the stronger bargaining position. It is of no consequence to the application of Article 13 whether it is the data holder or data recipient who has and wields a stronger bargaining position: it can be either of the two.

Recital 59 further explains when a contractual term should be considered to have been 'unilaterally imposed' on one of the contractors:

> This concerns take-it-or-leave-it situations where one party supplies a certain contractual term and the other enterprise cannot influence the content of that term despite an attempt to negotiate it.

On the basis of Article 13(7) and recital 59, it is submitted that the assessment to be made can be sub-divided into the following elements:

1. One of the contractors has, unilaterally, supplied the contractual term at issue;
2. The other contractor has tried to negotiate or otherwise influence the content of the contractual term; and
3. The latter contractor was unsuccessful in this attempt.

The second sentence of Article 13(7) puts the onus of proving that the contractual term was not 'unilaterally imposed' on the contractor who supplied it. This must pertain to the second and third element above. The contractor who supplied the contractual term at issue should thus be able to meet its burden of proof, and escape the scope of application of Article 13, either by proving that the other contractor never tried to negotiate or influence the term, or by proving that the term was meaningfully revised in response to objections made by the other contractor during negotiations. This interpretation finds further support in the next sentence of recital 59:

> A contractual term that is simply provided by one party and accepted by the other enterprise or a term that is negotiated and subsequently agreed in an amended form between contracting parties should not be considered to have been unilaterally imposed.

This has no effect on the burden of proof regarding the first element above, that is, that one of the contractors has, unilaterally, supplied the contractual term at issue. It seems this first element should be proven by the other party, in order for the burden of proof to shift with regard to the second and third elements.

Finally, the third sentence of Article 13(7) is an estoppel rule, under which the contracting party that supplied the contested contractual term is barred from reaping any potential benefits from the fact that the term is an unfair contractual term. This rule will probably find its typical application in situations where the infringer is trying to escape the contract by using unfairness as a sword or shield argument.

IV. UNFAIR CONTRACTUAL TERMS SHALL NOT BE BINDING

A. The Ambiguities of 'Not Binding'

In his writings, Ulf Bernitz has repeatedly revisited the issue of invalidity of contractual terms that constitute an infringement of competition law.[37] He has also repeatedly discussed the relationship between the Swedish transposition of the Unfair Terms Directive and general Swedish civil law on unfair contractual terms.[38] These are two very different variations of unlawfulness of contractual terms, and their enforcement also differs in significant ways. Indeed, the contract laws of Europe include many different nuances to the nullity, avoidability or other 'non-binding effect' of a contractual term which, for one reason or other, should not be fully upheld. There are also obvious differences between rules that can be privately enforced through litigation, where a claimant brings an action for a certain contractual term to be set aside, and rules that are publicly enforced, typically by public agencies issuing a prohibitive injunction against an enterprise to stop it from using a certain contractual term. Of course, both enforcement systems can be available in parallel in relation to the same rule, as is the case for Articles 101 and 102 TFEU.

Consequently, in order to understand what is meant, concretely, for a contractual term to be 'not binding' within the meaning of Article 13, it must first be asked how Article 13 is intended to be enforced. The two distinct questions are, therefore:

1. How might Article 13 of the Data Act be enforced?
2. What might, and should, 'not binding' mean in enforcement of Article 13?

B. Enforcement of Article 13

Implementation and enforcement are covered by Chapter IX (Articles 37–42) of the Data Act, but it is also relevant to consider the non-mandatory dispute settlement mechanism in Article 10. Beginning in Article 37, the Member States are instructed to 'designate one or more [new or existing] competent authorities to be responsible for the application and enforcement' of the Data Act. These competent authorities shall have power to hear complaints, conduct investigations, and to impose 'effective, proportionate and dissuasive financial penalties' on enterprises that have failed to fulfil their obligations under the Data Act. To that end, 'natural and legal persons shall have the right to lodge a complaint' with the competent authority under Article 38, and Member States shall 'lay down the rules on penalties . . . [and] ensure that they are implemented' under Article 40. Anyone affected by a decision taken by a competent authority shall, under Article 39(1), have the right to an effective judicial remedy in order to lodge an appeal against the decision. These Articles set out a framework for public enforcement for the purposes of safeguarding the rights of individuals in the Data Act.

[37] For example in Bernitz, *Marknadsrätt*, above note 6, 372–75; Bernitz, *Europarättens genomslag*, above note 1, 271–74; Bernitz and Henriksson, above note 9, 224–29.

[38] Bernitz, *Standardavtalsrätt*, above note 28, 180–82; Bernitz, *Europarättens tillämpning*, above note 13, 209–11.

Should, or must, there also be a system of private enforcement? This is less clear from Chapter IX,[39] but there are other provisions in the Data Act that reveal that it has been presupposed that private enforcement shall be available through the laws of the Member States. First, Article 10 of the Data Act instructs each of the Member States to set up a non-mandatory dispute settlement body which shall be able to hear disputes between users, data holders and data recipients, including disputes relating to Article 13.[40] Under Article 10(12), the decision of the dispute settlement body 'shall be binding on the parties only if the parties have explicitly consented to its binding nature prior to the start of the dispute settlement proceedings'. In other circumstances, therefore, it shall be understood as a recommendation. Further, under Article 10(13), the possibility of turning to a dispute settlement body set up according to Article 10 'does not affect the right of parties to seek an effective remedy before a court or tribunal of a Member State'. The existence of this dispute settlement mechanism, and its openness to dispute settlement in court or tribunal, must mean that the EU legislature has envisaged that private enforcement of Article 13 shall co-exist with public enforcement under Chapter IX.

Second, the Data Act is a regulation and thus, under Article 288 TFEU, directly applicable in the Member States, even between individuals. Provisions in the Data Act can have direct effect between individuals, and be privately enforceable, if with sufficient precision it confers a right on the claimant which corresponds to an obligation on the defendant (rather than on any other party, such as the Member State).[41] Article 13 seems to fulfil most of these criteria, but there is room for some discussion concerning the precision of paragraph 3. Undoubtedly, the black list offers enough precision to the types of contractual terms listed, but it may be argued that Article 13(3) is too general in its wording for private enforcement relying only on the direct applicability of the Data Act. One way to counter this possible *lacuna* is for the Member States to support private enforcement of Article 13 by introducing national legislation to that end. This could be a simple additional element in the process of setting up the dispute settlement body under Article 10. It can be added that, in the absence of harmonising EU legislation, the details of private enforcement will be governed by national law, albeit subject to general EU law principles of judicial protection.[42]

It is therefore concluded that the Data Act includes a system of public enforcement the basic tenets of which are set out in its Chapter IX, and presupposes that complementary private enforcement of its substantive rules is available in the Member States, supported by the dispute settlement body to be set up in accordance with Article 10.

[39] Art 39(2) says that '[w]here a competent authority fails to act on a complaint, any affected natural and legal person shall . . . either have the right to an effective judicial remedy or access to review by an impartial body with the appropriate expertise'. The latter alternative, to have the failure to act reviewed by an impartial body, is evidently another public enforcement mechanism. The former, having a right to an effective judicial remedy, is less clear-cut and may be satisfied by either a public or private enforcement mechanism. In isolation, this provision suggests private enforcement of art 13 of the Data Act is possible, but not necessary.

[40] Data Act art 10(1) mentions ch IV, which consists of art 13.

[41] Case C-253/00, *Antonio Muñoz y Cia SA and Superior Fruiticola SA v Frumar Ltd and Redbridge Produce Marketing Ltd*, EU:C:2002:497.

[42] See note 35.

C. What Does 'Not Binding' Mean?

For the purposes of public enforcement of Article 13 under Chapter IX of the Data Act, national competent authorities will have power to penalise parties who infringe Article 13 by imposing unfair contractual terms on the other party. It can further be assumed that national competent authorities may have power to issue prohibitive injunctions against the use of such contractual terms by an enterprise.

However, fines and prohibitive injunctions issued by a public agency do not mean that a party upon whom an unfair contractual term has been imposed will thereby escape that contractual term. To that end, the contractual term must be altered, avoided, or declared null and void on the basis of national private law. Granted, the parties may also re-negotiate the contract to this end, and the infringing contractor may have a strong incentive to do so in order to escape periodic penalties imposed under Article 37(5)(d) that will be payable until the infringement is ended. Still, the national competent authority may have failed to act, or the action taken may not have led to a re-negotiation. In such circumstances, to what effect may victimised contractors invoke, in private enforcement, that the unfair contractual term is 'not binding' on them?

The recitals of the Data Act offer no further guidance in this respect and there is as yet no case law of the Court of Justice on the Data Act. Can there be guidance in case law on adjacent EU law rules? Article 101(2) TFEU concerns B2B relations, but it is a public policy rule with a stronger wording, saying that agreements in breach of that Article are automatically void. Therefore, there is reason to be cautious of parallels to Article 101(2). It is equally problematic to draw parallels from case law on Article 6(1) of the Unfair Terms Directive. With regard to the meaning of 'not binding' it may be tempting to make inferences from that case law, but at the same time there may be aspects to this case law which should probably not be transposed from the B2C context of the Unfair Terms Directive to the B2B context of Article 13 of the Data Act. With this said, to find guidance on the more general meaning of 'not binding' under Article 13 of the Data Act it may be rewarding to extrapolate from the case law on both Article 101(2) TFEU and Article 6(1) of the Unfair Terms Directive, with the caution advised.

As regards Article 101(2) TFEU, it is settled that contractual clauses that are contrary to Article 101 TFEU are automatically null and void *ex tunc*.[43] Bernitz has explained that 'nullity in European competition law is of a strong, absolute character . . . [and] has effect *erga omnes*'.[44] This means it can be relied on by anyone. He further refers to the DCFR, which includes a rule on voidness of a contract which infringes a fundamental principle of law in its Article II-7:301. Nonetheless, Bernitz stressed that nullity as a private law concept may be interpreted slightly differently in the Member States and that this will have an influence on national courts irrespective

[43] Case 48/72, *SA Brasserie de Haecht v Wilkin-Janssen (Haecht II)*, EU:C:1973:11.

[44] Bernitz, *Europarättens genomslag*, above note 1, 278. The text cited is also published as Ulf Bernitz, 'The Sanction of Voidness Under Article 82 EC and Its Relation to the Right to Damages' in Ariel Ezrachi (ed), *Article 82 EC: Reflections on its Recent Evolution* (Oxford, Bloomsbury Publishing, 2009).

of the fact that it should be regarded as an autonomous EU law concept for the purposes of Article 101 TFEU.

Turning to Article 6(1) of the Unfair Terms Directive, the Court of Justice has consistently held that it 'is a mandatory provision which aims to replace the formal balance which the contract establishes between the rights and obligations of the parties with an effective balance which re-establishes equality between them'.[45] As a consequence, the Court has further held, Member States are precluded from allowing national courts to 'revise the content of that term instead of merely setting aside its application'.[46] To that end, the unfair contractual term 'must be regarded, in principle, as never having existed, so that it cannot have any effect'.[47] Indeed:

> such a finding must allow the restoration of the legal and factual situation that the consumer would have been in if that unfair term had not existed, by inter alia, creating a right to restitution of advantages wrongly obtained, to the consumer's detriment, by the seller or supplier on the basis of that unfair term.[48]

Further, the Court of Justice has consistently held, a national court must *ex officio* raise the unfair nature of a contractual term, within the meaning of the Unfair Terms Directive, and not make it an obligation of the consumer to invoke unfairness.[49] It can be concluded from this case law that the meaning of an unfair term being 'not binding' under the Unfair Terms Directive has been interpreted, just as nullity under Article 101(2) TFEU, to be automatic and as having effect *ex tunc*.

As Bernitz has indicated, that case law on the Unfair Terms Directive is driven by consumer protection.[50] By contrast, and while the Data Act partly seeks to protect consumers, Article 13 of the Data Act concerns B2B relations, albeit in the interests of consumers as well as enterprisees. Parallels between the two can only be made with caution. I would also advise caution in relation to Article 101(2) TFEU, which is a public policy rule of EU law. In sum, this attempt to find guidance in adjacent rules of EU law is interesting but inconclusive.

A more promising alternative is to seek inspiration in the DCFR, being an expression of contract law traditions in Europe. While Bernitz pointed to DCFR Article II-7:301 as a parallel to Article 101(2) TFEU, for our purposes we might focus instead on DCFR Article II-9:408 which connects to Article II-9:405 on the meaning of unfairness in B2B contracts. In the explanations to Article II-9:408, the authors state that the effect of 'not binding' in relation to an unfair term is unilateral, in the sense

[45] Case C-168/05, *Elisa María Mostaza Claro v Centro Móvil Milenium SL*, EU:C:2006:675; Case C-618/10, *Banco Español de Crédito, SA v Joaquín Calderón Camino*, EU:C:2012:349.

[46] *Camino*, above note 45, para 71.

[47] Joined Cases C-154/15 and C-307/15, *Francisco Gutiérrez Naranjo v Cajasur Banco SAU, Ana María Palacios Martínez v Banco Bilbao Vizcaya Argentaria SA (BBVA), Banco Popular Español SA v Emilio Irles López and Teresa Torres Andreu*, EU:C:2016:980; Case C-520/21, *Arkadiusz Szcześniak v Bank M SA*, EU:C:2023:478.

[48] *Gutiérrez Naranjo and others*, above note 47, para 66.

[49] Joined cases C-240/98 to C-244/98, *Océano Grupo Editorial SA v Roció Murciano Quintero (C-240/98) and Salvat Editores SA v José M Sánchez Alcón Prades (C-241/98), José Luis Copano Badillo (C-242/98), Mohammed Berroane (C-243/98) and Emilio Viñas Feliú (C-244/98)*, EU:C:2000:346; Case C-473/00, *Cofidis SA v Jean-Louis Fredout*, EU:C:2002:705; *Camino*, above note 45. See also Bar and Clive, above note 19, 655.

[50] Bernitz, *Europarättens tillämpning*, above note 13, 191.

that it is only not binding on the victimised party but remains binding on the infringer.[51] Indeed, this reflects the wording of Article 13(1), according to which an unfair contractual term shall not be binding on the contractor upon whom it was imposed. By contrast, under Article 13(6), third sentence, '[t]he contracting party that supplied the contested contractual term may not argue that the term is an unfair contractual term'. The DCFR continues to explain:

> Not binding means that no legal effects can be based on such a term: neither any rights against the other party [that is, on the party upon whom it was imposed] nor any exclusion or limitation of rights or defences . . . whereas it may be invoked against the supplier of the term, if the other party so desires.[52]

This means that the rule is not null and void, but only inapplicable against the party upon whom it was imposed. This inapplicability is not automatic and courts must not give it effect *ex officio*; rather, it must be invoked. It does not take effect *ex tunc*, but *ex nunc*, that is, it takes effect when invoked. This DCFR perspective on 'not binding' does neither carry the weight of public policy rules (for which it reserves Article II-7:301) nor the consumer protection perspective. This makes it more easily transferrable to a B2B context, where the contractual freedom of the parties is given further leeway.[53] It is therefore submitted that DCFR Article II-9:408 might serve as a better yardstick to the meaning of 'not binding' under Article 13 of the Data Act than the parallels to other EU law rules that were explored above. The latter are probably too far-reaching for the purposes of the Data Act. At least, in the absence of case law indicating a very strong meaning to the concept of 'not binding' in the Data Act, the DCFR version offers a more nuanced approach to how the Court of Justice might interpret this concept.

V. SEVERABILITY OF UNFAIR CONTRACTUAL TERMS

The legal consequences of the fact that a contractual term is not binding on one of the parties further includes the implications of this for the other terms of the contract. Is it meaningful to uphold the remaining parts of the contract, or will it fail in its entirety? With regard to Article 13 of the Data Act, and provided that the interpretation in the previous section is accepted, this may be of slightly less concern than in instances where a stringent concept of nullity applies. Nevertheless, the issue of severability may arise in situations where the 'not binding' effect of Article 13 is invoked, and the consequences of this for the contract can be expected to be quite similar to those where stringer nullity applies. Comparisons with such situations, for which there is case law of the Court of Justice, can therefore help courts to manage the severability issue.

For the purposes of Article 101 TFEU, it has long been settled that the consequences of nullity are governed by national law. In his PhD thesis of 1969,[54] Bernitz

[51] Bar and Clive, above note 19, 654.
[52] ibid 655.
[53] Data Act recs 43, 59, 61.
[54] Bernitz, *Marknadsrätt*, above note 6, 373.

could point to the earliest EU case on this point, *STM*, where it was first held that: 'The automatic nullity in question only applies to those parts of the agreement affected by the prohibition, or to the agreement as a whole if it appears that those parts are not severable from the agreement itself.'[55]

More recently, in *CEPSA*, the Court further held:

> the consequences, for all other parts of the agreement or for other obligations flowing from it, of the nullity are not a matter for [EU] law. It is [for the national court] to determine, in accordance with the national law applicable, the extent and consequences, for the contractual relation as a whole, of the nullity of certain contractual clauses under Article [101(2) TFEU].[56]

Bernitz has explained that if the contractual term which is null and void has a limited role in the contract as a whole, the remaining parts of the contract should remain in force between the parties. However, if the infringing term was central to the contract, it will likely be voidable in its entirety. Difficult cases will be decided on the basis of national law, which may include certain differences between the Member States.[57]

The same applies under Article 6(1) of the Unfair Terms Directive, which stipulates that 'the contract shall continue to bind the parties upon those terms if it is capable of continuing in existence without the unfair terms'. As seen, the Court of Justice does not allow national courts to revise an unfair term in order to make it fair (or at least 'not unfair' within the meaning of the Directive), but the Court does allow for the national courts to replace the unfair contractual term with an underlying supplementary provision of national law. Indeed, the Court of Justice has encouraged national courts to do so.[58]

Similarly, under the DCFR Article II-9:408(2): 'If the contract can reasonably be maintained without the unfair term, the other terms remain binding on the parties.' It is explained in the DCFR that the 'purpose of this provision [is] simply to strike out the unfair term so that the other side [that is, the party upon whom an unfair term was imposed] is not deprived of the advantages of a contract'.[59] If the contract is 'legally viable' without the unfair term, or if it is possible to use 'a default rule or statutory background to fill the gap', the remaining parts of the contract will continue in force. However, if 'the unfair term is essential for the contract' and cannot be replaced in this manner, the contract must be abandoned.[60]

These sources paint a coherent picture which should apply also to the Data Act. Along the same lines Article 13(7) stipulates: 'Where the unfair contractual term is severable from the remaining terms of the contract, those remaining terms shall be

[55] Case 56/65, *Société Technique Minière (LTM) v Maschinenbau Ulm GmbH (MBU)*, EU:C:1966:38.

[56] Case C-279/06, *CEPSA Estaciones de Servicio SA mot LV Tobar e Hijos SL*, EU:C:2008:485 para 79. See also eg Case 319/82, *Société de Vente de Ciments et Bétons de l'Est SA v Kerpen & Kerpen GmbH und Co KG*, EU:C:1983:374; Case 10/86, *VAG France SA v Établissements Magne SA*, EU:C:1986:502; Case C-230/96, *Cabour SA and Nord Distribution Automobile SA v Arnor 'SOCO' SARL, supported by Automobiles Peugeot SA and Automobiles Citroën SA*, EU:C:1998:181.

[57] Bernitz and Henriksson, above note 9, 228.

[58] Case C-26/13, *Árpád Kásler and Hajnalka Káslerné Rábai v OTP Jelzálogbank Zrt*, EU:C:2014:282 paras 80–85.

[59] Bar and Clive, above note 19, 654–55.

[60] ibid 656.

binding.' Similarly, in recital 62: 'If a contractual term is declared to be unfair, the contract concerned should continue to apply without that term, unless the unfair contractual term is not severable from the other terms of the contract.' The precise details of this will be for national courts to decide on the basis of national law.

VI. CONCLUSIONS AND REFLECTIONS

In this final section, findings above will be summarised in response to the concrete legal questions posed in the Introduction. Thereafter, there will be some final reflections on Article 13 of the Data Act and EU contract law, in light of some thoughts by Ulf Bernitz.

First, contractual terms are 'unfair' within the meaning of Article 13 only if they *grossly* deviate from good commercial practice, thereby constituting an abuse of the contractor upon which they are imposed. It is therefore clear that the prohibition is restricted in scope and should be expected also to be used restrictively.

Second, a contractual term has been 'imposed' on a contractor if:

1. One of the contractors has, unilaterally, supplied the contractual term at issue;
2. The other contractor has tried to negotiate or otherwise influence the content of the contractual term; and
3. The latter contractor was unsuccessful in this attempt.

The contractor who supplied a contractual term has the onus of proving that it is not 'unilaterally imposed' on the other, either by proving that the other contractor never tried to negotiate or influence the term, or by proving that the term was meaningfully revised in response to objections made by the other contractor during negotiations.

Third, the Data Act includes a system of public enforcement the basic tenets of which are set out in its Chapter IX, and presupposes that complementary private enforcement of its substantive rules is available in the Member States, supported by the dispute settlement body to be set up in accordance with Article 10. With regard to such private enforcement in the national courts, the details of when a contractual term is 'not binding' are probably less strictly governed by EU law under the Data Act than under Article 101(2) TFEU and the Unfair Terms Directive. It has been submitted that a better yardstick in B2B relations is DCFR Article II-9:408, under which '[n]ot binding means that no legal effects can be based on such a term: neither any rights against the [party upon whom it was imposed] nor any exclusion or limitation of rights or defences [of that party]'.[61]

Fourth, under Article 13(7), '[w]here the unfair contractual term is severable from the remaining terms of the contract, those remaining terms shall be binding'. As explained in the DCFR, an assessment of severability should focus on whether the contract is 'legally viable' without the unfair term, including if it is possible to use 'a default rule or statutory background to fill the gap', or if, by contrast, 'the unfair term is essential for the contract' and cannot be replaced in this manner.[62]

[61] ibid 655.
[62] ibid 656.

In the course of this exploration of Article 13 of the Data Act, a recurring theme has been the balance between the contractual freedom of the parties and the need for regulation in order to sustain a well-functioning market. Recital 59 of the Data Act thus pays tribute to 'the principle of contractual freedom as an essential concept in business-to-business relationships'. The Commission similarly stressed in its Impact Assessment Report that the prohibition against unfair terms should not be construed as being in conflict with the principle of contractual freedom:

> As a matter of principle, the contractual parties are free to negotiate the terms and conditions of the contract. Simply having a situation where one contractual party is able to obtain a better deal reflecting its stronger bargaining power does not mean that such contract terms are unfair. . . . The unfairness test looks thus at specific clauses of a contract to check whether they go beyond being simply disadvantageous and are abusive, putting an excessive burden on one party. Only such clauses are considered as an excessive use of a strong imbalance of bargaining power between the parties and consequently will be qualified as unfair and deprived of legal effect.[63]

In spite of these pledges of allegiance to contractual freedom, Article 13 can be seen as an intrusion into that contractual freedom. The idea is, however, that an imbalance between the parties will obfuscate the contractual freedom of the weaker party. Contractual freedom, as it is understood in the Data Act, is thus seen as an individual freedom rather than as an abstract freedom pertaining to the commercial sphere as a whole. In the DCFR, the authors similarly stress that Article II-9:405, the model rule on unfair contractual terms in B2B contracts, was drafted to apply only when one party has imposed its pre-set terms on the other, thereby restricting the latter's contractual freedom.[64]

It was suggested in the introduction that the overarching theme of the works of Ulf Bernitz is the balancing, through regulation, of commercial freedom against its negative side effects. Above, an expression of this balancing act has been explored, namely Article 13 of the Data Act. Should the parties enjoy full freedom to contract on data sharing, or is there reason to intervene? Bernitz defined the freedom of contract as the freedom to decide with whom to contract (as in *Sky Österreich*) but also as a freedom 'to give to the contract a content on which both parties can agree'.[65]

The capacity to agree is what is targeted in Article 13. It has been concluded that this intervention into the freedom of contract is intended to protect parties from being coerced into unfair contractual terms. In fact, and perhaps paradoxically, Article 13 (and other rules on unfairness in contractual relations) aims to rectify contractual freedom in situations where this freedom has been undermined by one of the parties. As seen above, such attempts at protecting a 'real' freedom of contract must be seen in context, and both legislators and adjudicators must proceed with care. For the protection of consumers, far-reaching regulatory intervention is now considered an important part of safeguarding social values in the market economy. For the proper functioning of the internal market, competition law makes it possible to intervene

[63] Commission SWD(2022) 34 final, above note 25, 166–67.
[64] Bar and Clive, above note 19, 641.
[65] ibid 26.

against abusive contracts and against contracts that distort competition. Article 13 of the Data Act contributes to this body of EU contract law by making it possible to safeguard effective data sharing by intervening against abusive terms in B2B data sharing contracts. However, just as with the other rules of EU contract law already touched upon, Article 13 is restricted in scope and should be expected also to be used restrictively. This is a common trait to EU contract law: Its rules have the function of intervening to protect specified interests, and are narrowly framed in order to keep within those limits. Indeed, as touched upon above, the EU does not have general legislative competence in private law.[66] Therefore, EU law excursions into contract law are scarce. Whether this is good or bad is a discussion to be saved for another time.

In his writings, Ulf Bernitz explored the broad theoretical brushstrokes of political economy of the market as well as the nitty-gritty of concrete rules that regulate our market economy. Bernitz examined the works of historical scholars but never failed to be up-to-date on recent trends in the literature or to ensure that Swedish academics and practitioners were informed of the wider European debate. Indeed, one of his trademark expressions was to 'take the research home': to be part of the international discussions of EU law scholars and practitioners, and to take findings back to be presented to the Swedish lawyers who might have difficulty keeping up as they were busy with urgent local tasks and discussions. In this, Ulf Bernitz was, is and will remain an example.

[66] See note 1.

11

The Meta *Judgment on GDPR*

JENS FEJØ*

I. INTRODUCTION

THE *META* JUDGMENT TO be discussed here was handed down by the European Court of Justice (ECJ) on 4 July 2023. It started by an action taken by the German Federal Cartel Office, the Bundeskartellamt, against Facebook's so-called 'off Facebook' treatment. While the case was initiated as a national competition law case in Germany, the ECJ handed down some interesting, important and decisive points in reference to the interface between the General Data Protection Regulation from 2016 – in short, the GDPR – and competition law. The judgment came to provide vital guidance for platforms where collecting data from users is a crucial part of the business strategy.

It should be added that Facebook is one of the most valuable companies in the world and is one of the big seven big tech companies together with Apple, Alphabet (owner of Google), Microsoft, Amazon, Tesla and Nvidia.

II. THE BACKGROUND OF THE CASE

A. Factual Circumstances

Meta Platforms Ireland operates the online social network Facebook within the European Union and promotes services that are free of charge for private users. Within the European Union, other undertakings of the Meta group offer other online services, including Instagram, WhatsApp, Oculus and earlier also Masquerade.

Facebook's business model is based on financing through online advertising, which is tailored to the individual users of the social network according, inter alia, to their consumer behaviour, interests, purchasing power and personal situation.

Such advertising is made possible by the production of detailed profiles in respect of the network users and the users of the online services offered at the level of the

* This chapter is a further development of an article written in Danish together with Andrej Savin in *Altinget*, September 2023.

Meta group. Data are first provided by the users directly when they make use of the Facebook website from when signing up for the online service – namely, Facebook membership. In addition to that, other user-- and device-related data are collected from other services provided by the Meta group; while the Meta group also collects data from other companies and services that are not connected to the Facebook ecosystem through various technologies such as cookies, or by the use of 'like' buttons and so on. The data collected are linked to the profiles of its users to enhance Facebook's advertising business. The aggregate view of these data allows detailed conclusions to be drawn on those users' preferences and interests.

For the processing of data, Meta Platforms Ireland relies on user agreements to which the users of Facebook adhere when they click on the 'sign up' button, thereby accepting the general terms of conditions drawn up by Facebook. Acceptance of those terms is necessary to be able to use Facebook.

Regarding the processing of personal data, these general terms refer to Facebook's data and cookie policies. According to those policies, Meta Platforms Ireland collects user- and device-related data about user activities on and off Facebook and links those data with the Facebook accounts of the users concerned.

The off Facebook data relating to activities outside the social network are data concerning visits to third-party webpages and apps, which are linked to Facebook through programming interfaces, 'Facebook Business Tools', as well as data concerning the use of other online services belonging to the Meta group, including Instagram, WhatsApp, Oculus and, earlier, Masquerade.

B. The German Administration and Court Case

The Bundeskartellamt imposed far-reaching restrictions on Facebook in the processing of user data and required Facebook to adapt its general terms in such a way that it was made clear that those data would not be collected or linked with Facebook user accounts or used without the consent of the users concerned. Further, the Bundeskartellamt clarified that such a consent is not valid if it is formulated as a condition for using the social network.

The Bundeskartellamt based its decision on the fact that the processing of the data of the users concerned constituted an abuse of the company's dominant position on the market for online social networks for private users in Germany within the meaning of paragraph 19(1) of the GWB (a national provision parallel to Article 102 of the Treaty on the Functioning of the European Union (TFEU)).

Meta Platforms (Facebook) brought an action against the Bundeskartellamt's decision to the Oberlandesgericht Düsseldorf (the Higher Regional Court in Düsseldorf), and this Court decided to refer several questions to the ECJ relating to the interpretation of the provisions of the GDPR.

C. Questions to the ECJ from the German Oberlandesgericht

The questions put forward by Oberlandesgericht Düsseldorf to the ECJ mainly concerned four issues:

1. The competence of a competition authority in relation to the GDPR;
2. the prohibition in the GDPR on processing sensitive personal data and the conditions applicable to consenting to their use;
3. the lawfulness of the processing of personal data in the light of certain justifications;
4. and, last, the validity of consent to the processing of personal data given to an undertaking in a dominant position.

III. THE META CASE IN FRONT OF THE ECJ

A. The ECJ's Handling of the Case

The ECJ composed itself in the Grand Chamber with 15 judges, which is a strong indication from the side of the Court regarding the calibre of the case. Then, the Court debated – in unusual depth – the issues that were raised in the case and came up with very explicit and in-depth answers. This contribution must limit itself to only a few of the highlights of that judgment. However, the European Court's answers to the questions – as they were rephrased by the Court itself – were not to be misunderstood.[1]

i. The Competence of a Competition Authority in Relation to the GDPR

Relating to these four issues, the European Court found, as a starting point, that a national competition authority of a Member State may find – in the context of the examination of an abuse of a dominant position by an undertaking – that that undertaking's general terms of use relating to the processing of personal data and the implementation thereof are not consistent with the GDPR, where that finding is necessary to establish the existence of such an abuse of a dominant position. In this context, the competition authority has a duty of sincere cooperation with the supervisory authorities of the GDPR. However, in the absence of a) any objection or of b) any reply at all within a reasonable time from such GDPR supervisory authorities, the national competition authority may conduct its own GDPR investigation.

ii. The Prohibition in the GDPR on Processing Sensitive Personal Data and the Conditions Applicable to Consenting to Their Use

Second, the ECJ looked at Article 9 of the GDPR that deals with processing of special categories of personal data. Here, the Court was rather strict and specifically pointed to Article 9 (paragraph 1), which concentrates on the processing of personal data revealing such as racial or ethnic origin, political opinions, religious or philosophical beliefs, and the processing of genetic or biometric data for the purpose of uniquely identifying a natural person or data concerning a person's sex life or sexual orientation.

On this, the Court stated that Article 9 (paragraph 1) of the GDPR must be interpreted as meaning that, where the user (the consumer) visits websites or apps to which

[1] C-251/21 *Meta Platforms and Others v Bundeskartellamt* (4 July 2023), ECLI:EU:C:2023:537.

one or more of the categories in Article 9 relate, and, as the case may be, enters personal information into these such as when registering or when placing online orders, the linking of all those data with the user's social network account and the use of those data by that operator (Facebook) must be regarded as 'processing of special categories of personal data', which is, in principle, prohibited subject to the derogations provided for in Article 9 (paragraph 2).

In this context, this primarily means that there is a need for an explicit consent on the part of the user.

iii. The Lawfulness of the Processing of Personal Data in Light of Certain Justifications

The next issue taken up by the ECJ was the provision in Article 6 (paragraph 1) of the GDPR. That provision deals with lawfulness of processing and spells out that processing shall be lawful only if and to the extent that at least one of the following applies.

Subsequently, six possibilities for exception are enumerated:

> (a) The consumer has given consent to the processing of his or her personal data for specific purposes;
>
> (b) processing is necessary for the performance of a contract to which the consumer is a party or in order to take steps at the request of the consumer prior to entering into a contract;
>
> (c) processing is necessary for compliance with a legal obligation to which the controller [Facebook] is subject;
>
> (d) processing is necessary in order to protect the vital interests of the consumer or of another natural person;
>
> (e) processing is necessary for the performance of a task carried out in the public interest or in the exercise of official authority vested in the controller [Facebook];
>
> (f) processing is necessary for the purposes of the legitimate interests pursued by the controller [Facebook] or by a third party, except where such interests are overridden by the interests or fundamental rights and freedoms of the data subject [the consumer], which require protection of personal data, in particular, where the data subject is a child.
>
> Further, possibility (f) shall not apply to processing carried out by public authorities in the performance of their tasks.

Let us go straight to the conclusion of the Court's well considered contemplations here, which is that, for being applicable for each of the six possible exemptions, the requirements therein must be fulfilled in their entirety.

But they are simply, bit by bit, being rejected by the ECJ and, further on, one can add that the ECJ – even though this is at preliminary ruling – goes deep into the facts of Facebook's handling of the various possible exceptions and subsequently rejects them all.

One of the rejections hereto might be of special interest, which is that of the exemption dealing with the requirement that the data subject (the consumer) has given *consent* to the processing.

iv. The Validity of Consent to the Processing of Personal Data Given to an Undertaking in a Dominant Position

The ECJ finds that the fact that the operator of an online social network (Facebook) holds a dominant position on the market for online social networks does not, as such, preclude the users of such a network from being validly able to consent within the meaning of the GDPR to the processing of their personal data by that operator (Facebook). However, the ECJ does find that it is an import factor in obtaining the *validity* of a *consent* to processing personal data given to an undertaking in a dominant position that it is *freely given* by the user, which is for that *operator* (Facebook) *to prove*.

The clear statement, regarding the burden of proof, must be seen as far reaching in the sense that, if Facebook or other similar companies cannot prove that the consent was validly given by the user towards the company in a dominant position, then the competition law consequences may come into play – those being prohibition, heavy fines and compensation to competitors, customers and consumers.

IV. CONSEQUENCES OF THE *META* JUDGMENT

Of importance for the judgment is first and foremost the clarification that it brings as to when platforms may legally treat data of behavioural action for targeting advertisements in cases where there is no explicit or precise consent. But legal handling of data must be based on one of the grounds in Article 6 in the GDPR (consent, necessary for the performance of a contract, necessary for the purposes of the legitimate interest pursued by the controller [Facebook], etc) Furthermore, this clearly is in contrast with how platforms traditionally have acted when collecting a generic consent that would cover a variety of different situations, including connecting data from the collectors' own companies with data from third parties, or, if there is no such consent or its validity may be problematic, to base its treatment on other grounds found in Article 6 in the GDPR. For a long period of time, Facebook's preferred foundation for handling data under the GDPR has been consent-based, and, until this judgment was handed down, it only had a few consequences to be worried about in this connection.

The first indication, however, of obstacles to Facebook and other companies from comparable fields already came about with a variety of national cases. Among these, just to mention a few, was an Austrian case that has given ground for preliminary questions from the Oberster Gerichtshof in Austria to the ECJ in the *Schrems v Facebook* case.[2] This case was lodged on 20 July 2021 but has still not yet been decided by the ECJ (and further on by the Austrian Oberster Gerichtshof). Also, an Irish case is worth mentioning in this regard, where the Irish Data Protection Commission (DPC) ended two inquiries into Meta Ireland[3] by putting a fine on Meta Ireland for breaches

[2] Case C-446/21, *Maximilian Schrems v Facebook Ireland Ltd*, ECLI:EU:C:2024:834.
[3] DPC Inquiry Reference: IN-18-5-5, 31.12.2022.

of the GDPR relating to its Facebook service and putting a fine on Meta Ireland for breaches in relation to its Instagram services. Meta Ireland was also directed to bring its data processing operations into compliance within a period of three months.

The key issue in these cases has been the fact that Facebook and similar companies arbitrarily collect data that is applied for appointing direct advertising based on the consumers' behaviour and has done that by forcing the consumers to accept conditions that allow this to happen or, otherwise, would have denied the consumers access to the platforms. The reason for Facebook being fined in the Irish case was that the authority, the DPC, found that Meta Ireland was not entitled to rely on the contract legal basis in Article 6 GDPR in connection with the delivery of behavioural advertising as part of its Facebook and Instagram services. The DPC found that Facebook's processing of users' data in purported reliance on the 'contract' as a legal basis amounted to a contravention of Article 6 of the GDPR.

Although the still-pending Austrian case in front of the ECJ may bring new and further clarifications to the far-reaching main points, the *Meta* judgment from 4 July 2023 has already brought so much clarity that the judgment can be seen as a 'game changer'.

The *Meta* judgment from July 2023 has thus, as its first essential contribution, put stress on sensitive personal information, which has entailed that, when Facebook collects information concerning consumers from non-Facebook ecosystem websites (eg, through the applications of cookies or through Facebook's 'Like' button on third party websites), this is done without the specific acceptance or consent of the consumer. Hence, when a consumer leaves sensitive information in places such as those related to health or to political websites, that are not connected to Facebook, nevertheless, Facebook uses the data generated from this. Obviously, the consumer can accept that such data may be applied. However, exactly here lies the core of the finding of the ECJ: the Court's central conclusion is that it cannot be deduced from the mere fact that a consumer by his or her simple visit to such places or apps has published his or her personal information on himself or herself in relation to Article 9(1)(e) of the GDPR.

Facebook will, after the *Meta* judgment of July 2023, have to make a big change in Europe to live up to the legal requirements so clearly spelled out by the ECJ if it still wants to collect sensitive data. Those requirements, especially in relation to a correctly informed acceptance, will undoubtedly be difficult to fulfil. The traditional ordinary consent from the consumers is far from satisfactory in this respect.

Another improvement for the consumers can be found in the limitations introduced by ECJ by its stringent interpretation of the requirement of 'necessity', that is, when processing of personal data is 'necessary'. As the ECJ spells out in point 97 of the judgment:

> As regards, in the first place, point (b) of the first subparagraph of Article 6(1) of the GDPR, that provision provides that processing of personal data is lawful if it is `necessary for the performance of a contract to which the data subject is party or in order to take steps at the request of the data subject prior to entering into a contract.

The ECJ's view on this 'necessity' is immediately found in paragraphs 98 and 99, which state:

> In that regard, in order for the processing of personal data to be regarded as necessary for the performance of a contract, within the meaning of that provision, it must be objectively indispensable for a purpose that is integral to the contractual obligation intended for the data subject. The controller [here Facebook] must therefore be able to demonstrate how the main subject matter of the contract cannot be achieved if the processing in question does not occur. The fact that such processing may be referred to in the contract or may be merely useful for the performance of the contract is, in itself, irrelevant in that regard. The decisive factor for the purposes of applying the justification set out in point (b) of the first subparagraph of Article 6(1) of the GDPR is rather that the processing of personal data by the controller must be essential for the proper performance of the contract concluded between the controller and the data subject and, therefore, that there are no workable, less intrusive alternatives.

In regard to personalisation of the processing, the ECJ has accepted that it might be useful for the consumer but nevertheless finds in paragraph 102:

> As regards, first, the justification based on personalised content, it is important to note that, although such a personalisation is useful to the user, in so far as it enables the user, inter alia, to view content corresponding to a large extent to his or her interests, the fact remains that, subject to verification by the referring court, personalised content does not appear to be necessary in order to offer that user the services of the online social network. Those services may, where appropriate, be provided to the user in the form of an equivalent alternative which does not involve such a personalisation, such that the latter is not objectively indispensable for a purpose that is integral to those services.

The ECJ thus basically spells out that personalisation is not covered by ordinary contractual fulfilment and must either be covered by specific informed consent or by one of the other foundations (which also seems unlikely to appear). This may be regarded as a hard blow to Facebook's usually personalised business model.

However, the GDPR does allow data treatment being covered by Facebook's legitimate interests. The GDPR thus spells out in Article 6(1)(f) that processing shall be lawful where it is necessary for the purposes of the legitimate interests pursued by the controller, except where such interests are overridden by the interests or fundamental rights and freedoms of the data subject, which require protection of personal data, in particular, in cases where the data subject is a child, and the ECJ accepts, in paragraph 115 regarding personalised advertising, that, according to recital 47 of the GDPR, the processing of personal data for direct marketing purposes may be regarded as carried out for a legitimate interest of the controller. However, the Court, at the same time, finds, in paragraph 112, that

> as can be seen from recital 47 of the GDPR, the interests and fundamental rights of the data subject may in particular override the interest of the data controller where personal data are processed in circumstances where data subjects do not reasonably expect such processing.

Or, plainly stated, data processing of an unknowable user acting in good faith and not being attentive as to the many complicated ways in which data may be collected, combined, and applied is a violation. The Court formulates it in the concluding paragraph 126 on that issue:

> Point (f) of the first subparagraph of Article 6(1) of the GDPR must be interpreted as meaning that such processing can be regarded as necessary for the purposes of the legitimate interests pursued by the controller or by a third party, within the meaning of that provision, only on condition that the operator has informed the users from whom the data have been collected of a legitimate interest that is pursued by the data processing, that such processing is carried out only in so far as is *strictly necessary* for the purposes of that legitimate interest and that it is apparent from a balancing of the opposing interests, having regard to all the relevant circumstances, that the interests or fundamental freedoms and rights of those users do not override that legitimate interest of the controller or of a third party. (emphasis added)

One could ask whether Facebook's economic interest and Facebook's business model based on advertisement are such legitimate interest. This is dealt with by the Court in ground 117 stating:

> In this regard, it is important to note that, despite the fact that the services of an online social network such as Facebook are free of charge, the user of that network cannot reasonably expect that the operator of the social network will process that user's personal data, without his or her consent, for the purposes of personalised advertising. In those circumstances, it must be held that the interests and fundamental rights of such a user override the interest of that operator in such personalised advertising by which it finances its activity, with the result that the processing by that operator for such purposes cannot fall within the scope of point (f) of the first subparagraph of Article 6(1) of the GDPR.

Once again, a strong blow to Facebook´s traditional business model.

Last the issue of consent is a point dealt with by the ECJ in the judgment. The Court formulates the issue as such:

> whether point (a) of the first subparagraph of Article 6(1) and Article 9(2)(a) of the GDPR must be interpreted as meaning that consent given by the user of an online social network to the operator of such a network may be regarded as satisfying the conditions of validity laid down in Article 4(11) of that regulation, in particular the condition that that consent must be freely given, where that operator holds a dominant position on the market for online social networks´. The Court at the outset states in ground 147 that `In that regard, it should be noted that, admittedly, the fact that the operator of an online social network, as controller, holds a dominant position on the social network market does not, as such, prevent the users of that social network from validly giving their consent, within the meaning of Article 4(11) of the GDPR, to the processing of their personal data by that operator.[4]

However, the Court subsequently goes on in paragraph 148 to state:

> The fact remains that . . . such a circumstance must be taken into consideration in assessing whether the user of that network has validly and, in particular, freely given consent, since

[4] See also section III.A.iv above.

> that circumstance is liable to affect the freedom of choice of that user, who might be unable to refuse or withdraw consent without detriment, as stated in recital 42 of the GDPR.

Further, the Court continues in paragraph 149:

> Furthermore, the existence of such a dominant position may create a clear imbalance, within the meaning of recital 43 of the GDPR, between the data subject and the controller, that imbalance favouring, inter alia, the imposition of conditions that are not strictly necessary for the performance of the contract, which must be taken into account under Article 7(4) of that regulation. In that context, it must be borne in mind that, . . . it does not appear, subject to verification by the referring court, that the processing at issue in the main proceedings is strictly necessary for the performance of the contract between Meta Platforms Ireland and the users of the social network Facebook.

This brings the ECJ to the conclusion on that issue in paragraph 150:

> Thus, those users must be free to refuse individually, in the context of the contractual process, to give their consent to particular data processing operations not necessary for the performance of the contract, without being obliged to refrain entirely from using the service offered by the online social network operator, which means that those users are to be offered, if necessary for an appropriate fee, an equivalent alternative not accompanied by such data processing operations.

Hence, the Court does not put the consumer in a 'take it or leave it' position but puts requirements on Facebook in relation to a reasonable solution. The Court itself has an additional point of view in the following ground:

> Moreover, given the scale of the processing of the data in question and the significant impact of that processing on the users of that network as well as the fact that those users cannot reasonably expect data other than those relating to their conduct within the social network to be processed by the operator of that network, it is appropriate, within the meaning of recital 43, to have the possibility of giving separate consent for the processing of the latter data, on the one hand, and the off Facebook data, on the other. It is for the referring court to ascertain whether such a possibility exists, in the absence of which the consent of those users to the processing of the off Facebook data must be presumed not to be freely given.

In other words, to make the service operational, informed consent should be collected specifically for those kinds of activities (off of Facebook activities) that originally gave rise to the case.

V. CONCLUDING REMARKS

The *Meta* judgment of July 2023 is important and far reaching. It has a direct consequence that Facebook and other similar platforms collecting personal data for advertising purposes must scrutinise the ECJ's judgment and make important changes in their daily operations towards their users and their customers. The judgment should, however, further be seen as considering two very important developments.

The first one is the environment around another important earlier judgment by the ECJ, the first *Schrems* judgment,[5] whereby the possibility of transatlantic data transfer has been made rather complicated to the clear detriment of the social network platforms, including Facebook.

The second new development will be the full implementation of the Digital Market Act[6] enforced by the European Commission, whereby Meta has been designated as one of the several 'gatekeepers', thereby being required to ensure full compliance with the Digital Market Act obligations for its platform services.

However, in my view, the judgment of July 2023 may be important in an even more far-reaching perspective, as it may possibly be seen as creating a broader direction for the future. It thus seems clear that Facebook and other IT behemoths' behaviour in the US has led to so much power for those companies that the US public regulators, prosecutors and courts have had great difficulties in administering the regulation and supervision of big tech companies. In Europe, as this judgment and maybe other activities in the European Union demonstrate, there seems to be established a virtual halt for the unlimited behaviour of the big tech companies. It is to be seen, of course, what will be the next step – or, better, *steps* – in the regulation of and fight against unlimited abuses by big tech companies.

The *Meta/Facebook* judgment is certainly a most obvious starting point for a new development in Europe. The fact that the ECJ has taken a very close look at Facebook's behaviour within the GDPR field and has practically prohibited Facebook from continuing its traditional collecting of sensitive data is a strong indication of European willingness to address the perceived problems.

At the same time, the ECJ has made it possible for competition law authorities to deal with transgressions of the GDPR as competition law violations. Competition law sanctions are not to be ignored in relation to the European law. We know that the US authorities have investigated the big tech companies, but it seems very clear that the US antitrust authorities have not been able to address the possibly dangerous behaviour of the big tech companies.

On the grounds of the clear difficulties for the US public prosecutors and courts in administering their supervision to restrict the power and behaviour of Facebook and other tech behemoths, the European Union may take the lead in the future for more adequate regulation of big tech companies. An intensified cooperation between US and European authorities in handling the tech industry may, however, be seen as necessary and unavoidable, and this should certainly be welcomed. One might, at the same time, think that alternative forms of regulation of the fast-developing big tech companies may be a consequence of this judgment.

[5] Case C-311/18, *Data Protection Commissioner v Facebook Ireland Limited and Maximillian Schrems*, Judgment of the ECJ (Grand Chamber) of 16 July 2020), ECLI:EU:C:2020:559.

[6] Regulation (EU) 2022/1925 of the European Parliament and of the Council of 14 September 2022 on contestable and fair markets in the digital sector and the Implementing Regulation, OJ 2022 L 265/1.

12

Protecting Gatekeepers Against Double Jeopardy: Is the Digital Markets Act Aligned with Article 50 of the EU Charter of Fundamental Rights?

HELENE ANDERSSON

UNDER BOTH EU LAW and the European Convention on Human Rights, companies are protected from being tried or punished twice for the same conduct. This chapter explores whether the introduction of the Digital Markets Act, and its concurrent application with existing EU competition rules, provides adequate safeguards against double jeopardy.

I. INTRODUCTION

Under the Digital Markets Act (the DMA),[1] companies that meet certain thresholds are designated as gatekeepers and need to comply with the strict rules set by the regulation in relation to the 'core platform services' that they offer.[2] A gatekeeper who fails to comply with the new rules or disagrees with the European Commission (the Commission) on how they should be interpreted has a lot to risk. Just like under the EU competition rules, non-compliance may come at a high price. The Commission has the authority to impose fines of up to 10 per cent of a company's annual global turnover.[3] For repeat offenders, the fines may be up to 20 per cent of their annual

[1] Regulation (EU) 2022/1925 of the European Parliament and of the Council of 14 September 2022 on contestable and fair markets in the digital sector and amending Directives (EU) 2019/1937 and (EU) 2020/1828 (Digital Markets Act), [2022] OJ L 265/1.

[2] The core platform services are listed in Article 2(2) of the DMA.

[3] The European Commission's Statement of Objections in the Google AdTech case concerning the alleged abuse of dominance under Article 102 TFEU suggests that the Commission may be prepared to require structural remedies, including divestitures, where this is considered necessary to restore effective competition or, in the context of the Digital Markets Act (DMA), to ensure fair and contestable markets. In its Statement of Objections, the Commission indicated its preliminary view that behavioural remedies

global turnover and the Commission may also impose structural remedies, such as divestiture orders.

Although the DMA is said to pursue objectives distinct from those of EU competition law, the Commission's own reasons for proposing the legislation suggest otherwise. In its DMA proposal, the Commission acknowledged that the regulation's ultimate aim is to prevent harms such as higher prices, reduced quality and diminished choice and innovation – all outcomes that closely mirror the concerns addressed by EU competition rules.[4] This overlap is further underscored by the fact that many of the DMA's obligations are directly inspired by recent antitrust cases brought by the Commission against companies now designated as gatekeepers.[5] When drafting the proposal in 2020, the Commission drew heavily from its enforcement experience in high-profile abuse of dominance cases involving major tech firms such as Meta, Apple and Google.[6]

While these companies must now abide by the regime set up by the DMA, preventing them from engaging in activities that are similar or even identical to those considered abusive by the Commission under Article 102 of the Treaty of the Functioning of the European Union (the TFEU), the DMA also makes it clear that its application is without prejudice to the application of national and EU competition rules. In theory, the same behaviour may thus be sanctioned twice – both under the DMA and national or EU competition rules.

Article 38 of the DMA partially addresses this issue by removing the power of national competition authorities to pursue a competition case once the Commission has initiated an investigation under the DMA. However, the DMA does not prevent the Commission from launching an investigation when an infringement decision has already been made by a national competition authority, nor does it prevent the Commission from initiating its own antitrust investigation. Consequently, it is essential to determine whether, and under what circumstances, such parallel investigations

---

would likely be insufficient to address the competition concerns identified, in particular the risk that Google could continue engaging in allegedly self-preferencing conduct or develop new forms of such conduct. The Commission therefore expressed the preliminary assessment that only the divestiture of part of Google's advertising technology services could effectively resolve the identified conflicts of interest within the adtech supply chain (Case AT.40670). See: https://ec.europa.eu/commission/presscorner/detail/en/ip_23_3207. On 5 September 2025, the Commission adopted a prohibition decision in the same case, imposing a fine of €2.95 billion and ordering Google to bring the infringement to an end. The Commission found that Google had abused its dominant position in parts of the online advertising technology stack by favouring its own services to the detriment of competing adtech providers, advertisers and publishers. The decision requires Google to propose measures to ensure compliance and eliminate the conflicts of interest identified, while indicating that structural remedies, including potential divestiture, may be considered if behavioural measures prove insufficient to effectively end the infringement. Google has since proposed a number of compliance measures aimed at modifying its adtech practices, which do not include divestiture.

[4] European Commission, *Proposal for a Regulation of the European Parliament and of the Council on contestable and fair markets in the digital sector (Digital Markets Act)* COM(2020) 842 final, Explanatory Memorandum, 1–2.

[5] ibid, 4–5; see also European Commission, *Impact Assessment Report Accompanying the DMA Proposal* SWD(2020) 363 final, Annexes 1–2.

[6] For example, Case AT.39740 – *Google Shopping*; Case AT.40462 – *Amazon Marketplace*; Case AT.40411 – *Apple App Store Rules*.

might be subject to the prohibition against double jeopardy as outlined in Article 50 of the Charter of Fundamental Rights of the European Union ('the Charter').

II. PURSUING PARALLEL INVESTIGATIONS UNDER THE DMA AND NATIONAL OR EU COMPETITION RULES

When the Commission designates a company as a gatekeeper and that gatekeeper engages in market conduct prohibited by the DMA concerning a core platform service, the Commission is likely to address and sanction such conduct under the DMA. This approach is advantageous because it eliminates the need to define a relevant market or prove dominance or abuse. However, there may be instances where the Commission opts to pursue a case under Article 102 TFEU, or potentially under both frameworks. Such situations might arise, for example, when a gatekeeper engages in practices that are partially covered by the DMA but extend beyond its prohibitions or when the conduct involves both a core platform service and another product or service. Also national competition authorities may want to launch investigations against gatekeepers under their national competition rules and/or Articles 101 and 102 TFEU.

Recital 11 addresses the relationship between the DMA and the competition rules, acknowledging that Articles 101 and 102 TFEU and the corresponding national competition rules have as their objective the protection of undistorted competition on the market. According to the recital, the DMA pursues an objective that is complementary to, but different from that objective as the regulation aims to ensure that markets where gatekeepers are present are and remain *contestable and fair*, independently from the actual, potential or presumed effects of the conduct of a gatekeeper on competition on a given market. According to the recital, the DMA therefore aims to protect a different legal interest from that protected by the competition rules and it should therefore apply without prejudice to their application. This is also reflected in Article 1(6) of the DMA. Despite the wording of the article, this does not mean that the powers of the national competition authorities, the NCAs, to apply the competition rules remain unfettered.

Also the operating parts of the regulation deal with this matter. Article 38 of the DMA lays down rules on cooperation and coordination between the Commission and the NCAs. According to Article 38(2), NCAs are required to inform the Commission of any investigations that are launched against gatekeepers,[7] and just as under Article 11(6) of Regulation 1/2003,[8] the NCAs are relieved of their powers to pursue an investigation against a gatekeeper if the Commission decides to open an investigation under Article 20 of the DMA. On the same note, an NCA may not open an investigation

[7] The NCAs shall inform the Commission of any enforcement of the rules referred to in Article 1(6) of the DMA, that is Articles 101 and 102 TFEU, Regulation 139/2004 and national competition rules (i) mirroring Articles 101 and 102 TFEU, (ii) prohibiting other forms of unilateral conduct and (iii) on merger control.

[8] Council Regulation (EC) No 1/2003 of 16 December 2002 on the implementation of the rules on competition laid down in Articles 81 and 82 of the Treaty [2003] OJ L1, 4 January, 1–25.

under national or EU competition rules when the Commission is pursuing an investigation under Article 20 of the DMA.

This means that (the wording of) the DMA allows for parallel investigations of the same conduct in the following situations. There is nothing in the DMA explicitly preventing:

1. The Commission from investigating the same conduct both under the DMA and the EU competition rules.
2. The Commission from investigating a certain conduct after an NCA has closed an investigation against the gatekeeper concerning the conduct in question.
3. An NCA from launching an investigation against a gatekeeper after the Commission has closed an investigation against the gatekeeper concerning the conduct in question.

The risk of parallel proceedings is further underlined by the digital nature of the criteria used to determine whether a company qualifies as a gatekeeper, which means that a company's status can change rapidly. For instance, on 23 April 2025, just 18 months after the initial designation of gatekeepers, Meta was undesignated for its online intermediation service, Facebook Marketplace.[9] Conversely, a company will quickly be designated a gatekeeper once the thresholds are met. This means that a national competition authority may have closed an antitrust investigation against a company which is then designated a gatekeeper for that product or service. In such case, the Commission might see itself empowered to prohibit the conduct in question and enforce the DMA against the company.

While the DMA does not explicitly prevent parallel conducts in the situations described above, the regulation is a piece of secondary legislation and may not be given an interpretation that runs contrary to primary EU legislation and more specifically Article 50 of the Charter protecting individuals against double jeopardy. This is also acknowledged in the DMA, as Recital 86 states that the Commission and NCAs shall coordinate their enforcement efforts to ensure respect for the principle. However, the wording suggests that the legislator was primarily concerned with the risk of a company being subjected to disproportionate penalties, not two different proceedings. The recital emphasises that appropriate levels of fines and periodic penalty payments should be established for non-compliance with the gatekeepers' obligations and breaches of procedural rules, subject to appropriate limitation periods and in accordance with the principles of proportionality and *ne bis in idem*.

However, as will be discussed in the following, the *ne bis in idem* principle also applies in situations where authorities conduct parallel investigations, even if these do not result in the imposition of sanctions in both cases. Thus, while the regulation

[9] The decision follows a request submitted by Meta on 5 March 2024 to reconsider the designation of Marketplace. Following a careful assessment of Meta's arguments and because of Meta's additional enforcement and continued monitoring measures to counteract the business-to-consumer use of Marketplace, the Commission found that Marketplace had less than 10,000 business users in 2024. Meta therefore no longer meets the relevant threshold giving rise to a presumption that Marketplace is an important gateway for business users to reach end users. See https://ec.europa.eu/commission/presscorner/detail/en/ip_25_1085.

acknowledges the risk of double jeopardy, it does not necessarily provide sufficient safeguards against it. Before examining the application of the principle to cases concerning the DMA, the following section presents a brief overview of the relevant Charter provision and whether it is even applicable to the sanctions imposed under the DMA or the competition rules.

III. ARTICLE 50 OF THE CHARTER AND THE PROTECTION AGAINST DOUBLE JEOPARDY

Article 50 of the Charter establishes the right to protection against double jeopardy, declaring that no one shall 'be liable to be tried or punished again in criminal proceedings for an offence for which he or she has already been finally acquitted or convicted within the Union in accordance with the law'.

Thus, the principle, which protects individuals from being tried or prosecuted twice, only applies to criminal proceedings. For the article to apply in relation to the DMA and/or the competition rules, the sanctions available therefore need to be considered criminal in character. While Article 23(5) of Regulation 1/2003 declares that any fines imposed by the Commission for infringements of the EU competition rules shall not be considered criminal, it is clear by now that this statement is outdated and that the fines imposed by the Commission in relation to competition law infringements do meet the *Engel* criteria once established by the European Court of Human Rights (the Strasbourg Court) to determine whether an offence is criminal or not.[10]

Thus, in *Toshiba*, the Court of Justice of the European Union (the ECJ or the Court of Justice) simply declared that the *ne bis in idem* principle must be observed in the proceedings for the imposition of fines under competition law.[11] As the sanctions available under the DMA mirror those in Regulation 1/2003 and may even be stricter, the same would apply to proceedings under the DMA.

In March 2022, the ECJ delivered two landmark rulings on the *ne bis in idem* principle and its application in competition cases. These two rulings, *bpost* and *Nordzucker*, establish that no derogations are allowed from Article 50 of the Charter in cases concerning the application of identical rules or rules that pursue the same objective. Where the two pieces of legislation pursue different objectives, derogations from the prohibition against double jeopardy may be acceptable, but only under certain conditions. The two cases are presented in more detail below and will then be examined through the lens of the European Convention for the Protection of Human Rights and Fundamental Freedoms (ECHR) to determine whether the EU standard meets the ECHR standard in this respect.

[10] *Engel and Others v the Netherlands*, Application no 5100/71; 5101/71; 5102/71; 5354/72; 5370/72. Here the European Court of Human Rights established that to determine whether an offence is criminal in character, regard should be had to the legal classification of the offence under national law, the intrinsic nature of the offence, and the degree of severity of the penalty which the person concerned is liable to incur.

[11] Case C-17/10, *Toshiba Corporation and Others v Úřad pro ochranu hospodářské soutěže*, EU:C:2012:72, para 94.

IV. THE COURT OF JUSTICE'S RULING IN *NORDZUCKER*

A. The Case Before the National Court

The two German sugar producers Nordzucker and Südzucker were investigated by both the German and the Austrian competition authorities for participation in a market sharing cartel affecting the German and Austrian markets. In both investigations, the authorities relied on a phone call made between the sales managers of the two sugar producers.[12]

By a final decision of 18 February 2014, the German authority found that Nordzucker, Südzucker and a third German sugar producer had infringed Article 101 TFEU and the corresponding provisions of German competition law. The authority imposed a fine of EUR 195 million on Südzucker. The decision included details of the phone call where the sales managers of Nordzucker and Südzucker discussed activities related to the Austrian market.

By a decision of 15 May 2019, the Oberlandesgericht Wien (Regional Court of Appeal, Vienna) dismissed the action brought by the Austrian competition authority seeking to impose a fine on the two sugar producers on the ground, inter alia, that the agreement concluded during the disputed telephone call had already been the subject of a sanction imposed by the German competition authority and that a new sanction would therefore be contrary to the *ne bis in idem* principle. The decision was appealed to the Austrian Supreme Court, which in turn decided to seek guidance from the Court of Justice.

B. The Questions of Interpretation

In its referral to the ECJ, the Austrian court inquired, among other things, whether Article 50 of the Charter prevents a national competition authority from initiating proceedings under Article 101 TFEU and its national equivalent for conduct that has restricted competition within its Member State, when a competition authority from another Member State has already addressed that conduct in a final decision against the undertaking for an infringement of Article 101 TFEU. In this context, the referring court sought clarification on the criteria relevant for determining whether the two national competition authorities have adjudicated the same facts.

C. Assessment by the ECJ

In its reply to the Austrian court, the Court of Justice starts out by reiterating that the *ne bis in idem* principle is a fundamental principle of EU law which is now laid down in Article 50 of the Charter and that for this principle to apply, the proceedings or penalties must be of a criminal nature.[13] Here, the Court notes that it has already

[12] Case C-151/20, *Bundeswettbewerbsbehörde v Nordzucker AG and Others*, EU:C:2022:203, para 16.

[13] Case C-151/20, *Bundeswettbewerbsbehörde v Nordzucker AG and Others*, EU:C:2022:203, paras 28 and 29.

held in the past that the principle must be respected in proceedings relating to fines for infringements of the competition rules.[14]

i. Criteria Triggering the Prohibition against Double Jeopardy

The Court of Justice recapitulates what has been said concerning the two *bis* and *idem* criteria, as the application of the principle requires not only that the penalties are of a criminal nature but also that these two conditions are met. First, there must be a previous final decision that has been issued on the merits (the *bis* condition). Second, the previous decision and the subsequent procedure or decision must relate to the same act/conduct (the *idem* condition). Here, the ECJ notes that the decision of the German authority was adopted following an assessment of the substance of the case and that it is now final – the *bis* condition is therefore fulfilled.[15]

As regards the *idem* condition, the Court of Justice notes that the legal persons are the same in both proceedings, Nordzucker and Südzucker. It then turns to the question of whether the offence is the same in the two proceedings, noting that it is not sufficient that the circumstances are similar, but that they must be identical. According to the Court of Justice, the assessment of whether the object or effect of the conduct in question was anti-competitive cannot be made in the abstract but must be made with regard to (i) the territory and the product market actually affected by the conduct, and (ii) the period during which the conduct in question had such an anti-competitive object or effect.[16]

The ECJ notes, moreover, that it is for the referring court to determine whether the facts are identical. While leaving this assessment to the national court, the ECJ nevertheless notes that it is apparent from the case-file that the questions posed by the referring court relate more specifically to the fact that the Austrian competition authority's action is based on a particular fact, namely the telephone conversation between the two companies' sales managers during which the Austrian sugar market was raised, a call which had already been mentioned in the German authority's final decision.

The ECJ clarifies that simply mentioning a factual circumstance related to another Member State in an NCA's decision does not automatically mean that this factor triggered the proceedings or was a key element of the infringement.[17] Instead, it must be assessed whether the NCA relied on that factual element to (i) establish the infringement, (ii) determine the liability of the person involved, and, if applicable, (iii) impose a penalty. Only then can the infringement be considered as extending to the territory of the other Member State.

The Court of Justice leaves it to the referring court to determine, by assessing all the relevant circumstances, whether the German competition authority's final decision was intended to establish and penalise the cartel also in so far as it concerned

[14] Ibid., para 32. The Court refers here to its judgment in C-17/10, *Toshiba Corporation and Others v Úřad pro ochranu hospodářské soutěže*, EU:C:2012:72, para 94.

[15] Case C-151/20, *Bundeswettbewerbsbehörde v Nordzucker AG and Others*, EU:C:2022:203, para 35.

[16] ibid, para 41.

[17] ibid, para 41.

the effects on the Austrian sugar market. Here, the ECJ provides some guidance on how such an examination should be carried out, explaining that the Austrian court must examine the legal assessments made by the German competition authority and whether or not the facts taken into account in the decision related exclusively to the German market. The ECJ further notes that it is also relevant to establish how the fine was calculated; whether it was based solely on the turnover achieved in Germany or whether the turnover in Austria was also considered when calculating the fine.

If the national court were to find that the German authority neither established nor penalised the cartel on account of its anti-competitive object or effect in Austria, it would have to find that the Austrian authority's action does not relate to the same facts as those on which the German authority's final decision was based. That, in turn, would mean that the *bis* condition is not fulfilled. Conversely, the *bis* condition would be deemed to be fulfilled – and the principle thus applicable – if the German competition authority had considered the object or effect of the cartel not only on the German market but also on the Austrian market.

Where the *bis* condition is fulfilled, it must also be determined whether a limitation of the right can be justified under Article 52 of the Charter, the Court of Justice continues.[18]

ii. The Possibility to Limit the Right

The ECJ notes that the protection against being punished or prosecuted twice for the same offence is not absolute but may be limited under certain circumstances. Article 52(1) of the Charter governs limitations and allows for the limitation of a Charter right if such restriction is provided for by law and respects the essence of the right or freedom in question. Furthermore, subject to the principle of proportionality, a limitation may only be made if it is necessary and genuinely meets either (i) objectives of general interest recognised by the European Union or (ii) the need to protect the rights or freedoms of others.

The Court of Justice notes that Regulation 1/2003, which governs the application of the competition rules in the EU, establishes a close link between the application of the EU competition rules and the corresponding national rules. Not only does the regulation require NCAs to apply national competition law in parallel with the EU competition rules, but the application of the national rules cannot also then lead to a different outcome than Article 101 TFEU. Thus, if a practice capable of affecting trade between Member States is compatible with Article 101 TFEU, the NCA is prevented from finding that the practice is contrary to the national equivalent of the Treaty article.[19] The implication of this compulsory link between national rules and Article 101 TFEU is that when two NCAs are investigating and sanctioning the same cartel, they are necessarily pursuing the same public interest objective, namely to ensure that competition in the internal market is not distorted by agreements, decisions of associations of undertakings or concerted practices.

[18] ibid, para 49.
[19] ibid, para 55.

In that regard, the ECJ makes the important statement of principle that the cumulation of procedures and penalties which have identical aims and objectives, and which concern the same aspects of a given procedure can in no circumstances be justified under Article 52(1) of the Charter. Such a limitation of the protection against double jeopardy is therefore never justified.[20]

By contrast, the Court of Justice considers that Article 50 does not preclude a national competition authority from initiating proceedings against an undertaking and imposing a fine on that undertaking for an infringement of Article 101 TFEU or an equivalent national provision on account of conduct which had an anti-competitive object or effect in that Member State, even though a competition authority of another Member State has already mentioned that conduct in a final decision against that undertaking, provided that the latter decision is not based on a finding of an anti-competitive object or effect in the territory of the first Member State. Thus, if those requirements are met, there is no restriction on the *ne bis in idem* principle. A decision to impose a fine in the second Member State would thus not even constitute a limitation of the right.

V. THE COURT OF JUSTICE'S RULING IN *BPOST*

A. The Case before the National Court

The *bpost* case concerns the parallel application of competition rules and rules governing postal regulation.[21] Bpost is the leading provider of postal services in Belgium. It offers postal delivery services to end customers (private individuals and businesses), but also to so-called mail preparation firms, which are consolidators that provide services upstream of the postal distribution service by preparing mail and delivering the mailings. In 2010, bpost made some adjustments to its pricing system towards these consolidators. Previously, pricing had been based on the total number of items sent through the intermediary, regardless of who the original sender was, but the price change introduced a 'sender-based' model instead. Now the price, and more specifically any volume discounts, were instead based on the volume of mailings that each individual sender passed through the intermediary.

In July 2011, the Belgian post and telecommunications authority found that bpost had violated the prohibition against discriminatory pricing and imposed a fine of EUR 2.3 million.[22] According to the decision, the new pricing system unjustifiably discriminated between direct customers and intermediaries. The decision explicitly stated that the Belgian regulator had not addressed the application of the competition rules.[23] In March 2016, the decision was overturned by the Brussels Court of Appeal on the grounds that the pricing at issue was not considered discriminatory.

[20] ibid, para 57.
[21] Case C-117/20, *bpost SA v Autorité belge de la concurrence*, EU:C:2022:202.
[22] Contrary to Article 144 bis and 144 ter, para 1, point 5 of the Law of 21 March 1991 on the reform of certain public commercial undertakings.
[23] Case C-117/20, *bpost SA v Autorité belge de la concurrence*, EU:C:2022:202, para 10.

In the meantime, the Belgian competition authority had investigated bpost's pricing practices. In 2012 it found that the pricing system infringed Article 102 TFEU and its Belgian equivalent and imposed a fine of nearly EUR 38 million on bpost. According to the competition authority, the tariff system had (i) an exclusionary effect on consolidators and bpost's potential competitors and (ii) a loyalty building effect on its main clients that would increase barriers to entry to the market.[24] When setting the amount of the fine, the competition authority had considered the fines previously imposed on bpost by the Belgian post and telecom authority. In its decision, the competition authority had not assessed whether bpost's behaviour was discriminatory.

In November 2016, the competition authority's decision was annulled by the Brussels Court of Appeal, which held that it violated the *ne bis in idem* principle. The Belgian Court of Cassation subsequently annulled the judgment and referred the case back to the Court of Appeal, which this time chose to request a preliminary ruling from the Court of Justice.

B. The Questions Referred to the Court of Justice

In its request for a preliminary ruling, the Belgian court sought clarification on whether Article 50 of the Charter precludes a competition authority from imposing a fine on a legal person for infringing EU competition law when that same conduct has already been the subject of a final decision in proceedings under sector-specific rules aimed at liberalising the postal market.

C. Assessment by the Court of Justice

Just as in *Nordzucker*, the Court of Justice begins by observing that the *ne bis in idem* principle is a fundamental principle of EU law, that it is now enshrined in Article 50 of the Charter, but also that the provision contains a right equivalent to that provided for in Article 4 of Protocol No 7 to the ECHR. Since Article 52(3) of the Charter links it to the ECHR, Article 50 and its prohibition against double jeopardy must be given the same meaning and scope as the ECHR provision. The Charter standard can thus not fall short of the ECHR standard the ECJ observes.

i. Conditions for the Ne Bis in Idem Principle to Apply

The Court of Justice further notes that Article 50 governs criminal proceedings,[25] and leaves it to the referring court to determine whether the procedures and penalties in question are of a criminal nature. Here, it recalls that, in making that assessment, the national court must take account of three criteria: (i) the legal classification of the offence under national law; (ii) the nature of the offence; and (iii) the penalties which

[24] ibid, para 12.
[25] ibid, para 24.

may be imposed.[26] It then notes that the referring court considers that the penalties in question are of a criminal nature and that the principle may therefore apply.[27]

However, the ECJ notes, the application of the principle requires that two additional conditions are met. First, there must be a previous final decision that has been issued on the merits (the *bis* condition). Second, the previous decision and the subsequent procedure or decision must relate to the same factual circumstances (the *idem* condition).

In that regard, the ECJ finds that the *bis* condition is satisfied, since the proceedings brought by the post and telecommunications authority have been concluded by a final decision. As regards the *idem* condition, the ECJ notes that the two proceedings concern the same legal person, bpost. It then turns to the requirement that the facts must also be the same. According to the ECJ, this means a set of concrete circumstances which are 'inextricably linked together and which have resulted in the final acquittal or conviction of the person concerned'.[28] The principle does not apply where the circumstances are merely similar – they must be identical.[29] The ECJ further notes that the question of how the circumstances and the protected legal interest are characterised under national law is irrelevant to the assessment of whether they constitute a single act. This is because the protection offered by the Charter may not vary from one Member State to another.

The ECJ once again leaves it to the referring court to determine whether the facts which were the subject of the two proceedings were identical. Should the national court find that that is the case, the parallel proceedings constitute a restriction of the fundamental right guaranteed by Article 50 of the Charter, the ECJ concludes.

ii. The Possibility to Limit the Right

Just as it did in *Nordzucker*, the ECJ acknowledges that the protection against double jeopardy is not absolute but may be limited under certain circumstances. Article 52(1) of the Charter allows for the limitation of a Charter right if such restriction is provided for by law and respects the essence of the right or freedom in question. Furthermore, subject to the principle of proportionality, a limitation may only be made if it is necessary and genuinely meets either (i) objectives of general interest recognised by the European Union or (ii) the need to protect the rights or freedoms of others, the Court of Justice declares.

In that regard, the Court of Justice notes that it appears that the two Belgian authorities dealt with the cases in accordance with Belgian law and that any limitation is therefore provided for by law. However, the Court of Justice leaves that final assessment to the referring court. It then goes on to assess whether the limitation corresponds to an objective of general interest. Here, it observes that the two

[26] The Court of Justice refers to its decision in *Bonda*, Case C-489/10, EU:C:2012:319, but the three criteria were already developed in 1976 by the European Court of Human Rights in its judgment of 8 June 1976 in *Engel v Netherlands*, Application Nos 5100/71; 5101/71; 5102/71; 5354/72; 5370/72.

[27] Case C-117/20, *bpost SA v Autorité belge de la concurrence*, EU:C:2022:202, para 28.

[28] ibid, para 27. See also the ruling of the Strasbourg Court in *Sergey Zolotukhin v Russia*, Application No 14939/03.

[29] Case C-117/20, *bpost SA v Autorité belge de la concurrence*, EU:C:2022:202, para 36.

legislations both pursue two distinct but legitimate objectives. While the sectoral legislation aims to liberalise the internal market in postal services, the competition rules aim to prevent distortions of competition in the internal market.[30] The first two criteria thus appear to be met. The additional burden which the duplication of proceedings represents may thus be justified by the two objectives pursued.

What remains is the assessment of proportionality. According to the Court of Justice, this means that the duplication of procedures and penalties must not go beyond what is appropriate or necessary to achieve the legitimate objectives pursued by the two sets of legislation. Thus, where there is a choice between several appropriate measures, recourse must be had to the least onerous and the disadvantages caused must not be disproportionate to the aims pursued. Nor must that duplication constitute an unreasonable burden for the individual.[31] Once again, the Court of Justice notes that it is for the referring court to make that assessment.

Here, it acknowledges the need to address a certain conduct from different aspects, declaring that public authorities can legitimately choose complementary legal responses to certain conduct that is harmful to society through different procedures forming a coherent whole to address different aspects of the social problem involved. This provided that the accumulated legal responses do not represent an excessive burden for the individual concerned. The ECJ therefore acknowledges that a limitation may be justified where the two authorities have taken measures against bpost which pursue complementary objectives and concern different aspects of the same behaviour.[32] Important factors in that assessment are the existence of clear and specific rules making it possible, on the one hand, to foresee the acts which may be the subject of parallel proceedings and, on the other, to coordinate the two proceedings. Thus, the ECJ notes, the national court must consider whether (i) such coordination has taken place, (ii) the two proceedings are close in time and (iii) the competition authority, when setting the fine, has considered the sanctions already imposed on bpost by the post and telecom authority.

While the Court of Justice considers that it is for the referring court to make this assessment, it makes a few clarifications to provide the national court with a useful answer. It thus notes that the Belgian telecommunications legislation provides for coordination and communication between the authorities concerned. Furthermore, the Court of Justice notes that there is a sufficiently close temporal link between the two procedures. The Belgian post and telecommunications authority took its decision on 20 July 2011 and the competition authority on 10 December 2012. Finally, the Court of Justice notes that the fact that the fine imposed on bpost by the competition authority was higher than the fine previously imposed on it by the Belgian post and telecommunications authority does not affect the assessment of proportionality. While the ECJ declares that it is for the national court to make the actual assessment, the guidance that it provides appears to leave the Belgian court with limited room for manoeuvre.

[30] ibid, para 46.
[31] ibid, para 49.
[32] ibid, para 50.

D. Conclusion of the Court of Justice

Finally, the Court of Justice notes that Article 50 of the Charter allows a competition authority to impose a fine on a legal person for an infringement of Article 102 TFEU even if that person has already been the subject of a final decision or proceedings for the same act in respect of an infringement of sectoral rules aimed at liberalising the market in question. This is provided that the national rules are clear and transparent and allow undertakings active on the market to foresee which acts or omissions that may lead to parallel proceedings and penalties under the two sets of legislation. Furthermore, the two procedures must have been carried out in a sufficiently coordinated manner and close enough in time. Finally, the aggregate sanctions must be proportionate to the gravity of the infringement.

VI. CONCLUSIONS FROM THE TWO RULINGS

The following conclusions can be drawn from the two Grand Chamber rulings. First, where the two parallel proceedings concern the application of rules that pursue the same objective, a limitation of the right can never be justified. Thus, if both the *bis* and the *idem* conditions are met, a duplication of proceedings is by necessity a violation of the Charter right.

Second, where the two parallel proceedings concern the application of rules that pursue distinct but complementary objectives, it is possible to limit the right under certain circumstances. Thus, a duplication of proceedings may be justified if there are clear and specific rules making it possible for the individual, on the one hand, to foresee the acts which may be the subject of parallel proceedings and, on the other, for the authorities to coordinate the two proceedings to ensure that any sanctions imposed are proportionate. In the specific case, the national court must consider whether (i) such coordination has taken place, (ii) the proceedings are close in time and (iii) the sanction imposed by the second authority is not considered excessive given the sanction already imposed.

This view taken by the Court of Justice allegedly aligns the EU rules to their ECHR equivalent and more specifically the stance taken by the Strasbourg Court in *A & B v Norway* delivered in 2016.[33] The question is whether there is alignment or if the ECJ establishes a standard that deviates somewhat from its ECHR equivalent.

[33] *A & B v Norway*, Judgment of 15 November 2016, Applications nos 24130/11 and 29758/11. That said, the two courts maintain a slightly different methodological approach while ultimately reaching the same conclusion. The Strasbourg Court recognises the possibility of parallel proceedings only when they are complementary and can be viewed as a single set of proceedings. In principle, no exceptions or limitations to this rule are permitted under the ECHR. Conversely, in *bpost*, the Court of Justice explicitly affirms the acceptance of dual proceedings, referring to the notion of a 'coherent whole'. In addition, the Court of Justice treats the duplication of proceedings as a restriction on the *ne bis in idem* principle, subjecting it to the Article 52(1) Charter test and a set of conditions heavily influenced by ECHR case-law.

VII. NE BIS IN IDEM UNDER THE ECHR

Before examining the Strasbourg Court's position in *A and B v Norway*, it is helpful to look back to an earlier and highly influential ruling. In February 2009, the Grand Chamber of the Strasbourg Court issued its landmark judgment in *Sergey Zolotukhin v Russia*,[34] where it was asked to provide a harmonised interpretation of the concept of the 'same offence' – the *idem* element of the *ne bis in idem* principle.

The Strasbourg Court's ruling in *Zolotukhin* sent shockwaves across Europe, as it was widely understood to establish that Article 4 of Protocol No 7 to the ECHR prohibits Contracting States from operating so-called double-track enforcement systems. Under such systems, which are common in several European states, a single act – such as submitting incorrect information on a tax return – could result in both administrative and criminal penalties.

A. *Zolotukhin v Russia*: The Strasbourg Court Tightens the Reins

The case concerns the legality of administrative and criminal proceedings brought against a Russian soldier, Mr Zolotukhin. On the morning of 4 January 2002, he was taken to a police station to explain how he had managed to bring his girlfriend into a restricted military area. While at the station, Mr Zolotukhin was reportedly intoxicated, used offensive language toward the officers and threatened to kill one of them. As a result, he was sentenced to three days of administrative detention for swearing in public and ignoring police warnings, in violation of the Code of Administrative Offences.

A few weeks later, authorities opened a separate criminal case against him, accusing him of disorderly conduct, including resisting a public official maintaining public order under the Criminal Code. Mr Zolotukhin was eventually convicted. He later filed a complaint with the Strasbourg Court, arguing that facing both administrative and criminal proceedings for essentially the same conduct violated Article 4 of Protocol No 7 to the ECHR, which protects individuals against being tried or punished twice for the same offence.

In its ruling, the Strasbourg Court acknowledged that its past approach had been inconsistent, noting that it had previously applied 'several different approaches' to determining whether the offences a person was prosecuted for were the same.[35] Whereas one approach had been to focus on the 'same conduct' another had been to focus on the fact that a certain conduct can constitute several offences. An example of the latter was *Oliveira*,[36] where the applicant had been convicted first of failing to control her vehicle and subsequently of negligently causing physical injury. Her car had veered onto the other side of the road, hitting one car and then colliding with a second, whose driver had sustained serious injuries. The Strasbourg Court found that the facts of the case were a typical example of a single act constituting various offences,

[34] *Sergey Zolotukhin v Russia*, Judgment of 10 February 2009, Application no 14939/03. See para 78.
[35] ibid, para 70.
[36] *Oliveira v Switzerland*, Judgment of 30 July 1998, Application no 84/97.

whereas Article 4 of Protocol No 7 only prohibited people from being tried twice for the same offence. Yet another approach had put emphasis on 'the essential elements' of the two offences. In addition to highlighting its own inconsistencies, the Strasbourg Court also observed that international legal instruments protecting against double jeopardy use varying language to express the concept.[37]

The Strasbourg Court then emphasised that the principles of legal certainty, foreseeability and equality before the law prevent it from departing from established case-law without good reason. At the same time, it reaffirmed that the ECHR is a living instrument that must be interpreted in light of current conditions. It further noted that focusing solely on the legal classification of offences is too narrow and fails to adequately protect individual rights. If the assessment were limited to whether the offences had different legal labels, it could undermine the protection offered by Article 4 of Protocol No 7, rather than ensuring that protection is practical and effective, as required under the ECHR. Based on this reasoning, the Strasbourg Court concluded that the Convention prohibits a second prosecution or trial where the second offence arises from the same facts, or facts that are substantially the same, as those already judged.[38]

Although the Strasbourg Court aimed to bring clarity and consistency to its approach, its ruling had the opposite effect. This is because it introduced uncertainty regarding the permissibility of imposing multiple types of sanctions on the same individual – a practice common in cases like tax fraud and other financial or economic crimes, known as double-track enforcement. The ECJ, for example, appeared to interpret the ruling as limiting the use of such systems. In the landmark *Åkerberg Fransson* case,[39] the ECJ held that a system allowing an individual to face both criminal prosecution for tax fraud and a tax surcharge for the same conduct would violate the principle of *ne bis in idem*, provided that the surcharge could be classified as a criminal penalty. Although the ECJ did not explicitly reference the *Zolotukhin* ruling, it is likely that the Strasbourg Court's reasoning influenced its decision.

Against this background, the Strasbourg Court was later called upon to assess the legality of the Norwegian system for enforcing their tax rules and took the opportunity to refine its approach towards double-track enforcement systems by re-interpreting the *bis* criterion.

B. *A and B v Norway*: A U-turn or a Refinement of Previous Case-Law?

Facing strong pressure from Contracting States defending their use of double-track enforcement systems, the Grand Chamber of the Strasbourg Court revisited its interpretation of the *ne bis in idem* principle in *A and B v Norway*. In this case, the two applicants had been subjected to administrative tax surcharges for failing to declare certain income in their tax returns. In addition, they faced parallel criminal

[37] *Sergey Zolotukhin v Russia*, Judgment of 10 February 2009, Application no 14939/03, para 79.
[38] ibid, para 81.
[39] Case C-617/10, *Åklagaren v Hans Åkerberg Fransson*, EU:C:2013:105. Following the ruling of the Strasbourg Court in *A & B v Norway*, the ECJ later revised its view in *Menci*, Case C-524/15, EU:C:2018:197.

proceedings and were convicted of tax fraud based on the same omissions. Arguing that the imposition of both administrative and criminal sanctions for the same conduct violated their right not to be tried or punished twice for the same offence, the applicants complained to the Strasbourg Court.

In its ruling, the Strasbourg Court observed that both prior to and following *Zolotukhin*, it had acknowledged the permissibility, to a certain extent, of different authorities imposing distinct sanctions for the same conduct, despite the presence of a final decision. In instances where such practices were accepted, the Strasbourg Court regarded the combination of sanctions as a unified whole, rendering it artificial to consider the situation as a duplication of proceedings. Although the sanctions were imposed by separate authorities in different proceedings, the Strasbourg Court found a sufficiently close connection between them, both in terms of substance and timing.[40]

It then proceeded to examine several cases involving Sweden and Finland where it had identified infringements of the principle, noting that in those cases, the criminal and the administrative sanctions had been imposed by different authorities without the proceedings being in any way connected: both sets of proceedings followed their own separate course and became final independently of each other. Moreover, neither of the sanctions had been taken into consideration by the other court or authority in determining the severity of the sanction, nor was there any other interaction between the relevant authorities. More importantly, under the Finnish system 'the tax penalties had been imposed following an examination of an applicant's conduct and his or her liability under the relevant tax legislation, which was independent from the assessments made in the criminal proceedings'.[41]

Before turning to the facts of the case at hand, the Strasbourg Court made several important observations. First, it noted that the prohibition of double jeopardy was not originally part of the ECHR but was introduced through Protocol No 7. It also pointed out that several Contracting States had not ratified this protocol, and that some of those which had done so included reservations or interpretative declarations – stating that the term 'criminal' should be understood in accordance with their respective national laws.

The Strasbourg Court further acknowledged the observation made by the Advocate General in *Åkerberg Fransson*, who had noted that dual-track enforcement systems – where both administrative and criminal sanctions are applied for the same offence – are widespread among EU Member States, particularly in areas such as taxation, environmental protection, and public safety.[42] Notably, six Contracting States had formally intervened in the proceedings before the Strasbourg Court, underscoring the broader significance of the case.[43]

No doubt aware of the pressure, the Grand Chamber acknowledged that the object of Article 4 of Protocol No 7 is to prevent the injustice of a person being prosecuted or punished twice for the same criminalised conduct. It declared that the safest way

[40] *A & B v Norway*, Judgment of 15 November 2016, Applications nos 24130/11 and 29758/11, para 113.
[41] ibid, para 114.
[42] ibid, para 118. Reference is made to the opinion of Advocate General Cruz Villalón in Case C-617/10, *Åklagaren v Hans Åkerberg Fransson*, EU:C:2012:340.
[43] *A & B v Norway*, Judgment of 15 November 2016, Applications nos 24130/11 and 29758/11, para 119.

to ensure compliance with Article 4 of Protocol No. 7 was to establish a single-track procedure 'enabling the parallel strands of legal regulation of the activity concerned to be brought together, so that the different needs of society in responding to the offence can be addressed within the framework of a single process'.[44] However, it did not outlaw legal systems which took an integrated approach to the social wrongdoing in question, and in particular an approach involving parallel stages of legal response by different authorities and for different purposes. A fair balance had to be struck between duly safeguarding the interests of the individual protected by the *ne bis in idem* principle, on the one hand, and accommodating the particular interest of the community in being able to take a calibrated regulatory approach in the area concerned, on the other.[45]

Turning to the Norwegian system, the Strasbourg Court declared that, for it to consider it compliant with the ECHR, the respondent state needed to convincingly demonstrate that the dual proceedings in question were closely connected both in substance and time. This meant that the objectives pursued, and the methods used to achieve them should essentially be complementary and occur within a linked timeframe. Additionally, the potential consequences of structuring the legal treatment of the conduct in this manner must be proportionate and foreseeable for those affected. Material factors for determining whether there was a sufficiently close connection in substance included whether the:

1. different proceedings pursued complementary purposes and therefore addressed different aspects of the social misconduct involved;
2. duality of the proceedings concerned was a foreseeable consequence, both in law and in practice;
3. relevant sets of proceedings were conducted in such a manner as to avoid as far as possible any duplication in the collection as well as the assessment of the evidence, notably through adequate interaction between the various competent authorities to bring about that the establishment of facts in one set was also used in the other set; and
4. a sanction imposed in the proceedings which became final first was taken into account in those which became final last, so as to prevent the individual concerned bearing an excessive burden.

Moreover, the temporal connection needed to be sufficiently close to shield individuals from uncertainty and delay, preventing proceedings from becoming excessively prolonged. If the connection in time is weak, the burden on the state increases to explain and justify any delays that may result from how the proceedings are conducted, the Strasbourg Court declared.[46]

The national authorities had determined that the applicants' conduct warranted two separate responses: an administrative penalty and a criminal sanction. The administrative penalty – a tax surcharge – was intended to serve as a general deterrent and to compensate the state for the substantial work and costs incurred by the tax

[44] ibid, paras 123 and 130.
[45] ibid, para 124.
[46] ibid, para 134.

authorities in detecting inaccurate tax declarations. The criminal conviction, on the other hand, was not only deterrent in nature but also punitive, addressing the same wrongful conduct, now further characterised by the element of culpable fraud.

Importantly, when sentencing the applicants, the domestic court considered the fact that an administrative penalty had already been imposed. The dual proceedings, including the possibility of cumulative penalties, were foreseeable in the circumstances, and the findings from one set of proceedings were used to inform the other. Finding no indication that the applicants had suffered disproportionate prejudice or injustice and concluding that there was a sufficiently close connection – both in substance and in time – between the two proceedings, the Strasbourg Court held, by 16 votes to one, that there had been no violation of the ECHR.

VIII. DOES THE EU STANDARD MEET ITS ECHR EQUIVALENT?

With the Lisbon Treaty, the EU aligned its fundamental rights protection more closely with the ECHR. Not only has the EU committed to acceding to the Convention,[47] but the level of protection provided under the Charter must not fall below that guaranteed by the ECHR. According to Article 52(3) of the Charter, rights that correspond to those in the ECHR must be interpreted with the same meaning and scope. The Charter may only diverge from the ECHR where it offers more extensive protection. In this way, the ECHR sets a minimum standard – or a 'floor' – for fundamental rights protection within the EU. It is therefore important to assess whether the standard established by the ECJ in *bpost* and *Nordzucker* aligns with the standard set by the ECHR.

A first observation is that the two ECJ rulings differ in several respects from the Strasbourg Court's ruling in *A and B v Norway*, making direct comparisons difficult. Contrary to the situation in *bpost* where the company were fined under both the competition rules and sectoral legislation, the ECHR jurisprudence examines and assesses dual enforcement systems where the legislations in place serve to achieve the same ultimate goal – for example to guarantee a well-functioning tax system – but where the sanctions imposed are of different types and serve complementary objectives. Thus, in *A & B v Norway*, the Strasbourg court acknowledged that the (i) tax surcharge was intended to serve as a general deterrent and to compensate the state for the substantial work and costs incurred by the tax authorities in detecting inaccurate tax declarations, and (ii) criminal conviction was not only deterrent in nature but also punitive, addressing the same wrongful conduct, now further characterised by the element of culpable fraud.

Admittedly, there is earlier case-law that is more comparable. In *Oliveira*,[48] the applicant was first convicted by the police magistrate for failing to control her vehicle as she had not adapted her speed to the road conditions. Subsequently, she was convicted by the criminal courts of causing physical injury by negligence. The fact that the two cases concerned two different offences led the Strasbourg Court to

[47] Article 6(2) of the Treaty on the European Union.

[48] *Oliveira v Switzerland*, Judgment of 30 July 1998, Application no 84/97.

conclude that there was no violation of Article 4 of Protocol No 7. A few years later, the Strasbourg Court came to another conclusion in *Franz Fischer v Austria*,[49] where the applicant had, whilst driving under the influence of drink, knocked down a cyclist who was fatally injured. After hitting the cyclist, the applicant drove off without stopping to give assistance. Finding him guilty of a number of road traffic offences, the St Pölten District Administrative Authority ordered him to pay fines with imprisonment in default. He was later convicted under the Criminal Code and sentenced to six months' imprisonment for causing death by negligence. Here the Strasbourg Court took note of the fact that the applicant had first been convicted by the administrative authority for drunken driving and later convicted of causing death by negligence with the special element of 'allowing himself to become intoxicated'. This made the Strasbourg Court reach the conclusion that there had been a violation of Article 4 of Protocol No 7 of the ECHR.

In *Zolotukhin*, the Strasbourg Court acknowledged that it had previously applied several approaches towards the prohibition against double jeopardy. It noted that one approach had been to look at the offence rather than the underlying facts, only prohibiting people from being tried twice for the same offence. Through the ruling in *Zolotukhin*, this approach was abandoned. There, the Strasbourg Court declared that focusing solely on the legal classification of offences is too narrow and fails to adequately protect individual rights. If the assessment were limited to whether the offences had different legal labels, it could undermine the protection offered by Article 4 of Protocol No 7, rather than ensuring that protection is practical and effective. Based on this reasoning, the Strasbourg Court concluded that the Convention prohibits a second prosecution or trial where the second offence arises from the same facts, or facts that are substantially the same, as those already judged.[50]

While the Strasbourg Court arguably adopted a more restrained approach in its ruling in *A & B v Norway*, its assessment remains grounded in an evaluation of the factual circumstances rather than the formal classification of the offences. At the same time, the calibrated approach now taken by the court reflects a desire among the Contracting States to retain the flexibility to impose multiple types of sanctions serving different purposes on certain forms of conduct. It could therefore be argued that the Strasbourg Court's limitation of what it had previously established in *Zolotukhin* is not directly applicable to the circumstances in *bpost*, which did not deal with different types of sanctions but rather with different types of offences, and that allowing subsequent proceedings where the facts are the same would be to set a standard that falls below the ECHR standard.

On the other hand, the Strasbourg Court does acknowledge that the principle is not accepted by all Contracting States, giving it a weaker status than other ECHR rights. Furthermore, its findings in *A and B v Norway* are couched in a general, more principled manner, focusing on closeness in substance and time, and not expressly limiting the application of its findings to situations such as that in the case at hand. Thus, the Strasbourg Court declares that:

[49] *Franz Fischer v Austria*, Judgment of 29 May 2001, Application no 37950/97.
[50] *Sergey Zolotukhin v Russia*, Judgment of 10 February 2009, Application no 14939/03, para 81.

> Article 4 of Protocol No. 7 does not exclude the conduct of dual sets of proceedings, even to their term, provided that certain conditions are fulfilled. In particular, for the Court to be satisfied that there is no duplication ('bis') of trial or punishment as proscribed by Article 4 of Protocol No. 7, the respondent State must demonstrate convincingly that the dual sets of proceedings in question have been sufficiently closely connected in substance and in time. In other words, it must be shown that they have been combined in an integrated manner so as to form a coherent whole. This implies not only that the purposes pursued and the means used to achieve them should in essence be complementary and linked in time, but also that the possible consequences of organising the legal treatment of the conduct concerned in such a manner should be proportionate and foreseeable for the persons affected.[51]

While the jurisprudence of the Strasbourg Court is typically less principled and more tied to the facts of the case at hand than the jurisprudence of the EU Courts, it may be assumed that the Strasbourg Court is not altogether pleased with the fragmented approach adopted earlier and now seeks to achieve a more common standard. On that basis, much suggests that the Charter standard set by the ECJ in *bpost* and *Nordzucker* would be considered to meet the ECHR standard.

For a parallel application of the DMA and EU or national competition rules, it is thus necessary that:

1. The two proceedings pursue complementary purposes and therefore address different aspects of the social misconduct involved;
2. the duality of the proceedings concerned is a foreseeable consequence, both in law and in practice;
3. the two proceedings are combined in an integrated manner and there is a sufficient connection in time between them;
4. the proceedings are conducted in such a manner as to avoid as far as possible any duplication in the collection as well as the assessment of evidence, notably through adequate interaction between the various competent authorities to bring about that the establishment of facts in one set was also used in the other set; and
5. the sanction imposed in the proceedings which becomes final first is taken into account in that which becomes final second, so as to prevent the individual concerned from bearing an excessive burden.

IX. THE OBJECTIVE OF THE DMA

A crucial criterion is thus that the two proceedings pursue different but complementary objectives and address different aspects of the social misconduct involved. According to the Commission, its application of Article 102 TFEU over the past couple of decades has undeniably highlighted the need for ex-ante regulation. The cases and types of abuses identified by the Commission have also inspired the drafting of the DMA and the obligations now imposed on gatekeepers. However, the legal

[51] *A & B v Norway*, Judgment of 15 November 2016, Applications nos 24130/11 and 29758/11, para 130.

basis for the DMA is Article 114 TFEU, which governs the internal market, rather than Article 103 TFEU, which pertains to the Union's competition rules.

The regulation is also purported to pursue different objectives than the EU competition rules. Recital 7 states that it aims to contribute to the proper functioning of the internal market by establishing rules to ensure contestability and fairness in the digital sector and by eliminating existing or potential fragmentation in the specific areas covered by the DMA. The recitals also address the relationship between the DMA and competition rules, acknowledging that the regulation is intended to complement the enforcement of competition rules and shall therefore apply without prejudice to EU or national competition rules.

Thus, according to recital 11, the DMA pursues an objective that is complementary to but different from that of protecting competition in any given market. The objective, according to the recital, is to ensure that markets where gatekeepers are present are and remain contestable and fair, independently from the actual, potential or presumed effects of the conduct of a given gatekeeper covered by the DMA on competition on a given market.

This raises the question of whether the Commission or the legislator is correct in asserting that the objectives of the DMA differ from those of competition law. It is generally assumed that most markets characterised by effective competition are also contestable. Admittedly, there has been ongoing debate about the role of fairness and whether it should be explicitly incorporated into competition policy and legislation.[52] Contestability, by contrast, appears to be a more inherent element of traditional competition rules. When the Commission presented its proposal to the DMA, it declared that 'unfair practices and lack of contestability lead to inefficient outcomes in the digital sector in terms of higher prices, lower quality, as well as less choice and innovation to the detriment of European consumers'.[53] This no doubt echoes the objectives of the EU competition rules.

When examining the sanctions available under both sets of legislation, they are essentially identical and appear to serve identical purposes, allowing the Commission to impose fines and decide on behavioural or structural remedies on companies infringing the rules.

From the ECJ's rulings in *Nordzucker* and *bpost* we know that there is no room for derogation from the *ne bis in idem* principle if the two cases concern the application of rules that are either identical or that pursue identical objectives. We also know that if, as in the case of *bpost*, two pieces of legislation pursue different objectives, there is some room, albeit limited, to investigate and sanction a certain conduct twice. In *Nordzucker* both cases concerned the application of Article 101 TFEU, and in *bpost* one case concerned the application of the postal regulation and the other the application of 102 TFEU, two set of rules pursuing clearly diverging aims.[54]

[52] See eg D Gerard, A Komninos and D Waelbroeck (eds), *Fairness in EU Competition Policy: Significance and Implications* (Brussels, Bruylant, 2020) and F Ducci and M Trebilcock, 'The Revival of Fairness Discourse in Competition Policy' (2019) 64(1) *The Antitrust Bulletin*, 79.

[53] European Commission, *Proposal for a Regulation of the European Parliament and of the Council on contestable and fair markets in the digital sector (Digital Markets Act)* COM(2020) 842 final, Explanatory Memorandum, 1–2, https://eur-lex.europa.eu/legal-content/EN/TXT/?uri=celex:52020PC0842.

[54] Albeit not necessarily complementary.

Here, there is a clear link between Article 102 TFEU and the DMA and the two are no doubt intertwined, ultimately pursuing the same objectives: lower prices, higher quality, as well as better choice and innovation to the benefit of European consumers. In addition, the sanctions available mirror each other and appear to serve the same objectives. It is uncertain whether the Court should or would consider the two pieces of legislation to pursue distinct objectives. In *bpost*, it was easy to establish that the regulations at hand did not pursue the same objectives. The liberalisation of the postal sector is clearly distinct from the objective to ensure undistorted competition and the two sets of rules are enforced by authorities with distinct roles and mandates.

As for the relationship between the competition rules and the DMA, the DMA springs from the competition rules and DG COMP is the designated enforcer of both sets of rules.[55] The link between the antitrust cases and the DMA cannot be ignored, this especially since the Court has acknowledged, for example in its recent ruling in *Google Shopping*,[56] that the behaviour struck down by the Commission and which is now also regulated through the DMA, does in fact amount to abuse of dominance.

While the wording of the DMA thus appears to provide some room for parallel proceedings, the Commission and the national competition authorities should tread carefully in order to ensure that the rights of the companies involved are safely protected. It should also be reminded that even if the Strasbourg Court does provide some room for dual-track enforcement systems, it is also pointing to the fact that the surest manner of securing compliance with Article 4 of Protocol No 7 is the provision, at some appropriate stage, of a single-track procedure enabling the parallel strands of legal regulation of the activity concerned to be brought together, so that the different needs of society in responding to the offence can be addressed within the framework of a single process.

X. ALLOWING PARALLEL PROCEEDINGS COMES AT A COST

Anyone who has been subject to a competition law investigation knows that this is a painful, time-consuming and costly experience, no matter if the case ends with an infringement decision or is closed without further action. The resources that the company will have to invest to cooperate fully with the authority to avoid the risk of having to pay a hefty fine for obstruction,[57] are often without proportions.

Being designated as a gatekeeper under the DMA comes with significant additional obligations. Gatekeepers must not only adapt their behaviour and business practices to meet the DMA's strict requirements, but also establish a dedicated compliance function within their organisation.[58] They are subject to extensive reporting obligations, which go beyond simply ensuring compliance – they must also demonstrate

[55] Together with the Directorate General for Communications Networks, Content and Technology (DG CONNECT).

[56] Case C-48/22 P, *Google and Alphabet v Commission (Google Shopping)*, EU:C:2024:726.

[57] The company risks having to pay up to 1 per cent of the group's annual global turnover, see Article 23(1) of Regulation 1/2003 and Article 30(3) of the DMA.

[58] Article 28 of the DMA.

compliance.[59] This includes regularly collecting, organising and submitting detailed information to the Commission about their activities and the steps they are taking to meet regulatory obligations. These reports enable the Commission to closely monitor compliance efforts and assess the effectiveness of the measures implemented by gatekeepers.

Article 50 of the Charter declares that no one should be tried for the same offence twice, implying that not only should you be protected against having to pay fines in two parallel proceedings, but you should also be protected from having to be subject to not only one but two parallel proceedings. This reflects the findings of the Strasbourg Court in *Zolotukhin* where it declared that the right is not confined to the right not to be punished twice, but that it covers also the right not to be prosecuted or tried twice. According to the Strasbourg Court this right thus contains three distinct guarantees, providing that, for the same offence, no one should be (i) liable to be tried, (ii) tried or (iii) punished twice.[60]

In addition, the Strasbourg Court has established that courts should consider whether the relevant sets of proceedings are conducted in such a manner so as to avoid as far as possible any duplication in the collection and assessment of evidence, this to assure that the establishment of facts in one set of proceedings is replicated in the other. That said, it is equally important to consider the risks that a company's defence rights are not properly safeguarded. If the authorities are allowed to exchange evidence without proper procedural safeguards or if they are allowed to gather evidence not strictly related to the investigation at hand. Thus, any collection and exchange of evidence needs to be assessed carefully before it is executed.

While the Court of Justice, drawing inspiration from the Grand Chamber's ruling in *A and B v Norway*, appears to permit the duplication of proceedings in certain limited circumstances, it is crucial that such exceptions remain narrowly confined. The Strasbourg Court has recognised that legislators may address socially harmful conduct through complementary legal responses pursued via different procedures – so long as these measures form part of a coherent whole and do not place an excessive burden on the individual.

In *A and B v Norway*, the issue concerned the combination of administrative and criminal proceedings, each targeting different aspects of the same conduct. However, it is more difficult to justify exposing an individual to two distinct administrative proceedings, particularly where the purported division of objectives appears, at least to some extent, artificial. This raises legitimate questions about whether the goals pursued under the DMA truly differ in substance from those underlying EU competition law. To conclude, the Commission and the national competition authorities must shoulder their responsibilities with care and not overstep the boundaries of their powers.

[59] Article 11 of the DMA.

[60] *Sergey Zolotukhin v Russia* (GC), Judgment of 10 February 2009, Application no 14939/03, para 110. This statement has been reiterated in several subsequent rulings including in *A & B v Norway* (GC), Judgment of 15 November 2016, Applications nos 24130/11 and 29758/11, para 110.

13

Enforcement Design for the New EU Law of the Digital Economy: Centralised, Decentralised or Lopsided?

ANTONINA BAKARDJIEVA ENGELBREKT

THE UNION'S EFFORTS FOR establishing a level-playing field in today's digital, data-driven economy[1] have brought about major changes in the regulatory frameworks of nearly all areas of EU market law. The substantive rules of EU competition, consumer and intellectual property law have been considerably reshaped, either through amendments of existing legislative instruments, or through judicial interpretation ensuring that the rules are better adapted to the new reality of digital marketing, digital content and ubiquitous communication networks.[2] In parallel, with the Digital Services Package, the Union rolled out novel specially tailored rules aiming at reining in the excessive power of gatekeeping platforms and imposing higher responsibilities on online intermediaries. This extensive upgrade of substantive standards and obligations has been both praised and criticised from a number of perspectives.[3] What is indisputable, however, is that the actual impact of the new rules

[1] The concepts and labels seeking to capture the essence of the ongoing transformation of the economy are many. Besides 'digital' and 'data-driven' economy, the notion 'attention economy' has been used to describe the increasing economic value of the arguably most scarce human resource 'attention' and ultimately 'time'. On the attention economy see, Tim Wu, Blind Spot: The Attention Economy and the Law (2019) 82 *Antitrust LJ* 771; Tim Wu, *The Attention Merchants: The Epic Scramble to Get Inside our Heads* (Columbia University, Faculty Books, 2016).

[2] For competition law, see eg the Google Shopping case, C-48/22 P *Google and Alphabet* ECLI:EU:C:2024:726; for consumer law, see Directive (EU) 2019/2161 as regards the better enforcement and modernisation of Union consumer protection rules, OJ L 328, 18.12.2019, pp 7–28 (Omnibus Directive); for copyright, Directive (EU) 2019/790 on copyright and related rights in the Digital Single Market (Digital Copyright Directive).

[3] See Martin Eifert, Axel Metzger, Heike Schweitzer and Gerhard Wagner, 'Taming the Giants: the DMA/DSA Package' (2021) 58 *Common Market Law Review* 987–1028; Rupprecht Podszun, 'From Competition Law to Platform Regulation – Regulatory Choices for the Digital Markets Act' (2023) 17(1) *Economics* 1; Pablo Ibáñez Colomo, 'The Draft Digital Markets Act: A Legal and Institutional Analysis' (2021) 12(7) *Journal of European Competition Law & Practice* 561–75; Peter Alexiadis and Alexandre de Streel, 'The EU's Digital Markets Act: Opportunities and Challenges Ahead' (2022) 23(2) *Bus L Int'l* 163.

will greatly depend on the effectiveness and appropriateness of the instruments for their enforcement, both novel and already existing.[4]

The Digital Markets Act (DMA) and the Digital Services Act (DSA) advance a new architecture of enforcement, bringing about visible concentration of enforcement powers in the Commission, apparently in contrast to the previously prevailing trend of decentralised and network-based enforcement in e.g. EU competition, consumer and data protection law.[5] This trend towards centralisation is explained by the focus of the new legislation on large-scale players in the digital economy – gatekeeping platforms under the DMA, and very large online platforms (VLOPs) and very large online search engines (VLOSEs) under the DSA. At the same time, the Commission is far from being alone in the process of enforcement. It will be performing its enforcement tasks in a densely populated institutional environment, and is expected to continue to interact with competent national authorities, as well as with existing and novel enforcement networks, relevant Union agencies, national and Union courts. This chapter explores the role of these 'other' institutional actors, who are supposed to support the Commission in its role of chief enforcer. It asks, more specifically, in what ways the Digital Services Package impacts the position of national authorities in the enforcement of EU digital market law; and what place, if any, does the new legislation assign to existing and new enforcement networks. The Union has been promoting for decades a model of coordinated decentralised enforcement. Does the Digital Services Package signal a more enduring shift away from this model?[6] Or is it just a matter of fine-tuning the mix between centralised and decentralised enforcement in light of past experiences?

In the rest of the chapter, first, I outline the enforcement architecture under the two main legislative instruments in the Digital Services Package, the DMA and the DSA,[7] describing briefly the role of the Commission and the role assigned to national

[4] Pieter Van Cleynenbreugel, 'The Commission's Digital Services and Markets Act Proposals: First Step Towards Tougher and More Directly Enforced EU Rules?' (2021) 28(5) *Maastricht Journal of European and Comparative Law* 667–86; Giorgio Monti and Alexander De Streel, 'Improving EU Institutional Design to Better Supervise Digital Platforms' (2022) CERRE, January 2022, available at: https://cerre.eu/publications/improving-eu-institutional-design/; Alexandre De Streel et al, 'Implementing the DMA: Substantive and Procedural Principles' (2024) CERRE, available at: https://cerre.eu/publications/implementing-the-dma-substantive-and-procedural-principles/.

[5] See for competition law Maartje de Visser, *Network-Based Governance in EC Law* (Oxford, Hart Publishing, 2009); Imelda Maher, 'Regulation and Modes of Governance in EC Competition Law: What's New in Enforcement?' (2007) 31 *Fordham International Law Journal* 1713; for consumer law Cristina Poncibò, 'Networks to Enforce European Law: The Case of the Consumer Protection Cooperation Network' (2012) (35) *Journal of Consumer Policy* 175; for data protection Francesca Bignami, 'Trans-Governmental Networks vs Democracy: The Case of the European Information Privacy Network' (2005) 26 *Michigan Journal of International Law* 807.

[6] An already ongoing tendency of moving enforcement to Brussels has been well observed in the literature. See Miroslava Scholten, 'Mind the Trend! Enforcement of EU Law Has Been Moving to 'Brussels' (2017) 24(9) *Journal of European Public Policy* 1348.

[7] See Regulation (EU) 2022/1925 of the European Parliament and of the Council of 14 September 2022 on contestable and fair markets in the digital sector (Digital Markets Act); Regulation (EU) 2022/2065 of the European Parliament and of the Council of 19 October 2022 on a Single Market for Digital Services (Digital Services Act). Both acts use the term National Competent Authorities without specifying the type of authorities.

competent authorities (NCAs).[8] I also discuss whether the two regulations leave some place for old and new networks of enforcement authorities. Second, I look back at the history of the network model of enforcement and recall the reasons for its advancement across EU policy domains from the early 1990s onwards. More concretely, I provide a concise account of the main features and the institutional dynamic of two networks of central importance for the enforcement of EU internal market law, which are also of relevance for the enforcement of the new EU digital legislation, namely the European Competition Network (ECN) and the Consumer Protection Cooperation Network (CPC Network). Based on various academic and expert evaluations of the performance of these networks, I seek to elicit to what extent the networks have lived up to expectations and what their stories tell us about the strengths and weaknesses of coordinated decentralised enforcement. In a final section, I return to the institutional framework for the enforcement of the Digital Services Package. The analysis focuses on the question whether and in what ways past experiences have influenced the enforcement architecture of the new EU law of the digital economy. Has the right balance been struck between centralised and decentralised enforcement? Or can we discern a new pattern emerging of what could be dubbed 'lopsided enforcement'?

I. THE NEW ENFORCEMENT ARCHITECTURE OF EU DIGITAL MARKET LAW

As already stated at the outset, the Digital Services Package entrusts considerable new enforcement powers to the Commission, in some instances, surprisingly, even upon the explicit insistence of the Member States. At the same time, the enforcement design is more multi-layered than it appears at first sight.

A. Centralisation as a Distinctive Feature

Both the DMA and the DSA famously empower the Commission to be a central enforcer – and in the case of the DMA even the sole enforcer – of the new rules and obligations.

i. The Commission Under the DMA

Under the DMA, the Commission is granted exclusive powers to designate gatekeeping platforms (Article 17 DMA). It is furthermore the chief institution mandated to monitor compliance and initiate investigations, and the sole institution empowered to establish infringements and impose the significant sanctions and structural

[8] Different EU documents use the abbreviation NCAs with different meaning – either National Competent Authorities or National Competition Authorities. In this chapter, NCAs will be used as an acronym for the more generic term National Competent Authorities, but it may, depending on the context, also signify National Competition Authorities.

remedies envisaged by the Regulation in case of non-compliance.[9] Although the DMA is worded in a way to minimise the perception of kinship with EU competition law, the many connections – genealogical, teleological and institutional – are hard to conceal. The substantive obligations set out in the DMA stem, quite conspicuously, from cases driven by the Commission on the basis of EU competition law. The objectives of the DMA to ensure fair and contestable markets in the digital economy, despite the efforts to demonstrate difference, are in fact closely related, if not fully identical, with those of EU competition law.[10] Finally, and most importantly for our purposes, institutionally, the big part of the responsibilities for enforcing the DMA unmistakably falls on Directorate-General for Competition (DG COMP). The Legislative Financial Statement accompanying the Commission proposal for a DMA identified three so-called leading DGs – DG COMP, DG GROW and DG CONNECT. The Statement made a preliminary estimate that as many as 80 full time equivalents (FTEs) would be needed at the Commission level, either to be redeployed within the respective DGs or in the form of additional allocations, to ensure that compliance with the Regulation is adequately monitored and obligations are enforced.[11] Although DG CONNECT has been the driving force behind the DMA, following the entry into force of the Regulation, it appears that DG COMP is the DG assigned most significant new manpower, as being tasked to shoulder DMA enforcement. DG CONNECT is focusing on the DMA's compliance pillar.[12]

ii. *The Commission Under the DSA*

In the context of the DSA, the Commission does not enjoy the same exclusive powers. However, with respect of large-scale operators, its prerogatives are similar to those under the DMA. First, the Commission has the sole power of identifying and designating the two categories of large actors having special responsibilities under the Regulation, namely VLOPs and VLOSEs.[13] The Commission is also the exclusive enforcer of key obligations of VLOPs and VLSEs related to systemic risk under Section 5

[9] See Recital (91) and Article 38(7) second sentence DMA. Pursuant to Article 30 DMA, the Commission can impose fines of up to 10 per cent of a company's annual turnover (Article 30(1) DMA) and has the possibility of imposing even higher fines, of up to 20 per cent of the gatekeeper's worldwide turnover, in case of recidivism (Article 30(2) DMA).

[10] Imelda Maher, 'Institutional Design of Enforcement under the DMA: No Solo Run for the Commission' (2025) 12(2) *Journal of Antitrust Enforcement* 273–79. According to Petit, '[t]he proposed Digital Markets Act (DMA) is in substance a sector-specific competition law', see Nicolas Petit, 'The Proposed Digital Markets Act (DMA): A Legal and Policy Review' (2021) 12(7) *Journal of European Competition Law & Practice* 529; see also Helene Andersson's contribution to this book.

[11] Legislative Financial Statement, in Commission Proposal for a Regulation of the European Parliament and of the Council on contestable and fair markets in the digital sector (Digital Markets Act) COM(2020) 842 final, 71–72; Brussels, 15.12.2020.

[12] Catarina Martins and Christophe Carugati, 'Insights for successful enforcement of Europe's Digital Markets Act', Bruegel, Blogpost, 22 May 2022, available at: www.bruegel.org/blog-post/insights-successful-enforcement-europes-digital-markets-act#:~:text=The%20staffing%20scenarios%20imply%2C%20respectively,613%20million%20and%20605%20staff; Paul-John Loewenthal, Cristina Sjödin and Folkert Wilman, Institutional Report, in: EU Digital Economy: General Framework (DSA/DMA) and Specialised Regimes, XXXI FIDE (Fédération Internationale pour le Droit Européen) Congress, Katowice 2025, Congress Publications, Vol 2, 204–05 (hereinafter FIDE Digital Economy, Institutional Report 2025) 237, https://doi.org/10.31261/PN.4295.

[13] See Article 33 DSA.

of Chapter III DSA. It is also the prime enforcer of other (non-key) obligations of these actors (Article 56(4) DSA). With respect of VLOPs and VLOSEs, the Regulation grants the Commission substantial investigatory powers, including powers to initiate an investigation into a suspected infringement, to conduct interviews and inspections, request information and so on (Articles 66–69 DSA). In the course of the investigation, it can decide on interim measures and take commitments (Articles 70–71 DSA). In terms of sanctioning powers, most consequentially, the Commission can impose on the non-compliant provider of VLOPs and VLOSEs a fine of up to 6 per cent of the latter's worldwide annual turnover (Articles 73–74 DSA).

The move towards furnishing the Commission with own enforcement powers in a domain other than competition law is quite remarkable and one might say even unique.[14] It is noteworthy that in the original proposal for a Digital Services Regulation, the Commission had envisaged more limited enforcement powers for itself and greater responsibilities for national authorities. Yet, in the course of negotiations, Member States argued, rather unusually, for higher degree of centralisation and greater empowerment of the Commission.[15]

The leading directorate under this Regulation is more clearly DG CONNECT. In the Impact Assessment to the proposal for DSA, the estimated manpower under the preferred option with an EU-level Board and engagement of the Commission in monitoring and enforcement, was 50 to 65 FTE, including Commission participation in the Board.[16] As noted, the final governance arrangement was further tilted towards empowering the Commission. Following the entry into force of the DSA, the supervision and enforcement at the Commission level has been institutionally organised through a Platforms Directorate set up within DG CONNECT, assisted by the Legal Service. By the end of 2023, the Commission had spent around 27 million euros on this task and the responsible team consisted of 69 persons.[17]

[14] Cf FIDE Digital Economy, Institutional Report 2025, above note 12, which states that 'the centralised supervision and enforcement of those instruments [the DMA and the DSA] by the Commission makes those pieces of digital services legislation unique as compared to other pieces of digital services legislation'. However, if we acknowledge the genetic connection between the DMA and EU competition law, the centralisation of enforcement powers within the Commission is less remarkable for the DMA, and truly unique only for the DSA. See in this sense Martin Husovec, General Report, EU Digital Economy: general framework (DSA/DMA) and specialised regimes, XXXI FIDE Congress, Katowice 2025, Congress Publications, Vol 2, (hereinafter FIDE General Report 2025) 26. The Institutional Report draws a comparison with other pieces of EU legislation governing digital services, namely the Audiovisual Media Services Directive (Directive (EU) 2018/1808), the Platform to Business Regulation (Regulation (EU) 2019/1150), and the Terrorist Content Online Regulation (Regulation (EU) 2021/784), which all rely on a decentralised enforcement by NCAs. See FIDE Digital Economy, Institutional Report 2025, above note 12, 181.

[15] 'The reason for this difference probably lies in the fact that the DMA was always intended to be monitored and enforced solely by the Commission, while the DSA's supervision and enforcement mechanism was altered during the legislative negotiations as a result of which the Commission was given primary responsibility for designation, supervision and enforcement of very large online platforms and very large online search engines', FIDE Digital Economy, Institutional Report 2025, above note 12, 182, also at 205.

[16] Commission, Impact Assessment part I, accompanying the document 'Proposal for a Regulation of the European Parliament and the Council on a Single Market For Digital Services (Digital Services Act) and amending Directive 2000/31/EC', SWD(2020) 348 final, Brussels, 15.12.2020.

[17] FIDE Digital Economy, Institutional Report 2025, above note 12, 205 with reference to Commission, Report on the overall annual costs incurred for the fulfilment of the Commission's tasks pursuant to Regulation (EU) 2022/2065 in the period from 16 November 2022 until 31 December 2023 and the total amount of the annual supervisory fees charged pursuant to Article 6(4) of Commission Delegated Regulation (EU) 2023/1127 in 2023, COM(2024) 523, 6 November 2024.

The concentration of powers in the hands of the Commission in both DMA and DSA has been justified by the structure and particular dynamics of the digital economy, where due to a number of specific, well-studied economic effects (notably network effects and economies of scale and scope), few large actors gain disproportionate power to control users' data and shape the modalities of digital services to their own advantage.[18] Only a competent and well-endowed enforcer of the size and capacity of the Commission, so the argument goes, would be in a position to exert credible pressure on the GAFAM (Google, Apple, Facebook (now Meta), Amazon and Microsoft) giants and convince (or force) them into compliance. The fact that these mega-actors are not European undertakings, but global players with their base typically in the USA is an additional reason to see the Commission as the most natural prime enforcer of the new legislation. Another important advantage with a centralised approach, especially in view of the pan-European reach of the addressees of the DMA and partly of the DSA, is avoiding the risk of regulatory fragmentation.[19]

B. Continued Role for National Authorities?

Yet despite the visible shift towards centralisation in the enforcement architecture of EU digital market law, it would be too hastened to proclaim the end of decentralised enforcement. As commentators have noted, even in the highly centralised enforcement framework of the DMA, enforcement is 'no solo run' for the Commission.[20] The institutional set up of enforcement of both DMA and DSA involves national authorities on many levels.

i. National Authorities Under the DMA

In the framework of the DMA, first, NCAs are expected to support the Commission in its enforcement role vis-à-vis gatekeepers. Upon request by the Commission, NCAs must provide information, assist in carrying out interviews and conduct inspections within their respective jurisdictions (Articles 21–23 DMA). Experts from NCAs may be appointed to monitor compliance with DMA obligations (Article 26 DMA). Although the DMA does not name the authorities, leaving the choice to the Member States, given the close interrelationship with EU competition law discussed above, it is clear that the competent authorities will typically be national competition authorities. At some points in the Act, the legislator refers specifically to 'the national authorities of the Member States enforcing the rules under Article 1(6) DMA)', which makes it even clearer that the task falls on national competition authorities. This clarification

[18] Michael L Katz and Carl Shapiro, 'Network Externalities, Competition, and Compatibility' (1985) 75 *Am. Econ. Rev.* 421; Carl Shapiro and Hal R Varian, *Information Rules: A Strategic Guide to the Network Economy* (Boston, Harvard Business School Press, 1999).

[19] FIDE Digital Economy, Institutional Report 2025, above note 12, 237.

[20] Maher, above note 10; Florian Wagner-von Papp, 'Digital Antitrust and the DMA: In Praise of Institutional Diversity' (2024) 12 *Journal of Antitrust Enforcement* 338–44.

is made in particular with regard to authorities entrusted with receiving information from third parties (Article 27 DMA).[21]

Second, the DMA does not prevent the continued application by NCAs of EU competition law (Articles 101 and 102 TFEU) and of national 'rules prohibiting anti-competitive agreements, decisions by associations of undertakings, concerted practices and abuses of dominant positions'; that is, national competition law which corresponds to EU competition law. Such application can be directed at gatekeepers, provided the requirements of EU or national competition law are met, notably of anti-competitive agreements or abuse of dominant position (Article 1(6)(a) DMA).

Moreover, NCAs can also enforce, in respect of gatekeepers, national competition rules prohibiting 'other forms of unilateral conduct insofar as . . . they amount to the imposition of further obligations on gatekeepers' (Article 1(6)(b) DMA). Obviously, it is a question of obligations that are both substantively different and pursue different objectives from those laid down in the DMA (cf Article 1(5) DMA). Such national rules can, however, be applied only 'provided that this application does not violate EU law in other respects'. To prevent conflicting decisions, Article 1(7) DMA further stipulates that '[n]ational authorities shall not take decisions which run counter to a decision adopted by the Commission under this Regulation'. Again, the DMA does not name the authorities, but typically this would be national competition authorities.

Third, and importantly, the DMA opens a possibility for NCAs to conduct, on their own initiative, investigations into cases of non-compliance by gatekeepers with their main obligations under the DMA, to the extent the non-compliance takes place on their territory.[22] This mandate engages most immediately NCAs into the enforcement of the DMA. Since the provision refers to a 'national competent authority enforcing the rules referred to in Article 1(6)' it is clear that this prerogative is reserved for national competition authorities. Interestingly, however, the opportunity is conditioned on competence and powers being provided for in national law. This construction is unusual and quite remarkable. Instead of establishing common rules and principles for such enforcement powers of NCAs, the DMA leaves the choice between a passive and a proactive role in the enforcement of the new DMA obligations to national lawmakers.[23]

If one wants to trace the origin of this rule, a look at the legislative history of the DMA is in order. It is noteworthy that the Commission proposal was based on strict exclusiveness of the Commission's enforcement powers and contained nothing

[21] While theses authorities have full discretion as to whether to react to this information, in case a national competition authority determines that there may be an issue of non-compliance with the DMA, it shall transfer that information to the Commission. See FIDE Digital Economy, Institutional Report 2025, above note 12, 237.

[22] Article 38(7) DMA stipulates: '7. Where it has the competence and investigative powers to do so under national law, a national competent authority of the Member States enforcing the rules referred to in Article 1(6) may, on its own initiative, conduct an investigation into a case of possible non-compliance with Articles 5, 6 and 7 of this Regulation on its territory. Before taking a first formal investigative measure, that authority shall inform the Commission in writing.'

[23] See FIDE Digital Economy, Institutional Report 2025, above note 12, 237. On developments in the Netherlands, see Jasper Van den Boom, Friso Bostoen and Giorgio Monti, 'The Netherlands: DMA Enforcement Paradise?' (2024) *TILEC Discussion Papers* 6, https://papers.ssrn.com/sol3/papers.cfm?abstra.

about NCAs' prerogatives to initiate investigations in gatekeepers' non-compliance with DMA obligations.[24] However, in the course of legislative deliberations, considerable pressure was exerted by a group of national competition authorities calling themselves 'Friends of an effective DMA'. The group consisted of the competition authorities of Germany, France and the Netherlands, all of them boasting exemplary track-records of active enforcement of European and national competition law in general, and vis-à-vis global digital companies in particular. This group argued vocally that the enforcement of the DMA has much to gain from assigning greater role to national authorities.[25] One can see the group as a sort of 'coalition of the willing', to use a term that has become popular in other domains of European politics. In a letter to the Commission, the group proposed full parallelism of enforcement powers between national authorities and the Commission and basing DMA enforcement on the kind of horizontal enforcement cooperation familiar from Regulation 1/2003 and managed through the ECN. The group's proposal was not followed in full. In the final text of Regulation 2022/1925 the Commission still preserved its exclusive enforcement powers. However, the proposal led to the model of optional partial empowerment of NCAs through national law, as set out in Article 38(7).[26]

ii. National Authorities Under the DSA

The reliance on national authorities is much more extensive in the DSA. Member States are required to designate one or more competent authorities to be responsible for the supervision of intermediary service providers (ISPs) and for enforcement of the Regulation (Article 49 DSA). One of these authorities has to be designated as national Digital Services Coordinator (DSC). Given the broad scope of subject matter covered by the Regulation, assigning tasks to a plurality of authorities within one Member State is expected to be the rule rather than the exception. However, in case of multiple competent authorities, Member States have to ensure that the tasks of those

[24] See Article 1, Commission proposal for a Digital Markets Act (above note 11), cf. Impact Assessment Report accompanying the Commission proposal for a Regulation of the European Parliament and of the Council on contestable and fair markets in the digital sector (Digital Markets Act), SWD(2020) 363 final, Brussels, 15.12.202, part I (hearinafter DMA Impact Assessment), para 402.

[25] See B Le Meire, P Altmaier and M Keijzer, 'Strengthening the Digital Markets Act and Its Enforcement', non-paper, p 6, 'Centralising certain powers at the EU level, for example designating globally active gatekeepers improves effectiveness and reduces fragmentation. However, the importance of the digital markets for our economies is too high to rely on one single pillar of enforcement only. Therefore, a larger role should be played by national authorities in supporting the Commission. This does require sufficient enforcement capacity and expertise, especially in the area of competition enforcement, but possibly also beyond, e.g. as regards market regulation, data analysts and IT experts'.

[26] See the following statement in the institutional report for the 2025 FIDE Congress: 'Despite calls by the Member States' national competition authorities ('NCAs') during the legislative process to provide for a joint application of the DMA by the Commission and NCAs, NCAs do not have full-fledged enforcement powers under the DMA', FIDE Digital Economy, Institutional Report 2025, above note 12, 237. For further analysis see Alba Ribera Martínez, 'The Decentralisation of the DMA's Enforcement System' (2024) Kluwer Competition Blog, 17 June 2024, https://legalblogs.wolterskluwer.com/competition-blog/the-decentralisation-of-the-dmas-enforcement-system/. See Wagner-von Papp's critique of the inconsistency in the mix between centralised and decentralised approach in the DMA. Wagner-von Papp, above note 20, 338–44.

authorities and the DSC are clearly defined and that the authorities cooperate closely and effectively. In any event, the DSC is responsible for coordinating the authorities' actions under the Regulation.[27]

The DSA takes an asymmetric approach to regulation and enforcement. While it centralises in the Commission enforcement powers in respect of large-scale actors (VLOPs and VLOSEs), with respect of smaller ISPs, the Regulation builds on a model of decentralised enforcement cooperation between NCAs close to what is familiar from other areas of Internal Market law such as data protection or consumer law. Furthermore, the centralisation of enforcement powers with respect of large-scale actors is not comprehensive, but is limited to obligations related to avoiding and mitigating systemic risk (Chapter III, Section 5 DSA). Concerning other obligations of VLOPs and VLOSEs the enforcement competences are shared between the Commission and Member States through their NCAs. NCAs have the competence to supervise and enforce non-key obligations under the DSA in respect of large actors established on their territory. However, once the Commission decides to initiate an investigation, its powers take precedence and DSCs are relieved from their powers to supervise and enforce (Article 66(3) DSA). In any case, the Commission and Member States, through their NCAs and DSCs, are expected to supervise and enforce the DSA in close cooperation (Article 56(3) DSA).

Given the greater reliance on decentralised enforcement, the DSA sets out more detailed obligations for Member States regarding their national responsible authorities. NCAs are required to have considerable investigatory powers (Article 51 DSA) and be able to impose proportionate, effective and dissuasive penalties that can reach a considerable size (Article 52 DSA).[28] Importantly, the DSA stipulates rather stringent requirements that Member States have to observe when defining the mandate and framework conditions for the work of their DSCs. Thus, Member States must ensure that the authorities acting as DSCs shall perform their tasks under the Regulation in an 'impartial, transparent and timely manner' (Article 50 DSA). The Member States shall further see to it that the DSCs have all the necessary resources to carry out their tasks, including sufficient technical, financial and human resources. Last, but not least, as has become common for recent EU regulatory initiatives, the DSA sets out a strongly worded requirement as to the national authority's independence.[29] Importantly, this independence is backed up by an obligation for the Member States to ensure sufficient budgetary autonomy for the competent authority (Article 50(3) DSA).

These new common standards as to the enforcement powers of NCAs are a novelty in the domain of digital services regulation. As is well known, the DSA builds on

[27] Cf Recital 110 and Article 49(2) DSA.

[28] The sanctions on VLOPs and VLOSEs can be of a size comparable with those under the DMA, with a relatively high ceiling of 6 per cent of the worldwide turnover of ISPs in case of violation of obligations under the DSA, or up to 1 per cent in case of failure to provide requested information or submit to inspections (cf Article 52 DSA).

[29] Pursuant to Article 50(3) DSA, '[w]hen carrying out their tasks and exercising their powers in accordance with this Regulation, the Digital Services Coordinators shall act with *complete independence*. They shall remain *free from any external influence*, whether direct or indirect, and shall neither seek nor take instructions from any other public authority or any private party' (emphasis added).

the E-commerce Directive,[30] which contained few specific requirements for Member States as to the organisation of enforcement. As a consequence of this deference, the disparity of enforcement instruments and approaches under the Directive has been pervasive. The DSA shows a much greater ambition in this respect.

C. Continued Role for Enforcement Networks?

The two Regulations retain some role for enforcement networks as well, with the DSA relying more visibly on a network-like infrastructure of enforcement.

i. Enforcement Networks Under the DMA

For the DMA, enforcement networks remain relevant in several respects, which mirror the role of national authorities in DMA enforcement. First, given that the DMA does not preclude national competition authorities from applying EU competition law vis-à-vis gatekeeping platforms, such application remains subject to the rules of Regulation 1/2003 and of the ECN cooperation mechanism. Article 1(7) DMA sets out: 'The Commission and Member States shall work in close cooperation and coordinate their enforcement actions on the basis of the principles established in Articles 37 and 38.'

Article 38 is devoted to cooperation and coordination with NCAs (or, as specified in the Article,'national competent authorities enforcing competition rules'). The provision specifies that the cooperation and information exchange between these authorities and the Commission shall take place through the ECN.[31] Thus, the ECN is interlocked with enforcement under the DMA and provides infrastructure for coordination of enforcement actions between national competition authorities and the Commission.

Another way of engaging existing networks in the enforcement of the DMA is through giving representatives of the most relevant bodies and networks a place in the High-Level Group for the DMA, where each network participates with a maximum of six representatives (Article 40 DMA).[32] The networks and bodies that are accorded a place in the High-Level Group are: (a) the Body of the European Regulators for Electronic Communications, BEREC (b) the European Data Protection Supervisor (EDPS) and the European Data Protection Board (EDPB); (c) the ECN; (d) the CPC Network and (e) the European Regulatory Group of Audiovisual Media Regulators (ERGA). Each network has to decide internally on the procedures for nominating their representatives into the High-Level Group. However, it is clear that the representation of each network has to be at a high level, that is, head of national

[30] Directive 2000/31/EC on certain legal aspects of information society services, in particular electronic commerce, in the Internal Market, OJ L 178, 17.7.2000, pp. 1–16.

[31] Article 38(1) Cooperation and coordination with national competent authorities enforcing competition rules.

[32] According to Article 40(2) each group shall participate with an equal number of representatives not exceeding a total number of 30.

agencies or equivalent, and that the nominated members act as representatives of the respective network.[33] The High-Level Group is chaired by the Directors General of DG CONNECT and of DG COMP.[34] The role of the High-Level Group is chiefly advisory. The idea is obviously to ensure that regulation and enforcement break the existing silos, enabling exchange of expertise and perspectives, and a holistic view on the regulatory landscape.[35]

ii. Enforcement Networks Under the DSA

When it comes to the DSA, as indicated above, the Act relies to a much greater extent on horizontal cooperation between NCAs, especially in the supervision and enforcement vis-à-vis small and medium-size operators. The DSCs are conceived as nodes in an enforcement network, with the Commission having the role of a mediator, facilitator and supervisor. To support decentralised enforcement, the DSA puts in place mechanisms for mutual assistance and cross-border cooperation between DSCs (Articles 57 and 58 DSA). Mutual assistance occurs foremost in the form of exchange of information between DSCs and through a duty of DSCs of establishment to inform DSCs of destination about investigatory and enforcement measures undertaken with respect of specific ISPs (Article 57 DSA). Cross-border cooperation implies possibilities for the DSC in one Member State to request the DSC in another Member State to undertake investigatory and enforcement measures against an ISP established on its territory in case of suspected infringement of DSA obligations negatively affecting service recipients in the first Member State (Article 58 DSA).

The DSCs are more formally connected within a novel body, the European Board for Digital Services (Article 61 DSA). The Board is conceived as an independent advisory group composed of one representative from each national DSC and tasked with upholding the consistency and effectiveness of enforcement cooperation, coordinating and contributing to guidelines and analysis and assisting the DSCs and the Commission in the supervision of VLOPs and VLOSEs.[36] The choice of the term Board probably seeks to project greater authority and capacity for cohesive action. However, the Board is not a body with legal personality and has no powers to adopt binding decisions. Such an option had been discussed in the drafting process, but had not been pursued further.

One alternative, considered during the drafting of the DMA, has been to give the Board under the DSA coordinating functions also in respect of the regulatory activity under the DMA. However, this option was discarded. In the Impact Assessment to the DMA, the Commission underscores the 'very different objectives of the two sets of rules and corresponding expertise and competences required from the competent

[33] See comments of Roberto Viola, Director General of DG CONNECT and chair of the first meeting of the High-Level Group, Minutes, 1st meeting of the High-Level Group for the DMA, 12 May 2023.

[34] See Commission decision on setting up the High-Level Group for the Digital Markets Act, C(2023) 1833 final, Brussels, 23.3.2023.

[35] FIDE Digital Economy, Institutional Report 2025, above note 12.

[36] See also DMA Impact Assessment, above note 24, para 411.

enforcement bodies'.[37] The Commission furthermore underlines that while the implementation and enforcement of harmonised rules under the DMA is to be ensured at the EU level by the Commission who has the necessary means and expertise, the DSA relies on a decentralised approach, where the focus of regulatory compliance activities is on the competent national DSCs.[38] This difference in approach has been, however, reduced by the greater empowerment of the Commission in the final version of the DSA.

Summing up, while the Digital Services Act preserves to a greater extent than the DMA the importance of national authorities and enforcement networks, there is no denying that the evolving enforcement architecture of the new EU of the digital economy differs significantly from the previous governance model of horizontal decentralised enforcement familiar from EU competition, consumer and data protection law. Indeed, a 2025 FIDE institutional report authored by Commission officials notes the increased role of the Commission in a whole array of new digital regulations, and suggests that 'we might be witnessing the emergence of a new model for the enforcement of "Big Tech"-related internal market legislation in which the Commission plays a central role'.[39]

Against this background, a legitimate question is whether there is something in the experiences from decentralised enforcement accumulated during the last two decades that has informed and influenced the new institutional design of enforcement of EU digital market law. Have these experiences brought about a certain disenchantment with the romantic vision of network-based enforcement models based on mutual learning and mutual trust?[40] This question will be analysed in the next part of this chapter by looking at two enforcement networks that in their subject matter have close connections with the new EU digital market law.

II. LOOKING BACK: THE EVOLUTION OF DECENTRALISED ENFORCEMENT AND LESSONS FROM ENFORCEMENT NETWORKS IN EU COMPETITION AND CONSUMER LAW (ECN AND THE CPC NETWORK)

The idea about decentralised network-based enforcement of EU internal market law can be traced back to the beginning of the 1990s. Starting from the 2000s, this governance model gained traction and saw a steady expansion across a number of EU policy

[37] See DMA Impact Assessment, above note 24, para 410. 'As regards the possible integration of the new Commission powers under the Digital Markets Act and responsibilities of the Board envisaged under the DSA it is important to note the very different objectives of the two sets of rules and corresponding expertise and competences that may be required from the competent enforcement bodies to ensure compliance with the respective rules'.

[38] DMA Impact Assessment, above note 24, 411–12.

[39] FIDE Digital Economy, Institutional Report 2025, above note 12, 204–05.

[40] Christian Joerges and Jürgen Neyer, 'From Intergovernmental Bargaining to Deliberative Political Processes: The Constitutionalisation of Comitology' (1997) (3) *European Law Review* 273. Cf Anne-Marie Slaughter, 'The Real New World Order: The State Strikes Back' (1997) 76(5) *Foreign Affairs* 183; Anne-Marie Slaughter, *A New World Order* (Princeton, Princeton University Press, 2004); Charles Sabel and Jonathan Zeitlin, 'Learning from Difference: The New Architecture of Experimentalist Governance in the EU' (2008) 14(3) *European Law Journal* 271.

domains. While a countermovement of so-called 'agencification', that is, delegating enforcement powers to European agencies, has been noted more recently, many of the newly built European bodies still rely on a web of national enforcement entities and can best be described as 'networked agencies'.[41]

To be able to adequately assess the experiences from decentralised network-based enforcement, in this section, I first go back to the advent of this enforcement approach and revisit the policy reasons and expectations underlying its rise. Then, I offer a necessarily concise review of the experiences from two of the most important enforcement networks in the EU internal market law – the ECN and the CPC Network, trying to gauge the main strengths and weaknesses encountered as well as the reasons for the differential performance of the two networks.

A. The Shift to Horizontal, Network-Based Enforcement

There are two major developments in the early 1990s that arguably explain the rise of enforcement networks. The first relates to the decisive steps taken by the Union at the time towards completing the Single Market. Propelled by the dynamic unleashed by the Single European Act, the Community famously drew up an ambitious Internal Market programme based on the principle of mutual recognition, and including, crucially, the dismantling of border controls. The new approach, outlined among others in the influential Sutherland Report on Completing the Single Market,[42] implied greater reliance on the supervisory and enforcement authorities of the Member States, thus shifting the focus from policy-making and lawmaking to ensuring the effective enforcement of commonly agreed laws and policies. As is well known, decentralised enforcement in the EU has traditionally been based on the principle of national procedural and institutional autonomy. Although this principle has been progressively constrained by the doctrines of equivalence and effectiveness elaborated by the Court of Justice of the European Union (CJEU), Member States have in principle been considered free to follow their own institutional choices and traditions; something that resulted in widely divergent institutional and procedural frameworks.[43]

Enforcement networks were consequently conceived as a way of bridging the institutional diversity between national authorities and ensuring greater degree of coherence in enforcement. The Sutherland report identified a 'cooperative approach to enforcement' as 'the single most important way of reinforcing mutual confidence

[41] Miroslava Scholten, Michiel Luchtman and Elmar Schmidt, 'The Proliferation of EU Enforcement Authorities: A New Development in Law Enforcement in the EU', in Miroslava Scholten and Michiel Luchtman (eds), *Law Enforcement by EU Authorities: Implications for Political and Judicial Accountability* (Cheltenham, Edward Elgar, 2017).

[42] 'The Internal Market after 1992: Meeting the Challenge. Report presented to the Commission by the High-Level Group on the functioning of the Internal Market presided over by Peter Sutherland' (Sutherland Report), 28 October 1992, SEC (1992) 2044.

[43] See Michal Bobek, 'Why There Is No Principle of "Procedural Autonomy" of the Member States', in Bruno de Witte and Hans-W Micklitz (eds), *The European Court of Justice and the Autonomy of The Member States* (Antwerp, Intersentia, 2011).

between Member States and the Commission'.[44] Such approach was to be based on 'groups of contact points between the Member States and the Commission', to deal with the application of internal market rules, and creating a 'permanent framework for administrative partnership'.[45] The approach was embraced by the Commission and by the Council.[46] In a follow up to the Sutherland report, the Commission charted a plan for developing operational arrangements for cooperation and information exchange and organising the work of competent officials designated by Member States 'on the basis of networks'.[47]

The other seminal, and largely parallel, development that arguably prompted the growth of enforcement networks was the then forthcoming Eastward Enlargement of the Union. The Union enlargement to the East was famously launched with the conclusions of the Copenhagen Council in 1993 and unfolded in the time-span between 1993 and 2013. Whereas the Union had undergone several previous enlargements, the Eastward Enlargement was of such proportions that it posed unique structural and constitutional challenges for the Union. With the accession of 10 new Member States, the Union nearly doubled its size in terms of number of states, territory and population. More importantly, at the end of the process, the EU came to encompass economies and polities, which in their historical paths and institutional legacies differed considerably from the previous Member States.[48] This dramatically increased diversity of socio-economic, legal and institutional legacies brought clearly a risk for diminished coherence and effectiveness of decentralised enforcement, and ran, somewhat paradoxically, counter to the ambitions of Internal Market completion.[49]

Enforcement networks were embraced as a governance arrangement offering solution to both problems. They were seen as a tool to cope with the risk of 'system entropy' associated with exponentially increased diversity in the decentralised enforcement of EU legislation. For the newly acceded Member States, the networks were supposed to work as platforms for mutual learning, gradual adaptation and socialisation.[50] Overall, cooperation within the networks was expected to enhance mutual understanding and trust between Member State authorities and the Commission and bring about greater coherence and effectiveness in enforcement practice.

[44] See Recommendation 31, The Internal Market after 1992: Meeting the Challenge. Report presented to the Commission by the High-Level Group on the functioning of the Internal Market presided over by Peter Sutherland (Sutherland Report), 28 October 1992, SEC (1992) 2044.

[45] ibid, Recommendation 32.

[46] See Commission communication to the Council of 22 December 1993 'Making the most of the Internal Market': Strategic Programme, (COM(93) 632 final); Council Resolution of 16 June 1994 on the development of administrative cooperation in the implementation and enforcement of Community legislation in the internal market, OJ C 179, 1.7.1994, 1.

[47] Communication from the Commission to the Council and the European Parliament, The operation of the Community's Internal Market after 1992. Follow-up to the Sutherland report, SEC(92) 2277 final, Brussels, 2 December 1992, para 22.

[48] Frank Schimmelfennig and Uli Sedelmeier, 'Governance by Conditionality: EU Rule Transfer to the Candidate Countries of Central and Eastern Europe' (2004) 11(4) *Journal of European Public Policy* 661.

[49] Fritz Scharpf, 'The Double Asymmetry of European Integration. Or: Why the EU Cannot Be a Social Market Economy' (2009) MPIfG Working Paper 09/12.

[50] Jeffrey Checkel, *International Institutions and Socialization in Europe* (Cambridge, CUP, 2007); Jeffrey Checkel, 'Sanctions, Social Learning and Institutions' (1999) Arena Working Papers no 11.

B. Comparing Two Enforcement Networks

Indeed, in the years that followed, a veritable web of networks with different enforcement functions was rolled out, connecting national authorities and enforcement bodies with each other and with corresponding units of the Commission, or with specially created European agencies.[51] Among the many enforcement networks launched in the aftermath of the Sutherland report, the ECN and the CPC Network take pride of place. The two networks are probably the most prominent enforcement networks in the EU Internal (or Single) Market having broad, horizontal, non-sectoral scope of operation, the first one in the domain of EU competition law, and the second one in the area of EU consumer law.[52]

i. History and Main Features of the Networks

The networks were launched within the span of only two years: the ECN in 2003 and the CPC Network in 2004. They were established upon the initiative of the Commission, through formal EU legal acts; in the first case Council Regulation 1/2003[53] giving effect to the Treaty rules on competition, and in the second case Council and Parliament Regulation 2006/2004 on consumer protection cooperation (CPC Regulation),[54] later on replaced by Regulation 2017/2934/EU (New CPC Regulation).[55] Thus, it is a question of formal, institutionalised or 'incorporated' networks.[56]

The ECN was launched as a result of a meticulously prepared 'modernisation' reform of EU competition law enforcement culminating in Regulation 1/2003. One of the architects of the modernisation reform called it a 'legal and cultural revolution'.[57]

[51] Renaud Dehousse, 'Regulation by Networks in the European Community: The Role of European Agencies' (1997) 4(2) *Journal of European Public Policy* 246–61, 254; David Levi-Faur, 'Regulatory Networks and Regulatory Agencification: Towards a Single European Regulatory Space' (2011) 18(6) *Journal of European Public Policy* 810–29, at 813.

[52] For a more detailed comparative account of the two networks see Antonina Bakardjieva Engelbrekt, 'Coherence in Diversity? Exploring the Institutional Dynamic of Enforcement Networks in the EU Internal Market' in Martin Belov (ed), *Representative Democracy in Flux?* (Abingdon, Routledge, 2025) 197–247.

[53] Council Regulation (EC) No 1/2003 of 16 December 2002 on the implementation of the rules on competition laid down in Articles 81 and 82 of the Treaty [2003] OJ L 1/1. The Regulation provides the fundament for the enforcement cooperation. The 'nuts and bolts' of network cooperation were set out in soft law instruments, i.e., two Commission Notices and a Joint Statement by the Council and the Commission, giving additional weight to the ECN. Commission Notice on cooperation within the Network of Competition Authorities, OJ C 101, 27 April 2004, 43–53; Commission Notice on the cooperation between the Commission and the courts of the EU Member States in the application of Articles 81 and 82 EC [2004] OJ C 101/54; Joint Statement of the Council and the Commission on the Functioning of the Network of Competition Authorities, Interinstitutional File 2000/0243(CNS), Brussels, 10 December 2002 (hereinafter Joint Statement).

[54] Regulation (EC) No 2006/2004 on cooperation between national authorities responsible for the enforcement of consumer protection laws [2004] OJ L 364/1 (hereinafter the CPC Regulation).

[55] Regulation (EU) 2017/2394 on cooperation between national authorities responsible for the enforcement of consumer protection laws and repealing Regulation (EC) No 2006/2004 [2017] OJ L 345/1; applying as of 17 January 2020 (hereinafter the New CPC Regulation).

[56] On the concept of 'incorporated networks' see Burkard Eberlein and Abraham Newman, 'Escaping the International Governance Dilemma? Incorporated Transgovernmental Networks in the EU' (2008) 21 *Governance* 25; Bakardjieva Engelbrekt, above note 52.

[57] Claus-Dieter Ehlermann, 'The Modernization of EC Antitrust Policy: A Legal and Cultural Revolution' (2000) 37 *Common Market Law Review* 537–90.

Indeed, the reform advanced a remarkable voluntary devolution of enforcement powers on the part of the European Commission in the only area of EU law and policy where it enjoyed such powers.[58] At the same time, it brought about previously unseen empowerment of national competition authorities, putting them on a par with the Commission and entrusting them with a new role of active and responsible enforcers of EU competition law. The launching of the CPC Network through the CPC Regulation stirred far less excitement, although it can also be seen as a minor revolution. In an area where previously Member States enjoyed almost full discretion, that is, consumer law enforcement, the CPC Regulation now required national governments to equip specially designated public authorities with adequate enforcement powers to curb cross-border infringements of EU consumer protection laws, setting minimum standards for such powers. Both reforms ushered the Union into the complex world of Member States' institutional and enforcement frameworks, leaving previously dominant doctrines of national procedural and institutional autonomy largely in the past.[59]

The two revolutions had many traits in common, and in the legislative history of the CPC Regulation one can clearly see that the reform of competition law enforcement had served as an inspiration for the one of consumer law enforcement.[60] In both domains the most distinctive institutional innovation was the setting up and the subsequent promotion of enforcement networks, linking national public authorities with each other and with the Commission. Public authorities with enforcement powers were required to cooperate within the networks, inter alia by exchanging information and assisting in investigations undertaken by their counterparts in other Member States, signalling a transition to a decentralised but coordinated model of enforcement in the Internal Market.

The two reforms had, at least partly, common genealogy. As noted above, a major driving force for the creation of enforcement networks in these, as well as in other domains, had been the then imminent Eastward Enlargement of the Union. The Union's expansion with ten new Member States was obviously expected to put a strain on the capacity of the Commission to act as a sole enforcer of EU competition law, or to supervise enforcement at the national level through the classical Community method in the field of consumer law.[61] Enlargement prepared the ground for the reforms also in another important respect. Following the Copenhagen accession criteria, the Candidate Countries (CCs) were required to put in place institutions with the capacity to implement and enforce the Community *acquis*. Through the mechanisms of soft pre-accession conditionality, the CCs were, thus, set on a course of wide-ranging institutional reforms resulting in a whole array of competition and consumer agencies that later became constitutive units in the new enforcement networks.[62]

[58] Lee McGowan and Stephen Wilks, 'The First Supranational Policy in the European Union: Competition Policy' (1995) 28 *European Journal of Political Research* 141.

[59] Bobek, above note 43.

[60] European Commission, Proposal for a Regulation on cooperation between national authorities responsible for the enforcement of consumer protection laws, COM(2003) 443 final, 22.

[61] Joanne Scott and David M Trubek, 'Mind the Gap: Law and New Approaches to Governance in the European Union' (2002) 8(1) *European Law Journal* 1.

[62] Antonina Bakardjieva Engelbrekt, 'Grey Zones, Legitimacy Deficits and Boomerang Effects: On the Implications of Extending the Acquis to Central and Eastern Europe' in Nils Wahl and Per Cramér (eds), *Swedish Yearbook of European Law*, vol 1 (Oxford, Hart Publishing, 2006) 1–36.

Obviously, the two Regulations boosted considerably public law enforcement in the two EU policy domains. The impact has been particularly consequential in the area of consumer law. Whereas enforcement by public authorities had been the predominant model of competition law enforcement at both EU and Member States level, consumer law has in many national jurisdictions been defined as an area of civil or private law, relying largely on private enforcement through consumer and business organisations. Thus, the CPC Regulation brought about not just an increase of EU intervention in the sphere of national procedural law and institutions. It also implied a powerful shift from private to public enforcement and increased reliance on public authorities in the enforcement mix at the national level; a change that was praised by the Commission, but met considerable resistance in some Member States.[63]

Yet, despite the common origins and direction of the reforms, there were also major differences due to the specific characteristics of the two domains. Probably the most important difference has to do with the role of the Commission in the respective network. As is well known, in the area of EU competition law, the Commission, while supporting the empowerment of national competition authorities, retained substantial enforcement powers and a secure position of control over NCAs enforcement actions . In contrast, the Commission had practically no own powers to enforce EU consumer law and the setting up of the CPC Network did not change this state of affairs.[64]

This difference relates in turn to the different constitutional status of the two policy areas. Whereas regulating competition in the Internal Market is an exclusive EU competence, recognised as one of the central pillars of the European economic constitutions, with its dedicated powerful directorate (DG COMP), consumer policy is a shared competence, which made a hesitant entry in the Treaties in the 1980s and with changing institutional affiliations.[65] Partly as a consequence of the above, the two Regulations differ in ambit and scope of application. Whereas Regulation 1/2003 focuses narrowly on the two Treaty provisions of Articles 101 and 102 TFEU, Regulation 2006/2004, as now Regulation 2017/2394, apply to a thicket of EU consumer law directives and regulations, with sometimes disparate objectives, subject matter and scope.

This difference in regulatory scope is mirrored in the number and type of public authorities participating in the two networks. In the case of the ECN, each Member

[63] See Commission proposal, COM(2003) 443 final, para 34; cf Antonina Bakardjieva Engelbrekt, 'The Impact of the UCP Directive on National Fair Trading Law and Institutions: Gradual Convergence or Deeper Fragmentation?' in Ulf Bernitz and Caroline Jorgensen (eds), *Marketing and Advertising Law in a Process of Harmonisation* (Oxford, Hart Publishing, 2017) 119–69, 161. On the resistance in Germany and the slowly emerging acceptance for the need of public enforcement see Rupprecht Podszun, Christoph Busch and Frauke Henning-Bodewig, 'Consumer Law in Germany: A Shift to Public Enforcement?' (2019) 2 *EuCML* 75.

[64] For a more detailed review see Bakardjieva Engelbrekt, above note 52.

[65] Whereas initially, there was a separate DG for Health and Consumers (DG SANCO), later on, consumer policy had its home with DG Justice and nowadays the responsibilities are divided between DG Justice and DG Internal Market. Indicative of this uncertainty is also the fate of the executive agency tasked to ensure administrative support for the Union's consumer policy. On this see Bakardjieva Engelbrekt, above note 52, 215.

State has as a rule one single competition authority, often with high status and independence, which also represents the country in the ECN.[66] Not so in the case of the CPC Regulation. The broad scope of consumer policy entails that different regulatory and enforcement functions are at the national level often divided among multiple authorities of varying size, status and place in the national system of public administration, including ministries, trade inspections and independent agencies, and in some Member States with federal structure, authorities at regional or local level. To ensure efficiency and cohesion within the Network, the CPC Regulation required Member States to designate one authority as a Single Liaison Office (SLO). Yet, Member States were likewise asked to list all competent authorities that have responsibilities under one or more of the legislative instruments covered by the Regulation. The resulting list is impressive, one report estimating the total number of registered competent authorities to be more than 300.[67]

ii. Evaluating Network Performance

In the years following their establishment, the two networks were subject to multiple evaluations authored by academic writers, the Commission and external experts.

a. Evaluating ECN Performance

The volume of such evaluations was particularly high with respect of the ECN, probably due to the importance of competition law and policy in the European integration project, but also due to the unexpected and somewhat counterintuitive shift from centralised to decentralised enforcement. While the results from these evaluations inevitably vary, there has been a striking consensus around a positive assessment of the ECN. The modernisation reform was almost invariably found to be a major success, increasing the rate and effectiveness of EU competition law enforcement, promoting mutual learning and trust, and raising the level of expertise and quality of enforcement.

Some years after launching the modernisation reform, the Commission published the first Report on the functioning of Regulation 1/2003, which was overwhelmingly positive about the cooperation within the Network and generally, the effects of the reform.[68] In the accompanying document to the Report, the Commission described Regulation 1/2003 as a 'landmark change in the way the European competition law is enforced' and praised the ECN as 'an innovative model of governance

[66] Giorgio Monti, 'Independence, Interdependence and Legitimacy: The EU Commission, National Competition Authorities, and the European Competition Network' (2014) *EUI Working Papers Law*, 2014/01, 10–11.

[67] See ex-post evaluation of the Consumer Programme 2007–13 and mid-term evaluation of the Consumer Programme 2014–20 – Final report. Part 1 Mid-term evaluation of the Consumer Programme 2014–20, 2018 https://op.europa.eu/en/publication-detail/-/publication/3aefdcef-22af-11e9-8d04-01aa75ed71a1. For transparency, it should be noted that the author of this chapter has participated as an expert in this evaluation.

[68] Communication from the Commission, Report on the functioning of Regulation 1/2003 COM(2009) 206 final, 29 April 2009 (hereinafter Commission Report Regulation 1/2003, 2009). According to the report, by the end of March 2009, more than 1000 cases had been pursued on the basis of the EC competition rules and more that 300 envisaged decisions announced by NCAs.

for the implementation of Community law by the Commission and Member State authorities'.[69] In the next Report of 2014 on the occasion of the tenth anniversary of the modernisation reform, the assessment remained unwaveringly positive.[70] The Commission boasted 'a considerable enforcement record, with more than 780 enforcement decisions applying the EU competition rules, underpinned by policy and horizontal work to enhance cooperation'.[71] Between 1 May 2004 and 31 December 2012 NCAs had reported 1,334 investigations and 646 envisaged decisions, while in that period the Commission reported 228 investigations and 88 decisions.[72] This positive assessment was confirmed in the most recent evaluation of Regulation 1/2003 of 2024. In the Commission Staff Working Document one can read:

> The decentralised application of Articles 101 and 102 TFEU is considered very positively. As can be seen from the evidence collected during the evaluation, Regulation 1/2003 has been both very effective in fulfilling the general objective of effective and uniform application of Articles 101 and 102 TFEU compared to a situation where the Regulation 17 framework would apply, and efficient in terms of net outcomes for businesses, NCAs and consumers associated with the Regulations. NCAs have become fundamental forces in EU competition law enforcement.[73]

Concerning participation and engagement of NCAs and the functioning of enforcement cooperation more generally, the first Commission report describes a harmonious relationship between NCAs, a smoothly functioning mechanism of case allocation and lack of conflicts between network members. The Commission underlines the permanent exchange of views, taking place within the Network, often in an informal manner, that 'has established confidence and trust between network members, increased the expertise and promoted convergence'. The ECN is presented as an achievement 'widely recognised by the legal and business community'. Despite non-insignificant divergencies in the institutional design and enforcement approach of NCAs, the Commission asserts that a common competition culture has indeed emerged through the network, something that has explicitly been the objective when launching the ECN.[74] Relating to the role of the ECN, the evaluation of 2024 states: 'The ECN as a network to exchange information and best practices has proven to be fundamental in promoting an effective decentralised enforcement and allowing cross-fertilisation between authorities'.[75]

[69] Commission Staff Working Document accompanying the Report on the functioning of Regulation 1/2003 SEC(2009) 574 final, 29 April 2009 (hereinafter Commission SWD Regulation 1/2003, 2009) 83, 89.

[70] Commission Communication, 'Ten Years of Antitrust Enforcement under Regulation 1/2003: Achievements and Future Perspectives', COM (2014) 453 Brussels, 9.7.2014 (hereinafter Commission Communication Regulation 1/2003, 2014); European Commission, Enhancing Competition Enforcement by the Member States Competition Authorities. Institutional and Procedural Issues, SWD (2014) 231, Brussels 9.7.2014, accompanying the Commission Communication 2014 (hereinafter Commission SWD Regulation 1/2003, 2014).

[71] Commission Communication Regulation 1/2003, 2014, above note 70, para 4.

[72] Wouter PJ Wils, 'Ten Years of Reg. 1/2003' (2013) 4 *Journal of European Competition Law & Practice* 295.

[73] European Commission, Evaluation of Regulations 1/2003 and 773/2004, SWD(2024) 216 final, Brussels, 5.9.2024, 228 (hereinafter Commission Evaluation, 2024).

[74] Commission Report Regulation 1/2003, 2009, above note 68, para 249, p 74.

[75] Commission Evaluation, 2024, above note 73, 228.

These Commission assessments are broadly confirmed by academic studies. According to a 2010 study by Cengiz, the statistical data on the enforcement activity of NCAs provide evidence of high and relatively equivalent engagement of national authorities in the application of EU competition law irrespective of agency size or jurisdiction.[76] Furthermore, empirical studies building on questionnaires and semi-structured interviews with representatives of NCAs in the ECN, document an almost uniform high appreciation for the work of the network, which is interpreted as a 'testimony to shared ownership and the vision of the ECN as a joint enterprise'.[77] The positive evaluation is confirmed by a 2021 study of Francesca Vantaggiato, Hussein Kassim and Kathryn Wright. To the question what could be improved in the Network, many respondents are reported to have replied 'more of it'.[78]

b. Evaluating the CPC Network

The results for the CPC Network were not quite as positive. Especially in the first decade of its existence, the interest of national authorities to engage in enforcement cooperation was lukewarm, to say the least.

Under the CPC Regulation, the Commission was obliged to produce biennial reports based on periodic reporting by the Member States along specific indicators, including the number of mutual assistance requests issued, number of requests received and number of uses of the IT tool, developed to facilitate information exchange. A first Commission report published in 2009[79] acknowledged the contribution of the CPC Network for raising the level of enforcement of EU consumer protection law throughout the Union, but also noted a series of shortcomings. In particular, two years after the entry into effect of the Regulation, significant number of the notified national authoritiess were either not connected or not actively using the system, thus not issuing requests for mutual assistance. Not all authorities had gained access to the IT tool, and among those having access, one-third were still not actively using the tool.[80] Correspondingly, the number of mutual assistance requests was relatively low – a total of 317 in 2007 and 384 in 2008. The same, or largely similar, problems were identified in the second biennial report, showing that many authorities 'rarely or never' used the CPC cooperation mechanisms. What is more, 'some of the most active players of the first years had reduced their engagement'.[81] The third (and last) biennial

[76] Firat Cengiz, 'Multi-Level Governance in Competition Policy: The European Competition Network' (2010) 35(5) *European Law Review* 660, 668.

[77] See Hussein Kassim and Kathryn Wright, 'The European Competition Network: A European Regulatory Network with a Difference' (2010) Paper delivered at the 32nd EGPA Annual Conference, Toulouse, France, 8–10 September 2010, 14.

[78] See Francesca Vantaggiato, Hussein Kassim and Kathryn Wright, 'Internal Network Structures as Opportunity Structures: Control and Effectiveness in the European Competition Network' (2021) 28(4) *Journal of European Public Policy* 571, 583–84.

[79] See Report from the Commission to the European Parliament and to the Council on the application of Regulation (EC) No 2006/2004, COM(2009) 336 final, Brussels, 2.7.2009 (hereinafter: First Commission Report CPC Regulation 2009).

[80] First Commission Report CPC Regulation 2009, ibid.

[81] Report from the Commission to the European Parliament and to the Council on the application of Regulation (EC) 2006/2004, COM(2012) 100 final, Brussels, 12.3.2012 (hereinafter: Second Commission Report CPC Regulation 2012), 12, 9.

report showed results not much different than the preceding two reports with continued modest number of exchanges.[82] A similarly bleak picture of underdeveloped and poorly used mechanism of mutual assistance was revealed in an external report in 2012;[83] broadly confirmed by a consumer programme evaluation in 2018.[84]

The other important indicator for the effectiveness of enforcement cooperation within the CPC Network is the timely handling of information and enforcement requests. The initially set time-limit of 14 days[85] proved problematic and the First Commission Report concluded that mutual assistance requests were taking 'longer and longer to be closed' with information requests being closed in an average of between 81 and 148 days in 2008.[86] Subsequent Operational Guidelines set more realistic benchmarks of three months for handling information requests and nine to 12 months for enforcement measures requests.[87] Yet, even these exceedingly generous targets proved too ambitious and were not met.[88]

Apart from being a clear sign of deficient effectiveness of enforcement cooperation, low numbers of exchanges are certainly strong evidence of lacking engagement of national authorities in the activity of the Network. Furthermore, the biennial reports showed that informal contacts between case handlers were rather the exception than the rule.[89] Importantly, in contrast to the ECN, the competent authorities participating in the CPC Network, show only moderate appreciation of the activities of the Network and the effects of the CPC cooperation for increasing the effectiveness of enforcement.[90]

c. Explaining Differential Outcomes

Different explanations for the differential results from network cooperation through the ECN and the CPC Network have been advanced in evaluation reports and in the scholarly literature. Some see the strength of the ECN to derive foremost from the Commission's decision to share its monopoly over enforcement within a regime in

[82] Report from the Commission to the European Parliament and to the Council on the application of Regulation (EC) 2006/2004, COM(2014) 439 final, Brussels, 1.7.2014 (hereinafter: Third Commission Report CPC Regulation 2014).

[83] (External) evaluation of the Consumer Protection Cooperation Regulation, Final Report submitted by the Consumer Policy Evaluation Consortium (CPEC), 17 December 2012 (hereinafter External Evaluation Report 2012 CPC Regulation).

[84] European Commission, Ex-post evaluation of the Consumer Programme 2007–2013 and mid-term evaluation of the Consumer Programme 2014–2020 – Final report, Part 2 – Ex-post evaluation of the Consumer Programme 2007-2013, 2018, available at: https://op.europa.eu/en/publication-detail/-/publication/3aefdcef-22af-11e9-8d04-01aa75ed71a1.

[85] Commission Decision 2007/76/EC implementing Regulation (EC) No 2006/2004 [2007] L 32/192; Cf. Commission Decision 2011/141/EU amending Commission Decision 2007/76/EC [2011] L 59/63.

[86] First Commission Report CPC Regulation 2009, above note 79, 7.

[87] Impact Assessment accompanying the document Proposal for a Regulation of the European Parliament and of the Council on cooperation between national authorities responsible for the enforcement of consumer protection laws, Brussels, SWD (2016) 164 final (hereinafter: Impact Assessment New CPC Regulation), 15.

[88] See European Commission, Ex-post evaluation, Final report, Part 2, above note 84, 56. The results are similar for the period 2014–2017, Ex-post evaluation, Final report, Part 1, available at https://op.europa.eu/en/publication-detail/-/publication/5e9ee253-22b0-11e9-8d04-01aa75ed71a1/language-en, 76.

[89] Second Commission Report CPC Regulation 2012, above note 81, 10.

[90] See a rate of 3.4 on a scale of 5 for the CPC Network, European Commission, Ex-post Evaluation, Final report, Part 2, above note 84.

which DG COMP has been historically central.[91] In addition, the preserved central role of the Commission in the ECN, is considered as a source of authority and stability. The Commission's retained power is in this view projected onto the NCAs, strengthening their self-confidence and appreciation for the Network. The Commission itself sees the key to the 'major success' of the ECN to lie in the possibility for network members to share knowledge and experiences in a confidential manner. This has, in the view of the Commission 'triggered a very open and constructive dialogue with the national competition authorities which fosters the coherent application of Articles 81 and 82 EC'.[92] In a similar vein Cengiz speaks of the 'emergence of an extensive informal communication culture between the competition officials'.[93] Related to this, is the closed character of the Network and the limited number of officials that participate in the communication.[94]

On a deeper level, scholars point to the special character of competition law and its quasi-constitutional status in the EU. According to Cseres competition law has become 'deeply rooted in the economic constitutions of its Member States'.[95] This arguably translates into greater commitment and a sense of a shared mission. Kassim and Wright also stress that what distinguishes the ECN from other European Regulatory Networks is 'the perception of the network as a shared enterprise'.[96] These analyses feed into Peter Haas's theory of epistemic communities, which provides probably the most convincing explanation for the success of the ECN. Haas defines epistemic communities as networks 'of professionals with recognized expertise and competence in a particular domain and an authoritative claim to policy-relevant knowledge within that domain or issue-area'.[97] According to him, an epistemic community can consist of any kind of experts or professionals, who have (i) a shared set of normative and principled beliefs; (ii) shared causal beliefs; (iii) shared notions of validity and (iv) a common policy enterprise.[98]

Applying this definition to the area of competition policy, the existence of a strong epistemic community in competition law and policy, becomes immediately apparent. Indeed, the prominent position of competition law in the EU integration project and the sheer volume of Commission and European Court of Justice (ECJ) decisions in the field have been providing employment and intellectual occupation to a whole array of practitioners, public officials and academics, sharing the values and principles of

[91] Kassim and Wright, above note 77, 8.

[92] Commission SWD Regulation 1/2003, 2009, above note 69, para 268; Commission Report Regulation 1/2003, 2009, above note 68, para 29.

[93] Cengiz, above note 76, 669.

[94] See Imelda Maher and Oana Stefan, 'Competition Law in Europe: The Challenge of a Network Constitution', in OD Prosser and T Rawlings (eds), *The Regulatory States: Constitutional Implications* (Oxford, OUP, 2010) 187–88.

[95] Katalin Cseres, 'Competition Law Enforcement Beyond the Nation State: A Model for Transnational Enforcement Mechanisms?' in Hans-W Micklitz and Andrea Wechsler (eds), *The Transformation of Enforcement: European Economic Law in a Global Perspective* (Oxford, Hart Publishing, 2016) 338. On competition law as part of the European economic constitution see David Gerber, *Law and Competition in Twentieth-Century Europe* (Oxford, Clarendon Press, 2001).

[96] Kassim and Wright, above note 77, 14.

[97] Peter Haas, 'Introduction: Epistemic Communities and International Policy Coordination' (1992) 46 *International Organization* 1, 3.

[98] ibid.

EU competition law and building a tightly knit professional community. This community has been informally existing already before the setting up of the ECN, but the Network provided a welcome platform, exacerbating the intensity of communication and the strong sense of common purpose of this community.[99]

The CPC Network has been far less subject to scholarly scrutiny, but both internal and external reports and evaluations have sought to provide some explanations for the generally disappointing results from its functioning.[100] Attention was initially directed foremost to practical impediments, such as insufficient resources at national level and differences in competent authorities' capabilities. The 'fairly broad scope of the CPC Regulation's annex' was brought up in several reports, as well as complex and diverging institutional frameworks and long communication lines, causing delays in handling of requests and ultimately undermining confidence in the CPC Network.[101] The degree of 'fragmentation' with an excessive number of participating authorities was confirmed as a major barrier also in subsequent reports.[102]

More fundamentally, the reports highlighted that the CPC Network has not succeeded in developing a 'corporate identity' and gaining high profile.[103] The reports thus identify a potentially crucial difference between the two networks. The CPC Network cannot tap into a strong epistemic community in the same way as the ECN. This is prevented by the lower profile of consumer protection as a policy area, the broad and patchy scope of the policy domain with national institutional choices gravitating in different degree to public or private enforcement. The more limited role of the Commission in the enforcement of EU consumer law and in the CPC Network is also a likely explanation for the weaker commitment to cooperation of NCAs, something pointed out in some of the reports.[104]

III. EXPLORING NETWORK DYNAMICS

The evaluations discussed above are based on a variety of qualitative and quantitative data, but they provide typically a rather static picture of the networks in a given evaluation period. At the same time, what is interesting to capture is the dynamic generated within each network throughout a longer stretch of time. This dynamic can arguably be studied along two dimensions. A first relevant dimension is the dynamic toward horizontal or vertical empowerment. The question to be examined here is to what extent the activities within the network contribute to strengthening the participating

[99] See Frans van Waarden and Michaela Drahos, 'Courts and (Epistemic) Communities in the Convergence of Competition Policies' (2002) 9(6) *Journal of European Public Policy* 91; cf Maher and Stefan, above note 94, 188; Cengiz, above note 76.

[100] See the biennial reports on the CPC Regulation (n 79, n 81, n 82); cf BEUC (The European Consumer Organisation), 'Strengthening the Coordinated Enforcement of Consumer Protection Rules: The Revision of the Consumer Protection Coordination (CPC) Regulation' (2022) www.beuc.eu/position-papers/strengthening-coordinated-enforcement-consumer-protection-rules (hereinafter BEUC).

[101] Second Commission Report CPC Regulation 2012, above note 81, 14. External Evaluation Report CPC Regulation, above note 83, 76–77.

[102] European Commission, Ex-post evaluation, Final Report, Part 1, above note 88, 30.

[103] First Commission Report CPC Regulation 2009, above note 79, 8.

[104] See Third Commission Report CPC Regulation 2014, above note 82, 5; cf BEUC, above note 100.

national authorities on a horizontal plane, or to shifting power vertically from the national to the EU level, notably to the Commission. Interestingly, when the ECN was set up, predictions would run in both directions. The second relevant dimension concerns the question whether the networks develop into a platform for equal engagement of all participating units or, alternatively, whether we can observe skewed engagement, or uneven participation in enforcement activities.

A. Between Horizontal and Vertical Empowerment

i. Horizontal and Vertical Empowerment in the ECN

As highlighted from the outset, the ECN represents an unusual example of actual divestment of powers from the Commission to NCAs and correspondingly of empowerment of NCAs. This was well acknowledged by NCAs, which according to Cengiz, 'enthusiastically agreed with the enhancement of their enforcement powers under the new regime'.[105] Likewise, Kassim and Wright conclude that 'the evidence points to a strengthening of competition agencies (and national courts), where NCAs have been empowered, individually and collectively'.[106]

Importantly, horizontal empowerment does not appear to constitute a one-time act, which is completed with the setting up of the Network. Rather it emerges as a continuous dynamic inherent in the logic and design of the enforcement cooperation mechanism. Its practical realisation is enabled by the fact that the ECN quickly assumed a central role in formulation of new competition policy, part of these policy-setting functions then being directed at strengthening the enforcement powers of the NCAs. Thus, a rather efficient mechanism for enhancement of NCAs powers gradually takes shape, building on two components (i) first, gathering evidence about the diversity in enforcement competences, powers and procedures of NCAs, and second (ii) calling for increased convergence of enforcement systems and upgrading of NCAs powers. In combination, these two components have been used as a successful leverage of the position of NCAs.

This dynamic can be clearly discerned starting already from the first Report on the functioning of Regulation 1/2003, where the Commission draws attention to the divergence of national enforcement systems on aspects such as 'fines, criminal sanctions. . .the power to impose structural remedies, as well as the ability of Member States' competition authorities to formally set enforcement priorities'.[107] This divergence is singled out as the main reason for suboptimal level of practical cooperation between NCAs.[108] This signal was then followed by the setting up of a designated Working Group within the ECN on the powers of competition authorities,

[105] Cengiz, above note 76, with reference to the summary of observations to the European Commission, White Paper on Reform of Regulation 17, Summary of the Observations, February 29, 2000.

[106] Kassim and Wright, above note 77, 17.

[107] Commission Report Regulation 2003/1, 2009, above note 68, p 7.

[108] Commission SWD Regulation 1/2003, 2009, above note 69, paras 200–07; cf Cengiz, above note 76, 670.

which produced two reports on Investigative Powers and Decision-making Powers of NCAs.[109] Based on the reports, the ECN adopted Recommendations, which, together with supportive Commission evaluation reports,[110] eventually led to a Commission proposal for a new legislative instrument harmonising and enhancing the powers of NCAs.[111]

The final result, the so-called ECN+ Directive declares its objective to be 'to empower the competition authorities of the Member States to be more effective enforcers [of EU competition rules]'[112] and incorporates literally all proposals advanced within the auspices of the ECN (either as Working Group reports or recommendations). It establishes a common minimum of investigative and enforcement powers set at a high level, including powers to issue interim measures, to impose structural remedies, to set the size of the penalty at a sufficiently deterrent level with a common minimum set at 10 per cent of the undertaking's total turnover.

Of particular significance in terms of empowerment is the strongly worded obligation that the ECN+ Directive stipulates viz the Member States to ensure that NCAs have sufficient resources and qualified staff to perform their tasks effectively. This obligation is backed by a transparency duty, namely an obligation for NCAs to periodically report to a governmental or parliamentary body on their activities, funding and staff changes.[113] Arguably, most importantly, the ECN+ Directive sets out an unambiguous obligation for the Member States to provide fundamental guarantees for the independence of competition authorities as one of the essential conditions for ensuring a 'truly common competition law enforcement area' (Recitals 5 and 8; Article 4(1)). The concept of independence is defined in dual terms: independence from political influence, as well as from any other external influence, such as influence from market actors. Moreover, Member States are obliged to put in place clear, transparent and fair procedures for selection, recruitment, appointment and dismissal of NCA officials (Article 4(3)(4) Directive 1/2019).[114]

It appears plain from the above that the transition from a centralised to decentralised enforcement has unleashed a dynamic of horizontal empowerment – and one

[109] ECN Working Group on Cooperation Issues and Due Process, Report on Decision-making Powers, 31 October 2012 and Report on Investigative Powers, 31 October 2012; both reports are available at https://competition-policy.ec.europa.eu/system/files/2021-07/decision_making_powers_report_en.pdf.

[110] The recommendations are available on the webpage of the ECN https://competition-policy.ec.europa.eu/antitrust-and-cartels/european-competition-network/documents_en, 09 December 2013. See also Commission Communication Regulation 1/2003, 2014 and Commission SWD Regulation 1/2003, 2014, above note 70.

[111] European Commission, Proposal for a Directive to empower the competition authorities of the Member States to be more effective enforcers and to ensure the proper functioning of the internal market COM(2017) 142 final.

[112] Directive (EU) 2019/1 of the European Parliament and of the Council of 11 December 2018 to empower the competition authorities of the Member States to be more effective enforcers and to ensure the proper functioning of the internal market, OJ L 11, 14.1.2019, pp 3–33.

[113] On the issue of funding see also Resolution of the Meeting of Heads of the European competition authorities of 16 November 2010 'Competition authorities in the European Union – the continued need for effective institutions'.

[114] Whereas strengthening the independence of competition authorities from national governments has many advantages, its advancement as an unquestionable premise of the institutional set up of competition policy has been discussed. See Monti, above note 66.

can say self-empowerment – of NCAs. The question is whether such empowerment has been at the expense of loss of powers on the part of the Commission. Already from the inception of the ECN, many saw in this initiative a disguised attempt by the Commission to in fact increase its own powers, an agency escape of sorts.[115] Initial empirical studies based on interviews with national representatives in the ECN did not confirm this thesis. Nevertheless, interviewees overwhelmingly describe the role of the Commission as still being 'in the driver's seat'.[116]

Indeed, the powers of the Commission in the network, as coded in the original set up of Regulation 1/2003 continue to be significant. The Commission occupies central place in the system of case allocation between competent authorities and is considered an authority 'particularly well placed' to handle most cases of economic significance.[117] Importantly, the Commission has the power of taking over a case from a NCA and requiring the NCA to close its investigation or proceedings.[118] Furthermore, the Commission has a privileged position in cases involving 'genuine uncertainty', presenting 'novel or unresolved questions' or when new types of agreements and practices arise.[119] This organisation of the division of work within the ECN appears to foster the authority of the Commission.[120] The way information exchange is designed, likewise puts the Commission in a position of oversight, if not control, over NCAs.[121] To be sure, analyses of the ECN show that the Commission has not used these powers so far, in particular the power under Article 11(6), or only infrequently.[122] Nevertheless, the very existence of Article 11(6) in particular is an unmistaken marker of a hierarchical structure and the Commission's top position in it.

In terms of internal operation, it is again no question that the Commission and DG COMP are at the centre of ECN activity. DG COMP is the main contact point for the national competition authorities. The Commission sets the agenda for the plenary meetings and a representative of the ECN unit of DG COMP chairs the meetings, even though NCAs are consulted too.[123] Based on her analysis of ECN from the perspective of NCAs from CEE Member States, Cseres finds that the 'ECN mechanisms are tilting towards hierarchical governance modes'.[124]

[115] See Stephen Wilks, 'Agencies, Networks, Discourses and the Trajectory of European Competition Enforcement' (2007) 3(2) *European Competition Journal* 437, 440.

[116] Kassim and Wright, above note 77.

[117] If the allegedly anti-competitive agreement(s) or practice(s) 'have effects on competition in more than three Member States'. See para 14 Commission Notice on Cooperation, above note 53.

[118] See Article 11(6) Regulation 1/2003; Cengiz calls this provision 'one of the central pillars of [the] previous centralised enforcement regime'. See Cengiz, above note 76, 644.

[119] See Recital 14, Regulation 1/2003; Recital 38, Regulation 1/2003. See Vantaggiato, Kassim and Wright, above note 78, 583.

[120] Vantaggiato, Kassim and Wright, above note 78, 583.

[121] See Article 11(3) Regulation 1/2003. On these information exchanges as 'monitoring channels' for the Commission see Cengiz, above note 76, 667. For a similar point see Poncibò, above note 5, 181.

[122] For possible explanations for this self-restraint see Kassim and Wright, above note 77, 15–16.

[123] Kassim and Wright, above note 77. Vantaggiato, Kassim and Wright claim that the ECN structure is too complex and open and therefore does not allow domination by the Commission. Vantaggiatto, Kassim and Wright, above note 78.

[124] Cseres, above note 95, 338.

One might ask whether the ECN+ Directive, by empowering NCAs is not reducing the power of the Commission. Yet, in this respect, the effect is rather one of common, joint self-empowerment for both the Commission and the NCAs. The 'power cake' is not redistributed between the Commission and the NCAs, it is increased for all participants in the Network. When the link of NCAs with their governments is weakened, the pull around the Commission can be expected to increase. Therefore, with enhanced independence and resources for NCAs, the Commission can see itself as the centre of a more powerful institutional conglomerate. If there is any loss of power, it would potentially be for national governments (both at the national level and in the Council) as locos for defining competition policy. Seen from the above, the dynamic within the ECN seems to work towards empowerment on both horizontal and vertical plane.[125]

ii. Horizontal and Vertical Empowerment in the CPC Network

Although the CPC Network has clearly proven far less successful than its competition counterpart, what is remarkable is that it appears to have triggered a broadly similar horizontal dynamics towards empowerment of national competent authorities. The original CPC Regulation 2006/2004 set out certain minimum powers that national authorities needed to have in order to ensure the effective enforcement of EU consumer law in cases of cross-border infringements, but these were not particularly demanding requirements.

As seen above, the first reports on the functioning of the CPC Network saw the main reasons for the suboptimal performance of the Network to lie foremost in practical barriers to cooperation, such as large number, incongruent competences and insufficient resources of national authorities. However, the attention was soon redirected to legal barriers to cooperation and in particular to the diversity in national authorities' enforcement powers. In subsequent reports, diversity surfaced as the single most important reason for the deficient performance of the Network,[126] which prompted further studies in the same direction.[127] Thus, in a manner similar to the ECN, diversity in the powers and status of national authorities is pressed on as a major explanation for the inefficiency of the system for enforcement cooperation and used as justification for new legislative initiatives seeking to harmonise and ratchet up national authorities' powers.

Following a Commission proposal in 2016, a new Regulation 2017/2394 was indeed adopted on 12 December 2017.[128] The Commission in its press release described

[125] According to Sauter, 'it is clear that the Commission is profiting from the new system, but also that the NCAs are empowered both by modernization and by collaborating in the ECN'. See Wolf Sauter, *Coherence in EU Competition Law* (Oxford, OUP, 2016), 169. Cf Cengiz, above note 76, 670.

[126] See Third Commission Report CPC Regulation 2014, above note 82.

[127] See Study on Enforcement Authorities' Powers and National Procedural Rules in the Application of Regulation 2006/2004/EC on Consumer Protection Cooperation, Studio Grimaldi in 2014; see also Support study for the Impact Assessment on the review of the CPC Regulation 2006/2004/EC, Final report submitted on 04 November 2015 by the CPEC.

[128] See Commission Proposal for a new Regulation on cooperation between national authorities responsible for the enforcement of consumer protection laws, Brussels, COM(2016) 283 final; Impact Assessment, Brussels, COM(2016) 283 final (hereinafter: Impact Assessment New CPC Regulation).

the new Regulation as giving 'sharper teeth for EU consumer protection'.[129] In a subsequent and related move, the powers of national authorities were additionally enhanced by the modernisation reform of EU consumer law following the New Deal for Consumers through the Enforcement and Modernisation Directive.[130] The details in the new instruments cannot be presented here. Suffice to say that the main direction of empowerment is parallel to that in the ECN. The New CPC Regulation defines in much stronger and exacting terms than the original Regulation the investigative powers to be granted to competent authorities.[131] Concerning enforcement powers, the arsenal of sanctions and remedies at the disposal of competent authorities is substantially expanded, including penalties and fines for infringements covered by the Regulation,[132] which following the Enforcement and Modernisation Directive, can reach up to 4 per cent of traders' annual turnover in cases of widespread infringements.[133]

Still, there are aspects in which the reforms propelled by the two networks differ significantly. In contrast to the ECN+ Directive, the New CPC Regulation while mentioning the need for sufficient resources, formulates this rather vaguely.[134] Most importantly, there is nothing in Regulation 2017/2394 about the status of the competent consumer protection authorities. Whereas the ECN+ Directive makes a very strong point about NCAs independence, the New CPC Regulation remains silent on the position of competent authorities in the system of government of the Member State.[135] Apparently, consumer protection does not have the same political clout as competition policy and is not seen to warrant comparable guarantees of agency independence.[136]

Summing up, as a result of the reform, national consumer protection authorities could see themselves empowered and emboldened in their task as national watchdogs. In this, the logic of horizontal empowerment is similar in the CPC Network as in the ECN. As stated in the BEUC report 'the CPC-Network is a chain which is as strong as its weakest link'. Consequently, strengthening the component parts of the Network, i.e. national consumer CPC authorities, is expected to strengthen the whole network and EU consumer law enforcement in general.[137]

In respect of vertical empowerment, given the very different origin and background of the CPC Network, a relevant question is whether it has developed in a different way from the ECN. After all, in the case of the CPC Network, the Commission has no enforcement powers of its own and the setting up of the CPC Network did not formally

[129] European Commission, CPC Factsheet – sharper teeth for EU Consumer Protection, 17 January 2020, https://commission.europa.eu/law/law-topic/consumer-protection-law/consumer-protection-cooperation-regulation_en.

[130] Directive (EU) 2019/2161.

[131] Article 9(3)(a)–(d) New CPC Regulation. Special powers are accorded for investigations and enforcement in the context of digital markets, see Article 9(4)(g).

[132] Under the old Regulation the power to impose penalties was only required for violation of an injunctive order and not as a direct sanction of an infringement.

[133] See Articles 1, 3 and 6 Directive (EU) 2019/2161 (Omnibus Directive), amending Directives 93/13/EEC; 2005/29/EC and 2011/83/EU.

[134] See Recital 4, Article 5(4) New CPC Regulation. This prompts the European Consumer Organization BEUC, in a report on the New CPC Regulation, to suggest that the Commission should carefully monitor budgetary allocations to CPC authorities. See BEUC, above note 100, 26.

[135] BEUC, above note 100, 23–24.

[136] For a critique in this respect see BEUC, above note 100, 23–24.

[137] BEUC, above note 100, 22.

change this. The original CPC Regulation envisaged mainly horizontal exchange of information and requests for enforcement measures between national authorities, where the Commission was to act chiefly as a moderator (Article 9(2) Regulation 2006/2004). Competent authorities could invite the Commission to participate in the coordinated action, but this possibility was formulated in weak terms.[138] Therefore, in contrast to the ECN, observers describe the CPC Network mostly as a decentralised cooperation system where the Commission has 'a limited role'.[139]

Nevertheless, a closer look at the operation of the CPC Network shows that the Commission has with time come to assume a more central role than apparent at first sight and this role has arguably been expanding. Probably due to the variation of national authorities participating in the Network and the broad diversity of their portfolios, design and working modes, bringing some operational efficiency into the Network would essentially be impossible without the Commission's disciplining role. Partly through the vehicle of the regular reports required under Article 21 Regulation 2006/2004, the Commission assumed a sort of pace-setting function within the Network, identifying flaws and proposing new initiatives. Given that the periodic reports revealed systemic deficiencies in the horizontal exchange between national authorities, relatively early on, calls for a more centralised and coordinated course of action were advanced, where the role of the Commission would naturally become stronger. The reports sent a strong signal suggesting enhancement of the Commission's powers and position in the CPC Network.[140]

In response, the New CPC Regulation 2017/2394 made a clear step towards centralisation with new provisions on coordinated investigation and enforcement in cases of so-called 'widespread infringements' and 'widespread infringements with Union dimension' (Chapter IV Regulation 2017/2394). These are, in the first category, infringements that harm the collective interests of consumers in at least three Member States, and in the second one, infringements harming consumer interests in at 'least two-thirds of the Member States, accounting, together, for at least two-thirds of the population of the Union' (Article 4(3)). If the competent authorities in the case of widespread infringements cannot agree on one authority to act as a coordinator, they may ask the Commission to take on that role. The Commission can itself coordinate actions in case of widespread infringements with Union dimension, but after consulting with relevant competent authorities (Article 17(3) and (4)).

Interestingly, the original proposal for a revised Regulation (Section II) sought to grant the Commission independent power to launch coordinated action without having to consult national authorities in the states concerned. Moreover, it envisaged granting the Commission wide-ranging powers of adopting implementing acts on a number of points concerning the institutional design of the cross-border cooperation within the CPC Network.[141] Obviously, the Commission envisioned a more precise

[138] See Article 9(3) and Article 10 Regulation 2006/2004.

[139] BEUC, above note 100, 7.

[140] The 2014 Commission Report emphasised that respondents to the public consultation were 'generally supportive for the Commission to have a more active role in the CPC network'. See Third Commission Report CPC Regulation 2014, above note 82, 6.

[141] See Draft Articles 10, 11(5), 12(5), 13(6), 15(7), 20, 27, 31(3), 31(4), 34(6), 35(5), 36(2), 37(4), 39(3), 43(4), 46(2).

and juridified framework for the system of enforcement cooperation. These proposals were, however, bluntly rejected by the Council under the label of 'simplification of the enforcement mechanism'.[142] It appears that while Member States in principle agree on the need for more effective tools to counteract widespread cross-border consumer law infringements, they are reluctant to vest too broad powers in the hands of the Commission.

As a result of this trimming of the original Commission proposal, the New CPC Regulation leaves essentially the responsibility for public enforcement to the EU Member States. The Commission still cannot itself launch a coordinated action and must rely on the investigative and enforcement powers, and on the engagement, of national authorities. Decisively, the Commission lacks adequate resources to effectively engage in the cooperation mechanism set up by the Regulation. The outcome is a fragmented enforcement landscape which is criticised as not particularly effective in curbing serious and widespread cross-border consumer law infringements.[143]

In sum, like the ECN, the CPC Network has generated both horizontal and vertical dynamic towards strengthening the Commission's role in the Network. In both dimensions, diversity is a crucial factor. Diversity of national authorities' enforcement powers is used as an argument for harmonisation and ratcheting up of those powers. At the same time, the plurality and excessive diversity of participating national authorities create internal fragmentation, which naturally calls for stronger leadership and coordination. The Commission has tried to procure a more formalised legal framework for exercising such leadership role, but these efforts have not resonated positively with the Member States. It appears that consumer protection does not command the same authority in the Union political spectrum and attempts to shift more powers to the supranational level meet with resistance.

B. Equal or Skewed Engagement in Decentralised Enforcement?

The second relevant dimension along which network dynamic can be usefully analysed relates to the equality of participation and engagement of the constitutive units. The notion of network is associated with an assumption of equivalent units having equal and even weight in the network. However, a closer look at internal network dynamic might reveal a different picture of skewed engagement, or uneven participation in enforcement activities.

i. Equality of Engagement in the ECN

In the area of competition law enforcement, such uneven pattern of engagement has been evidenced in more recent empirical surveys of the ECN conducted by Vantagiatto et al. In particular, analysis of informal contacts between officials of

[142] See Council, General approach on the Proposal for a regulation on cooperation between national authorities responsible for the enforcement of consumer protection laws, 6187/17 Brussels, 10 February 2017.

[143] BEUC, above note 100, 10.

NCAs has indicated different levels of engagement of national competition authorities. The study finds that certain NCAs play a more active role in the Network than others, in terms of authorities actually instituting enforcement proceedings, but also authorities that are being sought by their peers for expert advice and experience-sharing. The authorities most often consulted appeared to be those with highest level of resources and experience, which often coincides with number of cases handled. Most intense outgoing contacts from NCAs were typically from agencies with intermediate level of resources and experience, which is interpreted in the sense that the network is used as a compensation for insufficient own resources.[144] Furthermore, recent analyses discern a trend of closer regional cooperation between NCAs based on geographic proximity.[145] This may signal a positive horizontal dynamic but also an emerging variable geometry of network cooperation.

Additional evidence of uneven engagement is provided by empirical studies focused on the position of the NCAs from the new Member States from CEE in the ECN. These states have been lacking robust experience in market economy and competition law and policy and one objective with creating the Network was, in fact, to serve as a platform for socialising and learning for the public officials from these states.[146] At the same time, the authorities in the new Member States were expected to be less active in the ECN, something that could arguably create a varied-speed cooperation. The initial study by Kassim and Wright did not seem to confirm these misgivings. The Network was highly appreciated by officials from both old and new Member States, by experienced agencies and competition law novices alike.[147]

However, subsequent studies focusing specifically on the participation of the CEE countries in the ECN reveal a different picture, suggesting that, with few exceptions, the authorities in these Member States are passive participants and essentially, on the receiving end of policy recommendations and guidance as to enforcement activity.[148] A different nuance is added by an insightful analysis into the ways comprtition authorities from some Central and East European countries (CEECs) are interpreting the criterion of 'effect on trade', which is the decisive trigger for applying EU competition law.[149] The study shows that in the "new" Member States from CEE, there is a practice of overly narrow interpretation of this requirement with the result of many cases being treated as national and therefore not EU law relevant infringements. According to the authors, competition authorities from the studied new Member States tended to 'systematically avoid the application of EU competition rules, and thus avoid the

[144] Vantaggiato, Kassim and Wright, above note 78, 584.

[145] 'There is an opposite trend of greater decentralisation in the emergence of regional NCA cooperation agreements. These may well assist in consolidating and building on trust found in the ECN. Provided they operate in a complementary fashion, within the confines of sincere cooperation, then we can expect further NCA cooperation to occur across the EU'. Maher and Hosseini report of such regional agreements between eg the Nordic countries. Imelda Maher and Mina Hosseini, 'Cooperation between National Competition Authorities: An overview of EU and national case law' (2024) e-Competitions, 18 January 2024. The text of the cooperation agreement between the Nordic countries can be found here www.konkurrensverket.se/globalassets/dokument/om-oss/nordiskt-avtal-om-samarbete-i-konkurrensfragor.pdf.

[146] See Cengiz, above note 76, 664.

[147] Kassim and Wright, above note 77, 14 with reference to replies to question 29 of their survey.

[148] Cseres, above note 95, 338.

[149] See Article 3 Regulation 1/2003.

scrutiny of the Commission and other NCAs within the ECN'.[150] This was partly acknowledged in the latest – generally, once again, overwhelmingly positive – evaluation of Regulation 1/2003.[151]

ii. Equality of Engagement in the CPC Network

Turning to the CPC Network, in terms of equality of participation, the first two biennial reports on the CPC Regulation provided tables with distribution of mutual assistance requests across Member States, showing widely skewed patterns of engagement and use of the system. Although a formal analysis of intensity of use has not been performed, it is evident that among the countries least engaged in network cooperation are the countries with more limited resources or experience in consumer protection policy, or where the latter is not accorded political priority. Member States from CEE are systematically underrepresented in these statistics.[152]

A similar uneven pattern of participation transpires from the rate of attendance of network meetings, showing that certain Member States are systematically absent from CPC Committee meetings.[153] The impression is confirmed by the statistics from another form of participation in Network cooperation, namely exchanges of officials under the so-called Karolus programme. Here as well, participation is highly unbalanced, with relatively low rate of participation of countries that were expected to be the prime beneficiaries of the programme, notably Member States from CEE.[154] Conversely, information in the periodic reports on coordinated enforcement action shows that a few authorities – those in the Netherlands, Italy, Sweden and UK (before Brexit) – have recurrently been in the lead of such initiatives.

Renewed evidence of the uneven distribution of engagement in enforcement cooperation is provided in the latest information gathering report on the CPC Regulation from 2022. The report contains rich data about the rate of participation of Member State authorities in each of the cooperation mechanisms envisaged by the New CPC Regulation. The report identifies three groups of Member States, depending on their

[150] Marco Botta, Alexandr Svetlicinii and Maciej Bernatt, 'The Assessment of the Effect on Trade by the National Competition Authorities of the "New" Member States: Another Legal Partition of the Internal Market?' (2015) 52(5) *Common Market Law Review* 1247, 1249, 1252.

[151] 'However, it was also noted, from an academic background, that in certain countries there appeared to be a reluctance to apply the effect on trade concept and, consequently, Articles 101 and 102 TFEU. A small minority view expressed in the study also considered that the concept is applied inconsistently and may be used in a discretionary manner'. See Commission Evaluation, 2024, above note 73, 232.

[152] See First and Second Commission Reports CPC Regulation (n 79, n 81). Starting from the Third Report such statistics is regrettably no longer presented, cf. Third Commission Report CPC Regulation 2014, above note 82.

[153] This can be ascertained from a sample of attendance records from the CPC Committee meetings during the years 2009–19. Such records are publicly accessible through the Comitology register. The records are rather imperfect, since following the Covid19-pandemic meetings take place chiefly online. But between 2009 and 2019 meetings took place in person in Brussels. A review of the summary records for this period shows that for example Greece was hardly ever present at meetings. Other countries such as Cyprus, Croatia, Lithuania and Romania, were often absent, or represented by their Permanent Representation, arguably indicating lower engagement with the Committee work.

[154] Records on such exchanges are available in the reports of the executive agency CHAFEA, that used to provide funding for such exchanges. The rate of participation of CEE authorities as beneficiaries is higher in exchanges on the General Product Safety Directive compared to the CPC.

engagement. In the first group figure Member States whose national authorities are frequent senders and recipients of information, mutual assistance and enforcement requests. In the second group the rate of engagement is average. In the third group fall Member States whose activity is barely registered, with only a few instances of participation on either the giving or the receiving end of information and enforcement assistance.[155] Clearly, there are Member States that are left on the periphery of network cooperation with some national authorities not having performed a single action within the evaluation period.

This classification feeds into previous studies of cooperation between national authorities in enforcement networks. Thus, Polak and Versluis distinguish between the categories 'leaders' and 'laggards' and note the corrosive effect divergent degrees of compliance and engagement can have for mutual trust.[156] The data reported above suggest that a classification into three groups of typified roles in enforcement networks might be more accurate, namely: 'activists', 'followers' and 'shirkers'. Authorities in Member States with greater experience, resources and track record of effective enforcement are recognised as leaders, and acquire a more authoritative position in the network. They are the ones often entrusted with leading working groups, or coordinated actions. These authorities are also the preferred hosts for exchange of officials. The second group, the followers, is made up of authorities that shy away from taking on the leadership role themselves, probably due to limited resources and experience, but are still interested in cooperation. For them the network could be a resource, strengthening their enforcement capacity. The third, and potentially most problematic group, the shirkers, consists of authorities that avoid and try to minimise their participation in the enforcement cooperation.

Interestingly, rather than seeking to turn this dynamic, the New CPC Regulation appears to tacitly acknowledge and embrace it, adapting the design of decentralised enforcement accordingly. While enhancing the powers of national authorities, the New Regulation, less conspicuously, introduced changes in the distribution of powers within the CPC Network. As mentioned above, the Regulation strengthened the role of the Commission in several respects, notably in cases of widespread infringements with Union dimension.[157] In addition, and arguably, more consequentially for the success of coordinated enforcement, the focus of the Network has generally been redirected from mutual assistance between authorities to concerted actions coordinated by a competent national authority, or by the Commission, when designating a coordinator proves difficult. More specifically, the New Regulation formalised the practice of so-called 'sweeps', an institutional innovation born spontaneously within the CPC Network, partly in response of the experienced limitations of horizontal

[155] European Commission: Directorate-General for Justice and Consumers, IPSOS, Tetra Tech, VVA, Hausemer, P. et al., Information gathering for assisting the European Commission in complying with its obligations under Article 40 ('reporting') of Regulation (EU) 2017/2394 on Consumer Protection Cooperation – Final report, 2024, https://data.europa.eu/doi/10.2838/569634.

[156] Josine Polak and Esther Versluis, 'The Virtues of Interdependence and Informality: An Analysis of the Role of Transnational Networks in the Implementation of EU Directives', in Sara Drake and Melanie Smith (eds), *New Directions in the Effective Enforcement of EU Law and Policy* (Cheltenham, Edward Elgar, 2016) 117.

[157] See Article 17(2)–(4) Regulation 2017/2394.

cross-border cooperation.[158] In a 'sweep' exercise, willing national authorities join forces in a concerted investigation, typically coordinated by the Commission.[159] While in some sweeps almost all national authorities are said to have been involved, in others, only half of the authorities have been active. The reformed model of cooperation in the CPC Network has recently been praised by commentators, who acknowledge, however, that 'there is a difference between the expected functioning of the network and its actual operation'.[160]

C. An Emerging Pattern of Lopsided Enforcement?

The developments described above can be seen as signs of a more general disenchantment with the decentralised model of enforcement, or, to put it more positively, maybe of arriving at a more sober and realistic idea of what could be expected from the horizontal dimension of enforcement cooperation. While ratcheting up national authorities' powers was advanced as a way of achieving coherence and equivalence between network entities, there is arguably a growing realisation that the diversity of national public authorities in terms of institutional set-up, resources, expertise and commitment is more enduring than initially thought. In addition, a renewed attention to the importance of independence and institutional integrity in the context of rule-of-law backsliding in some Member States has demonstrated that the expected convergence around a positive public authority model, is slow to emerge.[161] It can be conjured that this realisation leads to greater acceptance of institutional design of enforcement which allows for variable geometry of network engagement and leaning more openly on the capacity and resources of the Commission working jointly with groups of active and well-endowed national authorities.

The distinction between horizontal and vertical empowerment introduced at the outset suggests a binary logic, as do the notions of centralisation and decentralisation. Such representation appears, however, to be simplistic. At a closer look, the dynamics within the two networks reveals a more complex pattern of what could be called 'lopsided' enforcement cooperation. Empowerment is neither running exclusively vertically towards the Commission, nor is it neatly horizontally distributed across the participating public authorities. Rather, the network enforcement model leaves space for uneven engagement of Member State authorities. As a consequence, the authorities of certain Member States with greater capacity and resources tend to

[158] 'Sweeps' are defined as 'concerted investigations of consumer markets through simultaneous coordinated control actions to check compliance with, or to detect infringements of, Union laws that protect consumers' interests' (Article 3(16) Regulation 2017/2394). The evolution of this instrument supports theories of experimentalist governance, demonstrating that network governance can work as 'incubator' for innovatory regulatory techniques. See Sabel and Zeitlin, above note 40.

[159] See Article 29 Regulation 2017/2394. Unless otherwise agreed upon by the competent authorities involved, sweeps shall be coordinated by the Commission. The record of conducted sweeps reported on the Commission's website shows an average of two sweeps per year.

[160] Monti and De Streel, above note 4.

[161] Maciej Bernatt, 'Rule of Law Crisis, Judiciary and Competition Law' (2019) 46(4) *Legal Issues of European Integration* 345–62.

assume a more central role, either jointly, or together with the Commission, whereas others are involved less actively, or not at all.

IV. THE INSTITUTIONAL DESIGN OF THE NEW EU DIGITAL LAW: HAS WISDOM BEEN DRAWN FROM PAST EXPERIENCES?

If we return to the two main instruments in the Digital Services Package, a relevant question to ask is to what extent the accumulated experiences from the enforcement networks analysed above have informed and influenced the enforcement design of the new EU law of the digital economy. Although the enforcement architecture set out in the DMA and the DSA presents many fascinating aspects worth deeper analysis, here only three features will be highlighted.

A. Increased Centralisation

First, as stated already from the outset, the institutional design of enforcement of the new EU digital law is characterised by increased centralisation and vertical empowerment of the Commission. While this choice is motivated chiefly by the large-scale actors that are targeted by the new regulations, there is also considerable evidence from the two decades of network-based enforcement that a strong engagement on the part of the Commission is a necessary condition for the success of both centralised and decentralised enforcement. The empowerment of NCAs through the modernisation reform of EU competition law and Regulation 1/2003 did not diminish the role of the Commission, which has continued to exercise considerable authority and act as a guarantor for the stability and success of the ECN. The CPC Network, which was initially based on a model of horizontal cross-border cooperation between national authorities, according only a modest role to the Commission, showed disappointing results. With time, however, the Commission has assumed a more central position and its engagement has proven instrumental for mobilising national authorities and intensifying enforcement of EU consumer laws through coordinated investigations and enforcement actions. In this light, the step towards vesting own enforcement powers in the Commission under the DSA, although limited to VLOPs and VLSEs, constitutes a continuation of an already existing trend and appears as a logical and well thought through move.

B. Preserved Role for Decentralised Enforcement

Second, despite the visible tilt towards centralisation, the institutional design of the Digital Services Package preserves a role for national authorities and enforcement networks and this aligns with the wisdom that can be derived from two decades of enforcement cooperation within ECN and CPC Network. In the case of the DMA, the genetic connection with EU competition law and the many intertwining objectives of the two sets of rules makes the reliance on the ECN only natural and probably existential. Despite a massive shift back towards concentration of, in most respects exclusive, powers in the Commission, the DMA still seeks to involve NCAs by assigning to them a number of supporting tasks in the course of DMA investigations and enforcement by the Commission. The DMA also appears to have the ambition of using the synergies with EU competition law and the well-oiled infrastructure of the ECN.[162] This is certainly a wise choice, because the tightly knit community of competition law experts can be an invaluable ally to the Commission in the enforcement of the DMA. The many competition-law-and-policy 'savvies' affiliated to both public and private institutions have been eagerly engaged in the process of drafting of the DMA and in the initial phases of its interpretation, implementation and application. The effective enforcement of the DMA can clearly only gain from tapping into the knowledge and engagement of this community. This is visible in the records from the first meetings of the High-Level Group for the DMA, where the representatives of the ECN are enthusiastic participants.[163]

The reliance on a network model of enforcement is more extensive for the DSA. As mentioned at the outset, the Act assigns to the Commission a central role in monitoring compliance and enforcement of the DSA rules vis-à-vis large-scale online platforms and search engines, leaving, however, the enforcement of DSA obligations in respect of other actors largely to a decentralised network-based model of cross-border cooperation (Article 58 DSA). In this part, the challenges of putting in place an adequate institutional design for DSA enforcement cooperation show considerable kinship with those under the New CPC Regulation, raising the question whether there is something to learn from the experience of the CPC Network. This question is all the more relevant because the institutional landscape 'on the ground' in the Member States reveals similar diversity and plurality of national competent authorities as in the consumer protection domain. The scope of the DSA is, if possible, even broader and more disparate than that of the CPC Regulation. Digital services take an endless variety of shapes and guises and are regulated from a number of perspectives. The DSA thus represents a legislative instrument without a clear place in the legal and administrative system of the Member States. Correspondingly, as noted by one commentator, there 'were no pre-existing regulators in the area'.[164]

For Member States, the choice has, thus, been between assigning additional tasks to an already existing regulator, or setting up a new public authority focused exclusively on the enforcement of the DSA. Most Member States have followed the first route allocating the function of DSC to existing authorities, mainly telecommunications and media regulators, but also competition and consumer authorities. Many States have further opted for designating more than one competent authority in addition to their DSC. In this approach, the variety is even greater, including data protection, consumer and other sectoral authorities. Some commentators see this diversity as offering positive complementarity of expertise and perspectives.[165] However, in view

[162] Cf Article 37 and in particular, Article 38 DMA.
[163] See Minutes, Second meeting of the High-Level Group for the DMA, 27 November 2023, CNECT.F.1/GCCOMP.J.1/VR.
[164] Husovec, FIDE Digital Economy, General report, above note 14.
[165] ibid 50.

of the above-described experiences from the CPC Network, excessive diversity should rather be seen as a source of concern as it may indicate a difficulty for an epistemic community to emerge with coherent vision and commitment to effective enforcement.

Given these realities, it is probably not surprising that designating DSCs has proven to be no trivial matter for the Member States. One year after the DSA entered into force, ten Member States had still not designated their DSC and other competent authorities. In April 2025, the Commission filed infringement actions against five Member States for failing to designate national DSCs and fulfil their obligations under the DSA.[166] Rather than outright obstruction, this 'feet-dragging' may signal certain institutional fatigue at the national level. The constant influx of new legislation with at times intersecting and partly overlapping areas of application, presents a challenge for the internal systemic coherence of national law and public administration. While enforcement networks were once introduced as an institutional innovation to help coordinate the enforcement actions of national authorities across Member States, the abundance of regulatory instruments seems now to require efforts for ensuring coordination between different authorities within one single Member States.[167] The trend towards mega agencies, combining competences in several policy fields, originally spurred by budgetary considerations, appears increasingly as a rational way of cutting through the growing complexity of the evolving regulatory landscape.[168] Arrangements such as the Digital Regulation Cooperation Forum in the UK and the Digital Regulation Cooperation Platform in the Netherlands are other examples of innovative institutional design prompted by the same need.[169] To be sure, it is not easy to bridge the institutional diversity and to impose unitary solutions. Nevertheless, in the continued work on the implementation and enforcement of the DSA, finding ways of welding an expert community with sufficiently coherent views about the objectives and main principles of the DSA seems to be key to the successful enforcement of the Act. This should be the most important task and most valuable contribution of the European Board for Digital Services.

C. Towards Lopsided Enforcement?

Third, and finally, both the DMA and the DSA, appear to include, either consciously or subconsciously, features that move the institutional design toward what I labelled 'lopsided enforcement', that is, an enforcement model where national authorities that possess greater regulatory experience, resources and expertise are allowed to engage more actively and to be a driving force of enforcement in close collaboration

[166] See European Commission, Press release, 5 May 2025, Brussels, available at: https://ec.europa.eu/commission/presscorner/detail/en/ip_25_1081.

[167] See de Streel and Monti, above note 4.

[168] On the experience in the Netherlands see Annetje T Ottow, 'Erosion or Innovation? The Institutional Design of Competition Agencies – A Dutch Case Study (2014) 2(1) *Journal of Antitrust Enforcement* 25–43; see also Anna Piszcz, '(Too) Many Policies Under One Roof? About the Integration of Competition Law Enforcement and Sectoral Regulation Within One Authority' (2024) VIII(1) *Market and Competition Law Review* 33–62.

[169] See de Streel and Monti, above note 2.

with the Commission. In the case of the DMA, this pattern is exhibited partly in the possibility, pursuant to Article 38(7) DMA, for willing Member States to empower their national authorities to be active in the initiation of investigations under the DMA. On the one hand, this construction can be interpreted as a sign of necessary realism, accepting the fact that despite considerable efforts towards coherence of institutional structures and enforcement cultures, substantial divergences between Member States will continue to exist. As seen from the evaluations of the ECN reviewed above, the uneven engagement in the activity of the network has been an acknowledged and maybe inevitable element in the dynamic of network cooperation. Therefore, it may only be rational to allow, and even urge, stronger and better equipped national authorities to carry the brunt of complex and costly investigations against large players in the digital economy, and act as side-kicks to the Commission especially in its prime enforcement role. On the other hand, such a construction potentially opens the road to greater fragmentation and stratification between Member States and their authorities, abandoning the original vision of horizontal cooperation partnership between equals. More problematically, it arguably risks leaving market developments in more passive Member States under the radar of DMA enforcement.

For Member States' lawmakers the choice of whether to equip their competent authorities with new tasks of initiating investigations against gatekeepers under Article 38(7) DMA has probably been the most consequential decision in the process of national implementation of the DMA. The majority of Member States appears to have eventually opted for empowering their competition authorities to conduct investigations into possible non-compliance with obligations under Articles 5, 6 and 7 DMA on their territories.[170] Hungary has been the first country to take this step. Among the activist Member States unsurprisingly are the 'friends of an effective DMA' – Germany, France and the Netherlands. Italy and Denmark have also joined the group.[171] There are, however, Member States that have preferred not to make use of this prerogative, probably concerned about possible costs of such additional enforcement activity. In Sweden, a special investigator who had the task to propose changes in Swedish legislation with the view of implementing the DMA proposed to furnish the Swedish Competition Agency with powers under Article 38(7) DMA. The Agency itself has argued in favour of being entrusted with such powers. However, the government did not consider such changes necessary, inferring that the DMA represents a new regulatory approach and it would be advisable to first gain some experience from its application and then see whether there is a need of special investigatory powers into DMA infringements taking place on Swedish territory.[172] Other states that have taken a similar 'wait and see' approach are Croatia, Lithuania and Finland.[173] Even if the predominant part of the Member States has chosen to introduce this option in

[170] See Report from the Commission to the Council and the European Parliament, Annual report on Regulation (EU) 2022/1925, COM(2025) 166 final, Brussels, 25.4.2025.

[171] See Klimat- och näringslivsdepartementet, Nya bestämmelser i anslutning till konkurrensregelverket, Regeringskansliet, Promemoria, KN2023/03687, 18.08.2023, 41.

[172] Prop. 2023/24:154 Kompletterande bestämmelser till nya unionsregler på konkurrensområdet, 28.

[173] One may speculate whether such self-restraint may be intended to signal less zealous enforcement climate, and hence, more attractive business environment with respect of major digital operators.

their national legislation,[174] it can still be expected that only a small group of these authorities will have the time and capacity to actually employ these new powers.

An additional tilt towards lopsided enforcement can result as a – probably unintended - consequence from the design of the High-Level Group for the DMA. The group is to be composed following the principle of equal representation of the five participating networks and bodies, with each network having the right to nominate six representatives. This model may generate an internal dynamic in these networks of nominating representatives primarily from national authorities with demonstrated competence, high reputation and solid funding. This can, in turn, create additional incentives for some of the already active national authorities to intensify their rate of engagement in the enforcement of EU Digital Markets law.[175] Interestingly, at the fourth meeting of the High-Level Group for the DMA, the representative of the ECN informed on an evolving practice of Joint Investigation Teams, which are established through memoranda of understanding between the Commission and various NCAs.[176] At the same time, in such a model, a passive and disinterested national public enforcer can escape the pressure of being an active partner in the scheme of enforcement cooperation.

In the case of the DSA, a lopsided pattern of enforcement may be expected to ensue as a result of the diversity in institutional set-up and the disparity in resources and engagement between DSCs and other designated national authorities; a development familiar from the CPC Network. The institutional design of enforcement appears to anticipate and prepare for such dynamic. First, as indicated earlier, in respect of VLOPs and VLOSEs obligations other than those under Section 5 Chapter III DSA, competent national authorities retain the power to monitor compliance, initiate investigations and impose sanctions, provided that the Commission has not already launched an investigation of its own (Article 56(4) DSA). Although the prerogative of launching an investigation belongs to any DSC, it can be expected that some national authorities will more readily assume the leader role than others.

Furthermore, Article 60 DSA outlines the mechanism for an enforcement tool called 'joint investigations', or coordinated investigations, as it is named in the title of Section 2 of Chapter IV DSA. This mechanism resembles the coordinated actions under the CPC Regulation. Joint investigations are to be launched and led by the DSC

[174] See comments from a representative of the ECN in the High-Level Group, 'The ECN noted that the national competition authorities . . . are following DMA closely and many of them are now empowered to conduct investigations under the DMA on their own territory'. Minutes, Third Meeting High-Level Group for the DMA, 22 May 2024, CNECT.F.1/GC COMP.J.2/VR, Ref. Ares(2024)4864235 - 05/07/2024.

[175] For instance, the representatives for the CPC Network are currently: a high-level official from the Danish Consumer Ombudsman; the Director General of the General Directorate of Economic Inspections, Belgium; the Director General at the Ministry of Economic Development, Slovenia; the Director General of the French Directorate General for Competition Policy, Consumer Affairs and Fraud Control; and the Chair of the Irish Competition and Consumer Protection Commission. The representatives for the ECN are currently the Director General of the Austrian Federal Competition Authority; the Chairman of Netherlands Authority for Consumers and Markets; the Chairman of the Antimonopoly Office of the Slovak Republic; the President of the Spanish National Commission of Markets and Competition (CNMC); the Chairman of the Polish Office for the Protection of Competition and Consumers; and the Director General of the Danish Competition and Consumers Authority.

[176] Minutes, High-Level Group for the DMA, 4th Meeting, 7 March 2025, CNECT.F/DNB/AM COMP.J/MK/VR, Ref. Ares(2025)2877401 - 09/04/2025.

of establishment either on its own initiative or upon recommendation of the Board acting upon the request of at least three DSCs alleging infringement affecting recipients in their Member States. Also here, it could be anticipated that some DSCs will be more active than others.

To overcome possible reluctance and 'shirking' on the part of DSCs of establishment in less engaged Member States, the DSA envisages possibility to involve the Board and the Commission, through a procedure of so-called referrals. The purpose of this procedure appears to be foremost to sustain consistency (cf 'consistency mechanism'). However, the Regulation stops short of empowering the Commission to take over investigations and lead investigations when the case concerns ISPs of normal size and scale. This deferent approach is probably preferred in order not to overburden the Commission with investigations of smaller-scale operators. However, it does not seem to acknowledge and incorporate the lessons from years of experience of decentralised enforcement, notably the dysfunctionalities in the work of the CPC Network. National authorities under the DSA will inevitably show even greater diversity in subject matter, regulatory mandate, expertise and resources. Therefore, there is a risk of seriously skewed enforcement activity across Member States and respectively, of some Member State authorities fully defecting from their enforcement mandate. Without a hands-on Commission mandate to intervene, including through taking over an enforcement file, there is a risk for 'grey' and 'dark' zones of the Internal Market where ISPs can operate under the radar of EU digital services law enforcement.

To conclude, while enforcement of internal market law has oscillated between centralisation and decentralisation, more recent developments seem to raise the question whether we are not observing a trend toward a lopsided enforcement, where certain competent authorities emerge as activists and set the tone, whereas others are more of observers and passive beneficiaries of the cooperation between the activists and the Commission. This development seems to be in line with a dynamic of uneven engagement in the enforcement cooperation within the ECN and the CPC Network, identified in the preceding section. It is submitted that the effects of this enforcement trend have to be followed carefully in order to intercept early signals of possible negative fragmentation and corroding effects. It is, however, also possible that this enforcement a *pleusieur vitesses* might generate positive dynamics based on best practices and regulatory, or rather enforcement, competition.

Part V

New and Old Challenges to EU Market Law: Intellectual Property and Competition Law

14

Resale Price Maintenance: Antitrust Review of Vertical Agreements

LARS HENRIKSSON

I. INTRODUCTION

JUSTIFICATION FOR ANTITRUST ENFORCEMENT regarding vertical agreements remains a contentious issue – especially when a comparison is made between US antitrust law and EU competition law.

A controversial and straightforward statement by Easterbrook in 1984 heralded later US case law on antitrust in vertical agreements: '[n]o practice a manufacturer uses do distribute its products should be a subject of serious antitrust attention'.[1] Easterbrook held that vertical agreements almost never threaten competition. Likewise, Bork warned already in 1966 about being over-reliant on per se-rules and advocated for a rule of reason approach.[2] In fact, Bork went even further and argued for per se legality of *all* vertical agreements. In a fiery statement against formalistic application of the Sherman Act he argued that

> [m]uch of the Sherman Act's doctrinal chaos is attributable to judicial and scholarly fondness for impossibly broad statements of the *per se* rule. The warmth and security that sweeping, absolutist formulations offer is likely to prove here, as in other areas of the law, the forerunner of icy intellectual demise.[3]

These few examples illustrate undoubtedly, the US continued disbelief in per se-rules in antitrust for vertical agreement, which may appear to stand in stark contrast to the EU/EEA competition rules of old. Notwithstanding the Atlantic division, that old

[1] FH Easterbrook, 'Vertical Arrangements and the Rule of Reason' (1984) 53(1) *Antitrust Law Journal*, thirty-second annual spring meeting: Part II (21–23 March 1984), 135–73.

[2] RH Bork, 'The Rule of Reason and the Per Se Concept: Price Fixing and Market Division' (1966) 75(3) *The Yale Law Journal* 373–475. See also RH Bork, *The Antitrust Paradox: A Policy at War with Itself* (New York, Basic Books, 1978).

[3] Bork, 'The Rule of Reason', above note 2, 377.

stance in the EU law appears to linger on to date although a gradual shift in application of the old rules is noticeable.[4]

In this Article, the focus will be on the method under EU law to distinguish certain severe restrictions which by their very nature are deemed anti-competitive agreements from those that may generate restrictive effects *in casu*. There is no counterpart in EU law to the US rule of reason or per se-rules. Instead Article 101 TFEU outlines a different approach and methodology for assessment. All agreements between undertakings, decisions by associations of undertakings and concerted practices which may affect trade between Member States, and which have as their object or effect the prevention, restriction or distortion of competition within the internal market are prohibited, subject to the possibility for undertakings to justify such agreements under Article 101(3) TFEU. It follows from the wording of the legislation that restrictions can appear in the form of either having as their object *or* effect the restriction, distortion or prevention of competition. According to the CJEU, the difference between the two relates merely to appreciate the objective seriousness of the practice concerned. In characterising an agreement the focus will, consequently, be on how to determine the means of proving it. As such, EU competition law does not recognise an American rule of reason, by virtue of which there should be undertaken an integrated weighing of the pro- and anti-competitive effects of an agreement when it is to be characterised as a 'restriction of competition' under Article 101(1) TFEU.[5]

In European competition law, the procedures for justifying restrictive agreements under Article 101(3) TFEU has changed considerably over the years. Initially, the Commission was the sole competent body to issue individual exemptions for restrictive agreements alongside of which there was an extensive practice of issuing so-called 'negative clearances' for agreements. Such clearances essentially only eliminated the risk for administrative fines but did not entail a binding exemption and thereby making it possible for the Commission to revisit such restrictions at a later stage. The great number of applications for individual exemptions lead to the need to adopt 'block' exemption regulations, whereby groups of agreement of similar function and nature were exempted and provided a safe harbour from the far-reaching general prohibitions of restrictive agreements that by its definition also covers those agreements with pro-competitive effects.[6] Also, the major reform that followed the expansion of the EU in 2004, Regulation 1/2003[7] made inter alia Article 101(3) TFEU

[4] See DD Sokol, 'The Transformation of Vertical Restraints: Per Se Illegality, the Rule of Reason and Per Se Legality' (2014) 79(3) *Antitrust Law Journal* 1003–16.

[5] See case C-307/18, *Generics (UK) Ltd and Others v Competition and Markets Authority*, ECLI:EU:C:2020:52, para 104.

[6] In view of the large number of notifications submitted to the Commission it was considered desirable already in 1965 that, in order to facilitate the task of the Commission, it should be enabled to declare by way of regulation that the general prohibition does not apply to certain categories of agreements and concerted practices, see Regulation No 19/65/EEC of 2 March of the Council on application of Article 85 (3) of the Treaty to certain categories of agreements and concerted practices, OJ 36, 6/3/1965, pp 533–35, and Council Regulation (EC) No 1215/1999 of 10 June 1999 amending Regulation No 19/65/EEC on the application of Article 81(3) of the Treaty to certain categories of agreements and concerted practices, OJ L 148, 15/6/1999, pp 1–4.

[7] Council Regulation (EC) No 1/2003 of 16 December 2002 on the implementation of the rules on competition laid down in Articles 81 and 82 of the Treaty, OJ L 1, 4.1.2003, pp 1–25.

generally applicable so that undertakings could rely on that provision without notifying agreements to the Commission.

One of the EU block exemption regulations is the Vertical Block Exemption Regulation (VBER)[8] that covers agreements entered into between undertakings on different levels of the distribution chain, for example distribution agreements, agency agreements and so on. Although vertical agreements generally are considered pro-competitive, terms and conditions in, for example, a distribution agreement main contain obligations imposed upon the distributor that limits its possibilities to freely set its prices or how and where to sell or offset the products or services. These terms can vary in seriousness and depending on their impact on competition, they can either be excluded from the safe harbour of the VBER, or render the exemption non-applicable for the entire agreement (so-called 'hardcore' restrictions), necessitating a need to make an individual assessment under Article 101(3) TFEU.

II. RPMS IN EU COMPETITION LAW

A long-standing 'hardcore' restriction in EU competition law concerns vertical agreements that restrict the buyer's ability to determine its sale prices. Pursuant to Article 4 VBER, the imposition of minimum or fixed resale prices remains prohibited under the revised 2022 VBER, whereas the maximum and genuinely recommended prices are considered less restrictive and even unharmful. Typically, such measures emerge most commonly in distribution agreements where a producer sells through resellers, intermediaries or other agents whilst seeking to control downstream pricing or distribution, often aiming for maintaining a brand image of exclusivity, to prevent cannibalising amongst resellers, free-riding or simply just a tool to control distributors. Regardless of the possible motivations behind such contractual obligations they all are met with the same legal presumption; they are inherently harmful to competition. As such, they do not warrant the safe harbour of the block exemption and are even presumed detrimental in terms of economic efficiency.

A. The Design of Vertical Price Controls in the EU

RPMs can be achieved in several direct or indirect ways. The vertical guidelines list measures such as fixing resale margins, maximum levels of discounts, making rebates conditional on observance of price levels, minimum advertised prices (MAPs), linking prices across competitors, threats, warnings, sanctions and so on.[9] In law, the overall quandary is whether such practices can – or even should – be presumed to generate negative competitive effects. If so, it may motivate a presumption of

[8] Commission Regulation (EU) 2022/720 of 10 May 2022 on the application of Article 101(3) of the Treaty on the Functioning of the European Union to categories of vertical agreements and concerted practices, C/2022/3015, OJ L 134, 11.5.2022, pp 4–13 ('the VBER').

[9] See Commission Notice – Guidelines on vertical restraints 2022/C 248/01, C/2022/4238, OJ C 248, 30.6.2022, pp 1–85 ('the VBER Guidelines'), para 196.

illegality, with or without the possibility to confute the presumption. If not, a rule of reason approach would be better suited. In EU competition law, that would translate to plaintiffs or authorities needing to demonstrate a credible theory of competitive harm and actual or at least potential effects *in casu* according to the rules of burden and standards of proof.

Early EU case law and policy indicates an ostensibly strict approach to RPMs,[10] where this practice was viewed not only to have restrictive effects, but also amounted to restrictions of object of sorts, rendering assessment of market shares and actual effects redundant. From an enforcement perspective, it may appear compelling to lean against such a finding, which is also truly plaintiff friendly and easy to litigate. Classifying an agreement as anti-competitive by its very nature implies that it could never yield any pro-competitive effects – such severe restrictions always generate an impediment to competition and, by extension, economic efficiency. Dealing with such restrictions would significantly alleviate the investigation burden of the competition authorities and may in extreme cases reduce the inquiry to laying bare the mere existence of the said restriction. However, following the judgment in *Cartes Bancaires*,[11] the headroom for findings of restriction of object has been lowered considerably.

While the 2010 vertical guidelines were quite laconic on pro-competitive economic efficiencies resulting from RPMs, the 2022 version provides several tangible new examples of pro-competitive effects of RPMs. Further, it is now explicitly stated that although RPMs may not enjoy the safe harbour of the VBER, it may still be justified under Article 101(3) TFEU. At the outset, this reasonably implies that it becomes questionable to continue categorising RPMs as *hardcore* restrictions. Moreover, does this mean that the notion of 'hardcore' in law has been reduced to a procedural presumption rule subject to extensive rebuttal possibilities, or does this black-listed practice still go beyond procedure indicating a substantive anti-competitive character of such restrictions? Nonetheless, it is evident that – at some point – it is necessary to assess the effects of individual RPMs, viewed in the commercial and economic context where they are applied. The true differences between restrictions of object, severe restraints and hardcore restrictions are therefore both theoretically and practically important to clarify in law.

The need for further clarity is prompted by the ruling in *Super Bock*, where the Commission's revised or complemented view on efficiencies in relation to RPMs

[10] In Council Regulation 1215/1999, providing the legal foundation for the VBER, it is stated that 'severe anticompetitive vertical restraints like minimum and fixed resale prices and certain types of territorial protection should be excluded from the application of the regulation irrespective of the market share of the undertaking concerned', Council Regulation (EC) No 1215/1999 of 10 June 1999 amending Regulation No 19/65/EEC on the application of Article 81(3) of the Treaty to certain categories of agreements and concerted practices, OJ L 148, 15/06/1999 pp 1–4, at 9. See also eg case 243/83, *SA Binon & Cie v SA Agence et messageries de la presse*, ECLI:EU:C:1985:284, para 44, and particularly case 311/85, *ASBL Vereniging van Vlaamse Reisbureaus v ASBL Sociale Dienst van de Plaatselijke en Gewestelijke Overheidsdiensten*, ECLI:EU:C:1987:418, para 17. Further, a similar approach was applied in case C-27/87, *SPRL Louis Erauw-Jacquery v La Hesbignonne SC*, ECLI:EU:C:1988:183, para 15.

[11] Case C-67/13 P, *Groupement des cartes bancaires (CB) v European Commission*, ECLI:EU:C:2014:2204. The ECJ held that it is required to demonstrate a 'sufficient degree of harm to competition that it may be found that there is no need to examine their effects'. Otherwise, the Commission would not have to prove actual effects of an agreement which in no way is established – by its very nature – to be harmful to the proper functioning of normal competition (para 58).

appears to have been essentially affirmed in 2023 by the CJEU. The court held that a finding of restriction by object with regard to fixing minimum resale prices 'may only be made after having determined that that agreement presents a sufficient degree of harm to competition, taking into account the nature of its terms, the objectives that it seeks to attain and all of the factors that characterise the economic and legal context of which it forms part'.[12] Nevertheless, this could also be construed more narrowly as simply reiterating the court's view in *Cartes Bancaires*, which would leave the question of the need to uphold the presumption rule for RPMs unanswered – or at least the actual extent of the presumption.

In contrast to horizontal agreements, the case law on vertical agreements have been quite scarce – presumably because of the inherent difficulties of firmly establishing the anti-competitive effects of such agreements. Also, vertical agreements are in themselves less problematic than horizontal agreements; the vast majority of such agreements have as their primary object to bring product and services to the market – not to distort competition. In the context of, for example, distribution agreements, it may therefore at the outset prove difficult to demonstrate that they by their nature are capable of restricting, distorting or preventing competition. This does not rule out that vertical agreements – or terms therein – may generate such effects with the economic and legal context that they operate, and that those effects are not outweighed by efficiencies.

Compared with US antitrust law, the treatment of RPMs in EU both systems share a general concern at the outset against RPMs and minimum prices. With regard to the ruling in *Leegin*[13] there has been considerable development in the US that stands in contrast to the then nearly century-old *Dr. Miles Medical*,[14] which affirmed that vertical restraints should be assessed by rule of reason, as opposed to the earlier formalistic per se approach, much in line with what legal antitrust scholars had advocated for decades earlier. In can to some extent be argued that *Dr. Miles* had become obsolete long before *Leegin*, bearing in mind the court's approach gradually moved away for the per se-rules in vertical restraints.[15] Also, already the handling in US antitrust law of RPMs that followed from the *Colgate* doctrine that entailed the firm's right to freely choose its business partners made it compatible with Section 1 of the Sherman Act for a firm to unilaterally announce its minimum retail pricing policy, and thereafter legally simply refuse to sell to distributors who would not comply with that policy.[16] Although US antitrust case law may not have been entirely straightforward in light of these cases, it appears safe to conclude that after *Leegin*, the rule of reason has paved the way for a more nuanced approach towards RPMs and has had significant impact for stakeholders and undertakings in the US.[17]

[12] Case C-211/22, *Super Bock Bebidas*, ECLI:EU:C:2023:529, para 43.

[13] *Leegin Creative Leather Products, Inc v PSKS, Inc*, 551 US 877 (2007).

[14] *Dr. Miles Medical Co v John D. Park & Sons Co*, 220 US 373 (1911).

[15] *cf Standard Oil Co of New Jersey v United States*, 221 US 1 (1910), *United States v Colgate & Co*, 250 US 300 (1919), *Continental Television v GTE Sylvania*, 433 US 36 (1977), *State Oil Co v Khan*, 522 US 3 (1997) and *Verizon Communications v Law Offices of Curtis V. Trinko, LLP*, 540 US 398 (2004).

[16] cf *United States v Colgate & Co*, 250 US 300 (1919).

[17] For an overview and analysis of the market effects following Leegin, see GT Gundlach and RT Krotz, 'Resale Price Maintenance: Implications of Marketing Trends for the Colgate Doctrine and the Leegin Factors' (2020) 39(1) *Journal of Public Policy & Marketing* 48–61.

In EU/EEA, however, there still remains a legal uncertainty associated with the underlying theory of harm justifying enforcement or presumption rules, and what a presumption or restriction by object should actually cover. In Sweden, the Swedish Competition Authority, *Konkurrensverket* (KKV) has motivated investigations and given prioritisation to such cases merely because the competition may be restricted if resellers are prevented from 'freely setting their prices to end customers', echoing the legislative motivations of yesteryears without much of further qualification.[18] Paradoxically as it may seem, the KKV's assessment of the cases have still been aligned with the effects-based approach and in seemingly practice moving away from approached akin to per se treatment.[19]

There are indeed important differences between the notions of restriction of object, severe restraints, and hardcore restrictions within the meaning of EU/EEA competition law with regard to vertical agreements. Overly theoretical as it may seem, any differences between these concepts will still matter in litigation and is of utmost importance about the legislator's true view on the matter and corresponding legitimate expectations amongst undertakings in the market place. An excessively strict approach may generate type I errors (excessive enforcement), whereas, at the outset, the risk for type II errors (under-enforcement) seems to be of lesser concern. Nonetheless, a good balance between the two error types should always be adhered to.

B. RPMs in Vertical Agreements Under Assessment by the CJEU – *Super Bock*

The Commission has earlier had a strict view on RPMs in vertical agreements – even so far that it has been regarded as a restriction by object, resounding the older case law from the CJEU.[20] Pursuant to inter alia the rulings in *Allianz Hungária Biztosító*,[21] *Cartes Bancaires*,[22] *Maximima Latvija*[23] and *Budapest Bank*[24] it has become growingly uncertain whether RPMs merits such a categorisation.

> In *Super Bock*, the beverage company Super Bock Bebidas SA had for more than a decade on a regular basis fixed and imposed, universally and without change, on all distributors, the terms of business which they were required to comply with when reselling products that it had sold to them, which included maintenance of resale prices. The purpose of the

[18] Despite this concern, however, in cases KKV dnr 764/202 – *Tura Scandinavia AB*, and KKV dnr 156/2021 – *Carl Hansen & Søn Møbelfabrik A/S* the KKV did not find any evidence of an 'extensive price control procedure' viewed together with small sales volumes.

[19] See eg KKV dnr 559/2013 – *13:e Protein Import AB*, 2014-10-30, where the KKV employed an effects-based analysis that revealed – seeming based on the very low market shares – that the RPM was not harmful. Nb, as mentioned above regarding the structure of Article 101 TFEU, there is generally not per se findings of infringement in EU competition law.

[20] See the accompanying document to the De Minimis Notice, Commission Staff Working Document, Guidance on restrictions of competition 'by object' for the purpose of defining which agreements may benefit from the De Minimis Notice, SWD(2014) 198 final, 3/6/2015.

[21] Case C-32/11, *Allianz Hungária Biztosító Zrt. m.fl. mot Gazdasági Versenyhivatal*, ECLI:EU:C:2013:160.

[22] Case C-67/13, *Groupement des cartes bancaires (CB) v European Commission*, ECLI:EU:C:2014:1958.

[23] Case C-345/14, *SIA 'Maxima Latvija' v Konkurences padome*, ECLI:EU:C:2015:784.

[24] Case C-228/18, *Gazdasági Versenyhivatal v Budapest Bank Nyrt. and Others*, ECLI:EU:C:2020:265.

> practice was to ensure a stable and consistent minimum price level throughout national market. Minimum resale prices were transmitted to and were subsequently in general followed by distributors. The requirements imposed on resellers were upheld by a system of monitoring and tracking of prices including mandatory reporting to Super Bock. A practice of penalising measures was employed vis-à-vis distributors that did not comply with the minimum prices, such as removal of financial incentive, refusal to supply or replenish stock etc., making the distributors risk to lose positive margins on sales of the beverages. The Autoridade da Concorrência held this practice to constitute an infringement of Article 101 TFEU and its Portuguese national counterpart.[25]

The dispute in *Super Bock* essentially concerned the Portuguese competition authority's finding of unlawful anti-competitive agreement in the form of fixing of prices and other reselling terms, be it by direct and indirect means, for the concerned beverage distribution sector covering almost the entire Portuguese territory.

Now, it doesn't follow from *Super Bock* if, and if so how, the competition authority had assessed the possible justification of the anti-competitive agreement under Article 101(3) TFEU or its national counterpart. That must, however, have been ruled out – seemingly based upon the finding of the restrictive nature of the practice under scrutiny. Prior to the ruling in Super Bock, there also appear to have been some uncertainty if a hardcore restriction within the meaning of the VBER should be equated to a restriction by object under Article 101(1) TFEU.

C. The 'Hardcore' Restriction Under the VBER

RPMs are explicitly regulated in the Commission's VBER.[26] The so-called 'hardcore' restrictions are regulated in Article 4 VBER, which lists a number of restrictions that removes the benefit of the block exemption for the entirety of the agreement. In Article 4(1) regulates severe restriction that concerns vertical agreements which, directly or indirectly, in isolation or in combination with other factors under the control of the parties, have *as their object* to restrict of the buyer's *ability to determine its sale price*. The key focus is whether the seller is directly or indirectly imposing an obligation upon the buyer to adhere to a minimum or fixed price level. The imposition of a maximum price sale price or the provision of a recommended price is not considered to be restrictive, as long as such contract terms do not in practice amount to a fixed or minimum sale price as a result of pressure from, or incentives offered by, any of the parties. The anti-competitive concerns of RPMs are therefore the minimum and fixed prices in vertical agreements.

The legal uncertainty has primarily related to what effects will follow from categorising an agreement – or elements thereof – as a hardcore restriction. Also, there appears to exist some doubts relating to the true meaning of a hardcore restriction.

[25] Case C-211/22, *Super Bock Bebidas*, ECLI:EU:C:2023:529, paras 13–14.

[26] Commission Regulation (EU) 2022/720 of 10 May 2022 on the application of Article 101(3) of the Treaty on the Functioning of the European Union to categories of vertical agreements and concerted practices, C/2022/3015, OJ L 134, 11.5.2022, pp 4–13.

Absent provisions in law, it is for the courts to rule on the effects of categorising a restriction in vertical agreements as 'hardcore'. It can be interpreted in several ways.

i. A Narrow Approach Concerned with the Applicability of the VBER

First, and in a more limited sense, a narrow interpretation of hardcore restrictions can be viewed to relate just to whether the BER is applicable to the agreement alone. A finding of a hardcore restriction then relates to whether the agreement should enjoy the safe harbour of the BER. Moreover, it can be viewed as a distinction from the excluded restrictions enshrined in Article 5 VBER, which exclude the VBER for certain specific restrictive obligations whilst the BER remains valid for the remainder of the agreement. By contrast, the existence of hardcore restrictions renders the block exemption inapplicable to the agreement in its entirety. Still, it does not say anything about whether the agreement would be incapable of being exempted under Article 101(3) TFEU despite it does not qualify for a group exemption. At the outset, this appears the most logical consequence bearing in mind that VBER does not apply to certain vertical agreements between competitors as defined in Article 2(4) VBER and those situations when seller and buyer's market share thresholds are exceeded as outline in Article 3 VBER. In those situations there is no knock-on effect on the subsequent assessment under Article 101(3) TFEU.

ii. Presumption of Illegality of Hardcore Restrictions Based Upon Its Effects

Second, a wider interpretation of hardcore restrictions could be that not only does it exclude the application of the VBER to the agreement in question, but it also creates a presumption of the agreement being unqualified for an exemption under Article 101(3) TFEU. Although the purpose of VBER is to exempt restrictive agreements from the general prohibition in Article 101(1) TFEU, the exemption is based upon the ubiquitous net pro-competitive effects of vertical agreements, whereas some restrictions would still be harmful to consumers because the restrictions are too severe or serious. Also, the VBER explicitly states that the regulation should not exempt restrictions for which it cannot be assumed with sufficient certainty that they satisfy the conditions of Article 101(3) of the Treaty (paragraph 16). That would, however, impose a double evidentiary burden on the undertakings concerned as they need to only justify the applicability of Article 101(3) TFEU, but also then that the criteria therein are met. From a procedural point of view, this would, nonetheless, be undesirable. Despite it may in practice be difficult to justify the restriction under an individual assessment, there is no support in law for a negative presumption that needs to be rebutted. Formally, therefore, it is an altogether other matter that it may in practice prove difficult to meet the criteria under Article 101(3) TFEU.

iii. Equating 'Hardcore' Restrictions with Restriction 'By Object'

Third, a stricter view of hardcore restrictions entailing a wide and extensive interpretation would be that they are equated to restrictions of object, whereby they by their very nature are to be regarded as anti-competitive and that it would be superfluous to assess the agreement under Article 101(3) TFEU or even appraising any anti-competitive effects. The mere existence of a certain type of restriction could therefore be regarded so detrimental to competition and ultimately to consumers that regardless of legal and economic context, relevant market, market size or turnover the restriction is so malignant that there is no acceptable justification whatsoever for its existence. If so, this would considerably alleviate the competition authority's evidentiary burden, and the assessment may be reduced to a simple finding of the existence of the restriction in question. From a legal certainty point of view this calls at the very least for firm and reliable based upon extensive experience and undisputable economic theory of harm that the restriction can safely be qualified as such.[27]

D. The Commission's Current (?) Approach to RPMs

The Commission appears to have favoured the third and wide interpretation. As late as 2022, the Commission held that

> [s]ince resale price maintenance ('RPM') is a hardcore restriction . . . , *and a restriction by object* under Article 101(1) of the Treaty, the agency relationship should not be misused by suppliers to circumvent the application of Article 101(1) of the Treaty.[28]

Strangely, authority for that finding is not found in case law, but only in the Commission's own staff working paper.[29] Confusing as it may seem, the Commission also notes that hardcore restrictions not necessarily [sic!] fall within the scope of Article 101(1) of the Treaty and that undertakings may indeed demonstrate pro-competitive effects under Article 101(3) TFEU in an individual case.[30] That would essentially mean that RPMs *not* by its very nature can be regarded as anti-competitive, but following an individual assessment they could be either or. Such a statement instead appears to bear all the hallmarks of an effects-based approach rendering it unnecessarily unclear how RPMs should be categorised in law. After all, an agreement cannot reasonably be simultaneously regarded as restriction by object and effect. The alternative nature of the legal requirement in Article 101(1) TFEU – as indicated by the conjunction 'or' – follows from established case law and implies a two-step approach where it is first necessary to consider the object of the agreement. If it cannot be established a restriction by object, an effects-based analysis should follow.[31] From a due procedure

[27] To this effect, cf AG Wahl opinion in case C-67/13, *Groupement des cartes bancaires (CB) v European Commission*, ECLI:EU:C:2014:1958, paras 55–56.

[28] Guidelines, above note 9, para 45 (emphasis added).

[29] See ibid para 179, and Commission Staff Working Document, Guidance on restrictions of competition 'by object' for the purpose of defining which agreements may benefit from the De Minimis Notice, 25 June 2014, SWD(2014) 198 final, p 4.

[30] Guidelines, above note 9, paras 181–82.

[31] See case C-345/14, *SIA 'Maxima Latvija' v Konkurences padome*, ECLI:EU:C:2015:784, para 16, case 56/65, *Société Technique Minière (LTM) v Maschinenbau Ulm GmbH (MBU)*, ECLI:EU:C:1966:17, case C-306/20, *SIA 'Visma Enterprise' v Konkurences padome*, ECLI:EU:C:2021:935, paras 55–56, case C-228/18, *Gazdasági Versenyhivatal v Budapest Bank Nyrt. and Others*, ECLI:EU:C:2020:265, para 33 and case C-373/14 P, *Toshiba Corporation v European Commission*, ECLI:EU:C:2016:26, para 24. See also case C-439/09, *Pierre Fabre Dermo-Cosmétique SAS v Président de l'Autorité de la concurrence och Ministre de l'Économie, de l'Industrie et de l'Emploi*, ECLI:EU:C:2011:649, para 34, and case C-32/11, *Allianz Hungária Biztosító Zrt. m.fl. mot Gazdasági Versenyhivatal*, ECLI:EU:C:2013:160, para 33.

point of view, it is therefore of utmost importance to distinguish between such type of restrictions.

A finding of restriction by object does considerably alleviates the competition authority evidentiary and investigation burden because it entails that it is not necessary to examine its effects on competition. Absent a restriction by object, the consequences of the agreement must be considered and the CJEU has held that it is necessary to find that those factors are present which show that competition has in fact been prevented, restricted or distorted to an appreciable extent for it to be caught by the prohibition.[32]

E. The CJEU's Ruling Hardcore Restrictions V Restrictions by Object

The main question in *Super Bock* related to whether the concept of 'restriction of object' is capable of covering – and, if so, under what conditions – a vertical agreement fixing minimum resale prices. Specifically, in the request for a preliminary ruling, the Tribunal da Relação de Lisboa sought clarification on several legal concepts of relevance to the case at hand. Apart from clarification of the concepts of agreement and effect on trade between Member States, the Portuguese court asked, in essence, whether Article 101(1) TFEU must be interpreted as meaning that the finding that a vertical agreement fixing minimum resale prices constitutes a 'restriction of competition by object' may be made without first examining whether that agreement raises a sufficient level of harm to competition or whether it may be presumed that such an agreement, of itself, presents such a degree of harm.

i. The Starting Point for Restrictions by Object: To be Applied Restrictively

Bearing in mind that there is no need to consider the effects of a restriction where its anti-competitive object is established, it is essentially from a legal certainty point of view to carefully distinguish such practices from those whose effects must be assessed to be considered harmful to competition. In this regard, the CJEU has consistently held that the concept of 'restriction by object' must be interpreted restrictively. It should be limited to certain types of coordination between undertakings that reveal a sufficient degree of harm to competition rendering it superfluous to examine their effects.[33]

Vertical agreements are generally pro-competitive because their prime objective is most often to put goods or services on the market. As such, they are therefore at the outset considerably less problematic than horizontal agreements which are entered into between competitors that are active on the same level of the distribution chain.

[32] See joined cases C-501/06 P, C-513/06 P, C-616/06 P and C-519/06 P, *GlaxoSmithKline Services and Others v Commission and Others*, ECLI:EU:C:2009:610, para 55. See also case C-8/08, *T-Mobile Netherlands BV, KPN Mobile NV, Orange Nederland NV and Vodafone Libertel NV v Raad van bestuur van de Nederlandse Mededingingsautoriteit*, ECLI:EU:C:2009:343, paras 28, 30.

[33] Case C-211/22, *Super Bock Bebidas*, ECLI:EU:C:2023:529, para 32, case C-345/14, *SIA 'Maxima Latvija' v Konkurences padome*, ECLI:EU:C:2015:784, para 18, and case C-306/20, *SIA 'Visma Enterprise' v Konkurences padome*, ECLI:EU:C:2021:935, para 60.

The CJEU has consequently underlined that vertical agreements *by their nature* are often less damaging to competition than horizontal agreement. Regardless thereof, the CJEU also acknowledges that in some cases they may still have 'particularly significant restrictive potential'.[34] In line with this general remark, the court has emphasised that it does not rule out the possibility that also vertical agreements can amount to a restriction by object. The legal criterion to be applied for horizontal and vertical agreements alike is whether the agreement in itself presents a sufficient degree of harm to competition, and it is for the national court to ascertain this *in casu*.[35]

ii. *The Criteria for Establishing Restriction by Object: No Major Novelties*

It could be argued that the preliminary ruling in *Super Bock* is not particularly helpful and merely reiterating existing case law on the matter of restriction by object. Horizontal and vertical agreements are, however, different in nature and most often do they pursue different main objectives. They will inescapably entail different market effects that may restrictive, distort or prevent competition in different ways. Although there is a clear interest for the court not to create unwarranted safe harbours that can be exploited by creative contracting by undertakings in order to escape the general prohibition in Article 101 TFEU, the different natures of agreements should in itself should merit a better analysis toolbox. So far, the CJEU has been reluctant to elaborate on *how* to more specifically establish the decisive criterion on 'sufficient degree of harm'.

Some guidance is, however, still provided by the court: Pursuant to the ruling in *Allianz Hungária Biztosító*, the court indicates that regard must be had to

(1) the content of its provisions;

(2) its objectives and the economic and the legal context of which it forms a part, with due regard to the nature of the goods or services affected; as well as

(3) the actual conditions of the functioning and structure of the market or markets in question.[36]

This comprehensive approach also eliminates a possible circular reasoning. If the contract stipulate adherence to a minimum price level, it is evident that the object of that contract clause is to establish a minimum price that is adhered to by the distributor. This contractual object is not the same as a restriction by object. In other words, just because the contract fixes a price the question of whether the fixed or minimum price is restriction of competition cannot be answered without appraising this in its proper context. Therefore although the object of a contractual terms may restrict price setting it is not automatically a restriction by object.

[34] Case C-211/22, *Super Bock Bebidas*, ECLI:EU:C:2023:529, para 33.

[35] Case C-211/22, *Super Bock Bebidas*, ECLI:EU:C:2023:529, para 34, case C-67/13, *Groupement des cartes bancaires (CB) v European Commission*, ECLI:EU:C:2014:1958, para 57 and case C-306/20, *SIA 'Visma Enterprise' v Konkurences padome*, ECLI:EU:C:2021:935, para 59.

[36] Case C-211/22, *Super Bock Bebidas*, ECLI:EU:C:2023:529, para 35, case C-32/11, *Allianz Hungária Biztosító Zrt. m.fl. mot Gazdasági Versenyhivatal*, ECLI:EU:C:2013:160, para 36.

iii. De-categorising a 'By Object' Restrictions to 'By Effect' Restrictions

The court has also underlined that where the parties to the agreement rely on its pro-competitive effects, those effects *must*, as elements of the context of that agreement, be taken into account. However, the court raises the bar considerably for such an assessment: it requires that such effects are demonstrated, deemed relevant, and intrinsic to the agreement concerned, and sufficiently significant. If so, those effects *may* [sic!] give rise to reasonable doubt as to whether the agreement concerned caused a sufficient degree of harm to competition.[37]

From an enforcement perspective, it still appears to be little guidance on the matter of how to distinguish the 'object' from 'effect'. Again, from a legal certainty point of view, this remains unsatisfactory considering both the potential draconic consequences of such a finding, and the fact that the CJEU appears to place a considerable heavy burden on the undertakings to be able to rebut a finding of restriction of object. If successful, that would still only lead to that the enforcement agency would have to carry out an effects-based analysis. It is most unclear why it is justified to not only to have a general unclear rule to place an agreement in the 'object box', whilst requiring quite specific and comprehensive evidence to get out of it.

The rebuttal possibility also appears to get entangled or confused with the efficiency and pro-competitive arguments that are to be carried out under Article 101(3) TFEU. If the undertaking would be successful in raising doubts against a finding of restriction by object – where does it leave the parties in terms of litigation? If it merely ends up in effects-based analysis, it appears to be a disproportionate burden for the undertaking just to accomplish a proper analysis by the authority. If it is tantamount to an argumentation for individual exemption it would seriously shift the balance between the authority and the defendant that may not be compatible with the division of burden of proof laid down in Regulation 1/2003. Naturally, on the one hand, it cannot reasonably be sufficient for the undertakings to make unsubstantiated claims for efficiencies to de-categorise the agreement as a 'by object' restriction. Still, on the other hand, the now seriously high standard of proof appears disproportionate.

iv. Equating 'Hardcore' Restrictions With 'By Object' Restrictions?

Returning to the question of whether a hardcore restriction could or even should be regarded as tantamount to a restriction by object. The CJEU appears not to rule out the possibility, although the court has settled on a requirement that the existence of a hardcore restriction must be taken into account upon making the overall assessment on sufficient degree of harm to competition. It is therefore one – albeit important – element of the legal context of the appraisal, however *not* a sole decisive one: it does not exempt the court or the enforcement authority to carry out the assessment on sufficient degree of harm to competition.[38]

[37] Case C-211/22, *Super Bock Bebidas*, ECLI:EU:C:2023:529, para 36, and case C-307/18, *Generics (UK) Ltd and Others v Competition and Markets Authority*, ECLI:EU:C:2020:52, paras 103, 105 and 107.

[38] Case C-211/22, *Super Bock Bebidas*, ECLI:EU:C:2023:529, paras 38–39.

The CJEU clarifies that the *sole* purpose of Article 4 of the VBER is to exclude certain vertical restrictions from the scope of a block exemption.[39] The hardcore restrictions listed in the VBER does not indicate that such restrictions must be categorised as either restriction 'by object' or 'by effect'. Hardcore restrictions and restrictions by object are not conceptually interchangeable and do not necessarily overlap. Whether a hardcore restriction amounts to a restriction by object must therefore be appraised on a case-by-case basis. In that regard it is not sufficient to base a finding of restriction by object on a hypothesis thereof – the assessment laid down by the CJEU must still made in full.[40] Therefore the legal consequence of the existence of a hardcore restriction appear to entail a more narrow interpretation as indicated above.

It is remarkable that the Commission seems to have deviated from the long-standing opinion on the status of hardcore restrictions and restrictions by object. The Commission itself conceded that they are not interchangeable a do not necessarily overlap – a fact that the CJEU acknowledged, as mentioned above. This does, however, stand in contrast to the existing guidance documents and this (new?) stance has so far regrettably not trickled down to be clarified in the guidance papers. Even before the ruling in *Super Bock*, Jones et al cautioned against an overreliance of hardcore restrictions to be equated as restrictions by object. They also questioned the Commission's earlier stance not only as a matter of law because a list of object restraints cannot be codified, and it appeared insupportable to dissuade undertakings from the making efficiency claims under Article 101(3) TFEU by creating a rule akin to the American *per se*-rules.[41]

It therefore follows from *Super Bock* that the existence of a hardcore restriction *does not automatically* lead to a finding of a restriction by object. The legal criterion has therefore not changed in substance. A finding of restriction by object should still be done restrictively and be reserved to severe cases. That being said, hardcore restrictions remain problematic to the proper function of competition as defined in EU law. The existence thereof is an important, perhaps even the most important, but still not the sole decisive, element of the assessment leading up to a finding of an anti-competitive agreement.

III. RPMS IN SWEDISH COMPETITION LAW

In the Swedish case *Tapwell*, the ruling in *Super Bock* has recently led to the first major decision on fines associated with RPMs. In light of the CJEU's latest ruling it is notable that the KKV still relies on the findings of old that certain RPMs were equated to restrictions by object. The case is currently under appeal and not finally decided yet. Still, it illustrates well the difficulties of how to more precisely handle

[39] Case C-211/22, *Super Bock Bebidas*, ECLI:EU:C:2023:529, para 40. See also Article 4(a)VBER, recital 15. Similar considerations applied for Article 4(a) of Regulation No 2790/1999, recital 10, and Article 4(a) of Regulation No 330/2010.

[40] Case C-211/22, *Super Bock Bebidas*, ECLI:EU:C:2023:529, paras 41–42.

[41] A Jones, B Sufrin and N Dunne, *Jones & Sufrin's EU Competition Law*, 8th edn (Oxford, Oxford University Press, 2023) 263.

severe restrictions under Article 101 TFEU and the problems associated with classifying hardcore restrictions as 'by object' restrictions or whether such restrictions are better appraised under the effects-based approach.

Following a dawn raid, the manufacturer of inter alia kitchen and bathroom mixers (faucets) Tapwell was fined 16.900.000 SEK (≈ €1.450.000). It is the first decision where the newly established *Super Bock*-doctrine was applied in Sweden for RPMs vis-à-vis Tapwell's resellers and distributors.[42] By contrast, the NCA decided earlier to close an investigation in the *Protein* case based upon what appeared to be a finding that a RPM-scheme was *in substance* incapable of harming competition bearing in mind the low market shares whilst opening up for a effects-based reasoning years before the revised view of RPMs by the Commission.[43]

The case is considerably comprehensive, and the key finding of infringement relates to the undisputed fact that Tapwell employed a pricing strategy for the distribution of its products that entailed the setting of minimum or fixed prices by Tapwell against its resellers. Those pricing terms were also generally accepted by the distributors. Although confidential, Tapwell asserted that it held a quite modest market share on the relevant market, even lower than the five per cent threshold for de minimis agreements for horizontal agreement and thereby definitively lower than the 15 per cent threshold for vertical agreements.[44] Neither the Competition authority, nor Tapwell could provide any certain facts to objectively establish the true market share for Tapwell. Nonetheless, and disputed by Tapwell, the KKV held that although the market shares were low, but growing, they still surpassed the threshold for the NAAT-test in relation to Article 101 TFEU and the national Swedish criterion of appreciability (Sw. *märkbarhetskriteriet*).[45]

The KKV's assessment of the restriction essentially concerned Tapwell's pricing primarily towards two of its major customers and, by extension, also Tapwell's general pricing strategy that in substance was aimed at maintaining resell prices at a minimum level. If that is ultimately held true by the courts, it would constitute a hardcore restriction under Article 4(a) VBER. The KKV found, however, that this also amounted to a restriction by object. It follows from *Super Bock* that such restrictions may indeed exist in vertical agreements in general and for hardcore restrictions in particular, although there is not per se prohibition. It is therefore of specific interest *how* the KKV arrived at its conclusion in *Tapwell.*

The competition authority heeded off its analysis by referring to the established fact that restrictions of competition do not need to entail actual effects. Referring to *T-Mobile*, the KKV held that in order for an agreement to be regarded as having an anti-competitive object, it is *sufficient* that it has the *potential* (Sw. *är ägnat*) to have a negative impact on competition. This finding is entirely in line with older

[42] Case KKV dnr 122/2021, *Tapwell AB – VVS-produkter*, currently under appeal to the Patent and Market Court.

[43] KKV dnr 559/2013 – *13:e Protein Import AB*, 2014-10-30.

[44] Cf Notice on agreements of minor importance which do not appreciably restrict competition under Article 101(1) of the Treaty on the Functioning of the European Union (De Minimis Notice), OJ C 291/01, 30/8/2014, pp 1–4.

[45] Cf Commission Notice – Guidelines on the effect on trade concept contained in Articles 81 and 82 of the Treaty, OJ C 101, 27/04/2004, pp 81–96.

EU case law, whereby the agreement under scrutiny must simply be *capable* in an individual case, having regard to the specific legal and economic context, of resulting in the prevention, restriction or distortion of competition within the common market.[46]

A. The Assessment of the Restrictive Agreement's Potential

The question is then what such a 'potential' entails. Before attributing to much weight to this concept, it is important to recollect that the wording of *T-Mobile* been superseded by later case law on how more precisely to establish a restriction by object. The relevant criterion to apply is nowadays therefore not a simple assessment of an agreement's potential, but – as outlined in *Super Bock* – whether the agreement in itself presents a sufficient degree of harm to competition. Arguably, this is a higher threshold for the authority to meet than a mere finding of potential, which is also confirmed by the requirement of that restrictions by object should be applied restrictively.

As already stated above, there are several elements to consider that jointly would build up and support a finding of restriction by object. Notably, however, the KKV's assessment does not appear to follow the established procedure by the CJEU. Instead of assessing the legal and economic context to support the nature of the restriction, the KKV appear to have favoured a method that did not incorporate all the elements on test required procedure, especially not analysing the restriction as such within its economic and legal context. The latter would instead be relevant for rebuttal of the presumption illegality that would follow from the restriction's intrinsic potential of harm to competition.

With reference to current EU case law, the competition authority held that although the fact that the effects of the agreement should not be taken into account, there may under certain conditions, within the legal and economic context, be reasons to consider pro-competitive effects, but the undertaking claiming such effects have the burden of proving the existence of such effects.[47] This is in itself a correct interpretation, but it pre-supposes that the authority has, with regard to the standards or proof whilst adhering the method prescribed by the CJEU, firmly arrived at the conclusion that the restriction is anti-competitive by object. In establishing a restriction by object it is still possible for the undertakings concerned to rely on pro-competitive effects and it is also mandatory to take such assertions into considerations, subject to the standards laid down in *Super Bock*. It is, however, not a rebuttal of finding of an anti-competitive restriction, but an integral part of the assessment leading up to such a finding. Markedly, the assessment of pro-competitive effects is here akin to, but not the same as, the positive effects that may be asserted under Article 101(3) TFEU.

[46] See case C-8/08, *T-Mobile Netherlands BV, KPN Mobile NV, Orange Nederland NV and Vodafone Libertel NV v Raad van bestuur van de Nederlandse Mededingingsautoriteit*, ECLI:EU:C:2009:343, para 31.

[47] See case C-307/18, *Generics (UK) Ltd and Others v Competition and Markets Authority*, ECLI:EU:C:2020:52, para 105, case C-211/22, *Super Bock Bebidas*, ECLI:EU:C:2023:529, para 36, and particularly case C-591/16, *P.H. Lundbeck A/S and Lundbeck Ltd v European Commission*, ECLI:EU:C:2021:243, para 137.

Considering such effects is aimed at distinguishing 'by object' restrictions from 'by effect' restrictions. As such, the purpose of assessing pro-competitive effects is, consequently, dissimilar in this early stage of the appraisal.

Next, the KKV underlined correctly that the appraisal of restrictive agreements does not entail a rule of reason by virtue of which there should be undertaken a weighing of the pro- and anti-competitive effects of an agreement when it is to be characterised as a 'restriction of competition' under Article 101(1) TFEU. Although that statement is for certain established and true, it is nonetheless unclear what relevance it carries for the assessment at hand. There are indeed differences between the structures of Article 101 TFEU and the US Sherman Act and in the assessment of categorising severity of restrictions, the CJEU held that considering pro-competitive effects 'is intended not to undermine characterisation as a "restriction of competition" within the meaning of Article 101(1) TFEU, but merely to appreciate the objective seriousness of the practice concerned and, consequently, to determine the means of proving it'.[48] Therefore, it says very little about how to establish a 'by object' restriction in the case at hand.

B. The Stepwise Approach in Tapwell

The KKV then went to analyse the restriction in question. Instead of the assessment prescribed in *Super Bock*, the KKV advocated for a *stepwise approach*, whereby the first step would be to isolated analysis of the content and objective of the agreement. However, the test laid down by the CJEU does not support this procedure but rather an integrated and comprehensive overall assessment of which the content and objective of the agreement is one part, but not the sole decisive one.

Both Article 101(1) TFEU and Chapter 2, section 1 of the Swedish Competition Act list a number of examples of agreements that are caught by the prohibition. However, the KKV then explicitly underlined that such agreements are typically restrictions by object, seemingly even viewed isolated. There is no authority presented for this conclusion and the decision offers no arguments in favour thereof. This finding of the KKV lacks proper legal support and deviates considerably from the ruling in *Super Bock*.

i. *The Prima Facie Findings of Restriction 'By Object'*

For the sake of argumentation – let us assume that the purpose of the contracts terms employed by Tapwell were to impose an obligation upon the distributors to adhere to a minimum price level and that this obligation – forming part of the wider distributorship agreement – is caught by Article 4(a) as a hardcore restriction. Does this automatically lead to a finding of restriction by object? Pursuant to the ruling in

[48] Cf case C-307/18, *Generics (UK) Ltd and Others v Competition and Markets Authority*, ECLI:EU:C:2020:52, para 104.

Super Bock the answer must be in the negative. The KKV is, however and contrary thereto, still of the opinion that

> the agreements, which involve vertical price control, fall into the category of agreements whose harmful effects, based on previous experience, are widely recognised and easily identifiable. . . . The agreements are therefore of such a nature that they are, prima facie, likely to restrict competition, i.e., they constitute a practice with the object of restricting competition.[49]

Although in part redacted in the decision on grounds of business secrets, the argument may still have reinforced by the supplementary objective for Tapwell to increase its profits, as well as the fact that the distributors did not object to the obligation with the view to uphold their margins. However, whether the purpose of making profit is at all an antitrust concern seems doubtful and also not something that the KKV held against Tapwell as such. After all, all private undertakings must reasonably be presumed to engage in market activities for the pursuit of profits whilst performing economic activity within the meaning of EU competition law. What then remains is the isolated objective to maintain the reseller's prices at a minimum level, that is, a standard hardcore restriction.

All in all, the KKV appears to rely solely on the *prima facie finding* of the existence of an RPM, which ostensibly has been regarded as a 'by object' restriction.

ii. The Relevance of the Economic and Legal Context

However, the KKV then carries out the *next step* in its analysis for establishing the existence of a 'by object' restriction. Not as an integral part of the overall assessment of the nature of restrictiveness, but as a step design to explore whether the economic legal context can rebut the prima facie finding of restrictiveness. In the view of the KKV, it is widely recognised that RPMs have harmful effects on competition.

The KKV maintains that such agreements have, in *earlier* case law of the CJEU, been found to be harmful to competition by their very nature. KKV also refers to the list of examples enshrined in Chapter 2, Section 1 of the Swedish Competition Act and Article 101 TFEU and seems to favour the interpretation that those are restrictions by object. Furthermore, the KKV correctly asserts that RPMs are generally regarded as hardcore restrictions of competition. Finally, and perhaps more unclear, the KKV avows without any further qualification that agreements which directly or indirectly establish a minimum sale price fall into the category of practices where there is substantial experience of their restrictive effects on competition.[50]

iii. The Pro-competitive Effects of RPMs and its Significance

Notably, the authority does not mention the fact that in the Commission's Guidelines for assessing hardcore restrictions there are also a number of potential pro-competitive

[49] KKV decision in *Tapwell*, paras 504–05.
[50] KKV decision in *Tapwell*, paras 514.

effects of RPMs. It is correct that the RPMs generally have restrictive effects on competitions, which is also why they are categorised as hardcore restrictions.[51] This general tough stance against RPMs is generally in line with economic theory.[52] Nonetheless, the Commission has underlined that RPMs in individual cases may also lead to efficiencies, in particular where it is supplier driven. In the context of exemption under Article 101(3) TFEU, undertakings may therefore rely on an efficiency defence for RPM, although pursuant to the burden of proof, they must be able to substantiate this with concrete evidence and show that all the conditions of Article 101(3) are fulfilled in the individual case. There mere fact RPM may more often lead to restrictions justifies its classification as a hardcore restriction, but it cannot be held that such agreements by their very nature always generate negative effect on competition. This fact alone illustrates why the CJEU does not equate hardcore restrictions with restrictions by object.

The Commission lists four examples in the Guidelines that could justify even minimum, or fixed prices This could therefore be justified in a context when a new product is introduced on the market, to co-ordinate short-term low-price campaigns, to prevent a reseller from using a product as a loss leader damaging the brand name. Also in contexts of complex products, RPMs may allow retailer to provide additional pre-sales services and to prevent free-riding. In cases of low market power these considerations are particularly relevant.[53]

iv. The Reliance on 'By Object' Restrictions Instead of Effects-based Analysis

The logic behind categorising an agreement as a 'by object'-restriction is that there is no need to assess the effects of the agreement on competition. Since such agreements are by their very nature incapable of generating pro-competitive effects and it can be presumed that they would never satisfy the criteria for individual exemption under Article 101(3) TFEU. Notwithstanding, Article 101 TFEU does not prevent undertakings from arguing efficiency defences under Article 101(3) TFEU, which is why the presence of a restriction by object will remain a presumption of illegality – not a per se-finding thereof. It does, as already mentioned, considerably alleviate the competition authority's investigation burden because they are not required to appraise any direct or indirect, actual or potential, negative effects of the agreement in question.

Although the undertaking is technically not prevented from presenting evidence in support of an exemption, the existence of a 'by object' restriction should imply an unsurmountable task for undertakings to demonstrate that the four cumulative criteria for exemption are fulfilled – otherwise the agreement is wrongly classified and should have been assessed as a 'by effect'-restriction.

Naturally, from an enforcement point of view it appears quite compelling to categorise agreements as restrictions by object bearing in mind that scarce investigation resources can then be minimised and the likelihood for succeeding to uphold

[51] See specifically VBER Guidelines, above note 9, para 196.

[52] See T Staahl Gabrielsen, BO Johansen and TL Lømo, 'Resale Price Maintenance in Two-sided Markets' (2018) 66(3) *The Journal of Industrial Economics* 570–609.

[53] See Article 2 of Council Regulation (EC) No 1/2003 of 16 December 2002 on the implementation of the rules on competition laid down in Articles 81 and 82 of the Treaty, OJ L 1, 4.1.2003, pp 1–25, and VBER Guidelines, above note 9, para 197.

the decisions on appeal increases considerably. From a legal certainty standpoint, however, it is of utmost importance not to fall into the Type I-error trap. Naturally, harmful restrictions should not go unsanctioned in order to avoid the Type II-error. Both types of error risk, however, to undermine the legitimacy of the competition law. Admittedly, it is never an easy task to strike the correct balance between these interests. Still, this is precisely why due process and adherence to proper methods matters. Applied wrongly it may lead to unwarranted fines or harm to competition, depending on type of error. This is furthermore the very reason for being restrictive and tread carefully in claiming restrictions by object.

In *Tapwell*, it cannot be ruled out that the pricing strategy under an effects-based analysis would be deemed anti-competitive and restrictive and thereby prohibited. The body of facts and circumstances presented in the KKV's decision, viewed in its entirety, appears to speak in favour of such a finding. This also means that such a finding can very well be well-founded and robust. This also, however, would imply that although the KKV in such a case had fulfilled the standard of proof, there would be a reversal of the burden of evidence to the undertakings to demonstrate that the criteria under Article 101(3) (or its national counterpart) are satisfied.

Instead of carrying out an effects-based analysis, the finding of illegal agreement revolves around the question of the existence of a restriction by object. As mentioned above, it appears clear that the authority has deviated in important aspects from the method laid down in *Super Bock* and relied on a step-by-step analysis combined with an (unfounded) automatic categorisation of a hardcore restriction as a restriction by object. This stepwise approach seems to tangle up efficiency claims aimed at justifying the agreement as an exemption or at the very least to de-categorise it as 'hardcore' with a means to rebut the general per se-like categorisation as 'by object' restriction. Also, instead of carrying out an integrated analysis that included the legal and economic context *in casu*, those facts and circumstances are instead to analysed with the view to verify if there are any aspects that may rebut the already established restriction by object. Naturally, this then puts the entire analysis on the wrong track from the beginning and the analysis is then limited only to finding elements that may rebut a prima facie-assumption instead of finding the elements that would build up a finding of restriction by object.

The decision is arguably illusorily clear. It is by all standards a well-written and carefully carried out assessment that re-arranged under an effects-based approach very well may hold water. Still, the reliance on the squeezing the agreement into the 'by object' box seriously deprives the undertaking the possibility of justifying the agreement under examination and diverts attention from competitive effects to matters of formality. From an enforcement perspective it is questionable whether this stance is optimal bearing in mind that it is a perilous litigation strategy to rely solely on the categorisation instead of carefully evaluating the market effects.[54] After all, it

[54] This would not be the first time the KKV has relied on restrictions by object alone. In *AQM*, the KKV relied on an assessment that entailed both an 'by object' and 'by effect' analysis in the alternative. However, after having lost the case before the Stockholm District Court, the authority relied entirely on the matter of restriction by object on appeal to the Market and Patent Court of Appeal. The appellate court disagreed with the KKV, and since an ancillary restriction (non-compete clause) to an M&A-agreement could not, as such, be regarded as a restriction by object, the KKV's claim was dismissed. See case PMÖD 2017:18, *Konkurrensverket v Alfa Quality Moving Aktiebolag*, 29/11/2017.

is far from clear that the KKV's stance on the isolated matter of 'by object' restriction will be upheld. If the agreement cannot be classified as such, it can be argued that there is not adequate supportive evidence for such anti-competitive effects that need to be demonstrated for it to be prohibited. Hence, putting all procedural eggs into one basket by relying entirely on the existence of restriction by object may prove to be a venturesome strategy. In fact, absent a restriction by object, this also leaves the door open to argue that the agreement is in fact covered by the VBER and that the RPM is not even a hardcore restriction if the undertaking were to be able to demonstrate such facts and circumstances as envisaged by the Commission in the Guidelines.

The ruling in *Super Bock* is clear insofar an assessment must be made regarding the content of its provisions, its objectives and the economic and the legal context of which it forms a part, with due regard held to the nature of the goods or services affected as well as the actual conditions of the functioning and structure of the market or markets in question. It is nowadays also clear from *Super Bock* that hardcore restrictions do not automatically amount to a restriction by object.

Although seemingly not entirely in line with the CJEU's ruling, the KKV's stance is, however, to a considerable extent understandable bearing in mind that the Commission prior to *Super Bock* regarded RPM as *generally* constituting a restriction by object.[55] The Commission's non-binding guidance document has, however, not been updated since 2015 and is regrettably still displayed as fully valid and reflecting the current state of law. On appeal, it will be of great interest to see how the courts will handle the matter of hardcore restrictions. The CJEU has clarified important aspects of how to assess such restrictions and courts will most certainly take this into consideration.

[55] See the accompanying document to the De Minimis Notice, Commission Staff Working Document, Guidance on restrictions of competition 'by object' for the purpose of defining which agreements may benefit from the De Minimis Notice, SWD(2014) 198 final, 3/6/2015.

15

Traces of a Trojan Horse: How EU Trade Mark Law Interacts with Unfair Competition

ANNETTE KUR

I. INTRODUCTION

ONE ACHIEVEMENT RANKING PROMINENTLY in Ulf Bernitz's academic legacy concerns his vision of what he called 'Market Law', that is, his vision of Intellectual Property, Unfair Marketing Practices and Competition (Antitrust) Law as elements of one overarching concept.[1] This chapter written in his honour addresses a segment out of that larger tableau, namely the relationship between trade mark and unfair competition law. More specifically, the issue is considered in the light of jurisprudence of the Court of Justice of the European Union (CJEU), thereby connecting it with legal integration in the European Union (EU) and thus another one of Ulf's favourite topics.

As a starting point, I borrow a metaphor from Ansgar Ohly, who remarked that the CJEU's case law extending the realm of (harmonised) trade mark law into an area previously solely governed by (non-harmonised) unfair competition law had a Trojan horse-effect:[2] it resulted in an erosion of trade mark law's traditional right-holder-centric orientation towards formal, abstract criteria which, although being grounded on a prototypical image of market needs and reactions, often fail to respond to the complexities of market reality. Of course, different from the ancient royal city, trade mark law was not burnt down and looted by antagonistic forces thirsty for revenge. On the contrary – the invasion is a friendly one. The hidden cargo entering the secluded premises proved fruitful where it peacefully mingled with the formerly isolated incumbents, smoothly increasing the level of harmonisation and making

[1] Ulf Bernitz. *Marknadsrätt. En komparativ studie av marknadslagstiftningens utveckling och huvudlinjer* (Stockholm, Jurist- och samhällsvetareförbundets förlag, 1969).

[2] Ansgar Ohly and Annette Kur, 'Lauterkeitsrechtliche Einflüsse auf das Markenrecht' [2020] *Gewerblicher Rechtsschutz und Urheberrecht (GRUR)* 457–71, 458.

room for fair and balanced measures in situations that are not amenable to rigid solution schemes. That could be the happy, non-Homeric end of the tale. However, the story is not finished yet; certain risks and drawbacks remain. First, this concerns situations where the invasion has not fully achieved its goals, that is, where the need to modulate the expansion of trade mark law by a good portion of fairness-oriented thinking is not fully realised. Second, the incorporation of adjacent territory by the invigorated power may go too far, meaning that issues are subjected to EU trade mark law that should remain at the disposal of national courts and legislatures.

The following chapter traces the manner in which EU trade mark law is moulded under the influence of unfair competition-inspired thinking. The process of 'carrying the horse into the city' most evidently and massively started with the development of the CJEU's 'functions' jurisprudence, which is considered first (Section II). Even earlier than that, the CJEU did apply certain concepts borrowed from unfair competition law in trade mark law's core area of assessing likelihood of confusion (Section III). Extended protection for trade marks having a reputation is another example of merging standards of trade mark and unfair competition law (Section IV), and the same applies to the limitations (Section V). The picture is concluded by examples of situations when the CJEU too rigidly tried to impose its integrative scheme, ignoring the limits of its own competence (Section VI). The article ends with a summary and a warning that in spite of an overall positive picture, the CJEU in its more recent trade mark law decisions showed a disquieting degree of insensitivity towards the needs of competitors and the public at large, thus indicating that the friendly invasion has not yet settled for a finite, secure status quo (Section VII).

II. DOUBLE IDENTITY AND THE TRADE MARK FUNCTIONS

A. Background and CJEU Jurisprudence

Before EU trade mark law harmonisation, discussing trade mark functions and the extent of their protection was a frequent topic in the specialised literature of some Member States, such as Italy,[3] Switzerland,[4] Germany[5] and also Sweden.[6] The general

[3] See eg Adriano Vanzetti, 'Funzione e Natura Giuridica del Marchio' (1961) I *Riv Dir Comm* 16, which seems to have been the first publication on the issue in Europe; see also Vito Mangini, 'Competition and Monopoly in Trademark Law: An EEC Perspective' [1980] *International Review of Intellectual Property and Competition Law (IIC)* 591–614, 60 et seq).

[4] Alois Troller, 'Wesen und Unwesen der Marke', in Wolfgang Hefermehl, Rudolf Nirk and Harry Westermann (eds), *Festschrift für Philipp Möhring* (Munich, Beck Verlag, 1965) 291–314.

[5] In Germany, the discussions were heavily influenced by the approach taken towards international exhaustion. See in particular Friedrich-Karl Beier, 'Territorialität des Markenrechts und internationaler Wirtschaftsverkehr' (1968) *GRUR International* 8–17, 13 et seq; English version in (1970) *IIC* 48–72. See further Friedrich-Karl Beier and Ulrich Krieger, 'Wirtschaftliche Bedeutung, Funktion und Zweck der Marke' [1976] *GRUR International* 125–28; Ludwig Heydt, 'Parallelimporte und Warenzeichenrecht' [1969] *GRUR* 450–67; Rolf Sack, 'Die Rechtlichen Funktionen des Warenzeichens' [1972] *GRUR* 402–12 (Part I); 445–53 (Part II); Walter Oppenhoff, 'Wandel der Markenrechtskonzeption?' [1973] *GRUR International* 333–436; Frauke Henning-Bodewig and Annette Kur, *Marke und Verbraucher*, Vol I (Weinheim, VCH, 1988) 227–58.

[6] See in particular Lars Pehrson, *Varumärke från konsumentsynpunkt.En rättsvetenskaplig studie* (Stockholm, Liber Förlag, 1981).

tenor of those discussions was that, while trade marks perform a number of relevant functions in the market place, their legal protection under trade mark law was basically limited to the function of indicating origin. When in the 1980s, the potential of trade marks to communicate much more than origin became increasingly apparent, the governing approach was criticised inter alia because a number of other functions were neglected that might be more important economically, thus alienating the law from commercial reality.

After harmonisation, the discussions became moot for a while, because most of the issues where a 'modern' solution had been prevented by the strict focus on the origin function – protection vis-à-vis dissimilar products; 'isolated' transfer of marks; exhaustion – were settled by positive law in the Trade Mark Directive (TMD) (104/89) and the Community Trademark Regulation (CTMR). However, they came back with new vigour after the CJEU started to develop its own version of the functions doctrine. The background lay in the so-called double identity clause (identical marks being used in relation to identical products) which under a literal interpretation not only provides protection against acts of counterfeiting, but also against use which correctly refers to the trade mark for the purpose of identification of the product to which it applies (referential use). In early decisions, the CJEU either did not address the issue – pointing instead to the limitations[7] – or seemed to indicate that the scope of application of the double identity clause must be limited to instances when unauthorised use by a third party risks jeopardising the essential function of the mark to guarantee the origin of goods or services.[8] Finally, however, in *L'Oréal v Bellure*, the CJEU stated that the account taken of the trade mark functions as the yardstick for measuring the reach of the double identity clause not only included

> the essential function of the trade mark, which is to guarantee to consumers the origin of the goods or services, but also its other functions, in particular that of guaranteeing the quality of the goods or services in question and those of communication, investment or advertising.[9]

In the actual decision this meant that use of the plaintiffs' precious perfume brands on a chart juxtaposing those brands with those of cheap 'smell-alikes' fell into the ambit of the general clause, obliging the national court to assess whether one of the additional functions listed by the CJEU was negatively affected.[10] Fears that this would lead to basically unlimited protection of trade marks against any kind of use for referential purposes were however soothed soon thereafter, when the CJEU in its decisions

[7] CJEU Case C-355/96, *Silhouette International Schmied v Hartlauer Handelsgesellschaft* [1998] ECR I-04799; CJEU Case C-63/97, *BMW v Karel Deenik* [1999] ECR I-00905; CJEU Case C-228/03, *Gillette v LA Laboratories* [2005] ECR I-02337.

[8] See CJEU Case C-2/00, *Hölterhoff v Freiesleben (Sun Spirit and Context Cut)* [2002] ECR I-04187, para 16 (not mentioning the term 'functions', but instead referring to the interests protected under trade mark law); Case C-206/01, *Arsenal v Reed* [2002] ECR I-10273, paras 47 to 51; Case C-48/05, *Adam Opel v Autec* [2007] ECR I-01017, para 24.

[9] Case C-487/07, *L'Oréal v Bellure* [2009] ECR I-05185, para 58.

[10] ibid, para 63. In addition, the CJEU pointed out in para 65 that the legitimacy of the use made of the mark also depended on its compatibility with Art 3a of the Directive 84/450/EEC on Misleading and Comparative Advertising (now: Art 4 of Directive 114/2006/EC on Misleading and Comparative Advertising (MCAD)).

concerning use of adwords (*Google and Google France*;[11] *Interflora*[12]) signalled that the additional functions cannot be invoked against conduct which neither jeopardises the origin function[13] nor materially affects the visibility of the competitor's trade mark,[14] or otherwise substantially compromises the trade mark's ability to attract and maintain customers'[15] prejudices. Such measures must be tolerated irrespective of the fact that they are contrary to the interests of the trade mark holder and may force them to react in order to maintain their position on the market.[16]

B. Evaluation

The functions doctrine succinctly illustrates the Trojan horse-effect addressed in the introduction. If the CJEU had stuck with its initial approach to limit the application of the double identity clause to cases when the essential trade mark function was jeopardised, the ambit of harmonised trade mark law, and thus the Court's area of supervisory competence, would have been limited accordingly. Mere referential use would have remained in the domain of national law.[17] By choosing the broader approach, and thus adopting a larger concept of what fell into the realm of harmonised – or, in the case of the CTMR (now: European Union Trade Mark Regulation, EUTMR), even unified – trade mark law, the CJEU effectively claimed authority over a number of issues that are adjacent to, but not necessarily form a genuine part of trade mark law. In the adword cases, the CJEU remained conscious of the responsibility assumed thereby: Instead of applying a one-sided, pro-rightholder biased kind of property logic, the Court in those decisions remained sensitive towards the parameters of free and fair competition.

Viewed in that light, the functions doctrine is helpful as a tool for fashioning fair and balanced solutions. Initial fears that it may be a magic weapon permitting trade mark holders to prevail in any situation they consider as detrimental to their commercial interests[18] are not sustained by a close analysis of the case law. It is true, however, that commitments to the principles of sound competition like in the adword cases are

[11] CJEU Joined Cases C-236/08 to C-238/08, *Google France v Louis Vuitton et al.* [2010] ECR I-02417. See further CJEU Case C-278/08 *BergSpechte v Guni* [2010] ECR I-02517; CJEU Case C-91/09, *Eis.de v BBY Vertriebsgesellschaft* [2010] ECR I-00043; Case C-588/08, *Portakabin v Primakabin* [2010] ECR I-06963; Case C-324/09, *L'Óréal v eBay* [2011] ECR I-06011.

[12] CJEU Case C-323/09, *Interflora v Marks & Spencer* [2011] ECR I-08625.

[13] C-236 to 238/08, *Google and Google France*, para 90. The origin function is said to be jeopardised where the ad is vague to such an extent on the origin of the goods or services at issue that average internet users are unable to determine whether the advertiser is economically linked to the proprietor of the mark.

[14] C-236 to 238/08, *Google and Google France*, para 97; see also C-323/09, *Interflora v Marks & Spencer*, para 59.

[15] C-323/09, *Interflora v Marks & Spencer*, para 63.

[16] ibid, para 64.

[17] That is of course different in areas where unfair competition law, including practices between businesses (B2B) have been harmonised, as in the case of the MCAD.

[18] See in particular Jacob LJ in *L'Oréal v Bellure* [2010] EWCA Civ 535, para 30, stating that there is nothing in the legislation about functions, that they are conceptually vague and ill-defined, and lead to overbroad protection. In the same vein, Martin Senftleben, 'Trade Mark Protection – a Black Hole in the IP Galaxy' (Editorial) [2011] *IIC* 383–87; a critical approach is also taken by Ansgar Ohly [2011] *GRUR* 1131 (commenting on C-323/09, *Interflora v Marks & Spencer*).

not always found in CJEU decisions. Furthermore, the definitions of the advertising and investment functions proffered by the CJEU are convoluted and cumbersome;[19] they hinder transparency of decision-making rather than furthering it.[20] It is therefore highly commendable that after amendment of EU trade mark law in 2016, most of the critical cases can be solved on the basis of the newly introduced limitation for referential use. Lastly, the functions jurisprudence becomes dangerous when it is invoked by the CJEU as a justification to extend its area of competence even further into the realm of non-harmonised unfair competition law, as is addressed below (Section VI).

III. LIKELIHOOD OF CONFUSION

A. Background and CJEU Jurisprudence

In trade mark law's core area of likelihood of confusion, the legal objectives pursued are closely related to the fight against consumer deception, emerging from a need of competitors and members of the relevant public to be protected against fraudulent misuse of signs identifying the commercial source of goods or services. Nevertheless, the common origin of the two fields did not prevent that they were clearly separated in theory and in practice. Although the approaches have changed over time and varied between states, it can be contended that already when European harmonisation was in its infancy, it was taken for granted that the notion of 'indicating and guaranteeing commercial origin' in the meaning of trade mark law does not conform to a strictly unfair competition/consumer protection-informed approach. In CJEU jurisprudence, it was acknowledged since the early 1990s that trade marks already fulfil their essential function if they guarantee control by one undertaking, that is, if and as long as the proprietor of the mark has the final say about whether, how and by whom goods or services bearing the mark are released on the common market.[21] Consumers' awareness of the source or the correctness of their assumptions about the identity of the trade mark proprietor are not relevant for the purpose.[22] In that sense, the primary objective of trade mark law is about safeguarding the owner's exclusive position on a specific market. Protection of consumer interests is a welcome reflex, but not the genuine goal of the protection conferred.

The distinction thus made between trade mark law and consumer protection can also impact the manner of assessing likelihood of confusion. In the light of what was said before, a trade mark law-specific interpretation of that notion is typically informed by the goal of safeguarding the position of the trade mark holder against undue inferences and thus by a normatively defined agenda, and not primarily by an effort to investigate the actual perception of consumers. Furthermore, in view of

[19] See C-236 to C-238/08, *Google and Google France*, para 91, 92 for the advertising function and C-323/09, *Interflora v Marks & Spencer* para 60, 62 for the investment function.

[20] More extensively on this see Annette Kur, 'Trade Marks Function, Don't They? CJEU Jurisprudence and Unfair Competition Principles' [2014] *IIC* 434–53.

[21] See CJEU case C-10/89, *CNL-Sucal v. HAG (HAG II)* [1990] ECR I-3711, para 14 and even more clearly CJEU case C-9/93, *IHT v Ideal Standard* [1994] ECR I-2789, para 30.

[22] CJEU case, C-259/04 *Elizabeth Emanuel* [2006] ECR I-3089, para 48.

registration proceedings, it is particularly obvious that assessment of likelihood of confusion in trade mark law must proceed in a different manner than in the context of unfair competition/marketing practices. Administrative agencies must be able to operate on the basis of abstract, formalised schemes which allow a high number of cases being handled in a brief time-span, with the proceedings being geared towards legal certainty and foreseeability rather than offering room for flexibility and contextualism. Because, and as long as, the concept of likelihood of confusion remains the same in administrative and infringement proceedings, the assessment is guided by abstract, normative considerations also in the latter framework. Thus, at least in Germany, courts and authorities regularly emphasise that assessing likelihood of confusion is ultimately a matter of law,[23] with actual consumer perception constituting only one, although important, factor in the appraisal.

Different from that, likelihood of confusion in the jurisprudence of the CJEU is essentially regarded as a matter of fact. Of course, the CJEU as well recognises that in administrative proceedings the authorities must base their decisions on the 'paper form' of a mark and cannot – at least not as a regular matter – include circumstantial evidence concerning the use of one or both signs on the market. In infringement proceedings, however, the CJEU is open towards such evidence. For instance, in *Specsavers* the CJEU confirmed that it complies with EU trade mark law to take account in infringement proceedings of the fact that a trade mark registered in black and white is used in green colour, thus potentially enhancing the risk of confusion with another sign likewise used in green.[24] In line with that, the CJEU remarked in *O2 v Hutchinson* that administrative proceedings and infringement suits may be subject to different forms of assessing likelihood of confusion.[25] Regarding the relevant public, the CJEU declared in *Meyer v Klijsen*[26] that the global appreciation of factors contributing to likelihood of confusion[27] must proceed from the perspective of 'the average consumer of the category of products concerned . . . deemed to be reasonably well-informed and reasonably observant and circumspect',[28] thus referencing a benchmark developed as a counter-model to the 'inattentive consumer' previously prevalent in German unfair competition law.[29]

On the other hand, the CJEU also declared that the assessment must be based on the 'imperfect picture' that the average consumer has in mind, as the chance rarely exists to make a direct comparison between the different marks.[30] Accordingly, it cannot be excluded that, for example, mere aural similarity creates a likelihood of

[23] Established principle; see eg German Federal Supreme Court (BGH), 5 December 2012, I ZR 85/11 (*Culinaria/Villa Culinaria*) para 67.

[24] CJEU case C-252/12, *Specsavers v ASDA Stores*, EU:C:2013:577, para 41.

[25] CJEU case C-553/06, *O2 Holdings v Hutchinson* [2008] ECR I-04231, paras 65, 66.

[26] CJEU case C-342/97, *Schuhfabrik Meyer v Klijsen* [1999] ECR I-03819. The dispute concerned a conflict between the trade marks 'Lloyd's' and 'Loints' for shoes. The referring court (District Court, Munich) explained that according to general rules applying in trade mark law, the junior mark would have to be considered infringing, while the court doubted that consumers would actually confuse both signs.

[27] Those factors were first defined in Case C-251/95, *Sabèl v Puma*, [1997] ECR I-6191, para 23, with reference to the tenth recital in the preamble of the TMD (104/1989): '[The] global appreciation of the visual, aural or conceptual similarity of the marks in question, must be based on the overall impression given by the marks, bearing in mind, in particular, their distinctive and dominant components'.

[28] C-342/97, *Meyer v Klijsen*, para 26.

[29] In Case C-210/96, *Gut Springenheide and Tusky* [1998] ECR I-4657, para 31; see already – somewhat less explicitly – Case C-251/95, *SABEL v Puma* [1997] ECR I-6191, para 23.

[30] C-342/97, *Meyer v Klijsen*, para 26; Case C-251/95, *SABEL v Puma* [1997] ECR I-6191, paras 22, 23.

confusion.[31] Furthermore, in accordance with a statement in the Directive's preamble, the CJEU regularly emphasises that likelihood of confusion arises more easily when the mark, either per se or by acquisition, enjoys a highly distinctive character.[32] In practice this means that marks enjoying a high degree of public awareness and market share have a wider scope of protection than others. The empirical soundness of the underlying assumption is questionable, as customers' familiarity with a sign can rather be expected to reduce their liability to errors than having the opposite effect. This hints at a normative understanding which, instead of being strictly oriented towards a factual evaluation, includes elements of legal policy, such as rewarding the efforts and investment of entrepreneurs to create 'strong' marks.[33]

Remarkably, in the opposite situation – when marks, or elements of which they consist, are 'weak' or even non-distinctive, the CJEU's readiness to include normative elements into the considerations is less pronounced. True, the Court regularly states that marks with a low degree of distinctiveness do not enjoy strong protection, and that the relevant public in their overall appreciation is not likely to attach importance to 'weak' elements. However, the CJEU regularly rejects the view that, if allegations of likelihood of confusion are solely based on the similarity or identity of non-distinctive elements of a complex mark, likelihood of confusion must be denied.[34] In the Court's opinion, the legal concept of 'weakness' of such elements is 'not a factor which influences the perception which the consumer has of the similarity of the signs'.[35] In other words, in these situations the CJEU insists that the assessment of likelihood of confusion is an entirely factual exercise devoid of normative considerations. That position is not only inconsistent with the approach vis-à-vis 'strong' marks, which, as pointed out before, is apparently based on normative reasoning. It also clashes with the principle set forth in trade mark law that protection of non-distinctive and descriptive marks must be denied. That principle does not lose its prescriptive force simply because such protection is claimed indirectly, for non-protectable elements forming part of a sign that also comprises distinctive features. Consequently, different from what the CJEU contended, the holder of the trade mark consisting of the entirely descriptive term 'Roslagspunsch' – whose registrability was solely based on the graphic elements added to those words – should not be able to successfully invoke the right vis-à-vis the equally descriptive term 'Roslagsöl'.[36]

B. Evaluation

The overview of CJEU jurisprudence on likelihood of confusion provides a mixed picture. On the one hand, the CJEU, by treating the assessment of likelihood of

[31] C-342/97, *Meyer v Klijsen*, para 28.

[32] Established principle since; first articulated in C-251/95, *SABEL v Puma*, para 24.

[33] Annette Kur and Martin Senftleben, *European Trade Mark Law* (Oxford, Oxford University Press, 2017) 5.152, at 326.

[34] See Case C-235/05 P, *L'Oréal v OHIM (FLEXI AIR/FLEX)*, paras 39 to 47; C-42/12 P, *Vaclav Hrbek v OHIM (alpine/alpine pro)*, paras 56 to 62.

[35] C-235/05 P, *L'Oréal v OHIM*, para 42; C-42/12 P, *Vaclav Hrbek v OHIM*, para 61.

[36] For the opposite position endorsed by the CJEU see Case C-705/17, *Hansson (Roslangspunsch/Roslagsöl)* EU:C:2019:481.

confusion essentially as a matter of fact, brings trade mark law closer to unfair competition law with its orientation towards market reality and actual consumer perception. Inter alia, the affinity between both fields is signalled by the CJEU's literal adoption of the 'average consumer' benchmark, which applies horizontally in trade mark law and marketing practices law, notably in the Unfair Commercial Practices Directive (UCPD). In line with that approach the CJEU tends to oppose the application of principles which are regarded as rigid and formalised. On the other hand, the Court is also ready to some extent to accept – if only tacitly – rules of appreciation which are founded on normative rather than factual, empirically verifiable considerations. This concerns in particular the principle that the scope of protection of marks increases with the degree of recognition that is acquired on the market. Vice versa, the CJEU refutes a normative analysis when conflicts arise between signs which include non-distinctive or descriptive elements, and ignores the risk that by including such elements into the comparison of the overall impression produced by those signs, indirect protection might be granted to elements falling under the absolute grounds for refusal.

IV. EXTENDED PROTECTION

A. Background and CJEU Jurisprudence

Extended protection for trade marks having a reputation – or, to use a more traditional term, famous marks – is no new phenomenon. In the Nordic countries, pertinent provisions even formed part of trade mark law already since the 1960s.[37] From the 1980s at the latest, a consensus was growing in Europe and worldwide that using marks with a high level of public awareness as a vehicle to promote one's own goods is problematic under the aspect of honest business practices, irrespective of whether this provokes a likelihood of confusion.[38]

After harmonisation, several CJEU decisions have elaborated on the notion of trade marks having a reputation and on the scope of protection enjoyed. Concerning the latter aspect, the CJEU pointed out that the infringer's actions must establish a mental link between the sign used and the trade mark.[39] For that aim, a number of factors must be considered.[40] For further assessment, a distinction is made

[37] S 6(2) of the (uniform) Nordic trade mark laws enacted in the 1960s. The law included the so-called 'Kodak rule', prohibiting unfair taking advantage of famous trade marks, and the 'rat poison' rule, prohibiting use damaging the reputation of a famous mark. By contrast, Germany only introduced such protection in the course of implementing the Trade Mark Directive; before that, trade mark protection was strictly limited to identical or similar goods or services. If a practical need for protection against use of a mark for dissimilar goods arose, German Courts until the 1980s took resort to a specific variety of tort under the 'general clause' of civil tort law, s 823 BGB.

[38] One might also say that granting extended protection of trade marks which are highly recognised in the market is but a logical step further in a system that, already in the context of likelihood of confusion, honours the value inherent in highly distinctive marks by increasing their scope of protection.

[39] CJEU cases C-408/01, *Adidas-Salomon and Adidas Benelux* [2003] ECR I-12537, para 30; C-102/07, *adidas and adidas Benelux* [2008] ECR I-02439, para 42; C-252/07, *Intel Corp v CPM United* [2008] ECR I-08823, para 41.

[40] C-252/07, *Intel*, para 42.

between inflicting detriment on the reputation or distinctive character of the mark, and the taking of unfair advantage. In the former case, it must be established by objective evidence that use of the sign impacts, or is likely to impact, the economic behaviour of the relevant public.[41] As such changes are difficult to impossible to ascertain or predict with some precision, the option is of small practical value. In the case of taking unfair advantage, an infringement is found if the use of a sign which is identical or similar to a mark with a reputation 'rides on the coat-tails' of that mark

> in order to benefit from its power of attraction, its reputation and its prestige, and to exploit, without paying any financial compensation and without being required to make efforts of his own in that regard, the marketing effort expended by the proprietor of that mark in order to create and maintain the image of that mark.[42]

Furthermore, where it has been established prima facie by the proprietor of a mark having a reputation that unfair advantage has been taken of the mark, the option remains for the alleged infringer to show that the use was made with due cause.[43] The assessment of that concept includes not only 'objectively overriding reasons but may also relate to the subjective interests of a third party',[44] such as activities that may be considered as 'natural extensions' of one's core business – such as the selling of non-alcoholic beverages, including energy drinks – for a café owner[45] or, in particular, use made for the purpose of drawing the attention of the relevant public to alternative offers, such as use of a mark for keyword advertising.[46]

The evaluation informed by 'due cause' constitutes a clear example of flexible, unfair competition law-inspired thinking. Unfortunately, the CJEU does not always observe its own precepts to the full extent. In *L'Oréal v Bellure*,[47] the CJEU only mentioned the requirement of unfair advantage being shown, without considering 'due cause' as a potential justification for alluding to signs which allegedly shared an important characteristic – the smell – with the precious perfume brands they sought to resemble, without creating a likelihood of confusion.[48]

Another point of concern regards the relationship between extended protection including 'due cause' and the catalogue of limitations. This became apparent, though only indirectly, in the Inditex decision.[49] The underlying dispute concerned use of the trade mark Zara on gift cards offered as prize in a prize draw organised as a marketing measure by the defendant, an internet and telephone service provider, in Spain.

[41] C-252/07, *Intel*, para 77; Case C-383/12 P, *Environmental Manufacturing v OHIM (Wolf Jardin)*, EU:C:2013:741, para 37.
[42] C-487/07, *L'Oréal v Bellure*, para 49.
[43] CJEU case C-65/12, *Leidseplein Beheer v Red Bull*, EU:C:2014:49, para 44.
[44] C-65/12, *Leidseplein v Red Bull*, para 45.
[45] As in the dispute underlying C-65/12 *Leidseplein v Red Bull*.
[46] C-323/09, *Interflora v Marks & Spencer*, para 91.
[47] C-487/07, *L'Oréal v Bellure*.
[48] It would arguably be better to convey the relevant information in a more neutral form. However, in the same decision, the CJEU de facto prohibited giving such information – even if only vis-à-vis retailers – by way of juxtaposing the precious brands and the small-alikes, by applying the restriction following from Art 3a(1)(h) (now: Art 4(g)) MCAD in a very broad manner. See below, s V.A.
[49] CJEU case C-361/22, *Inditex v Buongiorno Myalert*, EU:C:2024:17.

Zara filed an infringement suit, based on extended protection. The claim had been rejected by the courts of first and second instance. Being seized with an appeal on points of law, the Tribunal Supremo referred to the CJEU the question whether the limitation for referential use, now set forth in Article 14(1)(c) TMD and EUTMR was different – broader – in its content than the earlier version of the limitations applying at the time when the conflict arose. The answer to that question was obviously positive; it was the clear intention of the EU legislature to broaden the scope of the limitations.[50] More remarkable than that is the fact that the CJEU did not consider it worthwhile to emphasise that, in view of 'due cause', the question posed was not relevant for the decision, as the balancing exercise to be conducted under that criterion does not depend on the wording of the limitations at a given time. Though the issue was addressed at least briefly – responding to an argument by the plaintiff which did, however, not mention 'due cause' – the Court limited itself to contending that the question posed was, after all, not manifestly absurd.[51] This could nourish doubts as to the breadth of considerations of which account may be taken for assessing due cause, thus diminishing the provision's flexibility. More specifically, it could encourage the assumption by the Spanish Court that due to the narrow wording of the limitation, the fact that the gift card was indeed offered as a prize by the defendant cannot be invoked as a justification for using the mark. That result stands in clear contrast to the *Interflora*[52] and *Leidseplein*[53] decisions, where the advantage taken had been considered justified for reasons that did not – and still do not – explicitly figure in the catalogue of limitations.

B. Evaluation

With its elements of 'taking (unfair) advantage' and 'without due cause', the provision on extended protection of marks having a reputation is basically capable of encompassing a fruitful combination of trade mark law-oriented and unfair competition law-inspired thinking. However, the scheme thus conceived only works as it should if all elements are given equal weight and thorough consideration. It is important not to terminate the analysis once the taking of advantage has been confirmed. Furthermore, the balancing effect of 'due cause' is severely curtailed if its application were restricted to what, at a given point in time, is set forth in the limitations. The scope of protection offered under the clause to marks having a reputation is considerably stronger than that under the double identity clause or likelihood of confusion; as a corollary, the alleged infringer must have access to the whole range of reasons that may justify its actions in the light of fair and sound competition. It is true that the questions referred in *L'Oréal v Bellure*[54] and in *Inditex*[55] were not geared towards 'due

[50] ibid, para 47.

[51] ibid, paras 31 to 35; more explicit on the relationship between extended protection and the limitations see Opinion by Advocate General Szpunar, EU:C:2023:653, para 56 et seq.

[52] C-323/09, *Interflora v Marks & Spencer*.

[53] C-65/12, *Leidseplein v Red Bull*.

[54] C-487/07, *L'Oréal v Bellure*.

[55] C-361/22, *Inditex v Buongiorno Myalert*.

cause'; the Court therefore, at least formally, did not have an opportunity to address that point which might have been crucial in both cases. However, the CJEU has often claimed it as its privilege or duty to give advice that may be useful to the referring court, even beyond the questions posed.[56] Considering the paramount importance of CJEU decisions and the responsibility conferred thereby, it is unfortunate that the chance was missed here.

V. LIMITATIONS

A. Background and CJEU Jurisprudence

While in the case of extended protection, the balancing instrument ('due cause') is integrated within the provision itself, it is for the limitations to provide a scheme of grounds for justifications in the case of violations of the double identity clause or the event of likelihood of confusion. Following the continental European tradition, the limitations are set forth in a closed catalogue instead of an open 'fair use' clause. Furthermore, they are subject to the condition of being compatible with honest business practices.

The latter requirement was defined by CJEU jurisprudence in a negative way. Thus, commercial activities covered by the limitations are not compatible with honest practices if they (a) give the impression that there is a commercial connection between the third party and the trade mark owner; (b) affect the value of the trade mark by taking unfair advantage of its distinctive character or repute; (c) entail the discrediting or denigration of the mark; or (d) where the third party presents its product as an imitation or replica of the product bearing the trade mark of which it is not the owner.[57] Those criteria are adapted from Article 4 MCAD and thus from a piece of EU marketing practices regulation.[58] Different from what is generally expected of such imports, the criteria do not have a softening effect, but are rather meant to reinforce the efficiency of protection by controlling the safe spaces granted under the limitations. Thus, the first to third elements quoted above basically reiterate criteria under which infringement is found; if applied strictly, they could superimpose findings of infringement on situations basically covered by the limitations, rendering the latter largely moot in practice. Even more problematic is the fourth element quoted above, which was inserted into the MCAD[59] due to heavy lobbying by inter alia the French perfume industry. In order to safeguard the purpose of the limitations, prudent interpretation is therefore necessary. For instance, it should be clear that 'giving the impression of there being a commercial connection' cannot be confirmed simply for the reason that the analysis of factors contributing to a likelihood of confusion has led to a positive result.[60] Instead, the question must be posed whether that risk is

[56] For instance, in C-48/05, *Opel v Autec*.

[57] C-228/03, *Gillette v LA Laboratories* [2005] ECR I-02337, para 49.

[58] Art 4 MCAD is explicitly referenced in Art 10(3)(f) TMD and Art 9(3)(f) EUTMR insofar as use of marks in comparative advertising is concerned.

[59] Originally: Art 3a(1)(h); now Art 4(g) MCAD.

[60] See CJEU case C-100/02, *Gerolsteiner Brunnen v Putsch (Gerri/KERRY Springs)*, [2004] ECR I-00691 para 27.

disproportionally high in comparison to the interests safeguarded by the pertinent limitation.[61] The same kind of proportionality assessment should be carried out in the case of alleged taking of advantage or inflicting detriment. Concerning the prohibition to present products as replicas or imitations of a product bearing a trade mark, a competition-sensitive approach means that the application is restricted to presentations actually using the incriminated words. Unfortunately, however, the CJEU applied the corresponding provision in the MCAD more broadly, declaring in *L'Oréal Bellure* that it not only covers advertisements 'which explicitly evoke the idea of imitation or reproduction', but also those which 'are capable of implicitly communicating such an idea to the public at whom they are directed'.[62]

The modes of use covered by the limitations originally concerned use of one's own name or address, use of a sign which is descriptive of the characteristics or other properties of the goods or services, and use which is necessary to indicate the purpose of a product to serve as spare part or accessory. In the course of the 2016 law reform, the provisions were changed to some extent: the use of one's name was restricted to personal names of natural persons,[63] non-distinctive signs were added to the limitation concerning use for descriptive purposes, and the limitation concerning use to indicate purpose was complemented by use 'for the purpose of identifying or referring to goods or services as those of the proprietor of that trade mark' (referential use).

As a matter of principle, the legal situation thus became more user-friendly than previously. However, the practical impact of those changes also depends on the courts' – and in particular the CJEU's – willingness to apply them in a spirit of openness for countervailing interests. The negative effects produced by lack of such openness were demonstrated by the CJEU's decision in *Audi v GQ*.[64] The dispute concerned the manufacturing and marketing by a Polish firm of radiator grilles to be used as spare parts for older Audi models. The Audi logo – four interlocking rings – is displayed on the original grille. Instead of that logo, a hollow device was affixed on the grilles on which the logo could be mounted by the car owners themselves. In the lawsuit filed by Audi, the Warszaw District Court referred the questions to the CJEU whether the defendant's actions could be considered as use to indicate purpose, and whether there was any trade mark infringement in the first place. Regarding infringement, the CJEU declared that the defendant's use of the mark was 'liable to affect one or more functions of the trade mark',[65] but left that to be decided by the referring court. Concerning the first question, however, the CJEU clearly excluded any possibility of invoking the limitations, holding that indication of purpose could only be done by an explicit statement accompanying the marketing of the grille, but not by

[61] The CJEU (ibid, para 26) does not refer to proportionality, but instead declares that national court must 'carry out an overall assessment of all the relevant circumstances'. In the actual case, which concerns bottled drinks, this means that the circumstances to be taken into account include 'in particular the shape and labelling of the bottle in order to assess, more particularly, whether the producer of the drink bearing the indication of geographical origin might be regarded as unfairly competing with the proprietor of the trade mark.'

[62] C-487/07, *L'Oréal v Bellure*, para 75.

[63] Thereby overruling CJEU case C-245/02, *Anheuser Busch*, paras 78, 79 where the Court had declared that the limitation also applied to trade names.

[64] CJEU case C-334/22, *Audi v GQ*, EU:C:2024:76.

[65] ibid, para 49.

the shape as such.[66] The reasoning fails to be convincing. Whether or not the limitation applies should depend on the perception by the relevant public rather than the option being categorically excluded as a matter of law, and it cannot be excluded that in the eyes of the public, the grille as marketed by the defendant sent exactly the same message as a written statement (eg 'this grille is meant for Audi cars'). It must be added here that Audi was not the first decision when such doubtful reasoning was adopted by the CJEU. A similar argument was already used in *Opel v Autec*,[67] when the CJEU held that affixing the miniature version of Opel's figurative mark ('Opel Blitz') on true-to-scale car models could not benefit from the limitation allowing use of marks so as to describe the properties of the product (in this case: to represent an Opel car). In the view of the CJEU, the fact that affixing the sign formed part of the imitation excluded such an interpretation.[68]

In *Opel v Autec*, the failure to recognise that use of the sign on the car model could have double purposes – serving as part of the reproduction and as an indication of the brand forming its object – did not have negative repercussions for the maker of the car model, as the CJEU, based on the assessment by the referring court, denied an encroachment of the origin function.[69] The same result could be reached in the Audi case; this lies now in the hands of the Polish court.

B. Evaluation

There is a general understanding that at least in its previous version, the catalogue of limitations was too narrow to provide an effective counterweight to the scope of protection enjoyed by trade marks, especially in view of the absolute kind of protection conferred under the double identity clause. Indeed, one reason for developing the functions doctrine lay in the lack of an adequately tailored arsenal of limitations, motivating the CJEU to look for other balancing instruments. By contrast, where adequate limitations were available, the CJEU did not bother to investigate the encroachment of functions, but directly proceeded to apply the written law.[70] Thus, it can be expected that after the limitations have been extended in the course of the 2016 law reform, the focus of legal assessment can shift (back) from the functions doctrine to the written law. However, the overview given under A shows that satisfactory results are not guaranteed. First, by relying heavily on the criteria adopted from the MCAD, the efficient application of the limitations may be hampered by an overly strict approach towards what is deemed compatible with honest commercial practices. Second, the CJEU's failure to recognise that, under specific circumstances which are for the national court to evaluate, the appearance of products themselves may be perceived by the relevant public as an indication of product characteristics or of purpose, unduly narrows the range of case scenarios covered by the limitations.

[66] ibid, paras 57, 58.
[67] CJEU case C-48/05, *Adam Opel v Autec* [2007] ECR I-01017.
[68] ibid, para 44.
[69] ibid, paras 24, 25.
[70] For instance, in C-63/97, *BMW v Deenik*, or C-355/96, *Silhouette*.

In that situation, relief can only be expected (again) from the functions doctrine, depending on the willingness of courts to embark on that route.

VI. INVADING ADJACENT TERRITORY?

In most of the situations critically examined above, the deficiencies noted were due to the fact that the CJEU did not fully realise – or did not make use of – the opportunities provided under the friendly invasion of trade mark law by the Trojan cargo of flexible, unfair competition-oriented principles. Before concluding our roundtrip in the invaded premises, two cases are reported that point in the opposite direction, of the CJEU venturing into adjacent territory, arguably without a solid construction shielding its activities.

The terrain into which such excursions are undertaken is known as unfair commercial practices among businesses (B2B). Unlike unfair commercial practices vis-à-vis consumers (B2C), it has not been harmonised as yet.[71] The distinction is rather subtle, and overlaps are frequent. The same is true for B2B marketing practices and trade mark law. For instance, using a competitor's trade mark as adword falls within the ambit of non-harmonised B2B unfair competition law (unless it is misleading in the meaning of Article 6(2)(a) of the UCPD); at the same time, it is a potential case of infringement to be assessed under EU trade mark law.[72] As the relevant fields are basically independent from each other, following similar but independent goals, there is no formal hierarchy between them. This means that national courts are not bound to CJEU rulings when adjudicating conflicts on the basis of B2B unfair competition law. However, in the interest of consistency of the law, national courts are unlikely to deviate from those rulings even when applying unfair competition law, unless there are special reasons to do so. That way, the Trojan horse-effect reaches into areas which, formally, are declared as non-harmonised ('cold harmonisation'). Nevertheless, the CJEU in those cases remains within the limits of its legal competence; the occurrence of indirect effects does not delegitimise its rulings.

The situation is different if the relevant issue is not addressed by harmonised trade mark law. In such cases, there is no legitimate basis for the CJEU to fashion a solution.[73] The mere fact that the conflict involves a trade mark does not suffice. If the CJEU nevertheless assumes competence, they overstep the borders of the place allocated to them within the legal system. The problem persists even where the result may basically appear acceptable in its substance.

The issue is illustrated by the following cases. The first dispute arose between two Belgian firms, Martin Y Paz (MYP) and Gauquie, over a figurative sign depicting the letter 'N' and the wordmark 'NATHAN BAUME' for certain leather goods.[74] Due

[71] See Recital 6 of Directive 29/2005/EC on Unfair Commercial Practices (UCPD).

[72] As follows inter alia from Case C-53/06, *O2 v Hutchinson* and C-487/07, *L'Oréal v Bellure*.

[73] The CJEU showed keen awareness of those limits in case C-23/01, *Robeco v Robelco* [2003] ECR I-10913, holding that use of a sign to identify and distinguish businesses (instead of goods or services) only falls under national law. The practical effects of that distinction were subsequently narrowed in C-245/02 *Budweiser* and, in particular, C-17/06, *Céline* [2007] ECR I-07041.

[74] Case C-661/11, *Martin Y Paz v Gauquie*, EU:C:2013:577.

to circumstances developing over time, the signs were used by both firms, with MYP using them for small leather goods, while Gauquie used them for shoes and handbags. No written contract existed between the firms. After NYP – allegedly without informing Gauquie – had filed and obtained a registration of the signs with the Benelux IP Office, they started suing Gauquie for trademark infringement, claiming the sole right to use the mark even for products which, during the period of shared use, were offered under the marks by Gauquie. Gauquie counterclaimed, seeking a verdict prohibiting MYP from exercising their rights against them. The Brussels court of appeals contended that under Belgian law, NYP's actions amount to an act of unfair competition, to the effect that the infringement claim cannot proceed. To dispel doubts in that regard, the court asked the CJEU whether the result was compatible with EU law. The CJEU denied the claim, arguing that resolution of trade mark conflicts is completely harmonised by Articles 5 to 7 (now: Articles 10 to 15) TMD.[75] As Gauquie was obviously unable to invoke one of the limitations in Article 6 (now: Article 14) TMD, and given that the marks and the articles for which they were registered and used by the parties were identical, the only way to escape liability for infringement would be to establish that the trade mark functions were not jeopardised.[76] No place was left in the assessment for considering whether the circumstances of MYP's acquisition and exercise of the right made its actions unfair. The CJEU thereby ignored its lacking competence in matters of B2B unfair competition law. It went unnoticed that the 'complete harmonisation' to which the Court referred is not limitless. In particular, while harmonised law regulates the scope of protection conferred by registration of a mark, it does not address the case in point, namely whether under special circumstances the exercise of the right may amount to misuse. Clearly, the CJEU would have to accept that trade mark infringement claims must be rejected if exercising the right constitutes abuse of a dominant market position under Article 102 TFEU. If that is taken for granted, there is no plausible reason to posit that misuse in the meaning of unfair competition law – which in the area concerned remains under the sole authority of national law – should be treated differently.

In the second case to be reported here, the CJEU's lack of respect for the limits of its own competence is even more obvious. The dispute concerned forklift trucks made and marketed outside the EU by Mitsubishi under its trade mark. The defendant bought a number of the articles, and, during warehouse proceedings before being released into intra-EU commerce, deleted the trade mark Mitsubishi and replaced it with its own mark. The CJEU, upon referral by the Brussels court of appeal, declared that the defendant's action amounted to trade mark infringement.[77] The counterarguments following from the explicit restriction of harmonisation to use of marks for the purpose of distinguishing goods or services, or the CJEU's own previous ruling that in order to find for infringement, the infringer must have used the mark in his own commercial communication[78] were waved off. Disregarded were also the Advocate

[75] ibid, para 54.

[76] ibid, para 58.

[77] Case C-129/17, *Mitsubishi*, EU:C:2018:594. For more details, see critical comment by Roland Knaak and Annette Kur [2018] *GRUR* 1120–24.

[78] C-236 to 238/08, *Google and Google France*, para 56.

General's warnings who, after a thorough analysis – inter alia interpreting the law under semantic, historical and teleological aspects and considering the trade mark functions – arrived at the result that there is no tenable way to argue that deletion of marks, especially when it is happening outside EU (or EEA) commerce, fell within the ambit of harmonised trade mark law.[79] The CJEU, however, considered it sufficient that removal of the mark constituted 'active conduct' of the defendant.[80] Furthermore, they postulated a 'right to control import' by the trade mark holder,[81] notwithstanding the fact that the law only grants such rights in regard to products bearing the protected mark (which was not the case here). Finally, they proffered a number of arguments based on the trade mark functions.[82] The arguments about jeopardising the origin function are unconvincing, given that it was never meant to actually indicate origin in the sense that consumers are informed about which company actually made an article to which a mark is affixed.[83] The arguments concerning the advertisement and, in particular, the investment function, make more sense. However, where those arguments operate without a basis in the corpus of harmonised trade mark law, they simply substitute national unfair competition law by the CJEU's opinion about what is conducive to fairness of marketing practices among entrepreneurs. In other words, the decision marks a step towards substantive harmonisation of an area which was deliberately left non-harmonised, without any parallel competence having been allocated to the CJEU under trade mark law.

Details from the decision suggest that this step was taken consciously. The Advocate General noted that during the hearing, the Commission had argued that 'in the absence of harmonisation of the provisions on unfair competition between undertakings in the EU, the rights of trade mark proprietors should be strengthened judicially'.[84] The Advocate General clearly rejected such prompts, remarking that the

> gradual creation of the internal market necessitates acceptance that, where there are no measures harmonising national laws, differences between those laws are legitimate until such time as that situation is rectified by legislative action on the part of the EU.[85]

Obviously, the CJEU was less shy to grasp what it may have seen as a welcome opportunity to expand their area of control at the cost of national diversities.

VII. CONCLUSIONS

The tour d'horizon offered in this chapter dedicated to the memory of Ulf Bernitz has shown how, in a number of instances, unfair competition-oriented thinking and principles of trade mark law have mingled and, where the chances thus offered are fully and adequately realised, are able to produce fruitful results. While that is an overall

[79] Opinion by Advocate General Campos Sánchez-Bordona, 18 April 2028, EU:C:2028:292, paras 50 to 60 and 68 to 71.
[80] C-129/17, *Mitsubishi*, para 48.
[81] ibid, para 42.
[82] ibid, paras 43 to 47.
[83] See already above s III.A.
[84] Opinion by AG Campos Sánchez-Bordona, para 91.
[85] ibid.

positive picture, there are also reasons for concern. On the one hand, that applies to the CJEU's sometimes rather generous neglect of the limits of its own competence, as addressed under Section VI. On the other hand, the CJEU's handling of conflicts lying at the fringes of trade mark protection and thus typically calling for openness towards overarching concerns is sometimes clouded by a narrow, right-holder oriented view. Examples of that approach are found in *L'Oréal v Bellure*,[86] or, more recently, in *Audi v GQ*.[87] The latter decision is all the more unfortunate as it completely ignores the general importance of strengthening the secondary market for repair of used articles, which according to the EU Commission's statement at the occasion of introducing the Union-wide repair clause through the recast of the Design Directive, is meant to contribute to the aim of bolstering the transition to a circular economy.[88] Of course, this does not mean – as insinuated by the CJEU – that the repair clause inserted into design law should apply by analogy in trade mark law.[89] However, proceeding from the principle often highlighted by the CJEU itself, that the genuine aim of trade mark protection is to support and maintain undistorted competition, the attitude towards overarching goals that the EU legislature strives to achieve must necessarily leave an imprint also on the interpretation of trade mark law. It clashes with that understanding if the interpretation as in *Audi*, without cogent reason, bars any access to applying the limitations. The misgivings raised thereby become even stronger when, as was equally done in *Audi*, the CJEU emphasises that the limitations are the only place within the provision that allows balancing the interests of the parties involved and of the general public, while no account can be taken of such considerations in the framework of assessing infringement.[90] Submitting that the CJEU did not intend by that statement to overrule a substantial part of their own case law, the second part of that statement is obviously wrong as the Court itself has repeatedly declared that it is precisely the aim of the functions doctrine to weigh the interests concerned already when assessing infringement, so as to enable balanced decisions. Therefore, the damage done can, and hopefully will, be controlled.[91] Nevertheless, the disquieting signals sent by this and other decisions[92] by the CJEU call for a better, more thoughtful use of judicial powers in an environment which no longer resembles a fortified city with firmly closed walls, but rather a space which has chosen to open the enclosure for elements of unfair competition law, and, for its own good, ought to fully realise and embrace the consequences.

[86] C-487/07, *L'Oréal v Bellure*; above s IV.A.

[87] C-334/22, *Audi v GQ*; above s V.A.

[88] Art 19 of the Design Directive (recast); Art 20a of the amended EU Design Regulation. See press release by the Commission at the occasion of the provisional agreement between the Council and the European Parliament on the repair clause, www.consilium.europa.eu/de/press/press-releases/2024/02/02/circular-economy-council-and-parliament-strike-provisional-deal-on-the-right-to-repair-directive/. Further on this aspect see Anna Tischner, 'Marken- und Designrechte – Freund oder Feind, comment on Audi v. GQ' [2024] GRUR 249–54.

[89] C-334/22, *Audi v GQ*, para 29; see already Case C-500/14, *Ford v Wheeltrims*, EU:C:2016:680, para 42.

[90] C-334/22, *Audi v GQ*, para 29.

[91] Indeed, after completing this text, the Warszaw court decided that there was no encroachment of the trade mark functions and thus no infringement; see Okręgowy w Warszawie XXII Wydział Własności Intelektualnej (District Court Warszaw XXII Intellectual Property Division), 24 June 2024, *Audi v Senkowski*. The decision is currently under appeal.

[92] For instance by C-361/22, *Inditex*, which seems to ignore the breadth and importance of the 'due cause' defence, as pointed out above (s V.A).

16

Clinical Trials Data: Transparency versus Exclusivity, the Case of an Inverted Pendulum?

FRANTZESKA PAPADOPOULOU SKARP

I. INTRODUCTION

OWNERSHIP, ACCESSIBILITY AND USE of data have become one of the central concerns of the contemporary intellectual property law debate. Although 'data' is used as an all-encompassing term expected to cover different forms of information contained, irrespective of its format and practical use, it is obvious that its precise nature and actual application impose the consideration of regulatory aspects that are intended to complement and at times even complicate the overarching regulatory regime.[1]

The case of medical data and in particular of clinical trial data is both very interesting and at the same time utterly complicated.[2] Due to its close connection to the regulation of access and use of patient data but also due to its decisive role in the marketing authorisation of medical products, it raises a number of legal issues.[3] The regulation of medical data in the European Union (EU) is currently undergoing significant changes, both directly and indirectly. These changes stem from the revision of

[1] Regulation (EU) 2023/2854 of the European Parliament and of the Council of 13 December 2023 on harmonized rules on fair access to and use of data and amending Regulation (EU) 2017/2394 and Directive (EU) 2020/1828 (Data Act) [2023] OJ L 2023/2854, 22.12.2023. For an analysis of the EU regulatory framework regarding data, see Björn Lundqvist, *Regulating the Data-Driven Economy under EU Law – Access and Transfer of Data* (Cambridge, Cambridge University Press, 2023) 260. See also Björn Lundqvist, 'An Access and Transfer Right to Data – from a Competition Law Perspective' (2023) 11 *Journal of Antitrust Enforcement* i57, i71.

[2] See Johanna Chamberlain and Andreas Kotsios, 'Data Protection Beyond Data Protection Regulation' in *Dataskyddet 50 år – Historia, aktuella problem och framtid* (2024) Stiftelsen Juridisk Fakultetslitteratur, available at: www.lawpub.se/utgava/633, 397.

[3] See, for instance, Regulation (EU) 2016/679 of the European Parliament and of the Council of 27 April 2016 on the protection of natural persons with regard to the processing of personal data and on the free movement of such data, and repealing Directive 95/46/EC (General Data Protection Regulation) [2016] OJ L 119/1.

EU pharmaceutical legislation presented in April 2023,[4] as well as from the entry into application of the Clinical Trials Regulation (CTR) in January 2022, which aims to harmonise the regulation of clinical trials across the EU.[5]

Clinical trials are research studies that test medical, surgical or behavioural intervention in patients.[6] These trials are the primary means for researchers to determine if a new form of treatment or prevention, such as a new drug, diet or medical device, is safe and effective in the way it claims to be. Clinical trials data is the data produced as a result of or during the process of such trials.[7] Such data is included in the dossier submitted to the competent authority in order for medicinal products to acquire a marketing authorisation and be placed on the market. The EU agency with a central role in this process is the European Medicines Agency, a decentralised agency of the EU responsible for the scientific evaluation, supervision and safety monitoring of medicines in the EU.[8]

Clinical trials data is naturally of central importance when evaluating the efficiency and safety of pharmaceuticals while it also constitutes the end-result of particularly expensive and time-consuming research endeavours. Clinical trials are estimated to cost approximately $48 to $225 million, while the timeframe necessary in order to complete a full set of tests is between 10 to 15 years.[9]

The value encompassed in the production of this data has been recognised as a protectable subject-matter on an international level in Article 39(3) of the TRIPS Agreement.[10] Until the day of writing, the protection of clinical trials data is provided on an EU level by the Medicines Directive 2001/83.[11]

[4] Proposal for a Regulation of the European Parliament and of the Council laying down Union procedures for the authorization and supervision of medicinal products for human use and establishing rules governing the European Medicines Agency, amending Regulation (EC) No 1394/2007 and Regulation (EU) No 536/2014, and repealing Regulation (EC) No 726/2004, Regulation (EC) No 141/2000, and Regulation (EC) No 1901/2006. See also Proposal for a Directive of the European Parliament and of the Council on the Union code relating to medicinal products for human use, and repealing Directive 2001/83/EC and Directive 2009/35/EC.

[5] Regulation (EU) No 536/2014 of the European Parliament and of the Council of 16 April 2014 on clinical trials on medicinal products for human use, and repealing Directive 2001/20/EC [2014] OJ L 158/1.

[6] On the important role clinical trials play in the public health system, see European Medicines Agency (EMA), *External Guidance on the Implementation of the European Medicines Agency Policy on the Publication of Clinical Data for Medicinal Products for Human Use*, EMA/90915/2016, version 1.4 (15 October 2018) 8. www.ema.europa.eu/en/documents/regulatory-procedural-guideline/external-guidance-implementation-european-medicines-agency-policy-publication-clinical-data_en-3.pdf.

[7] See the definition by the EMA, 'Glossary – Clinical Trial' www.ema.europa.eu/en/glossary/clinical-trial.

[8] On the role and mandate of the EMA, see, for example, I Abed, R Gonzalez-Quevedo, M Mura, M Dias, S da Rocha Dias and J García Burgos, 'Commentary on the European Medicines Agency's Extended Mandate: Protecting Public Health in Times of Crisis and Improving Availability of Medicines and Medical Devices' (2023) 89(1) *British Journal of Clinical Pharmacology* 5, 10.

[9] See, for instance, V Kandi and S Vadakedath, 'Clinical Trials and Clinical Research: A Comprehensive Review' (2023) 15(2) *Cureus* e35034.

[10] See, for instance, Eric M Solovy, 'Protection of Test Data Under Article 39.3 of the TRIPS Agreement: Advancements and Challenges After 25+ Years of Interpretation and Application' (2022) 43 *Northwestern Journal of International Law & Business* 55.

[11] Directive 2004/27/EC of the European Parliament and of the Council of 31 March 2004 amending Directive 2001/83/EC on the Community code relating to medicinal products for human use [2004] OJ L 136/34. The revision of the pharmaceutical regulatory framework was the result of extensive research on the impact of the earlier system and the needs of the pharmaceutical market. See, for instance, the studies that preceded the proposal: Technopolis Group, *Study Supporting the Evaluation and Impact Assessment of*

However, the legal regulation of clinical trials data is not limited to matters of protection and exclusivity but also to transparency requirements and the obligation to make data available to third parties. The applicable legal framework regulates how data submitted to the marketing authorisation authority may be shared by others, competitors or other interested third parties, as well as how this information is to be ultimately used by third parties.[12]

The new CTR (EU) No 536/20145 is expected to contribute to increased transparency in the area of clinical trials.[13] The establishment of the Clinical Trials Information System (CTIS), the new portal that will centralise the collection of clinical trial data, is expected to further contribute to the harmonisation of the legal status of clinical data.[14]

The benefits of a increased access to clinical data have long been recognised by the global community. Governments, international organisations and researchers specifically point to the value of accessibility of clinical trial data from the perspective of safety of clinical trial participants, society as a whole, the efficiency of public health systems as well as of scientific progress. A very important perspective in this regard is the possibility to resort to an independent scientific verification of medicinal products confirming their safety and efficacy. At the same time, access to clinical data is coherent to an ethical dimension, since it reduces the duplication of clinical trials, and in particular such that have been considered unsuccessful. In this regard, it aligns well with the declaration on transparency of the International Committee of Medical Journal Editors[15] and the World Medical Association's Declaration of Helsinki.[16]

Furthermore, it contributes to an enhanced general trust of patients in clinical trials as processes as well as in medicinal products as such. The use of Artificial Intelligence (AI) and other innovative data analysis technologies, using raw data as a starting point, has revealed a new world of potential and has accentuated the potential value of data as such. New technologies allow data to be used in risk modelling, counterfactual simulation, drug repurposing and development.[17]

---

the General Pharmaceutical Legislation – Evaluation Report (2022); Technopolis Group, *Study Supporting the Evaluation and Impact Assessment of the General Pharmaceutical Legislation – Impact Assessment Report* (2022); Technopolis Group, *Future-Proofing Pharmaceutical Legislation – Study on Medicine Shortages* (2021); Technopolis Group and Ecorys, *Study to Support the Evaluation of the EU Orphan Regulation* (2019); Copenhagen Economics, *Study on the Economic Impact of Supplementary Protection Certificates, Pharmaceutical Incentives and Rewards in Europe* (2018); Technopolis Group and Ecorys, *Study on the Economic Impact of the Paediatric Regulation, Including Its Rewards and Incentives* (2016).

[12] On the importance and special role of clinical trials, see Kandi and Vadakedath, above note 9.

[13] Regulation (EU) 536/2014 of the European Parliament and of the Council of 16 April 2014 on clinical trials on medicinal products for human use, and repealing Directive 2001/20/EC [2014] OJ L 158/1.

[14] EMA, *Revised CTIS Transparency Rules*, EMA/263067/2023 (5 October 2023).

[15] See, for instance, the Clinical Trials Registration procedure, www.icmje.org/about-icmje/faqs/clinical-trials-registration/.

[16] The World Medical Association developed the Declaration of Helsinki as a statement of ethical principles for medical research involving human participants following the atrocities by physicians conducting unethical medical research during the Second World War. Since the World Medical Association first adopted the Declaration of Helsinki in 1964, researchers, ethics review committees and governments around the world now rely on the document's high-level enduring principles to guide fundamental ethical considerations and decision-making.

[17] See, for instance, Institute of Medicine, *Sharing Clinical Trial Data: Maximizing Benefits, Minimizing Risk* (Washington, DC, The National Academies Press, 2015). The importance of guaranteeing the openness of clinical data has been invoked by the EU Ombudsman; see European Ombudsman, 'Decision on

While the need to protect the exclusivity on clinical data has been uncontested, that is, that another sponsor may not use this data to acquire marketing authorisation for its own medicinal product, access to the actual information contained in the clinical trials data has constituted a grey zone, and the lack of transparency in the operations of the EMA has been a central point of critique of the agency during the past two decades.[18]

Exclusivity on clinical trials data was stipulated early on and in a clear manner. Transparency and accessibility of information was left initially to be regulated under the general rules on the operation of the European Medicines Agency with rather controversial results.[19] Policies 0046[20] and 0070[21] under which transparency of clinical trials data was to be regulated did not provide the envisioned results, and thus a new more efficient means of regulation was deemed necessary.[22] Naturally, the industry has expressed strong concerns with regards to the rising level of openness, claiming it constitutes a threat for the innovative power of the pharmaceutical industry, endangering trade secret protection. At the same time, it is the pharmaceutical industry that has been the most active user of the accessibility of clinical data, seeking to find out more about the products of their competitors.[23]

Both extremes of the pendulum, the regulation of the exclusivity on the one hand, and on the other the accessibility of clinical trials data to third parties, have during the past few years been subject to considerable changes, the background of which is representative of the dilemmas posed with regards to the protection of data in general.

This chapter investigates the recent changes that have been made in the regulatory framework of clinical trials data, and that have affected both sides of the pendulum, both its accessibility as well as its actual protection/exclusivity. The author seeks to demonstrate that while the regulatory changes are part of parallel legislative processes, the correlation between transparency and exclusivity is not explicitly

---

Own-Initiative Inquiry OI/3/2014/FOR Concerning the Partial Refusal of the European Medicines Agency to Give Public Access to Studies Related to the Approval of a Medicinal Product' (8 June 2016) Case OI/3/2014/FOR, Report, para 71. Regarding the academic debate on the importance of transparency, see JPA Ioannidis, 'Why Most Clinical Research Is Not Useful' (2016) 13(6) *PLoS Medicine*1; VS Moorthy and others, 'Rationale for WHO's New Position Calling for Prompt Reporting and Public Disclosure of Interventional Clinical Trial Results' (2015) 12(4) *PLoS Medicine* 1.

[18] See, for instance, RE Löfstedt, 'Transparency at the EMA: More Evidence Is Needed' (2013) 47(3) *Therapeutic Innovation & Regulatory Science* 299, 300. See also G Verhenneman, *The Patient, Data Protection and Changing Healthcare Models* (vol 12, Antwerp, Intersentia, 2021), concerning how new models of healthcare promote greater openness of information.

[19] The EMA introduced two policies related to the transparency of clinical trials data, Policy 0043 and Policy 0070.

[20] EMA, 'European Medicines Agency Policy on Access to Documents (Related to Medicinal Products for Human and Veterinary Use)' (2010) Policy/0043, EMA/110196/2006.

[21] EMA, 'The European Medicines Agency Policy on Publication of Clinical Data for Medicinal Products for Human Use' (2014) Policy/0070, EMA/240810/2013.

[22] See, for instance, HMA/EMA Working Group on Transparency, *Guidance Document on the Identification of Commercially Confidential Information and Personal Data Within the Structure of the Marketing Authorization (MA) Application – Release of Information After the Granting of a Marketing Authorization*, EMA/484l1/2010 (2012).

[23] Peter Doshi and Tom Jefferson, 'The First 2 Years of the European Medicines Agency's Policy on Access to Documents: Secret No Longer' (2013) 173(5) *JAMA Internal Medicine* 380. See also *PTC Therapeutics International v EMA* (Case T-718/15 R, Order of the President of the General Court, 20 July 2016, ECLI:EU:T:2016:425) para 38.

identified as a vital one and a balancing of the pendulum between the two sides seems to still be a work in progress.[24]

II. REGULATING THE RIGHT TO USE SOMEONE ELSE'S CLINICAL TRIALS DATA

Data exclusivity is regulated in Article 39(3) of the TRIPS Agreement. This Article provides a minimum standard of protection according to which regulatory data, such data that is necessary in order to obtain a marketing authorisation for a medicinal product, is to be protected when undisclosed.

In the text of the TRIPS Agreement exclusivity to clinical trials data is subject to the lack of transparency. This interrelation of exclusivity versus transparency has not been considered in the protection awarded on an EU level by means of Article 10(a)(iii) of Directive No 2001/83 and Article 14 of Regulation No 726/2004. These two provisions make no reference to a separate requirement, that would subject data and market exclusivity to the precondition that clinical trials data is kept undisclosed. In fact, under Article 10(a)(iii) of the 2001/83 Directive, both the EMA and the national authorities are to refuse to accept clinical data that is already part of a previous marketing authorisation dossier for a new marketing authorisation application unless there is a 'letter of access', a written agreement including the authorisation of the data holder to the data user. Whether this data is disclosed or undisclosed is thus of no relevance for the exclusivity awarded.[25]

Under the current legal framework new medicinal products are granted an eight-year period of data protection, during which the marketing authorisation (MA) holder has the exclusive right to the clinical and preclinical data for the approved product, followed by two years of marketing protection during which third parties may use the data to support an application for their generic or competing products and such applications may be approved, but the product may not be placed on the market. Collectively, this data and marketing protection period provides a total of a 10-year period during which generic competition is unable to enter the market.[26]

A further one year of marketing protection (thus a total of 8+2+1 duration) is available if, during the first eight years after approval, the MA holder obtains authorisation for at least one additional indication, and the new product provides a significant clinical benefit compared to existing treatments for the new indication.[27]

[24] Frantzeska Papadopoulou, *Evergreening Patent Exclusivity in Pharmaceutical Products: Supplementary Protection Certificates, Orphan Drugs, Paediatric Extensions and ATMPs* (Oxford, Hart Publishing, 2021).

[25] Even if the information is publicly available it cannot be used to support a new marketing authorisation application. That per se restricts competitors to a considerable extent since what competitors wish is to be able to enter the market, without having to engage in the costly and lengthy clinical trials.

[26] Obviously, the choice of term of protection is rather arbitrary but had been considered as appropriate. The marketing authorisation procedure is a necessary step in the process of competition entering the market. It is however important to note that there might be other.

[27] Although in the new proposed system, the new structure of duration for market and data exclusivity is also considered to be appropriate and still competitive in relation to what is offered in other jurisdictions, it is not at all transparent how the calculations were made.

This system of data and market exclusivity has recently been revised, and a new legal framework with an adjusted duration of exclusivity is proposed.[28] The Commission proposes to reduce the baseline period of regulatory data protection from eight years to six years.[29] In the explanatory memorandum, it is underlined that this baseline protection 'remains competitive given what other regions offer'.[30]

The option related to a variable duration of regulatory data protection (split into a baseline of six years and additional periods) was preferred and considered 'a cost-effective way of achieving the objectives of improved access'.[31] The period of market exclusivity (eg the period during which a generic/biosimilar/hybrid of the initially authorised product cannot be placed on the market) remains a period of two years after the expiry of the relevant regulatory data protection period.

More specifically the proposal provides:

> An additional two years of data protection are available if the new product is released and continuously supplied in sufficient quantities to satisfy the need in all EU Member States in which the MA is valid, within two years from the date of the MA. For SMEs, not-for-profit entities and undertakings that have received five or fewer centralised MAs in the EU, the period for launch is extended to three years.
>
> An additional six months of data protection are available if, at the time of the initial MA application, the medicinal product addresses an unmet medical need. In this context, an unmet medical need is considered to be a life-threatening or severely debilitating disease for which there is either no medicinal product authorised in the EU or, despite the existence of authorised medicinal products, the indication remains associated with high morbidity or mortality. To be considered to address such a need, the new medicinal product must result in a meaningful reduction in morbidity or mortality for the relevant patient group.
>
> An additional six months of data protection are available if, for medicinal products containing a new active substance, the clinical trials supporting the initial MA application use an evidence-based comparator in accordance with scientific advice provided by the EMA.
>
> An additional year of data protection is available if, during the data protection period following authorisation, the MA holder receives an authorisation for an additional therapeutic indication for which there is a significant clinical benefit in comparison with existing

[28] Commission Staff Working Document, *Subsidiarity Grid Accompanying the Document Proposal for a Regulation of the European Parliament and of the Council Laying Down Union Procedures for the Authorisation and Supervision of Medicinal Products for Human Use and Establishing Rules Governing the European Medicines Agency, Amending Regulation (EC) No 1394/2007 and Regulation (EU) No 536/2014 and Repealing Regulation (EC) No 726/2004, Regulation (EC) No 141/2000 and Regulation (EC) No 1901/2006* (COM(2023) 193 final) (SEC(2023) 390 final) (SWD(2023) 192 final) (SWD(2023) 193 final).

[29] Directive proposal, Article 81(2).

[30] See *Impact Assessment Report and Executive Summary Accompanying the Revision of the General Pharmaceutical Legislation*, Directorate-General for Health and Food Safety (26 April 2023) SWD(2023) 192 final.

[31] See Commission Staff Working Document, *Subsidiarity Grid Accompanying the Document Proposal for a Directive of the European Parliament and of the Council on the Union Code Relating to Medicinal Products for Human Use, and Repealing Directive 2001/83/EC and Directive 2009/35/EC* (COM(2023) 192 final) (SEC(2023) 390 final) (SWD(2023) 192 final) (SWD(2023) 193 final).

therapies. This replaces the additional year of marketing protection available under the current regime.

The duration of data exclusivity is thus dependent on several other variables beyond the actual performance of clinical trials and collection of clinical data. Consequently, the right to protection recognised for the generation of data as such is deemed shorter than previously. Whether this is at all balanced under the context of the new proposal by means of the prolonged exclusivities available to sponsors for other related counter performances or whether this is a result of a conscious choice based on a general policy objective that data should be transparent, available and reusable as soon as possible remains to be seen.[32]

It is of course interesting to see how the new system will be applied in practice and what the effects of this fine-tuning would be. Shortening the term of exclusivity seems to be indicative of an overarching intent to provide for a broader accessibility and spread of clinical trials data, while at the same time considering that the rights of sponsors are accommodated in other ways.

III. TRANSPARENCY AND ACCESSIBILITY OF CLINICAL TRIALS DATA

During its first decades of operation, the EMA was subject to considerable critique related to the lack of transparency of its operations. The EMA applied a generalised policy of systematically denying third parties' access to documents that form part of the agency's decisions, namely documents and data that constitute part of the marketing authorisation dossiers.[33]

The overarching regulation of accessibility of documents held by institutions, bodies, offices and agencies of the EU is provided in Article 42 of the Charter of Fundamental Rights of the European Union[34] as well as in Article 15 of the Treaty on the Functioning of the European Union and in Regulation No. 1049/2001.[35]

While the general principle is that documents and thus also data should be made available to third parties, such access may be restricted on the basis of Article 4 of Regulation No 1049/2001. Article 4(2) provides that:

> The institutions shall refuse access to a document where disclosure would undermine the protection of: commercial interests of a natural or legal person, including intellectual property, court proceedings and legal advice, the purpose of inspections, investigations and audits, unless there is an overriding public interest in disclosure.

This provision constituted the overarching legal basis for EMA's previous restrictive policy with regards to third parties' access to documents. EMA opted for a general refusal to requests of access to trial reports and their corresponding protocols based

[32] Papadopoulou, above note 24, 136–88.

[33] See, for instance, European Ombudsman, 'EMA Policy on Publication of and Access to Clinical-Trial Data' (Letter, 13 May 2014).

[34] Charter of Fundamental Rights of the European Union [2010] OJ C 83/02.

[35] Regulation (EC) 1049/2001 of the European Parliament and of the Council of 30 May 2001 regarding public access to European Parliament, Council, and Commission documents [2001] OJ L 145/43.

on the commercial nature such documents might have. Under the context of the EMA operations, access to clinical trials data was in general considered to undermine the protection of commercial interests of natural or legal persons. This 'closed' approach was debated for a long time, and the EMA was under pressure to shift towards a policy of broader accessibility of data that would also allow third parties to contribute in the verification of marketing authorisation of medicinal products granted.[36]

Policy 0043, enacted in 2010, marked the shift from a 'closed' to a more open approach when it came to the accessibility of documents and data included in marketing authorisation dossiers. According to the said policy third parties would have the possibility to access clinical trials data and documents included in the marketing authorisation dossier. That meant in principle that documents and information could be made available after the request of a third party (reactive access). Thus, in order to gain access to clinical trials data one had to submit a relevant request to the EMA.

The EMA proceeded towards the direction of enhanced transparency by enacting some years later, in 2015, Policy 0070, according to which, when a medicinal product is granted marketing authorisation, the EMA has the authority to publish relevant data on the agency's online sharing portal. The arguments supporting increased transparency were various. On the one hand, extensive transparency allows companies, researchers and the general scientific community to learn from past projects, both from successes and failures, and also to test what works and does not, as well as to use data in further research and evaluate therapies and medicinal products.

Under Policy 0070, third parties are given the possibility to download clinical reports in formats that are searchable as well as receive access to anonymised patient data. In general, information included in clinical trial reports is to be readily and openly available with one notable exception, that of commercially confidential information (CCI). Sponsors are expected to indicate which part of the information contained in the clinical trials dossier qualifies as CCI. However, a mere classification as CCI will not suffice, the sponsor will have to provide the necessary justification to the agency. It will ultimately be a matter for the EMA to decide whether the justification of the classification as CCI is satisfactory or not while this is to proceed on a case-to-case basis.

In its annex, Policy 0070 lists information or documents that may be considered CCI, such as product development rationale, overviews of biopharmaceutics and clinical pharmacology, benefits and risks, conclusions, summaries of biopharmaceutical studies and clinical pharmacology studies and reports of biopharmaceutical studies. The list is indicative, and the fact that a document is included does not mean it will be per se accepted as CCI.[37] In cases where a sponsor requests part of the information contained in the clinical trials data to be classified as CCI, the sponsor needs to submit information as to which innovative features of the information that is included, what is the specific ongoing development programme that the proposed redaction relates to and finally information as to how the information redacted would constitute a

[36] Löfstedt, above note 18, 300.

[37] Annex 3, Policy 0070. See also EMA, External Guidance on the Implementation of the European Medicines Agency Policy on the Publication of Clinical Data for Medicinal Products for Human Use, EMA/90915/2016, version 1.3 (20 September 2017, published 22 September 2017).

potential risk to their legitimate economic interest. There is no general guideline as to how CCI would be determined and that means in turn that the protection of confidential information included in marketing authorisation dossiers is subject to a rather unpredictable regime. The general principle is that clinical data is not to be considered CCI except for in limited circumstances. 78 per cent of the requests for redaction on the basis of CCI have been rejected due to the lack of sufficient justification. A report published after the first year of implementation of the Policy revealed that over 3,000 clinical documents corresponding to regulatory procedures of 50 different medicinal products were made publicly available, with CCI redactions in the documents published amounting to only 0.01 per cent of the total pages published.[38]

The documents containing the most interesting and thus also valuable information in the marketing authorisation dossiers are the Clinical Study Reports (CSRs). This is where studies of medicinal products including the description as well as the clinical and statistical presentation are provided. Subjecting CSRs to the open access regime of Policy 0070 caused the pharmaceutical industry to argue that there are two main risks with such broad accessibility of documents, one related to the protection of patient data, and the other to the protection of pharmaceutical companies' confidential information. Sponsors fear that the information contained in the CSR is detailed enough (and thus critical enough) for it to provide third parties accessing it with a competitive advantage. Such documents and data could also potentially be used to support marketing authorisation application dossiers, in jurisdictions where national legislation fails to offer adequate data and market protection.

Access to documents under Policy 0070 is further regulated by means of the agency's terms and conditions. In fact, access to documents made available under Policy 0070 is subject to third parties' consent to terms of use, providing that accessed clinical reports shall be used only for academic and non-commercial research purposes. They will, at the same time, not be used to support MA applications anywhere in the world or as means of unfair competition.[39] Although this seems to provide sponsors with an additional layer of protection, sanctioning these terms of access might turn out to be a complicated endeavour. First, enforcing the terms of use would presuppose the sponsor knowing the identity of the party that accessed the information. The EMA has as a matter of principle declined to provide such information. Furthermore, the obligations are binding on the actual party accessing the information in the first place but the moment the information becomes publicly available, enforcement will concern third parties, and will thus become automatically much more complicated, if not even unnecessary.[40]

In fact, determining whether certain information/documents will be considered as CCI and thus redacted from the published documents or not has proven to be a complicated and difficult matter that ultimately became a question for the Court of

[38] See also Sergio Bonini, Hans-Georg Eichler, Noël Wathion and Guido Rasi, 'Transparency and the European Medicines Agency – Sharing of Clinical Trial Data' (2014) 371(26) *New England Journal of Medicine* 2452, 2455.

[39] For the terms of use, see EMA, 'Terms of Use' https://clinicaldata.ema.europa.eu/web/cdp/termsofuse.

[40] See Daria Kim, 'Transparency Policies of the European Medicines Agency: Has the Paradigm Shifted?' (2017) 25(3) *Medical Law Review* 456, 483. See also Daria Kim, *Access to Non-Summary Clinical Trial Data for Research Purposes Under EU Law* (vol 16, Munich Studies on Innovation and Competition, 2021).

Justice of the European Union (CJEU). The CJEU ruled for the first time on the question of the CCI status of documents submitted under the framework of a marketing authorisation application, in the cases of *PTC Therapeutics International v EMA* (C-175/18P)[41] and of *MSD Animal Health Innovation and Intervet International v EMA* (C-178/18P) on 22 January 2020.[42]

These cases constituted appeals of the rulings of the General Court concerning the EMA's decisions to make available documents and data (namely toxicology reports and CSRs), under Regulation No 1049/2001. The EMA decided to disclose the content of these reports to third parties, except for a limited part that was classified as CCI. According to the CJEU, the application of a general presumption of confidentiality is merely an option for the institution, body, office or agency concerned and the latter always retains the possibility of carrying out a specific and individual examination of the documents in question to determine whether they are protected, in whole or in part, by one or more of the exceptions laid down in Article 4 of Regulation No 1049/2001.

Consequently, the Court of Justice rejected the appellants' plea that the reports at issue were covered by a general presumption of confidentiality, noting that the EMA was not obliged to apply such a presumption to those reports and that the EMA had carried out a specific and individual examination, which had led it to redact certain passages. Another issue of interest was whether the EMA's decision to grant access to the reports at issue had undermined the appellants' commercial interests, an exception laid down in the first indent of Article 4(2) of Regulation No 1049/2001. The Court of Justice concluded that a person seeking to apply Article 4 of Regulation No 1049/2001 should establish the commercial interest at peril and at the same time also substantiate a clear risk related to this specific piece of data and not just a general argumentation of commercial interests.[43]

Naturally, the timing of accessibility of the data is also of immense importance for sponsors but also potentially for third parties. Clinical trials data must be submitted to the EMA within 30 days from the day the MA was granted, the procedure for granting marketing authorisation has been completed or the applicant has chosen to withdraw the application. Such data is made available with the exception of what is marked as a CCI.

The legal framework that introduced Policy 0070 could not be considered an easily accessible one, taking consideration of the number of guidelines and explanatory documents published since its entry into force and until today.[44]

[41] Case C-175/18 P, *PTC Therapeutics International Ltd v European Medicines Agency* (Judgment of 22 January 2020, ECLI:EU:C:2020:23 para 38.

[42] Case C-178/18 P — *MSD Animal Health Innovation GmbH and Intervet International BV v European Medicines Agency* (Judgment of the Court (Fourth Chamber) of 22 January 2020, ECLI:EU:C:2020:24 para 40-43.

[43] ECLI:EU:C:2020:23; ECLI:EU:C:2020:24, paras 51–53. See also paras 109, 117.

[44] Already in 2018, the EMA produced a detailed document including EMA (15 Oct 2018) External guidance on the implementation of the European Medicines Agency policy on the publication of clinical data for medicinal products for human use. EMA/90915/2016, version 1.4. www.ema.europa.eu/en/documents/regulatory-procedural-guideline/externalguidance-implementation-european-medicines-agency-policy-publication-clinical-data_en-3.pdf.

Furthermore it is rather difficult to conclude on an overarching evaluation of EMA's Policy 0700 due to its rather short period of application. Policy 0070 was suspended during the COVID-19 pandemic for all except COVID-19 medicines.[45] The clinical data packages for non-COVID-19 medicines published following the resumption were made available in January 2024 via EMA's clinical data website.[46] Nevertheless, what may be concluded is that parties that are overrepresented in the list of access requests are pharmaceutical companies and lawyers. Academics and researchers envisioned to be the most important users of the system turned out to be less interested in this possibility.

The Clinical Trials Directive (CTR) included very limited provisions on transparency and accessibility and those were concerned primarily with the exchange of information between national competent authorities.[47] Transparency and accessibility of documents that were part of the decentralised procedure have thus been dependent on national legislation and/or the practices and policies of national authorities. While EMA Policies 0043 and 0070 guaranteed the accessibility of clinical trials reports on an EMA level, these were not in any way binding on the operations of the national competent authorities. Thus, while the accessibility of data contained in centralised marketing authorisation documents gradually became the rule, the decentralised applications were subject to varying standards of transparency.

The CTR came to repeal the Clinical Trials Directive on 31 January 2022 and shifted the system towards guaranteeing among other things the same level of transparency and accessibility of documents irrespective of the choice of the MA application route.[48]

The Regulation does not have retroactive effect, and it applies thus only to medicinal products authorised after its entry into force. The entry into force of the CTR underlined the concerns of pharmaceutical companies that competitors will use the data accessed under the Regulation to support their own marketing authorisation applications, without their consent. Concerns have also been expressed as to the potentially earlier publication of clinical trials data.[49]

According to Article 81(5) CTR, data that is contained in the application dossier can be made publicly accessible even before any decision is reached if there is an 'overriding public interest in disclosure'. Articles 80 and 81 of the Regulation assign the EMA the task of creating an EU Portal and Database. The portal, named CTIS, was launched on 31 January 2022. This was also the date from which the transition period

[45] In line with the EMA, *Final Programming Document 2023–2025* and its Management Board meeting of 14–15 December 2022.

[46] See www.ema.europa.eu/en/human-regulatory-overview/marketing-authorisation/clinical-data-publication.

[47] Directive 2001/20/EC of the European Parliament and of the Council of 4 April 2001 on the approximation of the laws, regulations, and administrative provisions of the Member States relating to the implementation of good clinical practice in the conduct of clinical trials on medicinal products for human use [2001] OJ L 121/34. See Recital 9 and also art 11 concerning the accessibility of information and data between Member States.

[48] Regulation (EU) No 536/2014 of the European Parliament and of the Council of 16 April 2014 on clinical trials on medicinal products for human use, and repealing Directive 2001/20/EC Text with EEA relevance OJ L 158, 27.5.2014, pp 1–76.

[49] Ilse-Maria Nolan, Senior Director, Regulatory Affairs, PPD; Tracy Farrow, Director, Medical Writing, PPD; Rina Kacha, Senior Manager, Regulatory Affairs, PPD, Preparing for data transparency requirements of the new EU CTR, Vol 18, No 6, June 2021.

of one year for the application of the new rules was initiated. During the transition period, clinical trial sponsors could choose whether to submit an initial clinical trial application in line with the Clinical Trials Directive or under the CTR and through the CTIS. After the transition period elapsed, the CTIS became the single entry point for submission of data and information relating to clinical trials. The CTIS becomes thus a central transparency portal for the new clinical trials regime in Europe. It is a platform that, aside transparency and accessibility, facilitates the application for clinical trials authorisation procedures, in particular in the case of multinational clinical trials.[50]

Already a year after its entry into force, the new system was subject to a public consultation concluded in June 2023, with a special focus on the CTIS transparency rules. The results of the public consultation led to a fine-tuning of the system, with a focus on the revisions on the actual transparency regulations. The objective of these changes has been to make the system user-friendly.[51]

Under the CTR, there is a recognised legitimate interest in protecting information that the pharmaceutical companies use to develop new medical products. The CTR also employs the term 'commercially confidential information' without however further specifying the meaning and scope of this term.[52]

A transparent of the legal framework seems dependent on a clear definition of what constitutes a CCI. Yet this is missing. Neither Policy 0070 nor the CTR provide a clarification as to how this term is to be defined and interpreted in practice. The EMA's newly published draft guidance provides examples of information that may constitute commercially confidential information (CCI) for users of the Clinical Trials Information System (CTIS), including clinical trial sponsors and marketing authorisation applicants or holders. However, according to the guidance these categories are not automatically confidential and must be assessed on a case-by-case basis.

The examples include: the names of manufacturers or suppliers of the active substance or excipients, unless disclosure is required under existing pharmaceutical legislation (for example, in the case of certain biological products); and the quantitative composition of excipients in the investigational or authorised medicinal product; detailed information on the synthesis or manufacture of the active substance; detailed descriptions of the manufacturing and control processes for the investigational/authorised final product; information related to future development

[50] EMA, *Annex I: Guidance Document on How to Approach the Protection of Personal Data and Commercially Confidential Information While Using the Clinical Trials Information System (CTIS)*, EMA/194159/2023 (18 June 2024). See also EMA, *Q&A on the Protection of Commercially Confidential Information and Personal Data While Using CTIS*, EMA/898965/2022, version 2 (8 July 2024). See also EMA, *Guidance Document on How to Approach the Protection of Personal Data and Commercially Confidential Information While Using the Clinical Trials Information System (CTIS)*, EMA/212507/2021, version 2 (18 June 2024). See also EMA, *Revised CTIS Transparency Rules*, EMA/263067/2023 (5 October 2023).

[51] The feedback collected during the public consultation was provided by 204 stakeholders, including sponsors, CROs, academia, national competent authorities, ethics committees, health care professionals and patients organisations.

[52] EMA, *Guidance Document on How to Approach the Protection of Personal Data and Commercially Confidential Information While Using the Clinical Trials Information System (CTIS)*, version 2, EMA/212507/2021 (18 June 2024).

plans for indications other than the one under investigation and not yet disclosed in the public domain; new biomarkers or novel methodologies not yet qualified (to the extent that the information is not yet disclosed in the public domain); detailed information concerning innovative analytical methods as well as detailed information on the facilities and equipment available at the sponsor and at clinical sites.[53]

The evaluation of whether a given piece of information is innovative is to be performed in collaboration with experienced professionals having relevant expertise in the clinical research area and should consider whether the release of such information could undermine the economic interests or competitive position of the owner of the information. [54]

The CTR transparency rules are obviously inspired by Policy 0070 both in terms of the procedure and of the timeline for publication of data and documents being the time of the clinical trial application decision (irrespective of whether this is positive or negative). This is also in coherence with Article 81(5) of the CTR stating that no data from a clinical trial application dossier shall be publicly accessible before the decision on the clinical trial has been made, unless there is an overriding public interest; furthermore, overriding public interests apply only in exceptional circumstances, on an ad hoc basis, when the public interest in having information made publicly available may outweigh considerations that the same information should remain confidential; information on applications which did not reach the decision phase, have lapsed or have been withdrawn by the sponsors or have been considered not valid during evaluation, will continue to be exempted from publication.[55]

Neither in the EMA Policy 0070 nor in the CTR is the CCI defined in a satisfactory manner. In the EMA Policy 0070 it is provided that:

> CCI shall mean any information contained in the clinical reports submitted to the Agency by the applicant/MAH that is not in the public domain or publicly available and where disclosure may undermine the legitimate economic interest of the applicant/MAH.

While in the text of the CTR, CCI is referenced to as follows in Recital 68, which provides that:

> For the purposes of this Regulation, in general the data included in a clinical study report should not be considered commercially confidential once a marketing authorization has been granted, the marketing authorization has been completed, the application for marketing authorization has been withdrawn. In addition, the main characteristics of a clinical trial, the conclusion on Part I of the assessment report for the authorization of a clinical trial, the decision on the authorization of a clinical trial, the substantial modification of a clinical trial, and the clinical trial results including reasons for temporary halt and early termination, in general, should not be considered confidential.

[53] See also HMA/EMA, *Draft Guidance Document on the Identification of Personal Data and Commercially Confidential Information Within the Structure of the Marketing Authorisation Application (MAA) Dossier*, draft 3 (25 March 2024).

[54] Z Zemła-Pacud and G Lenarczyk, 'Clinical Trial Data Transparency in the EU: Is the New Clinical Trials Regulation a Game-Changer?' (2023) 54(5) *IIC Int Rev Ind Prop Copyr Law* 732–63.

[55] EMA, *Revised CTIS Transparency Rules*, EMA/263067/2023 (5 October 2023).

Article 81(4)(b) provides that the CTIS will be publicly open while:

> (b) protecting commercially confidential information, in particular through taking into account the status of the marketing authorisation for the medicinal product, unless there is an overriding public interest in disclosure.

As of 18 June 2024, the Revised CTIS transparency rules constitute the applicable rules of the Clinical Trial Information System.[56] All trials submitted on or after 18 June 2024 will have to follow the principles and timelines defined in the revised rules. In the Guidelines, the CCI is defined as any information submitted to CTIS which is not in the public domain, or publicly available, and where disclosure may undermine the legitimate economic interest or competitive position of the concerned entities, for example clinical trial sponsors, marketing authorisation applicants/holders or service providers.[57] Unfortunately the Guidelines do not not provide any further clarification to what is provided in the text of the CTR

The protection of CCI was also previously enabled via the use of a deferral mechanism with different options based on a categorisation of trials, acknowledging that clinical trials are different and contain different CCI, depending on the development phase of the investigational medicinal product being used. Categorisation of trials has been the basis for defining the applicable deferral timelines allowing sponsors to request to publish the relevant clinical trial information not at the time of the application decision, but rather at the end of the deferral period (a variable number of years after trial ends in EU/EEA), the submission of summary of results or CSRs, whatever occurred earlier. This allowed, for the delay of publication for certain types of trial data, including the protocol of clinical trials, for a period of up to seven years from the end of the trial in the EU/EEA. The system of deferral is abandoned under the new transparency rules of the EMA. This is also one of the key novelties of the revised system.

Policy 0070 focuses on the publication of clinical data while the CTR includes an overarching legislative framework for the authorisation and process of clinical trials in the EU in general and not only on transparency issues. It contains thus a much more comprehensive and complete legal framework. Furthermore, there is a difference in focus with regards the publication of clinical data. The EMA Policy 0070 concerns clinical data submitted in MA application procedures at the EMA after 1 January 2015 while CTR applies to clinical data produced under the framework

[56] EMA, *Guidance Document on How to Approach the Protection of Personal Data and Commercially Confidential Information While Using the Clinical Trials Information System (CTIS)*, version 2, EMA/212507/2021 (18 June 2024). These guidelines provide guidance to users on the revised Clinical Trials Information System (CTIS) transparency rules and on the protection of personal data and CCI submitted to CTIS, the EU database established in accordance with the requirements of Regulation (EU) 536/2014 (CTR). It should be read in conjunction with its Annex I. See EMA, *Annex I: Guidance Document on How to Approach the Protection of Personal Data and Commercially Confidential Information While Using the Clinical Trials Information System (CTIS)*, EMA/194159/2023 (18 June 2024).

[57] See also HMA/EMA, *Recommendations on Transparency Approved in November 2010 – Recommendations on Release of Information with Regard to New Applications for Medicinal Products Before and After Opinion or Decision on Granting of a Marketing Authorisation*, EMA/484118/2010. CCI potentially claimed by service providers is unlikely to appear in clinical trial information submitted in CTIS and will be subject to a particular degree of rigour when scrutinising its existence.

of clinical trials authorised under the legal framework of the CTR (and thus both centralised and decentralised marketing authorisations) after its entry into force 1 January 2022.[58]

A preliminary evaluation of the CTR and an overall evaluation of the system as such was published 4 July 2024.[59] In the evaluation survey, a total of 186 respondents participated (only 43 of them participated in the first one). The results of the evaluation reveal that respondents are preoccupied on the one hand with issues pertaining to some technical aspects,[60] but mainly on the lack of clarity of the system and the way the CTR interacts with the rest of the applicable framework, such as the clinical data sharing requirements under the European Health Data Space (EHDS) draft legislation, the In Vitro Diagnostic Medical Devices Regulation (IVDR)[61] and Medical Devices Regulation (MDR)[62] as well as the lack of an articulation relating to the CTR and its guidance on the one hand, and EMA Policies 046 and 0070 on the other.[63]

It seems also that the question of the scope of the transparency rules, that is, what kind of information/data is to be included, is not yet a settled one. The EMA has launched a pilot project to assess whether the analysis of 'raw data' from clinical trials by regulatory authorities improves the evaluation of marketing authorisation applications (MAAs) for new medicines as well as post-authorisation applications and to explore the practical aspects of the submission and analysis of such data. Raw data constitutes individual patient data from clinical studies in electronic structured format that is directly accessible for analysis and visualisation. Examples of raw data include records of original observations and measurements of clinical study participants, such as clinical laboratory results, imaging data and patient medical charts. Under the current MA system, the submission of raw data is not necessary.[64]

[58] EMA, 'Questions and Answers on the European Medicines Agency Policy on Publication of Clinical Data for Medicinal Products for Human Use' (2014) EMA/357536/2014 (hereinafter *Questions and Answers*) 6–7 (clarifying that the EMA's publication policy 'will serve as a useful complementary tool ahead of the implementation of the new Clinical Trials Regulation').

[59] European Commission, *EU Survey 2023 – Factual Summary Report: Targeted Consultation on the Implementation of the Clinical Trials Regulation (EU) 536/2014*, 1/39.

[60] See for instance, Increase the user friendliness of the system. • Facilitate the upload / download of the list of documents. • Implement missing specific functionalities (e.g. Change of the sponsor). • Generate notices and alerts via email. • Improve the design of the system platform. • Improvements in the system performance causing delays in the submissions. • Facilitate the submission of substantial modifications (SM) or additional member states. while others Clinical Trial Applications (CTA) are under evaluation.

[61] Regulation (EU) 2017/746 of the European Parliament and of the Council of 5 April 2017 on in vitro diagnostic medical devices, and repealing Directive 98/79/EC and Commission Decision 2010/227/EU.

[62] Regulation (EU) 2017/745 of the European Parliament and of the Council of 5 April 2017 on medical devices, amending Directive 2001/83/EC, Regulation (EC) No 178/2002 and Regulation (EC) No 1223/2009 and repealing Council Directives 90/385/EEC and 93/42/EEC

[63] Regulation (EU) 2017/746 of the European Parliament and of the Council of 5 April 2017 on in vitro diagnostic medical devices and repealing Directive 98/79/EC and Commission Decision 2010/227/EU (Text with EEA relevance) [2017] OJ L 117/176.

[64] EMA, *Information About the Raw Data Proof-of-Concept Pilot for Industry: Access to Raw Data for Marketing Authorization and Post-Authorization Applications Submitted to the* EMA, EMA/174598/2022 (24 October 2022). See also EMA, *Application of EMA's Transparency Principles to the Raw Data Proof-of-Concept Pilot*, EMA/949891/2022 (19 December 2022); EMA, *Questions and Answers About the Raw Data Proof-of-Concept Pilot for Industry: Scope, Terms of Participation and Data Submission Process*, EMA/658116/2022 (12 December 2023).

IV. CONCLUSIONS

The COVID-19 pandemic confirmed previously debated concerns on pharmaceutical product regulation mainly originating in a mismatch between the technical characteristics of modern pharmaceuticals, the structure of the pharmaceutical market, as well as the needs of contemporary public health systems on the one hand, and the regulatory regime they are expected to abide by on the other. It was thus to be expected that the post-COVID era would prioritise a general overview of the system, legislative changes and a fine-tuning of procedures that concern both the marketing authorisation as a process and the data and market exclusivity as well as the regulation of transparency and accessibility of documentation related to the marketing authorisation procedure.

Parallel to these legislative developments there is a general intensified political interest in increased transparency of clinical trials data, which must also be seen under the light of the overarching work on the accessibility and use of medical data under the EHDS. The EHDS is claimed to constitute the key pillar of the upcoming European Health Union and the first EU data space, and is thus indicative of the direction to be taken by future legislation in this field.[65] Despite the importance of this political agenda, it seems that the current evolution of clinical data regulation is still rather disconnected from the EHDS framework as well as from the overarching discussion on ownership of data and its treatment under the intellectual property regime. It is obvious that difficult legal issues may arise in the interface between these two legal systems.

In the process of promoting secondary use of medical data and thus achieving a more efficient and modern health system, data transparency and accessibility have become objectives of utmost importance. And while the system had from the start an interest in balancing the necessary production of clinical trials data with the rights of the sponsor by means of the protection provided for under the data and market exclusivity, priorities seem to have shifted towards keeping data out of the scrutiny of the public eye. Sponsors are exposed in a way they have never previously experienced, and their sole means of protection from disclosure is invoking the still rather unclear CCI status.

It is obvious that transparency and accessibility and, as a result, the effectiveness of the system as whole, will depend on how to discern between data to be publicly available and that classified as CCI. The starting point in this evaluation has been that data should per se be treated as information for which transparency and accessibility must be guaranteed in the marketing authorisation process. Thus, to succeed in extracting data as CCI, the sponsor must provide specific justification pertaining both to the nature of the data and to the potential commercial risks of it being made openly available. In this respect it may be argued that the use of AI data analytics will make it very difficult to assess a priori what the use of data may lead to and what the potential damages to the sponsor could amount to.[66]

[65] As recently as in spring 2024, the European Parliament and the Council reached a political agreement concerning the Commission proposal for the EHDS that focuses in particular in empowering individuals to take control of their health data and facilitate its exchange for the delivery of healthcare across the EU.

[66] The goal of the EHDS is to empower patients to access their health data in an electronic format, including from a different member state to the one in which they live, and allow health professionals

Undoubtedly, transparency has been approached on a more systematic and structural basis during the past few years in Policy 0070 as well as in the provisions of the CTR. Both instruments contribute to a more open system of access. Even though there are some deviations between the two,[67] the CTR seems to elaborate on and confirm the transparency rules introduced by Policy 0070. The most radical impact of the CTR is its scope, covering data in marketing authorisation procedures irrespective of the level of administration, central or national. In the post-CTR era, the decentralised applications will no longer fall outside the radar of transparency rules, and thus the impact of national legislation is gradually minimised to a considerable degree.

Despite the recent rich production of guidelines and supporting documents having as their main objective to clarify the legal framework under which data is expected to be made available as well as attempting to specify the role of the CTIS in this respect, it is only by means of its practical application that we will be able to identify potential gaps in the system and provide the necessary fine-tuning.[68]

In this respect, what is particularly interesting is certainly the definition of the term CCI. Without clear and transparent rules as to what constitutes CCI the legal framework will not fulfil the requirements of legal certainty, and the practical application will still vary depending on the discretion authority applying it. Thus, introducing a harmonised view between the practices of EMA and that of the national authorities might turn out to be a chimaera.

At the same time, the revisions provided for under the Pharmaceutical Package are indicative of the political will to further adjust (and in fact limit), the duration of data protection. In other words, the actual production of clinical data seems now to be worthy of a much more limited duration of exclusivity. Data is thus not only to be transparent and openly accessible; third parties should also be given the possibility to re-use it under more generous terms and on a timely manner.

These recent developments in the protection of clinical trials data two decades after its first introduction are characteristic of the dilemmas that have characterised it from the start, that is, how much exclusivity on data is enough to compensate for the expensive and lengthy clinical trials, while at the same time guaranteeing transparency and broader accessibility and thus the possibility to verify clinical trials and to avoid their unnecessary duplication.

The new system makes promises of unparalleled transparency levels and it is thus only to be expected that this will in turn also raise the concerns of the innovative pharmaceutical industry. Moreover, at first glance, the noticeable, gradually ongoing shift towards greater access to clinical trials data within the EU seems to go hand-in-hand or maybe even be part of the rise of innovative data analysis technologies.

---

to consult their patients' files with their consent (so-called primary use), also from other EU countries. These electronic health records (EHR) would include patient summaries, electronic prescriptions, medical imagery and laboratory results. The law will make it possible to transfer health data safely to health professionals in other EU countries (based on MyHealth@EU infrastructure), for example when citizens move to another state. It will be possible to download the health record free of charge.

[67] See EMA, *Sponsor Handbook: Clinical Trials Information System (CTIS)*, version 4.0 (August 2024).

[68] See Revised CTIS Transparency Rules and Historical Trials: Quick Guide for Users CTIS Team, Data Analytics and Methods Taskforce (TDA), version 1.7 (updated 19 July 2024, to include slide 17 on SM change of sponsor).

The ever-expanding data accessibility not only benefits from, but also requires AI-powered capabilities to gather, normalise and analyse it in the interests of both public healthcare and drug R&D. Until now, the limited accessibility of data available for model training constituted considerable restraints to efficient implementation of such AI-driven projects.[69]

Regulating transparency while at the same time taking good consideration of the rights of sponsors is a difficult equation especially at a time where the value and potential practical uses of data is increasing exponentially due to the technological advancements in the field. The pharmaceutical market has always been a very complicated one to regulate, partly due to the burden of its historical overregulation, but also due to its special characteristics and the tendency these have to change over time. It is however clear that, the rapid technological evolution and the endless possibilities it provides for the processing and re-use of data, brings the regulation of data in the forefront of healthcare innovation.[70]

[69] Thomas Davenport and Ravi Kalakota, 'The Potential for Artificial Intelligence in Healthcare' (2019) 6(2) *Future Healthcare Journal* 94, 98. See also Shuroug Alowais and others, 'Revolutionizing Healthcare: The Role of Artificial Intelligence in Clinical Practice' (2023) 23(1) *BMC Medical Education* 689.

[70] The potential of AI in medical research is undeniable, the *New England Journal of Medicine* (NEJM) itself started a series of articles on 'AI in Medicine', stating that 'medicine stands out as one [field] in which there is tremendous potential' for AI along with 'equally substantial challenges'. Among these challenges is 'a mismatch between the data set with which an AI system was developed and the data on which it is being deployed'.

Index

www.ingramcontent.com/pod-product-compliance
Ingram Content Group UK Ltd.
Pitfield, Milton Keynes, MK11 3LW, UK
UKHW020234290926
15470UKWH00002B/528

9 781509 993376